Eighteenth-Century Poetry

Eighteenth-Century Poetry

An Annotated Anthology

Edited by

David Fairer and Christine Gerrard

BLACKWELL Publishers

Copyright © Blackwell Publishers Ltd 1999.
Introduction, notes and editorial apparatus copyright © David Fairer
and Christine Gerrard 1999.

First published 1999

2 4 6 8 10 9 7 5 3 1

Blackwell Publishers Ltd
108 Cowley Road
Oxford OX4 1JF
UK

Blackwell Publishers Inc.
350 Main Street
Malden, Massachusetts 02148
USA

British Library Cataloguing in Publication Data

A CIP catalogue record for this book is available from the British Library.

Library of Congress Cataloging-in-Publication Data

Eighteenth-century poetry: an annotated anthology/edited by David
Fairer and Christine Gerrard.
    p.   cm. – (Blackwell annotated anthologies)
    Includes bibliographical references (p.   ) and index.
    ISBN 0–631–20623–X (acid-free paper). – ISBN 0–631–20624–8 (acid-free paper)
    1. English poetry–18th century. I. Fairer, David. II. Gerrard,
Christine. III. Series.
PR1215.E54 1998
821'.508–dc21   98–6211
                                                      CIP

Typeset in 9.5pt on 11pt Ehrhardt
by York House Typographic Ltd, London
Printed in Great Britain by T. J. International, Padstow, Cornwall

This book is printed on acid-free paper

Contents
(Short Titles)

Selected Contents by Theme

5   Natural Description

6   Urban Description

7   Houses and Gardens

14 CONTEMPLATING DEATH

15 MADNESS

16 VISIONS

23   LYRICS

Alphabetical List of Authors

Introduction

The richness and variety of eighteenth-century poetry has become increasingly recognized in recent years. Thanks in large measure to Roger Lonsdale's pioneering volumes and to the many new discoveries in the field of women writers, the range of its voices has dramatically increased. We believe that the need has arisen for a verse anthology tailored to the requirements of students and teachers of eighteenth-century literature: one which consists of complete poems or books from poems, rather than extracts, and which supplies detailed introductory headnotes and full annotation.

This volume presents a collection of poems by forty poets chosen from the full range of the period 1700–1800, but excepting Blake, Wordsworth and Coleridge. Although their major early work was published before 1800 (notably *Lyrical Ballads* 1798, and Blake's *Songs of Innocence and Experience* 1789/1794), we have omitted them from this volume on the grounds that they are well represented in Romantic anthologies and would have demanded very considerable space. The 128 items collected here range from *The Choice* (1700) to work by Mary Robinson published in the *Morning Post* (1800). In the opening text the Reverend John Pomfret describes his ideal country estate, and in the final poem the radical Helen Maria Williams invokes the Creator as she looks down from a Swiss glacier. In many ways English poetry had travelled an equally long distance over those hundred years. But the trajectory is deceptive. The social satire of Swift, Gay and Pope was shouldered aside at mid-century by a young generation of early Romantics (Collins, the Wartons, Gray, Akenside), and in the sixties, with the work of Macpherson, Chatterton and Smart, English poetry recovered an older music of bard, minstrel and psalmist. Yet as the range of poetry expanded Pope never lost his influence, and in the hands of Johnson, Goldsmith and Crabbe the moralizing heroic couplet was enriched by a variety of new tones. In the 1780s, in the sonnets and elegies of Charlotte Smith and William Lisle Bowles, we hear the distinctive notes of Romantic melancholy; but it is useful to recall that in the opening decade of the century both Anne Finch and Isaac Watts were already adventuring with their imaginations. Where Finch and Watts may look forward to Wordsworth and Blake, Mary Robinson's late poems consciously return to Pope and Swift. Eighteenth-century poetry does not represent a single progressive development, but an ebb and flow of tastes, and a continuing debate over the nature and potential of poetry itself.

The rich diversity of verse forms employed by the poets of the eighteenth century is evident throughout this collection. The ambitious metrical experimentation of Collins, Smart, Macpherson and Burns runs counter to any idea that the century was dominated by the heroic couplet. Poets exploit a wide range of metrical resources, from the shaped paragraphs of Miltonic blank verse to percussive rhymed octosyllabics, the rhythms of primitive epic to the easy converse of the verse-letter, the lofty complexity of the Pindaric ode to the simplest song.

We do not pretend that our selection represents the 'best' 128 poems of the period (it is not that kind of anthology). But we do hope to have brought together the work of forty writers with particularly interesting voices, who engage with material that tests and rewards their poetic skill. As a matter of principle we have declined to offer extracts from poems, on the grounds that to remove an individual passage from its context is to sacrifice one of the most characteristic qualities of eighteenth-century verse: its fascination with transition and digression, and the relation of part to whole. Satirical portraits or set-piece descriptions are usually part of an argument, and the poet's craft is to work the varied elements into a whole, exploiting juxtapositions and shifts in tone to do so (Pope, Thomson and Cowper are especially skilled in this). Extracts can give a false impression of what a poet is trying to do, and eighteenth-century verse tends to become miniaturized and rather less ambitious as a result.

Some of the most interesting poetry of the period is to be found in its longer works. These are not always adequately represented in the anthology format, where several briefer poems or vivid extracts are likely to be preferred to a single more substantial piece. But the eighteenth century was a great age of poetic argument and exploration, in which poems develop ironies and insights over a wider range. Like good conversation or intense meditation, they shift direction and explore issues on a more extensive scale. Hence our principle of giving whole pieces only (either complete poems or a complete book of a larger work). This means, for example, that we include individual books from *Trivia*, *The Dunciad*, *The Seasons*, *The Wanderer*, *The Fleece*, *The Pleasures of Imagination*, *The Village* and *The Task*. The century is also particularly strong in those middle-length poems of between one and four hundred lines which tend to be excluded from anthologies in favour of several of their briefer competitors. We have therefore consciously made a feature of including some of these more substantial pieces, one result being that women poets are seen tackling more extensive and argumentative subjects. Items of this kind include Anne Finch's *Upon the Hurricane*, Mary Collier's *The Woman's Labour*, Mary Jones's *Of Desire*, Mary Leapor's *Epistle to Artemisia* and *Crumble-Hall*, Anna Laetitia Barbauld's *Corsica* and Ann Yearsley's *Clifton Hill*.

In our choice of texts we have tried to be both useful and adventurous, combining the familiar and unfamiliar. However, rather than pack in as many 'samples' from different authors as possible, we have mostly attempted to offer two or three poems by a single interesting author so as to give some idea of his or her range. We set the work of well-known figures (Pope, Swift, Thomson, Gray, Burns and Cowper) alongside exciting work by other writers, particularly women, with strong and distinctive voices. Several of these (Finch, Montagu, Leapor and Barbauld) are now recognized as major poets of the period and receive a corresponding amount of space in this volume. We have deliberately sought to bring the century's women poets into dialogue with the more established male writers. Rather than present them as a special group with characteristically 'feminine' concerns, we intentionally juxtapose them (Pope followed by Lady Mary, Stephen Duck by Mary Collier, Ann Yearsley by Robert Burns, Anna Barbauld by William Cowper, Charlotte Smith by William Lisle Bowles). This can be particularly helpful when a female poet supplies an indignant riposte to a poem by her male counterpart (Collier's *The Woman's Labour* in reply to Duck's *The Thresher's Labour*). Such alignments also illuminate the way in which women poets engage with, yet never slavishly emulate, male poetic models. Lady Mary Wortley Montagu offers a voice of commitment, indignation and sensitivity quite different from her detested Pope's: her landscape-poem *Epistle to Lord Bathurst* is a sharp reply to his *Epistle to Burlington*, and her own poem of frustrated love, *Epistle from Arthur Gray the Footman*, dramatically reworks the themes of *Eloisa to Abelard*. Although both Mary Jones and Mary Leapor engage admiringly with Popean forms, they draw them into new directions, giving the speaking voice a lighter, humorous sparkle.

Although we have tried to avoid any obvious thematized approach, we acknowledge that in the selected texts there is a discernible emphasis on certain issues, such as male–female relations, autobiography, the self and the natural world, social change, the politics and economics of landscape and pastoral, the passions, imagination, madness, beauty, nature and art, the recovery of the past, birth and death; and on certain modes such as loco-descriptive and meditative poetry, burlesque and mock-heroic, georgic, epistle, narrative, ode and elegy. Poets in the volume address similar topics or themes from radically different perspectives, and we have suggested a few such groupings on pp. x–xvi. We hope that readers will go on to establish their own connections and find relationships unperceived by the editors.

Editorial Procedures

In this age of instantly available text, when thousands of lines of poetry can be downloaded from a database directly into the classroom, an anthology has to justify itself by offering more than just a selection of poems. The emphasis must fall on the reliability of the text, the helpfulness of the annotation, and the general 'usability' of the volume. We hope that both the student and non-student reader will feel encouraged to move about amongst poems and authors, and develop a sense of the period's variety and range of voices. With this in mind we have taken advantage of the anthology format to encourage readers to investigate links or contrasts between texts.

In the layout we have avoided the anthology convention of ordering poets by strict chronology, either of birth-date or date of the first item. In this collection the order of an author's poems is generally chronological, but we have taken some liberty in grouping or juxtaposing poets where it was thought appropriate. This is not intended to be any kind of thematic organization, but one which will feel natural to a reader who gets to know the contents well.

Each writer is introduced by a headnote which is largely biographical (eighteenth-century poets had such fascinating lives), but which includes an indication of the character and significance of their work. The headnotes to individual poems record the source, date and something of the poem's textual history, along with further contextual information which may be of interest to the reader. We also offer on occasion a few critical pointers and suggest links with other poems in the anthology. We realize the dangers of crossing the line between editing and interpreting, but have tried to be helpful rather than coercive. Any critical hints are there to suggest further lines of thought and to stimulate discussion or disagreement. Eighteenth-century poems themselves often debate ideas, and we would like to encourage this.

The footnotes in this edition are perhaps more extensive than in most anthologies. As well as glossing words which have slipped out of common use or which take on more subtle nuances in their poetic context, we have exploited the opportunity the anthology gives of recording intertextual references within the volume. There is a considerable poetic dialogue going on during the century, of which the writers themselves were aware, and the notes draw attention to this dimension. The poets of the period can be highly allusive and they expected their readers to be alert to echoes of other writers. Interwoven allusions and parallels are often part of a poem's fabric, and we have recorded them quite liberally. We have not limited ourselves to the material in the volume, but have tried to do justice to the many echoes of the classical writers, the Bible, and that modern 'classic', Milton. Some poets such as Swift, Pope, Gray, Akenside or Chatterton supplied their own annotation, and we include this in the notes. In several cases where the poet's notes are frequent and long-winded we have had to be selective (and record the fact in the headnote).

The Text

The texts in this volume are presented as they were written or printed, without any silent modernization of spelling, capitalization or punctuation. We believe that readers do not want an easy-reading text which smooths out the original and makes it conform to present-day practice. This kind of editorial intervention risks wiping away nuances and details which, however minute, ought to register in the close reading of a poem. Spelling, capitalization and punctuation can all affect the rhythm of a line and therefore help direct its emphasis. Eighteenth-century practice in this area could vary greatly. The polarities are represented by the 1703 *Poems* of Sarah Fyge Egerton, in which some texts are punctuated with extraordinary heaviness, and the Wellesley manuscript of Anne Finch's *The Agreeable*, where there is no punctuation at all. These extreme cases have received some editorial adjustment (see the respective headnotes). In poetry texts standardization and consistency are not necessarily virtues, and we have been happy to allow occasional inconsistencies to stand. We want readers to notice a difference between (for example) the printing style of Collins's *Odes* (1747) and that of Dodsley's popular *Collection* of the following year (see headnote to Collins's *Ode to Evening*), and to appreciate the conventions or quirks of different texts. In the particular discipline of reading poetry it helps to be alert to minutiæ: better to notice things than to take things for granted.

The source of a text is given in the headnote, and all editorial interventions are recorded either in the footnotes or (if more extensive) in a separate textual note. We have selectively noted authorial revisions or variants between editions when these are likely to be of interest (limitations of space prevent us from giving them in full). Rather than produce an 'eclectic' text in which a poet's revisions are incorporated into an earlier copytext to form an amalgam, we have chosen to present in each case a specific printed or manuscript version. An individual decision has been taken for each poem. We have generally preferred the first edition or, for some poems, an early revised edition. These are the texts contemporary readers knew.

Acknowledgements

Eighteenth-century poets have been exceptionally well served by their twentieth-century editors, and it will be evident throughout how indebted we are to the rich inheritance of scholarship that has illuminated many of the writers gathered here. Even in those cases where our approach and conclusions differ from previous editors, we have been greatly helped by their discussion of editorial or interpretive problems, and our notes have often benefited from the investigations of previous scholars – far more so than we can possibly acknowledge individually. Our researches have been greatly assisted by librarians and keepers of collections, who have readily answered queries or made material available. We are especially grateful to the staff of the following libraries for their practical assistance: the Brotherton Collection and Special Collections, University of Leeds; the Bodleian Library, Oxford; the British Library; the John Rylands University Library of Manchester; the National Library of Scotland; and St Andrews University Library.

We want to extend our thanks to the many individuals who have helped us with suggestions or answers to queries, or by reading and commenting on draft material. Their assistance has been given freely and generously, and this collection owes a lot to their specialist knowledge: Professor John D. Baird; Dr Stephen Bending; John and Ann Bowers; Dr Chris Brooks; Dr Tim Burke; Dr Robin Gilmour; Simoney Girard; Dr John Goodridge; Colin Harris (Modern Papers Room, Bodleian Library); Dr William Hutchings; Dr Vivien Jones; Elizabeth Knight (Cowper & Newton Museum); Dr Oliver Pickering (Brotherton Library, University of Leeds); Dr David Richards; Hazel Robertson (National Library of Scotland); Professor Nicholas Roe; Dr Valerie Rumbold; Dr Jane Stabler; Alistair and Jennifer Stead; Gurion Taussig; Dr Andrew Wawn; Dr John Whale; Richard G. Williams (Lewis Walpole Library, Farmington, CT); and Karina Williamson.

Finally, we make grateful acknowledgement to the following for allowing us to print manuscript material in their collections: Princeton University (for Cowper's *On the Ice-islands* and *The Cast-away*); Wellesley College (for Anne Finch's *The Agreeable*); the Bodleian Library (for Anna Seward's *Colebrooke Dale*); and the Cowper & Newton Museum, Olney (for Cowper's *Yardley Oak*). In addition we are grateful to the University of Delaware Press for permission to make use of the text of Parnell's *Oft have I read*; to Oxford University Press for permission to print from their editions, Prior's *For His own Epitaph*, Swift's *Stella's Birthday, 1721* and *Verses on the Death of Dr Swift*, Burns's *Holy Willie's Prayer*, and the extract from Smart's *Jubilate Agno*; to the Master and Fellows of Pembroke College, Cambridge, for Gray's *Sonnet on the Death of Richard West*; and to Harvard University for the extract from Smart's *Jubilate Agno*. We want to record our particular thanks to the Marquis of Bath for permission to reproduce Prior's *For His own Epitaph*, to the Duke of Bedford for permission to reproduce Swift's *Stella's Birthday, 1721*, and to the Earl of Harrowby for permission to record manuscript readings from Lady Mary Wortley Montagu's poems.

John Pomfret (1667–1702)

The Choice (1700) made its obscure author John Pomfret instantly famous. As late as 1779 Dr Johnson remarked that 'Perhaps no composition in our language has been oftener perused'. Pomfret, the son of a Luton vicar, followed his father through Cambridge, then himself entered orders in 1688 and ended up as rector in his home county of Bedfordshire, first at Maulden (1695) then at Millbrook (1702). Pomfret had started writing poetry in his teens and published *Poems on Several Occasions* in 1699. *The Choice*, published the next year, was a runaway success, passing through three editions in its first year and four in its second. All of Pomfret's subsequent poems, ranging from pastoral love lyrics to apocalyptic pindarics, capitalized on their author's fame by proclaiming themselves to be 'By the Author of The Choice'. But Pomfret never repeated his success. He caught smallpox in London in 1702 and died at the young age of thirty-five. Johnson claimed that Pomfret had gone to the capital to try to clear his reputation (and hence improve his chances of preferment) with Henry Compton, Bishop of London, who apparently took exception to *The Choice*'s avowed preference for a mistress to a wife. The passage which compromised Pomfret was not biographical (he had married Elizabeth Wingate in 1692) but based on literary precedents such as Thomas Otway's more sexually explicit *Epistle to R.D.* of 1684.

The Choice is modelled loosely on Horace's Satire 2:6, which expresses the wish for 'a piece of land not over large', with a garden, a clear spring of water, a strip of woodland, and convivial conversation with friends far from the corruptions and extravagance of the city. Pomfret pays lip service to Horace's ethical imperatives of frugality, honesty and stoic indifference, and his speaker is also a pious Christian and a benevolent patriot. But *The Choice*'s huge success rested not on its inner moral message but on its physical depiction of 'blissful Ease and Satisfaction', an escapist fantasy of an English landed gentleman's life of rural leisure, reading books and enjoying fine wines with his male friends, free from everyday responsibilities – including wife and children. Pomfret reappropriated and made morally palatable for the 'polite' middle-class readers of William III's reign the epicurean poetry of rural retirement formerly monopolized by Cavalier and Restoration court poets. Johnson astutely summed up Pomfret as 'the favourite of that class of readers, who without vanity or criticism seek only their own amusement. His *Choice* exhibits a system of life adapted to common notions and equal to common expectations; such a state as affords plenty and tranquillity, without exclusion of intellectual pleasures.' The following text is that of the first edition.

The Choice

If Heav'n the grateful Liberty wou'd give,
That I might chuse my Method how to live:
And all those Hours propitious Fate shou'd lend,
In blissful Ease and Satisfaction spend.
   Near some fair Town I'd have a private Seat,   5
Built Uniform, not little, nor too great:
Better, if on a rising Ground it stood,
Fields on this side, on that a Neighb'ring Wood.
It shou'd within no other Things contain,
But what are Useful, Necessary, Plain: 10
Methinks, 'tis Nauseous, and I'd ne'er endure
The needless Pomp of gawdy Furniture:
A little Garden, grateful to the Eye,
And a cool Rivulet run Murmuring by:
On whose delicious Banks a stately Row   15
Of shady Lymes, or Sycamores, shou'd grow.
At th'end of which a silent Study plac'd,
Shou'd with the Noblest Authors there be grac'd.

Horace and *Virgil*, in whose mighty Lines,
Immortal Wit, and solid Learning Shines.   20
Sharp *Juvenal*, and am'rous *Ovid* too,
Who all the turns of Loves soft Passion knew:
He, that with Judgment reads his Charming Lines,
In which strong Art, with stronger Nature joyns,
Must grant, his Fancy do's the best Excel: 25
His Thoughts so tender, and exprest so well;
With all those Moderns, Men of steady Sense,
Esteem'd for Learning, and for Eloquence:
In some of These, as Fancy shou'd advise,
I'd always take my Morning Exercise.   30
For sure, no Minutes bring us more Content,
Than those in pleasing useful Studies spent.
    I'd have a Clear and Competent Estate,
That I might live Genteelly, but not Great.
As much as I cou'd moderately spend,   35
A little more sometimes t'oblige a Friend.
Nor shou'd the Sons of Poverty Repine
Too much at Fortune, they shou'd taste of Mine;
And all that Objects of true Pity were,
Shou'd be reliev'd with what my Wants cou'd spare;   40
For what our Maker has too largely giv'n,
Shou'd be return'd in gratitude to Heav'n.
A frugal Plenty shou'd my Table spread,
With healthy, not luxurious Dishes, fed:
Enough to satisfy, and something more   45
To feed the Stranger, and the Neighb'ring Poor.
Strong Meat indulges Vice, and pampering Food
Creates Diseases, and inflames the Blood.
But what's sufficient to make Nature Strong,
And the bright Lamp of Life continue long,   50
I'd freely take, and as I did possess
The bounteous Author of my Plenty bless.
    I'd have a little Cellar, Cool, and Neat,
With Humming Ale, and Virgin Wine Repleat.
Wine whets the Wit, improves its Native Force,   55
And gives a pleasant Flavour to Discourse;
By making all our Spirits Debonair,
Throws off the Lees, the Sedement of Care.
But as the greatest Blessing Heaven lends
May be debauch'd, and serve ignoble Ends;   60
So, but too oft, the Grapes refreshing Juice,
Does many mischievous Effects produce.

19 *Horace* (65–8 BC), Roman author of satires and epistles, notable for his self-portraiture as a good-humoured, tolerant, urbane country-lover; *Virgil* (70–19 BC), great Roman poet of the rurally inspired *Eclogues* and *Georgics* and the epic *Aeneid*.

21 *Juvenal* Early second-century Roman satirist notable for his bitter irony and lofty invective; *Ovid* (43 BC–AD 17), Roman love poet and author of the mythopoeic *Metamorphoses*.

27 *Moderns* Contemporary (as opposed to classical) authors.

33 *Clear* 'unencumbered by debt'; *Competent* 'generating sufficient income'.

54 *Humming* 'strong', 'frothy', a colloquial term; *Virgin* 'new'. In subsequent editions lines 53–4 were replaced by the more genteel 'I'd have a little Vault, but always stor'd / With the Best Wines, each Vintage cou'd afford'.

58 *Lees* The unpalatable sediment in a bottle of wine.

My House, shou'd no such rude Disorders know,
As from high Drinking consequently flow.
Nor wou'd I use what was so kindly giv'n, 65
To the dishonour of Indulgent Heav'n.
If any Neighbour came he shou'd be free,
Us'd with respect, and not Uneasy be,
In my Retreat, or to himself, or me.
What Freedom, Prudence, and Right Reason give, 70
All Men, may with Impunity receive;
But the least swerving from their Rules too much;
For what's forbidden Us, 'tis Death to touch.
That Life might be more comfortable yet,
And all my Joys refin'd, sincere and great, 75
I'd chuse two Friends, whose Company wou'd be
A great Advance to my Felicity.
Well born, of Humours suited to my own;
Discreet, and Men as well as Books have known.
Brave, Gen'rous, Witty, and exactly free 80
From loose Behaviour, or Formality.
Airy, and Prudent, Merry, but not Light,
Quick in discerning, and in Judging Right;
Secret they shou'd be, faithful to their Trust,
In Reasoning Cool, Strong, Temperate and Just. 85
Obliging, Open, without huffing, Brave;
Brisk in gay Talking, and in sober Grave.
Close in Dispute, but not tenacious, try'd
By solid Reason, and let that decide;
Not prone to Lust, Revenge, or envious Hate; 90
Nor busy Medlers with Intrigues of State.
Strangers to Slander, and sworn Foes to spight,
Not Quarrelsom, but Stout enough to Fight:
Loyal and Pious, Friends to *Cæsar* true
As dying Martyrs to their Maker too. 95
In their Society I cou'd not miss,
A permanent, sincere, substantial Bliss.
   Wou'd bounteous Heav'n once more indulge, I'd chuse
(For, who wou'd so much Satisfaction lose,
As Witty Nymphs in Conversation give) 100
Near some obliging Modest-Fair to live;
For there's that sweetness in a Female Mind,
Which in a Man's we cannot find;
That by a secret, but a pow'rful Art,
Winds up the Springs of Life, and do's impart 105
Fresh Vital Heat to the transported Heart.
I'd have her Reason, and her Passions sway,
Easy in Company, in private Gay.
Coy to a Fop, to the Deserving free,

80 *exactly* 'perfectly'.
84 *Secret* 'discreet'.
86 *huffing* 'boasting', 'blustering'.
88 *Close* 'rigorous'.

94 *Cæsar* King William III (d. 1702).
101 *Modest-Fair* 'pretty modest woman'.
109 *Coy* 'reserved'; *free* 'open', 'generous'.

Still constant to her self, and just to me.   110
A Soul she shou'd have for great Actions fit,
Prudence, and Wisdom to direct her Wit.
Courage to look bold danger in the Face,
No Fear, but only to be proud, or base:
Quick to advise by an Emergence prest,   115
To give good Counsel, or to take the best.
I'd have th'Expressions of her Thoughts be such,
She might not seem Reserv'd, nor talk too much;
That shows a want of Judgment, and of Sense:
More than enough, is but Impertinence.   120
Her Conduct Regular, her Mirth refin'd,
Civil to Strangers, to her Neighbours kind.
Averse to Vanity, Revenge, and Pride,
In all the Methods of Deceit untry'd:
So faithful to her Friend, and good to all,   125
No Censure might upon her Actions fall.
Then wou'd ev'n Envy be compell'd to say,
She goes the least of Womankind astray.
   To this fair Creature I'd sometimes retire,
Her Conversation wou'd new Joys inspire,   130
Give Life an Edge so keen, no surly Care
Wou'd venture to assault my Soul, or dare
Near my Retreat to hide one secret Snare.
But so Divine, so Noble a Repast,
I'd seldom, and with Moderation taste.   135
For highest Cordials all their Virtue lose,
By a too frequent, and too bold an use;
And what would cheer the Spirits in distress,
Ruins our Health when taken to Excess.
   I'd be concern'd in no litigious Jarr,   140
Belov'd by all, not vainly popular:
Whate'er Assistance I had power to bring
T'oblige my Country, or to serve my King,
Whene'er they call'd, I'd readily afford,
My Tongue, my Pen, my Counsel, or my Sword.   145
Law Suits I'd shun with as much Studious Care,
As I wou'd Dens, where hungry Lyons are;
And rather put up Injuries, than be
A Plague to him, who'd be a Plague to me.
I value Quiet, at a Price too great,   150
To give for my Revenge so dear a Rate:
For what do we by all our Bustle gain,
But counterfeit Delight for real Pain.
   If Heav'n a date of many years wou'd give,
Thus I'd in Pleasure, Ease, and Plenty live.   155
And as I near approach'd the Verge of Life,
Some kind Relation (for I'd have no Wife)
Shou'd take upon him all my Worldly Care,
While I did for a better State prepare.

---

115 *Emergence* 'emergency'.   **140** *litigious Jarr* 'legal dispute'.
130 *Conversation* 'company'.   **148** *put up* 'put up with'.

Then I'd not be with any trouble vex't,   160
Nor have the Evening of my Days perplext.
But by a silent, and a peaceful Death,
Without a Sigh, Resign my Aged Breath:
And when committed to the Dust, I'd have
Few Tears, but Friendly, dropt into my Grave.   165
Then wou'd my Exit so propitious be,
All Men wou'd wish to live and dye like me.

John Philips (1676–1709)

The name of John Philips is invariably linked with that of John Milton. Although previous poets had imitated Milton's style, it was Philips who adapted the Miltonic medium as a surprisingly flexible vehicle for contemporary political, descriptive and patriotic subject-matter. As a Winchester schoolboy Philips reputedly gained an 'exquisite delight' from reading Milton's verse for hours at a stretch while having his hair combed. The contrast between the sensual, pleasure-loving Philips and the sober Milton extended to politics. Philips (unlike the republican Milton) came from Tory Royalist stock. Born at Bampton, near Oxford, he spent his student years at Christ Church, where he gained a reputation for good fellowship and hard drinking. That he was often strapped for cash is suggested by his rueful self-portrait in *The Splendid Shilling*, a piece described by Joseph Addison as 'the finest burlesque poem in the British language'. Philips continued to experiment with the Miltonic style, adapting it first to the heroics of Marlborough in *Blenheim* (1705), then, far more innovatively, to two subjects very close to his heart – namely beer, in *Cerealia* (written around 1706 but not published as his until after his death), and *Cyder* (1708). Like Virgil's *Georgics*, Philips's English georgics combine practical agricultural advice with closely observed rural description and patriotic emotion. Philips, described by the admiring Thomson as 'Pomona's Bard', proved a powerful influence on several of the poets in this volume. John Gay's georgic *Wine* (1709) was the Philips-inspired precursor of his urban georgic *Trivia*, which also catches some of the burlesque qualities of *The Splendid Shilling*. Thomson's *The Seasons*, Dyer's *The Fleece* and Cowper's *The Task* are all indebted to Philips.

The Splendid Shilling

Dr Johnson dismissed the poem as a stylistic novelty which scored its points by 'degrad[ing] the sounding words and stately constructions of Milton by an application to the lowest and most trivial things'. But Philips's graphic self-portrait of the impoverished, socially isolated writer daily forced to fend off the bailiffs struck a note which resonated uncomfortably in Pope's *Dunciad*. Philips's poet, devoid of his comic vitality, would be a precursor of that later romantic icon, the solitary poet starving in his garret. See Richard Savage, and Mary Robinson, *The Poet's Garret*. The poem was first published without its author's permission in *A Collection of Poems* (1701). The text here is that of Philips's revised version, *The Splendid Shilling. An Imitation of Milton. Now First Correctly Published* (1705).

> Happy the Man, who void of Cares and Strife,
> In Silken, or in Leathern Purse retains
> A *Splendid Shilling*: He nor hears with Pain
> New Oysters cry'd, nor sighs for chearful Ale;
> But with his Friends, when nightly Mists arise, 5
> To *Juniper's*, *Magpye*, or *Town-Hall* repairs:
> Where, mindful of the Nymph, whose wanton Eye
> Transfix'd his Soul, and kindled Amorous Flames,
> *Chloe*, or *Phillis*; he each Circling Glass
> Wisheth her Health, and Joy, and equal Love. 10
> Mean while he smoaks, and laughs at merry Tale,
> Or *Pun* ambiguous, or *Conundrum* quaint.
> But I, whom griping Penury surrounds,
> And Hunger, sure Attendant upon Want,

Epigraph The 1705 title page carried the epigraph: '— Sing, Heavenly Muse, / Things unattempted yet in Prose or Rhime, / A Shilling, Breeches, and Chimera's Dire'. Cf. *Paradise Lost*, 1:6, 15.

1 *Happy the Man* This phrase, a translation of the first line of Horace's Epode 2, 'Beatus ille', introduced numerous English poems on country retirement. Cf. Pope, *Windsor-Forest*, 233.

6 A list of Oxford ale-houses.

12 *Conundrum quaint* 'ingenious riddle'.

With scanty Offals, and small acid Tiff   15
(Wretched Repast!) my meagre Corps sustain:
Then Solitary walk, or doze at home
In Garret vile, and with a warming puff
Regale chill'd Fingers; or from Tube as black
As Winter-Chimney, or well-polish'd Jet,   20
Exhale *Mundungus*, ill-perfuming Scent:
Not blacker Tube, nor of a shorter Size
Smoaks *Cambro-Britain* (vers'd in Pedigree,
Sprung from *Cadwalader* and *Arthur*, Kings
Full famous in Romantic tale) when he   25
O'er many a craggy Hill, and barren Cliff,
Upon a Cargo of fam'd *Cestrian* Cheese,
High over-shadowing rides, with a design
To vend his Wares, or at th'*Arvonian* Mart,
Or *Maridunum*, or the ancient Town   30
Eclip'd *Brechinia*, or where *Vaga*'s Stream
Encircles *Ariconium*, fruitful Soil,
Whence flow Nectareous Wines, that well may vye
With *Massic*, *Setin*, or renown'd *Falern*.
    Thus while my joyless Minutes tedious flow   35
With Looks demure, and silent Pace, a *Dunn*,
Horrible Monster! hated by Gods and Men,
To my aerial Citadel ascends;
With Vocal Heel thrice thund'ring at my Gates,
With hideous Accent thrice he calls; I know   40
The Voice ill-boding, and the solemn Sound.
What shou'd I do? or whither turn? amaz'd,
Confounded, to the dark Recess I fly
Of Woodhole; strait my bristling Hairs erect
Thro sudden Fear; a chilly Sweat bedews   45
My shud'ring Limbs, and (wonderful to tell!)
My Tongue forgets her Faculty of Speech;
So horrible he seems! his faded Brow
Entrench'd with many a Frown, and *Conic* Beard,
And spreading Band, admir'd by Modern Saints,   50
Disastrous Acts forebode; in his Right Hand
Long Scrolls of Paper solemnly he waves,
With Characters, and Figures dire inscrib'd
Grievous to mortal Eyes; (ye Gods avert

15 *scanty Offals* 'sparse meal'; *Tiff* 'weak liquor'.

21 *Mundungus* Foul-smelling tobacco.

23 *Cambro-Britain* A Welshman.

24 *Cadwalader* Last king of the Britons who reigned in the seventh century and defended Wales against the Saxons.

27–32 Philips praises Welsh towns (here given their Roman names) and Welsh fare.

27 *Cestrian* 'Cheshire'.

29 *Arvonian Mart* The market-town of either Aberavon or Caernarvon.

30 *Maridunum* Carmarthen.

31 *Eclip'd* 'called'; *Brechinia* Brecon; *Vaga* The River Wye.

32 *Ariconium* Hereford.

34 *Massic*, *Setin*, ... *Falern* Italian wines highly praised by classical poets.

36 *Dunn* 'bailiff'.

39 *Vocal* 'resounding'. He is kicking in the door.

44 *Woodhole* A recess in the wall used to store wood for fuel.

46 *wonderful to tell* A translation of Lat. *mirabile dictu*, used to preface strange or supernatural events.

49 *Conic* 'cone-shaped'.

50 *spreading Band* The bailiff's official neck-cloth, like that worn by clergyman or 'Modern Saints'.

Such Plagues from righteous Men!) behind him stalks 55
Another Monster, not unlike himself,
Sullen of Aspect, by the Vulgar call'd
A *Catchpole*, whose polluted Hands the Gods
With Force incredible, and Magick Charms
Erst have indu'd, if he his ample Palm 60
Should haply on ill-fated Shoulder lay
Of Debtor, strait his Body, to the Touch
Obsequious, (as whilom Knights were wont)
To some enchanted Castle is convey'd,
Where Gates impregnable, and coercive Chains 65
In Durance strict detain him, 'till in form
Of Mony, *Pallas* sets the Captive free.
    Beware, ye Debtors, when ye walk beware,
Be circumspect; oft with insidious Ken
This Caitif eyes your Steps aloof, and oft 70
Lies perdue in a Nook or gloomy Cave,
Prompt to enchant some inadvertent wretch
With his unhallow'd Touch. So (Poets sing)
Grimalkin to Domestick Vermin sworn
An everlasting Foe, with watchful Eye, 75
Lyes nightly brooding o'er a chinky gap,
Protending her fell Claws, to thoughtless Mice
Sure Ruin. So her disembowell'd Web
Arachne in a Hall, or Kitchin spreads,
Obvious to vagrant Flies: She secret stands 80
Within her woven Cell; the Humming Prey,
Regardless of their Fate, rush on the toils
Inextricable, nor will aught avail
Their Arts, nor Arms, nor Shapes of lovely Hue;
The Wasp insidious, and the buzzing Drone, 85
And Butterfly proud of expanded wings
Distinct with Gold, entangled in her Snares,
Useless Resistance make: With eager strides,
She tow'ring flies to her expected Spoils;
Then with envenom'd Jaws the vital Blood 90
Drinks of reluctant Foes, and to her Cave
Their bulky Carcasses triumphant drags.
    So pass my Days. But when Nocturnal Shades
This world invelop, and th'inclement Air

---

58 *Catchpole* The bailiff employed to make arrests; *polluted Hands* A phrase usually reserved for sacrilegious acts of desecration and murder.
59–67 This extended metaphor of enchantment and incarceration is loosely modelled on episodes in Spenser's chivalric *The Faerie Queene*, whose archaic diction Philips also imitates.
61 *haply* 'by chance'.
63 *Obsequious* 'compliant'; *whilom* 'formerly'.
66 *Durance* 'forced confinement'.
67 *Pallas* Athena, Greek goddess of wisdom, industry and war. She came to the rescue of classical heroes such as Hercules and Perseus.

69 *insidious Ken* 'covert gaze'.
70 *Caitif* 'miserable villain'.
71 *perdue* 'hidden'.
74 *Grimalkin* Sinister name for a female cat.
77 *Protending* 'stretching forth' (Lat. *protendo*); *fell* 'cruel'.
79 *Arachne* A spider, in Greek myth the name of a woman who challenged Athena to a weaving contest and was turned by her into a spider.
80 *Obvious* In the stronger sense of Lat. *obviam*, 'standing in the way of'.
82 *toils* 'nets'.

Persuades Men to repel benumming Frosts,   95
With pleasant Wines, and crackling blaze of Wood;
Me Lonely sitting, nor the glimmering Light
Of Make-weight Candle, nor the joyous Talk
Of loving Friend delights; distress'd, forlorn,
Amidst the horrors of the tedious Night,   100
Darkling I sigh, and feed with dismal Thoughts
My anxious Mind; or sometimes mournful Verse
Indite, and sing of Groves and Myrtle Shades,
Or desperate Lady near a purling Stream,
Or Lover pendent on a Willow-Tree: 105
Mean while I Labour with eternal Drought,
And restless Wish, and Rave; my parched Throat
Finds no Relief, nor heavy Eyes Repose:
But if a Slumber haply does Invade
My weary Limbs, my Fancy's still awake,   110
Thoughtful of Drink, and Eager in a Dream,
Tipples Imaginary Pots of Ale;
In Vain; awake, I find the settled Thirst
Still gnawing, and the pleasant Phantom curse.
    Thus do I live from Pleasure quite debarr'd,   115
Nor taste the Fruits that the Sun's genial Rays
Mature, *John-Apple*, nor the downy *Peach*,
Nor *Walnut* in rough-furrow'd Coat secure,
Nor *Medlar*, Fruit delicious in decay;
Afflictions Great! yet Greater still remain: 120
My *Galligaskins* that have long withstood
The Winter's Fury, and Encroaching Frosts,
By Time subdu'd, (what will not Time subdue!)
An horrid Chasm disclose, with Orifice
Wide, Discontinuous; at which the Winds   125
Eurus and *Auster*, and the dreadful Force
Of *Boreas*, that congeals the *Cronian* Waves,
Tumultuous enter with dire chilling Blasts,
Portending Agues. Thus a well-fraught Ship
Long sail'd secure, or thro th'*Ægean* Deep,   130
Or the *Ionian*, 'till Cruising near
The *Lilybean* Shoar, with hideous Crush
On *Scylla*, or *Charybdis* (dang'rous Rocks)
She strikes rebounding, whence the shatter'd Oak,

101 *Darkling* 'obscure', 'in the shade'. Cf. *Paradise Lost*, 3:39. Milton's self-portrait of his isolation and sensory deprivation (3:20–50) is the inspiration behind Philips's in 93–120.

103 *Indite* 'compose'.

117 *John-Apple* An apple kept for two years, at its best when withered and shrivelled.

119 *Medlar* Apple-like fruit, eaten only when decayed.

121 *Galligaskins* 'loose breeches'. Philips's friend Edmund Smith claimed (with mock solemnity) that the following simile was 'admirably pathetical, and shows very well the vicissitudes of sublunary things'.

126 *Eurus* The east wind; *Auster* The south wind.

127 *Boreas* The north wind; *Cronian Waves* Arctic Ocean. Cf. *Paradise Lost*, 10:290.

129 *Agues* 'fevers'.

132 *Lilybean* A promontory on the coast of Sicily.

133 *Scylla … Charybdis* A rock and a whirlpool which face each other in the Straits of Messina. In classical myth they were personified as monsters who devoured sailors.

So fierce a Shock unable to withstand,   135
Admits the Sea; in at the gaping Side
The crouding Waves Gush with impetuous Rage,
Resistless, Overwhelming; Horrors seize
The Mariners, Death in their Eyes appears,
They stare, they lave, they pump, they swear, they pray: 140
(Vain Efforts!) still the battering Waves rush in
Implacable, 'till delug'd by the Foam,
The Ship sinks found'ring in the vast Abyss.

140 *lave* 'bale out'.

Sarah Fyge Egerton (1670–1723)

To the embarrassment of her family, the young Sarah Fyge brought herself to public notice by publishing *The Female Advocate* (1686). The poem is a spirited and well-argued reply to Robert Gould's *Love Given O're* (1682), a satirical poem retailing the stereotype of woman's lustfulness and inconstancy. In response to his daughter's outspoken defence of women Thomas Fyge (d. 1706) sent her to live with relatives in the country (the subject of her poem, 'On my leaving London'), and she married Edward Field, an attorney. In 1700, her husband having died, Fyge returned to publishing poetry and contributed to two verse collections commemorating Dryden's death. In 1703 as 'Mrs. S. F.' she brought out her *Poems on Several Occasions, Together with a Pastoral*, and in the dedication to the prominent Whig patron Lord Halifax she describes them as 'some of the first Attempts of my unskilful Muse. Most of the Copies being writ, 'ere I could write Seventeen.' She also defends their subject-matter: 'I hope your Lordship is of my Opinion, that where the Circumstances do not make Love a Crime, the confessing it can be none. Besides, our Sex is confin'd to so narrow a Sphere of Action, that things of greater Consequence seldom fall within our Notices; so that Love seems the only proper Theme (if any can be so) for a Woman's Pen, especially at the Age they were writ in.' In the same year Sarah Egerton (as she had now become) was also suing for divorce from her second husband, the Reverend Thomas Egerton (d. 1720), a rich widower some twenty years older than herself. There were bitter accusations on both sides, but the suit was unsuccessful, and their difficult marriage drew the couple into public ridicule. During this time Egerton's poems reveal her love for 'Alexis' (an attorney's clerk, Henry Pierce). In *Secret Memoirs ... from the New Atalantis* (1709) Delarivière Manley mocked Egerton's poems (which had been reissued in 1706) for being concerned with 'strange things, foreign to all fashionable Understanding'. Indeed, some of them directly challenge the decorums of politeness and elegance that society demanded. Egerton stands out from her contemporaries for the laconic power with which she expresses her feelings and beliefs.

The Liberty

Egerton's subject here is personal and social (not political) freedom. The poem goes beyond teenage angst: she demands a mature autonomy for herself and her 'daring' pen, and issues a wider challenge to formality, custom and the 'Rules'. In refusing the role of infant girl that society would foist on her, she discovers a strong and direct language capable of challenging elegance and politeness, along with the system of values they represent. The text is from the first printing, *Poems on Several Occasions* (1703), pp. 19–21. Like several poems in that volume, the text of

The Liberty is very heavily punctuated: all lines are end-stopped (except for an oversight in line 34) and most lines are given a comma after the second stress (lines 1–4, for example, have commas after *one*, *lives*, *ever* and *taught*). This aural pointing suggests that a contemporary reader might have heard a more marked caesura (or break) in the five-stress line than we do; but for a modern reader the effect is distracting and cloying. In the following text eighteen lines have had such commas removed.

> Shall I be one of those obsequious Fools,
> That square their lives by Customs scanty Rules;
> Condemn'd for ever to the puny Curse,
> Of Precepts taught at Boarding-school, or Nurse,
> That all the business of my Life must be,   5
> Foolish, dull Trifling, Formality.
> Confin'd to a strict Magick complaisance,
> And round a Circle of nice visits Dance,
> Nor for my Life beyond the Chalk advance:

---

1 *obsequious* 'servile'.
7 *complaisance* 'desire to please'.

9 *the Chalk* 'the set course'. To 'chalk out' was 'to mark out, as a course to be followed' (*OED*, 'chalk' *v.* 4c). Cf. 'On my leaving London', 36n.

The Devil Censure stands to guard the same,   10
One step awry, he tears my ventrous Fame.
So when my Friends, in a facetious Vein,
With Mirth and Wit, a while can entertain;
Tho' ne'er so pleasant, yet I must not stay,
If a commanding Clock bids me away: 15
But with a sudden start, as in a Fright,
I must be gone indeed, 'tis after Eight.
Sure these restraints with such regret we bear,
That dreaded Censure can't be more severe,
Which has no Terror, if we did not fear;   20
But let the Bug-bear, timerous Infants fright,
I'll not be scar'd from Innocent delight:
Whatever is not vicious, I dare do,
I'll never to the Idol Custom bow,
Unless it suits with my own Humour too.   25
Some boast their Fetters of Formality,
Fancy they ornamental Bracelets be,
I'm sure they're Gyves and Manacles to me.
To their dull fulsome Rules, I'd not be ty'd,
For all the Flattery that exalts their Pride: 30
My Sex forbids I should my Silence break,
I lose my Jest, cause Women must not speak.
Mysteries must not be with my search Prophan'd,
My Closet not with Books, but Sweat-meats cram'd,
A little *China*, to advance the Show,   35
My *Prayer Book*, and *Seven Champions*, or so.
My Pen if ever us'd imploy'd must be,
In lofty Themes of useful Housewifery,
Transcribing old Receipts of Cookery:
And what is necessary 'mongst the rest,   40
Good Cures for Agues, and a cancer'd Breast,
But I can't here write my *Probatum est*.
My daring Pen will bolder Sallies make,
And like my self, an uncheck'd freedom take;
Not chain'd to the nice Order of my Sex,   45
And with restraints my wishing Soul perplex:
I'll blush at Sin, and not what some call Shame,
Secure my Virtue, slight precarious Fame.
This Courage speaks me Brave, 'tis surely worse,
To keep those Rules, which privately we Curse: 50
And I'll appeal to all the formal Saints,
With what reluctance they indure restraints.

21 *Bug-bear* 'any imaginary being invoked by nurses to frighten children' (*OED*).

28 *Gyves* 'fetters' (in the eighteenth century pronounced with a hard 'g' as in *go*).

29 *fulsome* 'odious'.

36 *Seven Champions* 'The Seven Champions of Christendom'. The story, from the Elizabethan romance by Richard Johnson, was popular as a children's chap-book in the eighteenth century.

39 *Receipts* 'recipes'.

42 *Probatum est* 'approval'.

45 *nice* 'fastidious'.

TEXTUAL NOTES

2 *their* there (*1703*); 28 *they're* their (*1703*); 34 *cram'd*, cram'd (*1703*); 36 *Seven* seven (*1703*).

On my leaving London, June the 29

This poem would seem to relate to Egerton's exile to the country after the publication of *The Female Advocate* (see Egerton headnote). In addressing Fate she speaks with a simplicity born out of emotional exhaustion, as if offering a retrospect at the conclusion of a tragic drama. But the effect of this epilogue is less a cathartic calm of mind than a lingering bitterness. The text is that of the first printing, *Poems on Several Occasions* (1703), pp. 23–4.

What cross impetuous Planets govern me,
That I'm thus hurry'd on to Misery;
I thought I had been bless'd, a while ago,
But one quick push, plung'd me all o'er in Woe.
My cruel Fate doth act the Tyrant's part,   5
And doth Torment me with a lingering smart;
To make me sensible of greater Pain,
Lets me take Breath, then screws the Rack again:
Ah! where's the Joy of such precarious Bliss,
That for one smiling short Parenthesis,   10
I must such tedious horrid Pangs indure,
And neither State will either kill or cure.
With all Submission, I my Fate implore,
Destroy me quite, or else Torment no more;
At least let not one glimps of Joy appear,   15
It only makes my Sufferings more severe.
No, here I'll Rule, not sue to you for this,
You cannot tantalize me now with Bliss;
For when you took my Father's love away,
Perverse as you, I'd not let others stay: 20
I was not so insensibly undone,
To hoord up Counters, when my Gold was gone.
Plunder'd of all, I now forsake the Place,
Where all my Joys, and all my Treasure was,
Ah do not now my wandering Footsteps Trace;   25
I left the Town, and all Divertisement,
And in a lonely Village am content.
Nor do I ask to be remov'd from hence,
Tho' Man and Beast are both of equal Sense:
I had not fled, but strongly forc'd by you,   30
In hast bid Mother, Sisters sad adieu.
I saw them last of all I knew in Town,
Yet all alike to me are Strangers grown;
I almost have forgot I e'er was there,
And the sad Accidents that brought me here.   35
Ah Fate! pursue me not in this Retreat,
Let me be quiet in this humble Seat:

1 *cross* 'adverse'.
10 *Parenthesis,* Parenthesis; (*1703*).
22 *Counters* Used in games of chance.
26 *Divertisement* 'entertainment'.

36 *Fate* This is the subject of Egerton's *The Fatality* (*Poems*, pp. 72–3): 'Ther's none the mystick Scrolls of Fate can read, / … just as they guide we tread. / In vain we say we this or that will do, / It cannot be unless they'll have it so'.

Let not my Friends know where to send to me,
Lest I grow pleas'd with their Civility.
I'd fain live unconcern'd, not pleas'd nor cross'd,   40
And be to all the busy World as lost.

TEXTUAL NOTE
This is another heavily punctuated poem (see headnote
to *The Liberty*): seven commas have been removed after
the second stress in lines 5, 6, 9, 12, 19, 25 and 29.

To One who said I must not Love

This poem focuses on the concept of passion as the motivating force of human life. Here love defeats all attempts to curb or discipline it, and as in Pope's *Eloisa to Abelard*, a later poem with which it repays comparison, Egerton's verses chart a woman's 'strugling Soul' (39) as she contemplates an impassive and absent lover. It was first printed in *Poems on Several Occasions* (1703), pp. 42–3, the text given here.

Bid the fond Mother spill her Infants Blood,
The hungry Epicure not think of Food;
Bid the *Antartick* touch the *Artick* Pole:
When these obey I'll force Love from my Soul.
As Light and Heat compose the Genial Sun,   5
So Love and I essentially are one:
E'er your Advice a thousand ways I try'd
To ease the inherent Pain, but 'twas deny'd;
Tho' I resolv'd, and griev'd, and almost dy'd.
Then I would needs dilate the mighty Flame,   10
Play the Coquet, hazard my dearest Fame:
The modish Remedy I try'd in vain,
One thought of him contracts it all again.
Weary'd at last, curst *Hymen*'s Aid I chose;
But find the fetter'd Soul has no Repose.   15
Now I'm a double Slave to Love and Vows:
As if my former Sufferings were too small,
I've made the guiltless Torture Criminal.
E'er this I gave a loose to fond Desire,
Durst smile, be kind, look, languish and admire,   20
With wishing Sighs fan the transporting Fire.
But now these soft Allays are so like Sin,
I'm forc'd to keep the mighty Anguish in;
Check my too tender Thoughts and rising Sighs,
As well as eager Arms and longing Eyes.   25
My Kindness to his Picture I refrain,
Nor now imbrace the lifeless lovely Swain.
To press the charming Shade tho' thro' a Glass,

5 *Genial* 'life-giving'.
10 *dilate* 'expand'.

14 *Hymen* Marriage.
22 *Allays* 'additional elements'.

Seems a Platonick breach of *Hymen*'s Laws,
Thus nicely fond, I only stand and gaze,   30
View the dear conq'ring Form that forc'd my Fate,
Till I become as motionless as that.
My sinking Limbs deny their wonted Aid,
Fainting I lean against my frighted Maid;
Whose cruel Care restores my Sense and Pain,   35
For soon as I have Life I love again,
And with the fated softness strive in vain.
Distorted Nature shakes at the Controul,
With strong Convulsions rends my strugling Soul;
Each vital String cracks with th'unequal Strife,   40
Departing Love racks like departing Life;
Yet there the Sorrow ceases with the Breath,
But Love each day renews th'torturing scene of Death.

29 *Platonick* The heightened, non-physical passion Egerton describes in *The Platonick*: 'My elevated Flame needs no supply, / But the nice subtil Fewel of the Eye: / In Contemplation all my Pleasure lies, / My Joys are pure Ideal Extacies' (*Poems*, p. 107).
30 *nicely fond* 'reserved in my affections'; *gaze*, gaze. (*1703*)

The Emulation

This attack on the twin tyranny of Law and Custom was first printed in *Poems on Several Occasions* (1703), pp. 108–9, the text given here. At the beginning of the eighteenth century the contentious term 'emulation' could encompass both the positive sense of 'an endeavour to equal or surpass others', but also a negative 'grudge against the superiority of others'. Much perhaps depended on which side was using it.

Say Tyrant Custom, why must we obey
The impositions of thy haughty Sway?
From the first dawn of Life, unto the Grave,
Poor Womankind's in every State, a Slave,
The Nurse, the Mistress, Parent and the Swain,   5
For Love she must, there's none escape that Pain;
Then comes the last, the fatal Slavery,
The Husband with insulting Tyranny
Can have ill Manners justify'd by Law;
For Men all join to keep the Wife in awe.   10
Moses, who first our Freedom did rebuke,
Was Marry'd when he writ the Pentateuch;
They're Wise to keep us Slaves, for well they know,
If we were loose, we soon should make them so.
We yeild like vanquish'd Kings whom Fetters bind,   15
When chance of War is to Usurpers kind;
Submit in Form; but they'd our Thoughts controul,
And lay restraints on the impassive Soul:
They fear we should excel their sluggish Parts,
Should we attempt the Sciences and Arts;   20
Pretend they were design'd for them alone,
So keep us Fools to raise their own Renown;
Thus Priests of old their Grandeur to maintain,
Cry'd vulgar Eyes would sacred Laws Prophane.

12 *Marry'd* To Zipporah (Exodus, 2:21–2); *Pentateuch* The first five books of the Old Testament, which include the Mosaic laws.
17 *in Form* 'with due ceremony'.
18 *impassive* 'invulnerable'; 'without feeling'.
19 *Parts* 'abilities'.

So kept the Mysteries behind a Screen,   25
Their Homage and the Name were lost had they been seen:
But in this blessèd Age, such Freedom's given,
That every Man explains the Will of Heaven;
And shall we Women now sit tamely by,
Make no excursions in Philosophy,   30
Or grace our Thoughts in tuneful Poetry?
We will our Rights in Learning's World maintain,
Wits Empire, now, shall know a Female Reign;
Come all ye Fair, the great Attempt improve,
Divinely imitate the Realms above: 35
There's ten celestial Females govern Wit,
And but two Gods that dare pretend to it;
And shall these finite Males reverse their Rules?
No, we'll be Wits, and then Men must be Fools.

36 The Muses were the nine daughters of Mnemosyne
(Memory).

37 Apollo, god of poetry and music, and Mercury, god of
eloquent speech and quick intellect.

TEXTUAL NOTES
  1 *obey* obey, (*1703*); **2** *Sway?* Sway; (*1703*); **14** *them so*
  them, so (*1703*); **20** *Arts;* Arts. (*1703*); **26** *Their* There
  (*1703*); **38** *Rules?* Rules, (*1703*).

Isaac Watts (1674–1748)

Isaac Watts, like his seven younger siblings, grew up steeped in the traditions of religious nonconformity. As a baby his mother nursed him on the steps of the Southampton jail where her husband was imprisoned for dissent. Isaac Watts senior, a tradesman and boarding-school keeper, instilled in his precocious son a lifelong commitment to religious devotion and education. As a small child Watts wrote Latin verse, and he continued his education in Greek, French and Hebrew at the local Free School. In 1690 he refused a scholarship to Oxford or Cambridge with its requisite allegiance to the articles of the Church of England and instead attended Thomas Rowe's dissenting academy at Newington Green, London. After completing his studies he took up a post as tutor to Sir John Hartropp's son in Stoke Newington, residential sector of London's wealthy dissenter population. In 1699 he became assistant pastor, and in 1702 pastor, at the fashionable Mark Lane church. Under his highly successful ministry (Watts was an inspiring preacher) the congregation swelled to over five hundred. As early as 1703 his health had begun to fail through overwork. Often incapacitated for weeks on end, he would be cared for in the homes of prominent Mark Lane families, notably Thomas Hollis and Sir Thomas and Lady Abney, until his death.

Watts was one of the most popular and prolific writers of his day. His textbooks on geography, astronomy, spelling, composition and grammar, logic and philosophy were used in Britain and America for more than a century. He virtually singlehandedly set the trend for congregational hymn-singing. The fervent poetry of hymns such as 'When I survey the wond'rous Cross' took the world of dissent by storm. Watts published four collections of verse, *Horae Lyricae* (1706), *Hymns and Spiritual Songs* (1707), *Divine Songs for the Use of Children* (1715) and *The Psalms of David Imitated* (1719). His preface to *Horae Lyricae* (like Thomson's later preface to *Winter*) rejects elegant secular rhymes for a sacred, sublime, passion-stirring poetic. 'If the Heart were first inflam'd from Heaven, and the Muse … only call'd in as an Assistant to the Worship, then the Song would end where the Inspiration ceases; the whole Composure would be of a Piece, all Meridian Light and Meridian Fervour'.

The Adventurous Muse disparages safe, dull, rulebound neoclassical verse. It proclaims the visionary Milton as an original genius and the greatest of poets. Watts, like a number of his contemporaries, considered the irregular Pindaric ode (of which this poem is an example) as the appropriate vehicle for lofty, bold sentiment. Although Watts is famed for his 'simplicity', many of the poems in *Horae Lyricae* are similarly complex, even baroque, metrical experiments. There are interesting parallels between this ode and Collins's *Ode on the Poetical Character*. The text is taken from the revised second edition of *Horae Lyricae* (1709), pp. 210–13, where it first appeared.

The Adventurous Muse

I

URANIA takes her morning Flight
   With an inimitable Wing:
Thro' rising Deluges of dawning Light
   She cleaves her wondrous way,
She tunes immortal Anthems to the growing Day;   5
Nor *Rapin* gives her Rules to fly, nor *Purcell* Notes to sing.

II

   She nor inquires, nor knows nor fears
Where lie the pointed Rocks, or where th'ingulphing Sand;
Climbing the liquid Mountains of the Skies
She meets descending Angels as she flies,   10

Title See *Paradise Lost*, 1:12–14: 'I thence / Invoke thy aid to my advent'rous song, / That with no middle flight intends to soar'.

1 URANIA The Heavenly Muse invoked by Milton in *Paradise Lost*, 1:6.

6 *Rapin* René Rapin (1621–87), influential French neoclassical critic, author of *Réflexions sur la Poétique* (1674); *Purcell* Henry Purcell (1659–95), highly accomplished English composer of both sacred and secular Restoration music, especially for the stage.

Nor asks them where their Country lies,
    Or where the Sea-marks stand.
Touch'd with an Empyreal Ray
She springs unerring upward to eternal Day,
    Spreads her white Sayls aloft, and steers   15
With bold and safe Attempt to the Celestial Land.

III

Whilst little Skiffs along the mortal Shores
    With humble Toyl in Order creep,
Coasting in sight of one anothers Oars,
    Nor venture thro' the boundless Deep.   20
    Such low pretending Souls are they
Who dwell inclos'd in solid Orbs of Skull;
    Plodding along their sober way,
The Snail o'ertakes them in their wildest Play,
While the poor Labourers sweat to be correctly dull.   25

IV

Give me the Chariot whose diviner Wheels
    Mark their own Rout, and unconfin'd
    Bound o'er the everlasting Hills,
And lose the Clouds below, and leave the Stars behind.
    Give me the Muse whose generous Force   30
      Impatient of the Reins
    Pursues an unattempted Course,
    Breaks all the Criticks Iron Chains,
And bears to Paradise the raptur'd Mind.

V

There *Milton* dwells: The Mortal sung   35
    Themes not presum'd by mortal Tongue;
    New Terrors and new Glories shine
In every Page, and flying Scenes Divine
Surprize the wond'ring Sense, & draw our Souls along.
    Behold his Muse sent out t'explore   40
The unapparent Deep where Waves of *Chaos* roar,
      And Realms of Night unknown before.
    She trac'd a glorious Path unknown,
Thro' Fields of heav'nly War, and Seraphs overthrown,
      Where his advent'rous Genius led: 45
Sovereign she fram'd a Model of her own,
    Nor thank'd the Living nor the Dead.
The noble Hater of degenerate Rhyme
Shook off the Chains, and built his Verse sublime,

---

13 *Empyreal* 'celestial'.
17 *Skiff* A small rowing boat.
21 *low pretending* 'unambitious'.
30 *generous* 'invigorating'.
32 *unattempted Course* Cf. 'Things unattempted yet in prose or rhyme' (*Paradise Lost*, 1:16).
41 *unapparent* 'invisible'.

44 A reference to the war in Heaven recounted in *Paradise Lost*, Book 6.
48–50 Milton's preface to the 1668 edition of *Paradise Lost* censures rhyming couplets and justifies blank verse – 'an example set, the first in *English*, of ancient liberty recovered to Heroic Poem from the troublesome and modern bondage of Rhyming'.

A Monument too high for coupled Sounds to climb.   50
   He mourn'd the Garden lost below;
   (Earth is the Scene for tuneful Woe)
    Now Bliss beats high in all his Veins,
    Now the lost *Eden* He regains,
Keeps his own Air, and triumphs in unrivall'd Strains.   55

VI

Immortal Bard! Thus thy own *Raphael* sings,
   And knows no Rule but native Fire:
All Heav'n sits silent while to his Sovereign Strings
   He talks unutterable Things;
With Graces Infinite his untaught Fingers rove   60
    Across the Golden Lyre:
    From every Note Devotion springs,
    Rapture and Harmony and Love
    O'erspread the list'ning Choir.

---

50 *coupled Sounds* i.e. rhyming couplets.
56 *Raphael* In *Paradise Lost* the angel sent by God to warn

Adam and Eve and to recount the war in Heaven and
Lucifer's fall.

Ambrose Philips (1674–1749)

Although Pope and Swift nicknamed Ambrose Philips 'Namby Pamby' on account of his saccharine verses to the children of the rich and powerful, both admired the poem that became known as the *Winter-Piece*. Philips, the fourth son of a draper from Shrewsbury, had already acquired a reputation as a poet when in 1705 he abandoned an academic career at Cambridge and entered the army. He fought in the Allied armies in Spain; on his return to England in 1707 he developed literary friendships with Addison, Steele and Swift. In 1709 six of his pastorals appeared in Tonson's *Miscellany* alongside four by Pope. The extravagant praise which the Whig wits lavished on Philips's pastorals, coupled with their neglect of Pope's, occasioned a notorious 'pastoral war'. Pope, Gay, Swift and other Tory wits ridiculed Philips (see Gay, *The Shepherd's Week*), though their hostility was as much political as literary, since Philips was an ardent Whig.

In January 1709 Philips had travelled to Copenhagen as secretary to Daniel Pulteney, the British envoy. A fortnight after his arrival, while Denmark was still in the grip of its worst frost for more than a century, he wrote to Swift that he was 'versifying in a sledge'. In April Philips sent the poem to Addison, who published it in *Tatler*, 12 (7 May 1709). Addison thought the original fifty-two-line version needed a conclusion. Philips rejected his suggestion of a 'moral topic' such as the difference between Danish and English manners. Instead he added the ten-line simile on Merlin which appeared in the 1710 reprinting of the *Tatler*. Ostensibly about the magical power of frost to change the landscape, this passage also allegorizes the transformative power of the poet's imagination. It accords with the self-reflexive character of the poem as a whole, which begins by asking questions about its own composition and ends by exposing the processes by which poetic illusions are created and shattered. *A Winter-Piece* anticipates a series of eighteenth-century poems featuring the poet/artist as enchanter. It also established a vogue for winter-pieces and is echoed in Thomson's *Winter*, Savage's *The Wanderer*, Cowper's *The Task* and Coleridge's *Frost at Midnight*.

The text given below is that of the 1710 duodecimo reprint of the *Tatler*. Substantive variants from the original 1709 *Tatler* folio are recorded in footnotes.

A Winter-Piece

An Epistle to the Earl of Dorset

Copenhagen, March 9, 1709.

From Frozen Climes, and endless Tracks of Snow,
From Streams that Northern Winds forbid to flow;
What Present shall the Muse to *Dorset* bring;
Or how, so near the Pole, attempt to sing?
The hoary Winter here conceals from Sight,   5
All pleasing Objects that to Verse invite.
The Hills and Dales, and the delightful Woods,
The Flowry Plains, and Silver Streaming Floods,
By Snow disguis'd, in bright Confusion lye,
And with one dazling Waste fatigue the Eye.   10
    No gentle breathing Breeze prepares the Spring,
No Birds within the Desart Region sing.
The Ships unmov'd the boist'rous Winds defie,
While rattling Chariots o'er the Ocean fly.
The vast *Leviathan* wants Room to play,   15

---

3 *Dorset* Philips's patron, Lionel Cranfield Sackville (1688–1765), seventh Earl and first Duke of Dorset, a staunch Whig and recent diplomat to Hanover.
7 *Dales* Vales (*1709*).
11 The ruling Cold retards the coming Spring (*1709*).
12 *Desart* 'barren'.
14 *Chariots* 'sleds'.
15 *Leviathan* Biblical name for a giant whale or sea monster.

And spout his Waters in the Face of Day.
The starving Wolves along the main Sea prowl,
And to the Moon in Icy Valleys howl.
For many a shining League the level Main
Here spreads it self into a Glassy Plain: 20
There solid Billows of enormous Size,
Alpes of green Ice, in wild Disorder rise.
   And yet but lately have I seen e'en here,
The Winter in a lovely Dress appear.
E'er yet the Clouds let fall the treasur'd Snow,   25
Or Winds begun thro' hazy Skies to blow,
At Ev'ning a keen Eastern Breeze arose;
And the descending Rain unsullied froze.
Soon as the silent Shades of Night withdrew,
The ruddy Morn disclos'd at once to View   30
The Face of Nature in a rich Disguise,
And brighten'd ev'ry Object to my Eyes:
For ev'ry Shrub, and ev'ry Blade of Grass,
And ev'ry pointed Thorn, seem'd wrought in Glass.
In Pearls and Rubies rich the Hawthorns show,   35
While through the Ice the Crimson Berries glow.
The thick-sprung Reeds the watry Marshes yield,
Seem polish'd Lances in a hostile Field.
The Stag in limpid Currents with Surprize,
Sees Chrystal Branches on his Forehead rise.   40
The spreading Oak, the Beech, and tow'ring Pine,
Glaz'd over, in the freezing Æther shine.
The frighted Birds the rattling Branches shun,
That wave and glitter in the distant Sun.
   When if a sudden Gust of Wind arise,   45
The brittle Forest into Atoms flies:
The crackling Wood beneath the Tempest bends,
And in a spangled Show'r the Prospect ends.
Or, if a Southern Gale the Region warm,
And by Degrees unbind the Wintry Charm,   50
The Traveller a miry Country sees,
And Journeys sad beneath the dropping Trees.
   Like some deluded Peasant, *Merlin* leads
Thro' fragrant Bow'rs and thro' delicious Meads;
While here inchanted Gardens to him rise,   55
And airy Fabricks there attract his Eyes,
His wand'ring Feet the Magick Paths pursue;
And while he thinks the fair Illusion true,
The trackless Scenes disperse in fluid Air,
And Woods, and Wilds, and thorny Ways appear: 60
A tedious Road the weary Wretch returns,
And, as He goes, the transient Vision mourns.

21 And there the Frozen Billows of enormous Size (*1709*).
26 Or stormy Winds thick hazy Weather blow (*1709*).
27 First, a keen Eastern Breeze at Ev'ning rose (*1709*).
37 *watry* slabby (*1709*).
42 *Æether* 'air'.
46 *Atoms* 'tiny particles'.
48 A spangled Show'r from every Tree descends (*1709*);

spangled 'glittering like sequins'.
53–62 These lines added in 1710.
53 *Merlin* The famously wilful magician of Arthurian
myth.
54 *Meads* 'meadows'.
56 *Fabricks* 'structures'.

Anne Finch (1661–1720)

Anne Finch, Countess of Winchilsea, lived much of her life in rural retirement beyond the sphere of politics and public affairs, but in her twenties she had been able to observe the drama of national events at close quarters during one of the most crucial periods of English history. What she saw left its mark on her poetry as much as nature did.

Anne Kingsmill, the third child of Sir William Kingsmill, was orphaned by the age of ten and brought up by relatives. In 1682 she became a Maid of Honour to Mary of Modena, the wife of James Stuart, Duke of York, and went to live at St James's Palace. It was there that she was wooed by Captain Heneage Finch (1657–1726), a Gentleman of the Bedchamber in the Duke's service, and the couple married in 1684. The following year, when James succeeded his brother Charles as King, the Finches became prominent members of the Court and might have looked for many years of favour and influence. But this was not to be. The political situation rapidly became unstable as James II began to impose his own Roman Catholicism on a Protestant nation and its institutions. In 1688, in a bloodless revolution, James was exiled to France, and his brother-in-law the Dutch William of Orange, a Protestant, was brought over as King William III, joint ruler with his wife Mary Stuart. An oath of allegiance was demanded, and those who refused to swear (the 'Nonjurors') were stripped of office and subject to fines or imprisonment. The Finches, both from Royalist Anglican families, remained loyal to James. Colonel Finch, as he now was, refused the oath, and he and his wife found themselves on the move, seeking refuge with various friends. In 1690 Finch's husband was arrested on a charge of Jacobitism (treasonably working to restore James), but after seven months the court case was abandoned. In comparison with this

drama, the remainder of her life was uneventful. The couple went to live at Eastwell Park in Kent, home of Colonel Finch's nephew, the young Earl of Winchilsea, and here Anne Finch lived for the rest of her life, delighting in her 'Arcadia' with its deerpark, fine old beeches and historic Elizabethan mansion (the beautiful grounds still survive). Colonel Finch took up antiquarian studies and actively encouraged his wife to write poetry. He proudly transcribed her verses and suggested subjects for her. Their childless marriage seems to have been a very happy one. The Stuart Queen Anne came to the throne in 1702 and Finch regained a place at Court as a Lady of the Bedchamber. In 1712, on the death of their nephew, she and her husband became the Fourth Earl and Countess of Winchilsea.

Finch's poetry circulated in manuscript, and 'Ardelia', as she called herself, was addressed in verse by Swift, Prior and Pope. Swift's *Apollo Outwitted* urged her to publish her poems. Some of them had found their way into the collections of the time, but it was not until 1713 that she brought out her own volume, *Miscellany Poems*, which included a heroic tragedy, *Aristomenes*. Lady Winchilsea wrote over 230 poems, many of which remained in manuscript. She was well represented in *Poems by Eminent Ladies* (1755), and by the nineteenth century, partly thanks to Wordsworth's praise, she had a secure reputation as a responsive observer of nature. But in recent years the full range and variety of her work has come to be more appreciated. The tensions and nuances in her verse are often working intelligently just beneath the surface, and in her hands wit unites verbal dexterity with imagination. Like Wyatt and Marvell, those other poets who had watched political manoeuvrings close at hand, Finch is acutely sensitive to ideas of integrity, alteration and deception.

The Spleen

On 26 August 1708 Lady Marow wrote to Lady Kay: 'I went to see Mrs. Fynch, she ill of the spleen. Lady Worsley has painted a pretty fire screen, and presented her with [it]; and, notwithstanding her ill-natured distemper, she was very diverting – Mrs. Fynch I mean' (*An English Letter Book*, ed. F. Bickley (1925), pp. 94–5). The illness of 'the Spleen', characterized by moodiness, irritability, depression and nightmares, was prevalent, even fashionable, at the beginning of the century, and Anne Finch was a notable sufferer. Its alternative name, 'the Vapours', linked it to the melancholy humour whose mists the organ of the spleen was meant to dispel. In the grip of 'the Spleen' imagination tended to function in

neurotic, unstable and self-deceiving ways, and Finch's lively diagnosis exploits these possibilities. Her poem became popular and helped establish the 'diverting' wit and creativity that went along with the other symptoms. Pope's Cave of Spleen (*The Rape of the Lock*, Canto IV) developed the humorous and grotesque aspects.

The poem was included in *A New Collection of Poems on Several Occasions*, ed. Charles Gildon (1701), pp. 60–70, and a revised text was separately published as *The Spleen, A Pindarique Ode. By a Lady. Together with A Prospect of Death: A Pindarique Essay* (London, 1709). (The second poem was by John Pomfret.) The version in Finch's *Miscellany Poems*

(1713), pp. 88–96, reverts to the *1701* text. The one given below is that of *1709*, whose readings suggest a power that is more furtive, contradictory, oppressive and internalized than the earlier version. Textual notes are given separately at the end.

What art thou, *Spleen*, which every thing dost ape?
    Thou *Proteus* to abuse Mankind,
    Who never yet thy hidden Cause cou'd find,
Or fix thee to remain in one continu'd Shape;
    Still varying thy perplexing Form,   5
    Now a dead Sea thoul't represent
    A Calm of stupid Discontent,
Then dashing on the Rocks wilt rage into a Storm:
Trembling sometimes thou dost appear,
    Dissolv'd into a panick Fear.   10
On Sleep intruding do'st thy Shadows spread,
    Thy gloomy Terrors round the silent Bed,
And crowd with boding Dreams the melancholy Head.
Or when the mid-night Hour is told,
And drooping Lids thou still do'st waking hold,   15
    Thy fond Delusions cheat the Eyes;
    Before 'em antick Spectres dance,
Unusual Fires their pointed Heads advance,
    And aiery Phantoms rise.
    Such was the monstrous Vision seen,   20
When *Brutus* (now beneath his Cares opprest,
And all *Rome*'s Fortunes rolling in his Breast,
    Before *Philippi*'s latest Field
Before his Fate did to *Octavius* yield)
    Was vanquish'd by the *Spleen*.   25

II
Falsly the mortal part we blame
Of our depress'd and pond'rous Frame,
Which till the first degrading Sin
Let thee its dull attendant in,
Still with the other did comply;   30
Nor clogg'd the active Soul, dispos'd to fly,
And range the Mansions of its native Sky:
    Nor whilst in his own Heaven he dwelt,
    Whilst Man his Paradise possest,
    His fertile Garden in the fragrant East,   35
    And all united Odours smelt,
    No pointed Sweets until thy Reign
    Cou'd shock the Sense, or in the face
A Flush, Unhandsome Colour place:
Now the *Jonquil* o'recomes the feeble Brain,   40

---

1 *ape* 'mimic'.

2 *Proteus* A minor sea-god in Homer's *Odyssey*, 4, who is able to assume different shapes in order to avoid answering questions.

20–5 Shakespeare, *Julius Caesar*, IV.iii, where on the eve of battle Brutus sees the ghost of the murdered Caesar.

26–32 The Spleen as a product of the Fall, when the body became mortal and grew separate from the soul.

30 *comply* 'act in accordance'.

37 *pointed Sweets* 'penetrating fragrances'.

40 *Jonquil* A sweetly scented narcissus.

We faint beneath the Aromatick pain,
Till some offensive scent thy Powers appease,
And Pleasure we resign for short and nauseous Ease.

III

New are thy Motions and thy Dress,
In every one thou dost possess: 45
Here some attentive secret Friend
Thy false Suggestions must attend,
Thy whisper'd Griefs, thy fancy'd Sorrows hear,
Breath'd in a Sigh, and witness'd by a Tear:
Whilst in the light and vulgar Crowd   50
Thy Slaves more clamorous and loud,
By laughter unprovok'd thy Influence too confess.
In the imperious *Wife* thou Vapours art,
Which from o'er-heated Passions rise
In clouds to the attractive Brain,   55
Until descending thence again
Thro' the o'er-cast and showring Eyes,
Upon the Husband's softned Heart,
He the disputed Point must yield,
Something resign of the contested Field;   60
'Till Lordly Man, born to Imperial Sway,
Compounds for Peace, to make his Right away
And Woman arm'd with *Spleen* do's servilely obey.

IV

The Fool, to imitate the Wits,
Complains of thy pretended Fits;   65
And Dulness, born with him would lay
Upon thy accidental Sway;
Because thou do'st sometimes presume
Into the ablest Heads to come,
That often Men of Thoughts refin'd,   70
Impatient of unequal Sense,
Such slow returns, where they so much dispense,
Retiring from the Crowd, are to thy Shades confin'd,
In me alas! thou dost too much prevail,
I feel thy force, while I against thee rail?   75
I feel my Verse decay, and my crampt Numbers fail.
Through thy black Jaundies I all Objects see,
As dark and terrible as thee;
My Lines decry'd, and my Imployment thought
An useless Folly, or presumptuous Fault;   80
While in the Muses Paths I stray.
While in their Groves, and by their Springs,

---

41 Cf. 'Die of a rose in aromatic pain' (Pope, *Essay on Man*, 1:200).

42 *offensive scent* Spirit of hartshorn, an ammonia solution used to alleviate headaches.

62 *make … away* 'legally transfer'.

66–7 *lay Upon* 'impute to'.

67 *accidental* 'occasional', 'not inherent'.

71 *unequal* 'insufficient'.

77–8 'Black Jaundice', a specific illness in which the spleen was implicated, is here a more general depressive melancholy. Jaundiced people reputedly had yellowed vision, and 'Black Jaundice' is here given an equivalent effect. Cf. the 'Black Melancholy' of Pope, *Eloisa to Abelard*, 165–70.

My Hand delights to trace unusual things,
And deviates from the known and common way
　　　　Nor will in fading Silks compose, 85
　　　　Faintly th'inimitable Rose:
Fill up an ill-drawn Bird, or paint on Glass
The Sovereigns blur'd and undistinguish'd Face,
The threatning Angel, and the speaking Ass.

V

　　　　Patron thou art of every gross abuse, 90
　　　　The sullen *Husband*'s feign'd excuse,
　　　　When the ill humour with his Wife he spends,
And bears recruited Wit and Spirits to his Friends.
　　　　The son of *Bacchus* pleads thy Power,
　　　　As to the Glass he still repairs, 95
　　　　Pretends but to remove thy Cares;
Snatcht from thy Shades one gay and smiling hour,
And drown thy Kingdom with a Purple Show'r.
　　　　When the Coquet whom every Fool admires,
　　　　Wou'd in variety be fair, 100
　　　　And shifting hastily the Scene,
　　　　From light impertinent and vain,
Assumes a soft and melancholy Air,
And of her Eyes rebates the wand'ring Fires,
The careless Posture, and the Head reclin'd; 105
　　　　The thoughtful and composed Face
Proclaiming the withdrawn and absent Mind,
　　　　Allows the Fop more liberty to gaze;
Who gently for the tender Cause enquires:
The Cause indeed is a defect in Sense; 110
But still the *Spleen*'s alledg'd, and still the dull Pretence.

VI

　　　　But these are thy fantastick Harms,
　　　　The tricks of thy pernicious Rage,
　　　　Which do the weaker sort engage;
Worse are the dire effects of thy more powerful Charms. 115
　　　　By thee Religion all we know
　　　　That should enlighten here below,
　　　　Is veil'd in darkness, and perplext
With anxious Doubts, with endless Scruples vext,
And some restraint imply'd from each perverted Text. 120
　　　　Whilst tast not, touch not what is freely given,
Is but the Niggard's Voice, disgracing bounteous Heaven.
　　　　From Speech restrain'd, by thy deceits abus'd,

85–9 Her art is not merely imitative, like silk embroideries, transparencies, etc.
89 Balaam's encounter with the angel who was seen only by his ass (Numbers, 22:21–35).
93 *recruited* 'freshly supplied'.
94 *Bacchus* Roman god of wine, often pictured holding purple grapes.
95 *still* 'continually'.
104 *rebates* 'reduces'.
112 *fantastick* 'fanciful'.
119 *Scruples* 'intellectual uncertainties'.
120–2 Religion that stresses niggardly restriction, rather than joy and generosity of spirit.
123 *abus'd* 'imposed on'.

To Desarts banish'd and in Cells reclus'd;
Mistaken Votaries to the Powers Divine,   125
While they a purer Sacrifice design
Do but the *Spleen* adore, and worship at thy Shrine.

VII
In vain to chase thee, every Art we try;
In vain all Remedies apply;
In vain the *Indian* Leaf infuse,   130
Or the pearch'd Eastern Berry bruise;
Some pass in vain those bounds, and nobler Liquors use.
Now Harmony in vain we bring,
Inspire the Flute, and touch the String;
From Harmony no help is had: 135
Musick but sooths thee, if too sweetly sad;
And if too light, but turns thee gladly mad.
Not skilful *Lower* thy Source cou'd find,
Or through the well–dissected Body trace
The secret and mysterious ways,   140
By which thou dost destroy and prey upon the Mind;
Tho' in the Search, too deep for Humane Thought,
With unsuccessful Toil he wrought,
'Till in pursuit of thee himself was by thee caught;
Retain'd thy Prisoner, thy acknowledg'd Slave,   145
And sunk beneath thy Weight to a lamented Grave.

124 *reclus'd* 'shut up'.
125 *Votaries* Those who have taken vows.
130 *Indian Leaf* Tea.
131 'grind the roasted coffee beans'.
134 *inspire* 'breathe into'.
138 *Lower* Richard Lower (1631–91), an outstanding
   physiologist and researcher in anatomy. He performed
   the first blood transfusion (with two dogs) in 1665.

TEXTUAL NOTES
   The main variants with *1701* are: 3 *hidden* (real *1701*);
37 *pointed* (arm'd *1701*); 44–5 (*lines reversed in 1701*);

46 (Now, in some Grove a list'ning friend, *1701*); **73**
confin'd (inclin'd *1701*); **74** *In* (O'er *1701*); **101** *shifting*
(changing *1701*); **127** *adore* (obey *1701*); **137** *gladly*
(gayly *1701*); **141** *destroy* (surprize *1701*); **146** *Weight*
(Chain *1701*). After **137** *1701* adds: 'Tho, the
Physicians greatest gains, / Although, his growing
wealth he sees / Daily encreas'd by Ladies Fees, / Yet
dost thou baffle all his studious pains'.
   Four changes have been made to the *1709* copytext:
8 *Then* (The *1709*); 29 *attendant in,* (attendant, in;
1709); 95 *to* (to to *1709*); 145 *acknowledg'd* (acknowledg
1709).

Upon the Hurricane

The Great Storm devastated Southern Britain during
the night of 26–7 November 1703, blowing down
houses, toppling steeples and causing huge losses at
sea. Eyewitness accounts were gathered by Daniel
Defoe in *The Storm: or, a Collection Of the most
Remarkable Casualties and Disasters, Which happen'd in
the Late Dreadful Tempest* (London, 1704). The
experience offered Finch a very different Nature from
that normally associated with her (most notably in *A
Nocturnal Rêverie*), and in this ode she is engaging
large forces and public issues. Her 'Great Disposer'
remains inscrutable, and her gestures towards reading
the hurricane as a punishment for the nation's bad
faith are countered by a sense that her world has
glimpsed an elemental chaos outside history. But she
is also fascinated by the play of forces itself and what

it means in society, politics and religion: the mingling
and dispersing, confining and releasing, joining and
severing. What happens when the fabric holding
everything in place is shaken?

The poem existed in manuscript in the summer of
1704, when Finch gave Elizabeth Rowe a copy. It was
printed in *Miscellany Poems* (1713), pp. 230–47, the
text given here, where it is immediately followed by a
paraphrase of Psalm 148. We have made a few slight
adjustments to the layout of the original, which is
occasionally inconsistent in indentation.

   The full title is: '*A Pindarick Poem Upon the
Hurricane in* November 1703, *referring to this Text in*
Psalm 148. ver. 8. Winds and Storms fulfilling his
Word'.

You have obey'd, you WINDS, that must fulfill
    The Great Disposer's righteous Will;
Throughout the Land, unlimited you flew,
Nor sought, as heretofore, with Friendly Aid
    Only, new Motion to bestow   5
Upon the sluggish Vapours, bred below,
Condensing into Mists, and melancholy Shade.
No more such gentle Methods you pursue,
But marching now in terrible Array,
    Undistinguish'd was your Prey: 10
    In vain the *Shrubs*, with lowly Bent,
    Sought their Destruction to prevent;
    The *Beech* in vain, with out-stretch'd Arms,
    Deprecates th'approaching Harms;
    In vain the *Oak* (so often storm'd)   15
    Rely'd upon that native Force,
    By which already was perform'd
    So much of his appointed Course,
    As made him, fearless of Decay,
    Wait but the accomplish'd Time   20
    Of his long-wish'd and useful Prime,
To be remov'd, with Honour, to the Sea.
    The strait and ornamental *Pine*
    Did in the like Ambition joyn,
    And thought his Fame shou'd ever last,   25
When in some Royal Ship he stood the planted Mast;
    And shou'd again his Length of Timber rear,
    And new engrafted Branches wear
    Of fibrous Cordage and impending Shrouds,
Still trimm'd with human Care, and water'd by the Clouds.   30
    But oh, you *Trees!* who solitary stood;
    Or you, whose Numbers form'd a Wood;
    You, who on Mountains chose to rise,
    And drew them nearer to the Skies;
    Or you, whom Valleys late did hold   35
    In flexible and lighter Mould;
You num'rous Brethren of the Leafy Kind,
    To whatsoever Use design'd,
    Now, vain you found it to contend
With not, alas! one Element your Friend;   40
Your Mother Earth, thro' long preceding Rains,
    (Which undermining sink below)
    No more her wonted Strength retains;
Nor you so fix'd within her Bosom grow,
That for your sakes she can resolve to bear   45
    These furious Shocks of hurrying Air;
But finding All your Ruin did conspire,

Title Cf. 'Fire, and hails; snow, and vapours; stormy wind
    fulfilling his word' (Psalms, 148:8).
1–2 These lines become a refrain. Cf. 187–8, 243–4.
10 *Undistinguish'd* i.e. no distinction was made.
16 *Force* 'strength'.

22 To become ships. Cf. Pope, *Windsor-Forest*, 383–4.
29 *Cordage* Ropes in the rigging; *Shrouds* Ropes
    supporting the mast.
40 *Element your Friend;* Element; your Friend (*1713*).
47 *All* 'everything'.

She soon her beauteous Progeny resign'd
To this destructive, this imperious Wind,
That check'd your nobler Aims, and gives you to the Fire.   50

Thus! have thy Cedars, *Libanus*, been struck
   As the lythe Oziers twisted round;
Thus! *Cadez*, has thy Wilderness been shook,
When the appalling, and tremendous Sound
   Of rattl'ing Tempests o'er you broke,   55
   And made your stubborn Glories bow,
When in such Whirlwinds the *Almighty* spoke,
Warning *Judea* then, as our *Britannia* now.
   Yet these were the remoter Harms,
Foreign the Care, and distant the Alarms: 60
   Whilst but sheltring Trees alone,
   Master'd soon, and soon o'erthrown,
   Felt those Gusts, which since prevail,
   And loftier Palaces assail;
   Whose shaken Turrets now give way,   65
With vain Inscriptions, which the Freeze has borne
Through Ages past, t'extol and to adorn,
   And to our latter Times convey
Who did the Structures deep Foundation lay,
   Forcing his Praise upon the gazing Croud,   70
   And, whilst he moulders in a scanty Shroud,
Telling both Earth and Skies, he when alive was proud.
   Now down at once comes the superfluous Load,
      The costly Fret-work with it yields,
   Whose imitated Fruits and Flow'rs are strew'd,   75
Like those of real Growth o'er the Autumnal Fields.
      The present Owner lifts his Eyes,
   And the swift Change with sad Affrightment spies:
   The Cieling gone, that late the Roof conceal'd;
   The Roof untyl'd, thro' which the Heav'ns reveal'd,   80
Exposes now his Head, when all Defence has fail'd.

      What alas, is to be done!
   Those, who in Cities wou'd from Dangers run,
      Do but encreasing Dangers meet,
And Death, in various shapes, attending in the Street;   85
      Where some, too tardy in their Flight,
      O'ertaken by a worse Mischance,
      Their upward Parts do scarce advance,
When on their following Limbs th'extending Ruins light.
   One half's interr'd, the other yet survives,   90
   And for Release with fainting Vigour strives;

51–8 'The voice of the Lord breaketh the cedars; yea, the Lord breaketh the cedars of Lebanon … The voice of the Lord shaketh the wilderness; the Lord shaketh the wilderness of Kadesh' (Psalm 29:5–8).

52 *Oziers* Pliant willows used in basket-weaving. (In *The Storm* several reports speak of large trees turned around.)

66 *Freeze* Classical frieze, here carrying a commemorative inscription.

68 *convey* convey; (*1713*).

74 *Fret-work* Decorative work in wood or plaster.

91 *fainting* 'weakening'.

Implores the Aid of absent Friends in vain;
With fault'ring Speech, and dying Wishes calls
Those, whom perhaps, their own Domestick Walls
By parallel Distress, or swifter Death retains. 95

O *Wells!* thy Bishop's Mansion we lament,
So tragical the Fall, so dire th'Event!
    But let no daring Thought presume
    To point a Cause for that oppressive Doom.
Yet strictly pious KEN! had'st Thou been there, 100
This Fate, we think, had not become thy share;
        Nor had that awful Fabrick bow'd,
        Sliding from its loosen'd Bands;
        Nor yielding Timbers been allow'd
        To crush thy ever-lifted Hands, 105
        Or interrupt thy Pray'r.
Those Orizons, that nightly Watches keep,
Had call'd thee from thy Bed, or there secur'd thy Sleep.
    Whilst you, bold Winds and Storms! his Word obey'd,
    Whilst you his Scourge the Great *Jehova* made, 110
And into ruin'd Heaps our Edifices laid.
    You *South* and *West* the Tragedy began,
As, with disorder'd haste, you o'er the Surface ran;
        Forgetting, that you were design'd
        (Chiefly thou *Zephyrus*, thou softest Wind!) 115
    Only our Heats, when sultry, to allay,
And chase the od'rous Gums by your dispersing Play.
        Now, by new Orders and Decrees,
        For our Chastisement issu'd forth,
    You on his Confines the alarmed *North* 120
            With equal Fury sees,
        And summons swiftly to his Aid
        Eurus, his Confederate made,
    His eager Second in th'opposing Fight,
    That even the Winds may keep the Balance right, 125
Nor yield increase of Sway to arbitrary Might.
        Meeting now, they all contend,
        Those assail, while These defend;
        Fierce and turbulent the War,
        And in the loud tumultuous Jar 130
        Winds their own Fifes, and Clarions are.
    Each Cavity, which Art or Nature leaves,
    Their Inspiration hastily receives;

96–108 The Bishop of Bath and Wells and his wife were killed in their palace by two chimney-stacks falling through their bedroom. Richard Kidder (1633–1703) had supplanted the popular Bishop Thomas Ken (1637–1711) in 1691, when the latter was deprived of his see as a Nonjuror (i.e. refusing to swear the oath of allegiance to William and Mary). Ken was noted for his charity and spirituality. Finch was not alone in seeing this as God's judgement (see *The Storm*, p. 271).

97 *dire th'Event* 'Too well I see and rue the dire event' (*Paradise Lost*, 1:134). Cf. Pope, *The Rape of the Lock*, 2:141.

112–26 In this passage on the four winds Finch may be hinting at the political manoeuvrings following the accession of Queen Anne in 1702. Her husband's cousin, Daniel Finch, Earl of Nottingham (later sixth Earl of Winchilsea), was forced to resign as Secretary of State in 1704.

115 *Zephyrus* The west wind.

117 *Gums* 'mists'.

120 *North* The north wind, known as Boreas.

123 *Eurus* The east wind.

133 *Inspiration* Literally, 'breathing in'.

Whence, from their various Forms and Size,
As various Symphonies arise,   135
Their Trumpet ev'ry hollow Tube is made,
And, when more solid Bodies they invade,
Enrag'd, they can no farther come,
The beaten Flatt, whilst it repels the Noise,
Resembles but with more outrageous Voice   140
The Soldier's threatning Drum:
And when they compass thus our World around,
When they our Rocks and Mountains rend,
When they our Sacred Piles to their Foundations send,
No wonder if our ecchoing Caves rebound;   145
No wonder if our list'ning Sense they wound,
When arm'd with so much Force, and usher'd with such Sound.
Nor scarce, amidst the Terrors of that Night,
When you, fierce Winds, such Desolations wrought,
When you from out his Stores the Great Commander brought,   150
Cou'd the most Righteous stand upright;
Scarcely the Holiest Man performs
The Service, that becomes it best,
By ardent Vows, or solemn Pray'rs addrest;
Nor finds the Calm, so usual to his Breast,   155
Full Proof against such Storms.
How shou'd the Guilty then be found,
The Men in Wine, or looser Pleasures drown'd,
To fix a stedfast Hope, or to maintain their Ground!
When at his Glass the late Companion feels,   160
That Giddy, like himself, the tott'ring Mansion reels!
The Miser, who with many a Chest
His gloomy Tenement opprest,
Now fears the over-burthen'd Floor,
And trembles for his Life, but for his Treasure more.   165
What shall he do, or to what Pow'rs apply?
To those, which threaten from on High,
By him ne'er call'd upon before,
Who also will suggest th'impossible Restore?
No; *Mammon*, to thy Laws he will be true,   170
And, rather than his Wealth, will bid the World adieu.
The Rafters sink, and bury'd with his Coin
That Fate does with his living Thoughts combine;
For still his Heart's inclos'd within a Golden Mine.

Contention with its angry Brawls   175
By Storms o'er-clamour'd, shrinks and falls;
Nor WHIG, nor TORY now the rash Contender calls.
Those, who but Vanity allow'd,
Nor thought, it reach'd the Name of Sin,
To be of their Perfections proud,   180
Too much adorn'd without, or too much rais'd within,
Now find, that even the lightest Things,

---

139 *Flatt* 'flat surface'.
151 'But who may abide the day of his coming? and who
    shall stand when he appeareth?' (Malachi, 3:2).
170 *Mammon* Worldly riches, memorably personified in

Paradise Lost, 1:679–88. 'Ye cannot serve God and
    mammon' (Matthew, 6:24).
182–3 Airy frivolities.

As the minuter parts of Air,
When Number to their Weight addition brings,
Can, like the small, but numerous Insects Stings,   185
Can, like th'assembl'd Winds, urge Ruin and Despair.

Thus You've obey'd, you Winds, that must fulfill
The Great disposer's Righteous Will:
Thus did your Breath a strict Enquiry make,
Thus did you our most secret Sins awake,   190
And thus chastis'd their Ill.

Whilst vainly Those, of a rapacious Mind,
Fields to other Fields had laid,
By Force, or by injurious Bargains join'd,
With Fences for their Guard impenetrable made;   195
The juster Tempest mocks the wrong,
And sweeps, in its directed Flight,
Th'Inclosures of another's Right,
Driving at once the Bounds, and licens'd Herds along.
The Earth agen one general Scene appears;   200
No regular distinction now,
Betwixt the Grounds for Pasture, or the Plough,
The Face of Nature wears.

Free as the Men, who wild Confusion love,
And lawless Liberty approve,   205
Their Fellow-Brutes pursue their way,
To their own Loss, and disadvantage stray,
As wretched in their Choice, as unadvis'd as They.
The tim'rous *Deer*, whilst he forsakes the Park,
And wanders on, in the misguiding Dark,   210
Believes, a Foe from ev'ry unknown Bush
Will on his trembling Body rush,
Taking the Winds, that vary in their Notes,
For hot pursuing Hounds with deeply bellowing Throats.

Th'awaken'd *Birds*, shook from their nightly Seats,   215
Their unavailing Pinions ply,
Repuls'd, as they attempt to fly
In hopes they might attain to more secure Retreats.
But, Where ye wilder'd Fowls wou'd You repair?
When this your happy Portion given,   220
Your upward Lot, your Firmament of Heaven,
Your unentail'd, your undivided Air,
Where no Proprietor was ever known,
Where no litigious Suits have ever grown,

---

191 *Ill* 'Evil'.

192–203 The move from open-field farming to enclosed fields was resulting in larger farms and the extinction of common rights. The enclosure movement accelerated after 1740 through parliamentary legislation.

199 *licens'd* 'allowed to roam'.

219 *wilder'd* 'bewildered'.

222 *unentail'd* 'without legal restrictions', unlike the enclosed land (192–5).

Whilst none from Star to Star cou'd call the space his Own;   225
    When this no more your middle Flights can bear,
    But some rough Blast too far above conveighs,
Or to unquitted Earth confines your weak Essays.
    Nor You, nor wiser Man cou'd find Repose,
        Nor cou'd our Industry produce   230
        Expedients of the smallest Use,
To ward our greater Cares, or mitigate your Woes.

      Ye *Clouds!* that pity'd our Distress,
      And by your pacifying Showers
    (The soft and usual methods of Success)   235
Kindly assay'd to make this Tempest less;
Vainly your Aid was now alas! employ'd,
In vain you wept o'er those destructive Hours,
In which the Winds full Tyranny enjoy'd,
      Nor wou'd allow you to prevail,   240
But drove your scorn'd, and scatter'd Tears to wail
      The Land that lay destroy'd.

Whilst You obey'd, you Winds! that must fulfill
    The just Disposer's Righteous Will;
    Whilst not the Earth alone, you disarray,   245
But to more ruin'd Seas wing'd your impetuous Way.

Which to foreshew, the still portentous *Sun*
Beamless, and pale of late, his Race begun,
Quenching the Rays, he had no Joy to keep,
In the obscure, and sadly threaten'd Deep.   250
Farther than we, that Eye of Heaven discerns,
And nearer plac'd to our malignant Stars,
Our brooding Tempests, and approaching Wars
      Anticipating learns.
    When now, too soon the dark Event   255
    Shews what that faded Planet meant;
Whilst more the liquid Empire undergoes,
More she resigns of her entrusted Stores,
The Wealth, the Strength, the Pride of diff'rent Shores
In one Devoted, one Recorded Night,   260
Than Years had known destroy'd by generous Fight,
      Or Privateering Foes.
    All Rules of Conduct laid aside,
    No more the baffl'd *Pilot* steers,

228 *Essays* 'attempts' (at flight).

232 *ward* 'avert'.

233 'We had a great Shower of Rain in the midd'st of the Storm' (Finch's note).

247 'The Ancients look'd upon the Sun (or Phoebus) as Prophetick' (Finch's note).

248 'One Day of the Summer before the Storm, we had an unusual Appearance of the Sun (which was observ'd by many People in several Parts of *Kent*). It was of a pale dead Colour, without any Beams or Brightness for some Hours in the Morning, altho' obstructed by no Clouds; for the Sky was clear' (Finch's note).

253 The European War of the Spanish Succession had recently begun, ended by the Treaty of Utrecht, 1713. England had declared war on France 4 May 1702.

257 *liquid Empire* The ocean.

260 *Devoted* 'doomed'; *Recorded* 'memorable' (literally, 'put on record').

Or knows an Art, when it each moment veers, 265
To vary with the Winds, or stem th'unusual Tide.
Dispers'd and loose, the shatter'd Vessels stray,
Some perish within sight of Shore,
Some, happier thought, obtain a wider Sea,
But never to return, or cast an Anchor more! 270
Some on the *Northern* Coasts are thrown,
And by congealing Surges compass'd round,
To fixt and certain Ruin bound,
Immoveable are grown:
The fatal *Goodwin* swallows All that come 275
Within the Limits of that dangerous Sand,
Amphibious in its kind, nor Sea nor Land;
Yet kin to both, a false and faithless Strand,
Known only to our Cost for a devouring Tomb.
Nor seem'd the HURRICANE content, 280
Whilst only Ships were wreckt, and Tackle rent;
The Sailors too must fall a Prey,
Those that Command, with those that did Obey;
The best Supporters of thy pompous Stile,
Thou far Renown'd, thou pow'rful BRITISH Isle! 285
Foremost in Naval Strength, and Sov'reign of the Sea!
These from thy Aid that wrathful Night divides,
Plung'd in those Waves, o'er which this Title rides.
What art thou, envy'd *Greatness*, at the best,
In thy deluding Splendors drest? 290
What are thy glorious Titles, and thy Forms?
Which cannot give Security, or Rest
To favour'd Men, or Kingdoms that contest
With popular Assaults, or Providential Storms!
Whilst on th'Omnipotent our Fate depends, 295
And They are only safe, whom He alone defends.
Then let to Heaven our general Praise be sent,
Which did our farther Loss, our total Wreck prevent.
And as our Aspirations do ascend,
Let every Thing be summon'd to attend; 300
And let the Poet *after God's own Heart*
Direct our Skill in that sublimer part,
And our weak Numbers mend!

272 *congealing* 'freezing'.
275 *Goodwin* The notorious Goodwin Sands at the entrance
to the Straits of Dover claimed thirteen ships of war
during the storm.
282 Fifteen hundred men were lost at sea. Defoe reckoned
eight thousand (*The Storm*, p. 156).

284 *Supporters* 'maintainers'; *Stile* 'official title' (to her
dominions, etc.). Cf. 288, **291**.
291 *Forms* 'ceremonies'.
301 *Poet after God's own Heart* An allusion to King David,
the original psalmist. Cf. 'I have found David … a man
after mine own heart, which shall fulfil all my will'
(Acts, 13:22)

A Nocturnal Rêverie

Finch's most frequently anthologized poem was a
favourite of Wordsworth, but in anthologizing it
himself he removed lines 17–20, perhaps because they
intruded on the natural description he so admired.
The single unfolding sentence that forms the poem
has a subtle variety of mood and tone. Parnell's *A
Night-Piece on Death* offers an interesting comparison
as a nocturnal meditation. Text from *Miscellany Poems*
(1713), pp. 291–3.

In such a *Night*, when every louder Wind
Is to its distant Cavern safe confin'd;
And only gentle *Zephyr* fans his Wings,
And lonely *Philomel*, still waking, sings;
Or from some Tree, fam'd for the *Owl*'s delight,   5
She, hollowing clear, directs the Wand'rer right:
In such a *Night*, when passing Clouds give place,
Or thinly vail the Heav'ns mysterious Face;
When in some River, overhung with Green,
The waving Moon and trembling Leaves are seen;   10
When freshen'd Grass now bears it self upright,
And makes cool Banks to pleasing Rest invite,
Whence springs the *Woodbind*, and the *Bramble*-Rose,
And where the sleepy *Cowslip* shelter'd grows;
Whilst now a paler Hue the *Foxglove* takes,   15
Yet checquers still with Red the dusky brakes:
When scatter'd *Glow-worms*, but in Twilight fine,
Shew trivial Beauties watch their Hour to shine;
Whilst *Salisb'ry* stands the Test of every Light,
In perfect Charms, and perfect Virtue bright: 20
When Odours, which declin'd repelling Day,
Thro' temp'rate Air uninterrupted stray;
When darken'd Groves their softest Shadows wear,
And falling Waters we distinctly hear;
When thro' the Gloom more venerable shows   25
Some ancient Fabrick, awful in Repose,
While Sunburnt Hills their swarthy Looks conceal,
And swelling Haycocks thicken up the Vale:
When the loos'd *Horse* now, as his Pasture leads,
Comes slowly grazing thro' th'adjoining Meads,   30
Whose stealing Pace, and lengthen'd Shade we fear,
Till torn up Forage in his Teeth we hear:
When nibbling *Sheep* at large pursue their Food,
And unmolested Kine rechew the Cud;
When *Curlews* cry beneath the Village-walls,   35
And to her straggling Brood the *Partridge* calls;
Their shortliv'd Jubilee the Creatures keep,
Which but endures, whilst Tyrant-*Man* do's sleep:
When a sedate Content the Spirit feels,
And no fierce Light disturbs, whilst it reveals;   40
But silent Musings urge the Mind to seek
Something, too high for Syllables to speak;
Till the free Soul to a compos'dness charm'd,
Finding the Elements of Rage disarm'd,

---

1 The refrain 'In such a night …' opens Act V of
Shakespeare's *The Merchant of Venice*.
2 Aeolus, ruler of the winds, kept them imprisoned in a
cave (Virgil, *Aeneid*, 1).
4 *Philomel* The nightingale.
13 *Woodbind* Any climbing plant: ivy, convolvulus or
honeysuckle; *Bramble-Rose* white trailing dog-rose.

19 *Salisb'ry* Finch's close friend, Anne Tufton
(1693–1757), married James Cecil, fifth Earl of
Salisbury, in 1709.
34 *Kine* 'cows'.
37 *Jubilee* A period of remission or release.

O'er all below a solemn Quiet grown,   45
Joys in th'inferiour World, and thinks it like her Own:
In such a *Night* let Me abroad remain,
Till Morning breaks, and All's confus'd again;
Our Cares, our Toils, our Clamours are renew'd,
Or Pleasures, seldom reach'd, again pursu'd.   50

To the Nightingale

The poem makes an interesting contrast with Keats's famous ode of 1819. Less confident of the 'viewless wings of Poesy', Finch perhaps sees the poet as more limited, and transcendence (33) more of a problem?

The relationship between words and sounds, brain and sense, is at the heart of the matter. Text from *Miscellany Poems* (1713), pp. 200–2.

Exert thy Voice, sweet Harbinger of Spring!
    This Moment is thy Time to Sing,
    This Moment I attend to Praise,
And set my Numbers to thy Layes.
    Free as thine shall be my Song;   5
    As thy Musick, short, or long.
Poets, wild as thee, were born,
    Pleasing best when unconfin'd,
    When to Please is least design'd,
Soothing but their Cares to rest;   10
    Cares do still their Thoughts molest,
    And still th'unhappy Poet's Breast,
Like thine, when best he sings, is plac'd against a Thorn.

She begins, Let all be still!
    Muse, thy Promise now fulfill!   15
Sweet, oh! sweet, still sweeter yet
Can thy Words such Accents fit,
Canst thou Syllables refine,
Melt a Sense that shall retain
Still some Spirit of the Brain,   20
Till with Sounds like these it join.
    'Twill not be! then change thy Note;
    Let Division shake thy Throat.
Hark! Division now she tries;
    Yet as far the Muse outflies.   25
    Cease then, prithee, cease thy Tune;
    Trifler, wilt thou sing till *June*?
Till thy Bus'ness all lies waste,
And the Time of Building's past!
    Thus we Poets that have Speech,   30
Unlike what thy Forests teach,
    If a fluent Vein be shown
    That's transcendent to our own,
Criticize, reform, or preach,
Or censure what we cannot reach.   35

15 The promise of lines 4–5.
16–21 Here punctuated as in *1713*. Editors turn this sentence into a direct question by supplying an exclamation mark after *yet* (16) and a question mark after *join* (21).

17 *Accents* 'expressive tones'.
19 *Melt* 'make tender'.
23 *Division* Fluid embellishment of a simple melody.

A Sigh

This deceptively simple lyric touches on some of the concerns of *To the Nightingale*: the relationship between thought and feeling, word and sound. It was already circulating by 1703 and was included in the anonymous *Poems on Several Occasions: Together with Some Odes* (1703), Delarivière Manley's *Court* *Intrigues, in a Collection of Original Letters, from the Island of the New Atalantis* (1711), and Richard Steele's *Poetical Miscellanies* (1714), pp. 45–6 (from which the text below is taken). It was omitted from *Miscellany Poems* (1713).

Gentle Air, thou Breath of Lovers,
    Vapour from a secret Fire,
Which by Thee it self discovers,
    Ere yet daring to Aspire.

Softest Note of whisper'd Anguish,   5
    Harmony's refined Part,
Striking, while thou seem'st to Languish,
    Full upon the Listner's Heart.

Safest Messenger of Passion,
    Stealing thro' a Crowd of Spies;   10
Who constrain the outward Fashion,
    Close the Lips, and watch the Eyes.

Shapeless Sigh! we ne'er can show thee,
    Fram'd but to assault the Ear:
Yet, ere to their Cost they know thee,   15
    Every Nymph may read thee — Here.

3 *discovers* The older meaning of 'reveals' is also present.   4 *Aspire* A play on 'breathe upon' (Lat. *adspiro*).

The Agreeable

In *Spectator*, 511 (1712) Addison gives three categories of women: *Beauties*, *Agreeables* and the *Ugly*. Finch's poem on the mystery of the 'Agreeable' locates this woman's power outside the traditional language of beauty. It provides an interesting gloss on Pope's *The Rape of the Lock* and *Epistle to a Lady*. The unique text is that in the Wellesley College Manuscript, given here. It is unpunctuated throughout: all punctuation is here supplied by the editors.

She is not fair, you cricticks of the Town
That court her smiles and tremble at her frown;
She is not fair, and tho' I burn like you
I to my better judgement will be true;
Nor cou'd a Painter borrow from her face   5
One line that might his fancied Venus grace;
No feature which might countenance the rest
Is perfect or superlative confest,
Nor is the vail by nature o'er 'em drawn
A milky white or more transparent Lawn;   10
Nor softer olive nor enlivening red
Is with due mixture or distinction spread.
Whence then without a charm that we can tell
Does all that's charming in Valleria dwell?

10 *Lawn* Fine linen.

What is th'agreeable with which she kills,   15
And wanting all, all Beauty's part fulfills?
That whenso'er she speaks, or looks, or moves,
Th'observer listens, sighs, admires, and loves,
And wonders at the unexpected smart,
Who sees no quiver tho' he feels the dart.   20
What is this power which we can n'er discry,
That nicely shuns not an illcouler'd eye
Nor does from disproportion fly?
What is this charm but somthing from the Soul
Which warms us whilst it shines, and influences the whole;   25
That mocks description, which can ne'er advance
Her all subduing mind drest à la negligence.

22 *nicely* 'fastidiously'.
26 *advance* 'praise excessively'.
27 *Her* MS has 'Their'; *à la negligence* 'The Fashionable

World is grown free and easie; our Manners, sit more
loose upon us: Nothing is so modish as an agreeable
Negligence' (Addison, *Spectator*, 119).

John Gay (1685–1732)

John Gay, like the shoe-shine boy in his poem *Trivia*, was an orphan. His mother died when he was nine, his father, by an ironic stroke of fate, on his tenth birthday. Previous generations of this once prosperous merchant family from Barnstaple in rural Devon had enjoyed an Oxford education, but at seventeen Gay was apprenticed to a London silk-mercer. If he found selling clothes to women demeaning (he returned home after two years), this early immersion in London commercial culture shaped both his literary imagination and his deferential social manner. Aaron Hill, his former school-fellow, provided Gay with hack-work answering readers' queries for his journal *The British Apollo* while he tried to make his way in the capital's literary scene. After publication of his poem *Wine* (1708), a comic spin-off from John Philips's *Cyder*, he entered Pope's literary circle, later becoming secretary of the Scriblerus Club and one of Pope's aides-de-camp in his war with the Whig wits. He also embarked on what became a perpetual quest for literary patronage. If his first post as secretary and domestic steward to the flamboyant sixty-one-year-old Duchess of Monmouth occasionally required him to don her silver and blue livery, it also gave him time to write *Rural Sports* (1713) and *The Shepherd's Week* (1714).

At the start of 1714 Gay became secretary to Lord Clarendon, Ambassador to the Court of Hanover. He tried hard to ingratiate himself with Britain's future royal family (the Elector became George I after Queen Anne's death in August), but the new Hanoverian regime failed to reward him, perhaps uneasy about *The Shepherd's Week*'s dedication to the now Jacobite Bolingbroke. As Gay watched other writers gain sinecures, in February 1715 he staged a highly successful one-act play, *The What D'Ye Call It*, a 'Tragi-Comi-Pastoral Farce' whose hybrid nature paved the way for *The Beggar's Opera*. *Trivia: Or, the Art of Walking the Streets of London* (1716) marked the culmination of the Scriblerians' shorter experiments in urban pastorals and georgics. The next year Gay collaborated with Swift and Pope on *Three Hours After Marriage*, a burlesque play satirizing Pope's enemies Colley Cibber and John Dennis. In the play's successful aftermath Gay lost no time in cultivating rising Whig politicians, notably William Pulteney, a close associate and future opponent of Robert Walpole, whom he accompanied on a continental tour.

Gay's *Poems on Several Occasions* (1720), a lucrative subscription edition listing 364 important names, marked a new high in his literary career. He invested £1,000 in South Sea stock, but his fantasy of becoming a landowner and MP in his native Devon collapsed, like thousands of other fantasies, when the South Sea Bubble burst.

In 1723 one of Gay's most distinguished patrons, the Earl of Burlington, secured him the sinecure of Commissioner of the Lotteries. He made a last futile bid for royal favour with his *Fables* (1727), a book of animal fables inscribed to the infant Prince William. The Court's response – the offer of the post of Gentleman Usher to the two-year-old Princess Louisa – outraged Pope and his friends, who applauded Gay's dignified refusal. But it was in the theatre that Gay's greatest success at last came. *The Beggar's Opera* (1728), a burlesque of popular Italian opera and a double-edged satire on the 'great men' who operated the racket of Whig power-politics, proved a phenomenal success, creating a ballad-opera craze and a new theatre-going audience. It also won Gay his independence. Its sequel, *Polly*, was banned prior to production, but a printed subscription edition probably earned Gay more than a staging of the play would have done. In his last years he went on to produce some less distinguished dramatic works plus a second series of *Fables*.

Gay, a short, pudgy man who had suffered intestinal problems all his life, died in 1732. Pope's epitaph on his friend's tomb in Westminster Abbey suggests a creature of paradox: 'Of Manners gentle, of Affections mild; / In Wit, a Man; Simplicity, a Child; / With native Humour temp'ring virtuous Rage, / Form'd to delight at once and lash the age'. David Nokes's biography (Oxford, 1995) has noted other self-contradictions: the rakish 'ladies-man' who never enjoyed intimacy with a woman, the opportunistic quester after patronage whose poems praised independence, the man who died worth more than £6,000 but never owned his own home. The ambiguities extend to his writing. Gay's characteristic work is a generic hybrid, a literary burlesque mingling high and low, classical and demotic idioms. In particular, it is Gay's enthusiastic recuperation of vernacular 'low' culture (folk-songs and ballads, urban pastimes, country superstitions) which makes for part of his enduring appeal.

The Shepherd's Week

The Shepherd's Week is the offspring of a literary dispute in the *Guardian* during 1713. Pope, annoyed by a series of Whig-directed essays praising Ambrose Philips's pastorals and slighting his own, took revenge in an anonymous follow-up article ironically praising Philips's 'beauties' (i.e. his clumsiest passages of rustic dialect). The incensed Philips is said to have hung up a rod in Button's coffee-house ready to use on Pope's back. Gay's ambivalent response was *The Shepherd's Week*. Its mock-archaic 'Proeme to the Courteous Reader' parodies Philips's preface, yet its criticism of pastoral poetry's obsession with a 'Golden Age' reflects awkwardly on Pope's own idealized neoclassical pastorals of 1711. *The Shepherd's Week* burlesques pastoral convention by comically mingling its various elements. In this poem Spenserian swains with rustic names discuss topics familiar from Theocritus's idylls as adapted by Virgil – the singing contest, the song of the forsaken maid, the lament for a dead friend. Yet their seriousness is in various ways undermined. The twelve months of Spenser's *Shepheardes Calendar* are bathetically contracted to the six working days (no Sunday in Christian England), and the critical apparatus of footnotes, prefatory material, scholarly glosses and alphabetical index (a familiar ploy of Scriblerian mock-pedantry) parodies the textual apparatus of Spenser's poem. Yet in demolishing pastoral conventions Gay was paving the way for a new poetry of rural realism, and eventually for the angry anti-arcadianism of Crabbe's *The Village* (1783). Gay's rustics survive their comic debunking with their dignity intact. *Friday; or, The Dirge*, a version of Virgil's lament for the dead Daphnis (Eclogue 5), exemplifies Gay's ability movingly to recreate the homely details of English rural life, its rituals and its folklore. Passages in *The Shepherd's Week* prefigure the writings of such labourer poets as Stephen Duck and Mary Collier. The text is that of the first, Ferd. Burleigh, edition of the poem of 1714. Gay's citations in Latin and Greek are here translated.

Friday; or, The Dirge
BUMKINET. GRUBBINOL.

BUMKINET.

WHY, *Grubbinol*, dost thou so wistful seem?
There's Sorrow in thy Look, if right I deem.
'Tis true, yon Oaks with yellow Tops appear,
And chilly Blasts begin to nip the Year;
From the tall Elm a Show'r of Leaves is born, 5
And their lost Beauty riven Beeches mourn.
Yet ev'n this Season Pleasance blithe affords,
Now the squeez'd Press foams with our Apple Hoards.
Come, let us hye, and quaff a cheery Bowl,
Let Cyder New *wash Sorrow from thy Soul*. 10

GRUBBINOL.

Ah *Bumkinet* ! since thou from hence wert gone,
From these sad Plains all Merriment is flown;
Should I reveal my Grief 'twould spoil thy Chear,
And make thine Eye o'erflow with many a Tear.

BUMKINET.

Hang Sorrow ! Let's to yonder Hutt repair, 15
And with trim Sonnets *cast away our Care*.

Title Gay's lengthy footnote to *The Dirge* offers a mock-pedantic debate over the origins of the term, claiming that it derives from the 'Teutonick *Dyrke Laudare*, to praise and extol', rather than the 'Latin *Dirige*'.

Caption *BUMKINET. GRUBBINOL.* Bumkinet, a comic diminutive of 'bumkin' (country bumpkin), also sounds like Ambrose Philips's shepherd Colinet. Grubbinol's name is a compound of 'grub' (to dig up) and 'Hobbinol', a shepherd's name used by both Spenser and Philips.

6 *riven* 'split'.

10 Gay throughout uses italics for proverbial phrases of Biblical or rural wisdom.

15 Gay's note cites Virgil, *Eclogues*, 5:10–11: 'Begin first, Mopsus, if you have any songs, about your flame Phyllis, or in praise of Alcon, or satirizing Codrus'.

15–16 'Hang sorrow and cast away care' had appeared as a refrain in a drinking song in John Playford's *Musical Companion* (1673).

Gillian of Croydon well thy Pipe can play,
Thou sing'st most sweet, *o'er Hills and far away.*
Of *Patient Grissel* I devise to sing,
And Catches quaint shall make the Vallies ring.   20
Come, *Grubbinol*, beneath this Shelter, come,
From hence we view our Flocks securely roam.

GRUBBINOL.

Yes, blithesome Lad, a Tale I mean to sing,
But with my Woe shall distant Valleys ring.
The Tale shall make our Kidlings droop their Head,   25
For Woe is me! — our *Blouzelind* is dead.

BUMKINET.

Is *Blouzelinda* dead? farewel my Glee!
No Happiness is now reserv'd for me.
As the Wood Pidgeon cooes without his Mate,
So shall my doleful Dirge bewail her Fate.   30
Of *Blouzelinda* fair I mean to tell,
The peerless Maid that did all Maids excell.
    Henceforth the Morn shall dewy Sorrow shed,
And Ev'ning Tears upon the Grass be spread;
The rolling Streams with watry Grief shall flow,   35
And Winds shall moan aloud — when loud they blow.
Henceforth, as oft as *Autumn* shall return,
The dropping Trees, whene'er it rains, shall mourn;
This Season quite shall strip the Country's Pride,
For 'twas in *Autumn Blouzelinda* dy'd.   40
    Where-e'er I gad, I *Blouzelind* shall view,
Woods, Dairy, Barn and Mows our Passion knew.
When I direct my Eyes to yonder Wood,
Fresh rising Sorrow curdles in my Blood.
Thither I've often been the Damsel's Guide,   45
When rotten Sticks our Fuel have supply'd;
There, I remember how her Faggots large,
Were frequently these happy Shoulders charge.
Sometimes this Crook drew Hazel Boughs adown,
And stuff'd her Apron wide with Nuts so brown;   50
Or when her feeding Hogs had miss'd their Way,
Or wallowing 'mid a Feast of Acorns lay;
Th' untoward Creatures to the Stye I drove,
And whistled all the Way — or told my Love.

17 *Gillian of Croydon* A ballad published in Tom
D'Urfey's *Pills to Purge Melancholy* (1706).
18 *o'er Hills and far away* The refrain of an old air,
'Jockey's Lamentation', first collected in *Pills to Purge
Melancholy* and later made famous by Gay himself, who
used it in his song 'Were I Laid on Greenland's Coast'
in *The Beggar's Opera.*
19 *Patient Grissel* An Elizabethan broadside ballad. Like
Chaucer's *Clerk's Tale,* it recounts how Griselda's
patience is severely tested by her husband.
20 *Catches* 'musical rounds'.
27 *Glee* 'Joy, from the *Dutch, Glooren,* to *recreate*' (Gay's
note). Gay's glossing of the term suggests it was
obsolete and comically archaic.
41–4 Parodies a celebrated passage in Pope's *Pastorals:*
'Wher-e'er you walk, cool Gales shall fan the Glade ...'
(*Summer,* 73–6).
42 *Mows* 'hay-stacks'.
49 *Crook* A shepherd's hook-ended stick.
53 *untoward* 'unruly'.

If by the Dairy's Hatch I chance to hie,   55
I shall her goodly Countenance espie,
For there her goodly Countenance I've seen,
Set off with Kerchief starch'd and Pinners clean.
Sometimes, like Wax, she rolls the Butter round,
Or with the wooden Lilly prints the Pound.   60
Whilome I've seen her skim the clouted Cream,
And press from spongy Curds the milky Stream.
But now, alas! these Ears shall hear no more
The whining Swine surround the Dairy Door,
No more her Care shall fill the hollow Tray,   65
To fat the guzzling Hogs with Floods of Whey.
Lament, ye Swine, in Gruntings spend your Grief,
For you, like me, have lost your sole Relief.
    When in the Barn the sounding Flail I ply,
Where from her Sieve the Chaff was wont to fly,   70
The Poultry there will seem around to stand,
Waiting upon her charitable Hand.
No Succour meet the Poultry now can find,
For they, like me, have lost their *Blouzelind.*
    Whenever by yon Barley Mow I pass,   75
Before my Eyes will trip the tidy Lass.
I pitch'd the Sheaves (oh could I do so now)
Which she in Rows pil'd on the growing Mow.
There ev'ry deale my Heart by Love was gain'd,
There the sweet Kiss my Courtship has explain'd.   80
Ah *Blouzelind*! that Mow I ne'er shall see,
But thy Memorial will revive in me.
    Lament, ye Fields, and rueful Symptoms show,
Henceforth let not the smelling Primrose grow;
Let Weeds instead of Butter-flow'rs appear,   85
And Meads, instead of Daisies, Hemlock bear;
For Cowslips sweet let Dandelions spread,
For *Blouzelinda*, blithsome Maid, is dead!
Lament ye Swains, and o'er her Grave bemoan,
And spell ye right this Verse upon her Stone.   90
Here Blouzelinda *lyes — Alas, alas!*
Weep Shepherds. — and remember Flesh is Grass.

GRUBBINOL.

Albeit thy Songs are sweeter to mine Ear,
Than to the thirsty Cattle Rivers clear;

55 *Hatch* 'gate'; *hie* 'go'.

58 *Pinners* Either a pinafore or a flat cap with a small ruffle.

60 She uses a butter print carved with a lily of the valley; *Pound* 'slab of butter'.

61 *clouted* 'clotted'.

73 *Succour meet* 'suitable care'.

76 *tidy* 'attractively neat'.

79 *ev'ry deale* 'completely'.

84 Gay's note cites *Eclogues*, 5:38–9: 'Instead of the soft violet and the gleaming narcissus, the thistle rises up and the sharp-spined thorn'.

86 *Hemlock* A poisonous umbrella-shaped weed.

90 Gay's note cites *Eclogues*, 5:42: 'And build a tomb, and on the tomb add this verse'.

92 *Flesh is Grass* Cf. Isaiah, 40:6 and 1 Peter, 1:24.

93 Gay's note cites *Eclogues*, 5:45–7 and 50–1: 'Your song, O divine poet, is to me like sleeping on grass to the weary, like quenching the thirst with a dancing stream of sweet water in hot weather. . . . But in turn I shall somehow sing you this song of mine, and raise your Daphnis to the stars'.

Or Winter Porridge to the lab'ring Youth,   95
Or Bunns and Sugar to the Damsel's Tooth;
Yet *Blouzelinda*'s Name shall tune my Lay,
Of her I'll sing for ever and for aye.
    When *Blouzelind* expir'd, the Weather's Bell
Before the drooping Flock toll'd forth her Knell;   100
The solemn Death-watch click'd the Hour she dy'd,
And shrilling Crickets in the Chimney cry'd;
The boding Raven on her Cottage sate,
And with hoarse Croaking warn'd us of her Fate;
The Lambkin, which her wonted Tendance bred,   105
Drop'd on the Plains that fatal Instant dead;
Swarm'd on a rotten Stick the Bees I spy'd,
Which erst I saw when Goody *Dobson* dy'd.
    How shall I, void of Tears, her Death relate,
While on her Dearling's Bed her Mother sate!   110
These Words the dying *Blouzelinda* spoke,
And *of the Dead let none the Will revoke.*
    Mother, quoth she, let not the Poultry need,
And give the Goose wherewith to raise her Breed,
Be these my Sister's Care — and ev'ry Morn   115
Amid the Ducklings let her scatter Corn;
The sickly Calf that's hous'd, be sure to tend,
Feed him with Milk, and from bleak Colds defend.
Yet e'er I die — see, Mother, yonder Shelf,
There secretly I've hid my worldly Pelf.   120
Twenty good Shillings in a Rag I laid,
Be ten the Parson's, for my Sermon paid.
The rest is yours — My Spinning-Wheel and Rake,
Let *Susan* keep for her dear Sister's sake;
My new Straw Hat that's trimly lin'd with Green,   125
Let *Peggy* wear, for she's a Damsel clean.
My leathern Bottle, long in Harvests try'd,
Be *Grubbinol*'s — this Silver Ring beside:
Three silver Pennies, and a Ninepence bent,
A Token kind, to *Bumkinet* is sent.   130
Thus spoke the Maiden, while her Mother cry'd,
And peaceful, like the harmless Lamb, she dy'd.
    To show their Love, the Neighbours far and near,
Follow'd with wistful Look the Damsel's Bier.
Sprigg'd Rosemary the Lads and Lasses bore,   135
While dismally the Parson walk'd before.
Upon her Grave their Rosemary they threw,
The Daisie, Butter-flow'r and Endive Blue.
    After the good Man warn'd us from his Text,

96 Gay's note cites Theocritus, *Idylls*, 8:83: 'Your singing is sweeter than the taste of honey'.
99 *Weather* A castrated ram.
101 *Death-watch* A beetle which makes a noise like a ticking clock, supposedly portending death.
105 *wonted Tendance* 'customary care'.
108 *Goody* An abbreviation of 'goodwife', used to address a married woman, usually in humble life.
120 *Pelf* 'treasure'.

129 *Ninepence bent* A country love-token.
135 *Rosemary* The herb of remembrance, sprigs of which were carried at funerals.
138 The daisy, buttercup and endive flower at different times of the year. Gay is parodying Philips's *Pastorals*, in which flowers bloom together regardless of season.
139 *Text* Ecclesiastes, 9:12: 'For man also knoweth not his time'.

That None could tell whose Turn would be the next;   140
He said, that Heav'n would take her Soul no doubt.
And spoke the Hour-glass in her Praise — quite out.
    To her sweet Mem'ry flow'ry Garlands strung,
O'er her now empty Seat aloft were hung.
With wicker Rods we fenc'd her Tomb around,   145
To ward from Man and Beast the hallow'd Ground,
Lest her new Grave the Parson's Cattle raze,
For both his Horse and Cow the Church-yard graze.
    Now we trudg'd homeward to her Mother's Farm,
To drink new Cyder mull'd, with Ginger warm.   150
For Gaffer *Tread-well* told us by the by,
Excessive Sorrow is exceeding dry.
    While Bulls bear Horns upon their curled Brow,
Or Lasses with soft Stroakings milk the Cow;
While padling Ducks the standing Lake desire,   155
Or batt'ning Hogs roll in the sinking Mire;
While Moles the crumbled Earth in Hillocks raise,
So long shall Swains tell *Blouzelinda*'s Praise.
    Thus wail'd the Louts, in melancholy Strain,
'Till bonny *Susan* sped a-cross the Plain;   160
They seiz'd the Lass in Apron clean array'd,
And to the Ale-house forc'd the willing Maid;
In Ale and Kisses they forget their Cares,
And *Susan Blouzelinda*'s Loss repairs.

142 Sermons were often timed with an hour-glass.
151 *Gaffer* Title used for an old man.
153 Gay's note cites *Eclogues*, 5:75–8: 'As long as the boar loves the mountain ridges and the fish the streams; as long as the bees feed on thyme and the crickets on dew, your honour, name and glories will always endure'.

Trivia: Or, the Art of Walking the Streets of London

In his three-book poem *Trivia* (1716) Gay returned to Virgil's *Georgics*, the model behind so many eighteenth-century long poems including his own earlier *Wine* and *Rural Sports*. *Trivia* exploits the comic incongruity of applying Virgil's instruction-manual style of 'advice to farmers' to contemporary city-dwellers. Gay may have been inspired by Swift's brief 'street-wise' poems, *A Description of the Morning* and *A Description of a City Shower*. Yet *Trivia*'s 1300 lines are more than a literary spoof. Their detailed evocation of the commercial, cultural and social dynamics of London parallels Virgil's creation of a complex, multi-faceted patriotic microcosm of Italy under Augustus Caesar. *Trivia* is less mock-georgic than modern georgic, investing London, in both its splendour and squalor, with its own mythology. Gay's 'walker' occupies a more marginal and detached social role than Virgil's farmer; but his 'benevolence' – a public-spirited sympathy for the poor and oppressed – makes him a similar symbol of social cohesion. Walking becomes not only a (mock) heroic enterprise fraught with hidden perils, but a metaphor for moral independence. Just as the gilded coach or sedan chair registers its occupant's moral depravity or corruption, the walker is 'Wrapt in my virtue, and a good *Surtout*' (overcoat). Gay's lightness of touch keeps the poem poised between the earnest and the absurd. Book 1 offers the walker practical advice on appropriate dress, implements, signs of changing weather etc. Book 3 paints a dramatic, sometimes sinister chiaroscuro of London by night. But Book 2, the longest, reproduced here, contains the most sustained description of London's variety.

Trivia was first published in January 1716, complete with a Scriblerian mock-pedantic textual apparatus of running side-notes, scholarly footnotes and index. All but one of the side-notes were removed for the *Poems on Several Occasions* (1720), when Gay added the long, important episode (Book 2: 99–220) of the boot-black's mythological origins, and this is the text given here. Gay's footnotes have been incorporated into the editorial annotations.

BOOK II

Of Walking the Streets by Day

THUS far the Muse has trac'd in useful lays,
The proper implements for wintry ways;
Has taught the walker, with judicious eyes,
To read the various warnings of the skies.
Now venture, Muse, from home to range the town,   5
And for the publick safety risque thy own.
   For ease and for dispatch, the morning's best;
No tides of passengers the street molest.
You'll see a draggled damsel, here and there,
From *Billingsgate* her fishy traffick bear;   10
On doors the sallow milk-maid chalks her gains;
Ah! how unlike the milk-maid of the plains!
Before proud gates attending asses bray,
Or arrogate with solemn pace the way;
These grave physicians with their milky chear,   15
The love-sick maid and dwindling beau repair;
Here rows of drummers stand in martial file,
And with their vellom thunder shake the pile,
To greet the new-made bride. Are sounds like these
The proper prelude to a state of peace?   20
Now industry awakes her busie sons,
Full charg'd with news the breathless hawker runs:
Shops open, coaches roll, carts shake the ground,
And all the streets with passing cries resound.
   If cloath'd in black, you tread the busy town,   25
Or if distinguish'd by the rev'rend gown,
Three trades avoid; oft in the mingling press,
The barber's apron soils the sable dress;
Shun the perfumer's touch with cautious eye,
Nor let the baker's step advance too nigh: 30
Ye walkers too that youthful colours wear,
Three sullying trades avoid with equal care;
The little chimney-sweeper skulks along,
And marks with sooty stains the heedless throng;
When small-coal murmurs in the hoarser throat,   35

Title In his index to the poem Gay defines 'Trivia', the deity he invokes in 1:5, as 'the Goddess of Streets and High-Ways'. The Latin word *trivium* means a crossroads or a street. The Roman moon-goddess Diana was worshipped at crossroads, like her more sinister Greek predecessor, Hecate. In Gay's day the plural form 'trivia' also meant 'matters appropriate to the elementary stages of education' – apt for the poem's instruction-manual tone. 'Trivia' meaning 'things of little consequence' was not yet in use in 1716, but the adjective 'trivial' (which Gay plays on) certainly was.
  10 *Billingsgate* The great London fishmarket.

11 *gains* Here, deliveries. Once paid, she would erase the chalk marks.
13–16 Asses' milk, considered good for invalids, was supplied fresh to the buyer's door.
17–19 Drummers came to the house to serenade the bride the morning after the wedding and would only leave after being paid.
18 *vellom* Vellum, or calf-skin, used for drums.
22 *hawker* 'newspaper seller'.
27 *mingling press* 'thronging crowd'.
33–5 Cf. Swift, *A Description of the Morning*, 11–12.
35 *small-coal* Charcoal to kindle domestic fires.

From smutty dangers guard thy threaten'd coat:
The dust-man's cart offends thy cloaths and eyes,
When through the street a cloud of ashes flies;
But whether black or lighter dyes are worn,
The chandler's basket, on his shoulder born,   40
With tallow spots thy coat; resign the way,
To shun the surly butcher's greasy tray,
Butchers, whose hands are dy'd with blood's foul stain,
And always foremost in the hangman's train.
 Let due civilities be strictly paid.   45
The wall surrender to the hooded maid;
Nor let thy sturdy elbow's hasty rage
Jostle the feeble steps of trembling age:
And when the porter bends beneath his load,
And pants for breath; clear thou the crouded road.   50
But, above all, the groping blind direct,
And from the pressing throng the lame protect.
You'll sometimes meet a fop, of nicest tread,
Whose mantling peruke veils his empty head,
At ev'ry step he dreads the wall to lose,   55
And risques, to save a coach, his red-heel'd shoes,
Him, like the miller, pass with caution by,
Lest from his shoulder clouds of powder fly.
But when the bully, with assuming pace,
Cocks his broad hat, edg'd round with tarnish'd lace,   60
Yield not the way; defie his strutting pride,
And thrust him to the muddy kennel's side;
He never turns again, nor dares oppose,
But mutters coward curses as he goes.
 If drawn by bus'ness to a street unknown,   65
Let the sworn porter point thee through the town;
Be sure observe the signs, for signs remain,
Like faithful land-marks to the walking train.
Seek not from prentices to learn the way,
Those fabling boys will turn thy steps astray;   70
Ask the grave tradesmen to direct thee right,
He ne'er deceives, but when he profits by't.
 Where fam'd *St. Giles*'s ancient limits spread,
An inrail'd column rears its lofty head,
Here to sev'n streets sev'n dials count the day,   75
And from each other catch the circling ray.
Here oft the peasant, with enquiring face,
Bewilder'd, trudges on from place to place;
He dwells on ev'ry sign with stupid gaze,

---

37 *dust-man* 'refuse collector'.

40 *chandler* 'candle-maker'.

46 *The wall surrender* 'give up your walking place close to the wall' – i.e. the safe, clean side of the pavement.

54 *mantling peruke* 'large wig'.

58 *powder* Used to dress wigs.

62 *kennel* 'gutter', 'drain'.

66 *sworn porter* A licensed member of the 'Fellowship or Society of Porters'; a more reliable source for directions than the apprentices of 69.

67–8 The distinctive pictorial signs hanging outside London shops helped orientate walkers.

73 The parish of St Giles, once known for its slums, was being revamped with some smart new streets here described.

74–6 Seven Dials, the hub of seven streets, was named after the seven sundials attached to its central column, one facing down each street. The sun was reflected onto the dials by mirrors.

Enters the narrow alley's doubtful maze,   80
Tries ev'ry winding court and street in vain,
And doubles o'er his weary steps again.
Thus hardy *Theseus* with intrepid feet,
Travers'd the dang'rous labyrinth of *Crete*;
But still the wandring passes forc'd his stay,   85
Till *Ariadne*'s clue unwinds the way.
But do not thou, like that bold chief, confide
Thy ventrous footsteps to a female guide;
She'll lead thee with delusive smiles along,
Dive in thy fob, and drop thee in the throng.   90
        When waggish boys the stunted beesom ply
To rid the slabby pavement; pass not by
E'er thou hast held their hands; some heedless flirt
Will over-spread thy calves with spatt'ring dirt.
Where porters hogsheads roll from carts aslope,   95
Or brewers down steep cellars stretch the rope,
Where counted billets are by carmen tost
Stay thy rash step, and walk without the post.
        What though the gath'ring mire thy feet besmear,
The voice of industry is always near.   100
Hark! the boy calls thee to his destin'd stand,
And the shoe shines beneath his oily hand.
Here let the Muse, fatigu'd amid the throng,
Adorn her precepts with digressive song;
Of shirtless youths the secret rise to trace,   105
And show the parent of the sable race.
        Like mortal man, great *Jove* (grown fond of change)
Of old was wont this nether world to range
To seek amours; the vice the monarch lov'd
Soon through the wide etherial court improv'd,   110
And ev'n the proudest Goddess now and then
Would lodge a night among the sons of men;
To vulgar Deitys descends the fashion,
Each, like her betters, had her earthly passion.
Then *Cloacina* (Goddess of the tide   115
Whose sable streams beneath the city glide)
Indulg'd the modish flame; the town she rov'd,
A mortal scavenger she saw, she lov'd;
The muddy spots that dry'd upon his face,

83–6 The Greek hero Theseus sought to kill the
    Minotaur, a monster half-man half-bull living in a
    labyrinth on the island of Crete. Ariadne, daughter of
    King Minos, gave him a ball of silken thread to unwind
    on his way into the labyrinth so that he could find his
    way out again.
88 *female guide* A prostitute or pickpocket.
90 *fob* 'watch pocket'.
91 *beesom* 'broom'.
92 *slabby* 'muddy'.
93 *held their hands* 'restrained their movements'; *heedless
    flirt* 'thoughtless flip or twirl'.
95 *hogsheads* Large barrels.

97 *billets* Logs of firewood; *carmen* 'carters'.
98 *without* 'outside'. The walking area and the carriage
    area were separated by a line of posts.
99–220 This digression on the mythological genesis of the
    shoe-shine boy was added in 1720.
102 *oily* See 162–6n.
107 *Jove* King of the gods (the Roman Jupiter), famed for
    his promiscuous sexual couplings with mortal women.
115 '*Cloacina* was a Goddess whose Image *Tatius* (a King of
    the *Sabines*) found in the common shore, and not
    knowing what Goddess it was, he called it *Cloacina* from
    the place in which it was found, and paid to it divine
    honours' (Gay). *Cloacina* From Lat. *cloaca*, 'sewer'.

Like female patches, heighten'd ev'ry grace: 120
She gaz'd; she sigh'd. For love can beauties spy
In what seems faults to ev'ry common eye.
   Now had the watchman walk'd his second round;
When *Cloacina* hears the rumbling sound
Of her brown lover's cart, for well she knows   125
That pleasing thunder: swift the Goddess rose,
And through the streets pursu'd the distant noise,
Her bosom panting with expected joys.
With the night-wandring harlot's airs she past,
Brush'd near his side, and wanton glances cast;   130
In the black form of cinder-wench she came,
When love, the hour, the place had banish'd shame;
To the dark alley arm in arm they move:
O may no link-boy interrupt their love!
   When the pale moon had nine times fill'd her space,   135
The pregnant Goddess (cautious of disgrace)
Descends to earth; but sought no midwife's aid,
Nor midst her anguish to *Lucina* pray'd;
No cheerful gossip wish'd the mother joy,
Alone, beneath a bulk she dropt the boy.   140
   The child through various risques in years improv'd,
At first a beggar's brat, compassion mov'd;
His infant tongue soon learnt the canting art,
Knew all the pray'rs and whines to touch the heart.
   Oh happy unown'd youths, your limbs can bear   145
The scorching dog-star, and the winter's air,
While the rich infant, nurs'd with care and pain,
Thirsts with each heat, and coughs with ev'ry rain!
   The Goddess long had mark'd the child's distress,
And long had sought his suff'rings to redress;   150
She prays the Gods to take the fondling's part,
To teach his hands some beneficial art
Practis'd in streets; the Gods her suit allow'd,
And made him useful to the walking croud,
To cleanse the miry feet, and o'er the shoe   155
With nimble skill the glossy black renew.
Each Power contributes to relieve the poor:
With the strong bristles of the mighty boar
Diana forms his brush; the God of day

120 *patches* Artificial beauty spots of black silk.

131 *cinder-wench* A girl employed to rake cinders.

134 *link-boy* A boy hired to light people's way along the streets.

138 *Lucina* Juno, queen of the gods, also goddess of childbirth. Her name means 'bringer of light' – the antithesis of Cloacina's furtive acts of procreation and birth.

139 *gossip* 'female friend'.

140 *bulk* A stall in front of a shop on or under which tramps often slept.

143 *canting art* The stock pleas used by beggars to solicit donations.

146 *dog-star* Sirius, brightest of the fixed stars. Its appearance in July to August was synonymous with oppressive heat.

151 *fondling* 'orphan'.

159 *God of day* Apollo, associated in Greek religion with the symbol of the tripod.

A tripod gives, amid the crouded way   160
To raise the dirty foot, and ease his toil;
Kind *Neptune* fills his vase with fetid oil
Prest from th' enormous whale; The God of fire,
From whose dominions smoaky clouds aspire,
Among these gen'rous presents joins his part,   165
And aids with soot the new japanning art:
Pleas'd she receives the gifts; she downward glides,
Lights in *Fleet-ditch*, and shoots beneath the tides.
    Now dawns the morn, the sturdy lad awakes,
Leaps from his stall, his tangled hair he shakes,   170
Then leaning o'er the rails, he musing stood,
And view'd below the black canal of mud,
Where common-shores a lulling murmur keep,
Whose torrents rush from *Holborn*'s fatal steep:
Pensive through idleness, tears flow'd apace,   175
Which eas'd his loaded heart, and wash'd his face;
At length he sighing cry'd; That boy was blest,
Whose infant lips have drain'd a mother's breast;
But happier far are those, (if such be known)
Whom both a father and a mother own: 180
But I, alas! hard fortune's utmost scorn,
Who ne'er knew parent, was an orphan born!
Some boys are rich by birth beyond all wants,
Belov'd by uncles, and kind good old aunts;
When time comes round, a Christmas-box they bear,   185
And one day makes them rich for all the year.
Had I the precepts of a Father learn'd,
Perhaps I then the coach-man's fare had earn'd,
For lesser boys can drive; I thirsty stand
And see the double flaggon charge their hand,   190
See them puff off the froth, and gulp amain,
While with dry tongue I lick my lips in vain.
    While thus he fervent prays, the heaving tide
In widen'd circles beats on either side;
The Goddess rose amid the inmost round,   195
With wither'd turnip tops her temples crown'd;
Low reach'd her dripping tresses, lank, and black
As the smooth jet, or glossy raven's back;
Around her waste a circling eel was twin'd,
Which bound her robe that hung in rags behind.   200
Now beck'ning to the boy; she thus begun,
Thy prayers are granted; weep no more, my son:
Go thrive. At some frequented corner stand,
This brush I give thee, grasp it in thy hand,

162–6 Shoes were blackened with a mixture of whale-oil
    and soot.
163 *God of fire* Vulcan.
168 *Fleet-ditch* The lower end of the Fleet River which
    flowed into the Thames. By Gay's time it was a
    common sewer.
174 Holborn Hill was 'fatal' because it lay on the route
    taken by condemned prisoners from Newgate Prison to
    execution at Tyburn.

185 *Christmas-box* A box passed round at Christmas (usually
    by apprentices and workmen) for gifts of money.
195–200 A parody of Virgil, *Aeneid*, 8:33–4, in which the
    reed-clad Father Tiber emerges from the water to
    address the hero. Cf. Pope, *Windsor-Forest*, 327–48;
    Swift, *A Description of a City Shower*, 63.

Temper the soot within this vase of oil, 205
And let the little tripod aid thy toil;
On this methinks I see the walking crew
At thy request support the miry shoe,
The foot grows black that was with dirt imbrown'd,
And in thy pocket gingling halfpence sound. 210
The Goddess plunges swift beneath the flood,
And dashes all around her show'rs of mud:
The youth strait chose his post; the labour ply'd
Where branching streets from *Charing-cross* divide;
His treble voice resounds along the *Meuse*, 215
And *White-hall* echoes — *Clean your Honour's shoes.*
    Like the sweet ballad, this amusing lay
Too long detains the walker on his way;
While he attends, new dangers round him throng;
The busy city asks instructive song. 220
    Where elevated o'er the gaping croud,
Clasp'd in the board the perjur'd head is bow'd,
Betimes retreat; here, thick as hailstones pour,
Turnips, and half-hatch'd eggs, (a mingled show'r)
Among the rabble rain: Some random throw 225
May with the trickling yolk thy cheek o'erflow.
    Though expedition bids, yet never stray
Where no rang'd posts defend the rugged way.
Here laden carts with thundring waggons meet,
Wheels clash with wheels, and bar the narrow street; 230
The lashing whip resounds, the horses strain,
And blood in anguish bursts the swelling vein.
O barb'rous men, your cruel breasts asswage,
Why vent ye on the gen'rous steed your rage?
Does not his service earn your daily bread? 235
Your wives, your children, by his labours fed!
If, as the *Samian* taught, the soul revives,
And, shifting seats, in other bodies lives;
Severe shall be the brutal coachman's change,
Doom'd in a hackney horse the town to range: 240
Carmen, transform'd, the groaning load shall draw,
Whom other tyrants with the lash shall awe.
    Who wou'd of *Watling-street* the dangers share,
When the broad pavement of *Cheap-side* is near?
Or who that rugged street would traverse o'er, 245
That stretches, O *Fleet-ditch*, from thy black shore
To the *Tow'r's* moated walls? Here steams ascend
That, in mix'd fumes, the wrinkled nose offend.
Where chandlers cauldrons boil; where fishy prey

205 *Temper* 'mix'.
214 *Charing-cross* One of the busiest parts of central London.
215 *Meuse* The Royal Mews stood in what is now Trafalgar Square.
222 *board* The pillory, the common punishment for perjury at this time.
228 *defend* 'fence off'. See 98n.

237–42 The Greek philosopher Pythagoras, born at Samos *c.*580 BC, preached the doctrine of metempsychosis, or transmigration of souls. See Thomson, *Spring*, 373.
238 *shifting seats* 'changing places' – with a pun on the coachman's occupational position.
243–4 Watling Street and Cheapside were busy main streets in the City.
245 'Thames-street' (Gay).

Hide the wet stall, long absent from the sea;   250
And where the cleaver chops the heifer's spoil,
And where huge hogsheads sweat with trainy oil,
Thy breathing nostril hold; but how shall I
Pass, where in piles *Cornavian* cheeses lye;
Cheese, that the table's closing rites denies,   255
And bids me with th'unwilling chaplain rise.
　　O bear me to the paths of fair *Pell-mell*,
Safe are thy pavements, grateful is thy smell!
At distance rolls along the gilded coach,
Nor sturdy carmen on thy walks encroach;   260
No lets would bar thy ways were chairs deny'd,
The soft supports of laziness and pride;
Shops breathe perfumes, thro' sashes ribbons glow,
The mutual arms of ladies, and the beau.
Yet still ev'n here, when rains the passage hide,   265
Oft' the loose stone spirts up a muddy tide
Beneath thy careless foot; and from on high,
Where masons mount the ladder, fragments fly;
Mortar, and crumbled lime in show'rs descend,
And o'er thy head destructive tiles impend.   270
　　But sometimes let me leave the noisie roads,
And silent wander in the close abodes
Where wheels ne'er shake the ground; there pensive stray,
In studious thought, the long uncrouded way.
Here I remark each walker's diff'rent face,   275
And in their look their various bus'ness trace.
The broker here his spacious beaver wears,
Upon his brow sit jealousies and cares;
Bent on some mortgage (to avoid reproach)
He seeks bye streets, and saves th' expensive coach.   280
Soft, at low doors, old letchers tap their cane,
For fair recluse, who travels *Drury-lane*;
Here roams uncomb'd the lavish rake, to shun
His *Fleet-street* draper's everlasting dun.
　　Careful observers, studious of the town,   285
Shun the misfortunes that disgrace the clown;
Untempted, they contemn the jugler's feats,
Pass by the *Meuse*, nor try the thimble's cheats.
When drays bound high, they never cross behind,

---

251 *heifer's spoil* The hard beef fat which the chandlers rendered down to tallow for candles.

252 *trainy oil* 'whale oil'.

254 *Cornavian* '*Cheshire* anciently so called' (Gay).

255–6 The domestic chaplain, in status above a servant but below family and guests, was expected to leave the dinner table before cheese and dessert.

257 *Pell-mell* 'Pall Mall'. Originally an avenue in which the game of pall mall was played. Vehicles were excluded but sedan-chairs allowed.

261 *lets* 'obstacles'.

263 *sashes* The shop fronts' sash-windows.

267–70 Many of the fashionable new Georgian houses were jerry-built.

277 *beaver* A broad-brimmed hat worn by businessmen.

282 *Drury-lane* A red-light district.

284 *Fleet-street* Later famous for newspapers, in Gay's time it housed drapers, sadlers and other shops; *dun* 'bailiff'.

286 *clown* 'peasant'.

287 *contemn* 'scorn'; *jugler* 'magician'.

288 'A cheat commonly practis'd in the streets with three thimbles and a little ball' (Gay). Bystanders were invited to bet on which cup covered the ball.

289 *drays* Horses pulling a brewer's cart.

Where bubbling yest is blown by gusts of wind: 290
And when up *Ludgate-hill* huge carts move slow,
Far from the straining steeds securely go,
Whose dashing hoofs behind them fling the mire,
And mark with muddy blots the gazing 'squire.
The *Parthian* thus his jav'lin backward throws,   295
And as he flies infests pursuing foes.
    The thoughtless wits shall frequent forfeits pay,
Who 'gainst the centry's box discharge their tea.
Do thou some court, or secret corner seek,
Nor flush with shame the passing virgin's cheek.   300
    Yet let me not descend to trivial song,
Nor vulgar circumstance my verse prolong;
Why should I teach the maid when torrents pour,
Her head to shelter from the sudden show'r?
Nature will best her ready hand inform,   305
With her spread petticoat to fence the storm.
Does not each walker know the warning sign,
When wisps of straw depend upon the twine
Cross the close street; that then the paver's art
Renews the ways, deny'd to coach and cart?   310
Who knows not that the coachman lashing by,
Oft with his flourish cuts the heedless eye;
And when he takes his stand, to wait a fare,
His horses foreheads shun the winter's air?
Nor will I roam, when summer's sultry rays   315
Parch the dry ground, and spread with dust the ways;
With whirling gusts the rapid atoms rise,
Smoak o'er the pavement, and involve the skies.
    Winter my theme confines; whose nitry wind
Shall crust the slabby mire, and kennels bind;   320
She bids the snow descend in flaky sheets,
And in her hoary mantle cloath the streets.
Let not the virgin tread these slipp'ry roads,
The gath'ring fleece the hollow patten loads;
But if thy footsteps slide with clotted frost,   325
Strike off the breaking balls against the post.
On silent wheel the passing coaches roll;
Oft' look behind, and ward the threatning pole.
In harden'd orbs the school-boy moulds the snow,
To mark the coachman with a dextrous throw.   330
Why do ye, boys, the kennel's surface spread,
To tempt with faithless pass the matron's tread?

---

290 *yest* 'foam'.
295 Parthian horsemen were said to hurl missiles backwards while pretending to retreat.
298 *tea* Either recycled tea, or a slang word for urine. Urinating in public was punishable by fine.
301 *trivial* See note to title.
308 *depend* 'hang'.
309 *close* 'narrow'.
314 In cold weather the horses rubbed their heads against unwary bystanders' clothes.

317 *atoms* 'particles'.
318 *involve* 'wreathe around', 'envelop'.
319 *nitry* 'impregnated with nitre'. Frost was thought to be caused by nitre (potassium nitrate) in the air.
320 *slabby mire* 'slush'.
324 *gath'ring fleece* 'compacting snow'; *patten* A platform worn beneath shoes to raise them above the mud.
328 *pole* 'carriage-pole'.
331–4 Boys concealed the gutter with a compacted layer of snow to trick passers-by into walking on it.

How can ye laugh to see the damsel spurn,
Sink in your frauds, and her green stocking mourn?
At *White*'s the harness'd chairman idly stands,   335
And swings around his waste his tingling hands:
The sempstress speeds to '*Change* with red-tipt nose;
The *Belgian* stove beneath her footstool glows;
In half-whipt muslin needles useless lie,
And shuttle-cocks across the counter fly.   340
These sports warm harmless; why then will ye prove,
Deluded maids, the dang'rous flame of love?
     Where *Covent-garden*'s famous temple stands,
That boasts the work of *Jones*' immortal hands;
Columns with plain magnificence appear,   345
And graceful porches lead along the square:
Here oft' my course I bend, when lo! from far,
I spy the furies of the foot-ball war:
The 'prentice quits his shop, to join the crew,
Encreasing crouds the flying game pursue.   350
Thus, as you roll the ball o'er snowy ground,
The gath'ring globe augments with ev'ry round.
But whither shall I run? the throng draws nigh,
The ball now skims the street, now soars on high;
The dext'rous glazier strong returns the bound,   355
And gingling sashes on the pent-house sound.
     O roving Muse, recal that wond'rous year,
When winter reign'd in bleak *Britannia*'s air;
When hoary *Thames*, with frosted oziers crown'd,
Was three long moons in icy fetters bound.   360
The waterman, forlorn along the shore,
Pensive reclines upon his useless oar,
Sees harness'd steeds desert the stony town;
And wanders roads unstable, not their own:
Wheels o'er the harden'd waters smoothly glide,   365
And rase with whiten'd tracks the slipp'ry tide.
Here the fat cook piles high the blazing fire,
And scarce the spit can turn the steer entire.
Booths sudden hide the *Thames*, long streets appear,
And num'rous games proclaim the crouded fair.   370
So when a gen'ral bids the martial train
Spread their encampment o'er the spacious plain;

---

333 *spurn* 'stumble'.

334 *frauds* 'tricks'.

335 *White's* A famous chocolate house and aristocratic gambling place in St James's Street.

337 '*Change* The New Exchange, on the south of the Strand, a fashionable clothes retail area.

338 *Belgian stove* A foot-warmer filled with burning charcoal.

339 To 'whip' is to sew by overcasting.

343–6 The church of St Paul's, Covent Garden, built in 1631 to designs by Inigo Jones (1573–1652). He also created rows of elegant arcades ('porches') on the north and east sides of the piazza.

355 The 'dext'rous' glazier presumably aimed to break windows which he was then hired to replace.

356 *pent-house* A sloping roof projecting from a building to shelter passers-by.

357–98 The Thames was frozen over for three months in the winter of 1709–10 and for a shorter time in 1715–16. Both occasions were marked by a 'frost-fair', which featured fairground booths, puppet-shows, bull- and bear-baiting, and the roasting of a whole ox on the ice.

359 *oziers* 'willow-shoots'.

Thick-rising tents a canvas city build,
And the loud dice resound thro' all the field.
    'Twas here the matron found a doleful fate: 375
Let elegiac lay the woe relate,
Soft as the breath of distant flutes, at hours
When silent ev'ning closes up the flow'rs;
Lulling as falling water's hollow noise;
Indulging grief, like *Philomela*'s voice. 380
    Doll ev'ry day had walk'd these treach'rous roads;
Her neck grew warpt beneath autumnal loads
Of various fruit; she now a basket bore,
That head, alas! shall basket bear no more.
Each booth she frequent past, in quest of gain, 385
And boys with pleasure heard her shrilling strain,
Ah *Doll*! all mortals must resign their breath,
And industry it self submit to death!
The cracking crystal yields, she sinks, she dyes,
Her head, chopt off, from her lost shoulders flies; 390
Pippins she cry'd, but death her voice confounds,
And pip-pip-pip along the ice resounds.
So when the *Thracian* furies *Orpheus* tore,
And left his bleeding trunk deform'd with gore,
His sever'd head floats down the silver tide, 395
His yet warm tongue for his lost consort cry'd;
Eurydice with quiv'ring voice he mourn'd,
And *Heber*'s banks *Eurydice* return'd.
    But now the western gale the flood unbinds,
And black'ning clouds move on with warmer winds, 400
The wooden town its frail foundation leaves,
And *Thames*' full urn rolls down his plenteous waves;
From ev'ry penthouse streams the fleeting snow,
And with dissolving frost the pavements flow.
    Experienc'd men, inur'd to city ways, 405
Need not the Calendar to count their days.
When through the town with slow and solemn air,
Led by the nostril, walks the muzled bear;
Behind him moves majestically dull,
The pride of *Hockley-hole*, the surly bull; 410
Learn hence the periods of the week to name,
Mondays and *Thursdays* are the days of game.
    When fishy stalls with double store are laid;
The golden-belly'd carp, the broad-finn'd maid,
Red-speckled trouts, the salmon's silver joul, 415
The joynted lobster, and unscaly soale,
And luscious 'scallops, to allure the tastes
Of rigid zealots to delicious fasts;
Wednesdays and *Fridays* you'll observe from hence,

380 *Philomela* The nightingale. See Thomson, *Spring*, 601n.
393–8 Orpheus, after failing to rescue his lover Eurydice
    from the underworld, returned to Thrace. His body
    was torn apart by the Thracian women, but his severed
    head floated down the river Hebrus still calling for his
    lost love. The story is found in Virgil, *Georgics*,
    4:520–7.

410 *Hockley-hole* Bear- and bull-baitings were held at
    Hockley-in-the-Hole.
414 *maid* 'young skate'.
415 *joul* 'head and shoulders'.
418 *zealots* Those who abstained from eating meat on the
    traditional Catholic fast days of Wednesday and Friday.

Days, when our sires were doom'd to abstinence.   420
  When dirty waters from balconies drop,
And dext'rous damsels twirle the sprinkling mop,
And cleanse the spatter'd sash, and scrub the stairs;
Know *Saturday*'s conclusive morn appears.
  Successive crys the seasons change declare,   425
And mark the monthly progress of the year.
Hark, how the streets with treble voices ring,
To sell the bounteous product of the spring!
Sweet-smelling flow'rs, and elder's early bud,
With nettle's tender shoots, to cleanse the blood: 430
And when *June*'s thunder cools the sultry skies,
Ev'n *Sundays* are prophan'd by mackrell cries.
  Wallnuts the fruit'rer's hand, in autumn, stain,
Blue plumbs and juicy pears augment his gain;
Next oranges the longing boys entice,   435
To trust their copper fortunes to the dice.
  When rosemary, and bays the Poet's crown,
Are bawl'd, in frequent cries, through all the town,
Then judge the festival of *Christmas* near,
Christmas, the joyous period of the year.   440
Now with bright holly all your temples strow,
With lawrel green, and sacred misletoe.
Now, heav'n-born Charity, thy blessings shed;
Bid meagre Want uprear her sickly head:
Bid shiv'ring limbs be warm; let plenty's bowle,   445
In humble roofs make glad the needy soul.
See, see, the heav'n-born maid her blessings shed;
Lo! meagre Want uprears her sickly head;
Cloath'd are the naked, and the needy glad,
While selfish Avarice alone is sad.   450
  Proud coaches pass, regardless of the moan
Of infant orphans, and the widow's groan;
While Charity still moves the walker's mind,
His lib'ral purse relieves the lame and blind.
Judiciously thy half-pence are bestow'd,   455
Where the laborious beggar sweeps the road.
Whate'er you give, give ever at demand,
Nor let old-age long stretch his palsy'd hand.
Those who give late, are importun'd each day,
And still are teaz'd, because they still delay.   460
If e'er the miser durst his farthings spare,
He thinly spreads them through the publick square,
Where, all beside the rail, rang'd beggars lie,
And from each other catch the doleful cry;
With heav'n, for two-pence, cheaply wipes his score,   465

421–3 Cf. Swift, *A Description of the Morning*, 7–8 and *A Description of a City Shower*, 19–20.

425 *crys* 'street-cries'.

432 Fresh mackerel went bad so quickly its sale was permitted on Sundays.

435–6 Children gambled their pennies for oranges on Shrove Tuesday.

437 *bays* The bay-laurel, whose leaves traditionally crowned the poet.

447 *heav'n-born maid* Charity.

460 *teaz'd* 'pestered'.

465 *wipes his score* 'pays his debts'.

Lifts up his eyes, and hasts to beggar more.
  Where the brass knocker, wrapt in flannel band,
Forbids the thunder of the footman's hand;
Th'upholder, rueful harbinger of death,
Waits with impatience for the dying breath; 470
As vultures, o'er a camp, with hov'ring flight,
Snuff up the future carnage of the fight.
Here canst thou pass, unmindful of a pray'r,
That heav'n in mercy may thy brother spare?
  Come, *F* *** sincere, experienc'd friend, 475
Thy briefs, thy deeds, and ev'n thy fees suspend;
Come, let us leave the *Temple*'s silent walls,
Me bus'ness to my distant lodging calls:
Through the long *Strand* together let us stray:
With thee conversing I forget the way. 480
Behold that narrow street which steep descends,
Whose building to the slimy shore extends;
Here *Arundel*'s fam'd structure rear'd its frame,
The street alone retains an empty name:
Where *Titian*'s glowing paint the canvas warm'd, 485
And *Raphael*'s fair design, with judgment, charm'd,
Now hangs the bell-man's song, and pasted here,
The colour'd prints of *Overton* appear.
Where statues breath'd, the work of *Phidias*' hands,
A wooden pump, or lonely watch-house stands. 490
There *Essex*' stately pile adorn'd the shore,
There *Cecil*'s, *Bedford*'s, *Villers*', now no more.
Yet *Burlington*'s fair palace still remains;
Beauty within, without proportion reigns.
Beneath his eye declining art revives, 495
The wall with animated picture lives;
There *Hendel* strikes the strings, the melting strain
Transports the soul, and thrills through ev'ry vein;
There oft' I enter (but with cleaner shoes)
For *Burlington*'s belov'd by ev'ry Muse. 500

467–8 In a house where someone had just died the doorknocker was wrapped in cloth to mute the sound.

469 *upholder* 'undertaker'.

475 *F****** William Fortescue, a lawyer friend of both Gay and Pope.

477 *Temple* The Inns of Court.

483–90 Arundel House, home of Thomas Howard, second Earl of Arundel (1585–1646), had once contained England's first large art collection. By Gay's time the house had been demolished: all that remained was a street named after it which ran down to the Thames.

485 *Titian* (*c*.1488–1576), great Venetian painter of mythical and Biblical scenes.

486 *Raphael* (1483–1520), Italian painter, designer and architect.

487 The bellman, who acted as night-watchman and town-crier, turned his announcements into verses which he left at houses he passed.

488 Henry and Philip Overton were well-known print-sellers.

489 *Phidias* (fifth century BC), Athenian sculptor.

491–2 Four more great Elizabethan houses on the site of the Strand which had been demolished as a result of new developments.

493–500 Richard Boyle, third Earl of Burlington, was a famous patron of architecture and the other arts, and a friend to both Gay and Pope (see Pope, *Epistle to Burlington*). From 1716 onwards he converted the Piccadilly house built for his great-grandfather, the first earl, into an elegant Palladian mansion.

497 *Hendel* George Frederic Handel (1685–1759), the German composer, settled in England in 1712. He lived at Burlington House 1712–16.

O ye associate walkers, O my friends,
Upon your state what happiness attends!
What, though no coach to frequent visit rolls,
Nor for your shilling chairmen sling their poles;
Yet still your nerves rheumatic pains defye,   505
Nor lazy jaundice dulls your saffron eye;
No wasting cough discharges sounds of death,
Nor wheezing asthma heaves in vain for breath;
Nor from your restless couch is heard the groan
Of burning gout, or sedentary stone.   510
Let others in the jolting coach confide,
Or in the leaky boat the *Thames* divide;
Or, box'd within the chair, contemn the street,
And trust their safety to another's feet,
Still let me walk; for oft the sudden gale   515
Ruffles the tide, and shifts the dang'rous sail.
Then shall the passenger too late deplore
The whelming billow, and the faithless oar;
The drunken chairman in the kennel spurns,
The glasses shatters, and his charge o'erturns.   520
Who can recount the coach's various harms,
The legs disjointed, and the broken arms?
    I've seen a beau, in some ill-fated hour,
When o'er the stones choak'd kennels swell the show'r
In gilded chariot loll; he with disdain   525
Views spatter'd passengers all drench'd in rain;
With mud fill'd high, the rumbling cart draws near,
Now rule thy prancing steeds, lac'd charioteer!
The dust-man lashes on with spiteful rage,
His pond'rous spokes thy painted wheel engage,   530
Crush'd is thy pride, down falls the shrieking beau,
The slabby pavement crystal fragments strow,
Black floods of mire th'embroider'd coat disgrace,
And mud enwraps the honours of his face.
So when dread *Jove* the son of *Phoebus* hurl'd,   535
Scarr'd with dark thunder, to the nether world;
The headstrong coursers tore the silver reins,
And the sun's beamy ruin gilds the plains.
    If the pale walker pant with weak'ning ills,
His sickly hand is stor'd with friendly bills: 540
From hence he learns the seventh-born doctor's fame,
From hence he learns the cheapest tailor's name.
    Shall the large mutton smoak upon your boards?
Such, *Newgate*'s copious market best affords.

---

504 The chairmen fitted the poles of their sedan-chairs into
   slings which made them easier to carry.
506 *saffron* i.e. yellow with jaundice.
510 *stone* 'kidney-stone'.
513 *contemn* 'despise'.
520 *glasses* 'windows'.
535–8 In Greek myth, Phaethon, son of Helios (the sun),
   took charge of his father's chariot but lost control,

driving so close to the earth that he parched and
blackened part of the planet. Zeus punished him by
striking him with a thunder-bolt.
540 *bills* 'fliers'.
541 The seventh son of a seventh son was a born healer,
   according to popular superstition.
543–50 A list of famous London markets.

Would'st thou with mighty beef augment thy meal?   545
Seek *Leaden-hall*; Saint *James*'s sends thee veal.
Thames-street gives cheeses; *Covent-garden* fruits;
Moor-fields old books; and *Monmouth-street* old suits.
Hence may'st thou well supply the wants of life,
Support thy family, and cloath thy wife.   550
    Volumes, on shelter'd stalls expanded lye,
And various science lures the learned eye;
The bending shelves with pond'rous scholiasts groan,
And deep divines to modern shops unknown:
Here, like the bee, that on industrious wing   555
Collects the various odours of the spring,
Walkers, at leisure, learning's flow'rs may spoil,
Nor watch the wasting of the midnight oil,
May morals snatch from *Plutarch*'s tatter'd page,
A mildew'd *Bacon*, or *Stagyra*'s sage.   560
Here saunt'ring prentices o'er *Otway* weep,
O'er *Congreve* smile, or over *D* * * sleep;
Pleas'd sempstresses the *Lock*'s fam'd *Rape* unfold,
And *Squirts* read *Garth*, 'till apozems grow cold.
    O *Lintot*, let my labours obvious lie,   565
Rang'd on thy stall, for ev'ry curious eye;
So shall the poor these precepts gratis know,
And to my verse their future safeties owe.
    What walker shall his mean ambition fix,
On the false lustre of a coach and six?   570
Let the vain virgin, lur'd by glaring show,
Sigh for the liv'ries of th'embroider'd beau.
    See yon bright chariot on its harness swing,
With *Flanders* mares, and on an arched spring;
That wretch to gain an equipage and place,   575
Betray'd his sister to a lewd embrace.
This coach that with the blazon'd 'scutcheon glows,

557 *spoil* 'acquire' (more easily than by studying hard at night).

559 *Plutarch* Greek historian and philosopher (*c.*AD 46–*c.*120), author of the *Moralia.*

560 *mildew'd Bacon* Sir Francis Bacon (1561–1626), scientist and philosopher, author of *The Advancement of Learning* and *The New Atlantis* (with a pun on the bacon more usually sold in markets); *Stagyra's sage* Aristotle (384–322 BC), Greek philosopher, was born at Stagira.

561 Thomas Otway (1652–85), whose tragedies, notably *The Orphan* and *Venice Preserv'd*, were famously moving.

562 *Congreve* William Congreve (1670–1729), author of the comedies *The Way of the World* and *Love for Love*; *D* * * John Dennis (1657–1734), critic and playwright, who attacked Pope and was ridiculed whenever possible by Pope, Gay and their friends.

563 Pope's *Rape of the Lock* in its five-canto version (1714) was still a new poem.

564 Sir Samuel Garth's *The Dispensary* (1699), a popular mock-heroic poem on the professional quarrel between the apothecaries and the physicians. 'Squirt', as Gay's note observes, was the name of an apothecary's boy in the poem; *apozems* Medicinal preparations made by infusion.

565 *Lintot* Bernard Lintot (1675–1736), the highly successful publisher of *Trivia*, among many other works; *obvious* 'in the way of', in the stronger sense of Lat. *obviam.*

574 Large coaches owned by the rich were drawn by strong horses from Flanders.

575 *equipage* A carriage with horses and attendant servants; *place* Sinecure or official position at Court or in government.

577 *blazon'd 'scutcheon* 'painted coat of arms'.

Vain of his unknown race, the coxcomb shows.
Here the brib'd lawyer, sunk in velvet, sleeps;
The starving orphan, as he passes, weeps;   580
There flames a fool, begirt with tinsell'd slaves,
Who wastes the wealth of a whole race of knaves.
That other, with a clustring train behind,
Owes his new honours to a sordid mind.
This next in court-fidelity excells,   585
The publick rifles, and his country sells.
May the proud chariot never be my fate,
If purchas'd at so mean, so dear a rate;
O rather give me sweet content on foot,
Wrapt in my virtue, and a good *Surtout*!   590

578 *coxcomb* 'cocky upstart'.   590 *Surtout* 'overcoat'.
583 *train* A retinue of servants or hangers-on.

Thomas Parnell (1679–1718)

Parnell, like his friend Swift, was a reluctant Irishman. His English parents Thomas and Anna, supporters of Cromwell, had moved to Ireland after the Restoration of Charles II in 1660. Parnell was early destined for the church. He entered Trinity College, Dublin at thirteen, took orders in 1704 and by 1706 had become archdeacon of Clogher. His earliest poetic efforts reflect both the piety and Whig bias of his family background. But after 1706 Parnell began to spend increasingly long spells in England. His friendship with Swift brought him into contact with the London literary world; first with the Whig writers Addison and Steele, then, as party divisions sharpened, with the Tory-affiliated witty Scriblerus Club of which he, along with Swift, Arbuthnot, Gay and Pope, formed the nucleus. The period between 1711 and 1714, which Parnell spent in England, was his happiest. During the spring and summer of 1714 he stayed at Pope's home at rural Binfield helping him to translate Homer's *Iliad*. Parnell, an excellent classical scholar, supported Pope's Homeric enterprise with other pieces: the *Essay on the Life, Writings and Genius of Homer* (1715) which prefaced Book I of Pope's *Iliad*, and a witty translation of *Homer's Battle of the Frogs and Mice* printed in 1717 with *The Life of Zoilus*, a thinly veiled satire on Pope's foe, the critic John Dennis. When the fall of the Tories in August 1714 forced Parnell back to Ireland he complained to Pope that he had been transplanted to 'unfertile ground. / Far from the joys that with my soul agree, / From wit, from learning – very far from thee'.

Even though Parnell had been writing poems since his early teens, he was remarkably diffident about publication. Without Swift and Pope's encouragement he might have published nothing. When he died aged thirty-nine (perhaps from the heavy drinking that began after his wife Anne Minchin's death in 1711) he had published only nine poems. Pope, to whom Parnell had entrusted his manuscripts, was determined to erect the 'best Monument I can' to his friend's memory. The twenty poems Pope selected for *Poems on Several Occasions* (1722) secured Parnell's literary reputation as the epitome of the polite Augustan style. Their elegant and urbane classicism encompasses both witty social comment and profound Christian sentiment. Claude Rawson and F. P. Lock's recent work on Parnell's manuscripts has recovered a rather different Parnell. In *Poems on Several Occasions*, Pope, for better or worse, had fashioned a poet in his own image, polishing, refining and cutting some of the more abrasive, political and vernacular qualities of Parnell's original manuscript drafts. The following selection, drawn from both *Poems on Several Occasions* and a recently discovered manuscript poem, attempts to convey the poet's range.

An Elegy, To an Old Beauty

This poem addresses a theme central to Pope's *Rape of the Lock* and Swift's 'Stella' poems, namely that women must learn to cultivate wisdom and good humour when their looks fade through age. Parnell's measured urbanity fails to render this advice any more palatable. First published in *Poems on Several Occasions*, from which this text is taken.

> In vain, poor Nymph, to please our youthful sight
> You sleep in Cream and Frontlets all the Night,
> Your Face with Patches soil, with Paint repair,
> Dress with gay Gowns, and shade with foreign Hair.
> If Truth in spight of Manners must be told,   5
> Why really *Fifty Five* is something old.
>   Once you were young; or one, whose Life's so long
> She might have born my Mother, tells me wrong.
> And once (since Envy's dead before you dye,)
> The Women own, you play'd a sparkling Eye,   10

2 *Cream* 'skin-cream'; *Frontlets* Bandages worn on the forehead at night to prevent wrinkles.

3 *Patches* Artificial beauty spots of black silk; *Paint* 'cosmetics'.

4 *foreign Hair* i.e. a wig.

10 *own* 'acknowledge'.

Taught the light Foot a modish little Trip,
And pouted with the prettiest purple Lip —
    To some new Charmer are the Roses fled,
Which blew, to damask all thy Cheek with red;
Youth calls the *Graces* there to fix their Reign,   15
And *Airs* by thousands fill their easy Train.
So parting Summer bids her flow'ry Prime
Attend the Sun to dress some foreign Clime,
While with'ring Seasons in Succession, here,
Strip the gay Gardens, and deform the Year.   20
    But thou (since Nature bids) the World resign,
'Tis now thy Daughter's Daughter's time to shine.
With more Address, (or such as pleases more)
She runs her Female Exercises o'er,
Unfurls or closes, raps or turns the Fan,   25
And smiles, or blushes at the Creature Man.
With quicker Life, as guilded Coaches pass,
In sideling Courtesy she drops the Glass.
With better Strength, on Visit-days she bears
To mount her fifty Flights of ample Stairs.   30
Her Mein, her Shape, her Temper, Eyes and Tongue
Are sure to conquer. — for the Rogue is young;
And all that's madly wild, or oddly gay,
We call it only pretty *Fanny*'s way.
    Let Time that makes you homely, make you sage,   35
The Sphere of Wisdom is the Sphere of Age.
'Tis true, when Beauty dawns with early Fire,
And hears the flatt'ring Tongues of soft Desire,
If not from Virtue, from its gravest Ways
The Soul with pleasing Avocation strays.   40
But Beauty gone, 'tis easier to be wise;
As Harpers better, by the loss of Eyes.
    Henceforth retire, reduce your roving Airs,
Haunt less the Plays, and more the publick Pray'rs,
Reject the *Mechlin* Head, and gold Brocade,   45
Go pray, in sober *Norwich* Crape array'd.
Thy pendent Diamonds let thy *Fanny* take,
(Their trembling Lustre shows how much you shake;)
Or bid her wear thy Necklace row'd with Pearl,
You'll find your *Fanny* an obedient Girl.   50
So for the rest, with less Incumbrance hung,
You walk thro' Life, unmingled with the young;
And view the *Shade* and *Substance* as you pass
With joint Endeavour trifling at the Glass,

---

14 *blew* 'blossomed'; *damask* 'make blush-coloured'.
15 *Graces* The three classical goddesses of grace and beauty.
16 *Airs* 'delightful manners'.
23 *Address* 'dexterity'.
27 *quicker* 'more animated'; *guilded* gilded (suggesting wealthy occupants).
28 *sideling* 'with a sidelong look'; *Glass* 'window'.
29 *Visit-days* Days assigned for social calls.

31 *Mein* 'manner'.
32 *Rogue* A term of endearment, here describing a lively girl.
40 *Avocation* 'distraction'.
42 Blindness was thought to give poets and musicians special 'visionary' powers.
45 *Mechlin Head* A decorative lace headdress.
46 *Norwich Crape* A plain worsted cloth made in Norwich.
54 *Glass* 'mirror'.

Or *Folly* drest, and rambling all her Days,   55
To meet her Counterpart, and grow by *Praise*:
Yet still sedate your self, and gravely plain,
You neither fret, nor envy at the Vain.
   'Twas thus (if Man with Woman we compare)
The wise *Athenian* crost a glittering Fair,   60
Unmov'd by Tongues and Sights, he walk'd the place,
Thro' Tape, Toys, Tinsel, Gimp, Perfume, and Lace;
Then bends from *Mars*'s Hill his awful Eyes,
And *What a World I never want?* he cries;
But cries unheard: For *Folly* will be free.   65
So parts the buzzing gaudy Crowd, and He:
As careless he for them, as they for him;
He wrapt in *Wisdom*, and they whirl'd by *Whim*.

60 *wise Athenian* Socrates, the famous Greek philosopher. The episode is recorded in Diogenes Laertius's *Lives of the Philosophers*, 2:25.

62 *Tape* 'ribbon'; *Gimp* A silk or cotton twist.
63 *Mars* The Roman god of war.

A Night-Piece on Death

The *Night-Piece* is Parnell's best-known poem. The poised gravity of its meditations on the universality of death finds an unmistakeable echo in Gray's *Elegy Written in a Country Church Yard* (1751). Parnell's nocturnal landscape of mouldering ruins, ravens and charnel-houses resurfaced in later 'graveyard' poems such as Robert Blair's *The Grave* (1743) and Edward Young's *Night Thoughts* (1742–5). Yet the *Night-Piece* checks and even undercuts its own Gothic frisson. It is Death who reprimands foolish man for frightening himself with macabre phantasms. Death, for the enlightened Christian, is but a passage to heaven. The poem thus moves steadily from images of darkness and entrapment to those of flight, transcendence and sublimity.

By the blue Tapers trembling Light,
No more I waste the wakeful Night,
Intent with endless view to pore
The Schoolmen and the Sages o'er:
Their Books from Wisdom widely stray,   5
Or point at best the longest Way.
I'll seek a readier Path, and go
Where Wisdom's surely taught *below*.
   How deep yon Azure dies the Sky!
Where Orbs of Gold unnumber'd lye,   10
While thro' their Ranks in silver pride
The nether Crescent seems to glide.
The slumb'ring Breeze forgets to breathe,
The Lake is smooth and clear beneath,
Where once again the spangled Show   15
Descends to meet our Eyes below.
The Grounds which on the right aspire,
In dimness from the View retire:
The Left presents a Place of Graves,

1 Candles supposedly burnt blue in the presence of spirits or as an omen of death.
4 *Schoolmen* Medieval scholastic theologians; *Sages* Classical philosophers. Parnell draws on both Christian and pagan intellectual traditions.

8 *surely* 'soundly'; *below* 'here on earth', perhaps with pun on 'below, in the grave'.
12 *nether Crescent* The moon, lit on its lower side.
15 *spangled* 'glittering like sequins'.

Whose Wall the silent Water laves.   20
That Steeple guides thy doubtful sight
Among the livid gleams of Night.
There pass with melancholy State,
By all the solemn Heaps of Fate,
And think, as softly-sad you tread   25
Above the venerable Dead,
Time was, like thee they Life possest,
And Time shall be, that thou shalt Rest.

   Those Graves, with bending Osier bound,
That nameless heave the crumbled Ground,   30
Quick to the glancing Thought disclose
Where *Toil* and *Poverty* repose.

   The flat smooth Stones that bear a Name,
The Chissels slender help to Fame,
(Which e'er our Sett of Friends decay   35
Their frequent Steps may wear away.)
A *middle Race* of Mortals own,
Men, half ambitious, all unknown.

   The Marble Tombs that rise on high,
Whose Dead in vaulted Arches lye,   40
Whose Pillars swell with sculptur'd Stones,
Arms, Angels, Epitaphs and Bones,
These (all the poor Remains of State)
Adorn the *Rich*, or praise the *Great*;
Who while on Earth in Fame they live,   45
Are sensless of the Fame they give.

   Ha! while I gaze, pale *Cynthia* fades,
The bursting Earth unveils the Shades!
All slow, and wan, and wrap'd with Shrouds,
They rise in visionary Crouds,   50
And all with sober Accent cry,
Think, Mortal, what it is to dye.

   Now from yon black and fun'ral Yew,
That bathes the Charnel House with Dew,
Methinks I hear a *Voice* begin;   55
(Ye Ravens, cease your croaking Din,
Ye tolling Clocks, no Time resound
O'er the long Lake and midnight Ground)
It sends a Peal of hollow Groans,
Thus speaking from among the Bones.   60

   When Men my Scythe and Darts supply,
How great a *King* of *Fears* am I!
They view me like the last of Things:
They make, and then they dread, my Stings.
Fools! if you less provok'd your Fears,   65
No more my Spectre-Form appears.

---

20 *laves* 'washes'.
22 *livid* 'leaden grey'.
23 *State* 'dignity'.
31 *glancing* 'momentary'.
43 *State* 'power', 'high rank'.
47 *Cynthia* Moon-goddess, here the moon.

48 *Shades* 'spirits of the dead'.
54 *Charnel House* 'funeral vault'.
61 The human imagination furnishes Death with his fearful weapons.
64 An echo of 1 Corinthians, 15:55: 'O death, where is thy sting? O grave, where is thy victory?'

Death's but a Path that must be trod,
If Man wou'd ever pass to God:
A Port of Calms, a State of Ease
From the rough Rage of swelling Seas.   70
    Why then thy flowing sable Stoles,
Deep pendent Cypress, mourning Poles,
Loose Scarfs to fall athwart thy Weeds,
Long Palls, drawn Herses, cover'd Steeds,
And Plumes of black, that as they tread,   75
Nod o'er the 'Scutcheons of the Dead?
    Nor can the parted Body know,
Nor wants the Soul, these Forms of Woe:
As Men who long in Prison dwell,
With Lamps that glimmer round the Cell,   80
When e'er their suffering Years are run,
Spring forth to greet the glitt'ring Sun:
Such Joy, tho' far transcending Sense,
Have pious Souls at parting hence.
On Earth, and in the Body plac't,   85
A few, and evil Years, they wast:
But when their Chains are cast aside,
See the glad Scene unfolding wide,
Clap the glad Wing and tow'r away,   90
And mingle with the Blaze of Day.

71 *sable Stoles* Long dark mourning robes.
72 *Cypress* A black thin crepe-like material, also the branches of the cypress tree hung up at funerals.
73 *Weeds* 'apparel'.
74 *Palls* Draperies hung over the coffin; *drawn* 'horse-drawn'. The 'Steeds' were covered with black cloths.
75–6 The hearse was surmounted with ostrich plumes and adorned with banners displaying the *'Scutcheons* (escutcheons or coats of arms) of the deceased's family.
77–8 *Nor ... nor* 'Neither ... nor'.
77 *parted* 'severed' (from the soul).
78 *wants* 'needs'.
90 *tow'r away* 'soar aloft' (an expression from hawking).

Oft have I read

The ironic tone of this anti-pastoral vignette strikingly anticipates George Crabbe's *The Village* (1783). The unique text of the poem is a manuscript in Parnell's own hand first printed in *The Collected Poems of Thomas Parnell*, ed. Claude Rawson and F. P. Lock (Newark, Del., 1989), pp. 421–2. We reprint their text here, but with punctuation added (there is none in the manuscript). We also expand 'ye' to 'the' and '&' to 'and'.

Oft have I read that Innocence retreats
Where cooling streams salute the summer Seats;
Singing at ease she roves the field of flowrs
Or safe with shepheards lys among the bowrs.
But late alas I crossd a country fare   5
And found No Strephon nor Dorinda there;
There Hodge and William Joynd to cully ned
While Ned was drinking Hodge and William dead;

5 *crossd* 'came upon'; *fare* 'fair'.
6 *Strephon ... Dorinda* Typical classical pastoral names.
7 *Hodge* A generic name for an English rural labourer; *cully* 'cheat'.

There Cicely Jeard by day the slips of Nell
And ere the night was ended Cicely fell.   10
Are these the Virtues which adorn the plain?
Ye bards forsake your old Arcadian Vein,
To sheep, those tender Innocents, resign
The place where swains and nymphs are said to shine;
Swains twice as Wicked, Nymphs but half as sage.   15
Tis sheep alone retrieve the golden age.

9 *slips* 'sexual lapses'.

12 *Arcadian* Arcadia was the region of Greece idealized by classical poets, synonymous with pastoral bliss.

16 *golden age* The myth of a primitive, innocent, idyllic life, first described by the Greek poet Hesiod. Cf. Thomson, *Spring*, 242–71.

Matthew Prior (1664–1721)

No author buried in Poet's Corner in Westminster Abbey boasts a tomb more splendid than Matthew Prior. His father George, a Westminster carpenter whose two brothers ran local taverns, managed to send his brilliant, imaginative son Matt, aged eight, to Westminster School. His death three years later curtailed the boy's education. Prior was spotted keeping the books at his uncle's tavern by Charles Sackville, the patron of Dryden and Congreve, who offered to pay his Westminster fees. Prior subsequently won a prestigious scholarship to St John's College, Cambridge. In 1690 he was appointed secretary to Lord Dursley at The Hague, and this was the start of a distinguished diplomatic career which included a key role in the negotations for the Treaty of Ryswick (1697) and the Treaty of Utrecht (1713). Between 1699 and 1702 he acted as travelling diplomatic agent to William III (who found his skill in languages invaluable) and helped to shape the Grand Alliance between England, Austria and Holland. He also produced a significant body of poetry, including the elevated Pindaric panegyric *Carmen Seculare* (1700), which heralded the new century under Williamite rule.

Although Prior joined the Whig Kit-Kat club in 1700, his belief in strong kingship soon led him into the Tory camp. His political influence was reduced by William's death that year: Queen Anne, William's successor, refused to trust one of such 'meane extraction'. During the following decade Prior became the most important English poet in the years between the death of Dryden (1700) and Pope's poetic maturity. Two collections of his verse appeared – the fifth part of Tonson's *Miscellanies* and *Poems on Several Occasions* (1709 and later editions). The fall of the Whig ministry in 1709 propelled Prior and his Tory friends back into power. By this stage he was collaborating with Swift on the *Examiner* and the pair went on long walks together, Swift to lose weight and Prior (described at this time as 'a thin, hollow-looked man, very factious in conversation') to gain it. 'Matt's Palace', Prior's fine house overlooking St James's Park, often hosted negotiations for the Treaty of Utrecht, popularly known as 'Matt's Peace'.

Prior was acting ambassador in Paris when Anne died and the Tories fell from office in August 1714. On his return to England in June 1715 he suffered the full consequences of the Whig purge. Placed under arrest, he refused to implicate his friends in charges of treason and corruption, and was punished by a year's confinement. Prior survived by making himself financially self-sufficient through his poetry. In 1718 Tonson published a lavish folio subscription edition of an expanded *Poems on Several Occasions*. Its 1,446 subscribers, from the middle classes as well as aristocracy, made Prior's fortune (perhaps upwards of £4,000). It enabled him finally to buy a country estate, Down Hall in Essex, co-purchased with Edward Harley in early 1721. Prior died unexpectedly a few months later before he had time to enjoy his new role as a Tory squire.

Prior's verse carried into the eighteenth century some of the characteristics of Restoration court poetry: its easy grace, its ability to wear its classical learning lightly, its scepticism, urbanity and sophisticated worldliness. Yet this represents only one side of his work. What he called his 'idle Tales' (such as *The Ladle* or *Paulo Purganti and his Wife*, about a wife's insatiable sexual desire) have a bawdy Chaucerian knowingness, and his love poetry was inspired by his tempestuous relationships with several mistresses. The more innocent *Henry and Emma*, 1708 (a recasting of the fifteenth-century ballad of *The Nut-Brown Maid*), became an international success. His *Ode Humbly Inscrib'd to the Queen* (1706), one of his most important public poems, established a century-long trend for Spenserian imitations, and he produced ambitious devotional and philosophical poems, *Solomon* and *Alma* (1718). His *Predestination* (1721) links Rochester's sceptical materialism to a vein of Christian pessimism. Many of Prior's poems testify to his continental connections, including his friendships with the French writers Boileau, Dacier and Fontenelle. His influence in turn on his friends Swift and Pope can be seen in their mock-heroic verse and in the tightly controlled expository couplets of the latter's *Essay on Man*. Prior claimed that had a diplomatic career not intervened he might have made poetry 'the Business of my Life', and not merely 'the Amusement of it'. His continual self-deprecation has perhaps too often been taken at face value.

For His own Epitaph

This poem was occasioned by the completion of a bust of Prior by Charles Coysevoux (1640–1720) which was later placed on his monument in Westminster Abbey (but without these verses). Date of composition (1714) is fixed by the reference to the writer's age. As a self-epitaph the poem repays comparison with Swift's *Verses on the Death of Dr Swift* and the final stanzas of Gray's *Elegy*. It was first printed posthumously under the title 'For my own Monument' in *Miscellaneous Works of … Matthew Prior* (1740). However, an earlier manuscript version of the text in the hand of Prior's secretary Adrian Drift exists under the title 'Mr: Prior for His own Epitaph' in vol. 27 of the Prior Papers in the library of the Marquis of Bath at Longleat, Wiltshire. This manuscript is reproduced as 'For His own Epitaph' in *The Literary Works of Matthew Prior*, ed. Wright and Spears, 1:409–10, from where we have taken the following text.

As Doctors give Physic by way of prevention,
    MATT alive and in health of his Tomb-stone took care;
For delays are unsafe, and his Pious Intention
    May haply be never fulfill'd by his Heir.

Then take MATTS word for it, the Sculptor is paid,   5
    That the Figure is fine pray believe Your own Eye,
Yet credit but lightly what more may be said,
    For we flatter our Selves, and teach Marble to lye.

Yet counting as far as to Fifty his Years,
    His Virtues and Vices were as other Mens are,   10
High Hopes he conceiv'd, and he smother'd great fears,
    In a Life party-coloured, half Pleasure half care.

Nor to Buisness a Drudge, nor to Faction a Slave,
    He strove to make Intrest and freedom agree.
In public Employments industrious and grave,   15
    And alone with his Friends, Lord, how merry was He.

Now in Equipage Stately, now humbly on foot,
    Both Fortunes he Try'd but to neither wou'd Trust,
And whirl'd in the round, as the Wheel turn'd about
    He found Riches had wings, and knew Man was but Dust.   20

This Verse little polish'd tho mighty sincere
    Sets neither his Titles nor Merit to view,
It says that his Relicks collected lye here,
    And no Mortal yet knows too if this may be true.

Fierce Robbers there are that infest the Highway   25
    So MATT may be kill'd and his Bones never found;
False Witness at Court, and fierce Tempests at Sea,
    So MATT may yet chance to be Hang'd, or be Drown'd.

If his Bones lye in Earth, roll in Sea, fly in Air
    To Fate We must yeild, and the things are the same,   30
And if passing Thou giv'st Him a Smile, or a Tear
    He cares not — Yet prythee be kind to his Fame.

4 Prior was unmarried and childless.   17 *Equipage* 'carriage and horses'.
12 *party-coloured* 'checkered'.

An Epitaph

First published in *Poems on Several Occasions* (1718), from which the following text is taken. Prior's model may have been the French Renaissance writer Jean de Gombauld's epigram on an undistinguished man, 'La Vie de Guillaume'. Jack and Joan's passive indifference to fortune's ups and downs is more puzzling. As well as exposing the problematics of epitaph-writing this poem subtly undermines the verse tradition celebrating self-sufficient quietism and the avoidance of extremes exemplified in Pomfret's *The Choice* (1700). There are also ironic parallels with Parnell's *A Night-Piece on Death* (1722) and Gray's *Elegy Written in a Country Church Yard* (1751).

> *Stet quicunque volet potens*
> *Aulæ culmine lubrico, &c.*   Senec.

Interr'd beneath this Marble Stone,
Lie Saunt'ring JACK, and Idle JOAN.
While rolling Threescore Years and One
Did round this Globe their Courses run;
If Human Things went Ill or Well;   5
If changing Empires rose or fell;
The Morning past, the Evening came,
And found this Couple still the same.
They Walk'd and Eat, good Folks: What then?
Why then They Walk'd and Eat again: 10
They soundly slept the Night away:
They did just Nothing all the Day:
And having bury'd Children Four,
Wou'd not take Pains to try for more.
Nor Sister either had, nor Brother: 15
They seem'd just Tally'd for each other.
   Their Moral and Oeconomy
Most perfectly They made agree:
Each Virtue kept it's proper Bound,
Nor Trespass'd on the other's Ground.   20
Nor Fame, nor Censure They regarded:
They neither Punish'd, nor Rewarded.
He car'd not what the Footmen did:
Her Maids She neither prais'd, nor chid:
So ev'ry Servant took his Course;   25
And bad at First, They all grew worse.
Slothful Disorder fill'd His Stable;
And sluttish Plenty deck'd Her Table.
Their Beer was strong; Their Wine was *Port*;
Their Meal was large; Their Grace was short.   30
They gave the Poor the Remnant-meat,
Just when it grew not fit to eat.
   They paid the Church and Parish-Rate;
And took, but read not the Receit:
For which They claim'd their *Sunday*'s Due,   35
Of slumb'ring in an upper Pew.
   No Man's Defects sought They to know;
So never made Themselves a Foe.
No Man's good Deeds did They commend;

Epigraph A line from Seneca's tragedy *Thyestes*: 'Let the mighty, if they will, walk the slippery heights of the Court'.

16 *Tally'd* 'exactly suited'.

17 *Moral* 'morality'.

31 *Remnant-meat* 'leftovers'.

34 *Receit* Presumably for the annual rent on their reserved pew in church.

So never rais'd Themselves a Friend.   40
Nor cherish'd They Relations poor:
That might decrease Their present Store:
Nor Barn nor House did they repair:
That might oblige Their future Heir.
    They neither Added, nor Confounded: 45
They neither Wanted, nor Abounded.
Each *Christmas* They Accompts did clear;
And wound their Bottom round the Year.
Nor Tear, nor Smile did They imploy
At News of Public Grief, or Joy.   50
When Bells were Rung, and Bonfires made;
If ask'd, They ne'er deny'd their Aid:
Their Jugg was to the Ringers carry'd;
Who ever either Dy'd, or Marry'd.
Their Billet at the Fire was found;.   55
Who ever was Depos'd, or Crown'd
    Nor Good, nor Bad, nor Fools, nor Wise;
They wou'd not learn, nor cou'd advise:
Without Love, Hatred, Joy, or Fear,
They led — a kind of — as it were: 60
Nor Wish'd, nor Car'd, nor Laugh'd, nor Cry'd:
And so They liv'd; and so They dy'd.

45 *Confounded* 'spent', 'wasted'.
48 *wound their Bottom* 'put their affairs in order'.
53 *Ringers* i.e. bell-ringers.

55 *Billet* 'firewood'. They contributed to public bonfires celebrating the deposition of one monarch or the crowning of another with total impartiality.

The Lady's Looking-Glass

The poem was first printed in *Poetical Miscellanies: The Fifth Part* (1704), the source of the following text. Subtitled 'In Imitation of a Greek Idyllium', the poem draws on Poem 4, 'A Comparison', by the Greek bucolic poet Moschus (fl. *c.*150 BC), describing a sudden storm at sea.

Celia and I the other Day
Walk'd o're the Sand-hills to the Sea:
The setting Sun adorn'd the Coast,
His Beams entire, his Fierceness lost;
And on the Surface of the deep,   5
The Winds lay only not asleep:
The Prospect and the Nymph were gay,
With silent Joy I heard her say,
That we shou'd walk there ev'ry Day.
    But oh! the Change! the Winds grew high,   10
Impending Tempests charge the Sky;
The Light'ning flies, the Thunder roars,
And big Waves lash the frighten'd Shoars.
Struck with the Horror of the Sight,
She turns her Head and wings her Flight,   15
And trembling, vows she ne'er again
Will press the Shore or see the Main.
    Look back at least once more, said I,
Thy self in that great Glass descry,
When thou art in good Humour drest,   20
When gentle Reason rules thy Breast,

The Sun upon the calmest Sea
Appears not half so bright as Thee:
'Tis then that with Delight I rove
Upon the boundless depth of Love;   25
I bless my Chain, I hand my Oar,
Nor think on all I left on Shoar.
But when vain Doubts and groundless Fear,
Do that dear foolish Bosom tear,
When the big Lip and wat'ry Eye   30
Tell me the rising Storm is nigh;
'Tis then thou art yon angry Main,
Deform'd by Winds, and dash'd by Rain;
And the poor Sailor that must try
Its Fury, labours less than I.   35
 Shipwreck'd, in vain to Land I make,
While Love and Fate still drive me back;
Forc'd to doat on Thee thy own way,
I chide Thee first and then obey.
Wretched when from Thee, vext when nigh,   40
I with Thee or without Thee die.

Non Pareil

The poem was first printed in *Miscellaneous Works of ... Matthew Prior* (1740), from which the following text is taken. Prior once more presents women as an ambivalent force of nature.

I

Let others from the town retire,
 And in the fields seek new delight;
My PHILLIS does such joys inspire,
 No other objects please my sight.

II

In Her alone I find whate'er   5
 Beauties a country-landscape grace;
No shades so lovely as Her hair,
 Nor plain so sweet as is Her face.

III

Lilies and roses there combine,
 More beauteous than in flow'ry field;   10
Transparent is Her skin, so fine,
 To this each crystal stream must yield.

IV

Her voice more sweet than warbling sound,
 Tho' sung by nightingale or lark,
Her eyes such lustre dart around,   15
 Compar'd to them the sun is dark.

V

Both light and vital heat they give,
 Cherish'd by Them my love takes root,

Title 'Without compare', 'unparalleled'.

From Her kind looks does life receive,
  Grows a fair plant; bears flow'rs, and fruit.   20

VI

Such fruit, I ween, did once deceive
  The common parent of mankind;
And made transgress our mother EVE:
  Poison its core, tho' fair its rind.

VII

Yet so delicious is it's taste,   25
  I cannot from the bait abstain,
But to th'inchanting pleasure haste,
  Tho' I were sure 'twou'd end in pain.

21 *ween* 'believe', 'think'.

On a Pretty Madwoman

The poem was first printed in *Miscellaneous Works of ... Matthew Prior* (1740), from which the following text is taken. The madness and death of Ophelia, heroine of Shakespeare's *Hamlet*, both moved and troubled the critics of Prior's day. Jeremy Collier (1698) was unsympathetic: 'such People ought to be kept in dark Rooms and without Company'. James Drake (1699) disagreed: 'Here Piety and Love concur to make her Affliction piercing and to impress her Sorrow more deep and lasting'. Prior gives this sympathetic view an ironic twist.

I

While mad OPHELIA we lament,
  And Her distraction mourn,
Our grief's misplac'd, Our tears mispent,
Since what for Her condition's meant,
  More justly fits Our Own.   5

II

For if tis happiness to be,
  From all the turns of Fate,
From dubious joy, and sorrow free;
OPHELIA then is blest, and we
  Misunderstand Her state.   10

III

The Fates may do whate'er they will,
  They can't disturb her mind,
Insensible of good, or ill,
OPHELIA is OPHELIA still,
  Be Fortune cross or kind.   15

IV

Then make with reason no more noise,
  Since what should give relief,
The quiet of our mind destroys,
Or with a full spring-tide of joys,
  Or a dead-ebb of grief.   20

19–20 *Or ... Or* 'Either ... Or'.

Jonathan Swift (1667–1745)

A number of Swift's characteristic traits were formed in infancy: his love–hate relationship with Ireland, his mistrust of physical intimacy and emotional dependency, and his contempt for lawyers. Swift's father, the least successful of four English lawyer brothers drawn to Ireland by profitable legal business, died seven months before he was born. As a child Swift relied on his uncles' charity and enjoyed only occasional contact with his mother, from whom he was parted for three years as a toddler when his wet-nurse smuggled him on a sea voyage to England. When, aged six, he was sent to Kilkenny grammar school south of Dublin, his mother and elder sister moved to Leicester. In early 1689 political unrest ended Swift's student career at Trinity College, Dublin. He was to spend most of the next decade at Moor Park in Surrey as secretary to Sir William Temple, the retired Whig diplomat and author. Temple inspired in his protégé both hero-worship and resentment. In May 1694, frustrated by his patron's reluctance to advance him politically, Swift moved to Dublin to be ordained in the Church of Ireland. But in June 1696 he returned to Temple's service, disillusioned by clerical life in the isolated prebend of Kilroot in predominantly Presbyterian Ulster, and by his rejection in marriage by 'Varina', Jane Waring. Moor Park fostered Swift's first poems – lofty Pindaric odes – and his earliest prose satires, *A Tale of a Tub*, *The Mechanical Operation of the Spirit* and *The Battle of the Books* (published together in 1704), primarily targeting religious dissent and the vacuous arrogance of modern writing.

After Temple's death in January 1699, Swift, still in search of a career, went to Ireland as the Earl of Berkeley's chaplain. He was disappointed of promotion to the vacant deanery of Derry, a failure which he interpreted as part of a lifelong pattern of slights and snubs, and had to settle instead for the vicarage of Laracor and a prebend at St Patrick's, Dublin. His first political pamphlet, *A Discourse of the Contests and Dissensions in Athens and Rome* (1701), mirrored his former patron's moderate Whig politics, expressing support for the Revolution Settlement and the belief in parliament's right to determine monarchical succession. After King William's death in 1702 Swift sought political advancement in England and established his reputation among Addison's Whig circle with the *Bickerstaff Papers* (1708), a wildly successful literary hoax against the quack astrologer John Partridge. But Swift's High Church principles sat uncomfortably with the demands being placed on him, and he was simultaneously producing four tracts on religion which supplied a serious critique of Whig policies. In 1710 Swift started to see his political ambitions realized when the incoming Tory administration, led by Henry St John (later Viscount Bolingbroke) and Robert Harley, Earl of Oxford, was quick to recognize how it could use his literary skills. Swift was invited into their intimate gatherings (a source of enormous pride to him). Now openly Tory, he became their chief propagandist, producing the *Examiner* and a series of political pamphlets, notably *The Conduct of the Allies* (1711), which helped move public opinion behind the peace negotiations culminating in the Treaty of Utrecht of 1713. These were Swift's golden days (recorded in his daily *Journal to Stella*) in which he revelled in his friendships with Pope, Gay and other members of the Scriblerus Club. Yet his Tory mentors, perhaps unable to overcome Queen Anne's dislike of Swift's indecency, could only secure for him the Deanery of St Patrick's Cathedral, Dublin, instead of the English preferment he so coveted. After the death of Anne and the collapse of Tory power in August 1714 Swift returned to Ireland, 'a place … hateful to me', where he settled permanently. Despite his professed contempt for the Irish he wrote numerous economic pamphlets on their behalf. The Dean's most remarkable achievement as Irish patriot was a series of pamphlets, the *Drapier's Letters* (1724), in which Swift, writing as 'MD, Drapier of Dublin', led the Irish to reject the English government's imposition of a debased copper coinage known as Wood's Halfpence. More characteristic, however, was the pessimism behind the *Modest Proposal* (1729), his bleakly ironic solution to the recent Irish famine.

Swift's most famous work, *Gulliver's Travels* (1726), did little to endear him to the English government. The opposition turned Swift's broad attacks on political corruption against Walpole's administration, yet the pervasive irony of the *Travels* extends beyond party-politics to a universal condemnation of corrupt human nature. It was from this work that Swift's reputation for misanthropy emerged – a reputation which his closing years did little to dispel. Increasingly debilitated by the deafness and giddiness caused by a disease of the inner ear he had suffered since youth, Swift spent his last decades in Dublin. A large body of his verse dates from this period. In August 1742 he was deemed insane and finally died in 1745.

Swift's early Pindaric odes indicate a serious poetic ambition, yet his subsequent output – mostly satirical, comic, personal and occasional verse, often in jog-trot eight-stress couplets (octosyllabics) – suggests a man who refused to take his poetry entirely seriously. His notorious scatological poems, of which *Strephon and Chloe* and *A Beautiful Young Nymph Going to Bed*, printed here, are two examples, have offended readers and divided critics. Recent feminist criticism has recuperated these poems, perceiving in Swift's intractably physical women a liberating challenge to male-constructed poetic fictions of female beauty.

Swift's verbal energy is precisely focused and he is suspicious of grand poetic gestures. In his hands poetry counters the shams and self-deceptions of those who idealize or romanticize life. He is on the watch for this in himself as much as in others.

A Description of the Morning

This poem, reproduced from *Tatler*, 9 (30 April 1709), where it first appeared, is an early example of the oxymoronic 'town eclogue' or 'urban georgic'. Swift applies a rural descriptive style to matters modern and unpoetic. Sir Richard Steele, the *Tatler's* editor,

heralded the poem as a new experiment in urban realism. The author has 'run into a Way perfectly new, and describ'd Things exactly as they happen: He never forms Fields, or Nymphs, or Groves, where they are not, but makes the Incidents just as they really appear.'

> Now hardly here and there an Hackney-Coach
> Appearing, show'd the Ruddy Morn's Approach.
> Now *Betty* from her Master's Bed had flown,
> And softly stole to discompose her own.
> The Slipshod 'Prentice from his Master's Dore,   5
> Had par'd the Street, and sprinkl'd round the Floor.
> Now *Moll* had whirl'd her Mop with dex'trous Airs,
> Prepar'd to scrub the Entry and the Stairs.
> The Youth with broomy Stumps began to trace
> The Kennel Edge, where Wheels had worn the Place.   10
> The Smallcoal-Man was heard with Cadence deep,
> Till drown'd in shriller Notes of Chimney-sweep.
> Duns at his Lordship's Gate began to meet;
> And Brickdust *Moll* had scream'd through half a Street.
> The Turn-key now his Flock returning sees,   15
> Duly let out a' Nights to steal for Fees.
> The watchful Bayliffs take their silent Stands;
> And School-boys lag with Satchels in their Hands.

1 *hardly* 'abruptly'; *Hackney-Coach* A coach and horses for hire; the city's version of the sun-god Apollo's chariot.
3 *Betty* A generic name for a maidservant.
6 *par'd the Street* 'scraped dirt from the street' (subsequent editions replaced 'Street' with 'Dirt'); *sprinkl'd* With fresh sawdust.
9–10 A note, perhaps by Swift, in Faulkner's edition of Swift's *Works* (1735), states that the youths were searching 'to find old nails'; *Kennel* 'gutter'. These gutter-scavengers were known as 'kennel-rakers'.
11 *Smallcoal-Man* A seller of coal for domestic fires. Cf. Gay, *Trivia*, 2:35.

13 *Duns* 'debt-collectors'.
14 *Brickdust* Moll is hawking powdered brick, used to sharpen knives. Like the coalman and sweep she is discoloured by her trade.
15 *Turn-key* 'jailer'; *Flock* An ironic pastoral epithet for his prisoners. He lets them roam at night to steal so they can pay his fees for supplying them with provisions and privileges. It was Swift who first suggested the idea (later developed by Gay) of a 'Newgate Pastoral'.
18 Cf. 'Then the whining schoolboy, with his satchel / And shining morning face, creeping like snail / Unwillingly to school' (Shakespeare, *As You Like It*, II. vii.145–7).

A Description of a City Shower

This poem, which first appeared in *Tatler*, 238 (17 October 1710), was widely admired. Swift remarked that 'They say 'tis the best thing I ever writ, and I think so too'. It parallels Virgil's celebrated description of the storm in *Georgics*, 1:316–34 and his advice on reading the signs of changing weather, 1:351–92. The poem's Virgilian hinterland extends to

Aeneid 2's description of the Trojan horse and Book 4's account of the rainstorm which forces Dido and Aeneas to take shelter – the passage that was used to introduce this poem in the *Tatler*. The squalid urban refuse catalogued in the closing triplet drives home the unheroic realities of modern city life. The text is from the original *Tatler*.

Careful Observers may fortel the Hour,
(By sure Prognosticks) when to dread a Shower:
While Rain depends, the pensive Cat gives o'er
Her Frolicks, and pursues her Tail no more.
Returning Home at Night, you'll find the Sink   5
Strike your offended Sense with double Stink;
If you be wise, then go not far to dine,
You'll spend in Coach-Hire more than save in Wine.
A coming Shower your shooting Corns presage,
Old Aches throb, your hollow Tooth will rage.   10
Sauntring in Coffee-house is *Dulman* seen,
He damns the Climate, and complains of Spleen.
    Mean while the *South* rising with dabbled Wings,
A sable Cloud athwart the Welkin flings,
That swill'd more Liquor than it could contain,   15
And, like a Drunkard, gives it up again.
Brisk *Susan* whips her Linen from the Rope,
While the first drizz'ling Shower is born aslope:
Such is that sprinkling which some careless Quean
Flirts on you from her Mop, but not so clean: 20
You fly, invoke the Gods, then turning, stop
To rail; she singing, still whirls on her Mop.
Nor yet the Dust had shun'd th'unequal Strife,
But, aided by the Wind, fought still for Life;
And wafted with its Foe, by violent Gust,   25
'Twas doubtful which was Rain, and which was Dust.
Ah! Where must needy Poet seek for Aid,
When Dust and Rain at once his Coat invade;
His only Coat, where Dust confused with Rain,
Roughen the Nap, and leave a mingled Stain.   30
    Now in contiguous Drops the Flood comes down,
Threat'ning with Deluge this *Devoted* Town:
To Shops in Crowds the daggled Females fly,
Pretend to cheapen Goods, but nothing buy.
The Templer spruce, while every Spout's a-broach,   35
Stays till 'tis fair, yet seems to call a Coach:
The tuck'd-up Sempstress walks with hasty Strides,
While Streams run down her oil'd Umbrella's Sides.
Here various Kinds, by various Fortunes led,

3 *depends* 'is impending'.
5 *Sink* 'sewer'.
9 *shooting Corns* 'shooting pains in your corns'.
10 *Aches* A disyllable, pronounced 'aitches'.
12 *Spleen* See headnote to Anne Finch, *The Spleen*.
13 *South* 'south wind'; *dabbled* 'mud-splashed'.
14 *Welkin* 'sky' (archaic).
17 *Linen* 'laundry'; *Rope* 'washing-line'.
18 *aslope* 'slantingly'.
19 *Quean* 'hussy'.
20 *Flirts* 'flicks'.
22 *rail* 'complain'.

27–30 Cf. John Philips, *The Splendid Shilling*, 120–5.
30 *Nap* 'smooth texture'.
31 *contiguous* 'continuous'.
32 *Devoted* Means both 'devout' (ironic) and 'doomed'.
    Swift amplifies the references to 'the Flood' and
    'Deluge' (31–2) to hint at God's original punishment
    for man's wickedness.
33 *daggled* 'spattered with mud'.
34 *cheapen* 'haggle over'.
35 *Templer* A law student at the Inns of Court; *a-broach*
    'streaming'.
38 *oil'd* Made of oiled silk, so waterproof.

Commence Acquaintance underneath a Shed,   40
Triumphant Tories, and desponding Whigs,
Forget their Feuds, and join to save their Wigs:
Box'd in a Chair the Beau impatient sits,
While Spouts run clatt'ring o'er the Roof by Fits,
And ever and anon with frightful Din   45
The Leather sounds, he trembles from within.
So when *Troy* Chair-men bore the Wooden Steed,
Pregnant with *Greeks*, impatient to be freed,
(Those Bully *Greeks*, who, as the Moderns do,
Instead of paying Chair-men, run them thro')   50
Laoco'n struck the Outside with his Spear,
And each imprison'd Hero quak'd for Fear.
    Now from all Parts the swelling Kennels flow,
And bear their Trophies with them as they go:
Filth of all Hues and Odors seem to tell   55
What Street they sail'd from, by the Sight and Smell.
They, as each Torrent drives, with rapid Force
From *Smithfield* or St. *'Pulchre*'s shape their Course,
And in huge Confluent join'd at *Snow-Hill* Ridge,
Fall from the *Conduit* prone to *Holborn-Bridge*.   60
Sweepings from Butchers Stalls, Dung, Guts and Blood,
Drown'd Puppies, stinking Sprats, all drench'd in Mud,
Dead Cats and Turnep-Tops come tumbling down the
    Flood.

41 The poem was published shortly after the fall of the
   Whigs and the formation of the Tory ministry. Cf.
   Anne Finch, *Upon the Hurricane*, 175–7.
43 *Chair* 'sedan chair'.
46 *Leather* 'leather roof'. The sound mimics the
   drumbeats of battle.
47–52 The Greeks entered Troy by hiding within a large
   wooden horse which the Trojans dragged through the
   city gate believing it to be a gift to the gods. The priest
   Laocoön, suspecting a plot, struck the horse and
   frightened the Greeks inside (*Aeneid*, 2:40–56). Swift
   may be drawing an ironic parallel between the feud of
   Greeks and Trojans and the party squabbling of Whigs
   and Tories.

49 *Bully* 'violently aggressive'.
53 *Kennels* 'gutters'.
58–60 The refuse from Smithfield, an open-air livestock
   market just north-west of the City, flowed down Cow
   Lane. At Holborn Conduit it met the rubbish coming
   down Snow Hill from the parish of St Sepulchre.
   Together it poured into the notorious Fleet Ditch at
   Holborn Bridge.
61–3 Swift's note in Faulkner's edition of his works (1735)
   comically inveighs against the modern practice of
   triplet rhymes, the last line of which was an alexandrine
   with two or more extra syllables. Here the lines
   appropriately mirror the tumbling, irregular movement
   of the rubbish heading towards the river.

Stella's Birthday, 1721

Swift first encountered Esther Johnson (1681–1728)
in 1689 at Moor Park, where her mother lived as a
friend of the Temple family. Swift helped in the girl's
early education, but this pedagogical relationship soon
developed into probably the most important and
enduring friendship in Swift's life. In 1701 he moved
'Stella' to Dublin accompanied by her companion,
Rebecca Dingley, and a predictable amount of gossip.
Swift, despite or because of the value he placed on
their friendship, never proposed marriage. He began
writing birthday poems for her in 1719, when she was
thirty-eight, and continued, barring two years, until
her last birthday in 1727. Their form mimics the royal

birthday odes turned out by the Whig Poet Laureate
Laurence Eusden. The name Stella (first used by
Swift in these poems) recalls the idealized mistress of
Sir Philip Sidney's sonnet-sequence *Astrophel and
Stella* (1591). Yet Swift characteristically draws
attention to what poetic tributes to a mistress usually
hide – her age, weight, wrinkles and grey hair – before
praising Stella's true moral virtues which passing
years strengthen rather than deface. Stella took these
poems in good heart (she transcribed three of them in
her commonplace book), yet recent feminist critics,
troubled by Swift's undermining of his friend's
physical self-esteem, would dispute Irvin Ehrenpreis's

assertion (*Swift*, 3:422) that Swift is 'strongest when he makes the visible decay of [Stella's] body into the groundwork of his affection'. The consumerist metaphors which pervade the following poem also seem disturbing in their implications. The text printed below, a copy of Stella's transcription of the poem in a manuscript volume in the possession of the Duke of Bedford, Woburn Abbey, is reproduced from *The Poems of Jonathan Swift*, ed. Harold Williams, 3 vols, 2nd edn (1958, 1966), 2:734–6.

All Travellers at first incline
Where'e'er they see the fairest Sign,
And if they find the Chambers neat,
And like the Liquor and the Meat
Will call again and recommend   5
The Angel-Inn to ev'ry Friend:
And though the Painting grows decayd
The House will never loose it's Trade;
Nay, though the treach'rous Rascal Thomas
Hangs a new Angel two doors from us   10
As fine as Dawbers Hands can make it
In hopes that Strangers may mistake it,
They think it both a Shame and Sin
To quit the true old Angel-Inn.
   Now, this is Stella's Case in Fact;   15
An Angel's Face, a little crack't;
(Could Poets or could Painters fix
How Angels look at thirty six)
This drew us in at first to find
In such a Form an Angel's Mind   20
And ev'ry Virtue now supplyes
The fainting Rays of Stella's Eyes:
See, at her Levee crowding Swains
Whom Stella freely entertains
With Breeding, Humor, Wit, and Sense,   25
And puts them to so small Expence,
Their Minds so plentifully fills,
And makes such reasonable Bills
So little gets for what she gives
We really wonder how she lives;   30
And, had her Stock been less, no doubt
She must have long ago run out.
   Then, who can think we'll quit the Place
When Doll hangs out a newer Face
Nail'd to her Window full in Sight   35
All Christian People to invite;
Or stop and light at Cloe's Head
With Scraps and Leavings to be fed.
   Then Cloe, still go on to prate

6 *Angel-Inn* In Swift's day one of the most common inn-signs.

9 *Thomas* Possibly a reference to Swift's imprudent Irish schoolmaster friend Thomas Sheridan.

11 *Dawber* 'sign-painter'.

18 *thirty six* Stella was in fact forty in 1721. Swift's repeated practice of subtracting a few years from Stella's age is perhaps a sly dig at a common habit in the middle-aged.

21 *supplyes* 'compensates for'.

23 *Levee* A morning audience.

24 *freely* 'liberally'.

37 *light* 'alight'; *Cloe's Head* Swift continues the inn-sign metaphor but then reverts in the next line to the actual contents of Cloe's head.

Of thirty six, and thirty eight;   40
Pursue thy Trade of Scandall picking,
Thy Hints that Stella is no Chickin,
Your Innuendo's when you tell us
That Stella loves to talk with Fellows
But let me warn thee to believe   45
A Truth for which thy Soul should grieve,
That, should you live to see the Day
When Stella's Locks must all be grey
When Age must print a furrow'd Trace
On ev'ry Feature of her Face;   50
Though you and all your senceless Tribe
Could Art or Time or Nature bribe
To make you look like Beauty's Queen
And hold for ever at fifteen.
No Bloom of Youth can ever blind   55
The Cracks and Wrinckles of your Mind,
All Men of Sense will pass your Dore
And crowd to Stella's at fourscore.

48 Cf. Pope, *The Rape of the Lock*, 5:26.   53 *Beauty's Queen* Venus.

Stella's Birthday, 1727

This was Swift's last birthday poem to Stella. Dated 'March 13, 1727' it was written a few weeks before he left Ireland for a visit to England. Stella's health, already poor, continued to deteriorate during Swift's absence. When Swift returned to Dublin in October, she was clearly dying. This moving tribute, published two months after Stella's death on 28 January 1728, is at once a birthday ode, a memorial to their friendship, and an epitaph. The text is that of *Miscellanies. The Last Volume* (dated 1727 but really March 1728), where the poem first appeared.

This Day, whate'er the Fates decree,
Shall still be kept with Joy by me:
This Day then, let us not be told,
That you are sick, and I grown old,
Nor think on our approaching Ills,   5
And talk of Spectacles and Pills;
To morrow will be Time enough
To hear such mortifying Stuff.
Yet, since from Reason may be brought
A better and more pleasing Thought,   10
Which can in spite of all Decays,
Support a few remaining Days:
From not the gravest of Divines,
Accept for once some serious Lines.
  Although we now can form no more   15
Long Schemes of Life, as heretofore;
Yet you, while Time is running fast,
Can look with Joy on what is past.
  Were future Happiness and Pain,

8 *mortifying* 'humiliating', with a pun on the word's primary meaning, 'causing death'.

A mere Contrivance of the Brain, 20
As Atheists argue, to entice,
And fit their Proselytes for Vice;
(The only Comfort they propose,
To have Companions in their Woes.)
Grant this the Case, yet sure 'tis hard, 25
That Virtue, stil'd its own Reward,
And by all Sages understood
To be the chief of human Good,
Should acting, die, nor leave behind
Some lasting Pleasure in the Mind, 30
Which by Remembrance will assuage,
Grief, Sickness, Poverty, and Age;
And strongly shoot a radiant Dart,
To shine through Life's declining Part.
    Say, *Stella*, feel you no Content, 35
Reflecting on a Life well spent?
Your skilful Hand employ'd to save
Despairing Wretches from the Grave;
And then supporting with your Store,
Those whom you dragg'd from Death before: 40
(So Providence on Mortals waits,
Preserving what it first creates)
Your gen'rous Boldness to defend
An innocent and absent Friend;
That Courage which can make you just, 45
To Merit humbled in the Dust:
The Detestation you express
For Vice in all its glitt'ring Dress:
That Patience under tort'ring Pain,
Where stubborn Stoicks would complain. 50
    Must these like empty Shadows pass,
Or Forms reflected from a Glass?
Or mere Chimæra's in the Mind,
That fly and leave no Marks behind?
Does not the Body thrive and grow 55
By Food of twenty Years ago?
And, had it not been still supply'd,
It must a thousand Times have dy'd.
Then, who with Reason can maintain,
That no Effects of Food remain? 60
And, is not Virtue in Mankind
The Nutriment that feeds the Mind?
Upheld by each good Action past,
And still continued by the last:
Then, who with Reason can pretend, 65
That all Effects of Virtue end?
    Believe me *Stella*, when you show
That true Contempt for Things below,
Nor prize your Life for other Ends

---

22 *Proselytes* 'converts'.
50 Stoic philosophy preached indifference to suffering.

53 *Chimæra* 'distorted fantasy'.
65 *pretend* 'claim'.

Than merely to oblige your Friends;   70
Your former Actions claim their Part,
And join to fortify your Heart.
For Virtue in her daily Race,
Like *Janus*, bears a double Face;
Looks back with Joy where she has gone,   75
And therefore goes with Courage on.
She at your sickly Couch will wait,
And guide you to a better State.
   O then, whatever Heav'n intends,
Take Pity on your pitying Friends;   80
Nor let your Ills affect your Mind,
To fancy they can be unkind.
Me, surely me, you ought to spare,
Who gladly would your Suff'rings share;
Or give my Scrap of Life to you,   85
And think it far beneath your Due;
You, to whose Care so oft I owe,
That I'm alive to tell you so.

---

74 *Janus* The Roman god of entrances and exits who gave his name to the start of the year. His symbol was a double-faced head looking both backwards and forwards.

A Beautiful Young Nymph Going to Bed

This poem was first published by John Roberts in December 1734 in a quarto pamphlet along with two other Swift poems, *Strephon and Chloe* and *Cassinus and Peter*, all three of which were probably composed in 1731. It carried the ironic subtitle 'Written for the Honour of the Fair *Sex*' and a Latin epigraph from Ovid's *Remedia Amoris*, 1:334: 'A woman is the least part of herself' (when all additions are removed). The poem, for all its shock value, belongs to a well-established literary tradition satirizing women's use of artificial beauty aids. A sequence of light comic epigrams on women losing their mouse-skin eyebrows and glass eyes had appeared in Swift's friend Matthew Prior's *Poems on Several Occasions* (1718). Closer in tone to the intense disgust registered in Swift's poem is an episode in *The Visions of … Quevedo … Burlesqu'd* (1702), in which an old man advises a naive young man that a prostitute's artificial charms conceal a repulsive body. The text is that of Roberts's 1734 quarto.

Corinna, Pride of *Drury-Lane*,
For whom no Shepherd sighs in vain;
Never did *Covent Garden* boast
So bright a batter'd, strolling Toast;
No drunken Rake to pick her up,   5
No Cellar where on Tick to sup;
Returning at the Midnight Hour;
Four Stories climbing to her Bow'r;
Then, seated on a three-legg'd Chair,

Title Perhaps an ironic parallel to Donne's famous Elegy *To His Mistris Going to Bed*. Both poems describe the process of a woman undressing.
1 *Corinna* A name widely used in pastoral poetry. Corinna was the subject of Ovid's erotic Latin poems, the *Amores*, as well as the name of a Greek lyric poetess; *Drury-Lane* A notorious haunt of prostitutes.
3 *Covent Garden* London's theatre and red-light district. See Gay, *Trivia*, 2:343–56.
4 *Toast* 'reigning beauty'.
6 *Tick* 'credit'.
9 *three-legg'd* Like its owner, the chair is missing a part.

Takes off her artificial Hair: 10
Now, picking out a Crystal Eye,
She wipes it clean, and lays it by.
Her Eye-Brows from a Mouse's Hyde,
Stuck on with Art on either Side,
Pulls off with Care, and first displays 'em,   15
Then in a Play-Book smoothly lays 'em.
Now dextrously her Plumpers draws,
That serve to fill her hollow Jaws.
Untwists a Wire; and from her Gums
A Set of Teeth completely comes.   20
Pulls out the Rags contriv'd to prop
Her flabby Dugs and down they drop.
Proceeding on, the lovely Goddess
Unlaces next her Steel-Rib'd Bodice;
Which by the Operator's Skill,   25
Press down the Lumps, the Hollows fill,
Up goes her Hand, and off she slips
The Bolsters that supply her Hips.
With gentlest Touch, she next explores
Her Shankers, Issues, running Sores,   30
Effects of many a sad Disaster;
And then to each applies a Plaister.
But must, before she goes to Bed,
Rub off the Dawbs of White and Red;
And smooth the Furrows in her Front,   35
With greasy Paper stuck upon't.
She takes a *Bolus* e'er she sleeps;
And then between two Blankets creeps.
With Pains of Love tormented lies;
Or if she chance to close her Eyes,   40
Of *Bridewell* and the *Compter* dreams,
And feels the Lash, and faintly screams;
Or, by a faithless Bully drawn,
At some Hedge-Tavern lies in Pawn;
Or to *Jamaica* seems transported,   45
Alone, and by no Planter courted;

11 *Crystal* Here in the literal rather than the metaphorical sense often used in love poetry.

17 *Plumpers* Pads carried in the mouth to fill out hollow cheeks. Corinna has lost her teeth through venereal disease.

22 *Dugs* 'breasts' (derogatory).

30 *Shankers* 'ulcers'; *Issues* Incisions made to drain pus from the body.

34 *Dawbs of White and Red* i.e. cosmetics.

35 *Front* 'forehead'. Cf. Parnell, *An Elegy, To an Old Beauty*, 2n.

37 *Bolus* A large, soft, easily swallowed medicinal pill.

39 *Pains of Love* Perhaps literally, i.e. the painful symptoms of venereal disease.

41 *Bridewell* A house of correction for female vagrants and prostitutes; *Compter* (pronounced 'counter') A prison for debtors and thieves.

43 *Bully* 'pimp'.

44 *Hedge-Tavern* A rough, squalid inn; *lies in Pawn* Having pawned her clothes and possessions, she is not fit to be seen in public.

45 *transported* Transportation was a common punishment for convicted felons and prostitutes, but Corinna is also, figuratively, 'transported' by her imagination. She may be dreaming of the plot of Gay's *Polly* (1729), in which the highwayman Macheath has been transported to the West Indies: his love Polly comes to seek him but is trapped in the house of an amorous planter.

46 '*Et longam incomitata videtur / Ire viam*' (Swift's note). This quotation from Virgil, *Aeneid*, 4:467–8 ('She seemed to be going on a long journey alone') describes the deserted Queen Dido's turbulent dream that precedes her suicide.

Or, near *Fleet-Ditch*'s oozy Brinks,
Surrounded with a Hundred Stinks,
Belated, seems on watch to lye,
And snap some Cully passing by;   50
Or, struck with Fear, her Fancy runs
On Watchmen, Constables and Duns,
From whom she meets with frequent Rubs;
But, never from Religious Clubs;
Whose Favour she is sure to find,   55
Because she pays 'em all in Kind.
    Corinna wakes. A dreadful Sight!
Behold the Ruins of the Night!
A wicked Rat her Plaister stole,
Half eat, and dragg'd it to his Hole.   60
The Crystal Eye, alas, was miss't;
And *Puss* had on her Plumpers p—st.
A Pigeon pick'd her Issue-Peas;
And *Shock* her Tresses fill'd with Fleas.
    The Nymph, tho' in this mangled Plight,   65
Must ev'ry Morn her Limbs unite.
But how shall I describe her Arts
To recollect the scatter'd Parts?
Or shew the Anguish, Toil, and Pain,
Of gath'ring up herself again?   70
The bashful Muse will never bear
In such a Scene to interfere.
Corinna in the Morning dizen'd,
Who sees, will spew; who smells, be poison'd.

47 *Fleet-Ditch* The notorious canal carrying sewage and garbage which emptied into the Thames. Cf. Swift, *A Description of a City Shower*, 58–63; Gay, *Trivia*, 2:168–212.
50 *Cully* 'dupe' (of her sexual charms).
51 *Fancy* 'imagination'.
52 *Duns* 'debt-collectors'.
53 *Rubs* 'unpleasant encounters'.
54 *Religious Clubs* Protestant dissenters and enthusiasts, or perhaps the societies for the reformation of manners.

56 *in Kind* i.e. with sexual favours.
57–62 Cf. Prior, *A Reasonable Afflictwn: On the Same*, 1–4: 'Helen was just slipt into Bed: / Her Eye-brows on the Toilet lay: / Away the Kitten with them fled, / As Fees belonging to her Prey'.
63 *Issue-Peas* Small round pellets inserted in surgical issues to keep them open.
64 *Shock* A standard name for a lap-dog. See Pope, *The Rape of the Lock*, 1:115.
73 *dizen'd* 'decked out'.

Strephon and Chloe

In 1732 Swift had ironically defended his controversial poem *The Lady's Dressing Room* by claiming that its exposure of female sluttishness would teach women to be clean. Chloe, heroine of *Strephon and Chloe* (first published in 1734: see headnote to previous poem), needs no lessons in hygiene: she is a well-scrubbed virgin, not a raddled whore. All that the naive Strephon discovers on their wedding night is that his immaculate goddess has normal bodily needs. The poem exposes the absurdity of male poetic fictions which idealize and etherealize women. Yet, as so often in Swift, reality is not always preferable to illusion, and it is debatable whether the conclusion, recommending sense and wit as a basis for marriage, emerges convincingly from the preceding narrative. The text is that of Roberts's 1734 quarto pamphlet.

Of *Chloe* all the Town has rung;
By ev'ry size of Poets sung:
So beautiful a Nymph appears
But once in Twenty Thousand Years.
By Nature form'd with nicest Care,   5
And, faultless to a single Hair.
Her graceful Mein, her Shape, and Face,
Confest her of no mortal Race:
And then, so nice, and so genteel;
Such Cleanliness from Head to Heel: 10
No Humours gross, or frowzy Steams,
No noisom Whiffs, or sweaty Streams,
Before, behind, above, below,
Could from her taintless Body flow.
Would so discreetly Things dispose,   15
None ever saw her pluck a Rose.
Her dearest Comrades never caught her
Squat on her Hams, to make Maid's Water.
You'd swear, that so divine a Creature
Felt no Necessities of Nature.   20
In Summer had she walkt the Town,
Her Arm-pits would not stain her Gown:
At Country Dances, not a Nose
Could in the Dog-Days smell her Toes.
Her Milk-white Hands, both Palms and Backs,   25
Like Iv'ry dry, and soft as Wax.
Her Hands the softest ever felt,
Tho' cold would burn, tho' dry would melt.
    Dear *Venus*, hide this wond'rous Maid,
Nor let her loose to spoil your Trade.   30
While she engrosseth ev'ry Swain,
You but o'er half the World can reign.
Think what a Case all Men are now in,
What ogling, sighing, toasting, vowing!
What powder'd Wigs! What Flames and Darts!   35
What Hampers full of bleeding Hearts!
What Sword-knots! What Poetic Strains!
What Billet-doux, and clouded Cains!
    But, *Strephon* sigh'd so loud and strong,
He blew a Settlement along: 40

7 *Mein* 'manner'.

8 *Confest her* 'showed her to be'.

9 *nice* 'fastidious'.

11 *Humours* 'vapours'; *frowzy* 'stale-smelling'.

12 *noisom* 'offensive'.

13 Cf. 'Licence my roving hands, and let them go, / Before, behind, between, above, below' (Donne, *To His Mistris*, 25–6).

16 *pluck a Rose* A euphemism for passing urine.

24 *Dog-Days* The hottest time of the year, July and August (when Sirius the Dog-star is in the ascendant).

28 As Swift notes, a parody of Sir John Denham's *Cooper's Hill* (1655), 191–2: 'Though deep, yet clear, though gentle, yet not dull, / Strong without rage, without ore-flowing full'.

29 *Venus* The Roman goddess of love.

33 *Case* 'state'.

33–8 A catalogue of fashionable lovers' tokens, also satirized in Pope's *Rape of the Lock*, 1:99–102; 4:123–4.

37 *Sword-knots* Decorative tassels tied to the hilt of a sword.

38 *Billet-doux* 'love letters'; *clouded Cain* A walking cane decorated with dark streaks.

40 *Settlement* 'marriage settlement'.

And, bravely drove his Rivals down
With Coach and Six, and House in Town.
The bashful Nymph no more withstands,
Because her dear Papa commands.
The charming Couple now unites;   45
Proceed we to the Marriage Rites.
    Imprimis, at the Temple Porch
Stood *Hymen* with a flaming Torch.
The smiling *Cyprian* Goddess brings
Her infant Loves with purple Wings;   50
And Pigeons billing, Sparrows treading,
Fair Emblems of a fruitful Wedding.
The Muses next in Order follow,
Conducted by their Squire, *Apollo:*
Then *Mercury* with Silver Tongue,   55
And *Hebe*, Goddess ever young.
Behold the Bridegroom and his Bride,
Walk Hand in Hand, and Side by Side;
She by the tender Graces drest,
But, he by *Mars*, in Scarlet Vest.   60
The Nymph was cover'd with her *Flammeum*,
And *Phoebus* sung th' *Epithalamium.*
And, last to make the Matter sure,
Dame *Juno* brought a Priest demure.
Luna was absent on Pretence   65
Her Time was not till Nine Months hence.
    The Rites perform'd, the Parson paid,
In State return'd the grand Parade;
With loud Huzza's from all the Boys,
That now the Pair must *crown their Joys.*   70
    But, still the hardest Part remains.
Strephon had long perplex'd his Brains,
How with so high a Nymph he might
Demean himself the Wedding-Night:
For, as he view'd his Person round,   75
Meer mortal Flesh was all he found:
His Hand, his Neck, his Mouth, and Feet
Were duly washt to keep 'em sweet;
(With other Parts that shall be nameless,
The Ladies else might think me shameless.)   80
The Weather and his Love were hot;

---

47 *Imprimis* 'in the first place' (a Latin term used to begin a list or inventory).
48 *Hymen* The Roman god of marriage, who carries a torch and veil.
49 *Cyprian Goddess* Venus.
50 *infant Loves* Cupids.
51 *treading* 'copulating'.
54 *Apollo* The Greek god of music and poetry.
55 *Mercury* The Roman god of eloquent speech, with a pun on the element mercury or quicksilver.
56 *Hebe* The cup-bearer of the gods, a personification of the Greek word for youth.

59 *Graces* Three goddesses who personify grace and beauty.
60 *Mars* The Roman god of war; *Scarlet Vest* Strephon is married in military uniform.
61 *Flammeum* 'A Veil which the *Roman* Brides covered themselves with, when they were going to be married' (Swift). It was originally flame-coloured.
62 *Phoebus* Apollo; *Epithalamium* A marriage song.
64 *Juno* Queen of the gods, wife of Jupiter.
65 *Luna* 'Diana, Goddess of Midwives' (Swift).
70 *crown their Joys* i.e. with a child.

And should he struggle; I know what —
Why let it go, if I must tell it —
He'll sweat, and then the Nymph may smell it.
While she a Goddess dy'd in Grain   85
Was unsusceptible of Stain:
And, *Venus*-like, her fragrant Skin
Exhal'd *Ambrosia* from within:
Can such a Deity endure
A mortal human Touch impure?   90
How did the humbled Swain detest
His prickled Beard, and hairy Breast!
His Night-Cap border'd round with Lace
Could give no Softness to his Face.

   Yet, if the Goddess could be kind,   95
What endless Raptures must he find!
And Goddesses have now and then
Come down to visit mortal Men:
To visit and to court them too;
A certain Goddess, God knows who,   100
(As in a Book he heard it read)
Took Col'nel *Peleus* to her Bed.
But, what if he should lose his Life
By vent'ring *on* his heav'nly Wife?
For *Strephon* could remember well,   105
That, once he heard a School-boy tell,
How *Semele* of mortal Race,
By Thunder dy'd in *Jove*'s Embrace;
And what if daring *Strephon* dies
By Lightning shot from *Chloe*'s Eyes?   110
   While these Reflections fill'd his Head,
The Bride was put in Form to Bed;
He follow'd, stript, and in he crept,
But, awfully his Distance kept.

   Now, *Ponder well ye Parents dear*;   115
Forbid your Daughters guzzling Beer;
And make them ev'ry Afternoon
Forbear their Tea, or drink it soon;
That, e'er to Bed they venture up,
They may discharge it ev'ry Sup;   120
If not; they must in evil Plight
Be often forc'd to rise at Night,
Keep them to wholsome Food confin'd,
Nor let them taste what causes Wind;
'Tis this (the Sage of *Samos* means,   125
Forbidding his Disciples Beans)

---

85 *dy'd in Grain* 'through and through'.

88 *Ambrosia* Sweet-smelling food of the gods.

100–2 Zeus gave the goddess Thetis to the mortal Peleus. He first had to wrestle with her before he could win her. Their son was Achilles.

107–8 Semele, daughter of Cadmus, King of Thebes, was made pregnant by Zeus ('Jove'). His jealous wife Hera (Juno) visited her in human disguise and persuaded her

to pray for Zeus to visit her in all the splendour of a god. This he did and Semele was consumed by his lightning.

112 *in Form* 'according to custom'.

114 *awfully* 'with awe'.

125–6 *Sage of Samos* The Greek philosopher Pythagoras, born at Samos *c.*580 BC. 'A well known Precept of *Pythagoras*, not to eat Beans' (Swift).

O, think what Evils must ensue;
Miss *Moll* the Jade will burn it blue:
And when she once has got the Art,
She cannot help it for her Heart;   130
But, out it flies, even when she meets
Her Bridegroom in the Wedding-Sheets.
Carminative and *Diuretick*,
Will damp all Passion Sympathetick;
And, Love such Nicety requires,   135
One *Blast* will put out all his Fires.
Since Husbands get behind the Scene,
The Wife should study to be clean;
Nor give the smallest Room to guess
The Time when Wants of Nature press;   140
    But, after Marriage, practise more
Decorum than she did before;
To keep her Spouse deluded still,
And make him fancy what she will.
    In Bed we left the married Pair;   145
'Tis Time to shew how Things went there.
Strephon, who had been often told,
That Fortune still assists the bold,
Resolv'd to make his first Attack:
But, *Chloe* drove him fiercely back.   150
How could a Nymph so chaste as *Chloe*,
With Constitution cold and snowy,
Permit a brutish Man to touch her?
Ev'n Lambs by Instinct fly the Butcher.
Resistance on the Wedding-Night   155
Is what our Maidens claim by Right:
And, *Chloe*, 'tis by all agreed,
Was Maid in Thought, and Word, and Deed,
Yet, some assign a diff'rent Reason;
That *Strephon* chose no proper Season.   160
    Say, fair ones, must I make a Pause?
Or freely tell the secret Cause.
    Twelve Cups of Tea, (with Grief I speak)
Had now constrain'd the Nymph to leak.
This Point must needs be settled first;   165
The Bride must either void or burst.
Then, see the dire Effect of Pease,
Think what can give the Colick Ease,
The Nymph opprest before, behind,
As Ships are toss't by Waves and Wind,   170
Steals out her Hand by Nature led,
And brings a Vessel into Bed:

---

128 *blue* i.e. poisonous.
133 *Carminative* 'Medicines to break Wind'; *Diuretick*
    'Medicines to provoke Urine' (Swift).
135 *Nicety* 'delicacy'.
139–40 I.e. she should always use the privy when answering
    a call of nature.

142 *Decorum* 'what is fitting'. Etymologically linked to
    'Decency' (308).
172 *Vessel* 'chamberpot'.

Fair Utensil, as smooth and white
As *Chloe*'s Skin, almost as bright.
   Strephon who heard the fuming Rill   175
As from a mossy Cliff distill;
Cry'd out, ye Gods, what Sound is this?
Can *Chloe*, heav'nly *Chloe* — ?
But, when he smelt a noysom Steam
Which oft attends that luke-warm Stream;   180
(*Salerno* both together joins
As sov'reign Med'cines for the Loins)
And, though contriv'd, we may suppose
To slip his Ears, yet struck his Nose:
He found her, while the Scent increas'd,   185
As *mortal* as himself at least.
But, soon with like Occasions prest,
He boldly sent his Hand in quest,
(Inspir'd with Courage from his Bride,)
To reach the Pot on t'other Side.   190
And as he fill'd the reeking Vase,
Let fly a Rouzer in her Face.
   The little *Cupids* hov'ring round,
(As Pictures prove) with Garlands crown'd.
Abasht at what they saw and heard,   195
Flew off, nor evermore appear'd.
   Adieu to ravishing Delights,
High Raptures, and romantick Flights;
To Goddesses so heav'nly sweet,
Expiring Shepherds at their Feet;   200
To silver Meads, and shady Bow'rs,
Drest up with *Amaranthine* Flow'rs.
   How great a Change! how quickly made!
They learn to call a Spade, a Spade.
They soon from all Constraint are freed;   205
Can see each other *do their Need*.
On Box of Cedar sits the Wife,
And makes it warm for *Dearest Life*.
And, by the beastly way of Thinking,
Find great Society in Stinking.   210
Now *Strephon* daily entertains
His *Chloe* in the homeli'st Strains;
And, *Chloe* more experienc'd grown,
With Int'rest pays him back his own.
No Maid at Court is less asham'd,   215
Howe'er for selling Bargains fam'd,
Than she, to name her Parts behind,
Or when a-bed, to let out Wind.
   Fair *Decency*, celestial Maid,

175–6 Mock-pastoral diction.
179 *noysom* 'offensive'.
181 Salerno in Italy housed a famous medical school.
191 *the* 'with' (*1734*).

192 *Rouzer* 'massive fart'.
202 *Amaranthine* 'never-fading'.
216 *selling Bargains* A joke which consisted of naming the 'Parts behind' in answer to a question.

Descend from Heav'n to Beauty's Aid;   220
Though Beauty may beget Desire,
'Tis thou must fan the Lover's Fire;
For, Beauty, like supreme Dominion,
Is best supported by Opinion;
If Decency brings no Supplies,   225
Opinion falls, and Beauty dies.
 To see some radiant Nymph appear
In all her glitt'ring Birth-day Gear,
You think some Goddess from the Sky
Descended, ready cut and dry: 230
But, e'er you sell your self to Laughter,
Consider well what may come after;
For fine Ideas vanish fast,
While all the gross and filthy last.
 O *Strephon*, e'er that fatal Day   235
When *Chloe* stole your Heart away,
Had you but through a Cranny spy'd
On House of Ease your future Bride,
In all the Postures of her Face,
Which Nature gives in such a Case;   240
Distortions, Groanings, Strainings, Heavings;
'Twere better you had lickt her Leavings,
Than from Experience find too late
Your Goddess grown a filthy Mate.
Your Fancy then had always dwelt   245
On what you saw, and what you smelt;
Would still the same Ideas give ye,
As when you spy'd her on the Privy.
And, spight of *Chloe*'s Charms divine,
Your Heart had been as whole as mine.   250
 Authorities both old and recent
Direct that Women must be decent;
And, from the Spouse each Blemish hide
More than from all the World beside.
 Unjustly all our Nymphs complain,   255
Their Empire holds so short a Reign;
Is after Marriage lost so soon,
It hardly holds the Honey-moon:
For, if they keep not what they caught,
It is entirely their own Fault.   260
They take Possession of the Crown,
And then throw all their Weapons down;
Though by the Politicians Scheme
Whoe'er arrives at Pow'r supreme,
Those Arts by which at first they gain it,   265
They still must practise to maintain it.
 What various Ways our Females take,
To pass for Wits before a Rake!
And in the fruitless Search pursue

---

224 *Opinion* 'reputation'.
228 *Birth-day Gear* Fine clothes worn on royal birthdays.
230 *ready cut and dry* 'ready-made'.
238 *House of Ease* The privy.

258 *Honey-moon* Here, the first month after marriage.
263 *Politician* Niccolò Machiavelli (1469–1527), author of
 The Prince, a cynical instruction in power-politics.

All other Methods but the true. 270
   Some try to learn polite Behaviour,
By reading Books against their Saviour;
Some call it witty to reflect
On ev'ry natural Defect;
Some shew they never want explaining, 275
To comprehend a double Meaning.
But, sure a Tell tale out of School
Is of all Wits the greatest Fool;
Whose rank Imagination fills,
Her Heart, and from her Lips distills; 280
You'd think she utter'd from behind,
Or at her Mouth was breaking Wind.
   Why is a handsome Wife ador'd
By ev'ry Coxcomb, but her Lord?
From yonder Puppet-Man inquire, 285
Who wisely hides his Wood and Wire;
Shews *Sheba*'s Queen completely drest,
And *Solomon* in Royal Vest;
But, view them litter'd on the Floor,
Or strung on Pegs behind the Door; 290
Punch is exactly of a Piece
With *Lorraine*'s Duke, and Prince of *Greece*.
   A prudent Builder should forecast
How long the Stuff is like to last;
And, carefully observe the Ground, 295
To build on some Foundation sound;
What House, when its Materials crumble,
Must not inevitably tumble?
What Edifice can long endure,
Rais'd on a Basis unsecure? 300
Rash Mortals, e'er you take a Wife,
Contrive your Pile to last for Life;
Since Beauty scarce endures a Day,
And Youth so swiftly glides away;
Why will you make yourself a Bubble 305
To build on Sand with Hay and Stubble?
   On Sense and Wit your Passion found,
By Decency cemented round;
Let Prudence with Good Nature strive,
To keep Esteem and Love alive. 310
Then come old Age whene'er it will,
Your Friendship shall continue still:
And thus a mutual gentle Fire,
Shall never but with Life expire.

284 *Coxcomb* 'conceited fop'.
287–92 All these are puppet-show characters.
292 *Lorraine's Duke* James Francis Stuart, the Old
   Pretender; *Prince of Greece* Alexander the Great.

305 *Bubble* 'dupe'.

Verses on the Death of Dr Swift, D.S.P.D.

Occasioned by Reading a Maxim in Rochefoucault

Dans l'adversité de nos meilleurs amis nous trouvons quelque chose, qui ne nous deplaist pas.
In the Adversity of our best Friends, we find something that doth not displease us.

Between 1730 and 1733 Swift wrote two 'auto-biographical' poems with similar titles: *Verses on the Death of Dr Swift* and *The Life and Genuine Character of Dr Swift*. The *Life* was published in 1733, the *Verses* (though probably written in 1731) not until 1738. The *Verses*, more than twice as long as the *Life*, and far more outspoken in their criticism of English and Irish politics, are widely regarded as the more interesting and significant of the two poems. Swift's friend Matthew Prior had already written his own epitaph (see *For His own Epitaph*), but Swift's poem is a characteristically more complex affair, involving not only a speculative fantasy of 'what my friends and enemyes will say on me after I am dead' (as he wrote to Gay in 1731) but an apologia for his life and works. The chief difficulty lies in gauging Swift's continually fluctuating tone, particularly in the final section when an 'impartial' member of a London tavern club offers a measured assessment of Swift's life and achievements. The claims he makes for Swift veer between the comically untrue to the unabashedly flattering. The reader can never be quite sure whether Swift is being ironic or sincere: he seems to be simultaneously constructing a genuine memorial to his life and character while exposing the vanity and absurdity of such an enterprise.

TEXTUAL NOTE

Irvin Ehrenpreis (*Swift*, 3:708–9) speculates that Swift had originally intended the *Verses* to be published after his death. But in 1738 he gave the manuscript to his acquaintance William King, who, on Pope's advice, edited out the more controversial and self-glorifying passages before the poem was published at a much reduced length, padded out with a section from the previously published *Life and Genuine Character*. Swift was not mollified by the poem's huge sale of several thousand copies. Angered by the expurgations, he quickly arranged for Faulkner, his Dublin printer, to publish his original text in February 1739 incorporating his own notes. Faulkner's edition, printed in haste, contained a number of blanks. Modern editors have managed to fill the gaps by consulting several extant hand-annotated copies of this and Faulkner's subsequent edition of the poem. The text printed here is the notable reconstruction by Harold Williams (*Poems of Jonathan Swift*, 2:551–72) using Faulkner's 1739 edition and contemporary manuscript notes. We have omitted most of Swift's lengthy footnotes, incorporating the factual information they contain into the editorial annotations.

> As *Rochefoucault* his Maxims drew
> From Nature, I believe 'em true:
> They argue no corrupted Mind
> In him; the Fault is in Mankind.
>   This Maxim more than all the rest   5
> Is thought too base for human Breast;
> "In all Distresses of our Friends
> "We first consult our private Ends,
> "While Nature kindly bent to ease us,
> "Points out some Circumstance to please us.   10
>   If this perhaps your Patience move
> Let Reason and Experience prove.
>   We all behold with envious Eyes,
> Our *Equal* rais'd above our *Size*;

Title The initials stand for 'Dean of St Patrick's, Dublin'. The epigraph is number 99 of the *Maxims* of Duc François de la Rochefoucauld (1613–80), which mercilessly expose self-interest as the spring of human conduct.

11 *move* 'provoke'.

Who wou'd not at a crowded Show,   15
Stand high himself, keep others low?
I love my Friend as well as you,
But would not have him stop my View;
Then let him have the higher Post;
I ask but for an Inch at most.   20
    If in a Battle you should find,
One, whom you love of all Mankind,
Had some heroick Action done,
A Champion kill'd, or Trophy won;
Rather than thus be over-topt,   25
Would you not wish his Lawrels cropt?
    Dear honest *Ned* is in the Gout,
Lies rackt with Pain, and you without:
How patiently you hear him groan!
How glad the Case is not your own!   30
    What Poet would not grieve to see,
His Brethren write as well as he?
But rather than they should excel,
He'd wish his Rivals all in Hell.
    Her End when Emulation misses,   35
She turns to Envy, Stings and Hisses:
The strongest Friendship yields to Pride,
Unless the Odds be on our Side.
    Vain human Kind! Fantastick Race!
Thy various Follies, who can trace?   40
Self-love, Ambition, Envy, Pride,
Their Empire in our Hearts divide:
Give others Riches, Power, and Station,
'Tis all on me an Usurpation.
I have no Title to aspire;   45
Yet, when you sink, I seem the higher.
In POPE, I cannot read a Line,
But with a Sigh, I wish it mine:
When he can in one Couplet fix
More Sense than I can do in Six: 50
It gives me such a jealous Fit,
I cry, Pox take him, and his Wit.
    Why must I be outdone by GAY,
In my own hum'rous biting Way?
    ARBUTHNOT is no more my Friend,   55
Who dares to Irony pretend;
Which I was born to introduce,
Refin'd it first, and shew'd its Use.
    ST. JOHN, as well as PULTNEY knows,

55 John Arbuthnot (1667–1735), author and physician to Queen Anne. He was a close friend of Swift and Pope and a member of the Scriblerus Club.

59 *ST. JOHN ... PULTNEY* Henry St John, first Viscount Bolingbroke (1678–1751), statesman, philosopher and historian, and an intimate friend of Pope and Swift, had led the Tory administration under Queen Anne. After the Hanoverian accession in 1714 he fled to the Pretender's service and was convicted of high treason, but in 1723 was granted a qualified pardon and returned to England, though he remained banned from his seat in the Lords. By 1731 he was masterminding the opposition to Walpole's Whig administration alongside William Pulteney (1684–1764), a former ally of Walpole, who had been dismissed from office in 1725. Together they edited the leading opposition journal, the *Craftsman*, which (as Swift acknowledges) was highly effective.

That I had some repute for Prose;   60
And till they drove me out of Date,
Could maul a Minister of State:
If they have mortify'd my Pride,
And made me throw my Pen aside;
If with such Talents Heav'n hath blest 'em   65
Have I not Reason to detest 'em?
   To all my Foes, dear Fortune, send
Thy Gifts, but never to my Friend:
I tamely can endure the first,
But, this with Envy makes me burst.   70
   Thus much may serve by way of Proem,
Proceed we therefore to our Poem.
   The Time is not remote, when I
Must by the Course of Nature dye:
When I foresee my special Friends,   75
Will try to find their private Ends:
Tho' it is hardly understood,
Which way my Death can do them good;
Yet, thus methinks, I hear 'em speak;
See, how the Dean begins to break: 80
Poor Gentleman, he droops apace,
You plainly find it in his Face:
That old Vertigo in his Head,
Will never leave him, till he's dead:
Besides, his Memory decays,   85
He recollects not what he says;
He cannot call his Friends to Mind;
Forgets the Place where last he din'd:
Plyes you with Stories o'er and o'er,
He told them fifty Times before.   90
How does he fancy we can sit,
To hear his out-of-fashion'd Wit?
But he takes up with younger Fokes,
Who for his Wine will bear his Jokes:
Faith, he must make his Stories shorter,   95
Or change his Comrades once a Quarter:
In half the Time, he talks them round;
There must another Sett be found.
   For Poetry, he's past his Prime,
He takes an Hour to find a Rhime: 100
His Fire is out, his Wit decay'd,
His Fancy sunk, his Muse a Jade.

---

61 *out of Date* Swift perhaps felt overtaken by the
   Craftsman.
62 Swift himself had covertly attacked Walpole in the
   Drapier's Letters and *Gulliver's Travels*, but he may be
   alluding to his role as Tory propagandist in the
   Examiner when he 'mauled' a previous Whig minister,
   Sidney Godolphin (1645–1712).
71 *Proem* 'introduction'.
76 *find* 'find something beneficial to'.
77 *hardly* 'with difficulty'.

80 *break* 'fail in health'.
83 *Vertigo* Swift suffered bouts of severe dizziness. See
   biographical headnote.
97 *talks them round* He exhausts all his stories and has to
   start telling them over again. Among the series of
   resolutions Swift had written in 1699 for 'When I come
   to be old' were 'Not to keep young company unless
   they really desire it' and 'Not to tell the same story over
   and over to the same people'.

I'd have him throw away his Pen;
But there's no talking to some Men.
    And, then their Tenderness appears, 105
By adding largely to my Years:
"He's older than he would be reckon'd,
"And well remembers *Charles* the Second.
    "He hardly drinks a Pint of Wine;
"And that, I doubt, is no good Sign. 110
"His Stomach too begins to fail:
"Last Year we thought him strong and hale;
"But now, he's quite another Thing;
"I wish he may hold out till Spring.
    Then hug themselves, and reason thus; 115
"It is not yet so bad with us."
    In such a Case they talk in Tropes,
And, by their Fears express their Hopes:
Some great Misfortune to portend,
No Enemy can match a Friend; 120
With all the Kindness they profess,
The Merit of a lucky Guess,
(When daily Howd'y's come of Course,
And Servants answer; *Worse* and *Worse*)
Wou'd please 'em better than to tell, 125
That, GOD be prais'd, the Dean is well.
Then he who prophecy'd the best,
Approves his Foresight to the rest:
"You know, I always fear'd the worst,
"And often told you so at first:" 130
He'd rather chuse that I should dye,
Than his Prediction prove a Lye.
Not one foretels I shall recover;
But, all agree, to give me over.
    Yet shou'd some Neighbour feel a Pain, 135
Just in the Parts, where I complain;
How many a Message would he send?
What hearty Prayers that I should mend?
Enquire what Regimen I kept;
What gave me Ease, and how I slept? 140
And more lament, when I was dead,
Than all the Sniv'llers round my Bed.
    My good Companions, never fear,
For though you may mistake a Year;
Though your Prognosticks run too fast, 145
They must be verify'd at last.
    "Behold the fatal Day arrive!
"How is the Dean? He's just alive.
"Now the departing Prayer is read:

108 Charles II died in 1685 when Swift was eighteen.
110 *doubt* 'suspect'.
111 *Stomach* 'appetite'.
117 *Tropes* 'metaphors'.
123 *Howd'y's* Enquiries after his health; *of Course* 'routinely'.

128 *Approves* 'commends'.
134 *over* 'up'.
145 *Prognosticks* 'predictions'.

"He hardly breathes. The Dean is dead.   150
"Before the Passing-Bell begun,
"The News thro' half the Town has run.
"O, may we all for Death prepare!
"What has he left? And who's his Heir?
"I know no more than what the News is,   155
"'Tis all bequeath'd to publick Uses.
"To publick Use! A perfect Whim!
"What had the Publick done for him!
"Meer Envy, Avarice, and Pride!
"He gave it all: — But first he dy'd.   160
"And had the Dean, in all the Nation,
"No worthy Friend, no poor Relation?
"So ready to do Strangers good,
"Forgetting his own Flesh and Blood?
     Now Grub-Street Wits are all employ'd;   165
With Elegies, the Town is cloy'd:
Some Paragraph in ev'ry Paper,
To *curse* the *Dean*, or *bless* the *Drapier*.
     The Doctors tender of their Fame,
Wisely on me lay all the Blame: 170
"We must confess his Case was nice;
"But he would never take Advice:
"Had he been rul'd, for ought appears,
"He might have liv'd these Twenty Years:
"For when we open'd him we found,   175
"That all his vital Parts were sound.
     From *Dublin* soon to *London* spread,
'Tis told at Court, the Dean is dead.
     Kind Lady *Suffolk* in the Spleen,
Runs laughing up to tell the Queen.   180
The Queen, so Gracious, Mild, and Good,
Cries, "Is he gone? 'Tis time he shou'd.
"He's dead you say; why let him rot;
"I'm glad the Medals were forgot.
"I promis'd them, I own; but when?   185
"I only was the Princess then;
"But now as Consort of the King,
"You know 'tis quite a different Thing.

---

151 *Passing-Bell* 'death-knell'.
165 *Grub-Street Wits* i.e. hack-writers.
168 Swift's note explains that as Dean Swift he will be
  'cursed' by government hacks, but remembered with
  gratitude by the people of Ireland for writing the
  Drapier's Letters (1724). See biographical headnote and
  407–30.
169 *tender* 'protective'.
171 *nice* 'delicate'.
173 *been rul'd* 'obeyed advice'.
177 Swift imagines himself dying in Ireland.
179 *Lady Suffolk* Henrietta Howard, Countess of Suffolk
  (1681–1767), Lady of the Bedchamber to Queen
  Caroline and former mistress of George II. She had

previously been good friends with Gay, Pope and Swift
(the Scriblerus Club met at her house), but by 1731 her
relationship with Swift had soured; *the Spleen* 'low
spirits'.
184 *Medals* In October 1726 Swift sent Mrs Howard a piece
  of Irish poplin woven in Indian style, which Princess
  (subsequently Queen) Caroline much admired. Swift
  sent her a substantial present of the material, refusing
  payment for it, but he never received from her the royal
  medals she had promised him in return. Queen
  Caroline died two years before the poem was printed.
  Swift's minutely detailed recollection of the episode in
  his notes suggests – though not without self-irony – a
  long-standing grudge.

Now, *Chartres* at Sir *Robert*'s Levee,
Tells, with a Sneer, the Tidings heavy:　　　　　　190
"Why, is he dead without his Shoes?"
(Cries *Bob*) "I'm Sorry for the News;
Oh, were the Wretch but living still,
And in his Place my good Friend *Will*;
Or, had a Mitre on his Head　　　　　　　　　　195
Provided *Bolingbroke* were dead.
　　Now *Curl* his Shop from Rubbish drains;
Three genuine Tomes of *Swift*'s Remains.
And then to make them pass the glibber,
Revis'd by *Tibbalds, Moore, and Cibber*.　　　　200
He'll treat me as he does my Betters.
Publish my Will, my Life, my Letters.
Revive the Libels born to dye;
Which POPE must bear, as well as I.
　　Here shift the Scene, to represent　　　　　205
How those I love, my Death lament.
Poor POPE will grieve a Month; and GAY
A Week; and ARBUTHNOTT a Day.
　　ST. JOHN himself will scarce forbear,
To bite his Pen, and drop a Tear.　　　　　　　210
The rest will give a Shrug and cry,
I'm sorry; but we all must dye.
Indifference clad in Wisdom's Guise,
All Fortitude of Mind supplies:
For how can stony Bowels melt,　　　　　　　　215
In those who never Pity felt;
When *We* are lash'd, *They* kiss the Rod;
Resigning to the Will of God.
　　The Fools, my Juniors by a Year,
Are tortur'd with Suspence and Fear.　　　　　220
Who wisely thought my Age a Screen,
When Death approach'd, to stand between:
The Screen remov'd, their Hearts are trembling,
They mourn for me without dissembling.

---

189 *Chartres* Francis Charteris (1675–1732), a gambler and fraudster who accumulated a vast fortune through usury and corruption. In 1730 he was convicted of raping his maidservant but later given a royal pardon, supposedly through the influence of Walpole, to whom (as Swift notes) he made himself useful 'either as Pimp, Flatterer, or Informer'; *Sir Robert* Walpole; *Levee* 'morning audience'.

191 *without his Shoes* To 'die in one's shoes' is slang for 'to be hanged'.

192 *Bob* A common nickname for Walpole.

194 *Will* William Pulteney. See 59n.

196 *Bolingbroke* See 59n. Walpole took a leading part in his impeachment in 1715.

197 *Curl* Edmund Curll (1675–1747), an unscrupulous publisher who traded in sex, scandal and hastily compiled 'memoirs', and who pirated both Swift and

Pope's works as well as advertising spurious volumes under Swift's name. See Pope, *The Dunciad*, 1:40.

200 *Tibbalds, Moore, and Cibber* All three had recently been attacked in Pope's *Dunciad*. 'Tibbald', or Lewis Theobald (1688–1744), the King Dunce in the first version of *The Dunciad*, was an editor and a translator of classical texts as well as an author of plays, essays and poems. James Moore Smythe (1702–34) was an overpraised young Irish writer, author of a play *The Rival Modes* (1727). Colley Cibber (1671–1757), who subsequently replaced Theobald in *The Dunciad*, was a playwright and actor-manager famous for his lively egotism and showmanship. In 1730 he had been appointed Poet Laureate.

215 The bowels were considered the seat of pity and compassion.

217 *kiss the Rod* 'accept chastisement'.

My female Friends, whose tender Hearts   225
Have better learn'd to act their Parts.
Receive the News in *doleful Dumps*,
"The Dean is dead, (*and what is Trumps?*)
"Then Lord have Mercy on his Soul.
"(Ladies I'll venture for the *Vole.*)   230
"Six Deans they say must bear the Pall.
"(I wish I knew what *King* to call.)
"Madam, your Husband will attend
"The Funeral of so good a Friend.
"No Madam, 'tis a shocking Sight,   235
"And he's engag'd To-morrow Night!
"My Lady *Club* wou'd take it ill,
"If he shou'd fail her at *Quadrill.*
"He lov'd the Dean. (*I lead a Heart.*)
"But dearest Friends, they say, must part.   240
"His Time was come, he ran his Race;
"We hope he's in a better Place.
   Why do we grieve that Friends should dye?
No Loss more easy to supply.
One Year is past; a different Scene;   245
No further mention of the Dean;
Who now, alas, no more is mist,
Than if he never did exist.
Where's now this Fav'rite of *Apollo*?
Departed; *and his Works must follow*:   250
Must undergo the common Fate;
His Kind of Wit is out of Date.
Some Country Squire to *Lintot* goes,
Enquires for SWIFT in Verse and Prose:
Says *Lintot*, "I have heard the Name: 255
"He dy'd a Year ago." The same.
He searcheth all his Shop in vain;
"Sir you may find them in *Duck-lane:*
"I sent them with a Load of Books,
"Last *Monday* to the Pastry-cooks.   260
"To fancy they cou'd live a Year!
"I find you're but a Stranger here.
"The Dean was famous in his Time;
"And had a Kind of Knack at Rhyme:
"His way of Writing now is past;   265
"The Town hath got a better Taste:
"I keep no antiquated Stuff;
"But, spick and span I have enough.
"Pray, do but give me leave to shew 'em;

---

227 *doleful Dumps* 'a melancholy state' (comically archaic term).

230 *Vole* Winning all the tricks in a card game.

238 *Quadrill* Quadrille, a popular four-handed game of cards.

249 *Apollo* The Greek god of poetry and music.

253 *Lintot* Bernard Lintot (1675–1736), bookseller, who published both Gay's and Pope's works (though not Swift's).

258 *Duck-lane* The London street where old books were sold.

259–60 Sheets of old books were used to wrap pies or line baking trays.

"Here's *Colley Cibber*'s Birth-day Poem.   270
"This Ode you never yet have seen,
"By *Stephen Duck*, upon the Queen.
"Then, here's a Letter finely penn'd
"Against the *Craftsman* and his Friend;
"It clearly shews that all Reflection   275
"On Ministers, is disaffection.
"Next, here's Sir *Robert*'s Vindication,
"And Mr. *Henly*'s last Oration:
"The Hawkers have not got 'em yet,
"Your Honour please to buy a Set?   280
    "Here's *Wolston*'s Tracts, the twelfth Edition;
"'Tis read by ev'ry Politician:
"The Country Members, when in Town,
"To all their Boroughs send them down:
"You never met a Thing so smart;   285
"The Courtiers have them all by Heart:
"Those Maids of Honour (who can read)
"Are taught to use them for their Creed.
"The Rev'rend Author's good Intention,
"Hath been rewarded with a Pension: 290
"He doth an Honour to his Gown,
"By bravely running *Priest-craft* down:
"He shews, as sure as GOD'S in *Gloc'ster*,
"That *Jesus* was a Grand Imposter:
"That all his Miracles were Cheats,   295
"Perform'd as Juglers do their Feats:
"The Church had never such a Writer:
"A Shame, he hath not got a Mitre!
    Suppose me dead; and then suppose
A Club assembled at the *Rose*;   300
Where from Discourse of this and that,
I grow the Subject of their Chat:
And, while they toss my Name about,
With Favour some, and some without;
One quite indiff'rent in the Cause,   305
My Character impartial draws:
    "The Dean, if we believe Report,
"Was never ill receiv'd at Court:
"As for his Works in Verse and Prose,

270 Cibber's royal birthday odes were ridiculed by Pope and his friends.
272 See Stephen Duck, headnote.
274 *Craftsman and his Friend* See 59n.
278 *Henly* The Reverend John Henley (1692–1756) was an eccentric independent preacher whose 'Oratory', a cross between theatre and pulpit, attracted fee-paying audiences at Lincoln's Inn Fields. He defended Walpole in his journal *The Hyp-Doctor*.
279 *Hawkers* 'pamphlet-sellers'.
281 *Wolston* Thomas Woolston (1670–1733), a freethinker deprived of his Cambridge fellowship and convicted of blasphemy for publishing works asserting an allegorical interpretation of scripture. King omitted this passage from the Bathurst edition because he thought Swift had confused Woolston with William Wollaston (1660–1724), a heterodox theologian patronized by Princess Caroline and her circle.
283 *Country Members* Members of Parliament up from the country.
293 *GOD'S in Gloc'ster* An old proverb alluding to the numerous monks in Gloucestershire.
300 *Rose* A fashionable tavern in Covent Garden.

"I own my self no Judge of those: 310
"Nor, can I tell what Criticks thought 'em;
"But, this I know, all People bought 'em;
"As with a moral View design'd
"To cure the Vices of Mankind:
"His Vein, ironically grave,   315
"Expos'd the Fool, and lash'd the Knave:
"To steal a Hint was never known,
"But what he writ was all his own.
      "He never thought an Honour done him,
"Because a Duke was proud to own him: 320
"Would rather slip aside, and chuse
"To talk with Wits in dirty Shoes:
"Despis'd the Fools with Stars and Garters,
"So often seen caressing *Chartres*:
"He never courted Men in Station,   325
"*Nor Persons had in Admiration*;
"Of no Man's Greatness was afraid,
"Because he sought for no Man's Aid.
"Though trusted long in great Affairs,
"He gave himself no haughty Airs: 330
"Without regarding private Ends,
"Spent all his Credit for his Friends:
"And only chose the Wise and Good;
"No Flatt'rers; no Allies in Blood;
"But succour'd Virtue in Distress,   335
"And seldom fail'd of good Success;
"As Numbers in their Hearts must own,
"Who, but for him, had been unknown.
      "With Princes kept a due Decorum,
"But never stood in Awe before 'em: 340
"He follow'd *David*'s Lesson just,
"*In Princes never put thy Trust*.
"And, would you make him truly sower;
"Provoke him with a *slave in Power*:
"The *Irish* Senate, if you nam'd,   345
"With what Impatience he declaim'd!
"Fair LIBERTY was all his Cry;

320 *own* 'acknowledge'.
323 *Stars and Garters* The insignia of the Order of the
    Garter. Opposition complaints about corruption in
    dispensing honours were widespread following the
    commoner Walpole's sumptuous investiture as Knight
    of the Garter in 1726.
326 *Admiration* 'awe'.
327 *no Man's Greatness* Walpole was satirically dubbed 'The
    Great Man'.
334 *Allies in Blood* 'relatives'.
340 A number of annotated copies of Faulkner's 1739
    edition insert the following (deeply ironic) lines at this
    point: 'And to her Majesty, God bless her, / Would
    speak as free as to her Dresser, / She thought it his
    peculiar Whim, / Nor took it ill as come from him.'

342 Psalm 146:3.
345 *Senate* 'parliament'.
347–54 Here Swift alludes to two episodes when his
    political outspokenness put a price on his head. In
    England in 1713 his last major Tory pamphlet, *The
    Public Spirit of the Whigs*, was deemed so seditious that
    the Whigs petitioned Queen Anne to offer a £300
    reward for the discovery of its author. In Ireland in
    1724 the English government offered the same reward
    to find out the author of the inflammatory *Drapier's
    Fourth Letter*, but 'in neither Kingdoms was the Dean
    discovered' (Swift).

"For her he stood prepar'd to die;
"For her he boldly stood alone;
"For her he oft expos'd his own.   350
"Two Kingdoms, just as Faction led,
"Had set a Price upon his Head;
"But, not a Traytor cou'd be found,
"To sell him for Six Hundred Pound.
    "Had he but spar'd his Tongue and Pen,   355
"He might have rose like other Men:
"But, Power was never in his Thought;
"And, Wealth he valu'd not a Groat:
"Ingratitude he often found,
"And pity'd those who meant the Wound: 360
"But, kept the Tenor of his Mind,
"To merit well of human Kind:
"Nor made a Sacrifice of those
"Who still were true, to please his Foes.
"He labour'd many a fruitless Hour   365
"To reconcile his Friends in Power;
"Saw Mischief by a Faction brewing,
"While they pursu'd each others Ruin.
"But, finding vain was all his Care,
"He left the Court in meer Despair.   370
    "And, oh! how short are human Schemes!
"Here ended all our golden Dreams.
"What ST. JOHN'S Skill in State Affairs,
"What ORMOND'S *Valour*, OXFORD'S Cares,
"To save their sinking Country lent,   375
"Was all destroy'd by one Event.
"Too soon that precious Life was ended,
"On which alone, our Weal depended.
"When up a dangerous Faction starts,
"With Wrath and Vengeance in their Hearts: 380
"*By solemn League and Cov'nant bound,*

361 *Tenor* 'habit'.

365–90 Internal conflicts within the Tory party, brewing since 1710, emerged openly in its last year in power (1713–14) when the High Tory Bolingbroke finally succeeded (27 July 1714) in wresting power from the more moderate Robert Harley, first Earl of Oxford (1661–1724). Swift, who had enjoyed friendships with both men, was in despair at party disintegration. Queen Anne's sudden death five days later (1 August) put an end to all Tory hopes. Swift left England for Dublin on 16 August, never to live in England again. On the accession of George I the Whigs were returned to power. They took revenge by removing all Tories from office and impeaching some, notably Oxford and Matthew Prior (see Matthew Prior, headnote), and began to intervene in church affairs. On 2 March 1715 Bolingbroke fled to France and entered the service of the Stuart Pretender.

370 *meer* 'complete'.

374 *Ormond* James Butler, second Duke of Ormonde

(1665–1745). As commander in chief of the allied forces from 1712 he helped bring about the Peace of Utrecht of 1713. He followed Bolingbroke into exile in 1715 and took part in the unsuccessful Stuart rising of that year.

377 *precious Life* Queen Anne's.

378 *Weal* 'prosperity'.

379 *Faction* The Whig party.

381 *solemn League and Cov'nant* A reference to the 1643 establishment of Scottish Presbyterianism by an agreement between the English parliament, the General Assembly of the Church of Scotland and the Westminster Assembly of English divines. The term 'Whig' was thought to derive from 'Whiggamore', a group of fanatical Scottish covenanters of the 1640s. Swift associates the modern Whigs with their purported origins in religious dissent, claiming in his note that after 1714 'The greatest Preferments in the Church in both Kingdoms were given to the most ignorant Men, Fanaticks were publickly caressed'.

"To ruin, slaughter, and confound;
"To turn Religion to a Fable,
"And make the Government a *Babel*:
"Pervert the Law, disgrace the Gown,   385
"Corrupt the Senate, rob the Crown;
"To sacrifice old *England*'s Glory,
"And make her infamous in Story.
"When such a Tempest shook the Land,
"How could unguarded Virtue stand?   390
    "With Horror, Grief, Despair the Dean
"Beheld the dire destructive Scene:
"His Friends in Exile, or the Tower,
"Himself within the Frown of Power;
"Pursu'd by base envenom'd Pens,   395
"Far to the Land of Slaves and Fens;
"A servile Race in Folly nurs'd,
"Who truckle most, when treated worst.
    "By Innocence and Resolution,
"He bore continual Persecution;   400
"While Numbers to Preferment rose;
"Whose Merits were, to be his Foes.
"When, *ev'n his own familiar Friends*
"Intent upon their private Ends;
"Like Renegadoes now he feels,   405
"Against him lifting up their Heels.
    "The Dean did by his Pen defeat
"An infamous destructive Cheat.
"Taught Fools their Int'rest how to know;
"And gave them Arms to ward the Blow.   410
"Envy hath own'd it was his doing,
"To save that helpless Land from Ruin,
"While they who at the Steerage stood,
"And reapt the Profit, sought his Blood.
    "To save them from their evil Fate,   415
"In him was held a Crime of State.
"A wicked Monster on the Bench,

384 *Babel* 'confused assembly', after the confusion of
    languages first spoken in the Biblical tower of Babel.
387 *old England's Glory* A favourite catchphrase of the
    opposition to Walpole.
388 *Story* 'history'.
393 Bolingbroke and Ormonde were in exile, Prior and
    Oxford were in custody.
394–5 Several libels accused Swift of Jacobitism. His
    correspondence was opened by government spies and
    he claimed that 'at Nights [he] was forced to be
    attended by his Servants armed'.
396 Ireland.
398 *truckle* 'submit', 'cringe'.
403–6 From Psalm 41:9: 'Yea, mine own familiar friend, in
    whom I trusted, which did eat of my bread, hath lifted
    up his heel against me.'

408–14 The 'Cheat' is William Wood, the Bristol
    ironmaster awarded the patent to coin Irish halfpence
    by Walpole's government in 1722. Here Swift again
    alludes (see above, 168; 347–54) to the success of his
    four *Drapier's Letters* in stiffening Irish resistance.
413 *Steerage* 'helm'.
417 *wicked Monster* William Whitshed (*c*.1656–1727), Chief
    Justice of the Common Pleas, a staunch Whig. In 1722
    Whitshed had prosecuted the printer of Swift's
    Proposal for the Universal Use of Irish Manufacture. In
    November 1724 he presided over the trial of John
    Harding, printer of the *Drapier's Fourth Letter*, who
    refused to divulge the author's identity. When the
    Grand Jury declined to condemn the *Letter* he angrily
    discharged them and ordered a new jury.

"Whose Fury Blood could never quench;
"As vile and profligate a Villain,
"As modern *Scroggs*, or old *Tressilian*;   420
"Who long all Justice had discarded,
"*Nor fear'd he* GOD, *nor Man regarded*;
"Vow'd on the Dean his Rage to vent,
"And make him of his Zeal repent;
"But Heav'n his Innocence defends,   425
"The grateful People stand his Friends:
"Not Strains of Law, nor Judges Frown,
"Nor Topicks brought to please the Crown,
"Nor Witness hir'd, nor Jury pick'd,
"Prevail to bring him in convict.   430
    "In Exile with a steady Heart,
"He spent his Life's declining Part;
"Where, Folly, Pride, and Faction sway,
"Remote from ST. JOHN, POPE, and GAY.
    "His Friendship there to few confin'd,   435
"Were always of the midling Kind:
"No Fools of Rank, a mungril Breed,
"Who fain would pass for Lords indeed:
"Where Titles give no Right or Power,
"And Peerage is a wither'd Flower,   440
"He would have held it a Disgrace,
"If such a Wretch had known his Face.
"On Rural Squires, that Kingdom's Bane,
"He vented oft his Wrath in vain:
"Biennial Squires, to Market brought;   445
"Who sell their Souls and Votes for Naught;
"The Nation stript go joyful back,
"To rob the Church, their Tenants rack,
"Go Snacks with Thieves and Rapparees,
"And, keep the Peace, to pick up Fees: 450
"In every Jobb to have a Share,
"A Jayl or Barrack to repair;
"And turn the Tax for publick Roads
"Commodious to their own Abodes.

---

420 *Scroggs … Tressilian* Sir William Scroggs (*c.*1623–83), Lord Chief Justice in 1678, was involved in the trials surrounding the Popish Plot. In 1681 he was removed from office. Sir Robert Tresilian, Chief Justice in 1381, tried John Ball and his followers after the suppression of the Peasants' Revolt and was hanged for treason in 1388.

422 *Nor fear'd he* GOD See Luke, 18:2: 'There was in a city a judge, which feared not God, neither regarded man.'

428 *Topicks* Subtle points of law.

431 *In Exile* 'In *Ireland*, which he had Reason to call a Place of Exile; to which Country nothing could have driven him, but the Queen's Death, who had determined to fix him in *England*' (Swift). The latter claim was untrue.

436 *midling* Swift boasted that he enjoyed no close friendships with peers or bishops in Ireland.

439–40 The Declaratory Act of 1720, designed to secure Ireland's dependence on England, had removed much of the constitutional power of the Irish peers.

445 *Biennial Squires* The Irish parliament met once every two years, to pass money bills. Day-to-day executive power was in the hands of the Lord Lieutenant.

448 *rack* 'raise the rent of'.

449 *Go Snacks* 'divide the loot'; *Rapparees* Irish bandits.

450 *keep the Peace* i.e. act as magistrates.

451 *Jobb* 'racket'.

452 *Barrack* The Irish had to pay for repairs to the barracks housing the British army in Ireland.

454 *Commodious to* 'to the advantage of'.

"Perhaps I may allow, the Dean   455
"Had too much Satyr in his Vein;
"And seem'd determin'd not to starve it,
"Because no Age could more deserve it.
"Yet, Malice never was his Aim;
"He lash'd the Vice but spar'd the Name.   460
"No Individual could resent,
"Where Thousands equally were meant.
"His Satyr points at no Defect,
"But what all Mortals may correct;
"For he abhorr'd that senseless Tribe,   465
"Who call it Humour when they jibe:
"He spar'd a Hump or crooked Nose,
"Whose Owners set not up for Beaux.
"True genuine Dulness mov'd his Pity,
"Unless it offer'd to be witty.   470
"Those, who their Ignorance confess'd,
"He ne'er offended with a Jest;
"But laugh'd to hear an Idiot quote,
"A Verse from *Horace*, learn'd by Rote.
    "He knew an hundred pleasant Stories,   475
"With all the Turns of *Whigs* and *Tories:*
"Was chearful to his dying Day,
"And Friends would let him have his Way.
    "He gave the little Wealth he had,
"To build a House for Fools and Mad: 480
"And shew'd by one satyric Touch,
"No Nation wanted it so much:
"That Kingdom he hath left his Debtor,
"I wish it soon may have a Better.

474 *Verse* 'line'; *Horace* (65–8 BC), Roman poet.
480 *House for Fools and Mad* Swift left a bequest earmarked for the construction of a mental institution in Dublin (the first in Ireland). St Patrick's Hospital opened in 1757, twelve years after Swift's death.

Alexander Pope (1688–1744)

Pope's Roman Catholic upbringing and severe physical disability (the stunted growth and hump back caused by spinal tuberculosis) excluded him from full participation in the society of his day. He compensated for a lack of formal schooling or a university education (denied Catholics) by voracious reading habits which fostered his intellectual independence and fuelled his fierce sense of poetic vocation. In this he was encouraged by his devoted elderly parents Alexander, a London linen-merchant, and his second wife Edith. The Pope family's move to rural Binfield near Windsor in 1700 (in compliance with the law debarring Catholics from residence within ten miles of the city) brought the intellectually precocious teenager into contact with his earliest group of friends and admirers, including the poet William Walsh and the distinguished dramatist William Wycherley. Pope was already displaying signs of his lifelong genius for close friendships, both male and female. It was during this period that he met Martha Blount, future dedicatee of *Epistle to a Lady*. As a teenager Pope was already writing mature verses. In 1709 Tonson's *Miscellanies: The Sixth Part* published his four *Pastorals* (beautifully polished imitations of Virgil's *Eclogues*), his modern English version of Chaucer's *Merchant's Tale*, and his *Episode of Sarpedon* translated from Homer's *Iliad*. In 1711 the eminent critic Joseph Addison praised his astonishingly confident *Essay on Criticism* as a 'Masterpiece in its Kind'. Yet Pope's early fame brought as many enemies as friends. The critic John Dennis, mocked in the *Essay*, produced the first of a barrage of critical attacks (see J. V. Guerinot, *Pamphlet Attacks on Alexander Pope, 1711–1744* (1969)), many of which depicted his physical deformity as the external manifestation of a warped and waspish soul.

The context of controversy within which Pope produced his major works was political as well as personal. In his early years he affected political neutrality and entered London literary society, making friends among Addison and Steele's Whig circle as well as with the Tory wits of the Scriblerus Club, who included Bolingbroke, Parnell, Gay and Swift. But by 1712 party divisions had become sharpened by the impending succession crisis and the Tory government's controversial peace negotiations to end the European war. In 1714 the death of Queen Anne and the succession of the pro-Whig Hanoverian George I ended Tory hopes and dispersed Pope's closest literary friends, driving Bolingbroke to France and Swift and Parnell to Ireland. Even Pope himself, whose *Windsor-Forest* (1713) could be read as a Jacobite piece, did not escape the new Whig government's scrutiny, and in 1723 he was forced to testify at the trial for treason of his close friend Francis Atterbury, Bishop of Rochester. Pope won his independence from political or royal patronage by shrewdly marketing his writing and he was the first poet to make a fortune by the sale of his works alone. In 1713 he embarked on an ambitious translation of Homer's *Iliad*, published by subscription, followed in 1720 by a similar translation of the *Odyssey* (1725–6). Pope underscored his poetic pre-eminence by issuing, while still in his twenties, the handsome *Works of Alexander Pope* (1717). The volume, which contains most of Pope's original work to that date, would have been impressive for a poet twice his age. Despite Pope's almost unswerving adherence to the heroic couplet, the contents testify to the sheer diversity of his poetic talent; from the poised urbanity of *The Rape of the Lock* to the passionate tension of *Eloisa to Abelard* and the patriotic prophecy of *Windsor-Forest*.

The 1717 *Works* contained little to indicate Pope's future role as a satirist. Thus the mock-epic *Dunciad* of 1728, his first major original work for over a decade, shocked some admirers who thought Pope's talents wasted in abusing a host of minor writers. Revenge may have been Pope's initial motive – especially on the poem's 'hero' Lewis Theobald, who had criticized Pope's Shakespeare edition in 1726 – yet even in its first version, *The Dunciad* was concerned with serious wider issues: the defence of cultural values against a growing commercialization of the arts.

Pope's output during the first half of the 1730s suggests a poet driven by competing impulses. The *Epistles to Several Persons* of 1731–5, while claiming to offer universal truths about human nature, bring into sharp focus the corruption of the entrenched Whig government. The identity of 'Timon' in the first of these four poems, *To Burlington*, embroiled Pope in public controversy. Before the scandal died down Pope had begun to publish (anonymously and to great acclaim) *An Essay on Man* (1733–4), a major four-book theodicy justifying 'the ways of God to man' through an investigation of the natural laws of the universe. Pope never completed his far larger scheme, the philosophical 'Opus Magnum', of which *An Essay on Man* and the *Epistles* were subsidiary parts. As the 1730s advanced he became increasingly involved in opposition politics and was outspoken in his attacks on the Walpole administration; in this he was fired by his close friendship with Bolingbroke, who was now masterminding the opposition's propaganda campaign, sometimes from Pope's Twickenham villa. Pope had moved to his house by the Thames in 1718, and during the 1730s his artistically cultivated gardens and much-loved subterranean grotto came to acquire a symbolic value. The *Imitations of Horace* (1733–8), satiric epistles modelled on the Roman poet Horace, dramatize Pope and his friends as the custodians of moral values and Twickenham as a refuge from worldly corruption and self-interest. The *Imitations*, in part autobiographical, continue the defence of Pope's role as a satirist initiated in his *Epistle to Dr Arbuthnot* (1735) and culminating in the *Epilogue to the Satires* of 1738. Here Pope finally dispenses with Horatian moderation, brands by name the villains of his age, and presents the satirist as a hero wielding his 'sacred Weapon' in truth's defence. These two dialogues represent the high-water mark of Pope's involvement in opposition politics. Even then, Pope continued to maintain independent friendships with men of different political persuasions. By 1740, however, he had become politically disillusioned. Shortly after Walpole's fall in 1742 appeared *The New Dunciad*, a fourth book to his original poem, charting the decay in the nation's spiritual and civic life during the intervening years. The *Dunciad in Four Books* (October 1743), with its apocalyptic vision of a civilization on the brink of ruin, possessed the majesty and grandeur of a true rather than a 'mock' epic. In his last years Pope incongruously sketched out plans for a serious national epic, *Brutus*, of which an eight-line fragment – in uncharacteristic blank verse – remains. But in the final months of 1743 Pope's health rapidly deteriorated. The end to what he had ruefully described as 'this long disease, my Life' came peacefully in May 1744.

'Good God! What an Incongruous Animal is Man? how unsettled in his best part, his soul; and how changing and variable in his frame of body? The constancy of the one, shook by every notion, the temperament of the other, affected by every blast of wind. What an April weather in the mind! In a word, what is Man altogether, but one mighty Inconsistency' (Pope–Caryll, 14 August 1713). Pope was fascinated by contradiction and paradox, and especially by the use and misuse of human energies. Around him he saw how pride, frustrated desires, lack of direction, or just plain stupidity, could warp human life and destroy its hopes, how farce and tragedy intermingle. He channelled his own enormous mental and moral vitality into the tight heroic couplet, just as in later years he would strap his wasting body into a canvas corset in order to be able to move about. For him the rhymed pentameter was an instrument on which he could play with endless subtlety of tone and rhythm: it was not constricting, but liberating – within its formal bounds it allowed every nuance to register. After Pope's death, when tastes were shifting towards more personal and visionary modes, and poets were turning to a variety of other verse forms, the Popean couplet remained influential, especially for the 'epistle' form (see Mary Jones, Mary Leapor and Helen Maria Williams), and for poems of social comment (Goldsmith and Crabbe). But many other writers in this volume draw on his work. The poet of 'correctness', 'sense', 'wit' and 'decorum' admired by earlier twentieth-century critics is now seen to be only a partial picture. More recent criticism has thankfully rediscovered the creative and imaginative excitements of reading Pope.

Windsor-Forest

Windsor-Forest draws on the poet's teenage experiences of life in the environs of Windsor Forest (an historic Royal hunting ground) as well as on a rich diversity of literary models from Virgil's *Georgics* to the Book of Isaiah. An early version existed by 1707. It was the Treaty of Utrecht (1713), bringing to an end the long European war, that prompted Pope to transform his poem into a panegyric on his country. It was dedicated to the Secretary-at-War, George Granville, Lord Lansdowne, who was instrumental (like a number of Pope's other friends) in negotiating the Tory-led Peace. The Tory, possibly Jacobite, bias of *Windsor-Forest* emerges in its literary antecedents (Royalist poems that combined scenic description with moral and political reflection, Sir John Denham's *Coopers Hill* and Edmund Waller's *On St James's Park*) and in its reading of history. Windsor, traditional seat of English kings, acts as the focal point for Pope's survey of British history. This moves from the oppressive rule of a 'foreign' tyrant, William the Conqueror (and by implication his recent namesake, Dutch William III), through the execution of the 'sacred' Charles I in 1649 and the evils of Civil War, to the Plague and Great Fire of London (1665–6), culminating in the War of the Spanish Succession (1701–13). Queen Anne's divine fiat, 'Let Discord cease!', ushers in Pope's swelling prophecy of a new age of imperial concord, modelled on Virgil's *Georgics* and *Aeneid*. Pope's linking of this vision to a continuing Stuart dynasty ('Peace and Plenty tell, a STUART reigns') is tendentious, given that the childless Anne, who died the following year, had no legal Stuart heirs. The line could continue only through the exiled Stuart pretender, 'James III'. Paradoxically, Pope's political partisanship enabled him here to speak as the voice of the nation, the unofficial laureate of peace. The poet-figure who roams the forest meditating on Britain's past and future expresses an optimistic patriotism that Pope never recaptured. His later satires dramatize a poet increasingly at odds with society under the Hanoverian Whig oligarchy.

Some recent critics, disturbed by *Windsor-Forest*'s imperialist overtones, have exposed the 'commodity fetishism' behind Pope's glamorizing of the spoils of foreign trade. Instead of liberating 'freed Indians' as the poem's conclusion prophesies, the Treaty of Utrecht's Asiento clause granted Britain a thirty-year monopoly on importing slaves into the Spanish colonies. Yet *Windsor-Forest* is no unthinking piece of jingoism. The life of the forest expresses Pope's vision of a complex postlapsarian world order, in which mankind's violent and warlike energies may be harnessed and redirected, though never eradicated. The poem acknowledges victims as well as victors.

Thus the hunting scenes, unlike those of many conventional eighteenth-century georgics, are memorable less for the robust joys of the chase than for the poignant brevity of hunted lives.

Windsor-Forest. To the Right Honourable George Lord Lansdown was first published in folio on 7 March 1713. The following text is that of the first edition. Pope's own 1713 notes are included.

> *Non injussa cano: Te nostræ,* Vare, *Myricæ*
> *Te Nemus omne canet; nec Phœbo gratior ulla est*
> *Quam sibi quæ* Vari *præscripsit Pagina nomen.*
>
> VIRG.

Thy Forests, *Windsor*! and thy green Retreats,
At once the Monarch's and the Muse's Seats,
Invite my Lays. Be present, Sylvan Maids!
Unlock your Springs, and open all your Shades.
Granville commands: Your Aid O Muses bring! 5
What Muse for *Granville* can refuse to sing?
　The Groves of *Eden*, vanish'd now so long,
Live in Description, and look green in Song:
These, were my Breast inspir'd with equal Flame,
Like them in Beauty, should be like in Fame. 10
Here Hills and Vales, the Woodland and the Plain,
Here Earth and Water seem to strive again,
Not *Chaos*-like together crush'd and bruis'd,
But as the World, harmoniously confus'd:
Where Order in Variety we see, 15
And where, tho' all things differ, all agree.
Here waving Groves a checquer'd Scene display,
And part admit and part exclude the Day;
As some coy Nymph her Lover's warm Address
Nor quite indulges, nor can quite repress. 20
There, interspers'd in Lawns and opening Glades,
Thin Trees arise that shun each others Shades.
Here in full Light the russet Plains extend;
There wrapt in Clouds the blueish Hills ascend:
Ev'n the wild Heath displays her Purple Dies, 25
And 'midst the Desart fruitful Fields arise,
That crown'd with tufted Trees and springing Corn,
Like verdant Isles the sable Waste adorn.
Let *India* boast her Plants, nor envy we

Epigraph 'I do not sing unbidden strains: it is of thee, Varus, our tamarisk trees shall sing, of thee all our groves. To Phoebus no page is more welcome than that which bears on its front the name of Varus' (Virgil, *Eclogues*, 6:9–12). 'Varus' is probably P. Alfenus Varus, a notable jurist and patron of letters.

2 In legend Windsor was the seat of King Arthur and his Knights of the Round Table. In the fourteenth century Edward III reconstructed the castle as a meeting place

for the Order of the Knights of the Garter. The castle was second only to Westminster Abbey as a repository for the bodies of English monarchs. The poets Denham and Cowley had lived close by.

3 *Sylvan Maids* Nymphs of stream and wood.

5 *Granville* See headnote. Granville was also a Royalist poet and dramatist who had celebrated James II.

23 *russet* 'reddish brown'.

The weeping Amber or the balmy Tree,   30
While by our Oaks the precious Loads are born,
And Realms commanded which those Trees adorn.
Not proud *Olympus* yields a nobler Sight,
Tho' Gods assembled grace his tow'ring Height,
Than what more humble Mountains offer here,   35
Where, in their Blessings, all those Gods appear.
See *Pan* with Flocks, with Fruits *Pomona* crown'd,
Here blushing *Flora* paints th'enamel'd Ground,
Here *Ceres'* Gifts in waving Prospect stand,
And nodding tempt the joyful Reaper's Hand,   40
Rich Industry sits smiling on the Plains,
And Peace and Plenty tell, a STUART reigns.
    Not thus the Land appear'd in Ages past,
A dreary Desart and a gloomy Waste,
To Savage Beasts and Savage Laws a Prey,   45
And Kings more furious and severe than they:
Who claim'd the Skies, dispeopled Air and Floods,
The lonely Lords of empty Wilds and Woods.
Cities laid waste, they storm'd the Dens and Caves
(For wiser Brutes were backward to be Slaves)   50
What could be free, when lawless Beasts obey'd,
And ev'n the Elements a Tyrant sway'd?
In vain kind Seasons swell'd the teeming Grain,
Soft Show'rs distill'd, and Suns grew warm in vain;
The Swain with Tears to Beasts his Labour yields, 55
And famish'd dies amidst his ripen'd Fields.
No wonder Savages or Subjects slain
Were equal Crimes in a Despotick Reign;
Both doom'd alike for sportive Tyrants bled,
But Subjects starv'd while Savages were fed.   60
Proud *Nimrod* first the bloody Chace began,
A mighty Hunter, and his Prey was Man.
Our haughty *Norman* boasts that barb'rous Name,
And makes his trembling Slaves the Royal Game.
The Fields are ravish'd from th'industrious Swains, 65
From Men their Cities, and from Gods their Fanes:
The levell'd Towns with Weeds lie cover'd o'er,

---

31 *Oaks* i.e. ships built of English oak; *precious Loads* Of valuable foreign spices.

33 *Olympus* The mountain home of the Greek gods.

37 *Pan* Greek god of shepherds; *Pomona* Roman goddess of fruit.

38 *Flora* Roman goddess of flowers; *enamel'd Ground* A metaphor for nature derived from art, referring to the technique of enamel-work on metal in which the first coating, or 'ground' of colour, supplied the background for decorative painting.

39 *Ceres* Roman goddess of crops.

42 STUART Queen Anne (1665–1714), reigned from 1702.

43–84 Pope describes the tyrannies practised after 1066 by the Norman kings, especially William I, who turned Windsor Forest into a royal hunting ground.

45 *Savage Laws* 'The Forest Laws' (Pope). These laws prescribed harsh punishments, such as blinding, for poachers. They were among the list of grievances which led to Magna Carta.

55 His crops are ravaged by the protected royal game.

61 *Nimrod* Genesis, 10:9 describes Nimrod, King of Babylon, as a 'mighty hunter'. But Biblical commentary characterized him as a despot.

65 'Alluding to the *New Forest*, and the Tyrannies exercis'd there by *William* the First' (Pope).

66 *Fanes* 'temples'.

67–72 Recalls God's curse on Babylon, Isaiah, 13:19–22.

The hollow Winds thro' naked Temples roar;
Round broken Columns clasping Ivy twin'd;
O'er Heaps of Ruins stalk'd the stately Hind; 70
The Fox obscene to gaping Tombs retires,
And Wolves with Howling fill the sacred Quires.
Aw'd by his Nobles, by his Commons curst,
Th'Oppressor rul'd Tyrannick where he *durst*,
Stretch'd o'er the Poor, and Church, his Iron Rod, 75
And treats alike his Vassals and his God.
Whom ev'n the *Saxon* spar'd, and bloody *Dane*,
The wanton Victims of his *Sport* remain.
But see the Man who spacious Regions gave
A Waste for Beasts, himself deny'd a Grave! 80
Stretch'd on the Lawn his second Hope survey,
At once the Chaser and at once the Prey.
Lo *Rufus*, tugging at the deadly Dart,
Bleeds in the Forest, like a wounded Hart.
Succeeding Monarchs heard the Subjects Cries, 85
Nor saw displeas'd the peaceful Cottage rise.
Then gath'ring Flocks on unknown Mountains fed,
O'er sandy Wilds were yellow Harvests spread,
The Forests wonder'd at th' unusual Grain,
And secret Transports touch'd the conscious Swain. 90
Fair *Liberty*, *Britannia*'s Goddess, rears
Her chearful Head, and leads the golden Years.
      Ye vig'rous Swains! while Youth ferments your Blood,
And purer Spirits swell the sprightly Flood,
Now range the Hills, the thickest Woods beset, 95
Wind the shrill Horn, or spread the waving Net.
When milder Autumn Summer's Heat succeeds,
And in the new-shorn Field the Partridge feeds,
Before his Lord the ready Spaniel bounds,
Panting with Hope, he tries the furrow'd Grounds, 100
But when the tainted Gales the Game betray,
Couch'd close he lyes, and meditates the Prey;
Secure they trust th'unfaithful Field, beset,
Till hov'ring o'er 'em sweeps the swelling Net.
Thus (if small Things we may with great compare) 105
When *Albion* sends her eager Sons to War,
Pleas'd, in the Gen'ral's Sight, the Host lye down
Sudden, before some unsuspecting Town,
The Young, the Old, one Instant makes our Prize,

---

71 *obscene* 'ill-omened', 'loathsome'.
72 *Quires* The chancel or 'choir', often screened off from the rest of the church.
76 *Vassals* Feudal subjects.
80 *deny'd a Grave* A knight who owned the land on which William I was to be buried protested and had to be paid off.
81 *second Hope* '*Richard*, second Son of *William* the Conqueror' (Pope).

83–4 William Rufus (William II) was accidentally killed by an arrow while hunting.
87 *unknown* i.e. because previously forbidden to them.
94 *purer Spirits* The body's animal spirits, which supposedly moved through the bloodstream.
101 *tainted* 'carrying animal scent'; *Gales* 'breezes'.

And high in Air *Britannia*'s Standard flies.   110
   See! from the Brake the whirring Pheasant springs,
And mounts exulting on triumphant Wings;
Short is his Joy! he feels the fiery Wound,
Flutters in Blood, and panting beats the Ground.
Ah! what avail his glossie, varying Dyes,   115
His Purple Crest, and Scarlet-circled Eyes,
The vivid Green his shining Plumes unfold;
His painted Wings, and Breast that flames with Gold?
   Nor yet, when moist *Arcturus* clouds the Sky,
The Woods and Fields their pleasing Toils deny.   120
To Plains with well-breath'd Beagles we repair,
And trace the Mazes of the circling Hare.
(Beasts, taught by us, their Fellow Beasts pursue,
And learn of Man each other to undo.)
With slaught'ring Guns th'unweary'd Fowler roves,   125
When Frosts have whiten'd all the naked Groves;
Where Doves in Flocks the leafless Trees o'ershade,
And lonely Woodcocks haunt the watry Glade.
He lifts the Tube, and levels with his Eye;
Strait a short Thunder breaks the frozen Sky.   130
Oft, as in Airy Rings they skim the Heath,
The clam'rous Plovers feel the Leaden Death:
Oft as the mounting Larks their Notes prepare,
They fall, and leave their little Lives in Air.
   In genial Spring, beneath the quiv'ring Shade   135
Where cooling Vapours breathe along the Mead,
The patient Fisher takes his silent Stand
Intent, his Angle trembling in his Hand;
With Looks unmov'd, he hopes the Scaly Breed,
And eyes the dancing Cork and bending Reed.   140
Our plenteous Streams a various Race supply;
The bright-ey'd Perch with Fins of *Tyrian* Dye,
The silver Eel, in shining Volumes roll'd,
The yellow Carp, in Scales bedrop'd with Gold,
Swift Trouts, diversify'd with Crimson Stains,   145
And Pykes, the Tyrants of the watry Plains.
   Now *Cancer* glows with *Phoebus'* fiery Car;
The Youth rush eager to the Sylvan War;
Swarm o'er the Lawns, the Forest Walks surround,
Rowze the fleet Hart, and chear the opening Hound.   150
Th'impatient Courser pants in ev'ry Vein,
And pawing, seems to beat the distant Plain,
Hills, Vales, and Floods appear already crost,
And ere he starts, a thousand Steps are lost.

111 *Brake* 'thicket'.

119 *Arcturus* The brightest star in the northern hemisphere. Stormy weather was thought to follow the brief period in September when it rose at dawn.

132 *Plovers* Small birds who swoop and dive over heathland. See Thomson, *Spring*, 24n.

139 *hopes* 'anticipates'.

147 The sun ('Phoebus') enters the constellation of Cancer on 22 June.

150 *opening* 'beginning to bark'.

151 *Courser* A swift horse.

See! the bold Youth strain up the threatning Steep,   155
Rush thro' the Thickets, down the Vallies sweep,
Hang o'er their Coursers Heads with eager Speed,
And Earth rolls back beneath the flying Steed.
Let old *Arcadia* boast her spacious Plain,
Th'Immortal Huntress, and her Virgin Train;   160
Nor envy *Windsor*! since thy Shades have seen
As bright a Goddess, and as chast a Queen;
Whose Care, like hers, protects the Sylvan Reign,
The Earth's fair Light, and Empress of the Main.
  Here, as old Bards have sung, *Diana* stray'd,   165
Bath'd in the Springs, or sought the cooling Shade;
Here arm'd with Silver Bows, in early Dawn,
Her buskin'd Virgins trac'd the Dewy Lawn.
Above the rest a rural Nymph was fam'd,
Thy Offspring, *Thames*! the fair *Lodona* nam'd,   170
(*Lodona*'s Fate, in long Oblivion cast,
The Muse shall sing, and what she sings shall last)
Scarce could the Goddess from her Nymph be known,
But by the Crescent and the golden Zone,
She scorn'd the Praise of Beauty, and the Care;   175
A Belt her Waste, a Fillet binds her Hair,
A painted Quiver on her Shoulder sounds,
And with her Dart the flying Deer she wounds.
It chanc'd, as eager of the Chace the Maid
Beyond the Forest's verdant Limits stray'd,   180
Pan saw and lov'd, and furious with Desire
Pursu'd her Flight; her Flight increas'd his Fire.
Not half so swift the trembling Doves can fly,
When the fierce Eagle cleaves the liquid Sky;
Not half so swiftly the fierce Eagle moves,   185
When thro' the Clouds he drives the trembling Doves;
As from the God with fearful Speed she flew,
As did the God with equal Speed pursue.
Now fainting, sinking, pale, the Nymph appears;
Now close behind his sounding Steps she hears;   190
And now his Shadow reach'd her as she run,
(His Shadow lengthen'd by the setting Sun)
And now his shorter Breath with sultry Air
Pants on her Neck, and fans her parting Hair.
In vain on Father *Thames* she calls for Aid,   195
Nor could *Diana* help her injur'd Maid.
Faint, breathless, thus she pray'd, nor pray'd in vain;
"Ah *Cynthia*! ah — tho' banish'd from thy Train,
"Let me, O let me, to the Shades repair,

---

159 *Arcadia* A region of Greece mythologized by poets as an ideal pastoral landscape.
160 *Immortal Huntress* Diana, goddess of the moon, was often depicted as a huntress, leading a train of huntress-nymphs.
162 *Queen* Anne was a keen hunter, following the chase in a chariot she drove herself.
168 *buskin'd* Shod in buskins, calf-high boots.

170 *Lodona* The river Loddon flows into the Thames near Binfield, Pope's childhood home. He modelled the following episode on stories in Ovid's *Metamorphoses*.
174 *Crescent* The crescent moon, Diana's emblem; *Zone* 'girdle'.
176 *Fillet* 'head-band'.
184 *liquid* 'clear' (Lat. *liquidus*).
198 *Cynthia* Diana.

"My native Shades — there weep, and murmur there.   200
She said, and melting as in Tears she lay,
In a soft, silver Stream dissolv'd away.
The silver Stream her Virgin Coldness keeps,
For ever murmurs, and for ever weeps;
Still bears the Name the hapless Virgin bore,   205
And bathes the Forest where she rang'd before.
In her chast Current oft the Goddess laves,
And with Celestial Tears augments the Waves.
Oft in her Glass the musing Shepherd spies
The headlong Mountains and the downward Skies,   210
The watry Landskip of the pendant Woods,
And absent Trees that tremble in the Floods;
In the clear azure Gleam the Flocks are seen,
And floating Forests paint the Waves with Green.
Thro' the fair Scene rowl slow the lingring Streams,   215
Then foaming pour along, and rush into the *Thames*.
    Thou too, great Father of the *British* Floods!
With joyful Pride survey'st our lofty Woods,
Where tow'ring Oaks their spreading Honours rear,
And future Navies on thy Banks appear.   220
Not *Neptune*'s self from all his Floods receives
A wealthier Tribute, than to thine he gives.
No Seas so rich, so full no Streams appear,
No Lake so gentle, and no Spring so clear.
Not fabled *Po* more swells the Poets Lays,   225
While thro' the Skies his shining Current strays,
Than thine, which visits *Windsor*'s fam'd Abodes,
To grace the Mansion of our earthly Gods.
Nor all his Stars a brighter Lustre show,
Than the fair Nymphs that gild thy Shore below: 230
Here *Jove* himself, subdu'd by Beauty still,
Might change *Olympus* for a nobler Hill.
    Happy the Man whom this bright Court approves,
His Sov'reign favours, and his Country loves;
Happy next him who to these Shades retires,   235
Whom Nature charms, and whom the Muse inspires,
Whom humbler Joys of home-felt Quiet please,
Successive Study, Exercise and Ease.
He gathers Health from Herbs the Forest yields,
And of their fragrant Physick spoils the Fields: 240
With Chymic Art exalts the Min'ral Pow'rs,
And draws the Aromatick Souls of Flow'rs.
Now marks the Course of rolling Orbs on high;
O'er figur'd Worlds now travels with his Eye.

---

207 *laves* 'washes'.
219 *Oaks* Oak forest used for shipbuilding. See Cowper,
    Yardley Oak, 96n.
221 *Neptune* Roman god of the sea.
225 *Po* The river in northern Italy.

231 *Jove* Jupiter, king of the gods.
240 *Physick* 'medicine'.
241 *exalts* 'refines'.
242 *draws* 'distils'.
244 *figur'd* 'depicted' (on a globe or a map).

Of ancient Writ unlocks the learned Store, 245
Consults the Dead, and lives past Ages o'er.
Or wandring thoughtful in the silent Wood,
Attends the Duties of the Wise and Good,
T'observe a Mean, be to himself a Friend,
To follow Nature, and regard his End. 250
Or looks on Heav'n with more than mortal Eyes,
Bids his free Soul expatiate in the Skies,
Amidst her Kindred Stars familiar roam,
Survey the Region, and confess her Home!
Such was the Life great *Scipio* once admir'd, 255
Thus *Atticus*, and *Trumbal* thus retir'd.
 Ye sacred Nine! that all my Soul possess,
Whose Raptures fire me, and whose Visions bless,
Bear me, oh bear me to sequester'd Scenes
Of Bow'ry Mazes and surrounding Greens; 260
To *Thames*'s Banks which fragrant Breezes fill,
Or where ye Muses sport on *Cooper*'s Hill.
(On *Cooper*'s Hill eternal Wreaths shall grow,
While lasts the Mountain, or while *Thames* shall flow)
I seem thro' consecrated Walks to rove, 265
And hear soft Musick dye along the Grove;
Led by the Sound I roam from Shade to Shade,
By God-like Poets Venerable made:
Here his first Lays Majestick *Denham* sung;
There the last Numbers flow'd from *Cowley*'s Tongue. 270
O early lost! what Tears the River shed
When the sad Pomp along his Banks was led?
His drooping Swans on ev'ry Note expire,
And on his Willows hung each Muse's Lyre.
 Since Fate relentless stop'd their Heav'nly Voice, 275
No more the Forests ring, or Groves rejoice;
Who now shall charm the Shades where *Cowley* strung
His living Harp, and lofty *Denham* sung?
But hark! the Groves rejoice, the Forest rings!
Are these reviv'd? or is it *Granville* sings? 280
 'Tis yours, my Lord, to bless our soft Retreats,
And call the Muses to their ancient Seats,
To paint anew the flow'ry Sylvan Scenes,

---

249 *Mean* 'moderate course'.

252 *expatiate* 'wander freely'.

255 *Scipio* Scipio Africanus (236–183 BC), the Roman general who defeated Hannibal. After his enemies tried to prosecute him with trumped-up charges, he left Rome and retired to his country estate.

256 *Atticus* Titus Pomponius (110–32 BC), friend and correspondent of Cicero. In 85 he left politically turbulent Rome for Athens (hence his name Atticus), where he built up his library in calm retirement. During the Civil Wars he maintained strict neutrality; *Trumbal* Sir William Trumbull (1639–1716), former Secretary of State, a friend of Pope living near Windsor Forest and the dedicatee of one of his *Pastorals*.

257 *Nine* The Muses.

262 *Cooper's Hill* A hill offering views of both London and Windsor. It was immortalized by Denham's poem of that title, one of the models for *Windsor-Forest*.

269 *Denham* Sir John Denham (1615–69), Royalist poet, whose house at Egham near Windsor, where he wrote his earliest poems, was confiscated by Parliamentary forces during the Civil War.

270 *Cowley* Abraham Cowley (1618–67), Royalist poet of lyric and epic verse. 'Mr. *Cowley* died at *Chertsey*, on the Borders of the Forest, and was from thence convey'd to *Westminster*' (Pope).

To crown the Forests with Immortal Greens,
Make *Windsor* Hills in lofty Numbers rise,   285
And lift her Turrets nearer to the Skies;
To sing those Honours you deserve to wear,
And add new Lustre to her Silver *Star*.
    Here noble *Surrey* felt the sacred Rage,
Surrey, the *Granville* of a former Age: 290
Matchless his Pen, victorious was his Lance;
Bold in the Lists, and graceful in the Dance:
In the same Shades the *Cupids* tun'd his Lyre,
To the same Notes, of Love, and soft Desire:
Fair *Geraldine*, bright Object of his Vow,   295
Then fill'd the Groves, as heav'nly *Myra* now.
    Oh wou'dst thou sing what Heroes *Windsor* bore,
What Kings first breath'd upon her winding Shore,
Or raise old Warriors whose ador'd Remains
In weeping Vaults her hallow'd Earth contains!   300
With *Edward*'s Acts adorn the shining Page,
Stretch his long Triumphs down thro' ev'ry Age,
Draw Kings enchain'd, and *Cressi*'s glorious Field,
The Lillies blazing on the Regal Shield.
Then, from her Roofs when *Verrio*'s Colours fall,   305
And leave inanimate the naked Wall;
Still in thy Song shou'd vanquish'd *France* appear,
And bleed for ever under *Britain*'s Spear.
    Let softer Strains Ill-fated *Henry* mourn,
And Palms Eternal flourish round his Urn.   310
Here o'er the Martyr-King the Marble weeps,
And fast beside him, once-fear'd *Edward* sleeps:
Whom not th' extended *Albion* could contain,
From old *Belerium* to the *German* Main,
The Grave unites; where ev'n the Great find Rest,   315
And blended lie th' Oppressor and th' Opprest!
    Make sacred *Charles*'s Tomb for ever known,
(Obscure the Place, and uninscrib'd the Stone)
Oh Fact accurst! What Tears has *Albion* shed,

288 *Silver Star* The insignia of the Order of the Garter (see 2n).

289 *Surrey* Henry Howard, Earl of Surrey (?1517–47), 'one of the first Refiners of the *English* poetry; famous in the Time of Henry the VIIIth for his Sonnets, the Scene of many of which is laid at Windsor' (Pope).

292 *Lists* The space where jousting tournaments were held.

295 *Geraldine* Lady Elizabeth Fitzgerald, to whom Surrey's love poems were reputedly addressed.

296 *Myra* The addressee of Granville's love poems.

301 *Edward* 'Edward III. born here' (Pope). Edward III (1312–77), founder of the Order of the Garter. In 1340 he assumed the title of King of France, incorporating the French lily into his arms. Six years later he destroyed the French army at Crécy.

305 *Verrio* Antonio Verrio (?1639–1707), Italian painter employed by Charles II at Windsor Castle. In St George's hall he painted the triumphal procession in which Edward III's son, the Black Prince, leads the King of France captive; *Colours fall* The paintings had started to fade owing to the leeching of mineral salts.

309 *Ill-fated Henry* Henry VI, murdered by the followers of Edward, Duke of York (subsequently Edward IV) in 1471. He was revered as a saint and martyr. His body was moved to Windsor in 1484.

312 *Edward* Edward IV.

314 *Belerium* The Latin name for Land's End in Cornwall.

317–18 Charles I, executed in 1649, was buried in St George's chapel without a funeral service. The exact location of his body remained unknown until 1813.

Heav'ns! what new Wounds, and how her old have bled?   320
She saw her Sons with purple Deaths expire,
Her sacred Domes involv'd in rolling Fire.
A dreadful Series of Intestine Wars,
Inglorious Triumphs, and dishonest Scars.
At length great ANNA said — Let Discord cease!   325
She said, the World obey'd, and all was *Peace*!
　　In that blest Moment, from his Oozy Bed
Old Father *Thames* advanc'd his rev'rend Head.
His Tresses dropt with Dews, and o'er the Stream
His shining Horns diffus'd a golden Gleam: 330
Grav'd on his Urn appear'd the Moon, that guides
His swelling Waters, and alternate Tydes;
The figur'd Streams in Waves of Silver roll'd,
And on their Banks *Augusta* rose in Gold.
Around his Throne the Sea-born Brothers stood,   335
That swell with Tributary Urns his Flood.
First the fam'd Authors of his ancient Name,
The winding *Isis*, and the fruitful *Tame*:
The *Kennet* swift, for silver Eels renown'd;
The *Loddon* slow, with verdant Alders crown'd: 340
Cole, whose clear Streams his flow'ry Islands lave;
And chalky *Wey*, that rolls a milky Wave:
The blue, transparent *Vandalis* appears;
The gulphy *Lee* his sedgy Tresses rears:
And sullen *Mole*, that hides his diving Flood;   345
And silent *Darent*, stain'd with *Danish* Blood.
　　High in the midst, upon his Urn reclin'd,
(His Sea-green Mantle waving with the Wind)
The God appear'd; he turn'd his azure Eyes
Where *Windsor*-Domes and pompous Turrets rise,   350
Then bow'd and spoke; the Winds forget to roar,
And the hush'd Waves glide softly to the Shore.
　　Hail Sacred *Peace*! hail long-expected Days,
Which *Thames*'s Glory to the Stars shall raise!
Tho' *Tyber*'s Streams immortal *Rome* behold,   355
Tho' foaming *Hermus* swells with Tydes of Gold,
From Heav'n it self tho' sev'nfold *Nilus* flows,

321–2 The Great Plague (1665) and the Great Fire (1666) of London.

323 *Intestine Wars* The English Civil War had ended with Charles II's defeat at Worcester in 1651. Pope perhaps alludes to the Monmouth rebellion (1685) and the civil uprisings in Ireland under Cromwell and William III.

328 Pope's personification of the River Thames is modelled on Virgil's description of Father Tiber (*Aeneid*, 8:33–4) and Spenser's account of the Thames and its tributaries in *Faerie Queene*, IV.xi.25–9.

330 *Horns* River-gods were often depicted with bull-like horns, symbolizing their strength and their roaring noise.

334 *Augusta* The Roman name for London during the

fourth century, recently used by Dryden and other poets to evoke imperial power.

337 *ancient Name* 'Tamesis' (so called by Julius Caesar). Camden's theory that this Latin name derived from its parent rivers Thame and Isis is wrong.

341 *Cole* The River Colne divides into channels round several islands before it joins the Thames.

343 *Vandalis* The River Wandle.

345 *Mole* The Mole purportedly runs underground for many miles, surfacing at Leatherhead in Surrey.

346 *Danish Blood* In 1016 the Danes were repulsed by Edmund Ironside at Otford on the Darent.

356 *Hermus* An Italian river praised in Virgil's *Georgics*.

357 *sev'nfold Nilus* The fertile Nile Delta.

And Harvests on a hundred Realms bestows;
These now no more shall be the Muse's Themes,
Lost in my Fame, as in the Sea their Streams.   360
Let *Volga*'s Banks with Iron Squadrons shine,
And Groves of Lances glitter on the *Rhine*,
Let barb'rous *Ganges* arm a servile Train;
Be mine the Blessings of a peaceful Reign.
No more my Sons shall dye with *British* Blood   365
Red *Iber*'s Sands, or *Ister*'s foaming Flood;
Safe on my Shore each unmolested Swain
Shall tend the Flocks, or reap the bearded Grain;
The shady Empire shall retain no Trace
Of War or Blood, but in the Sylvan Chace,   370
The Trumpets sleep, while chearful Horns are blown,
And Arms employ'd on Birds and Beasts alone.
Behold! th'ascending *Villa*'s on my Side
Project long Shadows o'er the Chrystal Tyde.
Behold! *Augusta*'s glitt'ring Spires increase,   375
And Temples rise, the beauteous Works of Peace.
I see, I see where two fair Cities bend
Their ample Bow, a new *White-Hall* ascend!
There mighty Nations shall inquire their Doom,
The World's great Oracle in Times to come;   380
There Kings shall sue, and suppliant States be seen
Once more to bend before a *British* QUEEN.
　　　Thy Trees, fair *Windsor*! now shall leave their Woods,
And half thy Forests rush into my Floods,
Bear *Britain*'s Thunder, and her Cross display,   385
To the bright Regions of the rising Day;
Tempt Icy Seas, where scarce the Waters roll,
Where clearer Flames glow round the frozen Pole;
Or under Southern Skies exalt their Sails,
Led by new Stars, and born by spicy Gales!   390
For me the Balm shall bleed, and Amber flow,
The Coral redden, and the Ruby glow,
The Pearly Shell its lucid Globe infold,
And *Phœbus* warm the ripening Ore to Gold.
The Time shall come, when free as Seas or Wind   395
Unbounded *Thames* shall flow for all Mankind,

361 *Volga* A reference to Charles XII of Sweden's recent war against Russia. See Johnson, *The Vanity of Human Wishes*, 192–222.

362 *Rhine* Marlborough's advance towards the Rhine Valley in 1704 culminated in the victorious Battle of Blenheim.

363 *Ganges* A reference to the recent wars of the Indian Mughal emperor, Aurangzeb.

366 *Iber* The River Ebro. An allusion to the Allies' victory at Saragossa in Spain, 1710; *Ister* The Danube.

376 *Temples rise* During Anne's reign fifty new churches were commissioned in London.

377 *two fair Cities* London and Westminster, then separate towns.

378 *Bow* The Thames curves between the two sites; *new White-Hall* Most of Whitehall Palace had burned down in the 1690s. Plans to rebuild it were never carried out.

382 A reference back to the appeal of the Dutch to Queen Elizabeth I for help in their struggle against Philip of Spain.

383–4 Oaks used for shipbuilding. Cf. Anne Finch, *Upon the Hurricane*, 15–22.

385 *Cross* The red cross of St George.

387 *Tempt* 'adventure upon'.

391 *Balm* The sap collected from cutting into tree bark.

394 *ripening Ore* It was thought that the sun ripened gold and precious stones beneath the earth. Cf. *Epistle to a Lady*, 289–90.

Whole Nations enter with each swelling Tyde,
And Oceans join whom they did first divide;
Earth's distant Ends our Glory shall behold,
And the new World launch forth to seek the Old.   400
Then Ships of uncouth Form shall stem the Tyde,
And Feather'd People crowd my wealthy Side,
While naked Youth and painted Chiefs admire
Our Speech, our Colour, and our strange Attire!
Oh stretch thy Reign, fair *Peace*! from Shore to Shore,   405
Till Conquest cease, and Slav'ry be no more:
Till the freed *Indians* in their native Groves
Reap their own Fruits, and woo their Sable Loves,
Peru once more a Race of Kings behold,
And other *Mexico's* be roof'd with Gold.   410
Exil'd by Thee from Earth to deepest Hell,
In Brazen Bonds shall barb'rous *Discord* dwell:
Gigantick *Pride*, pale *Terror*, gloomy *Care*,
And mad *Ambition*, shall attend her there.
There purple *Vengeance* bath'd in Gore retires,   415
Her Weapons blunted, and extinct her Fires:
There hateful *Envy* her own Snakes shall feel,
And *Persecution* mourn her broken Wheel:
There *Faction* roars, *Rebellion* bites her Chain,
And gasping Furies thirst for Blood in vain.   420
   Here cease thy Flight, nor with unhallow'd Lays
Touch the fair Fame of *Albion*'s Golden Days.
The Thoughts of Gods let *Granville*'s Verse recite,
And bring the Scenes of opening Fate to Light.
My humble Muse, in unambitious Strains,   425
Paints the green Forests and the flow'ry Plains,
Where Peace descending bids her Olives spring,
And scatters Blessings from her Dove-like Wing.
Ev'n I more sweetly pass my careless Days,
Pleas'd in the silent Shade with empty Praise;   430
Enough for me, that to the listning Swains
First in these Fields I sung the Sylvan Strains.

402–4 In 1710 four Iroquois Indian chiefs were granted a public audience by Queen Anne.

407 *freed Indians* From Spanish oppression.

409 *Race of Kings* The Incas. Cf. Joseph Warton, *The Dying Indian*.

411–20 Modelled on two descriptions in Virgil which allude to Augustus's recent victories: *Georgics*, 3:37–9, and *Aeneid*, 1:293–6.

418 *Wheel* Of fortune.

420 *Furies* In Greek myth, the pitiless female spirits of vengeance.

423 *Gods* Granville's poems celebrated the god-like qualities of James II.

432 Echoes the opening line of Pope's *Spring*. Virgil had likewise closed his *Georgics* with the first line of his *Eclogues*.

The Rape of the Lock

The Rape of the Lock originated in a practical joke that went wrong. Lord Petre, a highly eligible bachelor, had publicly cut off a lock of Arabella Fermor's hair. Both she and her family were outraged, and John Caryll, a mutual friend, suggested Pope write a comic poem to heal the rift between the two prominent Catholic families and 'laugh them together again'.

Influenced in part by recent instances of comic epics in French and English (Boileau's *Le Lutrin* and Samuel Garth's *The Dispensary*), Pope decided to treat the 'rape' of Arabella's lock as a theme on a par with the abduction of Helen of Troy, the event which occasioned the war between Greeks and Trojans immortalized in the epics of Homer and Virgil. In his early two-canto version, *The Rape of the Locke* (1712), Pope perfected the technique of shrinking epic events and apparatus to domestic miniatures. The protagonists go to war with scissors, bodkins and snuff, and the Baron's stratagems are inspired not by a deity but by coffee vapours. By 1714, when the full five-canto version appeared, Pope had expanded *The Rape of the Lock* into a scaled-down version of a complete epic by adding a supernatural machinery of invisible spirits drawn from Rosicrucian mysticism (a parallel to the classical deities, but more specifically to the heavenly and diabolic protagonists of Milton's *Paradise Lost*). He also added Belinda's arming, the battle of cards, and in Canto 4 that staple of epic tradition, a journey to the underworld. Throughout the poem Pope exploits the comic gap between heroic rhetoric and modern life, but the relationship between style and subject is far more fluid and complex than that of ridicule. Thus Belinda, floating down the Thames in Canto 2, is enhanced, rather than diminished, by her implied comparison to Shakespeare's Cleopatra. Pope never produced the full-length national epic that his admirers hoped for. *The Rape of the Lock*, and subsequently *The Dunciad*, may have confirmed what many of his contemporaries suspected: that the values of heroic epic were incompatible with the commercial and consumerist energies of the eighteenth century, symbolized by the luxuries that turn Belinda's dressing table into an exotic emporium.

In later life Arabella Fermor (?1690–1738) boasted of her immortalization as Belinda. She had been less pleased when the two-canto version first appeared, believing that its pervasive sexual innuendo cast a slur on her reputation. Recent criticism has correspondingly found *The Rape of the Lock* controversial in its treatment of women. Does Pope use Belinda sympathetically to explore the dilemma of upper-class young women trapped by society's superficial demands? Or is the poet of the closing lines, who triumphantly exhibits his own immortal *Lock*, really a more successful version of the Baron? Yet if Pope seems to invigorate misogynist clichés (on women's vanity, superficiality and sexual provocation) he also subjects them to authorial irony, and the language of the poem has a restless electric power that challenges obvious or predictable responses.

The text reproduced below is that printed in the 1717 *Works of Mr Pope*. It was here for the first time that Pope added thirty lines to Canto 5 containing Clarissa's speech, which a note in the *1751* edition claims was designed 'to open more clearly the moral of the Poem'.

CANTO I

What dire Offence from am'rous causes springs,
What mighty contests rise from trivial things,
I sing — This verse to C—, Muse! is due:
This, ev'n *Belinda* may vouchsafe to view:
Slight is the subject, but not so the praise,   5
If She inspire, and He approve my lays.
    Say what strange motive, Goddess! could compel
A well-bred Lord t'assault a gentle *Belle*?
Oh say what stranger cause, yet unexplor'd,
Cou'd make a gentle *Belle* reject a Lord?   10
And dwells such rage in softest bosoms then?
And lodge such daring souls in Little men?
    Sol thro' white curtains shot a tim'rous ray,
And op'd those eyes that must eclipse the day;
Now lapdogs give themselves the rowsing shake,   15
And sleepless lovers, just at twelve, awake:
Thrice rung the bell, the slipper knock'd the ground,
And the press'd watch return'd a silver sound.
Belinda still her downy pillow prest,
Her guardian *Sylph* prolong'd the balmy rest.   20
'Twas he had summon'd to her silent bed

---

3 *C*— John Caryll (*c*.1666–1736), a wealthy landowning Catholic friend of Pope's.

13 *Sol* The sun.

17 *the slipper knock'd* To summon the maid from downstairs.

18 *press'd watch* A repeater, which chimed the hour when pressed.

The Morning-dream that hover'd o'er her head.
A Youth more glitt'ring than a Birth-night Beau,
(That ev'n in slumber caus'd her cheek to glow)
Seem'd to her ear his winning lips to lay,   25
And thus in whispers said, or seem'd to say.
   Fairest of mortals, thou distinguish'd care
Of thousand bright Inhabitants of Air!
If e'er one vision touch'd thy infant thought,
Of all the Nurse and all the Priest have taught,   30
Of airy Elves by moonlight shadows seen,
The silver token, and the circled green,
Or virgins visited by Angel-pow'rs,
With golden crowns and wreaths of heav'nly flow'rs,
Hear and believe! thy own importance know,   35
Nor bound thy narrow views to things below.
Some secret truths from Learned Pride conceal'd,
To Maids alone and Children are reveal'd:
What tho' no credit doubting Wits may give?
The Fair and Innocent shall still believe.   40
Know then, unnumber'd Spirits round thee fly,
The light Militia of the lower sky;
These, tho' unseen, are ever on the wing,
Hang o'er the Box, and hover round the Ring:
Think what an Equipage thou hast in air,   45
And view with scorn two Pages and a Chair.
As now your own, our beings were of old,
And once inclos'd in Woman's beauteous mold;
Thence, by a soft transition, we repair
From earthly Vehicles to these of air.   50
Think not, when Woman's transient breath is fled,
That all her vanities at once are dead:
Succeeding vanities she still regards,
And tho' she plays no more, o'erlooks the cards.
Her joy in gilded Chariots, when alive,   55
And love of *Ombre*, after death survive.
For when the Fair in all their pride expire,
To their first Elements the Souls retire:
The Sprites of fiery Termagants in flame

---

23 *Birth-night Beau* Courtiers wore especially fine clothes to celebrate royal birthdays. See Swift, *Strephon and Chloe*, 227–30.

25–6 Cf. Satan whispering a dream in Eve's ear, *Paradise Lost*, 4:800–3.

30 I.e. superstitions.

32 Tokens of the elves' presence were silver coins and 'fairy circles' (round patterns on grass caused by fungus).

33–4 The imagery is that of paintings of the Annunciation depicting the Virgin Mary visited by the angel Gabriel.

39 *doubting Wits* Sceptics.

41–3 Cf. 'Millions of spiritual creatures walk the earth / Unseen, both when we wake, and when we sleep' (*Paradise Lost*, 4:677–8).

44 *Box* A theatre box; *Ring* The fashionable circular drive in Hyde Park.

45 *Equipage* A coach and horses with attendants.

46 *Chair* Sedan chair.

56 *Ombre* The fashionable card game which features in Canto 3.

58 *first Elements* The ancient theory that the universe consists of four primal elements – earth, air, water, fire – was originated by Empedocles (fifth century BC). In the system of the alchemist and physician Paracelsus (1493–1541) the elemental spirits were sylphs (air), gnomes or 'pygmies' (earth), nymphs (water) and salamanders (fire).

59 *Termagant* 'shrewish woman'.

Mount up, and take a *Salamander*'s name.   60
Soft yielding minds to water glide away,
And sip, with Nymphs, their elemental Tea.
The graver Prude sinks downward to a *Gnome*,
In search of mischief still on earth to roam.
The light Coquettes in *Sylphs* aloft repair,   65
And sport and flutter in the fields of air.
    Know farther yet; whoever fair and chaste
Rejects mankind, is by some *Sylph* embrac'd:
For Spirits, freed from mortal laws, with ease
Assume what sexes and what shapes they please.   70
What guards the purity of melting Maids,
In courtly Balls, and midnight Masquerades,
Safe from the treach'rous friend, and daring spark,
The glance by day, the whisper in the dark;
When kind occasion prompts their warm desires,   75
When music softens, and when dancing fires?
'Tis but their *Sylph*, the wise Celestials know,
Tho' *Honour* is the word with Men below.
    Some nymphs there are, too conscious of their face,
For Life predestin'd to the *Gnomes* embrace.   80
These swell their prospects and exalt their pride,
When offers are disdain'd, and love deny'd.
Then gay Ideas crowd the vacant brain,
While Peers and Dukes, and all their sweeping train,
And Garters, Stars, and Coronets appear,   85
And in soft sounds, *your grace* salutes their ear.
'Tis these that early taint the female soul,
Instruct the eyes of young Coquettes to roll,
Teach Infants cheeks a bidden blush to know,
And little hearts to flutter at a Beau.   90
    Oft' when the world imagine Women stray,
The *Sylphs* thro' mystic mazes guide their way,
Thro' all the giddy circle they pursue,
And old impertinence expel by new.
What tender maid but must a victim fall   95
To one man's Treat, but for another's Ball?
When *Florio* speaks, what virgin could withstand,
If gentle *Damon* did not squeeze her hand?
With varying vanities, from ev'ry part,
They shift the moving Toyshop of their heart;   100
Where Wigs with Wigs, with Sword-knots Sword-knots strive,
Beaus banish Beaus, and Coaches Coaches drive.
This erring mortals Levity may call,
Oh blind to truth! the *Sylphs* contrive it all.

---

60 *Salamander* A lizard-like creature once thought to live in fire.
62 *Tea* Then pronounced 'tay'. Cf. 3:8.
69–70 Cf. 'For spirits when they please / Can either sex assume' (*Paradise Lost*, 1:423–4).
73 *spark* A fashionable young man.
79 *face* 'beauty', but here also 'public reputation'.

85 *Garters, Stars* The insignia of the Order of the Garter: hence signs of noble rank.
94 *impertinence* 'triviality'.
100 *Toyshop* A 'fancy shop' selling trinkets (snuff boxes, scissors, etc.).
101 *Sword-knots* Decorative tassels tied to sword-hilts.

Of these am I, who thy protection claim,   105
A watchful Sprite, and *Ariel* is my name.
Late, as I rang'd the crystal wilds of Air,
In the clear Mirror of thy ruling Star
I saw, alas! some dread event impend,
E're to the main this morning Sun descend.   110
But heav'n reveals not what, or how, or where:
Warn'd by thy *Sylph*, oh pious Maid beware!
This to disclose is all thy guardian can.
Beware of all, but most beware of man!
    He said; when *Shock*, who thought she slept too long,   115
Leap'd up, and wak'd his mistress with his tongue.
'Twas then *Belinda*! if report say true,
Thy eyes first open'd on a Billet-doux;
Wounds, Charms, and Ardors, were no sooner read,
But all the Vision vanish'd from thy head.   120
    And now, unveil'd, the Toilet stands display'd,
Each silver Vase in mystic order laid.
First, rob'd in white, the nymph intent adores
With head uncover'd, the cosmetic pow'rs.
A heav'nly Image in the glass appears,   125
To that she bends, to that her eyes she rears;
Th' inferior Priestess, at her altar's side,
Trembling, begins the sacred rites of Pride.
Unnumber'd treasures ope at once, and here
The various off'rings of the world appear;   130
From each she nicely culls with curious toil,
And decks the Goddess with the glitt'ring spoil.
This casket *India*'s glowing gems unlocks,
And all *Arabia* breaths from yonder box.
The Tortoise here and Elephant unite,   135
Transform'd to Combs, the speckled, and the white.
Here files of Pins extend their shining rows,
Puffs, Powders, Patches, Bibles, Billet-doux.
Now awful Beauty puts on all its arms;
The fair each moment rises in her charms,   140
Repairs her smiles, awakens ev'ry grace,
And calls forth all the wonders of her face;
Sees by degrees a purer blush arise,
And keener lightnings quicken in her eyes.
The busy *Sylphs* surround their darling care,   145
These set the head, and those divide the hair,
Some fold the sleeve, while others plait the gown;
And *Betty*'s prais'd for labours not her own.

---

110 *main* 'ocean'.
115 *Shock* Common name for a lap–dog, perhaps deriving from the Icelandic 'Shough' breed.
118 *Billet-doux* 'love letter'.
121 *Toilet* 'dressing-table'.
135 I.e. tortoise-shell and ivory. In ancient Indian

mythology the earth was supported by an elephant who stood on a tortoise.
138 *Patches* Artificial beauty spots; *Bibles* Miniature decorative Bibles carried by ladies.
139 Pope parodies the arming of the epic hero before battle.
148 *Betty* A stock name for a lady's maid.

CANTO II

Not with more glories, in th' etherial plain,
The Sun first rises o'er the purpled main,
Than issuing forth, the rival of his beams
Lanch'd on the bosom of the silver *Thames.*
Fair nymphs, and well-drest youths around her shone,   5
But ev'ry eye was fix'd on her alone.
On her white breast a sparkling Cross she wore,
Which Jews might kiss, and Infidels adore.
Her lively looks a sprightly mind disclose,
Quick as her eyes, and as unfix'd as those: 10
Favours to none, to all she smiles extends,
Oft' she rejects, but never once offends.
Bright as the sun, her eyes the gazers strike,
And, like the sun, they shine on all alike.
Yet graceful ease, and sweetness void of pride,   15
Might hide her faults, if *Belles* had faults to hide:
If to her share some female errors fall,
Look on her face, and you'll forget 'em all.
    This nymph, to the destruction of mankind,
Nourish'd two Locks, which graceful hung behind   20
In equal curls, and well conspir'd to deck
With shining ringlets her smooth iv'ry neck:
Love in these labyrinths his slaves detains,
And mighty hearts are held in slender chains.
With hairy sprindges we the birds betray,   25
Slight lines of hair surprize the finny prey,
Fair tresses man's imperial race insnare,
And beauty draws us with a single hair.
    Th' advent'rous Baron the bright locks admir'd,
He saw, he wish'd, and to the prize aspir'd: 30
Resolv'd to win, he meditates the way,
By force to ravish, or by fraud betray;
For when success a Lover's toil attends,
Few ask, if fraud or force attain'd his ends.
    For this, e'er *Phœbus* rose, he had implor'd   35
Propitious heav'n, and ev'ry pow'r ador'd,
But chiefly Love — to Love an altar built,
Of twelve vast French Romances, neatly gilt.
There lay three garters, half a pair of gloves;
And all the trophies of his former loves.   40
With tender Billet-doux he lights the pyre,
And breathes three am'rous sighs to raise the fire.
Then prostrate falls, and begs with ardent eyes
Soon to obtain, and long possess the prize:
The Pow'rs gave ear, and granted half his pray'r,   45
The rest, the winds dispers'd in empty air.

---

25 *sprindges* Noose-like traps.
27 An allusion to Eve's luxuriant curls in *Paradise Lost*,
    4:304–7.

32 *By force … or fraud* The Greeks used both to capture
    Troy. See 3:149n.
35 *Phœbus* The sun.

But now secure the painted vessel glides,
The sun-beams trembling on the floating tydes,
While melting music steals upon the sky,
And soften'd sounds along the waters die.   50
Smooth flow the waves, the zephyrs gently play,
Belinda smil'd, and all the world was gay.
All but the *Sylph* — with careful thoughts opprest,
Th' impending woe sate heavy on his breast.
He summons strait his Denizens of air;   55
The lucid squadrons round the sails repair:
Soft o'er the shrouds aerial whispers breath,
That seem'd but zephyrs to the train beneath.
Some to the sun their insect-wings unfold,
Waft on the breeze, or sink in clouds of gold.   60
Transparent forms, too fine for mortal sight,
Their fluid bodies half dissolv'd in light.
Loose to the wind their airy garments flew,
Thin glitt'ring textures of the filmy dew;
Dipt in the richest tincture of the skies,   65
Where light disports in ever-mingling dies,
While ev'ry beam new transient colours flings,
Colours that change whene'er they wave their wings.
Amid the circle, on the gilded mast,
Superior by the head, was *Ariel* plac'd;   70
His purple pinions opening to the sun,
He rais'd his azure wand, and thus begun.
    Ye *Sylphs* and *Sylphids*, to your chief give ear,
Fays, *Fairies*, *Genii*, *Elves*, and *Dæmons* hear!
Ye know the spheres and various tasks assign'd,   75
By laws eternal, to th'aerial kind.
Some in the fields of purest *Æther* play,
And bask and whiten in the blaze of day.
Some guide the course of wandring orbs on high,
Or roll the planets thro' the boundless sky.   80
Some less refin'd, beneath the moon's pale light
Hover, and catch the shooting stars by night;
Or suck the mists in grosser air below,
Or dip their pinions in the painted bow,
Or brew fierce tempests on the wintry main,   85
Or o'er the glebe distill the kindly rain.
Others on earth o'er humane race preside,
Watch all their ways, and all their actions guide:
Of these the chief the care of Nations own,

---

47 *secure* 'carefree', also 'over-confident'.
51 *zephyrs* 'gentle breezes'.
55 *Denizens* 'inhabitants'.
56 *lucid* 'translucent'.
57 *shrouds* Ropes belonging to the boat's rigging.
64 See Charlotte Smith, *The Gossamer*.
70 *Superior* 'Taller' – typical of the epic hero.
71 *purple* 'brightly coloured' (Lat. *purpureus*).

73–4 Cf. God's speech to the angelic host in *Paradise Lost*, 5:600–1: 'Hear, all ye Angels, Progeny of Light, / Thrones, Dominations, Princedoms, Virtues, Powers'.
73 *Sylphids* Probably young sylphs. Not necessarily female (cf. 1:69–70).
77 *Æther* A medium lighter and more fluid than air which supposedly filled the upper regions of the sky.
86 *glebe* 'soil'.

And guard with Arms divine the *British* Throne.   90
   Our humbler province is to tend the fair;
Not a less pleasing, tho' less glorious care.
To save the powder from too rude a gale,
Nor let th' imprison'd essences exhale,
To draw fresh colours from the vernal flow'rs,   95
To steal from rainbows e're they drop in show'rs
A brighter wash; to curl their waving hairs,
Assist their blushes, and inspire their airs;
Nay oft', in dreams, invention we bestow,
To change a Flounce, or add a Furbelo.   100
   This day, black Omens threat the brightest fair
That e'er deserv'd a watchful spirit's care;
Some dire disaster, or by force, or slight;
But what, or where, the fates have wrapt in night.
Whether the nymph shall break *Diana*'s law,   105
Or some frail *China* jar receive a flaw,
Or stain her honour, or her new Brocade,
Forget her pray'rs, or miss a masquerade,
Or lose her heart, or necklace, at a Ball;
Or whether heav'n has doom'd that *Shock* must fall.   110
Haste then ye spirits! to your charge repair;
The flutt'ring fan be *Zephyretta*'s care;
The drops to thee, *Brillante*, we consign;
And *Momentilla*, let the watch be thine;
Do thou, *Crispissa*, tend her fav'rite Lock;   115
Ariel himself shall be the guard of *Shock*.
   To fifty chosen *Sylphs*, of special note,
We trust th' important charge, the Petticoat:
Oft' have we known that sev'nfold fence to fail,
Tho' stiff with hoops, and arm'd with ribs of whale.   120
Form a strong line about the silver bound,
And guard the wide circumference around.
   Whatever spirit, careless of his charge,
His post neglects, or leaves the fair at large,
Shall feel sharp vengeance soon o'ertake his sins,   125
Be stop'd in vials, or transfixt with pins;
Or plung'd in lakes of bitter washes lie,
Or wedg'd whole ages in a bodkin's eye:
Gums and Pomatums shall his flight restrain,
While clog'd he beats his silken wings in vain;   130
Or Alom-stypticks with contracting pow'r
Shrink his thin essence like a rivell'd flow'r:
Or as *Ixion* fix'd, the wretch shall feel
The giddy motion of the whirling Mill,

---

97 *wash* A cosmetic lotion.
100 *Furbelo* Pleated trimming on a gown.
105 *Diana* Goddess of chastity.
113 *drops* 'drop-earrings'.
115 *Crispissa* From Lat. *crispare*, 'to curl'.
119 *sev'nfold fence* The seven-layered petticoat with its whale-bone hoops parodies the epic shields described in Homer and Virgil.

121 *Form* From (*1717*).
129 *Pomatums* 'ointments'.
131 *Alom-stypticks* Astringent lotions designed to treat cuts and blemishes.
132 *rivell'd* 'shrivelled'.
133 *Ixion* In Greek myth Zeus bound King Ixion to a fiery wheel for trying to seduce his wife.
134 *Mill* Coffee mill.

In fumes of burning Chocolate shall glow,   135
And tremble at the sea that froaths below!
    He spoke; the spirits from the sails descend;
Some, orb in orb, around the nymph extend,
Some thrid the mazy ringlets of her hair,
Some hang upon the pendants of her ear;   140
With beating hearts the dire event they wait,
Anxious, and trembling for the birth of Fate.

141 *dire event* Cf. 'Too well I see and rue the dire event'
      (*Paradise Lost*, 1:134).

CANTO III

Close by those meads, for ever crown'd with flow'rs,
Where *Thames* with pride surveys his rising tow'rs,
There stands a structure of majestic frame,
Which from the neighb'ring *Hampton* takes its name.
Here *Britain*'s statesmen oft' the fall foredoom   5
Of foreign tyrants, and of nymphs at home;
Here thou, great *Anna*! whom three realms obey,
Dost sometimes counsel take — and sometimes Tea.
    Hither the heroes and the nymphs resort,
To taste a while the pleasures of a Court;   10
In various talk th'instructive hours they past,
Who gave the ball, or paid the visit last:
One speaks the glory of the *British* Queen,
And one describes a charming *Indian* screen;
A third interprets motions, looks, and eyes;   15
At ev'ry word a reputation dies.
Snuff, or the fan, supply each pause of chat,
With singing, laughing, ogling, and all that.
    Mean while declining from the noon of day,
The sun obliquely shoots his burning ray;   20
The hungry Judges soon the sentence sign,
And wretches hang that Jury-men may dine;
The merchant from th'*Exchange* returns in peace,
And the long labours of the Toilet cease —
Belinda now, whom thirst of fame invites,   25
Burns to encounter two adventrous Knights,
At *Ombre* singly to decide their doom;
And swells her breast with conquests yet to come.

3 *structure of majestic frame* Hampton Court, on the
   Thames 15 miles upstream from Westminster. The
   palace was built by Cardinal Wolsey and given to Henry
   VIII as a royal residence. It was enlarged by William
   III. At the Court of Queen Anne wits and politicians
   mingled there.
7 *three realms* England, Scotland and Ireland. The
   kingdoms of England and Scotland had been united by
   the Act of Union (1707).
18 *ogling* 'eyeing up'.

23 *Exchange* The Royal Exchange, London's financial
    centre.
27 *Ombre* A fashionable card game for three players. The
    principal player or ombre (Spanish for 'man') – here
    Belinda – sets out, with trumps of his choosing, to
    make more tricks than either of the other players. If he
    fails, his opponents are said to give 'codille' to the
    ombre. The play Pope describes can be reconstructed.
    See Twickenham edn, 2:383–92.

Strait the three bands prepare in arms to join,
Each band the number of the sacred nine.   30
Soon as she spreads her hand, th' aerial guard
Descend, and sit on each important card:
First *Ariel* perch'd upon a Matadore,
Then each, according to the rank they bore;
For *Sylphs*, yet mindful of their ancient race,   35
Are, as when women, wondrous fond of place.
　　Behold, four Kings in majesty rever'd,
With hoary whiskers and a forky beard:
And four fair Queens whose hands sustain a flow'r,
Th' expressive emblem of their softer pow'r;   40
Four Knaves in garbs succinct, a trusty band,
Caps on their heads, and halberds in their hand;
And particolour'd troops, a shining train,
Draw forth to combat on the velvet plain.
　　The skilful nymph reviews her force with care;   45
Let Spades be trumps, she said, and trumps they were.
　　Now move to war her sable Matadores,
In show like leaders of the swarthy Moors.
Spadillio first, unconquerable Lord!
Led off two captive trumps, and swept the board.   50
As many more *Manillio* forc'd to yield,
And march'd a victor from the verdant field.
Him *Basto* follow'd, but his fate more hard
Gain'd but one trump and one *Plebeian* card.
With his broad sabre next, a chief in years,   55
The hoary Majesty of Spades appears;
Puts forth one manly leg, to sight reveal'd;
The rest, his many-colour'd robe conceal'd.
The rebel-Knave, who dares his prince engage,
Proves the just victim of his royal rage.   60
Ev'n mighty *Pam* that Kings and Queens o'erthrew,
And mow'd down armies in the fights of *Lu*,
Sad chance of war! now, destitute of aid,
Falls undistinguish'd by the victor Spade!
　　Thus far both armies to *Belinda* yield;   65
Now to the Baron fate inclines the field.
His warlike *Amazon* her host invades,
Th' imperial consort of the crown of Spades.
The Club's black Tyrant first her victim dy'd,
Spite of his haughty mien, and barb'rous pride: 70
What boots the regal circle on his head,
His giant limbs, in state unwieldy spread;

30 *sacred nine* The Muses. At ombre each player holds nine
cards.
33 *Matadore* In ombre the name of the three cards of
highest value.
41 *succinct* 'girded up'.
42 *halberd* A spear and battle-axe combined.
46 *Let Spades be trumps* Cf. 'And God said, Let there be
light: and there was light' (Genesis, 1:3). Cf. also
Windsor-Forest, 325–6.

49 *Spadillio* The ace of spades.
51 *Manillio* The 2 of spades, which, when trumps are
black, is the card second highest in value.
53 *Basto* The ace of clubs, the third highest card.
61 *Pam* The knave of clubs, the highest card in loo,
another popular game.
67 *Amazon* A warrior-woman.

That long behind he trails his pompous robe,
And, of all monarchs, only grasps the globe?
   The Baron now his Diamonds pours apace;   75
Th' embroider'd King who shows but half his face,
And his refulgent Queen, with pow'rs combin'd,
Of broken troops an easy conquest find.
Clubs, Diamonds, Hearts, in wild disorder seen,
With throngs promiscuous strow the level green.   80
Thus when dispers'd a routed army runs,
Of *Asia*'s troops, and *Afric*'s sable sons,
With like confusion different nations fly,
In various habits, and of various dye,
The pierc'd battalions dis-united fall,   85
In heaps on heaps; one fate o'erwhelms them all.
   The Knave of Diamonds tries his wily arts,
And wins (oh shameful chance) the Queen of Hearts.
At this, the blood the virgin's cheek forsook,
A livid paleness spreads o'er all her look;   90
She sees, and trembles at th' approaching ill,
Just in the jaws of ruin, and *Codille*.
And now, (as oft' in some distemper'd state)
On one nice Trick depends the gen'ral fate.
An Ace of Hearts steps forth: The King unseen   95
Lurk'd in her hand, and mourn'd his captive Queen:
He springs to vengeance with an eager pace,
And falls like thunder on the prostrate Ace.
The nymph exulting fills with shouts the sky,
The walls, the woods, and long canals reply.   100
   Oh thoughtless mortals! ever blind to fate,
Too soon dejected, and too soon elate!
Sudden, these honours shall be snatch'd away,
And curs'd for ever this victorious day.
   For lo! the board with cups and spoons is crown'd,   105
The berries crackle, and the mill turns round:
On shining Altars of *Japan* they raise
The silver lamp; the fiery spirits blaze:
From silver spouts the grateful liquors glide,
And *China*'s earth receives the smoking tyde.   110
At once they gratify their scent and taste,
While frequent cups prolong the rich repaste.
Strait hover round the fair her airy band;
Some, as she sipp'd, the fuming liquor fann'd,
Some o'er her lap their careful plumes display'd,   115
Trembling, and conscious of the rich brocade.
Coffee, (which makes the politician wise,
And see thro' all things with his half-shut eyes)
Sent up in vapours to the Baron's brain
New stratagems, the radiant Lock to gain.   120

92 *Codille* See above, 27n.
105 *board* 'sideboard'.
106 *berries* 'coffee beans'.

107 *Altars of Japan* Lacquered tables. 'Japanning' was a highly fashionable finish to furniture.

Ah cease, rash youth! desist e'er 'tis too late,
Fear the just Gods, and think of *Scylla*'s fate!
Chang'd to a bird, and sent to flit in air,
She dearly pays for *Nisus*' injur'd hair!
But when to mischief mortals bend their will,   125
How soon they find fit instruments of ill?
Just then, *Clarissa* drew with tempting grace
A two-edg'd weapon from her shining case;
So Ladies in Romance assist their Knight,
Present the spear, and arm him for the fight.   130
He takes the gift with rev'rence, and extends
The little engine on his finger's ends:
This just behind *Belinda*'s neck he spread,
As o'er the fragrant steams she bends her head.
Swift to the Lock a thousand Sprites repair,   135
A thousand wings, by turns, blow back the hair;
And thrice they twitch'd the diamond in her ear;
Thrice she look'd back, and thrice the foe drew near.
Just in that instant, anxious *Ariel* sought
The close recesses of the Virgin's thought;   140
As on the nosegay in her breast reclin'd,
He watch'd th' Ideas rising in her mind,
Sudden he view'd, in spite of all her art,
An earthly Lover lurking at her heart.
Amaz'd, confus'd, he found his pow'r expir'd,   145
Resign'd to fate, and with a sigh retir'd.
The Peer now spreads the glitt'ring *Forfex* wide,
T'inclose the Lock; now joins it, to divide.
Ev'n then, before the fatal engine clos'd,
A wretched *Sylph* too fondly interpos'd;   150
Fate urg'd the sheers, and cut the *Sylph* in twain,
(But airy substance soon unites again)
The meeting points the sacred hair dissever
From the fair head, for ever, and for ever!
Then flash'd the living lightnings from her eyes,   155
And screams of horror rend th' affrighted skies.
Not louder shrieks to pitying heav'n are cast,
When husbands, or when lapdogs breathe their last;
Or when rich *China* vessels, fal'n from high,
In glittering dust, and painted fragments lie!   160
Let wreaths of triumph now my temples twine,
(The victor cry'd) the glorious prize is mine!
While fish in streams, or birds delight in air,
Or in a Coach and six, the *British* fair,

---

122 *Scylla* Pope's footnote alludes to Ovid, *Metamorphoses*,
   8, which tells how Scylla, daughter of King Nisus of
   Megara, cut off the magic lock from her father's hair
   and then delivered their city to King Minos of Crete,
   whom she loved. But the honourable Minos rejected
   her in disgust. As she desperately tried to follow his
   ship she was transformed to a seabird.
132 *engine* 'instrument'. See 149n.
142 *Ideas* 'images'.

143–6 Belinda no longer 'rejects Mankind' (1:68).
147 *Forfex* Latin for 'scissors'.
149 *fatal engine* Dryden's term for the wooden horse by
   means of which the Greeks penetrated Troy's defences
   (Dryden, *Aeneid*, 2:345).
152 Pope notes his echo of *Paradise Lost*, 6:330–1, in which
   Satan recovers from being stabbed by the angel
   Michael: '… but th'ethereal substance closed / Not
   long divisible'.

As long as *Atalantis* shall be read, 165
Or the small pillow grace a Lady's bed,
While visits shall be paid on solemn days,
When num'rous wax-lights in bright order blaze,
While nymphs take treats, or assignations give,
So long my honour, name, and praise shall live! 170
   What Time wou'd spare, from steel receives its date,
And monuments, like men, submit to fate!
Steel could the labour of the Gods destroy,
And strike to dust th'imperial tow'rs of *Troy*;
Steel could the works of mortal pride confound, 175
And hew triumphal arches to the ground.
What wonder then, fair nymph! thy hairs shou'd feel
The conqu'ring force of unresisted steel?

165 *Atalantis* Mary Delarivière Manley's slanderous *Secret Memoirs ... From the New Atalantis* (1709).
167–8 Fashionable evening visits. Wax candles were superior to the cheaper tallow-fat tapers.

171 *date* 'end'.
173 *labour of the Gods* Legend held that Apollo and Poseidon built the walls of Troy.

Canto IV

But anxious cares the pensive nymph opprest,
And secret passions labour'd in her breast.
Not youthful Kings in battel seiz'd alive,
Not scornful virgins who their charms survive,
Not ardent lovers robb'd of all their bliss, 5
Not ancient ladies when refus'd a kiss,
Not tyrants fierce that unrepenting die,
Not *Cynthia* when her Manteau's pinn'd awry,
E'er felt such rage, resentment and despair,
As thou, sad virgin! for thy ravish'd Hair. 10
   For, that sad moment, when the *Sylphs* withdrew,
And *Ariel* weeping from *Belinda* flew,
Umbriel, a dusky, melancholy sprite
As ever sully'd the fair face of light,
Down to the central earth, his proper scene, 15
Repairs to search the gloomy cave of *Spleen*.
   Swift on his sooty pinions flits the *Gnome*,
And in a vapour reach'd the dismal dome.
No chearful breeze this sullen region knows,
The dreaded East is all the wind that blows. 20
Here, in a grotto, sheltred close from air,
And screen'd in shades from day's detested glare,
She sighs for ever on her pensive bed,
Pain at her side, and *Megrim* at her head,

8 *Manteau* A loose upper garment.
16 *Spleen* A healthy spleen was believed to purge the body of melancholy vapours which would otherwise mount to the brain and cause 'the Spleen' or 'the Vapours', a fashionable malady in the eighteenth century. See headnote to Anne Finch, *The Spleen*.

17ff. Umbriel's journey into Belinda's body parallels the traditional descent of the epic hero to the underworld, as in *Aeneid*, 6.
24 *Megrim* 'migraine'.

Two handmaids wait the throne: alike in place,   25
But diff'ring far in figure and in face.
Here stood *Ill-nature* like an ancient maid,
Her wrinkled form in black and white array'd;
With store of pray'rs, for mornings, nights, and noons,
Her hand is fill'd; her bosom with lampoons.   30
There *Affectation*, with a sickly mien,
Shows in her cheek the roses of eighteen,
Practis'd to lisp, and hang the head aside,
Faints into airs, and languishes with pride;
On the rich quilt, sinks with becoming woe,   35
Wrapt in a gown, for sickness, and for show.
The fair ones feel such maladies as these,
When each new night-dress gives a new disease.
A constant vapour o'er the palace flies;
Strange phantoms rising as the mists arise;   40
Dreadful, as hermit's dreams in haunted shades,
Or bright, as visions of expiring maids.
Now glaring fiends, and snakes on rolling spires,
Pale spectres, gaping tombs, and purple fires:
Now lakes of liquid gold, *Elysian* scenes,   45
And crystal domes, and Angels in machines.
Unnumber'd throngs on ev'ry side are seen,
Of bodies chang'd to various forms by spleen.
Here living Teapots stand, one arm held out,
One bent; the handle this, and that the spout: 50
A Pipkin there like *Homer*'s Tripod walks;
Here sighs a Jar, and there a Goose-pye talks;
Men prove with child, as pow'rful fancy works,
And maids turn'd bottles, call aloud for corks.
Safe past the *Gnome* thro' this fantastic band,   55
A branch of healing Spleenwort in his hand.
Then thus address'd the pow'r — Hail wayward Queen!
Who rule the sex to fifty from fifteen:
Parent of vapours and of female wit,
Who give th' hysteric, or poetic fit,   60
On various tempers act by various ways,
Make some take physic, others scribble plays;
Who cause the proud their visits to delay,
And send the godly in a pett, to pray.
A nymph there is, that all thy pow'r disdains,   65
And thousands more in equal mirth maintains.
But oh! if e'er thy *Gnome* could spoil a grace,

---

25 *wait* 'attend'.

31 *mien* 'manner'.

40–6 Disturbing religious hallucinations were considered a symptom of the Spleen.

42 *expiring* Undergoing an ecstatic experience. See *Eloisa to Abelard*, 341n.

43 *spires* 'coils'. Cf. Savage, *The Wanderer*, 4:55–6.

45–6 The images derive from the extravagant stage effects in contemporary opera and pantomime. Theatrical 'machines' fly figures across the stage.

51 *Pipkin* A small earthenware cooking pot; *Homer's Tripod* Pope's note refers to *Iliad*, 18:372–9 describing Vulcan's wheeled cauldrons which move at his command.

56 Aeneas entered the underworld carrying a golden bough as his passport. Spleenwort was a herb thought to cure the spleen.

59–62 In contradiction to Pope, Anne Finch thought the Spleen a poetic liability. See *The Spleen*, 74–80.

62 *physic* 'medicine'.

Or raise a pimple on a beauteous face;
Like Citron-waters matrons cheeks inflame,
Or change complexions at a losing game;   70
If e'er with airy horns I planted heads,
Or rumpled petticoats, or tumbled beds,
Or caus'd suspicion when no soul was rude,
Or discompos'd the head-dress of a Prude,
Or e'er to costive lap-dog gave disease,   75
Which not the tears of brightest eyes could ease:
Hear me, and touch *Belinda* with chagrin;
That single act gives half the world the spleen.
    The Goddess with a discontented air
Seems to reject him, tho' she grants his pray'r.   80
A wondrous bag with both her hands she binds,
Like that where once *Ulysses* held the winds;
There she collects the force of female lungs,
Sighs, sobs, and passions, and the war of tongues.
A vial next she fills with fainting fears,   85
Soft sorrows, melting griefs, and flowing tears.
The *Gnome* rejoicing bears her gift away,
Spreads his black wings, and slowly mounts to day:
    Sunk in *Thalestris*' arms the nymph he found,
Her eyes dejected and her hair unbound.   90
Full o'er their heads the swelling bag he rent,
And all the furies issued at the vent.
Belinda burns with more than mortal ire,
And fierce *Thalestris* fans the rising fire.
O wretched maid! she spread her hands, and cry'd,   95
(While *Hampton*'s ecchos, wretched maid reply'd)
Was it for this you took such constant care
The bodkin, comb, and essence to prepare?
For this your Locks in paper durance bound,
For this with tort'ring irons wreath'd around?   100
For this with fillets strain'd your tender head,
And bravely bore the double loads of lead?
Gods! shall the ravisher display your hair,
While the Fops envy, and the Ladies stare!
Honour forbid! at whose unrival'd shrine   105
Ease, pleasure, virtue, all, our sex resign.
Methinks already I your tears survey,
Already hear the horrid things they say,
Already see you a degraded toast,
And all your honour in a whisper lost!   110
How shall I, then, your helpless fame defend?
'Twill then be infamy to seem your friend!
And shall this prize, th' inestimable prize,

---

69 *Citron-waters* Brandy flavoured with lemon peel.
71 *airy horns* i.e. imagined cuckold's horns.
75 *costive* 'constipated'.
77 *chagrin* 'annoyance' (pronounced 'shagreen').
82 *winds* They were given him by Aeolus, keeper of the
winds (*Odyssey*, 10:19–22).
89 *Thalestris* Queen of the warlike Amazons.

92 *furies* In Greek myth, pitiless female spirits of revenge.
98 *bodkin* Here, an ornamental hair-fastener.
99–102 Hairdressing techniques resonant of the torture-
chamber. Hair was crimped in heated irons and curled
in papers kept in place by pliable lead ties.
101 *fillet* 'headband'.
109 *toast* A reigning beauty to whom toasts are drunk.

Expos'd thro' crystal to the gazing eyes,
And heighten'd by the diamond's circling rays,   115
On that rapacious hand for ever blaze?
Sooner shall grass in *Hyde-park circus* grow,
And wits take lodgings in the sound of *Bow*;
Sooner let earth, air, sea, to *Chaos* fall,
Men, monkies, lap-dogs, parrots, perish all!   120
    She said; then raging to Sir *Plume* repairs,
And bids her Beau demand the precious hairs:
(Sir *Plume*, of amber Snuff-box justly vain,
And the nice conduct of a clouded Cane)
With earnest eyes, and round unthinking face,   125
He first the snuff-box open'd, then the case,
And thus broke out — "My Lord, why, what the devil?
"Z—ds! damn the Lock! 'fore Gad, you must be civil!
"Plague on't! 'tis past a jest — nay prithee, pox!
"Give her the hair — he spoke, and rapp'd his box.   130
    It grieves me much (reply'd the Peer again)
Who speaks so well should ever speak in vain.
But by this Lock, this sacred Lock I swear,
(Which never more shall join its parted hair;
Which never more its honours shall renew,   135
Clip'd from the lovely head where late it grew)
That while my nostrils draw the vital air,
This hand, which won it, shall for ever wear.
He spoke, and speaking, in proud triumph spread
The long-contended honours of her head.   140
    But *Umbriel*, hateful *Gnome*! forbears not so;
He breaks the viol whence the sorrows flow.
Then see! the nymph in beauteous grief appears,
Her eyes half languishing, half drown'd in tears,
On her heav'd bosom hung her drooping head,   145
Which, with a sigh, she rais'd; and thus she said.
    For ever curs'd be this detested day,
Which snatch'd my best, my fav'rite Curl away!
Happy! ah ten times happy had I been,
If *Hampton-Court* these eyes had never seen!   150
Yet am not I the first mistaken maid,
By love of Courts to num'rous ills betray'd.
Oh had I rather un-admir'd remain'd
In some lone isle, or distant Northern land;
Where the gilt Chariot never marks the way,   155
Where none learn *Ombre*, none e'er taste *Bohea!*

---

117 *Hyde-park circus* See 1:44n.

118 *sound of Bow* The area within range of the bells of St Mary-le-Bow, Cheapside, a commercial district in London's East End never frequented by fashionable 'town' wits of the West End.

121 *Sir Plume* Arabella Fermor's second cousin Sir George Browne. He was extremely annoyed by Pope's caricature.

124 *nice* 'skilled'; *clouded* With a fashionable marbled head.

127–9 Sir Plume foppishly uses modish swearwords.

128 *Z—nds* 'zounds', a corruption of 'God's wounds'.

133 'In allusion to *Achilles*'s oath in *Homer*' (Pope). The reference is *Iliad*, 1:234–44.

142 *viol* Alternative spelling of 'vial'.

147–76 Parodies Achilles's lament for Patroclus, *Iliad*, 18:79–111.

156 *Bohea* Finest black tea.

There kept my charms, conceal'd from mortal eye
Like roses that in desarts bloom and die.
What mov'd my mind with youthful Lords to rome?
O had I stay'd, and said my pray'rs at home! 160
'Twas this, the morning omens seem'd to tell;
Thrice from my trembling hand the patch-box fell;
The tott'ring China shook without a wind,
Nay, *Poll* sate mute, and *Shock* was most unkind!
A *Sylph* too warn'd me of the threats of fate, 165
In mystic visions, now believ'd too late!
See the poor remnants of these slighted hairs!
My hands shall rend what ev'n thy rapine spares:
These, in two sable ringlets taught to break,
Once gave new beauties to the snowy neck; 170
The sister-lock now sits uncouth, alone,
And in its fellow's fate foresees its own;
Uncurl'd it hangs, the fatal sheers demands;
And tempts once more thy sacrilegious hands.
Oh hadst thou, cruel! been content to seize 175
Hairs less in sight, or any hairs but these!

162 *patch-box* A box holding artificial beauty spots.　　　164 *Poll* Belinda's parrot.

CANTO V

She said: the pitying audience melt in tears.
But Fate and *Jove* had stopp'd the Baron's ears.
In vain *Thalestris* with reproach assails,
For who can move when fair *Belinda* fails?
Not half so fix'd the *Trojan* could remain, 5
While *Anna* begg'd and *Dido* rag'd in vain.
Then grave *Clarissa* graceful wav'd her fan;
Silence ensu'd, and thus the nymph began.
　　Say why are Beauties prais'd and honour'd most,
The wise man's passion, and the vain man's toast? 10
Why deck'd with all that land and sea afford,
Why Angels call'd, and Angel-like ador'd?
Why round our Coaches crowd the white glov'd Beaus,
Why bows the side-box from its inmost rows?
How vain are all these glories, all our pains, 15
Unless good sense preserve what beauty gains:
That men may say, when we the front-box grace,
Behold the first in virtue, as in face!
Oh! if to dance all night, and dress all day,
Charm'd the small-pox, or chas'd old age away; 20

5–6 *The Trojan* Aeneas, who, directed by the gods to leave Carthage, remained deaf to the pleas of his lover Queen Dido and her sister Anna (*Aeneid*, 4:296–436).

7–36 These lines were added in 1717. Pope's model is Sarpedon's death-or-glory speech to his friend Glaucus, *Iliad*, 12:310–28. (Pope had earlier translated this. See Twickenham edn, 1:450–1.)

14 *side-box* Gentlemen usually occupied the side-boxes in the theatre, from where they could view the ladies in the front-boxes facing the stage.

20 *small-pox* Lord Petre had died of the disease in 1713.

Who would not scorn what huswife's cares produce,
Or who would learn one earthly thing of use?
To patch, nay ogle, might become a Saint,
Nor could it sure be such a sin to paint.
But since, alas! frail beauty must decay,   25
Curl'd or uncurl'd, since Locks will turn to grey,
Since painted, or not painted, all shall fade,
And she who scorns a man, must die a maid;
What then remains, but well our pow'r to use,
And keep good humour still whate'er we lose?   30
And trust me, dear! good humour can prevail,
When airs, and flights, and screams, and scolding fail.
Beauties in vain their pretty eyes may roll;
Charms strike the sight, but merit wins the soul.
    So spoke the Dame, but no applause ensu'd;   35
Belinda frown'd, *Thalestris* call'd her Prude.
To arms, to arms! the fierce Virago cries,
And swift as lightning to the combate flies.
All side in parties, and begin th' attack;
Fans clap, silks russle, and tough whalebones crack;   40
Heroes and Heroins shouts confus'dly rise,
And base, and treble voices strike the skies.
No common weapons in their hands are found,
Like Gods they fight, nor dread a mortal wound.
    So when bold *Homer* makes the Gods engage,   45
And heav'nly breasts with human passions rage;
'Gainst *Pallas, Mars; Latona, Hermes* arms;
And all *Olympus* rings with loud alarms:
Jove's thunder roars, heav'n trembles all around;
Blue *Neptune* storms, the bellowing deeps resound;   50
Earth shakes her nodding tow'rs, the ground gives way,
And the pale ghosts start at the flash of day!
    Triumphant *Umbriel* on a sconce's height
Clap'd his glad wings, and sate to view the fight,
Prop'd on their bodkin spears, the Sprites survey   55
The growing combat, or assist the fray.
    While thro' the press enrag'd *Thalestris* flies,
And scatters deaths around from both her eyes,
A Beau and Witling perish'd in the throng,
One dy'd in metaphor, and one in song.   60
O cruel nymph! a living death I bear,
Cry'd *Dapperwit*, and sunk beside his chair.
A mournful glance Sir *Fopling* upwards cast,
Those eyes are made so killing — was his last:

---

37 *Virago* 'female warrior'.

45 Pope's note points to *Iliad*, 20:86–102, in which Aeneas
   invokes the gods to aid him in the fight against Achilles.

47 A catalogue of Greek gods. *Latona* Leto, mother of
   Apollo.

48 *Olympus* The Greek mountain home of the gods.

53 *sconce* A wall-mounted candle-holder and mirror.

55 *bodkin* Pope plays here on two meanings of bodkin: a
   needle and a dagger.

57 *press* 'throng'.

62 *Dapperwit* A rake in William Wycherley's comedy, *Love
   in a Wood* (1672).

63 *Sir Fopling* Sir Fopling Flutter, the affected fop in Sir
   George Etherege's comedy, *The Man of Mode* (1676).

64 As Pope's note observes, a line from Marc Antonio
   Buononcini's popular opera, *Camilla* (1706).

Thus on *Meander*'s flow'ry margin lies 65
Th' expiring *Swan*, and as he sings he dies.
    When bold Sir *Plume* had drawn *Clarissa* down,
Chloe stepp'd in, and kill'd him with a frown;
She smil'd to see the doughty Hero slain,
But, at her smile, the Beau reviv'd again. 70
    Now *Jove* suspends his golden scales in air,
Weighs the Men's wits against the Lady's hair;
The doubtful beam long nods from side to side;
At length the wits mount up, the hairs subside.
    See fierce *Belinda* on the Baron flies, 75
With more than usual lightning in her eyes:
Nor fear'd the Chief th' unequal fight to try,
Who sought no more than on his foe to die.
But this bold Lord with manly strength endu'd,
She with one finger and a thumb subdu'd: 80
Just where the breath of life his nostrils drew,
A charge of Snuff the wily virgin threw;
The *Gnomes* direct, to ev'ry atome just,
The pungent grains of titillating dust.
Sudden, with starting tears each eye o'erflows, 85
And the high dome re-echoes to his nose.
    Now meet thy fate, incens'd *Belinda* cry'd,
And drew a deadly bodkin from her side.
(The same, his ancient personage to deck,
Her great great grandsire wore about his neck 90
In three seal-rings; which after, melted down,
Form'd a vast buckle for his widow's gown:
Her infant grandame's whistle next it grew,
The bells she gingled, and the whistle blew;
Then in a bodkin grac'd her mother's hairs, 95
Which long she wore, and now *Belinda* wears.)
    Boast not my fall (he cry'd) insulting foe!
Thou by some other shalt be laid as low.
Nor think, to die dejects my lofty mind:
All that I dread is leaving you behind! 100
Rather than so, ah let me still survive,
And burn in *Cupid*'s flames, — but burn alive.
    Restore the Lock! she crys; and all around
Restore the Lock! the vaulted roofs rebound.
Not fierce *Othello* in so loud a strain 105
Roar'd for the handkerchief that caus'd his pain.
But see how oft' ambitious aims are cross'd,
And chiefs contend till all the prize is lost!
The Lock, obtain'd with guilt, and kept with pain,
In ev'ry place is sought, but sought in vain: 110
With such a prize no mortal must be blest,
So heav'n decrees! with heav'n who can contest?

---

65 *Meander* A winding river in Asia Minor.
71 *scales* The device of scales to weigh the outcome of battle is common in epic. Pope's note points to *Iliad*, 8 and *Aeneid*, 12. It also appears in *Paradise Lost*, 4:996–1004.
78–80 Plays with the sexual sense of 'die'.
83 *atome* 'particle'.
89 Pope's note refers to the history of Agamemnon's sceptre in *Iliad*, 2:100–9.
105–6 Cf. Shakespeare, *Othello*, IV.i.35–43.

Some thought it mounted to the Lunar sphere,
Since all things lost on earth are treasur'd there.
There Hero's wits are kept in pondrous vases,   115
And Beau's in snuff-boxes and tweezer-cases.
There broken vows, and death-bed alms are found,
And lover's hearts with ends of riband bound;
The courtier's promises, and sick man's pray'rs,
The smiles of harlots, and the tears of heirs,   120
Cages for gnats, and chains to yoak a flea;
Dry'd butterflies, and tomes of casuistry.
　　But trust the Muse — she saw it upward rise,
Tho' mark'd by none but quick, poetic eyes:
(So *Rome*'s great founder to the heav'ns withdrew,   125
To *Proculus* alone confess'd in view)
A sudden Star, it shot thro' liquid air,
And drew behind a radiant trail of hair.
Not *Berenice*'s Locks first rose so bright,
The heav'ns bespangling with dishevel'd light,   130
The *Sylphs* behold it kindling as it flies,
And pleas'd pursue its progress thro' the skies.
　　This the *Beau-monde* shall from the Mall survey,
And hail with music its propitious ray.
This, the blest Lover shall for *Venus* take,   135
And send up vows from *Rosamonda*'s lake.
This *Partridge* soon shall view in cloudless skies,
When next he looks thro' Galilæo's eyes;
And hence th' egregious wizard shall foredoom
The fate of *Louis*, and the fall of *Rome*.   140
　　Then cease, bright nymph! to mourn the ravish'd hair,
Which adds new glory to the shining sphere!
Not all the tresses that fair head can boast,
Shall draw such envy as the Lock you lost.
For, after all the murders of your eye,   145
When, after millions slain, your self shall die;
When those fair suns shall set, as set they must,
And all those tresses shall be laid in dust;
This Lock, the Muse shall consecrate to fame,
And 'midst the stars inscribe *Belinda*'s name!   150

114–22 Pope's note directs the reader to Ariosto's epic *Orlando Furioso* (1532), in which Astolfo travels to the moon in search of Orlando's lost wits.
117 *alms* Charitable gifts.
122 *tomes* 'heavy volumes'; *casuistry* Ethical debate in which minute particulars challenge larger principles.
125–6 The Roman historian Livy (1:16) describes how Romulus, Rome's mythic founder, died mysteriously, and Proculus, to pacify the people, claimed that he had been carried into heaven.
129 *Berenice* An Egyptian queen who offered the gods a lock of her hair to ensure her husband Ptolemy's safe return from war. When the lock mysteriously

disappeared the court astronomer claimed to have observed it as a trail of stars in the heavens. This is told (by the lock itself) in a Greek poem by Callimachus.
133 *Mall* A fashionable enclosed walk in St James's Park.
136 *Rosamonda's lake* A lovers' rendezvous in St James's Park.
137 *Partridge* John Partridge (1644–1715), a quack astrologer, author of staunchly Protestant almanacs prophesying the fall of the Pope and the death of Louis XIV of France. He was much mocked by Swift.
138 Galileo (1564–1642), the Italian astronomer, perfected the refracting telescope.

Eloisa to Abelard

As a young poet Pope was fascinated by Ovid's *Heroides*, a series of love letters in verse from abandoned women such as Dido and Phaedra, which had established the genre of the Ovidian 'heroic epistle', fashionable in England since Elizabethan times. While still in his teens Pope had translated the epistle from Sappho to Phaon, where he had exploited to the full the frustrated emotion and self-dramatization that had become associated with the genre. The historical Eloisa, or Héloïse, whose famous letters had recently been translated by John Hughes, was another such passionate, transgressive heroine. She was the niece of Fulbert, a twelfth-century canon of Notre Dame in Paris, and her secret affair with her teacher and spiritual mentor Peter Abelard (one of the greatest scholars of the Middle Ages) ended disastrously with his castration by ruffians and her lifelong immurement behind convent walls. Some time between 1715 and 1716, Pope, drawing heavily on Hughes's translation, wrote his own dramatic epistle exploring Eloisa's plight. In the words of the preface: 'It was many years after this separation, that a letter of *Abelard*'s to a Friend which contain'd the history of his misfortune, fell into the hands of *Eloisa*. This awakening all her tenderness, occasion'd those celebrated letters (out of which the following is partly extracted) which give so lively a picture of the struggles of grace and nature, virtue and passion'.

Pope's heroic couplets, with their tightly antithetical clauses, convey a sense of the speaker's entrapment within the conflicting memories of physical passion and the desire to bend her will to strict religious devotion. In the unequal struggle Eloisa fails to spiritualize her former love but instead eroticizes the spiritual in awakened memories of the sexual act. The poem's Gothic backdrop functions as a psychic landscape, a subjective projection of Eloisa's disturbed thoughts and dreams.

During the later eighteenth century, when Pope's supremacy came to be questioned, the imaginative and emotional power of *Eloisa to Abelard* remained popular. In 1756 Joseph Warton praised it as one of the three poems by which Pope would be remembered. It suited less well the critical tastes of some twentieth-century Pope scholars. Recent critical opinion, however, has been more divided, not least over the success or otherwise of the poem's projection of a female consciousness.

Pope first mentions *Eloisa to Abelard* in a letter to Martha Blount of 1716. In June 1717 he sent a copy of it to Turkey for his close friend but subsequent enemy Lady Mary Wortley Montagu, to whom he covertly alludes in the closing lines. As 'Eloisa to Abelard, an Epistle' it was first published in *The Works of Mr. Pope* (1717), from where the following text is taken.

> In these deep solitudes and awful cells,
> Where heav'nly-pensive, contemplation dwells,
> And ever-musing melancholy reigns;
> What means this tumult in a Vestal's veins?
> Why rove my thoughts beyond this last retreat? 5
> Why feels my heart its long-forgotten heat?
> Yet, yet I love! — From *Abelard* it came,
> And *Eloisa* yet must kiss the name.
>   Dear fatal name! rest ever unreveal'd,
> Nor pass these lips in holy silence seal'd. 10
> Hide it, my heart, within that close disguise,
> Where, mix'd with God's, his lov'd Idea lies.
> O write it not, my hand — The name appears
> Already written — wash it out, my tears!
> In vain lost *Eloisa* weeps and prays, 15
> Her heart still dictates, and her hand obeys.
>   Relentless walls! whose darksom round contains
> Repentant sighs, and voluntary pains:
> Ye rugged rocks! which holy knees have worn;
> Ye grots and caverns shagg'd with horrid thorn! 20

---

3 *melancholy* The visionary powers (for good or ill) of the melancholy temperament were traditional. See 24n.

4 *Vestal* A nun. The original 'vestal virgins' were the chaste priestesses of the Roman goddess Vesta.

12 *Idea* 'image'.

20 *horrid* 'bristling' (Lat. *horridus*). Cf. 'By grots, and caverns shag'd with horrid shades' (Milton, *Masque*, 429).

Shrines! where their vigils pale-ey'd virgins keep,
And pitying saints, whose statues learn to weep!
Tho' cold like you, unmov'd, and silent grown,
I have not yet forgot my self to stone.
Heav'n claims me all in vain, while he has part,   25
Still rebel nature holds out half my heart;
Nor pray'rs nor fasts its stubborn pulse restrain,
Nor tears, for ages, taught to flow in vain.
    Soon as thy letters trembling I unclose,
That well-known name awakens all my woes.   30
Oh name for ever sad! for ever dear!
Still breath'd in sighs, still usher'd with a tear.
I tremble too where-e'er my own I find,
Some dire misfortune follows close behind.
Line after line my gushing eyes o'erflow,   35
Led thro' a sad variety of woe:
Now warm in love, now with'ring in thy bloom,
Lost in a convent's solitary gloom!
There stern religion quench'd th'unwilling flame,
There dy'd the best of passions, Love and Fame.   40
    Yet write, oh write me all, that I may join
Griefs to thy griefs, and eccho sighs to thine.
Nor foes nor fortune take this pow'r away.
And is my *Abelard* less kind than they?
Tears still are mine, and those I need not spare,   45
Love but demands what else were shed in pray'r;
No happier task these faded eyes pursue,
To read and weep is all they now can do.
    Then share thy pain, allow that sad relief;
Ah more than share it! give me all thy grief.   50
Heav'n first taught letters for some wretches aid,
Some banish'd lover, or some captive maid;
They live, they speak, they breathe what love inspires,
Warm from the soul, and faithful to its fires,
The virgins wish without her fears impart,   55
Excuse the blush, and pour out all the heart,
Speed the soft intercourse from soul to soul,
And waft a sigh from *Indus* to the *Pole*.
    Thou know'st how guiltless first I met thy flame,
When Love approach'd me under Friendship's name;   60
My fancy form'd thee of Angelick kind,
Some emanation of th'all-beauteous Mind.
Those smiling eyes, attemp'ring ev'ry ray,
Shone sweetly lambent with celestial day:
Guiltless I gaz'd; heav'n listen'd while you sung;   65
And truths divine came mended from that tongue.

---

22 *weep* With the condensed moisture trickling down
  damp stone. Cf. *Windsor-Forest*, 311.
24 *forgot my self to stone* i.e. become statuesque with rapt
  contemplation. Cf. Milton's address to divine
  Melancholy: 'There held in holy passion still, / Forget
  thy self to marble' (*Il Penseroso*, 41–2).
46 *else* 'otherwise'.

56 *Excuse* 'remove the need for'.
58 *Indus* The major river of Pakistan.
61 *fancy* 'imagination'.
64 *lambent* 'softly radiant'.
66 'He was her Preceptor in Philosophy and Divinity'
  (Pope).

From lips like those what precept fail'd to move?
Too soon they taught me 'twas no sin to love.
Back thro' the paths of pleasing sense I ran,
Nor wish'd an Angel whom I lov'd a Man.   70
Dim and remote the joys of saints I see,
Nor envy them, that heav'n I lose for thee.
   How oft', when press'd to marriage, have I said,
Curse on all laws but those which love has made?
Love, free as air, at sight of human ties,   75
Spreads his light wings, and in a moment flies.
Let wealth, let honour, wait the wedded dame,
August her deed, and sacred be her fame;
Before true passion all those views remove,
Fame, wealth, and honour! what are you to Love?   80
The jealous God, when we profane his fires,
Those restless passions in revenge inspires;
And bids them make mistaken mortals groan,
Who seek in love for ought but love alone.
Should at my feet the world's great master fall,   85
Himself, his throne, his world, I'd scorn 'em all:
Not *Caesar*'s empress wou'd I deign to prove;
No, make me mistress to the man I love;
If there be yet another name more free,
More fond than mistress, make me that to thee!   90
Oh happy state! when souls each other draw,
When love is liberty, and nature, law:
All then is full, possessing, and possest,
No craving Void left aking in the breast:
Ev'n thought meets thought e'er from the lips it part,   95
And each warm wish springs mutual from the heart.
This sure is bliss (if bliss on earth there be)
And once the lot of *Abelard* and me.
   Alas how chang'd! what sudden horrors rise?
A naked Lover bound and bleeding lies!   100
Where, where was *Eloise*? her voice, her hand,
Her ponyard, had oppos'd the dire command.
Barbarian stay! that bloody hand restrain;
The crime was common, common be the pain.
I can no more; by shame, by rage supprest,   105
Let tears, and burning blushes speak the rest.
   Canst thou forget that sad, that solemn day,
When victims at yon' altar's foot we lay?
Canst thou forget what tears that moment fell,
When, warm in youth, I bade the world farewell?   110
As with cold lips I kiss'd the sacred veil,
The shrines all trembled, and the lamps grew pale:
Heav'n scarce believ'd the conquest it survey'd,
And Saints with wonder heard the vows I made.

---

102 *ponyard* 'dagger'.
104 *common* 'shared'; *pain* 'punishment' (Lat. *poena*) as well as the common English meaning.

106 Joseph Warton noted that 'it was difficult to speak of this catastrophe that befel Abelard with any dignity and grace: our poet however has done it'.

Yet then, to those dread altars as I drew,   115
Not on the Cross my eyes were fix'd, but you;
Not grace, or zeal, love only was my call,
And if I lose thy love, I lose my all.
Come! with thy looks, thy words, relieve my woe;
Those still at least are left thee to bestow.   120
Still on that breast enamour'd let me lie,
Still drink delicious poison from thy eye,
Pant on thy lip, and to thy heart be prest;
Give all thou canst — and let me dream the rest.
Ah no! instruct me other joys to prize,   125
With other beauties charm my partial eyes,
Full in my view set all the bright abode,
And make my soul quit *Abelard* for God.
  Ah think at least thy flock deserve thy care,
Plants of thy hand, and children of thy pray'r.   130
From the false world in early youth they fled,
By thee to mountains, wilds, and deserts led.
You rais'd these hallow'd walls; the desert smil'd,
And Paradise was open'd in the Wild.
No weeping orphan saw his father's stores   135
Our shrines irradiate, or emblaze the floors;
No silver saints, by dying misers giv'n,
Here brib'd the rage of ill-requited heav'n:
But such plain roofs as piety could raise,
And only vocal with the Maker's praise.   140
In these lone walls (their days eternal bound)
These moss-grown domes with spiry turrets crown'd,
Where awful arches make a noon-day night,
And the dim windows shed a solemn light;
Thy eyes diffus'd a reconciling ray,   145
And gleams of glory brighten'd all the day.
But now no face divine contentment wears,
'Tis all blank sadness, or continual tears.
See how the force of others pray'rs I try,
(O pious fraud of am'rous charity!)   150
But why should I on others pray'rs depend?
Come thou, my father, brother, husband, friend!
Ah let thy handmaid, sister, daughter move,
And, all those tender names in one, thy love!
The darksom pines that o'er yon' rocks reclin'd   155
Wave high, and murmur to the hollow wind,
The wandring streams that shine between the hills,
The grots that eccho to the tinkling rills,
The dying gales that pant upon the trees,
The lakes that quiver to the curling breeze;   160
No more these scenes my meditation aid,
Or lull to rest the visionary maid:

133 'He founded the Monastery' (Pope).
135 *stores* The monastery was not financed by taxation or
  confiscation.
142 *domes* 'edifices'.
144 Cf. 'And storied windows richly dight / Casting a dim
  religious light' (Milton, *Il Penseroso*, 159–60).

152–3 These lines play on the religious meanings of 'father'
  as priest, 'brother' as monk and 'sister' as nun.
162 *visionary* 'seeing visions'.

But o'er the twilight groves, and dusky caves,
Long-sounding isles, and intermingled graves,
Black Melancholy sits, and round her throws   165
A death-like silence, and a dread repose:
Her gloomy presence saddens all the scene,
Shades ev'ry flow'r, and darkens ev'ry green,
Deepens the murmur of the falling floods,
And breathes a browner horror on the woods.   170
    Yet here for ever, ever must I stay;
Sad proof how well a lover can obey!
Death, only death, can break the lasting chain;
And here ev'n then, shall my cold dust remain,
Here all its frailties, all its flames resign,   175
And wait, till 'tis no sin to mix with thine.
    Ah wretch! believ'd the spouse of God in vain,
Confess'd within the slave of love and man.
Assist me heav'n! but whence arose that pray'r?
Sprung it from piety, or from despair?   180
Ev'n here, where frozen chastity retires,
Love finds an altar for forbidden fires.
I ought to grieve, but cannot what I ought;
I mourn the lover, not lament the fault;
I view my crime, but kindle at the view,   185
Repent old pleasures, and sollicit new:
Now turn'd to heav'n, I weep my past offence,
Now think of thee, and curse my innocence.
Of all affliction taught a lover yet,
'Tis sure the hardest science to forget!   190
How shall I lose the sin, yet keep the sense,
And love th'offender, yet detest th'offence?
How the dear object from the crime remove,
Or how distinguish penitence from love?
Unequal task! a passion to resign,   195
For hearts so touch'd, so pierc'd, so lost as mine.
E'er such a soul regains its peaceful state,
How often must it love, how often hate!
How often, hope, despair, resent, regret,
Conceal, disdain — do all things but forget.   200
But let heav'n seize it, all at once 'tis fir'd,
Not touch'd, but rapt; not waken'd, but inspir'd!
Oh come! oh teach me nature to subdue,
Renounce my love, my life, my self — and you.
Fill my fond heart with God alone, for he   205
Alone can rival, can succeed to thee.
    How happy is the blameless Vestal's lot?
The world forgetting, by the world forgot.
Eternal sun-shine of the spotless mind!
Each pray'r accepted, and each wish resign'd;   210
Labour and rest, that equal periods keep;

177 *spouse of God* A nun became the bride of Christ. See
    217 and note.
189 *all* all, (*1717*).

190 *science* 'skill'.
191 *sense* Both 'meaning' and 'feeling'.
205 *fond* Both 'affectionate' and 'foolish'.

'Obedient slumbers that can wake and weep';
Desires compos'd, affections ever even,
Tears that delight, and sighs that waft to heav'n.
Grace shines around her with serenest beams,   215
And whisp'ring Angels prompt her golden dreams.
For her the Spouse prepares the bridal ring,
For her white virgins *Hymenæals* sing;
For her th'unfading rose of *Eden* blooms,
And wings of Seraphs shed divine perfumes;   220
To sounds of heav'nly harps, she dies away,
And melts in visions of eternal day.
    Far other dreams my erring soul employ,
Far other raptures, of unholy joy:
When at the close of each sad, sorrowing day,   225
Fancy restores what vengeance snatch'd away,
Then conscience sleeps, and leaving nature free,
All my loose soul unbounded springs to thee.
O curst, dear horrors of all-conscious night!
How glowing guilt exalts the keen delight!   230
Provoking Dæmons all restraint remove,
And stir within me ev'ry source of love.
I hear thee, view thee, gaze o'er all thy charms,
And round thy phantom glue my clasping arms.
I wake — no more I hear, no more I view,   235
The phantom flies me, as unkind as you.
I call aloud; it hears not what I say;
I stretch my empty arms; it glides away:
To dream once more I close my willing eyes;
Ye soft illusions, dear deceits, arise!   240
Alas no more! — methinks we wandring go
Thro' dreary wastes, and weep each other's woe;
Where round some mould'ring tow'r pale ivy creeps,
And low-brow'd rocks hang nodding o'er the deeps.
Sudden you mount! you becken from the skies;   245
Clouds interpose, waves roar, and winds arise.
I shriek, start up, the same sad prospect find,
And wake to all the griefs I left behind.
    For thee the fates, severely kind, ordain
A cool suspense from pleasure and from pain;   250
Thy life a long, dead calm of fix'd repose;
No pulse that riots, and no blood that glows.
Still as the sea, e'er winds were taught to blow,
Or moving spirit bade the waters flow;
Soft as the slumbers of a saint forgiv'n,   255
And mild as opening gleams of promis'd heav'n.
    Come *Abelard*! for what hast thou to dread?
The torch of *Venus* burns not for the dead;

212 Pope notes that this line appears in the poem
  Description of a Religious House by Richard Crashaw
  (?1613–49).
217 *Spouse* Christ. See 177n.
218 *Hymenæals* Marriage songs.
233–8 Cf. Virgil, *Aeneid*, 6:700–2, in which Aeneas tries to

embrace the ghost of his father Anchises: 'Three times
he tried to throw his arms round his neck; three times
the phantom, clasped in vain, fled from his hands, like
light breezes or a winged dream'.
258 *Venus* The Roman goddess of love.

Cut from the root my perish'd joys I see,
And love's warm tyde for ever stopt in thee.   260
Nature stands check'd; Religion disapproves;
Ev'n thou art cold — yet *Eloisa* loves.
Ah hopeless, lasting flames! like those that burn
To light the dead, and warm th'unfruitful urn.
    What scenes appear where-e'er I turn my view,   265
The dear Ideas, where I fly, pursue,
Rise in the grove, before the altar rise,
Stain all my soul, and wanton in my eyes!
I waste the Matin lamp in sighs for thee,
Thy image steals between my God and me,   270
Thy voice I seem in ev'ry hymn to hear,
With ev'ry bead I drop too soft a tear.
When from the Censer clouds of fragrance roll,
And swelling organs lift the rising soul;
One thought of thee puts all the pomp to flight,   275
Priests, Tapers, Temples, swim before my sight:
In seas of flame my plunging soul is drown'd,
While Altars blaze, and Angels tremble round.
    While prostrate here in humble grief I lie,
Kind, virtuous drops just gath'ring in my eye,   280
While praying, trembling, in the dust I roll,
And dawning grace is opening on my soul.
Come, if thou dar'st, all charming as thou art!
Oppose thy self to heav'n; dispute my heart;
Come, with one glance of those deluding eyes,   285
Blot out each bright Idea of the skies.
Take back that grace, those sorrows, and those tears,
Take back my fruitless penitence and pray'rs,
Snatch me, just mounting, from the blest abode,
Assist the Fiends and tear me from my God!   290
    No, fly me, fly me! far as Pole from Pole;
Rise *Alps* between us! and whole oceans roll!
Ah come not, write not, think not once of me,
Nor share one pang of all I felt for thee.
Thy oaths I quit, thy memory resign,   295
Forget, renounce me, hate whate'er was mine.
Fair eyes, and tempting looks (which yet I view!)
Long lov'd, ador'd ideas! all adieu!
O grace serene! oh virtue heav'nly fair!
Divine oblivion of low-thoughted care!   300
Fresh blooming hope, gay daughter of the sky!
And faith, our early immortality!
Enter each mild, each amicable guest;

259–60 Pope later removed this couplet alluding to
Abelard's castration.
263–4 An allusion to the Roman practice of placing lamps
in tombs.
269 *Matin* 'morning'.
272 *bead* Of a rosary, each bead 'told' in prayer.
273 *Censer* A vessel from which burning incense is wafted
during services.

284 *dispute* 'contend for'.
295 *quit* 'release you from'.
300 *low-thoughted care* Earthly troubles. Cf. '… and with
low-thoughted care / Confin'd and pester'd in this
pinfold here' (Milton, *Masque*, 6–7).

Receive, and wrap me in eternal rest!
   See in her Cell sad *Eloisa* spread,   305
Propt in some tomb, a neighbour of the dead!
In each low wind methinks a Spirit calls,
And more than Echoes talk along the walls.
Here, as I watch'd the dying lamps around,
From yonder shrine I heard a hollow sound.   310
Come, sister come! (it said, or seem'd to say)
Thy place is here, sad sister come away!
Once like thy self, I trembled, wept, and pray'd,
Love's victim then, tho' now a sainted maid:
But all is calm in this eternal sleep;   315
Here grief forgets to groan, and love to weep,
Ev'n superstition loses ev'ry fear:
For God, not man, absolves our frailties here.
   I come, ye ghosts! prepare your roseate bow'rs,
Celestial palms, and ever blooming flow'rs.   320
Thither, where sinners may have rest, I go,
Where flames refin'd in breasts seraphic glow.
Thou, *Abelard*! the last sad office pay,
And smooth my passage to the realms of day:
See my lips tremble, and my eye-balls roll,   325
Suck my last breath, and catch the flying soul!
Ah no — in sacred vestments may'st thou stand,
The hallow'd taper trembling in thy hand,
Present the Cross before my lifted eye,
Teach me at once, and learn of me to die.   330
Ah then, thy once-lov'd *Eloisa* see!
It will be then no crime to gaze on me.
See from my cheek the transient roses fly!
See the last sparkle languish in my eye!
Till ev'ry motion, pulse, and breath, be o'er;   335
And ev'n my *Abelard* belov'd no more.
O death all-eloquent! you only prove
What dust we doat on, when 'tis man we love.
   Then too, when fate shall thy fair frame destroy,
(That cause of all my guilt, and all my joy)   340
In trance extatic may thy pangs be drown'd,
Bright clouds descend, and Angels watch thee round,
From opening skies may streaming glories shine,
And Saints embrace thee with a love like mine.
   May one kind grave unite each hapless name,   345
And graft my love immortal on thy fame.
Then, ages hence, when all my woes are o'er,
When this rebellious heart shall beat no more;
If ever chance two wandring lovers brings

---

323 *last sad office* The last rites.

326 Cf. 'Her lips suck forth my soul' (Marlowe, *Dr Faustus*, V.i.96). Said of Helen of Troy.

341 *extatic* Ecstasy (Gk. *ekstasis*) was the blissful release of the soul from the body.

345 '*Abelard* and *Eloisa* were interr'd in the same grave, or in monuments adjoining, in the Monastery of the *Paraclete*: He died in the year 1142, she in 1163' (Pope).

To *Paraclete*'s white walls, and silver springs,   350
O'er the pale marble shall they join their heads,
And drink the falling tears each other sheds,
Then sadly say, with mutual pity mov'd,
Oh may we never love as these have lov'd!
From the full choir when loud *Hosanna*'s rise,   355
And swell the pomp of dreadful sacrifice,
Amid that scene, if some relenting eye
Glance on the stone where our cold reliques lie,
Devotion's self shall steal a thought from heav'n,
One human tear shall drop, and be forgiv'n.   360
And sure if fate some future Bard shall join
In sad similitude of griefs to mine,
Condemn'd whole years in absence to deplore,
And image charms he must behold no more,
Such if there be, who loves so long, so well;   365
Let him our sad, our tender story tell;
The well-sung woes shall sooth my pensive ghost;
He best can paint 'em, who shall feel 'em most.

---

356 *dreadful sacrifice* The Eucharist.
363–4 Throughout 1717 Pope's friend Lady Mary Wortley

Montagu was absent from England, having
accompanied her husband to Constantinople.

To Richard Boyle, Earl of Burlington
Of the Use of Riches

The poem belongs to a set of four verse epistles known variously as the *Epistles to Several Persons* (Pope's title) and the *Moral Essays* (the posthumous name given by Pope's editor William Warburton). Pope originally wrote and published *To Burlington*, *To Bathurst*, *To Cobham* and *Of the Characters of Women* separately between 1731 and 1735. But they also featured in plans for his 'Opus Magnum', an ambitious moral scheme Pope sketched out in his closing years to encompass his major poems. He intended the *Epistles* to supply a coda to the treatment of '*Ethics*, or practical Morality' in Book 4 of *An Essay on Man*. The prefatory 'Argument' to each *Epistle* carries some of the *Essay*'s philosophical concerns into the socioeconomic sphere. But the poems also reflect Pope's growing reputation as an outspoken satirist of Court and government. It is their blend of philosophical generalization, personal compliment and satiric *exemplum* which makes the *Epistles* so fascinating.

Pope was a personal friend of Richard Boyle, third Earl of Burlington (1694–1753), a wealthy and distinguished patron of art, music, literature and architecture. Burlington, who had studied architecture in Italy, spearheaded the English Palladian movement responsible for much elegant Georgian architecture including Burlington House in Piccadilly and his own villa at Chiswick. It is to Burlington as the incipient publisher of Palladio's *Designs of the Baths, Arches, Theatres, &c. of Ancient*

Rome that Pope dedicates his poem, which in the first edition was subtitled 'Of Taste'. The epistle moves swiftly from architecture to landscape gardening, a topic which had preoccupied Pope throughout the 1720s as he transformed his own Twickenham garden and supported William Kent and Charles Bridgeman in developing the new natural, irregular landscapes that were starting to displace the formal labour-intensive French designs satirized in *To Burlington*. Before he published a second edition, Pope, on Aaron Hill's suggestion, changed the subtitle to 'Of False Taste' – more appropriate for a poem preoccupied with ambitious failure of many kinds. For the dominant figure is not Burlington, but the imaginary 'Timon', whose fantastically convoluted house and gardens linger in the memory long after other passages are forgotten. The Timon portrait caused Pope much trouble. Public opinion identified his original as the Duke of Chandos, a millionaire whose pretentious house, Cannons, at Edgeware just outside London, shared some of the same features as Timon's villa. Once the identification had been made, it stuck – much to Pope's embarrassment.

The poem's final paragraph, modelled on Virgil's prophecy of a new Augustan age in *Aeneid*, 6, seems limited in comparison with *Windsor-Forest*'s outward-looking vision of Britain's future under Anne. Pope implies that it is now left to private landowners like Burlington to carry out 'Imperial Works' that are 'worthy *Kings*', since the monarch himself is uncultured and uninterested. The catalogue of projected civic works is undercut by Pope's footnote drawing attention to the real state of Britain – bridges unbuilt, roads neglected, jerry-built London churches sinking into marsh-land. By the close of the poem, nature, initially a benign presence to be admired and consulted, has become an invasive, threatening force which man must tame. As in *Windsor-Forest*, the balance between wilderness and civilization is always precariously maintained.

Epistle to Burlington was first published in folio in December 1731. It underwent major revision prior to its publication in Pope's *Works* of 1735 and 1736. Pope's final changes were embodied in the definitive edition of his poems (subsequently known as the

'death-bed edition'), which he was preparing in the months before he died on 30 May 1744. Pope left his unpublished manuscripts to his friend Lord Bolingbroke, and although the four *Epistles* were ready for publication, Bolingbroke suppressed the edition after complaints from the Duchess of Marlborough that the *Epistle to a Lady* satirized her as 'Atossa'. But a few copies escaped destruction. In 1748 the Knaptons (one of Pope's publishers) published a small edition of *Four Ethic Epistles by Alexander Pope, Esq*, which was the 'death-bed' edition with a special title page. The text of the copy in the British Library is reproduced below. We have been selective in our reproduction of Pope's notes.

> 'Tis strange, the Miser should his Cares employ,
> To gain those Riches he can ne'er enjoy:
> Is it less strange, the Prodigal should wast
> His wealth, to purchase what he ne'er can taste?
> Not for himself he sees, or hears, or eats;   5
> Artists must chuse his Pictures, Music, Meats:
> He buys for Topham, Drawings and Designs,
> For Pembroke Statues, dirty Gods and Coins;
> Rare monkish Manuscripts for Hearne alone,
> And Books for Mead, and Butterflies for Sloane.   10
> Think we all these are for himself? no more
> Than his fine Wife, alas! or finer Whore.
>   For what has Virro painted, built, and planted?
> Only to show, how many Tastes he wanted.
> What brought Sir Visto's ill got wealth to waste?   15
> Some Dæmon whisper'd, "Visto! have a Taste."
> Heav'n visits with a Taste the wealthy fool,
> And needs no Rod but Ripley with a Rule.
> See! sportive fate, to punish aukward pride,
> Bids Bubo build, and sends him such a Guide: 20
> A standing sermon, at each year's expence,
> That never Coxcomb reach'd Magnificence!

7 *Topham* Richard Topham (d. 1735) bequeathed his art collection and books to Eton College.

8 *Pembroke* Thomas Herbert, eighth Earl of Pembroke (1656–1733), collected sculptures and paintings for his Wilton estate.

9 *Hearne* Thomas Hearne (1678–1735), distinguished Oxford historian.

10 *Mead … Sloane* 'Two eminent Physicians; the one had an excellent Library, the other the finest collection in Europe of natural curiosities; both men of great learning and humanity' (Pope). Pope's friend Richard Mead (1673–1754) was Physician in Ordinary to George II. The vast collection of Sir Hans Sloane (1660–1753), President of the Royal College of Physicians, formed the core of the British Museum.

13 *Virro* An aesthete satirized by the Roman poet Juvenal (first century AD).

15 *Visto* A name derived from landscape gardening's vogue for the 'vista', or distant view.

18 *Ripley* Thomas Ripley (d. 1758) designed Walpole's seat at Houghton, Norfolk. 'This man was a carpenter, employ'd by a first Minister, who rais'd him to an Architect, without any genius in the art; and after some wretched proofs of his insufficiency in public Buildings, made him Comptroller of the Board of works' (Pope).

20 *Bubo* George Bubb Dodington. See *Epistle to Dr Arbuthnot*, 230n.

22 *Coxcomb* Cocky upstart.

You show us, Rome was glorious, not profuse,
And pompous buildings once were things of Use.
Yet shall (my Lord) your just, your noble rules   25
Fill half the land with Imitating Fools;
Who random drawings from your sheets shall take,
And of one beauty many blunders make;
Load some vain Church with old Theatric state,
Turn Arcs of triumph to a Garden-gate;   30
Reverse your Ornaments, and hang them all
On some patch'd dog-hole ek'd with ends of wall,
Then clap four slices of Pilaster on't,
That, lac'd with bits of rustic, makes a Front.
Shall call the winds thro' long Arcades to roar,   35
Proud to catch cold at a Venetian door;
Conscious they act a true Palladian part,
And if they starve, they starve by rules of art.
　　Oft have you hinted to your brother Peer,
A certain truth, which many buy too dear: 40
Something there is more needful than Expence,
And something previous ev'n to Taste — 'tis Sense:
Good Sense, which only is the gift of Heav'n,
And tho' no Science, fairly worth the seven:
A Light, which in yourself you must perceive;   45
Jones and Le Nôtre have it not to give.
　　To build, to plant, whatever you intend,
To rear the Column, or the Arch to bend,
To swell the Terras, or to sink the Grot;
In all, let Nature never be forgot.   50
But treat the Goddess like a modest fair,
Nor over-dress, nor leave her wholly bare;
Let not each beauty ev'ry where be spy'd,
Where half the skill is decently to hide.
He gains all points, who pleasingly confounds,   55
Surprizes, varies, and conceals the Bounds.
　　Consult the Genius of the Place in all;
That tells the Waters or to rise, or fall,
Or helps th'ambitious Hill the heav'ns to scale,
Or scoops in circling theatres the Vale,   60

23 'The Earl of Burlington was then publishing the Designs of Inigo Jones, and the Antiquities of Rome by Palladio' (Pope).

33 *Pilaster* A rectangular column projecting from a wall – decorative only.

34 *rustic* A stone surface artificially roughened.

36 *Venetian door* A door with side windows for lighting an entrance hall.

37 *Palladian* In the style of Andrea Palladio (1508–80), the Italian neoclassical architect whose designs, inspired by Vitruvius (see 194n), were first popularized in Britain by Inigo Jones, then by Burlington's neo-Palladian school.

38 *starve* 'freeze'.

44 *Science* 'acquired knowledge'; *seven* The seven liberal arts of the medieval curriculum.

46 Inigo Jones (1573–1652), founder of English neoclassical architecture; his work included Covent Garden piazza and the banqueting hall at Whitehall. André Le Nôtre (1613–1700) designed the formal, symmetrical gardens at Versailles and Fontainebleau.

49 *Grot* Stone grottos were a popular feature of the new picturesque style of landscaping.

55 *confounds* 'mixes'.

57 *Genius* 'guardian spirit'.

60 *theatres* 'tiers'.

Calls in the Country, catches opening glades,
Joins willing woods, and varies shades from shades,
Now breaks or now directs, th'intending Lines;
Paints as you plant, and, as you work, designs.
    Still follow Sense, of ev'ry Art the Soul,   65
Parts answ'ring parts shall slide into a whole,
Spontaneous beauties all around advance,
Start ev'n from Difficulty, strike from Chance;
Nature shall join you, Time shall make it grow
A Work to wonder at — perhaps a STOW.   70
    Without it, proud Versailles! thy glory falls;
And Nero's Terraces desert their walls:
The vast Parterres a thousand hands shall make,
Lo! COBHAM comes, and floats them with a Lake:
Or cut wide views thro' Mountains to the Plain,   75
You'll wish your hill or shelter'd seat again.
Ev'n in an ornament its place remark,
Nor in an Hermitage set Dr. Clarke.
    Behold Villario's ten-years toil compleat;
His Quincunx darkens, his Espaliers meet,   80
The Wood supports the Plain, the parts unite,
And strength of Shade contends with strength of Light;
A waving Glow the bloomy beds display,
Blushing in bright diversities of day,
With silver-quiv'ring rills mæander'd o'er —   85
Enjoy them, you! Villario can no more;
Tir'd of the scene Parterres and Fountains yield,
He finds at last he better likes a Field.
    Thro' his young Woods how pleas'd Sabinus stray'd,
Or sat delighted in the thick'ning shade,   90
With annual joy the red'ning shoots to greet,
Or see the stretching branches long to meet!
His Son's fine Taste an op'ner Vista loves,
Foe to the Dryads of his Father's groves,
One boundless Green, or flourish'd Carpet views,   95
With all the mournful family of Yews;
The thriving plants ignoble broomsticks made,
Now sweep those Alleys they were born to shade.

---

63 *intending* 'extending' (Lat. *intendere*, 'to stretch out').

70 STOW 'The seat and gardens of the Lord Viscount Cobham in Buckinghamshire' (Pope). Richard Temple, Viscount Cobham (1675–1749), addressee of the first of Pope's *Epistles to Several Persons*, transformed the formal gardens at Stowe into an unrivalled landscape whose buildings and monuments formed a political allegory of opposition Whig principles.

71 *Versailles* The French royal palace whose gardens were considered Le Nôtre's masterpiece.

72 The Roman emperor Nero's 'golden house' was covered with gold and jewels and surrounded by elaborate grounds with artificial lakes and woods.

73 *Parterres* Ornamental flower-beds forming regular patterns.

74 *floats* 'floods'.

78 Samuel Clarke (1675–1729) was a controversial theologian and scientist patronized by Queen Caroline. She installed his bust among a pantheon of English intellectuals in her 'Hermitage' in Richmond Gardens.

80 *Quincunx* A decorative group of five trees, four planted around the central tree; *Espaliers* Fruit trees trained across a frame.

89 *Sabinus* A name derived from the Sabine countryside near Rome.

94 *Dryads* Wood-nymphs.

96 'Pyramids of dark-green, continually repeated, not unlike a Funeral procession' (Pope).

At Timon's Villa let us pass a day,
Where all cry out, "What sums are thrown away!   100
So proud, so grand, of that stupendous air,
Soft and Agreeable come never there.
Greatness, with Timon, dwells in such a draught
As brings all Brobdignag before your thought.
To compass this, his building is a Town,   105
His pond an Ocean, his parterre a Down:
Who but must laugh, the Master when he sees,
A puny insect, shiv'ring at a breeze!
Lo, what huge heaps of littleness around!
The whole, a labour'd Quarry above ground.   110
Two Cupids squirt before: a Lake behind
Improves the keenness of the Northern wind.
His Gardens next your admiration call,
On ev'ry side you look, behold the Wall!
No pleasing Intricacies intervene,   115
No artful wildness to perplex the scene;
Grove nods at grove, each Alley has a brother,
And half the platform just reflects the other.
The suff'ring eye inverted Nature sees,
Trees cut to Statues, Statues thick as trees,   120
With here a Fountain, never to be play'd,
And there a Summer-house, that knows no shade;
Here Amphitrite sails thro' myrtle bow'rs;
There Gladiators fight, or die in flow'rs;
Un-water'd see the drooping sea-horse mourn,   125
And swallows roost in Nilus' dusty Urn.
  My Lord advances with majestic mien,
Smit with the mighty pleasure, to be seen:
But soft — by regular approach — not yet —
First thro' the length of yon hot Terrace sweat,   130
And when up ten steep slopes you've drag'd your thighs,
Just at his Study-door he'll bless your eyes.
  His Study! with what Authors is it stor'd?
In Books, not Authors, curious is my Lord;
To all their dated Backs he turns you round,   135
These Aldus printed, those Du Suëil has bound.
Lo some are Vellom, and the rest as good
For all his Lordship knows, but they are Wood.
For Locke or Milton 'tis in vain to look,

---

99 *Timon's Villa* 'This description is intended to comprize
the principles of a false Taste of Magnificence, and to
exemplify what was said before, that nothing but Good
Sense can attain it' (Pope).

103 *draught* 'scheme' (the meaning 'current of air' is post-
1760).

104 *Brobdignag* Brobdingnag, the land of giants in Book 2
of Swift's *Gulliver's Travels* (1726).

107–8 Cf. Lady Mary Wortley Montagu, *Verses Address'd to
the Imitator of Horace*, 79–80.

120 Pope had satirized the fashion for topiary in *Guardian*,
173 (29 September 1713).

123 *Amphitrite* A Greek sea-goddess.

126 *Nilus* A river-god.

136 *Aldus* Aldo Manucci (*c.*1450–1515), the Venetian who
printed many Greek and Roman classics for the first
time; *Du Suëil* Augustin Duseuil (1673–1746), Parisian
royal bookbinder.

These shelves admit not any modern book.   140
   And now the Chapel's silver bell you hear,
That summons you to all the Pride of Pray'r:
Light quirks of Musick, broken and uneven,
Make the soul dance upon a Jig to Heav'n.
On painted Cielings you devoutly stare,   145
Where sprawl the Saints of Verrio or Laguerre,
On gilded clouds in fair expansion lie,
And bring all Paradise before your eye.
To rest, the Cushion and soft Dean invite,
Who never mentions Hell to ears polite.   150
   But hark! the chiming Clocks to dinner call;
A hundred footsteps scrape the marble Hall:
The rich Buffet well-colour'd Serpents grace,
And gaping Tritons spew to wash your face.
Is this a dinner? this a Genial room?   155
No, 'tis a Temple, and a Hecatomb.
A solemn Sacrifice, perform'd in state,
You drink by measure, and to minutes eat.
So quick retires each flying course, you'd swear
Sancho's dread Doctor and his Wand were there.   160
Between each Act the trembling salvers ring,
From soup to sweet-wine, and God bless the King.
In plenty starving, tantaliz'd in state,
And complaisantly help'd to all I hate,
Treated, caress'd, and tir'd, I take my leave,   165
Sick of his civil Pride from Morn to Eve;
I curse such lavish cost, and little skill,
And swear no Day was ever past so ill.
   Yet hence the Poor are cloath'd, the Hungry fed;
Health to himself, and to his Infants bread   170
The Lab'rer bears: What his hard Heart denies,
His charitable Vanity supplies.
   Another age shall see the golden Ear
Imbrown the Slope, and nod on the Parterre,
Deep Harvests bury all his pride has plann'd,   175
And laughing Ceres re-assume the land.
   Who then shall grace, or who improve the Soil?
Who plants like BATHURST, or who builds like BOYLE.
'Tis Use alone that sanctifies Expence,

146 *Verrio* See *Windsor-Forest*, 305n; *Laguerre* Louis
   Laguerre (1663–1721), French artist who painted the
   elaborate ceilings at Blenheim Palace.
150 'This is a fact; a reverend Dean preaching at Court,
   threatened the sinner with punishment in "a place
   which he thought it not decent to name in so polite an
   assembly"' (Pope).
153 *Buffet* 'sideboard'.
154 *Triton* A merman.
156 *Hecatomb* A formal public sacrifice in ancient Greece.
160 *Sancho's dread Doctor* Recalls the scene in Cervantes's
   Don Quixote, 2:47, where Sancho Panza has his food
   spirited away.

161 *salvers* 'dishes'.
164 *complaisantly* 'courteously'.
169 'The *Moral* of the whole, where PROVIDENCE is justified
   in giving Wealth to those who squander it in this
   manner. A bad Taste employs more hands, and diffuses
   Expence more than a good one' (Pope).
176 *Ceres* Roman goddess of the fertile earth.
178 *BATHURST* Allen, Earl Bathurst (1685–1775), Tory peer
   and friend of Prior, Swift and Pope. Pope addressed to
   him the third of the *Epistles*. He was an enthusiastic
   tree-planter (see Lady Mary Wortley Montagu, *Epistle
   to Lord Bathurst*, 12n) *BOYLE* Burlington's family name.

And Splendor borrows all her rays from Sense.   180
   His Father's Acres who enjoys in peace,
Or makes his Neighbours glad, if he encrease;
Whose chearful Tenants bless their yearly toil,
Yet to their Lord owe more than to the soil;
Whose ample Lawns are not asham'd to feed   185
The milky heifer and deserving steed;
Whose rising Forests, not for pride or show,
But future Buildings, future Navies grow:
Let his plantations stretch from down to down,
First shade a Country, and then raise a Town.   190
   You too proceed! make falling Arts your care,
Erect new wonders, and the old repair,
Jones and Palladio to themselves restore,
And be whate'er Vitruvius was before:
Till Kings call forth th'Idea's of your mind,   195
Proud to accomplish what such hands design'd,
Bid Harbors open, public Ways extend,
Bid Temples, worthier of the God, ascend;
Bid the broad Arch the dang'rous Flood contain,
The Mole projected break the roaring Main;   200
Back to his bounds their subject Sea command,
And roll obedient Rivers thro' the Land:
These Honours, Peace to happy Britain brings,
These are Imperial Works, and worthy Kings.

194 *Vitruvius* Marcus Vitruvius Pollio, Roman architect during the Augustan age. His treatise *De architectura* was based on Hellenistic Greek practice and stressed simplicity and proportion. He influenced Palladio, and in turn the neo-Palladian movement.

195–204 'The poet, after having touched upon the proper objects of Magnificence and Expence, in the private works of great men, comes to those great and public works which become a Prince' (Pope). Pope's lengthy note here is an indictment of civic corruption under Walpole's administration. It complains about the shady deals surrounding the construction of Queen Anne's

London churches; about an unrepaired breach in the bank of the Thames; about the state of the nation's roads; and finally about Ripley's plans for a wooden Westminster bridge.

195 *Ideas* 'conceptions'.

200 *Mole* 'breakwater'.

202 *obedient Rivers* Canals.

204 Cf. Dryden's translation of *Aeneid*, 6:852: 'These are Imperial Arts, and worthy thee'. Pope's closing lines are indebted to Anchises's prophetic vision of imperial Rome under Augustus (6:847–53).

An Epistle To a Lady
Of the Characters of Women

The poem was first published in February 1735. Though last in order of composition, it was accorded second place among Pope's *Epistles to Several Persons* as the appropriate sequal to Epistle I. *Of the Knowledge and Characters of Men: To Richard Lord Cobham. Epistle to a Lady* is addressed to Martha ('Patty') Blount (1690–1763), the younger of two unmarried sisters from an old Catholic family, and Pope's former neighbours at Binfield. Pope had once flirted with both sisters but after 1718 his relationship with Patty grew intimate and intense. At one stage marriage seemed likely and rumour proclaimed her Pope's mistress. The absence of Martha Blount's

name from the title page of *Epistle to a Lady* reflects the problem of addressing a public epistle to a female friend. Whereas the other three *Epistles* are dedicated to male aristocrats with well-defined public roles, Martha Blount's virtues are private and domestic. Her own insistence that Pope suppress her name testifies to her shrewd awareness that for a woman, 'fame' and 'scandal' were closely linked – an association underscored by the poem's thinly veiled portraits of female notoriety and its assertion that 'Your Virtues open fairest in the shade'.

It seems anomalous that Pope should compliment his 'Lady' with a poem that can exempt her from the general opprobrium only by desexualizing her into 'a softer Man', as a mix of male and female virtues. Echoing Clarissa's advice in *The Rape of the Lock*, Pope advocates the cultivation of 'good humour' (one of Martha Blount's noted qualities) as an alternative to the lonely old age faced by the fading beauties of yesteryear. In this poem the misogynist undercurrents which in the *Rape* had remained elusive and unattributable are foregrounded by the first-person voice. Pope's need to explain female character according to his theory of the 'ruling passion' expounded in *An Essay on Man* and *To Cobham* leads to some dogmatic generalizations about women which provoked protests from several female contemporaries. Yet the poem's assertion that all female action derives from either 'Love of Pleasure' or 'Love of Sway' scarcely does justice to the complex psychological portraits of strong-willed but self-defeating women which dominate the poem, from

Narcissa who oscillates between devotion and debauchery, to Flavia who dies 'of nothing but a Rage to live'. Pope's sympathy with the rebellious, passionate female who is at odds with social convention, so evident in *Eloisa to Abelard*, here struggles with his satiric impulse. Three of the sketches – Atossa (115–50), Cloe (157–80) and Philomedé (69–87) – did not appear in the early versions of the poem, though they may have been drafted at that stage. Their omission perhaps mirrored Pope's fear of a scandal similar to that stirred up by his *Epistle to Burlington*. The portraits were first included in an edition of the *Epistles* which Pope was preparing in the months immediately preceding his death in 1744, a move which led indirectly to its suppression (see *To Burlington* headnote). The text reproduced below is that of the unique British Library copy of this 'death-bed' text.

Nothing so true as what you once let fall,
"Most Women have no Characters at all."
Matter too soft a lasting mark to bear,
And best distinguish'd by black, brown, or fair.
How many pictures of one Nymph we view,   5
All how unlike each other, all how true!
Arcadia's Countess, here, in ermin'd pride,
Is there, Pastora by a fountain side.
Here Fannia, leering on her own good man,
And there, a naked Leda with a Swan.   10
Let then the Fair one beautifully cry,
In Magdalen's loose hair and lifted eye,
Or drest in smiles of sweet Cecilia shine,
With simp'ring Angels, Palms, and Harps divine;
Whether the Charmer sinner it, or saint it,   15
If Folly grows romantic, I must paint it.
     Come then, the colours and the ground prepare!
Dip in the Rainbow, trick her off in Air,
Chuse a firm Cloud, before it fall, and in it
Catch, e'er she change, the Cynthia of this minute.   20
     Rufa, whose eye quick-glancing o'er the Park,

7 *Arcadia's Countess* Mary, Countess of Pembroke (1561–1621), sister of Sir Philip Sidney. She was both the dedicatee and reviser of his pastoral romance, *Arcadia*; *ermin'd pride* i.e. formal state robes.
8 *Pastora* A shepherdess.
9 *Fannia* An aristocratic Roman woman who committed adultery.
10 *Leda* The god Zeus, in the form of a swan, raped Leda and fathered Helen of Troy. The subject was popular among painters.
12 *Magdalen* Mary Magdalene, the penitent prostitute

who annointed Christ's feet and wiped them with her hair.
13 *Cecilia* Patron saint of music.
16 *romantic* 'fanciful', 'extravagant'.
17 *ground* 'background colour'. Cf. *Windsor-Forest*, 38n. Pope studied painting under his friend Charles Jervas.
20 *Cynthia* Diana, moon goddess and symbol of mutability.
21–8 'Instances of contrarieties ... in the *Affected*' (Pope).
21 *Rufa* Red-haired (the female form of 'Rufus'), suggesting lasciviousness.

Attracts each light gay meteor of a Spark,
Agrees as ill with Rufa studying Locke,
As Sappho's diamonds with her dirty smock;
Or Sappho at her toilet's greasy task,   25
With Sappho fragrant at an ev'ning Mask:
So morning Insects that in muck begun,
Shine, buzz, and fly-blow in the setting-sun.
  How soft is Silia! fearful to offend,
The Frail one's advocate, the Weak one's friend: 30
To her, Calista prov'd her conduct nice,
And good Simplicius asks of her advice.
Sudden, she storms! she raves! You tip the wink,
But spare your censure; Silia does not drink.
All eyes may see from what the change arose,   35
All eyes may see — a Pimple on her nose.
  Papillia, wedded to her am'rous spark,
Sighs for the shades — "How charming is a Park!"
A Park is purchas'd, but the Fair he sees
All bath'd in tears — "Oh odious, odious Trees!"   40
  Ladies, like variegated Tulips, show,
'Tis to their Changes half their charms we owe;
Their happy Spots the nice admirer take,
Fine by defect, and delicately weak.
  'Twas thus Calypso once each heart alarm'd,   45
Aw'd without Virtue, without Beauty charm'd;
Her Tongue bewitch'd as odly as her Eyes,
Less Wit than Mimic, more a Wit than wise:
Strange graces still, and stranger flights she had,
Was just not ugly, and was just not mad;   50
Yet ne'er so sure our passion to create,
As when she touch'd the brink of all we hate.
  Narcissa's nature, tolerably mild,
To make a wash, would hardly stew a child,
Has ev'n been prov'd to grant a Lover's pray'r,   55
And paid a Tradesman once to make him stare,
Gave alms at Easter, in a Christian trim,
And made a Widow happy, for a whim.
Why then declare Good-nature is her scorn,
When 'tis by that alone she can be born?   60
Why pique all mortals, yet affect a name?
A fool to Pleasure, yet a slave to Fame:

22 *Spark* Fashionable young man.
23 *Locke* John Locke (1632–1704), philosopher, author of
An Essay Concerning Human Understanding (1690).
24 *Sappho* Pope's name for Lady Mary Wortley Montagu,
who was notoriously careless in her dress.
25 *toilet* 'dressing table'.
26 *Mask* 'masquerade'.
28 *fly-blow* 'deposit their eggs'.
29–40 'Contrarieties in the *Soft-natured*' (Pope).
31 *Calista* The guilty heroine of Nicholas Rowe's tragedy
The Fair Penitent (1703); *nice* 'refined'.

37 *Papillia* From Lat. *papilio*, 'butterfly'.
43 *nice* 'discerning'.
45–52 'Contrarieties in the *Cunning* and *Artful*' (Pope).
45 *Calypso* The nymph in Homer's *Odyssey* who kept the
shipwrecked Odysseus on her island for seven years.
The name means 'one who conceals' (Gk. *kalypso*).
53–68 'In the *Whimsical*' (Pope).
53 *Narcissa* Cf. Narcissus, the handsome youth of Greek
myth who fell in love with his own image.
54 *wash* 'cosmetic lotion'.
57 *trim* 'mode', 'guise'.

Now deep in Taylor and the Book of Martyrs,
Now drinking citron with his Grace and Chartres.
Now Conscience chills her, and now Passion burns;   65
And Atheism and Religion take their turns;
A very Heathen in the carnal part,
Yet still a sad, good Christian at her heart.
　　See Sin in State, majestically drunk,
Proud as a Peeress, prouder as a Punk;   70
Chaste to her Husband, frank to all beside,
A teeming Mistress, but a barren Bride.
What then? let Blood and Body bear the fault,
Her Head's untouch'd, that noble Seat of Thought:
Such this day's doctrine — in another fit   75
She sins with Poets thro' pure Love of Wit.
What has not fir'd her bosom or her brain?
Caesar and Tall-boy, Charles and Charlema'ne.
As Helluo, late Dictator of the Feast,
The Nose of Hautgout, and the Tip of Taste;   80
Critick'd your wine, and analyz'd your meat,
Yet on plain Pudding deign'd at-home to eat;
So Philomedé, lect'ring all mankind
On the soft Passion, and the Taste refin'd,
Th'Address, the Delicacy — stoops at once,   85
And makes her hearty meal upon a Dunce.
　　Flavia's a Wit, has too much sense to Pray,
To Toast our wants and wishes, is her way;
Nor asks of God, but of her Stars to give
The mighty blessing, "while we live, to live."   90
Then all for Death, that Opiate of the soul!
Lucretia's dagger, Rosamonda's bowl.
Say, what can cause such impotence of mind?
A Spark too fickle, or a Spouse too kind.
Wise Wretch! with Pleasures too refin'd to please,   95
With too much Spirit to be e'er at ease,
With too much Quickness ever to be taught,
With too much Thinking to have common Thought:
You purchase Pain with all that Joy can give,
And die of nothing but a Rage to live.   100

63 *Taylor* Bishop Jeremy Taylor (1613–67), author of the widely read *Holy Living* (1650) and *Holy Dying* (1651); *Book of Martyrs* John Foxe's popular Protestant martyrology (1563).

64 *citron* Brandy flavoured with lemon peel; *his Grace* Philip, Duke of Wharton (1698–1731), a political maverick and president of the Hell-Fire Club; *Chartres* Francis Charteris, a notorious fraudster and rake – see Swift, *Verses on the Death of Dr Swift*, 189n.

69–86 'In the *Lewd* and *Vicious*' (Pope).

70 *Punk* 'prostitute'.

71 *frank* 'free' (in a sexual sense).

78 *Tall-boy* The foolish lover in Richard Brome's play *A Jovial Crew* (1641); *Charles* The generic name for a

footman; *Charlema'ne* Charlemagne (747–814), Christian emperor and warrior.

79 *Helluo* Glutton (Lat.).

80 *Nose of Hautgout* 'connoisseur of piquant flavours'; *Tip* 'epitome'.

83 *Philomedé* 'Laughter-loving' (Gk.). Homer applied the epithet to Aphrodite, goddess of love.

85 *Address* 'manner of addressing others'.

87–100 'Contrarieties in the *Witty* and *Refin'd* (Pope).

92 *Lucretia* The Roman wife who committed suicide after being raped by Sextus, son of King Tarquin; *Rosamonda's bowl* Legend held that Rosamond Clifford, mistress of Henry II, was forced by his queen to drink poison.

Turn then from Wits; and look on Simo's Mate,
No Ass so meek, no Ass so obstinate:
Or her, that owns her Faults, but never mends,
Because she's honest, and the best of Friends:
Or her, whose life the Church and Scandal share,   105
For ever in a Passion, or a Pray'r:
Or her, who laughs at Hell, but (like her Grace)
Cries, "Ah! how charming, if there's no such place!
Or who in sweet vicissitude appears
Of Mirth and Opium, Ratafie and Tears,   110
The daily Anodyne, and nightly Draught,
To kill those foes to Fair ones, Time and Thought.
Woman and Fool are two hard things to hit,
For true No-meaning puzzles more than Wit.
  But what are these to great Atossa's mind?   115
Scarce once herself, by turns all Womankind!
Who, with herself, or others, from her birth
Finds all her life one warfare upon earth:
Shines, in exposing Knaves, and painting Fools,
Yet is, whate'er she hates and ridicules.   120
No Thought advances, but her Eddy Brain
Whisks it about, and down it goes again.
Full sixty years the World has been her Trade,
The wisest Fool much Time has ever made.
From loveless youth to unrespected age,   125
No Passion gratify'd except her Rage.
So much the Fury still out-ran the Wit,
The Pleasure miss'd her, and the Scandal hit.
Who breaks with her, provokes Revenge from Hell,
But he's a bolder man who dares be well: 130
Her ev'ry turn with Violence pursu'd,
Nor more a storm her Hate than Gratitude.
To that each Passion turns, or soon or late;
Love, if it makes her yield, must make her hate:
Superiors? death! and Equals? what a curse!   135
But an Inferior not dependant? worse.
Offend her, and she knows not to forgive;
Oblige her, and she'll hate you while you live:
But die, and she'll adore you — Then the Bust
And Temple rise — then fall again to dust.   140
Last night, her Lord was all that's good and great,
A Knave this morning, and his Will a Cheat.
Strange! by the Means defeated of the Ends,
By Spirit robb'd of Pow'r, by Warmth of Friends,
By Wealth of Follow'rs! without one distress   145
Sick of herself thro' very selfishness!
Atossa, curs'd with ev'ry granted pray'r,

---

101 *Simo* An old man in Terence's comedy *Andria*.
110 *Ratafie* Cherry brandy.
115–50 Atossa was once considered a sketch of Sarah,
 Duchess of Marlborough, but the original is now
 believed to have been the eccentric, strong-willed
 Katherine, Duchess of Buckinghamshire (1682?–1743),
an illegitimate daughter of James II. Atossa was the
 daughter of Cyrus, King of Persia.
121 *Eddy* 'swirling'.
130 *be well* 'get on well with her'.
139–40 The Duchess erected elaborate monuments to her
 husband and son.

Childless with all her Children, wants an Heir.
To Heirs unknown descends th'unguarded store
Or wanders, Heav'n-directed, to the Poor.   150
    Pictures like these, dear Madam, to design,
Asks no firm hand, and no unerring line;
Some wand'ring touches, some reflected light,
Some flying stroke alone can hit 'em right:
For how should equal Colours do the knack?   155
Chameleons who can paint in white and black?
    "Yet Cloe sure was form'd without a spot —
Nature in her then err'd not, but forgot.
"With ev'ry pleasing, ev'ry prudent part,
"Say, what can Cloe want? — She wants a Heart.   160
She speaks, behaves, and acts just as she ought;
But never, never, reach'd one gen'rous Thought.
Virtue she finds too painful an endeavour,
Content to dwell in Decencies for ever.
So very reasonable, so unmov'd,   165
As never yet to love, or to be lov'd.
She, while her Lover pants upon her breast,
Can mark the figures on an Indian chest;
And when she sees her Friend in deep despair,
Observes how much a Chintz exceeds Mohair.   170
Forbid it Heav'n, a Favour or a Debt
She e'er should cancel — but she may forget.
Safe is your Secret still in Cloe's ear;
But none of Cloe's shall you ever hear.
Of all her Dears she never slander'd one,   175
But cares not if a thousand are undone.
Would Cloe know if you're alive or dead?
She bids her Footman put it in her head.
Cloe is prudent — would you too be wise?
Then never break your heart when Cloe dies.   180
    One certain Portrait may (I grant) be seen,
Which Heav'n has varnish'd out, and made a *Queen:*
The same for ever! and describ'd by all
With Truth and Goodness, as with Crown and Ball:
Poets heap Virtues, Painters Gems at will,   185
And show their zeal, and hide their want of skill.
'Tis well — but, Artists! who can paint or write,
To draw the Naked is your true delight:
That Robe of Quality so struts and swells,

148–50 The Duchess's five children all died before her.
155 *knack* 'trick'.
156 The chameleon changes colour in order to blend with
    its surroundings.
157–80 These lines had originally appeared separately as
    'Cloe: a character' in 1738. Pope's model may have
    been Henrietta Howard, Countess of Suffolk
    (1681–1767). See Swift, *Verses on the Death of Dr Swift,*
    179n.

170 *Chintz* Colourfully printed cotton; *Mohair* A silk fabric
    which imitated the fine feel of genuine goat's-wool
    mohair.
182 *Queen* Queen Caroline (1683–1737), wife of George II,
    much disliked by Pope as an ally of Walpole and Lord
    Hervey.
183 *The same for ever* 'Semper eadem' (Lat.), the motto of
    Elizabeth I and Queen Anne.
184 *Ball* The orb, part of the royal regalia.

None see what Parts or Nature it conceals.   190
Th'exactest traits of Body or of Mind,
We owe to models of an humble kind.
If QUEENSBERRY to strip there's no compelling,
'Tis from a Handmaid we must take a Helen.
From Peer or Bishop 'tis no easy thing   195
To draw the man who loves his God, or King:
Alas! I copy (or my draught would fail)
From honest Mah'met, or plain Parson Hale.
    But grant, in Public Men sometimes are shown,
A Woman's seen in Private life alone: 200
Our bolder Talents in full light display'd,
Your Virtues open fairest in the shade.
Bred to disguise, in Public 'tis you hide;
There, none distinguish 'twixt your Shame or Pride,
Weakness or Delicacy; all so nice,   205
That each may seem a Virtue, or a Vice.
    In Men, we various Ruling Passions find,
In Women, two almost divide the kind;
Those, only fix'd, they first or last obey,
The Love of Pleasure, and the Love of Sway.   210
    That, Nature gives; and where the lesson taught
Is but to please, can Pleasure seem a fault?
Experience, this; by Man's oppression curst,
They seek the second not to lose the first.
    Men, some to Bus'ness, some to Pleasure take;   215
But ev'ry Woman is at heart a Rake:
Men, some to Quiet, some to public Strife;
But ev'ry Lady would be Queen for life.
    Yet mark the fate of a whole Sex of Queens!
Pow'r all their end, but Beauty all the means.   220
In Youth they conquer, with so wild a rage,
As leaves them scarce a Subject in their Age:
For foreign glory, foreign joy, they roam;
No thought of Peace or Happiness at home.
But Wisdom's Triumph is well-tim'd Retreat,   225
As hard a science to the Fair as Great!
Beauties, like Tyrants, old and friendless grown,
Yet hate Repose, and dread to be alone,
Worn out in public, weary ev'ry eye,
Nor leave one sigh behind them when they die.   230
    Pleasures the sex, as children Birds, pursue,
Still out of reach, yet never out of view,
Sure, if they catch, to spoil the Toy at most,
To covet flying, and regret when lost:

193 Catherine Hyde, Duchess of Queensberry (1700–77),
    Gay's patron, a remarkably beautiful woman.
194 Helen of Troy's beauty provoked the Trojan wars.
198 *Mah'met* George I's Turkish servant; *Parson Hale*
    Pope's friend Dr Stephen Hales (1677–1761), a curate
    and eminent physiologist.

205 *nice* 'subtle'.
211 *That* i.e. 'Love of Pleasure'.
213 *this* 'Love of Sway'.

At last, to follies Youth could scarce defend,   235
It grows their Age's prudence to pretend;
Asham'd to own they gave delight before,
Reduc'd to feign it, when they give no more:
As Hags hold Sabbaths, less for joy than spight,
So these their merry, miserable Night;   240
Still round and round the Ghosts of Beauty glide,
And haunt the places where their Honour dy'd.
    See how the World its Veterans rewards!
A Youth of Frolicks, an old Age of Cards,
Fair to no purpose, artful to no end,   245
Young without Lovers, old without a Friend,
A Fop their Passion, but their Prize a Sot,
Alive, ridiculous, and dead, forgot!
    Ah! Friend! to dazzle let the Vain design,
To raise the Thought, and touch the Heart, be thine!   250
That Charm shall grow, while what fatigues the Ring
Flaunts and goes down, an unregarded thing.
So when the Sun's broad beam has tir'd the sight,
All mild ascends the Moon's more sober light,
Serene in Virgin Modesty she shines,   255
And unobserv'd the glaring Orb declines.
    Oh! blest with Temper, whose unclouded ray
Can make to morrow chearful as to day;
She, who can love a Sister's charms, or hear
Sighs for a Daughter with unwounded ear;   260
She, who ne'er answers till a Husband cools,
Or, if she rules him, never shows she rules;
Charms by accepting, by submitting sways,
Yet has her humour most, when she obeys;
Let Fops or Fortune fly which way they will;   265
Disdains all loss of Tickets, or Codille;
Spleen, Vapours, or Small-pox, above them all,
And Mistress of herself, tho' China fall.
    And yet, believe me, good as well as ill,
Woman's at best a Contradiction still.   270
Heav'n, when it strives to polish all it can
Its last best work, but forms a softer Man;
Picks from each sex, to make the Fav'rite blest,
Your love of Pleasure, our desire of Rest,
Blends, in exception to all gen'ral rules,   275
Your Taste of Follies, with our Scorn of Fools,
Reserve with Frankness, Art with Truth ally'd,
Courage with Softness, Modesty with Pride,
Fix'd Principles, with Fancy ever new;

---

239 *Hags* Witches. Cf. Burns, *Tam o' Shanter*, 115–78.

249 'Advice for their true Interest' (Pope). Here Pope addresses Martha Blount.

251 *Ring* See *Rape of the Lock*, 1:44n.

257 *Temper* 'equanimity'.

260 *Daughter* Earlier editions read 'Sister' – an obvious allusion to Martha Blount's more attractive sister Teresa.

266 *Tickets* Lottery tickets; *Codille* See *Rape of the Lock*, 3:27n.

268 Cf. *Rape of the Lock*, 3:157–60.

269 'The Picture of an estimable Woman, with the best kinds of contrarieties' (Pope).

272 *last best work* In Genesis, Eve is created after Adam.

Shakes all together, and produces — You.   280
　　Be this a Woman's Fame: with this unblest,
Toasts live a scorn, and Queens may die a jest.
This Phœbus promis'd (I forget the year)
When those blue eyes first open'd on the sphere;
Ascendant Phœbus watch'd that hour with care,   285
Averted half your Parents simple Pray'r,
And gave you Beauty, but deny'd the Pelf
That buys your sex a Tyrant o'er itself.
The gen'rous God, who Wit and Gold refines,
And ripens Spirits as he ripens Mines,   290
Kept Dross for Duchesses, the world shall know it,
To you gave Sense, Good-humour, and a Poet.

282 *Toasts* Celebrated beauties.
283 *Phœbus* Apollo, Greek god of sun and poetry (cf.
　289–90); *forget the year* Cf. Swift, *Stella's Birthday,*
　1721, 18n.
285 *Ascendant* Rising, hence astrologically dominant.

287 *Pelf* 'wealth'. Martha's parents lacked the money to
　supply her with a dowry.
289–90 Cf. *Windsor-Forest*, 394n.
291 *Dross* 'discarded impurities'.

An Epistle to Dr Arbuthnot

Pope wrote the poem in response to the tide of criticism which had greeted his recent incursion into personal and topical satire. The immediate provocation, as he confessed in his 'Advertisement' to the epistle, was the *Verses Address'd to the Imitator of Horace* (1733) by Lady Mary Wortley Montagu and Lord Hervey (see headnote to that poem), who chose to attack 'in a very extraordinary manner, not only my Writings … but my *Person, Morals*, and *Family*'. The episode brought into the open an issue which Pope had discussed at length with his Scriblerian friend John Arbuthnot (1667–1735), fellow-wit and formerly physician to Queen Anne. Was it artistically legitimate, morally defensible, or even satirically effective, to attack individuals by name? Arbuthnot urged Pope to reach the 'General Vice' by continuing to wage war on corrupt individuals.

An Epistle to Dr Arbuthnot is thus a defence of Pope's recent career as a satirist as well as an apologia for his life, friends, family, moral character and poetic calling. The colloquial intimacy of the first-person voice lends an impression of coherence to a poem which in structural terms is composed of curiously disparate parts. A number of passages had been written earlier – the portrait of Addison as 'Atticus' (1715), lines 283–304 (1732), the concluding lines on Pope's mother's illness (1731) – and were incorporated into the text. As the 'Advertisement' says, 'This Paper is a Sort of Bill of Complaint, begun many years since, and drawn up by snatches, as the several Occasions offer'd'. Recent critics have tended

to stress the inconsistencies between the various 'selves' that Pope dramatizes in the poem. The voice of the comic opening is modelled on Horace's half-vexed, half-amused attempts to flee from his hangers-on in his *Satire*, 1:9, and the tone is one of playful exasperation (his targets are so obtuse as to be unredeemable). Yet the poem contains another, earnestly impassioned voice, which presents the satirist as the champion of truth and morality fighting for 'Virtue's better end'. The satiric energy of the 'Sporus' portrait is at odds with the calm domestic piety of the poem's closing scenes. There is incongruity also in Pope's oblique presentation of his relationship to the publishing world (which dominates this poem as it did *The Dunciad*). He pours scorn on scribblers and would-be poets who rack their invention to earn a living in 'Grubstreet'. Yet Pope too wrote for a living, and it was his commercial acumen that rendered him immune to the vagaries of the aristocratic patrons his poem satirizes.

An Epistle to Dr Arbuthnot was written in September 1734. Pope may have intended to publish it in the second collected volume of his works the following year, but Arbuthnot's mortal illness led him to rush it into print on 2 January 1735. The text printed below is that of vol. 2 of the 1739 octavo *Works*, which contains the final revisions Pope made to the text in his lifetime. They include a much expanded portrait of 'Sporus' in 305–33. We have been selective in our reproduction of Pope's extensive notes.

Shut, shut, the door, good John! fatigu'd I said,
Tye up the knocker, say I'm sick, I'm dead.
The Dog-star rages! nay tis past a doubt,
All Bedlam, or Parnassus, is let out:
Fire in each eye, and papers in each hand,   5
They rave, recite, and madden round the land.
    What walls can guard me, or what shades can hide?
They pierce my thickets, thro' my Grot they glide,
By land, by water, they renew the charge,
They stop the chariot, and they board the barge.   10
No place is sacred, not the Church is free,
Ev'n Sunday shines no Sabbath-day to me:
Then from the Mint walks forth the Man of rhyme,
Happy! to catch me, just at Dinner-time.
    Is there a Parson, much be-mus'd in beer,   15
A maudlin Poetess, a rhyming Peer,
A Clerk, foredoom'd his father's soul to cross,
Who pens a Stanza when he should *engross*?
Is there, who lock'd from ink and paper, scrawls
With desp'rate charcoal round his darken'd walls?   20
All fly to Twit'nam, and in humble strain
Apply to me, to keep them mad or vain.
Arthur, whose giddy son neglects the Laws,
Imputes to me and my damn'd works the cause:
Poor Cornus sees his frantic wife elope,   25
And curses Wit, and Poetry, and Pope.
    Friend to my Life! (which did not you prolong,
The world had wanted many an idle song)
What *Drop* or *Nostrum* can this plague remove?
Or which must end me, a Fool's wrath or love?   30
A dire dilemma! either way I'm sped,
If foes, they write, if friends, they read me dead.
Seiz'd and ty'd down to judge, how wretched I!
Who can't be silent, and who will not lye:
To laugh, were want of goodness and of grace,   35
And to be grave, exceeds all Pow'r of face.
I sit with sad civility, I read
With honest anguish, and an aching head;
And drop at last, but in unwilling ears,

1 *John* John Searle, Pope's manservant.
2 The doorknocker was muffled if someone inside the
   house had recently died. Cf. Gay, *Trivia*, 2:467–8.
3 *Dog-star* Sirius, associated with oppressive summer
   heat thought to cause madness.
4 *Bedlam* The Hospital of St Mary of Bethlehem, a
   lunatic hospital in Bishopsgate, London; *Parnassus* The
   Greek mountain sacred to Apollo, god of poetry.
8 *Grot* Pope's subterranean garden grotto.
13 *the Mint* A sanctuary for debtors.
16 *maudlin* 'sentimental'.

18 *engross* 'copy formal documents'.
23 *Arthur* Arthur Moore, MP, a businessman whose son
   James Moore Smythe was a minor poet and dramatist.
   The son refused to remove some of Pope's verses from
   his comedy *The Rival Modes* (1727) after Pope
   withdrew his permission to include them.
25 *Cornus* From Lat. *cornu*, 'horn', the symbol of a
   cuckold.
29 *Drop or Nostrum* Medicines.
31 *sped* 'finished'.

This saving counsel, "Keep your piece nine years."   40
   Nine years! cries he, who high in Drury-lane
Lull'd by soft Zephyrs thro' the broken pane,
Rymes 'ere he wakes, and prints before *Term* ends,
Oblig'd by hunger, and request of friends:
"The piece you think is incorrect? why take it,   45
I'm all submission, what you'd have it, make it."
   Three things another's modest wishes bound,
My Friendship, and a Prologue, and ten pound.
   Pitholeon sends to me: "You know his Grace,
"I want a Patron; ask him for a Place."   50
Pitholeon libell'd me — "but here's a letter
"Informs you, Sir, 'twas when he knew no better.
"Dare you refuse him? *Curl* invites to dine,
"He'll write a *Journal*, or he'll turn *Divine*."
   Bless me! a packet. — "'Tis a stranger sues,   55
"A Virgin Tragedy, an Orphan Muse."
If I dislike it, "Furies, death and rage!
If I approve, "Commend it to the Stage."
There (thank my stars) my whole commission ends,
The Play'rs and I are, luckily, no friends.   60
Fir'd that the house reject him, "'S'death I'll print it,
"And shame the fools — your int'rest, Sir, with Lintot."
Lintot, dull rogue! will think your price too much:
"Not Sir, if you revise it, and retouch."
All my demurs but double his attacks,   65
At last he whispers, "Do, and we go snacks.
Glad of a quarrel, strait I clap the door,
Sir, let me see your works and you no more.
   'Tis sung, when Midas' Ears began to spring,
(Midas, a sacred person and a King)   70
His very Minister who spy'd them first,
(Some say his Queen) was forc'd to speak, or burst.
And is not mine, my friend, a sorer case,
When ev'ry coxcomb perks them in my face?
"Good friend forbear! you deal in dang'rous things,   75
"I'd never name Queens, Ministers, or Kings;
"Keep close to Ears, and those let asses prick,

---

40 *nine years* The length of time Horace advised writers to keep their manuscripts before publication.

41 *Drury-lane* A disreputable red-light district.

42 *Zephyrs* 'breezes': a pastoral poeticism.

43 *Term* Booksellers preferred to publish during legal terms, when courts were in session and more people were in town.

49 *Pitholeon* 'The name taken from a foolish Poet of Rhodes, who pretended much to *Greek*' (Pope). Pope may be alluding both to Leonard Welsted (see 375n) and to Thomas Cooke, another enemy, who translated the work of several Greek poets. See 108n.

53 Edmund Curll (1675–1747), a notorious publisher who pirated Pope's works.

54 *Journal* A scandal sheet; *turn Divine* Cooke was involved in religious controversy and Welsted was writing a treatise on Providence.

61 *house* 'playhouse'.

62 Bernard Lintot (1675–1736), bookseller, who published many of Pope's works.

66 *go snacks* 'share the profits'.

69 *Midas* Legendary king of Phrygia. He arbitrated a musical contest between Apollo and Pan, and foolishly judged Pan superior. Apollo gave him asses' ears, which he tried to conceal under a headdress.

74 *coxcomb* 'upstart fool'.

77 *Keep close to Ears* i.e. whisper your criticisms.

   "'Tis nothing" — Nothing? if they bite and kick?
Out with it, *Dunciad*! let the secret pass,
That secret to each fool, that he's an Ass: 80
The truth once told (and wherefore should we lie?)
The Queen of Midas slept, and so may I.
     You think this cruel? take it for a rule,
No creature smarts so little as a fool.
Let peals of laughter, Codrus! round thee break,   85
Thou unconcern'd canst hear the mighty crack:
Pit, box, and gall'ry in convulsions hurl'd,
Thou stand'st unshook amidst a bursting world.
Who shames a Scribler? break one cobweb thro',
He spins the slight, self-pleasing thread anew: 90
Destroy his fib or sophistry, in vain,
The creature's at his dirty work again,
Thron'd in the centre of his thin designs,
Proud of a vast extent of flimzy lines!
Whom have I hurt? has Poet yet, or Peer,   95
Lost the arch'd eye-brow, or Parnassian sneer?
And has not Colly still his lord, and whore?
His butchers Henley, his free-masons Moor?
Does not one table Bavius still admit?
Still to one Bishop Philips seem a wit?   100
Still Sappho — "Hold! for God-sake — you'll offend,
"No Names — be calm — learn prudence of a friend:
"I too could write, and I am twice as tall;
"But foes like these! — One Flatt'rer's worse than all;
Of all mad creatures, if the learn'd are right,   105
It is the slaver kills, and not the bite.
A fool quite angry is quite innocent.
Alas! 'tis ten times worse when they *repent*.
    One dedicates in high heroic prose,
And ridicules beyond a hundred foes;   110
One from all Grubstreet will my fame defend,
And more abusive, calls himself my friend.
This prints my *Letters*, that expects a bribe,
And others roar aloud, "Subscribe, subscribe."

---

85 *Codrus* A fictitious poet mocked by Virgil and Juvenal.
89–92 Swift's *Battle of the Books* (1704) had used the spider to symbolize the modern hack writer.
91 *sophistry* 'fallacious reasoning'.
96 *Parnassian* 'loftily poetic', from Parnassus, the sacred mountain of poetry.
97 *Colly* Colley Cibber (1671–1757), who replaced Theobald as hero of *The Dunciad* (see headnote to that poem).
98 *Henley* The Reverend John Henley (1692–1756), a showman and preacher. In 1729 he had delivered a sermon on the butcher's calling. See Swift, *Verses on the Death of Dr Swift*, 278n; *Moor* James Moore Smythe was apparently a freemason. See 23n.
99 *Bavius* A poet who attacked Horace and Virgil. Nothing by him survives.

100 Ambrose Philips became secretary to the Bishop of Armagh.
101 *Sappho* Lady Mary Wortley Montagu.
103 *twice as tall* Pope was 4' 6" tall.
106 *slaver* 'saliva' (of a rabid dog).
108 Probably a reference to Thomas Cooke (1703–56), poet and translator, who offended Pope in 1725–6 then wrote a letter of apology which Pope refused to accept.
112 Perhaps an allusion to Aaron Hill (1685–1750), a writer and indefatigable correspondent of Pope, who satirized him in *The Dunciad*. Hill expressed his determination not to let this spoil their friendship.
114 *Subscribe* Publication by subscription was a common practice, one from which Pope made great profits.

There are, who to my person pay their court, 115
I cough like *Horace*, and tho' lean, am short,
Ammon's great son one shoulder had too high,
Such *Ovid*'s nose, and "Sir! you have an Eye —
Go on, obliging creatures, make me see
All that disgrac'd my Betters, met in me. 120
Say for my comfort, languishing in bed,
"Just so immortal *Maro* held his head:"
And when I die, be sure you let me know
Great *Homer* dy'd three thousand years ago.
    Why did I write? what sin to me unknown 125
Dipt me in ink, my parents, or my own?
As yet a child, nor yet a fool to fame,
I lisp'd in numbers, for the numbers came.
I left no calling for this idle trade,
No duty broke, no father disobey'd. 130
The Muse but serv'd to ease some friend, not Wife,
To help me thro' this long disease, my Life,
To second, ARBUTHNOT! thy Art and Care,
And teach, the Being you preserv'd, to bear.
    But why then publish? *Granville* the polite, 135
And knowing *Walsh*, would tell me I could write;
Well-natur'd *Garth* inflam'd with early praise,
And *Congreve* lov'd, and *Swift* endur'd my lays;
The courtly *Talbot*, *Somers*, *Sheffield* read,
Ev'n mitred *Rochester* would nod the head, 140
And *St. John*'s self (great *Dryden*'s friends before)
With open arms receiv'd one Poet more.
Happy my studies, when by these approv'd!
Happier their author, when by these belov'd!
From these the world will judge of men and books, 145
Not from the *Burnets*, *Oldmixons*, and *Cooks*.
    Soft were my numbers; who could take offence
While pure Description held the place of Sense?

117 *Ammon's great son* Alexander the Great.

122 *Maro* Virgil.

135–41 'These are persons to whose account the Author charges the publication of his first pieces: Persons with whom he was conversant (and he adds belov'd) at 16 or 17 years of age: an early period for such acquaintance' (Pope).

135 *Granville* See headnote to *Windsor-Forest*.

136 *Walsh* William Walsh (1663–1708), poet and critic, one of Pope's earliest friends.

137 *Garth* Sir Samuel Garth (1661–1719), poet and physican, author of the mock-heroic *Dispensary* (1699).

138 *Congreve* William Congreve (1670–1729), poet and author of the witty comedies *Love for Love* (1695) and *The Way of the World* (1700).

139–41 A roll-call illustrating the range of Pope's political sympathies: Charles Talbot, Duke of Shrewsbury (1660–1718), prominent Whig statesman and Lord Treasurer; John, Baron Somers (1651–1716), head of the Whig party during the early years of Anne's reign; John, Earl of Mulgrave and Duke of Buckingham (1648–1721), Tory statesman whose poems Pope published in 1723; Francis Atterbury (1662–1732), Bishop of Rochester and Dean of Westminster, a Jacobite exiled in 1723 for aiding a plot to reinstate the Pretender; and Henry St John, Viscount Bolingbroke (1678–1751), leading Tory statesman and Jacobite sympathizer. Dismissed in 1714 and attainted, he fled to serve the Pretender in France. After being pardoned he returned to Britain and helped form the opposition to Walpole. He was one of Pope's closest friends.

146 *Burnet* Sir Thomas Burnet (1694–1753), son of the famous Bishop. A follower of Addison, he had attacked Pope over his Homer translation; *Oldmixon* John Oldmixon (1673–1742), Whig writer and popular historian who wrote (in Pope's words) 'secret and scandalous Histor[ies]'. He had pirated three of Pope's poems in *Court Poems* (1717); *Cook* See 108n.

Like gentle *Fanny*'s was my flow'ry theme,
A painted mistress, or a purling stream.   150
Yet then did *Gildon* draw his venal quill;
I wish'd the man a dinner, and sate still.
Yet then did *Dennis* rave in furious fret;
I never answer'd, I was not in debt.
If want provok'd, or madness made them print,   155
I wag'd no war with *Bedlam* or the *Mint*.
      Did some more sober Critic come abroad?
If wrong, I smil'd; if right, I kiss'd the rod.
Pains, reading, study, are their just pretence,
And all they want is spirit, taste, and sense.   160
Comma's and points they set exactly right,
And 'twere a sin to rob them of their mite.
Yet ne'er one sprig of laurel grac'd these ribalds,
From slashing *Bentley* down to pidling *Tibalds*:
Each wight, who reads not, and but scans and spells,   165
Each Word-catcher, that lives on syllables,
Ev'n such small Critics some regard may claim,
Preserv'd in *Milton*'s or in *Shakespear*'s name.
Pretty! in amber to observe the forms
Of hairs, or straws, or dirt, or grubs, or worms!   170
The things, we know, are neither rich nor rare,
But wonder how the devil they got there?
      Were others angry? I excus'd them too;
Well might they rage, I gave them but their due.
A man's true merit 'tis not hard to find,   175
But each man's secret standard in his mind,
That Casting-weight pride adds to emptiness,
This, who can gratify? for who can *guess*?
The Bard whom pilfer'd Pastorals renown,
Who turns a Persian tale for half a crown,   180
Just writes to make his barrenness appear,
And strains from hard-bound brains, eight lines a year;
He, who still wanting, tho' he lives on theft,
Steals much, spends little, yet has nothing left:

149 *Fanny* Lord Hervey. See 305–33n. He wrote a number of romantic verse epistles.

150 As Pope notes, this line is taken from Addison's poem *A Letter from Italy*.

151 *Gildon* Chàrles Gildon (1665–1724), who attacked Pope in *A New Rehearsal* (1714) in part for the sexual suggestiveness of *The Rape of the Lock*. Pope thought Gildon had co-authored with Dennis the unpleasant *True Character of Mr Pope* (1716).

153 *Dennis* John Dennis (1657–1734), a distinguished Whig critic and champion of Milton's verse who helped popularize the taste for the sublime. Pope had mocked Dennis's irascible temper in *An Essay on Criticism* (1711), the start of a long conflict between them.

163 *laurel* The crown of poetic achievement.

164 *Bentley* Richard Bentley (1662–1742), Master of Trinity College, Cambridge. A classical scholar who

attempted to restore the 'true' text of *Paradise Lost* on the assumption that the blind Milton's verse had been mistranscribed during dictation. Bentley is Pope's archetypal pedant; *Tibalds* Lewis Theobald (1688–1744), scholar and playwright, who praised Pope's poetry but questioned his ability as a Shakespeare editor. Theobald produced his own edition in 1734. He is the hero of the 1728 *Dunciad*.

165 *wight* 'person': an archaism.

177 *Casting-weight* 'counterbalance'.

179 *The Bard* Ambrose Philips, whose *Pastorals* were initially admired more than Pope's. The 'pilfering' is perhaps from Spenser. See headnote to Gay, *The Shepherd's Week*.

180 *Persian tale* Philips translated *Les Mille et Une Nuits* of Petit de la Croix. He was purportedly paid half-a-crown per section, the going rate for prostitutes.

And he, who now to sense, now nonsense leaning,   185
Means not, but blunders round about a meaning:
And he, whose fustian's so sublimely bad,
It is not Poetry, but prose run mad:
All these, my modest Satire bad *translate*,
And own'd, that nine such Poets made a *Tate*.   190
How did they fume, and stamp, and roar, and chafe?
And swear, not *Addison* himself was safe.
   Peace to all such! but were there One whose fires
True Genius kindles, and fair Fame inspires;
Blest with each talent and each art to please,   195
And born to write, converse, and live with ease:
Shou'd such a man, too fond to rule alone,
Bear, like the *Turk*, no brother near the throne,
View him with scornful, yet with jealous eyes,
And hate for arts that caus'd himself to rise;   200
Damn with faint praise, assent with civil leer,
And without sneering, teach the rest to sneer;
Willing to wound, and yet afraid to strike,
Just hint a fault, and hesitate dislike;
Alike reserv'd to blame, or to commend,   205
A tim'rous foe, and a suspicious friend;
Dreading ev'n fools, by Flatterers besieg'd,
And so obliging, that he ne'er oblig'd;
Like *Cato*, give his little Senate laws,
And sit attentive to his own applause;   210
While Wits and Templers ev'ry sentence raise,
And wonder with a foolish face of praise —
Who but must laugh, if such a man there be?
Who would not weep, if *Atticus* were he!
   What tho' my Name stood rubric on the walls,   215
Or plaister'd posts, with claps in capitals?
Or smoking forth, a hundred hawkers load,
On wings of winds came flying all abroad?
I sought no homage from the Race that write;

---

187 *fustian* 'inflated language'.

189 *translate* 'make comprehensible', with a pun on the religious meaning, 'elevate to heaven'.

190 *Tate* Nahum Tate (1652–1715), poet and dramatist who succeeded Dryden as Poet Laureate in 1692. Pope described him as 'a cold writer, of no invention' (1728 *Dunciad*, 1:102n).

192 *Addison* Joseph Addison (1672–1719), the distinguished Whig critic, poet and essayist whose journal the *Spectator* helped create and cater for the new middle-class 'polite' reader. In 1713 Pope wrote the prologue for his tragedy *Cato*, but by 1714 the two men, never close, became veiled adversaries when Addison and his 'little senate' of Whig writers praised Ambrose Philips's pastorals above Pope's, and one of their number, Thomas Tickell, produced a rival translation of Homer's *Iliad*, I. The following portrait of Addison as

Atticus (see *Windsor-Forest*, 256n) was originally sketched in 1715.

198 *Turk* Addison in the *Spectator* had likened Pope to a jealous Eastern monarch who could brook no literary rivals. Here Pope returns the compliment. Cf. 220.

201 *Damn with faint praise* Cf. Wycherley's prologue to *The Plain Dealer* : 'And, with faint Praises, one another Damn'.

209 *Cato* Addison, who held court among his protégés in Button's coffee-house, is ironically likened to the hero of his own play. Pope's prologue to *Cato* had included the line 'While *Cato* gives his little Senate laws'.

211 *Templers* Law students.

215–16 Booksellers pasted up the title pages of their wares as posters ('claps'). Pope's publisher Lintot was fond of using red ('rubric') letters on the title pages.

I kept, like *Asian* Monarchs, from their sight: 220
Poems I heeded (now be-rym'd so long)
No more than Thou, great GEORGE! a birth-day song.
I ne'er with wits or witlings past my days,
To spread about the itch of verse and praise;
Nor like a puppy, daggled thro' the town,   225
To fetch and carry sing-song up and down;
Nor at Rehearsals sweat, and mouth'd, and cry'd,
With handkerchief and orange at my side;
But sick of fops, and poetry, and prate,
To *Bufo* left the whole *Castalian* state.   230
    Proud, as *Apollo* on his forked hill,
Sate full blown *Bufo*, puff'd by ev'ry quill;
Fed with soft Dedication all day long,
Horace and he went hand in hand in song.
His Library, (where busts of Poets dead   235
And a true *Pindar* stood without a head)
Receiv'd of wits an undistinguish'd race,
Who first his judgment ask'd, and then a place:
Much they extoll'd his pictures, much his seat,
And flatter'd ev'ry day, and some days eat: 240
Till grown more frugal in his riper days,
He pay'd some bards with port, and some with praise.
To some a dry rehearsal was assign'd,
And others (harder still) he paid in kind.
Dryden alone (what wonder?) came not nigh,   245
Dryden alone escap'd this judging eye:
But still the great have kindness in reserve,
He help'd to bury whom he help'd to starve.
    May some choice Patron bless each gray goose quill!
May ev'ry *Bavius* have his *Bufo* still!   250
So when a Statesman wants a day's defence,
Or Envy holds a whole week's war with sense,
Or simple Pride for Flatt'ry makes demands,
May dunce by dunce be whistled off my hands!
Blest be the *Great*! for those they take away,   255
And those they left me; For they left me GAY;
Left me to see neglected Genius bloom,
Neglected die, and tell it on his tomb:
Of all thy blameless life the sole return

---

222 GEORGE King George II, for whom Cibber and others produced effusive birthday odes.

225 *daggled* 'traipsed through mud'.

228 *handkerchief and orange* Two items often carried by theatre-goers: handkerchiefs for tears, and oranges to eat or throw at the actors.

230 *Bufo* The Latin word for toad, here applied to a puffed-up literary patron. 'Bufo' is modelled in part on Charles Montagu, Earl of Halifax (1661–1715), a generous patron of poets but, in Pope's words, 'a pretender to taste'. Pope's chief inspiration is George Bubb Dodington, Baron Melcombe (1691–1762), a plump, ostentatiously vulgar Whig politician who gave patronage to a number of writers; *Castalian* The sacred spring on Mount Parnassus, hence poetic inspiration.

231 *forked hill* The twin peaks on Parnassus.

236 *Pindar* (518–after 446 BC), Greek poet distinguished for his lofty odes. Pope elsewhere mocks the fashion for collecting headless antiquities.

239 *his seat* Dodington's estate at Eastbury, Dorset, was lavishly decorated.

258 *Neglected ... tomb* In fact Gay received considerable help from patrons such as the Duke and Duchess of Queensberry, and on his death was worth at least £6,000. Pope wrote his friend's epitaph. See headnote to Gay.

My Verse, and QUEENSB'RY weeping o'er thy urn!　　　　260
　　Oh let me live my own, and die so too!
("To live and die is all I have to do:)
Maintain a Poets dignity and ease,
And see what friends, and read what books I please:
Above a Patron, tho' I condescend　　　　265
Sometimes to call a Minister my friend.
I was not born for Courts or great affairs;
I pay my debts, believe, and say my pray'rs;
Can sleep without a Poem in my head,
Nor know, if *Dennis* be alive or dead.　　　　270
　　Why am I ask'd, what next shall see the light?
Heav'ns! was I born for nothing but to write?
Has Life no joys for me? or, (to be grave)
Have I no friend to serve, no soul to save?
"I found him close with *Swift* — Indeed? no doubt　　　　275
"(Cries prating *Balbus*) something will come out.
'Tis all in vain, deny it as I will.
"No, such a Genius never can lie still;
And then for mine obligingly mistakes
The first Lampoon Sir *Will.* or *Bubo* makes.　　　　280
Poor guiltless I! and can I chuse but smile,
When ev'ry Coxcomb knows me by my *Style*?
　　Curst be the verse, how well so'er it flow,
That tends to make one worthy man my foe,
Give Virtue scandal, Innocence a fear,　　　　285
Or from the soft-ey'd Virgin steal a tear!
But he who hurts a harmless neighbour's peace,
Insults fall'n worth, or Beauty in distress,
Who loves a Lye, lame slander helps about,
Who writes a Libel, or who copies out:　　　　290
That Fop, whose pride affects a patron's name,
Yet absent, wounds an author's honest fame:
Who can *your* merit *selfishly* approve,
And show the *sense* of it without the *love*;
Who has the vanity to call you friend,　　　　295
Yet wants the honour injur'd to defend;
Who tells whate'er you think, whate'er you say,
And, if he lye not must at least betray:
Who to the *Dean*, and *silver bell* can swear,
And sees at *Cannon's* what was never there;　　　　300
Who reads, but with a lust to misapply,
Make Satire a Lampoon, and Fiction Lye.
A lash like mine no honest man shall dread,
But all such babling blockheads in his stead.

261–2 Taken from Denham's poem *Of Prudence* (1668): 'Learn to live well, that thou may'st dye so too; / To live and dye is all we have to do'.

270 John Dennis died shortly before the poem was published.

276 *Balbus* A Roman lawyer, here possibly Viscount Dupplin, an able politican known for his incessant small talk.

280 *Sir Will.* Sir William Yonge (d. 1755), a prominent Walpole supporter notorious for his dishonesty and superficial eloquence.

299–300 A reference to the identification of Pope's 'Timon' with the Duke of Chandos. See *Epistle to Burlington* headnote and lines 141 and 149.

Let *Sporus* tremble — "What? that thing of silk,   305
"*Sporus*, that mere white curd of Ass's milk?
"Satire or sense alas! can *Sporus* feel?
"Who breaks a butterfly upon a wheel?"
Yet let me flap this bug with gilded wings,
This painted child of dirt, that stinks and stings;   310
Whose buzz the witty and the fair annoys,
Yet wit ne'er tastes, and beauty ne'er enjoys:
So well-bred spaniels civilly delight
In mumbling of the game they dare not bite.
Eternal smiles his emptiness betray,   315
As shallow streams run dimpling all the way.
Whether in florid impotence he speaks,
And, as the prompter breathes, the puppet squeaks,
Or at the ear of *Eve*, familiar Toad,
Half froth, half venom, spits himself abroad,   320
In puns, or politicks, or tales, or lyes,
Or spite, or smut, or rymes, or blasphemies.
His wit all see-saw, between *that* and *this*,
Now high, now low, now master up, now miss,
And he himself one vile Antithesis.   325
Amphibious thing! that acting either part,
The trifling head, or the corrupted heart,
Fop at the toilet, flatt'rer at the board,
Now trips a Lady, and now struts a Lord.
Eve's tempter thus the Rabbins have exprest,   330
A Cherub's face, a reptile all the rest,
Beauty that shocks you, parts that none will trust,
Wit that can creep, and pride that licks the dust.
    Not Fortune's worshipper, nor Fashion's fool,
Not Lucre's madman, nor Ambition's tool,   335
Not proud, nor servile; be one Poet's praise,
That, if he pleas'd, he pleas'd by manly ways;
That Flatt'ry, ev'n to Kings, he held a shame,
And thought a Lye in verse or prose the same.

305–33 In the poem's original version this satirical portrait of the bisexual Lord Hervey was much shorter. The name was originally 'Paris', but 'Sporus' (a boy the emperor Nero kept for sexual gratification) took Pope's accusation further. John, Baron Hervey of Ickworth (1696–1743), fathered eight children with his wife, and he also competed with the Prince of Wales for the favours of Anne Vane. But his high voice and effeminate appearance called his sexual orientation into question, as did his passionate relationship with Stephen Fox, the young Lord Ilchester. Hervey was a Walpolian Court Whig. Appointed Chamberlain in 1730, he was Queen Caroline's confidant and Walpole's most trusted agent in the palace.
306 Asses' milk was often drunk by invalids, including Hervey and Pope.

314 *mumbling* Chewing softly with toothless gums. According to the Duchess of Marlborough, Hervey had 'not a tooth in his head'.
318 *prompter* Walpole.
319 Pope's note directs us to *Paradise Lost*, 4:800, which describes Satan 'Squat like a toad, close at the ear of Eve'. See also Lady Mary Wortley Montagu, *Verses Address'd to the Imitator of Horace*, 52–5.
328 *toilet* 'dressing table'; *board* 'sideboard', i.e. at dinner.
330 *Rabbins* Jewish doctrinal authorities.
333 *licks the dust* The fate of Milton's devils, *Paradise Lost*, 10:564–70.
335 *Lucre* 'monetary gain'.

That not in Fancy's maze he wander'd long,   340
But stoop'd to Truth, and moraliz'd his song:
That not for Fame, but Virtue's better end,
He stood the furious foe, the timid friend,
The damning critic, half approving wit,
The coxcomb hit, or fearing to be hit;   345
Laugh'd at the loss of friends he never had,
The dull, the proud, the wicked, and the mad;
The distant threats of vengeance on his head,
The blow unfelt, the tear he never shed;
The tale reviv'd, the lye so oft o'erthrown,   350
Th' imputed trash, and dulness not his own;
The morals blacken'd when the writings scape,
The libel'd person, and the pictur'd shape;
Abuse, on all he lov'd, or lov'd him, spread,
A friend in exile, or a father, dead;   355
The whisper, that to greatness still too near,
Perhaps, yet vibrates on his SOVEREIGN's ear —
Welcome for thee, fair Virtue! all the past:
For thee, fair Virtue! welcome ev'n the *last!*
    "But why insult the poor, affront the great?"   360
A knave's a knave, to me, in ev'ry state:
Alike my scorn, if he succeed or fail,
Sporus at court, or *Japhet* in a jayl,
A hireling scribbler, or a hireling peer,
Knight of the post corrupt, or of the shire;   365
If on a Pillory, or near a Throne,
He gain his Prince's ear, or lose his own.
    Yet soft by nature, more a dupe than wit,
Sapho can tell you how this man was bit:
This dreaded Sat'rist *Dennis* will confess   370
Foe to his pride, but friend to his distress:
So humble, he has knock'd at *Tibbald*'s door,
Has drunk with *Cibber*, nay has rhym'd for *Moor.*
Full ten years slander'd, did he once reply?
Three thousand suns went down on *Welsted*'s lye.   375
To please a Mistress one aspers'd his life;
He lash'd him not, but let her be his wife:

---

341 *stoop'd* 'swooped' (a hawking term).

343 *stood* 'withstood'.

349 *The blow unfelt* In 1728 an anonymous pamphlet *A Popp upon Pope*, sometimes attributed to Lady Mary Wortley Montagu, described a fictitious whipping inflicted on Pope.

351 *trash, and dulness* 'such as profane *Psalms, Court-Poems,* and other scandalous things, printed in his Name by *Curl* and others' (Pope).

353 *pictur'd shape* An illustration to the scurrilous *Pope Alexander's Supremacy* (1729) depicted him as a hunchbacked ape with a human face.

355 *friend in exile* Atterbury. See 139–41n.

363 *Japhet* Japhet Crook, a notorious forger, who in 1731 was punished by being pilloried and having his ears cut off.

365 *Knight … shire* i.e. a perjurer ('post-knight') or MP for the county ('Knight of the Shire').

370–1 In 1731 Pope helped promote a subscription edition of Dennis's works when the critic was old, ill and poor.

373 *Moor* See 23n.

375 *Welsted* Leonard Welsted (1688–1747), poet and translator of Longinus. In one satire he hinted that Pope had caused a woman's death.

Let *Budgel* charge low *Grubstreet* on his quill,
And write whate'er he pleas'd, except his will;
Let the two *Curls* of Town and Court, abuse   380
His father, mother, body, soul, and muse.
Yet why? that Father held it for a rule,
It was a sin to call our neighbour fool:
That harmless Mother thought no wife a whore:
Hear this, and spare his family, *James Moore!*   385
Unspotted names, and memorable long!
If there be force in Virtue, or in Song.
    Of gentle blood (part shed in Honour's cause,
While yet in *Britain* Honour had applause)
Each parent sprung — "What fortune, pray? —
    Their own,   390
And better got, than *Bestia*'s from the throne.
Born to no Pride, inheriting no Strife,
Nor marrying Discord in a noble wife,
Stranger to civil and religious rage,
The good man walk'd innoxious thro' his age.   395
No Courts he saw, no suits would ever try,
Nor dar'd an Oath, nor hazarded a Lye.
Un-learn'd, he knew no schoolman's subtile art,
No language, but the language of the heart.
By Nature honest, by Experience wise,   400
Healthy by temp'rance, and by exercise;
His life, tho' long, to sickness past unknown,
His death was instant, and without a groan.
O grant me, thus to live, and thus to die!
Who sprung from Kings shall know less joy than I.   405
    O Friend! may each domestick bliss be thine!
Be no unpleasing Melancholy mine:
Me, let the tender office long engage,
To rock the cradle of reposing Age,
With lenient arts extend a Mother's breath,   410
Make Languor smile, and smooth the bed of Death,
Explore the thought, explain the asking eye,
And keep a while one parent from the sky!
On cares like these if length of days attend,
May heav'n, to bless those days, preserve my Friend.   415
Preserve him social, chearful, and serene,
And just as rich as when he serv'd a QUEEN.
Whether that blessing be deny'd or giv'n,
Thus far was right, the rest belongs to Heav'n.

378 *Budgel* Eustace Budgell (1686–1737), Addison's cousin and a minor writer, who was accused of forging a will in his own favour. Budgell attacked Pope, believing him responsible for his exposure in the *Grub-Street Journal*.
380 *two Curls* The second is Lord Hervey.
381 'Mr. *Pope*'s Father was of a Gentleman's Family in Oxfordshire, the Head of which was the Earl of *Downe* …' (Pope). Pope's extended note is meant to challenge

Lady Mary Wortley Montagu, *Verses Address'd to the Imitator of Horace*, 20, but this paternal ancestry was wishful thinking.
391 *Bestia* A corrupt Roman consul who took bribes.
395 *good man* A generalized ideal embodied in Pope's father, Alexander Sr (1646–1717).
410 *lenient* 'soothing'; *Mother* Edith Pope (1643–1733) died eighteen months before publication of this poem.

The Dunciad, 1743

The publication of Pope's three-book *Dunciad* on 18 May 1728 stirred up a hornet's nest. Angry authors besieged the bookseller, anxious to discover whether Pope had satirized them in his new 'Poem of Dulness'. Rumours of its imminent publication had long been circulating. The previous month Pope had tested the waters of controversy with *Peri Bathous: Or the Art of Sinking in Poetry*, an ironic prose treatise on the absurd and bathetic in modern poetry, lavishly illustrated with appropriate quotations from current authors and critics. Both works were motivated in part by Pope's desire to revenge himself for fifteen years of attacks on his poetry, religion, politics, friendships and physical deformity.

The decline in cultural standards over which Pope's goddess Dulness presides expresses a wider political and spiritual malaise. *The Dunciad* appeared the year after George II had succeeded George I, thus lending a piquancy to 1:6 ('Still Dunce the second reigns like Dunce the first'), a line rendered even more audacious by Pope's gift of a copy of the 1729 revised version of the poem, *The Dunciad Variorum*, to George II. The King's neglect to read (or failure to understand) the work caused him famously to pronounce Pope 'a very honest man'. Neither George expressed any interest in literature, and George II's love of theatrical farce and spectacle helped set a new trend in the London theatres for the kind of mindless fare that had previously entertained fairground crowds.

Even before the poem first appeared, Pope had in mind further revisions. *The Dunciad Variorum* added a hundred lines, notably an expanded conclusion to Book 3 prophesying the coming of darkness and chaos. The poem was also given a weighty textual apparatus of pedantic footnotes, commentaries, prefaces, appendices and addenda which comically threaten to overwhelm the text itself. *The Dunciad* remained in this form until 1741, when Pope decided to produce a fourth book (published as *The New Dunciad*, 1742) to fulfil his prophecy of universal darkness. The intervening years had witnessed the ascendancy of Robert Walpole, George II's chief minister (whom Swift dubbed 'Bob, the Poet's Foe'), and this final book describes the viral spread of dullness through Britain's institutional bloodstream: schools, universities, the Church and the Court. The vision corresponds to the opposition's view of the nation in a state of terminal decline. In October 1743 a full and final version, *The Dunciad in Four Books*, was published. This incorporated the new fourth book alongside an extensive revision of the first three. The most notable change, however, was the dethronement as the poem's hero of Lewis Theobald, pantomime writer turned Shakespeare scholar, and the elevation in his place of Colley Cibber (1671–1757), actor, theatre manager and playwright. Although Pope and Cibber had recently crossed swords (in 1742 Cibber had ridiculed Pope in an unpleasant satire), the motive for his inclusion was not entirely personal. Cibber, a popular showman and a monster of egotism, had been appointed the nation's Poet Laureate in 1729, a perfect symbol for Pope of the debasement and commercialization of culture under the Hanoverian regime.

Book 1 describes Cibber's invocation of Dulness, the goddess's descent, and her proclamation that this new cultural hero will extend her reign to every part of the kingdom. Book 2 describes the 'heroic' games which celebrate the event among Grub Street authors (such as urinating, mud-diving, tickling and noise-making). In Book 3 Cibber is carried into the underworld where his spiritual father, Elkanah Settle, displays the past and prophesies the triumphant progress of Dulness from the City to the West End (the traditional route of the Lord Mayor's procession). Book 4 enacts the total victory of Dulness, who holds court to her followers in all walks of life. She summons the nations to her throne, and after conferring degrees and delivering her address the goddess yawns – and swallows everything in her vortex.

The Dunciad differs from the earlier *Rape of the Lock* in its use of the classical past. Whereas *The Rape* is a complete epic poem in miniature, the allusions in *The Dunciad* (perhaps appropriately for a poem concerned with a fragmenting civilization) are less extensive and coherent. The most frequently invoked epic poem is Virgil's *Aeneid*. Both poems treat of 'foundation' myths, but whereas *The Aeneid* tells of the founding of Rome from the ruins of Troy, *The Dunciad* charts the final establishment of Dulness's kingdom. In Pope's poem the Millennium has turned to Apocalypse, a theme heightened by the ironic allusions to a more recent epic, *Paradise Lost*, which in deploring the loss of one kingdom still holds out hope of a providential future. But in *The Dunciad* Dulness's 'uncreating word' brings universal darkness.

Yet, for all its prognostications of cultural decline, *The Dunciad* remains not only a comic, but also a highly creative and exuberant poem. Pope's Dulness is very far from dull (see his note to line 15), and this is what makes her so dangerous. She is indeed wildly creative, but her effects can be cheap and flashy. The fact that some modern criticism sees the poem as an imaginative celebration of her world suggests Pope's prophecy has been fulfilled, and that vivid pictures, shameless hype and easy popularity now take priority over sense and substance. In a world ruled by immediate universal information and infinitely exploitable images, we may be closer to Pope's cultural apocalypse than ever.

Conversely, the poem may make us suspicious of any literary canon, however idealistic, which needs to work by exclusion. Recent criticism has embraced a popular global culture as against a restrictive and traditional 'elite', and it has found the breaking down of cultural boundaries a wholly positive development.

To set out these two contrasting emphases is to suggest how the poem remains at the centre of a debate. In the two centuries after the poem's publication, the cultural values articulated in *The Dunciad* came to acquire an almost unquestioned

authority, and the literary canon tended to exclude those writers Pope mocked. But it is no accident that nearly all his dunces were Court Whigs or dissenters, and modern readers should be mindful that a Pope who could include a Daniel Defoe among his catalogue of duncess might be equally wrong about a John Dennis, an Aaron Hill, an Eliza Haywood or a Margaret Cavendish. On the other hand, the creative arts and media of today do offer striking duncely parallels...

The following text is taken from *The Dunciad in Four Books* (1743). A selection of Pope's notes is given in italics.

BOOK I

The Mighty Mother, and her Son who brings
The Smithfield Muses to the ear of Kings,
I sing. Say you, her instruments the Great!
Call'd to this work by Dulness, Jove, and Fate;
You by whose care, in vain decry'd and curst,   5
Still Dunce the second reigns like Dunce the first;
Say how the Goddess bade Britannia sleep,
And pour'd her Spirit o'er the land and deep.

    In eldest time, e'er mortals writ or read,
E'er Pallas issu'd from the Thund'rer's head,   10
Dulness o'er all possess'd her ancient right,
Daughter of Chaos and eternal Night:
Fate in their dotage this fair Ideot gave,
Gross as her sire, and as her mother grave,
Laborious, heavy, busy, bold, and blind,   15
She rul'd, in native Anarchy, the mind.

    Still her old Empire to restore she tries,
For, born a Goddess, Dulness never dies.
    O Thou! whatever title please thine ear,

1 The goddess Dulness and her chosen 'son', Colley Cibber. Pope suggests her kinship with the mysterious Cybele, or Magna Mater ('great mother'), worshipped in Greece and Rome as a protective fertility goddess. Her priests were self-castrated eunuchs, and her worshippers practised prophetic rapture.

2 *Smithfield* The London meat-market, location of the annual St Bartholomew's Fair. Pope's note complains that lowbrow fairground entertainments, 'formerly agreeable only to the taste of the Rabble', have now become 'the reigning pleasures of the Court and Town'.

6 *Dunce the second* Pope alludes to the series of untalented Poets Laureate (Shadwell, Tate, Eusden, Cibber), and by implication to the Hanoverian succession. George II had succeeded George I in 1727.

10 *Pallas* Athena, the Greek goddess of wisdom who sprang fully grown from the head of Zeus 'the Thund'rer'.

12 Cf. 'where eldest Night / And Chaos, ancestors of Nature, hold / Eternal anarchy' (*Paradise Lost*, 2:894–6).

15 *Dulness here is not to be taken contractedly for mere Stupidity, but in the enlarged sense of the word, for all Slowness of Apprehension, Shortness of Sight, or imperfect Sense of things. It includes (as we see by the Poet's own words) Labour, Industry, and some degree of Activity and Boldness: a ruling principle not inert, but turning topsyturvy the Understanding, and inducing an Anarchy or confused State of Mind.*

Dean, Drapier, Bickerstaff, or Gulliver!   20
Whether thou chuse Cervantes' serious air,
Or laugh and shake in Rab'lais' easy chair,
Or praise the Court, or magnify Mankind,
Or thy griev'd Country's copper chains unbind;
From thy Bœotia tho' her Pow'r retires,   25
Mourn not, my SWIFT, at ought our Realm acquires,
Here pleas'd behold her mighty wings out-spread
To hatch a new Saturnian age of Lead.
   Close to those walls where Folly holds her throne,
And laughs to think Monroe would take her down,   30
Where o'er the gates, by his fam'd father's hand
Great Cibber's brazen, brainless brothers stand;
One Cell there is, conceal'd from vulgar eye,
The Cave of Poverty and Poetry.
Keen, hollow winds howl thro' the bleak recess,   35
Emblem of Music caus'd by Emptiness.
Hence Bards, like Proteus long in vain ty'd down,
Escape in Monsters, and amaze the town.
Hence Miscellanies spring, the weekly boast
Of Curl's chaste press, and Lintot's rubric post: 40
Hence hymning Tyburn's elegiac lines,
Hence Journals, Medleys, Merc'ries, Magazines:
Sepulchral Lyes, our holy walls to grace,
And New-year Odes, and all the Grub-street race.
   In clouded Majesty here Dulness shone;   45
Four guardian Virtues, round, support her throne:

---

20 Names and titles, real and fictional, used by Swift. See Swift, biographical headnote.
21 Miguel de Cervantes (1547–1616), Spanish novelist, author of *Don Quixote*.
22 François Rabelais (?1494–?1553), earthy satirist, creator of the popular giants Gargantua and Pantagruel.
24 *copper chains* Swift's defence of Irish rights in the affair of 'Wood's Halfpence'. See Swift headnote and *Verses on the Death of Dr Swift*, 408–14n.
25 *Bœotia* A region of ancient Greece with proverbially stupid inhabitants.
28 In Rome, the rule of Saturn had been associated with the lost Golden Age.
29–30 *those walls* Bethlehem, or 'Bedlam', lunatic hospital (see *Epistle to Dr Arbuthnot*, 4n), close to Grub Street. James Monro was hospital physician.
31–2 The sculptor Caius Gabriel Cibber, father of Colley, was responsible for the two statues of lunatics over the gates of Bedlam.
37 *Proteus* A Greek god who escaped questioning by assuming different shapes. [*B*]*y* Proteus *must certainly be meant a hacknied Town scribler; and by his Transformations, the various disguises such a one assumes, to elude the pursuit of his irreconcilable enemy, the Bailiff.*
39 *Miscellanies* Poetry anthologies.

40 *Two Booksellers ... The former was fined by the Court of King's Bench for publishing obscene books; the latter usually adorned his shop with titles in red letters.* Edmund Curll (1675–1747) specialized in scandalous 'memoirs' and biographies, and in pirating the works of famous authors such as Pope and Swift. Bernard Lintot (1675–1736) was Pope's publisher. See *Epistle to Dr Arbuthnot*, 215–16n.
41 *Tyburn* Tyburn Hill, traditional site of public executions. Publishers did brisk business in criminals' 'confessions' and elegies on their deaths.
42 Journal titles.
43 *Sepulchral Lyes Is a just satyr on the Flatteries and Falshoods admitted to be inscribed on the walls of Churches, in Epitaphs.*
44 *New-year Odes Made by the Poet Laureate ... to be sung at Court on every New-year's day, the words of which are happily drowned in the voices and instruments.* Cibber's odes were widely ridiculed by opposition wits.
45 *In clouded Majesty* Cf. 'the Moon / Rising in clouded Majesty' (*Paradise Lost*, 4:606–7).
46 *guardian Virtues* The four traditional cardinal virtues: fortitude, temperance, prudence and justice. They featured in the pageantry of the Lord Mayor's Day.

Fierce champion Fortitude, that knows no fears
Of hisses, blows, or want, or loss of ears:
Calm Temperance, whose blessings those partake
Who hunger, and who thirst for scribling sake: 50
Prudence, whose glass presents th'approaching jayl:
Poetic Justice, with her lifted scale,
Where, in nice balance, truth with gold she weighs,
And solid pudding against empty praise.
Here she beholds the Chaos dark and deep,   55
Where nameless Somethings in their causes sleep,
'Till genial Jacob, or a warm Third day,
Call forth each mass, a Poem, or a Play:
How hints, like spawn, scarce quick in embryo lie,
How new-born nonsense first is taught to cry,   60
Maggots half-form'd in rhyme exactly meet,
And learn to crawl upon poetic feet.
Here one poor word an hundred clenches makes,
And ductile dulness new meanders takes;
There motley Images her fancy strike,   65
Figures ill pair'd, and Similies unlike.
She sees a Mob of Metaphors advance,
Pleas'd with the madness of the mazy dance:
How Tragedy and Comedy embrace;
How Farce and Epic get a jumbled race;   70
How Time himself stands still at her command,
Realms shift their place, and Ocean turns to land.
Here gay Description Ægypt glads with show'rs,
Or gives to Zembla fruits, to Barca flow'rs;
Glitt'ring with ice here hoary hills are seen,   75
There painted vallies of eternal green,
In cold December fragrant chaplets blow,
And heavy harvests nod beneath the snow.
All these, and more, the cloud-compelling Queen
Beholds thro' fogs, that magnify the scene.   80
She, tinsel'd o'er in robes of varying hues,
With self-applause her wild creation views;
Sees momentary monsters rise and fall,
And with her own fools-colours gilds them all.

48 *loss of ears* The common punishment for perjury, sedition or forgery.
50 Cf. Matthew, 5:6, 'Blessed are they which do hunger and thirst after righteousness: for they shall be filled'. In *1728* this line provoked accusations of blasphemy.
51–2 Prudence was traditionally pictured with a mirror, Justice with a pair of scales.
55–6 *That is to say, unformed things, which are either made into Poems or Plays, as the Booksellers or the Players bid most.*
57 *genial* 'life-giving'; *Jacob* Jacob Tonson (1656–1737), publisher; *Third day* The playwright's benefit night.
59 *quick* 'living'.
61 *Maggots* Also means 'whimsical fancies'.
63 *clenches* 'puns'.

64 *ductile* 'easily spun out'.
69–72 *Allude to the transgressions of the* Unities *in the Plays of such poets. For the miracles wrought upon* Time *and* Place, *and the mixture of Tragedy and Comedy, Farce and Epic.*
73 *In the lower Ægypt Rain is of no use, the overflowing of the Nile being sufficient to impregnate the soil. – These six verses represent the Inconsistencies in the descriptions of poets, who heap together all glittering and gawdy images, though incompatible in one season, or in one scene.*
74 *Zembla* Nova Zembla, a frozen Arctic island; *Barca* The Libyan desert.
77 *chaplets* Garlands of flowers.
79 *cloud-compelling* The Homeric epithet for Zeus.

'Twas on the day, when * * rich and grave,   85
Like Cimon, triumph'd both on land and wave:
(Pomps without guilt, of bloodless swords and maces,
Glad chains, warm furs, broad banners, and broad faces)
Now Night descending, the proud scene was o'er,
But liv'd, in Settle's numbers, one day more.   90
Now May'rs and Shrieves all hush'd and satiate lay,
Yet eat, in dreams, the custard of the day;
While pensive Poets painful vigils keep,
Sleepless themselves, to give their readers sleep.
Much to the mindful Queen the feast recalls   95
What City Swans once sung within the walls;
Much she revolves their arts, their ancient praise,
And sure succession down from Heywood's days.
She saw, with joy, the line immortal run,
Each sire imprest and glaring in his son: 100
So watchful Bruin forms, with plastic care,
Each growing lump, and brings it to a Bear.
She saw old Pryn in restless Daniel shine,
And Eusden eke out Blackmore's endless line;
She saw slow Philips creep like Tate's poor page,   105
And all the mighty Mad in Dennis rage.
    In each she marks her Image full exprest,
But chief in BAYS's monster-breeding breast;
Bays, form'd by nature Stage and Town to bless,
And act, and be, a Coxcomb with success.   110
Dulness with transport eyes the lively Dunce,
Remembring she herself was Pertness once.
Now (shame to Fortune!) an ill Run at Play
Blank'd his bold visage, and a thin Third day:
Swearing and supperless the Hero sate,   115

85 * * 'Thorold' (Sir George Thorold, Lord Mayor of
    London in 1719).
86 *The Procession of a Lord Mayor is made partly by land,
    and partly by water. – Cimon, the famous Athenian
    General, obtained a victory by sea, and another by land,
    on the same day, over the Persians and Barbarians.*
90 *Settle* Elkanah Settle (1648–1724). *Settle was poet to the
    City of London. His office was to compose yearly
    panegyrics upon the Lord Mayors, and verses to be spoken
    in the Pageants.*
91 *Shrieves* 'sheriffs'.
98 *Heywood* Thomas Heywood (d. 1641), author of Lord
    Mayor's pageants. Pope's note here confuses him with
    John Heywood (?1497–?1580), writer of comic
    interludes.
101 *Bruin* 'bear'. Bears supposedly licked their new-born
    offspring into shape.
103 William Prynne (1600–69), Puritan pamphleteer, was
    pilloried for writing *Histriomastix* (1633) against
    Charles I, and had his ears cut off; Daniel Defoe
    (1660–1731), dissenting pamphleteer and novelist, was

    pilloried for his ironic *The Shortest Way with the
    Dissenters* (1702).
104 *Eusden* Laurence Eusden (1688–1730), Poet Laureate
    from 1718 to his death; *Blackmore* Sir Richard
    Blackmore (1654–1729), Whig city poet and physician
    to William III and Anne. He was best known for a
    series of long wooden epics mocked by Pope and his
    friends.
105 *Philips* Ambrose Philips (see Philips, biographical
    headnote); *Tate* Nahum Tate (see *Epistle to Dr
    Arbuthnot*, 190n).
106 *Dennis* John Dennis (see *Epistle to Dr Arbuthnot*, 153n).
    Pope and Swift's *The Narrative of Dr Robert Norris*
    (1713) satirized Dennis as a raving madman.
108 *BAYS* i.e. Cibber, who as Poet Laureate wore the crown
    of bay laurel. The name suggests his descent from the
    inept playwright Bayes in Buckingham's *The Rehearsal*
    (1672), a role often played by Cibber.
110 Cibber was especially talented in comic roles such as
    the coxcomb ('cocky fool').
114 *Blank'd* 'made pale', 'put out of countenance'.

Blasphem'd his Gods, the Dice, and damn'd his Fate.
Then gnaw'd his pen, then dash'd it on the ground,
Sinking from thought to thought, a vast profound!
Plung'd for his sense, but found no bottom there,
Yet wrote and flounder'd on, in mere despair.   120
Round him much Embryo, much Abortion lay,
Much future Ode, and abdicated Play;
Nonsense precipitate, like running Lead,
That slip'd thro' Cracks and Zig-zags of the Head;
All that on Folly Frenzy could beget,   125
Fruits of dull Heat, and Sooterkins of Wit.
Next, o'er his Books his eyes began to roll,
In pleasing memory of all he stole,
How here he sipp'd, how there he plunder'd snug
And suck'd all o'er, like an industrious Bug.   130
Here lay poor Fletcher's half-eat scenes, and here
The Frippery of crucify'd Moliere;
There hapless Shakespear, yet of Tibbald sore,
Wish'd he had blotted for himself before.
The rest on Out-side merit but presume,   135
Or serve (like other Fools) to fill a room;
Such with their shelves as due proportion hold,
Or their fond Parents drest in red and gold;
Or where the pictures for the page attone,
And Quarles is sav'd by Beauties not his own.   140
Here swells the shelf with Ogilby the great;
There, stamp'd with arms, Newcastle shines complete:
Here all his suff'ring brotherhood retire,
And 'scape the martyrdom of jakes and fire:
A Gothic Library! of Greece and Rome   145
Well purg'd, and worthy Settle, Banks, and Broome.
   But, high above, more solid Learning shone,
The Classics of an Age that heard of none;
There Caxton slept, with Wynkyn at his side,

122 *abdicated* 'given up'.

126 *Sooterkins* According to folk myth, these were small
animals hatched by Dutch women who warmed
themselves with stoves under their petticoats.

129 *snug* 'secretly'.

131 Cibber's plays were heavily indebted to those of John
Fletcher (1579–1625), a prolific Jacobean dramatist.

132 *Frippery* 'cast-off clothes'. Cf. Cibber, *An Apology for
the Life of Mr Colley Cibber, Comedian* (1740): 'When I
fitted up an old play, it was as a good housewife will
mend old linnen, when she has not better employment'.
His play *The Nonjuror* (1718) owed something to
Molière's *Tartuffe* (1667).

133 *Tibbald* Lewis Theobald, former hero of *The Dunciad*,
edited Shakespeare (1734) in rivalry with Pope.

138 *red and gold* The special binding used for an author's
presentation copies.

140 Francis Quarles (1592–1644), author of the heavily
illustrated *Emblems* (1635).

141 John Ogilby (1600–76), author and printer, published
his own translations of Homer and Virgil in lavish folio.

142 *Newcastle* Margaret Cavendish, Duchess of Newcastle
(1623–73), prolific author of poems, plays, and a
distinguished biography of her husband. The folio
volumes were stamped with the family arms.

144 *jakes* 'lavatory'.

145 *Gothic* Here 'tasteless', 'uncivilized'.

146 *Settle* See 90n; *Banks* John Banks (?1650–?1696), writer
of historical tragedies; *Broome* Richard Brome (d.
1652?), dramatist, author of *A Jovial Crew*.

147 *more solid Learning Some have objected, that books of this
sort suit not so well with the library of our Bays, which
they imagine consisted of Novels, Plays, and obscene
books; but they are to consider, that he furnished his shelves
only for ornament.*

149 *Caxton* William Caxton (?1422–91), the first English
printer; *Wynkyn* Wynkyn de Worde (?d. 1535),
Caxton's principal assistant and successor.

One clasp'd in wood, and one in strong cow-hide;   150
There, sav'd by spice, like Mummies, many a year,
Dry Bodies of Divinity appear:
De Lyra there a dreadful front extends,
And here the groaning shelves Philemon bends.
　　Of these twelve volumes, twelve of amplest size,   155
Redeem'd from tapers and defrauded pies,
Inspir'd he seizes: These an altar raise:
An hecatomb of pure, unsully'd lays
That altar crowns: A folio Common-place
Founds the whole pile, of all his works the base: 160
Quartos, octavos, shape the less'ning pyre;
A twisted Birth-day Ode completes the spire.
　　Then he: Great Tamer of all human art!
First in my care, and ever at my heart;
Dulness! whose good old cause I yet defend,   165
With whom my Muse began, with whom shall end;
E'er since Sir Fopling's Periwig was Praise,
To the last honours of the Butt and Bays:
O thou! of Bus'ness the directing soul!
To this our head like byass to the bowl,   170
Which, as more pond'rous, made its aim more true,
Obliquely wadling to the mark in view:
O! ever gracious to perplex'd mankind,
Still spread a healing mist before the mind;
And lest we err by Wit's wild dancing light,   175
Secure us kindly in our native night.
Or, if to Wit a coxcomb make pretence,
Guard the sure barrier between that and Sense;
Or quite unravel all the reas'ning thread,
And hang some curious cobweb in its stead!   180
As, forc'd from wind-guns, lead itself can fly,
And pond'rous slugs cut swiftly thro' the sky;
As clocks to weight their nimble motion owe,
The wheels above urg'd by the load below:
Me Emptiness, and Dulness could inspire,   185
And were my Elasticity, and Fire.
Some Dæmon stole my pen (forgive th'offence)
And once betray'd me into common sense:
Else all my Prose and Verse were much the same;

153 *De Lyra* Nicholas de Lyra (?1270–1340), French theologian.

154 *Philemon* Philemon Holland (1552–1637), translator of classical authors.

156 *defrauded pies* See Swift, *Verses on the Death of Dr Swift*, 259–60n.

158 *hecatomb* A formal public sacrifice in ancient Greece.

159 *folio Common-place* 'huge scrap-book'. The volumes lessen in size ('Quartos, octavos').

167 *Sir Fopling* A character in Etherege's comedy *The Man of Mode*, here a reference to the bewigged fop acted by

Cibber in his first play *Love's Last Shift, or The Fool of Fashion* (1696).

168 *Butt* The Poet Laureate was traditionally entitled to a yearly cask ('butt') of wine. The bay-laurel crown is symbolic.

170 *byass* Cf. Dryden, *Mac Flecknoe*, 189–90: 'This is that boasted Byas of thy mind, / By which, one way, to dullness, 'tis inclined'. The metaphor comes from the game of bowls: the 'bias' is the weighting of the bowl which pulls it to one side.

182 *slugs* 'bullets'.

This, prose on stilts; that, poetry fall'n lame.   190
Did on the stage my Fops appear confin'd?
My Life gave ampler lessons to mankind.
Did the dead Letter unsuccessful prove?
The brisk Example never fail'd to move.
Yet sure had Heav'n decreed to save the State,   195
Heav'n had decreed these works a longer date.
Could Troy be sav'd by any single hand,
This grey-goose weapon must have made her stand.
What can I now? my Fletcher cast aside,
Take up the Bible, once my better guide?   200
Or tread the path by vent'rous Heroes trod,
This Box my Thunder, this right hand my God?
Or chair'd at White's amidst the Doctors sit,
Teach Oaths to Gamesters, and to Nobles Wit?
Or bidst thou rather Party to embrace?   205
(A friend to Party thou, and all her race;
'Tis the same rope at different ends they twist;
To Dulness Ridpath is as dear as Mist.)
Shall I, like Curtius, desp'rate in my zeal,
O'er head and ears plunge for the Commonweal?   210
Or rob Rome's ancient geese of all their glories,
And cackling save the Monarchy of Tories?
Hold — to the Minister I more incline;
To serve his cause, O Queen! is serving thine.
And see! thy very Gazetteers give o'er,   215
Ev'n Ralph repents, and Henly writes no more.
What then remains? Ourself. Still, still remain
Cibberian forehead, and Cibberian brain.
This brazen Brightness, to the 'Squire so dear;
This polish'd Hardness, that reflects the Peer;   220
This arch Absurd, that wit and fool delights;
This Mess, toss'd up of Hockley-hole and White's;
Where Dukes and Butchers join to wreathe my crown,
At once the Bear and Fiddle of the town.

---

193 *dead Letter* 'spiritless, ineffective writing'.

195 Cf. 'Had Heav'n decreed that I shou'd Life enjoy, / Heav'n had decreed to save unhappy Troy' (Virgil, *Aeneid*, 2:641–2, Dryden's translation).

197–8 Cf. 'If Troy's towers could be saved by strength of hand, by mine, too, had they been saved' (Virgil, *Aeneid*, 2:291–2).

198 *grey-goose weapon* i.e. writing quill.

202 *Box* 'dice-shaker'. Pope parodies Virgil, *Aeneid*, 10:773–4: 'Now let my right hand (for that is the god I worship) and this weapon which I am poised to throw, be favourable to me'.

203 *White's* A chocolate house and aristocratic gambling club; *Doctors* 'learned men'. The word was also slang for 'false dice'.

208 *George Ridpath, author of a Whig paper, called the Flying post; Nathanael Mist, of a famous Tory Journal.*

209 *Curtius* The legendary Roman soldier who rode fully armed into a mysterious hole in the Roman forum after an oracle had decreed that Rome's chief strength be thrown into it.

211 When the Gauls attacked Rome in 390 BC cackling geese alerted the Romans to their approach.

213 *Minister* Walpole.

215 *Gazetteers* The *Daily Gazetteer* was the chief organ of ministerial propaganda.

216 *Ralph* James Ralph (*c*.1705–62) had 'repented' his role as contributor to the *Daily Gazetteer* by subsequently writing for the opposition; *Henly* John Henley. See *Epistle to Dr Arbuthnot*, 98n.

222 *Hockley-hole* A famous bull- and bear-baiting venue.

224 *Fiddle* 'jester'. Cibber is both jester and victim.

O born in sin, and forth in folly brought! 225
Works damn'd, or to be damn'd! (your father's fault)
Go, purify'd by flames ascend the sky,
My better and more christian progeny!
Unstain'd, untouch'd, and yet in maiden sheets;
While all your smutty sisters walk the streets. 230
Ye shall not beg, like gratis-given Bland,
Sent with a Pass, and vagrant thro' the land;
Not sail, with Ward, to Ape-and-monkey climes,
Where vile Mundungus trucks for viler rhymes;
Not sulphur-tipt, emblaze an Ale-house fire; 235
Not wrap up Oranges, to pelt your sire!
O! pass more innocent, in infant state,
To the mild Limbo of our Father Tate:
Or peaceably forgot, at once be blest
In Shadwell's bosom with eternal Rest! 240
Soon to that mass of Nonsense to return,
Where things destroy'd are swept to things unborn.
    With that, a Tear (portentous sign of Grace!)
Stole from the Master of the sev'nfold Face:
And thrice he lifted high the Birth-day brand, 245
And thrice he dropt it from his quiv'ring hand;
Then lights the structure, with averted eyes:
The rowling smokes involve the sacrifice.
The op'ning clouds disclose each work by turns,
Now flames the Cid, and now Perolla burns; 250
Great Cæsar roars, and hisses in the fires;
King John in silence modestly expires:
No merit now the dear Nonjuror claims,
Moliere's old stubble in a moment flames.
Tears gush'd again, as from pale Priam's eyes 255
When the last blaze sent Ilion to the skies.

225 *This is a tender and passionate Apostrophe to his own works, which he is going to sacrifice, agreeable to the nature of man in great affliction; and reflecting like a parent on the many miserable fates to which they would otherwise be subject.*

229–30 I.e. these copies of Cibber's works are still fresh from the press, 'in sheets', while other copies are being sold in the streets.

231–2 *It was a practice so to give the Daily Gazetteer and ministerial pamphlets (in which this B. was a writer) and to send them Post-free to all the Towns in the kingdom.* Henry Bland (d. 1746) was one of the chief government propagandists.

233 *Ward* Ned Ward (1667–1731), author of the monthly *London Spy*.

234 *Mundungus* Cheap tobacco; *trucks* 'is bartered'.

236 See *Epistle to Dr Arbuthnot*, 228n.

238 *Limbo* The distant home of everything empty and useless (*Paradise Lost*, 3:493–7); *Tate* See *Epistle to Dr Arbuthnot*, 190n.

240 *Shadwell* Thomas Shadwell (?1642–92), Dryden's successor as Poet Laureate and hero of his *Mac Flecknoe*.

241–2 Cf. 'And to that mass of matter shall be swept / Where things destroyed with things unborn are kept' (Rochester, 'A Translation from Seneca's *Troades*, Act II, Chorus', 9–10).

244 The phrase characterizes Cibber as a consummate actor. Cf. 'the Master of the sev'nfold Shield' (Dryden's translation of Ovid, *Metamorphoses*, 13:2).

250–4 All plays or adaptations by Cibber: *Ximena*, based on Corneille's *Le Cid* (1712); *Perolla and Izadora* (1705); *Caesar in Egypt* (1724); *Papal Tyranny in the Reign of King John* (withdrawn 1735); and *The Nonjuror* (1718). The latter, partly indebted to Molière, satirized Catholics, nonjurors and other purported enemies of the House of Hanover.

255–6 In *Aeneid*, 2, Virgil describes how Priam, King of Troy ('Ilion'), wept over its destruction by the Greeks.

Rowz'd by the light, old Dulness heav'd the head;
Then snatch'd a sheet of Thulè from her bed,
Sudden she flies, and whelms it o'er the pyre;
Down sink the flames, and with a hiss expire.   260
    Her ample presence fills up all the place;
A veil of fogs dilates her awful face:
Great in her charms! as when on Shrieves and May'rs
She looks, and breathes herself into their airs.
She bids him wait her to her sacred Dome: 265
Well pleas'd he enter'd, and confess'd his home.
So Spirits ending their terrestrial race,
Ascend, and recognize their Native Place.
This the Great Mother dearer held than all
The clubs of Quidnuncs, or her own Guild-hall: 270
Here stood her Opium, here she nurs'd her Owls,
And here she plann'd th'Imperial seat of Fools.
    Here to her Chosen all her works she shews;
Prose swell'd to verse, verse loit'ring into prose:
How random thoughts now meaning chance to find,   275
Now leave all memory of sense behind:
How Prologues into Prefaces decay,
And these to Notes are fritter'd quite away:
How Index-learning turns no student pale,
Yet holds the eel of science by the tail: 280
How, with less reading than makes felons scape,
Less human genius than God gives an ape,
Small thanks to France, and none to Rome or Greece,
A past, vamp'd, future, old, reviv'd, new piece,
'Twixt Plautus, Fletcher, Shakespear, and Corneille,   285
Can make a Cibber, Tibbald, or Ozell.
    The Goddess then, o'er his anointed head,
With mystic words, the sacred Opium shed.
And lo! her bird, (a monster of a fowl,
Something betwixt a Heideggre and owl,)   290
Perch'd on his crown. "All hail! and hail again,
My son! the promis'd land expects thy reign.
Know, Eusden thirsts no more for sack or praise;
He sleeps among the dull of ancient days;
Safe, where no Critics damn, no duns molest,   295

258 *Thulè An unfinished poem of that name, of which one sheet was printed many years ago, by Amb. Philips, a northern author. It is an usual method of putting out a fire, to cast wet sheets upon it. Some critics have been of opinion that this sheet was of the nature of the Asbestos, which cannot be consumed by fire: But I rather think it an allegorical allusion to the coldness and heaviness of the writing.* Ambrose Philips's *Thulè* had been published in the *Freethinker*, 9 (1718).

262 *dilates* 'expands'.

263–4 Cf. 'Great in her Charms, as when the Gods above / She looks, and breaths herself into their Love' (Dryden's translation of Virgil, *Aeneid*, 2:591–2, describing Venus appearing in a vision to Aeneas).

266 *confess'd* 'acknowledged'.

270 *The* Quidnuncs, *a name given to the ancient members of certain political clubs, who were constantly enquiring* quid nunc? *what news?*

281 By 'benefit of clergy', a first offender's reading ability could exempt him from punishment.

286 *Tibbald* See 133n; *Ozell* John Ozell (d. 1743), a prolific translator of French and Italian works.

289–91 A parody of Matthew, 3:16, where the Holy Spirit descends like a dove on Christ's head.

290 *Heideggre* John James Heidegger (?1659–1749), a Swiss-born impresario who promoted masquerades and popular entertainments. He was notoriously ugly.

295 *duns* 'bailiffs'.

Where wretched Withers, Ward, and Gildon rest,
And high-born Howard, more majestic sire,
With Fool of Quality compleats the quire.
Thou Cibber! thou, his Laurel shalt support,
Folly, my son, has still a Friend at Court.   300
Lift up your Gates, ye Princes, see him come!
Sound, sound ye Viols, be the Cat-call dumb!
Bring, bring the madding Bay, the drunken Vine;
The creeping, dirty, courtly Ivy join.
And thou! his Aid de camp, lead on my sons,   305
Light-arm'd with Points, Antitheses, and Puns.
Let Bawdry, Bilingsgate, my daughters dear,
Support his front, and Oaths bring up the rear:
And under his, and under Archer's wing,
Gaming and Grub-street skulk behind the King.   310
    O! when shall rise a Monarch all our own,
And I, a Nursing-mother, rock the throne,
'Twixt Prince and People close the Curtain draw,
Shade him from Light, and cover him from Law;
Fatten the Courtier, starve the learned band,   315
And suckle Armies, and dry-nurse the land:
'Till Senates nod to Lullabies divine,
And all be sleep, as at an Ode of thine.

    She ceas'd. Then swells the Chapel-royal throat:
God save king Cibber! mounts in ev'ry note.   320
Familiar White's, God save king Colley! cries;
God save king Colley! Drury-lane replies:
To Needham's quick the voice triumphal rode,
But pious Needham dropt the name of God;
Back to the Devil the last echoes roll,   325
And Coll! each Butcher roars at Hockley-hole.
    So when Jove's block descended from on high
(As sings thy great forefather Ogilby)
Loud thunder to its bottom shook the bog,
And the hoarse nation croak'd, God save King Log!   330

296 *Withers* George Wither (1588–1667), Puritan pamphleteer and poet, imprisoned for sedition, 1660–3; *Gildon* See *Epistle to Dr Arbuthnot*, 151n.

297 *Howard* Edward Howard (fl. 1669), poet and dramatist.

298 *Fool of Quality* Lord Hervey (see *Epistle to Dr Arbuthnot*, headnote and 305–33n). He is possibly the 'Friend at Court' (300) and 'Aid de camp' (305).

304 *courtly Ivy* In his Appendix to the 1743 *Dunciad* Pope remarks on the propriety of adding ivy to the Laureate's crown: 'it is emblematical of the three virtues of a court poet in particular; it is *creeping, dirty,* and *dangling*'.

306 Hervey was particularly fond of these word games.

307 *Bawdry* 'obscenity'; *Bilingsgate* 'coarse language' (from Billingsgate fish-market).

309 *Archer* Thomas Archer (d. 1743) was responsible for the provision of gaming tables at Court.

311–18 Pope attacks George II's reign, rehearsing the accu-

sations that he neglected culture and learning (315) and was maintaining expensive foreign standing armies (316).

312 *Nursing-mother* 'And kings shall be thy nursing fathers, and their queens thy nursing mothers' (Isaiah, 49:23).

319 *Chapel-royal* The Voices and Instruments used in the service of the Chapel-royal being also employed in the performance of the Birth-day and New-year Odes.

323 *Needham* Mother Needham, a notoriously foul-mouthed procuress.

325 *Devil* The Devil Tavern in Fleet-street, where these Odes are usually rehearsed before they are performed at Court.

326 *Coll* A slang term for 'fool' or 'dupe'.

327 Pope alludes to the fable of the Frogs in John Ogilby's *The Fables of Aesop, Paraphrased in Verse* (1651). The frogs ask Jove for a King, but he gives them a useless wooden log. In response to their complaints he sends down a stork which devours them. Better the evil one knows?

Lady Mary Wortley Montagu (1689–1762)

Lady Mary Pierrepont, daughter of the first Duke of Kingston-upon-Hull, had wit, intelligence and beauty, and from her infancy she mixed easily in the company of her father's Whiggish political and literary friends. Beneath the dazzle, however, were private depths: imaginative richness and intellectual strength. She had a tenacious memory and was an omnivorous reader in her father's libraries. Like many girls of her age she devoured romances, but she also taught herself Latin and made herself proficient in other languages. Her father could be proud of her, and she held her own in a circle that included Congreve, Prior and Addison. There survive two albums of her juvenile poems, written in her early teens (see Grundy, *Yearbook of English Studies* (1977), pp. 91–107). Her doting parent, however, turned tyrant and in 1712 tried to force her into an arranged marriage; she resisted and to his fury eloped with Edward Wortley Montagu, MP (1678–1761), a scholarly and rather self-contained man with some poetical taste but also considerable political ambitions that could be forwarded by having a brilliant young wife at Court. There Lady Mary became the confidante of the Princess of Wales (later Queen Caroline) and a notable figure in the *beau monde* evoked in Pope's *Rape of the Lock*, enjoying the opportunities for malicious gossip and the circulating of witty verses. She relished the company of Pope and Gay, and under their influence she began to find a confident satirical voice in what became the *Six Town Eclogues* (1714–16). When her reign as a Court beauty was cut short by an attack of smallpox in December 1715, her reputation shifted towards her wit and poetic skills.

In 1716 her husband was appointed Ambassador to Turkey and Lady Mary travelled with him to Constantinople, where she took the opportunity to study the language and immerse herself in Turkish life. Out of this experience came the incomparable 'Embassy Letters' published after her death, which confirmed her as one of the century's great letter writers. In Turkey she also became interested in the effectiveness of smallpox inoculation, and after her return to England in 1718 she worked to popularize the practice there. Lady Mary once again moved easily in Court circles and grew especially close to the brilliant Lord Hervey (Pope's 'Sporus'). She wrote an unperformed play, 'Simplicity', based on Marivaux, and anonymously engaged in political controversy through her short-lived pro-Walpole paper, *The Nonsense of Common-Sense* (1737–8).

Her husband, thwarted in his political career and by the failure of his diplomatic mission, turned to his business dealings, and Lady Mary's marriage grew stale. She enjoyed liaisons and intrigue, and he accumulated vast wealth. By 1728 her friendship with Pope, who had for years been enchanted with her, turned to mutual hate, and during the 1730s she featured in his work as the slovenly 'Sappho', while he felt the lash of the satiric voice he had helped her to develop. During the summer of 1736 Lady Mary's life was jolted into a new direction by Francesco Algarotti (1712–64), a brilliant young Italian touring the courts and literary circles of Europe. Hervey and she became rivals for the love of this bisexual charmer, who left them both distraught when he set off for France in September. In 1739 Montagu left England, intending to live with Algarotti in Italy, but this plan never materialized, and for the next twenty-two years she lived abroad, in Venice, Avignon, Brescia and Padua, corresponding with the husband she was never to see again, and visited by many young men on the Grand Tour. She kept in touch with England and the literary world through her correspondence with her daughter (who as Lady Bute became the wife of the British Prime Minister). She had books shipped out to her, and especially enjoyed the novels of her favourite cousin, Henry Fielding. In the last year of her life she returned to England, and made a final flourish in a society curious to encounter the old woman who had once dazzled the world of Queen Anne. She died of breast cancer in August 1762.

As an aristocratic woman, Montagu was doubly inhibited from publishing her poetry, and she never did so under her own name. Much of her verses are concerned with the events of the moment and the people and activities of her own circle. When a poem was completed she would allow transcriptions to be circulated around her friends, and these would be read and exchanged with eagerness, spreading like a ripple of gossip from one to another. Curll's pirated *Court Poems* (see the headnote to *Saturday*) were an exception, and little of her poetry was published during her lifetime. Horace Walpole's *Six Town Eclogues. With some other Poems* (1747) printed just four pieces in addition to the eclogues, and the two poems included here from the *London Magazine* may have been sent to the editor with her approval. Certainly she was happy for visitors to copy material from the albums into which she had transcribed her verses. The most important of these is Harrowby Manuscript 256, compiled by Montagu from 1730, and the copytext favoured by Isobel Grundy in her excellent edition of the poetry (*Essays and Poems, and Simplicity, a Comedy*, ed. Robert Halsband and Isobel Grundy, Oxford: Clarendon Press, 1977). There is something to be said, however, for reproducing the earliest printed texts, as in the selection that follows.

They are the versions read by the literary public of the day and can be presented with very little editorial intervention, unlike her own transcripts, which although having the authority of her hand, need to be carefully emended by an editor. They have slips of the pen, awkward abbreviations, even careless omissions, and their punctuation has sometimes to be modified. In the texts given here any significant substantive variants (i.e. those involving a difference in wording) with the Harrowby MS as printed in Grundy's edition are noted, and on a few occasions the manuscript wording has been preferred. In two cases (*Epistle from Arthur Gray* and *Verses on Self-Murder*) the printed titles are markedly different and remind us of that element of notoriety that sharpened Montagu's reputation during her 'exile'. The major difference between the texts, however, lies in the accidentals (spelling, capitalization and punctuation), and in this the earliest printed texts offer some advantages to a modern reader. They too, as far as verbal readings are concerned, were based on manuscript copies, and when Walpole prints *The Lover* he notes that the addressee's name has been changed 'in the copies which she gives now'. He clearly prized his text as offering an authentic earlier reading. Anyone interested in Lady Mary's poetry ought to use the printed and manuscript versions side by side.

Saturday. The Small-Pox. Flavia.

This concluding poem of Montagu's *Six Town Eclogues* (published 1747) was written in the wake of her illness of December 1715. Her granddaughter's memoir is specific about the biographical element: 'The small-pox was a disorder which she had sufficient reason to dread: it carried off her only brother, and had visited her so severely that she always said she meant the Flavia of her sixth Town-Eclogue for herself, having expressed in that poem what her own sensations were while slowly recovering under the apprehension of being totally disfigured.' Certainly, Flavia's combination of pathos and pride does have an authentic ring. But the poem is also generically interesting. It was one of the fruits of Montagu's witty intimacy with Pope and Gay during 1715–16: Pope's satire on society beauties in *The Rape of the Lock* (1712–14) and Gay's street-wise *Trivia* (published January 1716) showed what could be done in reworking classical genres in modern dress, and in 1715 Montagu began working on some updated pastoral eclogues. Where Gay's *The Shepherd's Week* (1714) adopted a burlesque rusticity (see his *Friday; or, The Dirge*), Montagu's pastorals are elevated to the Court circle, where the naïve Arcadian shepherdess is transformed by the sophisticated mores of upper-class London. The other eclogues (*Monday. The Drawing-room*, *Tuesday. St James's Coffee-house*, *Wednesday. The Tete à Tete*, *Thursday. The Bassette Table* and *Friday. The Toilette*, this last largely written by Gay) move through a range of settings familiar to Pope's Belinda and her Baron. *Saturday* is in the tradition of the pastoral lament, and its refrain of 'no more!' recalls Pope's *Winter* from his 1709 *Pastorals* ('Fair *Daphne*'s dead, and Beauty is no more!', etc.).

The first three eclogues to be written (*Monday*, *Thursday*, *Friday*) appeared in a pirated edition as *Court Poems* (1716). All six were first published by Horace Walpole in *Six Town Eclogues. With some other Poems* (1747), and were soon reprinted in Dodsley's popular *Collection of Poems* (1748), 3:274–98. The text given here is 1747, with significant variants recorded from the Harrowby MS.

> The wretched FLAVIA on her couch reclin'd,
> Thus breath'd the anguish of a wounded mind;
> A glass revers'd in her right hand she bore,
> For now she shun'd the face she sought before.
>   'How am I chang'd! alas! how am I grown   5
> A frightful spectre, to myself unknown!
> Where's my Complexion? where my radiant Bloom,
> That promis'd happiness for Years to come?
> Then with what pleasure I this face survey'd!
> To look once more, my visits oft delay'd!   10
> Charm'd with the view, a fresher red would rise,
> And a new life shot sparkling from my eyes!
>   'Ah! faithless glass, my wonted bloom restore;
> Alas! I rave, that bloom is now no more!
> The greatest good the GODS on men bestow,   15
> Ev'n youth itself, to me is useless now.

There was a time (oh! that I could forget!)
When opera-tickets pour'd before my feet;
And at the ring, where brightest beauties shine,
The earliest cherries of the spring were mine.   20
Witness, O *Lilly*; and thou, *Motteux*, tell
How much Japan these eyes have made ye sell,
With what contempt ye saw me oft despise
The humble offer of the raffled prize;
For at each raffle still the prize I bore,   25
With scorn rejected, or with triumph wore!
Now beauty's fled, and presents are no more!
    'For me the Patriot has the house forsook,
And left debates to catch a passing look:
For me the Soldier has soft verses writ;   30
For me the Beau has aim'd to be a Wit.
For me the Wit to nonsense was betray'd;
The Gamester has for me his dun delay'd,
And overseen the card I would have paid.
The bold and haughty by success made vain,   35
Aw'd by my eyes have trembled to complain:
The bashful 'squire touch'd with a wish unknown,
Has dar'd to speak with spirit not his own;
Fir'd by one wish, all did alike adore;
Now beauty's fled, and lovers are no more!   40
    'As round the room I turn my weeping eyes,
New unaffected scenes of sorrow rise!
Far from my sight that killing picture bear,
The face disfigure, and the canvas tear!
That picture which with pride I us'd to show,   45
The lost resemblance but upbraids me now.
And thou, my toilette! where I oft have sat,
While hours unheeded pass'd in deep debate,
How curls should fall, or where a patch to place:
If blue or scarlet best became my face;   50
Now on some happier nymph your aid bestow;
On fairer heads, ye useless jewels glow!
No borrow'd lustre can my charms restore;
Beauty is fled, and dress is now no more!
    'Ye meaner beauties, I permit ye shine;   55
Go, triumph in the hearts that once were mine;
But midst your triumphs with confusion know,
'Tis to my ruin all your charms ye owe.
Would pitying Heav'n restore my wonted mien,
Ye still might move unthought-of and unseen.   60
But oh! how vain, how wretched is the boast

19 *ring* The fashionable carriage drive in Hyde Park.
20 *spring* Park (MS).
21 Charles Lillie ran a notable perfumery in The Strand;
    Peter Anthony Motteux (1663–1718), translator and
    dramatist, kept a fashionable shop in Leadenhall Street
    selling silks and oriental goods.
22 *Japan* Japanese lacquered ware.
25 *each ... the* (from MS; *1747* has 'the ... each').
28 *the house* Parliament.

33 *his dun delay'd* 'delayed taking his winnings'.
34 *overseen* 'failed to notice'; *paid* (from MS; *1747* has
    'play'd').
43 *killing* 'devastating'. The word could also mean
    'devastatingly beautiful' (cf. Pope, *The Rape of the Lock*,
    5:64), an appropriate irony.
58 *charms* (from MS; *1747* has 'arms'). Cf. Pope, *Epistle to
    a Lady*, 42.
59 *wonted mien* 'accustomed appearance'.

Of beauty faded, and of empire lost!
What now is left but weeping, to deplore
My beauty fled, and empire now no more!
   'Ye, cruel Chymists, what with-held your aid!   65
Could no pomatums save a trembling maid?
How false and trifling is that art ye boast;
No art can give me back my beauty lost.
In tears, surrounded by my friends I lay,
Mask'd o'er and trembling at the sight of day;   70
MIRMILLO came my fortune to deplore,
(A golden headed cane well carv'd he bore)
Cordials, he cried, my spirits must restore:
Beauty is fled, and spirit is no more!
   'GALEN, the grave; officious SQUIRT, was there,   75
With fruitless grief and unavailing care:
MACHAON too, the great MACHAON, known
By his red cloak and his superior frown;
And why, he cry'd, this grief and this despair?
You shall again be well, again be fair;   80
Believe my oath; (with that an oath he swore)
False was his oath; my beauty is no more!
   'Cease, hapless maid, no more thy tale pursue,
Forsake mankind, and bid the world adieu!
Monarchs and beauties rule with equal sway;   85
All strive to serve, and glory to obey:
Alike unpitied when depos'd they grow;
Men mock the idol of their former vow.
   'Adieu! ye parks! — in some obscure recess,
Where gentle streams will weep at my distress,   90
Where no false friend will in my grief take part,
And mourn my ruin with a joyful heart;
There let me live in some deserted place,
There hide in shades this lost inglorious face.
Ye, operas, circles, I no more must view!   95
My toilette, patches, all the world adieu!

66 *pomatums* 'scented ointments'.

70 *trembling* (from MS; *1747* has 'trembled').

71–82 Several prominent physicians seem to be alluded to here: MIRMILLO may be Richard Mead (1673–1754); GALEN may be John Woodward (1665–1728), here named after the great Greek physician at the imperial court in Rome; MACHAON is Sir Samuel Garth (1661–1719), author of a popular poem, *The Dispensary*

(1699). *Squirt* is slang for 'doctor' (*OED* s.n. 'squirt' *sb* 4b).

89–94 These lines recall Adam's despair after The Fall: 'O might I here / In solitude live savage, in some glade / Obscured, where highest woods impenetrable / To star or sunlight, spread their umbrage broad' (*Paradise Lost*, 9:1084–7).

Epistle from Arthur Gray the Footman, after his Condemnation for attempting a Rape

Lady Mary's friend Griselda Baillie (1692–1759) had married Alexander Murray in 1710, but the couple were legally separated four years later, and by 1721 Mrs Murray was living in her father's London house. It was there on 14 October that she was awakened at 4 a.m. by a young footman of the household armed with a pistol and sword, threatening rape. After keeping him talking she seized the pistol and rang for help as the man fled. The *Weekly Journal or Saturday's Post* for 21 October gave a vivid account ('At the same time with a vigorous Spring she fix'd her Feet upon his Breast, as he reclin'd himself, and over-turn'd him upon the Floor. The Noise his Head made against the Wainscot, her Shrieks, and ringing of the Bell, alarm'd the Family …'). After his trial at the Old Bailey on 7 December Gray was found guilty of burglary and felony and sentenced to be hanged. (The full story is reconstructed by Robert Halsband, '*Virtue in Danger*: The Case of Griselda Murray', *History Today* (October 1967), pp. 692–700.) The incident caused a frisson among Mrs Murray's friends and became the subject of a smutty comic ballad, 'Virtue in Danger', which was printed as a broadside and served only to increase Murray's embarrassment ('He lay'd his Sword close by her side; / Her heart went pit a pat: / You've but one weapon left, She cry'd, / Sure I can deal with that'). Montagu was almost certainly the author, and when she refused to

deny it, Murray's friendship turned to hate. The epistle printed below is in a very different vein, but it is perhaps equally remarkable as a response to her friend's situation. Here Lady Mary makes the man's frustrated love the subject for an Ovidian heroic epistle in the genre of Pope's *Eloisa to Abelard*. With the genders reversed, the speaker is once again the voice of passion nursing an illicit and impossible love. An imaginative identification with the footman's feelings combines with a satiric awareness of class difference to produce a poem that engages the reader's responses in a powerful way.

The poem was first published by Horace Walpole in *Six Town Eclogues. With some other Poems* (1747), and soon after reprinted in Dodsley's popular *Collection of Poems* (1748), 3:298–302. The text given here is 1747. There are only a few very minor substantive variants with the Harrowby MS.

> Read, lovely nymph, and tremble not to read,
> I have no more to wish, nor you to dread:
> I ask not life, for life to me were vain,
> And death a refuge from severer pain.
> My only hope in these last lines I try;   5
> I wou'd be pitied, and I then wou'd die.
>   Long had I liv'd as sordid as my fate,
> Nor curs'd the destiny that made me wait
> A servile slave: content with homely food
> The gross instinct of appetite pursued: 10
> Youth gave me sleep at night and warmth of blood.
> Ambition yet had never touch'd my breast;
> My lordly master knew no sounder rest;
> With labour healthy, in obedience blest.
> But when I saw — Oh! had I never seen   15
> That wounding softness, that engaging mien!
> The mist of wretched education flies,
> Shame, fear, desire, despair and love arise,
> The new creation of those beauteous eyes.
> But yet that love pursued no guilty aim,   20
> Deep in my heart I hid the secret flame.
> I never hop'd my fond desire to tell,
> And all my wishes were to serve you well.
> Heav'ns! how I flew, when wing'd by your command;
> And kiss'd the letters giv'n me by your hand.   25
> How pleas'd, how proud, how fond was I to wait,
> Present the sparkling wine, or change the plate!
> How when you sung, my soul devour'd the sound,
> And ev'ry sense was in the rapture drown'd!

Title *Gray* (Grey *1747*). The title in the Harrowby MS is 'Epistle From Arthur G —— y to Mrs M —— y'.

1 The *Saturday's Post* article reported that Gray 'wrote a Letter to Mrs. Murray from Newgate [prison], telling her, that as his Fault was only a Fault of raging Love, he hoped she would commiserate his Condition'.

7 *sordid* 'ignoble'.

28–9 *when you sung* Gay celebrated 'Sweet Tongu'd Murray' in 'Mr Popes Welcome from Greece', 61.

Tho' bid to go, I quite forgot to move;   30
— You knew not that stupidity was Love!
But oh! the torment not to be express'd,
The grief, the rage, the hell that fir'd this breast,
When my great rivals, in embroid'ry gay,
Sate by your side, or led you from the play.   35
I still contriv'd near as I cou'd to stand,
(The flambeau trembled in my shaking hand)
I saw, or thought I saw those fingers press'd,
For thus their passion by my own I guess'd,
And jealous fury all my soul possess'd.   40
Like torrents, Love and Indignation meet,
And madness wou'd have thrown me at your feet.
  Turn, lovely nymph (for so I wou'd have said)
Turn from those triflers who make Love a trade;
This is true passion in my eyes you see;   45
They cannot, no — they cannot love like me.
Frequent debauch has pall'd their sickly taste,
Faint their desire, and in a moment past:
They sigh not from the heart, but from the brain;
Vapours of vanity, and strong champagne.   50
Too dull to feel what forms, like yours, inspire,
After long talking of their painted fire,
To some lewd brothel they at night retire;
There pleas'd with fancy'd quality and charms,
Enjoy your beauties in a strumpet's arms.   55
Such are the joys those toasters have in view,
And such the wit and pleasure they pursue:
— And is this Love that ought to merit you?
Each opera-night a new address begun,
They swear to thousands what they swear to one.   60
Not thus I sigh — but all my sighs are vain —
Die, wretched ARTHUR, and conceal thy pain:
'Tis impudence to wish, and madness to complain.
  Fix'd on this view, my only hope of ease,
I waited not the aid of slow disease: 65
The keenest instruments of death I sought,
And death alone employ'd my lab'ring thought.
This all the night — when I remember well,
The charming tinkle of your morning bell!
Fir'd by the sound, I hasten'd with your tea,   70
With one last look to smooth the darksome way —
But oh! how dear that fatal look has cost!
In that fond moment my resolves were lost.
Hence all my guilt, and all your sorrows rise —

31 *stupidity* 'The Lady observ'd, that the Fellow, who was always esteemed the most stupid Wretch in the World, pleaded his amorous Cause with all imaginable Eloquence' (*Saturday's Post*). An older meaning of 'stupid' is also present here: 'in a state of stupor, deprived of one's faculties'.

56 *toasters* Rakish men who worship the current beauty.
66–7 The thoughts of suicide are Montagu's invention. At his trial Gray claimed he had heard another man in her room and had gone in armed to rescue her.

I saw the languid softness of your eyes;   75
I saw the dear disorder of your bed;
Your cheek all glowing with a tempting red;
Your night-cloaths tumbled with resistless grace;
Your flowing hair play'd careless round your face;
Your night-gown fasten'd with a single pin;   80
— Fancy improv'd the wond'rous charms within!
I fix'd my eyes upon that heaving breast,
And hardly, hardly I forbore the rest;
Eager to gaze, unsatisfied with sight,
My head grew giddy with the near delight!   85
— Too well you know the fatal following night!
    Th'extremest proof of my desire I give,
And since you will not love, I will not live.
Condemn'd by you, I wait the righteous doom,
Careless and fearless of the woes to come.   90
But when you see me waver in the wind,
My guilty flame extinct, my soul resign'd,
Sure you may pity what you can't approve,
The cruel consequence of furious Love.
Think the bold wretch that cou'd so greatly dare,   95
Was tender, faithful, ardent and sincere:
Think when I held the pistol to your breast,
Had I been of the world's large rule possest,
That world had then been yours, and I been blest!
Think that my life was quite below my care,   100
Nor fear'd I any hell beyond despair —
    If these reflections, tho' they seize you late,
Give some compassion for your ARTHUR's fate:
Enough you give, nor ought I to complain;
You pay my pangs, nor have I dy'd in vain!   105

105 *dy'd* At the intercession of some of Mrs Murray's
family, Gray's sentence was commuted on 23
December and he was transported to the West Indies.

The Lover: A Ballad

Lord Byron admired the poem for its relish of life. Quoting the fourth stanza, he wrote: 'what say you to such a Supper with such a woman? … Is not her '*Champagne and Chicken*' worth a forest or two? – Is it not poetry?' He read some of Lady Mary's love letters in manuscript, and in the English cantos of *Don Juan* (1819–24) he caught something of her aristocratic world, where wit and sex enlivened each other. *The Lover* may originally have been addressed to Richard Chandler (?1703–69), son of the Bishop of Durham, and Horace Walpole's subtitle when he printed it in *Six Town Eclogues. With some other Poems* (1747) was 'To Mr. C ——'. He noted: 'One of her many amours was with Mr Chandler … to whom she wrote that admirable Description of a Lover … though in the copies which she gives now she writes (Molly) meaning Miss Skerret' (*Walpole Correspondence*, 14:245). (Montagu's friend Molly Skerrett was Sir Robert Walpole's mistress, later wife.) Grundy dates the poem to the period 1721–5. The text below is that of 1747, with significant variants noted from the Harrowby MS.

1

At length by so much importunity press'd,
Take, C ——, at once, the Inside of my breast;
This stupid indiff'rence so often you blame,
Is not owing to nature, to fear, or to shame.
I am not as cold as a virgin in lead,   5
Nor is Sunday's sermon so strong in my head.
I know but too well how Time flies along,
That we live but few years, and yet fewer are young.

2

But I hate to be cheated, and never will buy
Long years of repentance for moments of joy.   10
Oh! was there a man (but where shall I find
Good sense and good nature so equally join'd?)
Wou'd value his pleasure, contribute to mine;
Not meanly would boast, nor would lewdly design;
Not over severe, yet not stupidly vain,   15
For I would have the power, tho' not give the pain.

3

No pedant, yet learned; not rake-helly gay,
Or laughing, because he has nothing to say;
To all my whole sex obliging and free,
Yet never be fond of any but me.   20
In public preserve the decorum that's just,
And shew in his eyes he is true to his trust;
Then rarely approach, and respectfully bow,
But not fulsomely pert, or foppishly low.

4

But when the long hours of public are past,   25
And we meet with Champagne and a Chicken at last,
May ev'ry fond pleasure that moment endear;
Be banish'd afar both discretion and fear!
Forgetting or scorning the airs of the crowd,
He may cease to be formal, and I to be proud,   30
Till lost in the joy, we confess that we live,
And he may be rude, and yet I may forgive.

5

And that my delight may be solidly fix'd,
Let the Friend and the Lover be handsomely mix'd,
In whose tender bosom my soul may confide,   35
Whose kindness can sooth me, whose counsel cou'd guide.
From such a dear Lover as here I describe,
No danger should fright me, no millions should bribe:
But till this astonishing creature I know,
As I long have liv'd chaste, I will keep myself so.   40

2 *C* —— (Molly) (MS).
14 *nor would* nor (MS).
17 *rake-helly* Like a rake-hell, a dissolute scoundrel.
19 *free* 'unreserved', 'generous'.
21 *decorum that's* Decorums are (MS).

24 *But ... or* Yet ... nor yet (MS); *pert* 'forward'; *foppishly low* 'exaggeratedly submissive'.
27 *moment* hour (MS)
35 *may* might (MS).

6

I never will share with the wanton coquet,
Or be caught by a vain affectation of wit.
The toasters and songsters may try all their art,
But never shall enter the pass of my heart.
I loath the lewd rake, the dress'd fopling despise: 45
Before such pursuers the nice virgin flies;
And as OVID has sweetly in parables told,
We harden like trees, and like rivers grow cold.

45 *fopling* The fashion victim, embodied in Sir Fopling
   Flutter in Etherege's *The Man of Mode* (1676).
46 *nice* 'discriminating'.
46–8 Women rescued from their male pursuers: Daphne

became a laurel tree (Ovid, *Metamorphoses*, 1:452–567)
and Arethusa a stream (5:572–641). Cf. the episode of
Lodona in Pope's *Windsor-Forest*, 171–206.
48 *grow* are (MS); Cf. *Hymn to the Moon*, 12.

An Epistle to Lord Bathurst

Allen, first Earl Bathurst (1684–1775), was for many
years one of Pope's closest friends. A larger-than-life
personality, with an unbounded appetite for food,
drink, sex and good company, he fathered seventeen
legitimate children, had many mistresses, and was
famed for his gregariousness and his passion for
designing and planting his estates. Pope was a
frequent guest at Cirencester Park and Richings,
where he advised Bathurst on gardening matters.
Montagu seems to have had a hot-and-cold affair with
Bathurst during the spring of 1725, and Grundy
would date this poem to later that year, linking it to his
flirtation with Henrietta Howard. Montagu presents
Bathurst as an impressionable and whimsical
character, and in doing so she anticipates the charges
Pope was to bring against aristocratic women in his

Epistle to a Lady, and which were traditionally linked
to the female sex. Likewise Bathurst's gardening
ambitions here prefigure the grandiose and spiritually
empty Timon of *Epistle to Burlington*. Montagu's
satiric imagination relishes the changeability she
detects in every aspect of Bathurst's life. An ironic
postscript: in 1730 when he heard news of Lady
Mary's being severely ill, he told Pope 'we have both
been her humble Admirers at different times. I am not
so changeable as you, I think of her now as I allways
did' (Bathurst to Pope, 19 September 1730).

Text from Dodsley's *Collection of Poems* (1st edn,
1748), 3:306–9, where it was first published as 'An
Epistle to Lord B——t'. The notes record significant
variants with the Harrowby MS.

How happy you! who vary'd joys pursue;
And every hour presents you something new!
Plans, schemes, and models, all Palladio's art,
For six long months have gain'd upon your heart:
Of colonades, of corridores you talk,   5
The winding stair-case, and the cover'd walk;
You blend the orders with Vitruvian toil,
And raise with wond'rous joy the fancy'd pile:
But the dull workman's slow-performing hand
But coldly executes his lord's command.   10
With dirt and mortar soon you grow displeas'd,

3 *Palladio* Andrea Palladio (1508–80), Italian architect,
  influenced the English 'Palladian' style of Burlington
  and Kent.
5 Describing the plans he and Bathurst had for
  Cirencester Park, Pope spoke of 'the Pavillions that are
  to glitter, the Colonnades that are to adorn them' (Pope
  to Digby, [May] 1722).
6 After line 6, MS has a couplet: 'Proportion'd Colums

strikes before your Eye, / Corinthian Beauty, Ionian
Majesty'.
7 *orders* The three orders of classical Greek architecture:
  Doric, Ionic, Corinthian. *Vitruvian* Marcus Vitruvius
  Pollio (first century AD), Roman Augustan architect,
  author of *De architectura* in ten books, regarded in the
  Renaissance as the ultimate classical authority. Cf.
  Pope, *Epistle to Burlington*, 191–4.

Planting succeeds, and avenues are rais'd,
Canals are cut, and mountains level made;
Bowers of retreat, and galleries of shade:
The shaven turf presents a lively green;   15
The bordering flow'rs in mystic knots are seen:
With studied art on nature you refine,
The spring beheld you warm in this design,
But scarce the cold attacks your fav'rite trees,
Your inclination fails, and wishes freeze.   20
You quit the grove, so lately you admir'd;
With other views your eager hopes are fir'd.
Post to the city you direct your way;
Not blooming paradise could bribe your stay:
Ambition shews you power's brightest side,   25
'Tis meanly poor in solitude to hide:
Tho' certain pains attend the cares of state,
A good man owes his country to be great;
Should act abroad the high distinguish'd part,
Or shew at least the purpose of the heart.   30
With thoughts like these the shining court you seek;
Full of new projects for almost a week;
You then despise the tinsel glittering snare;
Think vile mankind below a serious care:
Life is too short for any distant aim;   35
And cold the dull reward of future fame:
Be happy then, while yet you have to live;
And love is all the blessing heav'n can give.
Fir'd by new passion you address the fair;
Survey the opera as a gay parterre: 40
Young Cloe's bloom had made you certain prize,
But for a side-long glance from Celia's eyes:
Your beating heart acknowledges her pow'r;
Your eager eyes her lovely form devour;
You feel the poison swelling in your breast,   45
And all your soul by fond desire possess'd.
In dying sighs a long three hours are past;
To some assembly with impatient haste,
With trembling hope, and doubtful fear you move,
Resolv'd to tempt your fate, and own your love: 50
But there Belinda meets you on the stairs.
Easy her shape, attracting all her airs;
A smile she gives, and with a smile can wound;
Her melting voice has music in the sound;
Her ev'ry motion wears resistless grace;   55
Wit in her mien, and pleasure in her face:
Here while you vow eternity of love,
Cloe and Celia unregarded move.

---

12 Bathurst planted a thousand acres of woodland on his
Cirencester estate. See Maynard Mack, *Alexander Pope*,
pp. 382–3.

13 At Richings, Bathurst created a canal some 1,600 feet
long, and at Cirencester he had grandiose plans (never
executed) for linking the Rivers Thames and Severn.

15 *lively* living (MS).
23 *Post* 'hastily'.
40 *parterre* A formal flower-bed.
41–2 Bathurst is likened to the coquettes in Pope's *The
Rape of the Lock*, 1:95–8.
56 *mien* 'manner'.

> Thus on the sands of Afric's burning plains,
> However deeply made, no long impress remains;   60
> The lightest leaf can leave its figure there;
> The strongest form is scatter'd by the air.
> So yielding the warm temper of your mind,
> So touch'd by every eye, so tost by wind;
> Oh! how unlike has heav'n my soul design'd!   65
> Unseen, unheard, the throng around me move;
> Not wishing praise, insensible of love:
> No whispers soften, nor no beauties fire;
> Careless I see the dance, and coldly hear the lyre.
>   So num'rous herds are driven o'er the rock;   70
> No print is left of all the passing flock:
> So sings the wind around the solid stone:
> So vainly beat the waves with fruitless moan.
> Tedious the toil, and great the workman's care,
> Who dare attempt to fix impressions there: 75
> But should some swain more skillfull than the rest,
> Engrave his name upon this marble breast,
> Not rolling ages cou'd deface that name;
> Through all the storms of life 'tis still the same:
> Tho' length of years with moss may shade the ground,   80
> Deep, tho' unseen, remains the secret wound.

65 *has* (from MS; *1748* has 'the').
68 Cf. *The Rape of the Lock*, 1:76.

77 *upon this* on this cold (MS). Cf. *Eloisa to Abelard*, 24.

Verses Address'd to the Imitator of Horace

By 1733 relations between Montagu and Pope had become strained to breaking point. In a close-knit society through which anonymous satires circulated as easily as gossip, suspicions grew on both sides: Pope thought she was influencing or even writing some of the vicious attacks on him, and from her viewpoint it could hardly be an oversight that his *Dunciad* (1728) employed 'Lady Mary' as a synonym for prostitute. In the background may have been some disastrous confrontation like that recorded by Montagu's granddaughter during which Pope supposedly declared his love only to be met with Lady Mary's laughter. Whatever the ingredients of the quarrel, it was Pope who brought it to public notice, and the first of his *Imitations of Horace* (published under his name on 15 February 1733) included two couplets designed to wound both her and her intimate friend Hervey. The latter is briefly dismissed as an effeminate rhymester: 'The Lines are weak, another's pleas'd to say, / Lord *Fanny* spins a thousand such a Day', and Montagu makes the first of several appearances in Pope's verse as Sappho, the archetype of the passionate woman poet: 'From furious *Sappho* scarce a milder Fate, / P—x'd by her Love, or libell'd by her Hate'. The response of Hervey and Montagu was immediate, uncompromising and anonymous. *Verses Address'd to the Imitator of the First Satire of the Second Book of Horace. By a Lady*, published on 8 March, represents perhaps the most scabrous and stylish attack Pope had to suffer during a bombardment that lasted over thirty years (catalogued by J. V. Guerinot, *Pamphlet Attacks on Alexander Pope, 1711–1744* (1969)). Most of the poem is considered to be Montagu's (she never acknowledged it), but Hervey's manuscript corrections survive and some passages may be his. Pope believed that 'both sexes had a share in it, but which was uppermost, I know not. I pretend not to determine the exact method of this witty fornication.' For examples of Pope's retaliation, see *Epistle to Dr Arbuthnot*, 305–33, and *Epistle to a Lady*, 24–8.

In 1733 the poem appeared in handsome folio editions simultaneously through two publishers, Dodd and Roberts (the texts vary slightly); a second Dodd edition in octavo made some changes to accidentals, and a further folio Dodd edition (also 1733) was based on the first but with an additional couplet (lines 38–9). It is the latter text that is given here.

In two large Columns, on thy motly Page,
Where *Roman* Wit is stripe'd with *English* Rage;
Where Ribaldry to Satire makes pretence;
And modern Scandal rolls with ancient Sense:
Whilst on one side we see how *Horace* thought;   5
And on the other, how he never wrote:
Who can believe, who view the bad and good,
That the dull Copi'st better understood
That *Spirit*, he pretends to imitate,
Than heretofore that *Greek* he did translate?   10
    Thine is just such an Image of *his* Pen,
As thou thy self art of the Sons of Men:
Where our own Species in Burlesque we trace,
A Sign-Post Likeness of the noble Race;
That is at once Resemblance and Disgrace.   15
    Horace can laugh, is delicate, is clear;
You, only coarsely rail, or darkly sneer:
His Style is elegant, his Diction pure,
Whilst none thy crabbed Numbers can endure;
Hard as thy Heart, and as thy Birth obscure.   20
    If *He* has Thorns, they all on Roses grow;
Thine like rude Thistles, and mean Brambles show
With this Exception, that tho' rank the Soil,
Weeds, as they are, they seem produc'd by Toil.
Satire shou'd, like a polish'd Razor keen,   25
Wound with a Touch, that's scarcely felt or seen.
Thine is an Oyster-Knife, that hacks and hews;
The Rage, but not the Talent to Abuse;
And is in *Hate*, what *Love* is in the Stews.
'Tis the gross *Lust* of Hate, that still annoys,   30
Without Distinction, as gross Love enjoys:
Neither to Folly, nor to Vice confin'd;
The Object of thy Spleen is Human Kind:
It preys on all, who yield or who resist;
To Thee 'tis Provocation to exist.   35
    But if thou see'st a great and gen'rous Heart,
Thy Bow is doubly bent to force a Dart.
Nor Dignity nor Innocence is spar'd,
Nor Age, nor Sex, nor Thrones, nor Graves rever'd.
Nor only Justice vainly we demand,   40
But even Benefits can't rein thy Hand:
To this or that alike in vain we trust,
Nor find Thee less Ungrateful than Unjust.

1 *Columns* Pope's imitations of Horace were printed on the recto pages alongside the original Latin on the verso.

10 Pope had completed his translation of Homer in 1726.

13 *Burlesque* 'parodic mockery'.

16 *delicate* 'finely sensitive'. Pope took up this point in *Epilogue to the Satires*: 'But *Horace*, Sir, was delicate, was nice ...' (1:11–12).

19 *crabbed Numbers* 'harsh verses'. 'Crabbed' can also mean 'ill tempered' and 'physically crooked'.

20 *Birth obscure* See Pope, *Epistle to Dr Arbuthnot*, 381n.

23 *rank* 'fertile in excess', 'weed-producing'. The word also draws on its other meanings of 'offensive' and 'indecent'.

29 *Stews* 'brothels'.

30 *still annoys* 'is persistently offensive'.

36–7 'See *Taste*, an Epistle' (footnote). This alludes to Pope's alleged mockery of the Duke of Chandos in *Epistle to Burlington* (see headnote to that poem).

Not even Youth and Beauty can controul
The universal Rancour of thy Soul;   45
Charms that might soften Superstition's Rage,
Might humble Pride, or thaw the Ice of Age.
But how shou'dst thou by Beauty's Force be mov'd,
No more for loving made, than to be lov'd?
It was the Equity of righteous Heav'n,   50
That such a Soul to such a Form was giv'n;
And shews the Uniformity of Fate,
That one so odious, shou'd be born to hate.
    When God created Thee, one would believe,
He said the same as to *the Snake of Eve*;   55
To human Race Antipathy declare,
'Twixt them and Thee be everlasting War.
But oh! the Sequel of the Sentence dread,
And whilst you *bruise their Heel*, beware your Head.
    Nor think thy Weakness shall be thy Defence;   60
The Female Scold's Protection in Offence.
Sure 'tis as fair to beat who cannot fight,
As 'tis to libel those who cannot write.
And if thou drawst thy Pen to aid the Law,
Others a Cudgel, or a Rod, may draw.   65
    If none with Vengeance yet thy Crimes pursue,
Or give thy manifold Affronts their due;
If Limbs unbroken, Skin without a Stain,
Unwhipt, unblanketed, unkick'd, unslain;
That wretched little Carcass you retain: 70
The Reason is, not that the World wants Eyes;
But thou'rt so mean, they see, and they despise.
When fretful *Porcupine*, with rancorous Will,
From mounted Back shoots forth a harmless Quill,
Cool the Spectators stand; and all the while,   75
Upon the angry little Monster smile.
Thus 'tis with thee: — whilst impotently safe,
You strike unwounding, we unhurt can laugh.
Who but must laugh, this Bully when he sees,
A puny Insect shiv'ring at a Breeze?   80
One over-match'd by ev'ry Blast of Wind,
Insulting and provoking all Mankind.
    Is this the *Thing* to keep Mankind in awe,
To make those tremble who escape the Law?

---

50 *Equity* 'even-handedness'.

55 See Pope, *Epistle to Dr Arbuthnot*, 319n.

56–9 'And the Lord God said unto the serpent, Because thou hast done this, thou art cursed above all cattle, and above every beast of the field … And I will put enmity between thee and the woman, and between thy seed and her seed; it shall bruise thy head, and thou shalt bruise his heel' (Genesis, 3:14–15).

61 *Scold* 'one addicted to abusive language'.

70 *Carcass* A term Pope used of his own body: 'Were not my own Carcase (very little suited to my Soul) my

worst Enemy, were it not for the *Body of this Death*, (as St Paul calls it) I would not be separated from you' (to Lord Orrery, 10 May 1736).

73 Cf. *Hamlet*, I.v.20.

79–80 Cf. Pope, *Epistle to Burlington*, 107–8.

84–6 Pope is being reminded of boastful passages in his *Imitation*: 'Hear this, and tremble! you, who 'scape the Laws' (118); 'Satire's my Weapon … / Who-e'er offends, at some unlucky Time / Slides into Verse, and hitches in a Rhyme, / Sacred to Ridicule!' (69–80).

Is this *the Ridicule* to live so long, 85
The deathless Satire, and *immortal Song*?
No: like thy self-blown Praise, thy Scandal flies;
And, as we're told of Wasps, it stings and dies.
   If none do yet return th'intended Blow;
You all your Safety, to your Dullness owe: 90
But whilst that Armour thy poor Corps defends,
'Twill make thy Readers few, as are thy Friends;
Those, who thy Nature loath'd, yet lov'd thy Art,
Who lik'd thy Head, and yet abhor'd thy Heart;
Chose thee, to read, but never to converse, 95
And scorn'd in Prose, him whom they priz'd in Verse.
Even they shall now their partial Error see,
Shall shun thy Writings like thy Company;
And to thy Books shall ope their Eyes no more,
Than to thy Person they wou'd do their Door. 100
   Nor thou the Justice of the World disown,
That leaves Thee thus an Out-cast, and alone;
For tho' in Law, to murder be to kill,
In Equity the Murder's in the Will:
Then whilst with Coward Hand you stab a Name, 105
And try at least t'assassinate our Fame;
Like the first bold Assassin's be thy Lot,
Ne'er be thy Guilt forgiven, or forgot;
But as thou hate'st, be hated by Mankind,
And with the Emblem of thy crooked Mind, 110
Mark'd on thy Back, like *Cain*, by God's own Hand;
Wander like him, accursed through the Land.

88 This is true of bees, not wasps.
107–12 'Behold, thou hast driven me out this day from the face of the earth; and from thy face shall I be hid; and I shall be a fugitive and a vagabond in the earth; and it shall come to pass, that every one that findeth me shall slay me ... And the Lord set a mark upon Cain, lest any finding him should kill him' (Genesis, 4:14–15).

Verses on Self-Murder, address'd to —

The poem expresses Montagu's despair after Algarotti's departure from England on 6 September 1736. Four days later she wrote to him (in French) likening herself to Queen Dido deserted by Aeneas: 'I am a thousand times more to be pitied than the sad Dido, and I have a thousand more reasons to kill myself. But since until now I have not imitated her conduct, I believe that I shall live, either by cowardice or by strength of character.' The addressee would seem therefore to be Algarotti himself, but there is no evidence it was sent to him. Montagu circulated the poem privately amongst her friends. The verses were first printed (as 'by a Lady') in the *London Magazine* for June 1749, the text given here. It was followed by a corrective note from the editor: 'As it is to be suppos'd that we often differ from the sentiments of our correspondents, and sometimes disapprove them; so here we think this lady has suggested very immoral and pernicious advice; that she has not duly weighed that inimitable soliloquy of *Hamlet*, *To be, or not to be*, – nor the many excellent Tracts that have been publish'd against *Self-Murder*; and, what is worse, seems to have forgot her Maker and her Christianity.'

   In the Harrowby MS the poem is simply entitled '1736 Address'd to ——'. Significant variants are recorded.

With toilsome steps I pass thro' life's dull road,
No packhorse half so weary of his load;
And when this dirty journey shall conclude,
To what new realms is then my way pursu'd?

3 *shall* will (MS).

Say then, does the unbody'd spirit fly   5
To happier climes, and to a better sky?
Or sinking, mix with dust and kindred clay,
And sleep a whole eternity away?
Or shall this form be once again renew'd,
With all its frailties, and its hopes endu'd,   10
Acting once more, on this detested stage,
Passions of youth, infirmities of age?
    I see in *Tully* what the antients thought,
And read unprejudic'd what moderns taught;
But no conviction from my reading springs,   15
Most dubious in the most important things.
    Yet one short moment would at once explain,
What all philosophy has sought in vain;
Would clear all doubt, and terminate all pain.
Why then not hasten that decisive hour,   20
Still in my view, and ever in my power?
Why should I drag along this life I hate,
Without one thought to mitigate the weight?
Why this mysterious being forced t'exist,
When every joy is lost, and every hope dismist?   25
In chains and darkness wherefore should I stay,
And mourn in prison, while I keep the key.

7 *mix with dust and* mixes with its (MS).

13 In his theological dialogues, *De Natura Deorum* and *De Divinatione* (45–44 BC) Cicero expounded the competing views of three philosophical schools: Epicurean, Stoic and Academic.

24 *forced* force (*1749*). Harrowby MS reads 'Whence this misterious bearing to exist' (*bearing* = 'enduring').

A Hymn to the Moon

The poem is subtitled 'Written in *July* in an Arbour'. It was composed earlier than August 1740 (Grundy) and was printed under Montagu's name in the *London Magazine* for May 1750 (the text given here). In 1758 Algarotti asked her for a copy, which he printed in his 'Pensieri Diversi' (*Opere*, Venice (1792), 7:79–81), praising Montagu as occupying an honoured place on the 'English Parnassus'. There are no substantive variants with the Harrowby MS.

Thou silver deity of secret night,
    Direct my footsteps thro' the woodland shade;
Thou conscious witness of unknown delight,
    The lover's guardian, and the muses aid!

By thy pale beams I solitary rove,   5
    To thee my tender grief confide;
Serenely sweet, you gild the silent grove,
    My friend, my goddess, and my guide.

Ev'n thee, fair queen, from thy amazing height,
    The charms of young Endymion drew;   10
Vail'd with the mantle of concealing night;
    With all thy greatness, and thy coldness too.

10 *Endymion* The moon goddess fell in love with the handsome shepherd, Endymion. She caused him to sleep for ever so she could eternally enjoy his beauty.

12 Cf. *The Lover: A Ballad*, 48.

James Thomson (1700–1748)

James Thomson, a lowland Scot, had intended to follow his father into the Presbyterian ministry. But the protracted ten-year period he spent as a student at Edinburgh College (1715–25) witnessed the unmaking of a minister and the making of a poet. Thomson had written poems since boyhood, though his witty friends in the College's literary Grotesque Club dubbed him 'a dull fellow'. Yet there was nothing 'dull' about his rhapsodic blank verse paraphrase of one of the Psalms which he had been set as a routine divinity exercise. For the young Thomson poetry and piety were by no means incompatible, but, unable to conform to his tutor's mandate to 'keep a stricter rein upon his imagination, and express himself in language more intelligible to an ordinary congregation', he abandoned his divinity studies in February 1725. Like many ambitious young Scots in the aftermath of the 1707 Act of Union he sailed south to seek his fortune in London, where he found work as a tutor to Lord Binning's son – 'a low task', he complained, but it was one which gave him leisure to write poetry. *Winter*, published by John Millan on 8 April 1726, had been planned as a sequence of set 'winter-pieces' (see Ambrose Philips), but its close observation of the moods and movements of the natural world marked it out as something distinctly original. 'The images burn and live', remarked the literary patron Aaron Hill, who drew Thomson into his circle of writers, an association which encouraged Thomson to produce successively *Summer* (1727), *Spring* (1728) and, in 1730, *The Seasons* (including the new *Autumn*). *The Seasons* was one of the most popular and widely read poems through the eighteenth and nineteenth centuries.

Meanwhile Thomson had attracted the patronage of both Frances Thynne, Countess of Hertford, and the Lord Chancellor, Charles Talbot, who chose Thomson to accompany his son on the Grand Tour in 1730. Thomson's letters home reveal a man deeply disillusioned. His exposure to Europe confirmed rather than challenged his conviction of British superiority. Thomson's patriotism also informed his politics. *Britannia* (1729), a scathing diatribe against Walpole's pacific Spanish policy, inaugurated his close association with the dissident Whig 'Patriot' opposition which dominated his writing over the next decade. George Lyttelton, the leading Patriot politician and author who became Thomson's long-standing friend and patron, drew him to the notice of Frederick, Prince of Wales, who granted Thomson an annual pension after 1737. *Liberty* (1735–6), dedicated to Frederick, a five-book account of the rise and fall of liberty through history, proved far less popular than *The Seasons* despite its topical application. Thomson, who had already enjoyed modest success as a dramatist with *Sophonisba* (1731), went on to produce a number of politically charged historical tragedies, of which *Edward and Eleanora* (1738) was the first to be banned by Walpole's 1737 Stage Licensing Act. *Alfred* (1740), a masque first performed privately for Prince Frederick's household, gave the world the song 'Rule, Britannia'.

In March 1748 Thomson finally published his two-book Spenserian allegory, *The Castle of Indolence*, on which he had worked intermittently since 1732. The sensual, dream-like descriptions of Canto 1, coupled with its 'faery-world' of Spenserian archaism, fired the imagination of later Romantic poets such as Keats and Wordsworth. The personal nature of the allegory (Thomson depicts himself as an inmate of the Castle, which is abruptly destroyed in Canto 2) hints at some profound inner conflict. Outwardly plump and placid, Thomson harboured a private loneliness and guilt about some of his male friendships which he hoped might be assuaged by a late marriage to Elizabeth Young, a fellow Scot, whom he courted unsuccessfully in 1743. Thomson died a bachelor in August 1748. The next year William Collins's *Ode occasion'd by the Death of Mr Thomson* was the first of many poems to prove the extraordinary influence which Thomson's poetry was to exert over the next literary generation.

The Seasons

'I know no Subject more elevating, more amusing; more ready to awake the poetical Enthusiasm, the philosophical Reflection, and the moral Sentiment, than the *Works of Nature*', exclaimed Thomson in his idealistic Preface to the second edition of *Winter* (1726). 'But there is no thinking of these Things without breaking out into POETRY'. Thomson's choice of 'The Works of Nature' as source and centre of his poetic vision might seem a radical departure from the practice of his contemporaries. Yet the same Preface invokes time-honoured classical and especially Christian precedents for nature poetry – Virgil's *Georgics*, and sublime religious verse 'from *Moses* down to *Milton*'. Like his contemporaries Isaac Watts, Joseph Addison and Aaron Hill, Thomson admired the Old Testament as inspired Hebrew verse. But Milton far outweighs Moses as an influence on *The Seasons*. Other eighteenth-century poets had imitated

Milton's style without finding a subject–matter high enough to bear its weight (see John Philips). It was Thomson who reinvested Miltonic blank verse with an epic grandeur befitting the alternately beautiful and terrible workings of the forces of nature, its storms, floods and fires – a landscape in which vulnerable man only sometimes walks 'superior ... / Amid the glad Creation'.

The distinctive quality of Thomson's verse derives in large part from its Miltonic Latinate style, with its syntactic inversions and its play on the original senses of commonly used words (see notes). *The Seasons'* extraordinarily high frequency of verbs testifies to the dynamic, ever-changing shape of the natural world. The fluency with which the poem moves from one subject to another (including political and historical observations) acquires some coherence through the unifying 'I' of the solitary speaker-poet, who pauses, meditates, rhapsodizes and invites us to penetrate beyond the world of sensory surfaces with the 'eye' of imagination or intellectual understanding. Thomson, a keen student of science and admirer of Newton, believed that a knowledge of optic laws made a rainbow more, not less beautiful. Thomson's shifts in perspective, from the telescopic to the microscopic, confront the reader with the familiar made strange. Dr Johnson perceptively noted that 'The reader of *The Seasons* wonders that he never saw before what Thomson shews him'.

The contrast between *Spring*'s temperate mildness and the fierce extremes of *Winter* and *Summer* must inevitably be lost in reading only one of *The Seasons*. In *Spring* harmony rather than dissonance prevails: the 'informing Author' of nature is a 'SMILING GOD', not a storm-hurling Old Testament Jehovah. The chief source of pain and disruption is sexual desire – as befits a natural world caught in the throes of the mating season. Thomson's frequent periphrases – 'speckled Infant' (fish), 'peaceful People' (sheep), 'feather'd Youth' (birds) – imply a mutually interdependent relationship between mankind and the animal kingdom. Tenderness toward animals is only one facet of Thomson's benevolist philosophy (derived from Shaftesbury – see headnote to Akenside, *The Pleasures of Imagination*), which emphasizes the 'social feelings of the heart'. It is thus disquieting to find a passage in praise of vegetarianism followed by a spirited mock-heroic account of fishing and hunting. Of such ironic juxtapositions are *The Seasons* made, suggesting perhaps not the 'want of method' of which Dr Johnson complained, but a complex, multi-faceted vision of the world.

Thomson seemed unable to stop revising *The Seasons*. The poem expanded over twenty years to reflect his growing interests in foreign geography, politics, history and science, in the process losing some of its original delicacy and vigour. *Spring*, first published in 1729, is the least revised season. It acquired about one hundred extra lines in the 1744 version – the descriptions of fishing and of Lyttelton's Hagley Park, and the lines on happy virtuous love (1158–62). The 1746 duodecimo edition, the last to be revised by Thomson himself, has been used for the following text. The editors have made two emendations (see notes) and have standardized *tho'* and *thro'*, which mostly occur without the apostrophe. Other inconsistencies have been allowed to remain. Our notes have benefited from the full and meticulous annotation in James Sambrook's edition of *The Seasons*.

Spring

Come, gentle SPRING, Ethereal Mildness, come,
And from the Bosom of yon dropping Cloud,
While Music wakes around, veil'd in a Shower
Of shadowing Roses, on our Plains descend.
 O HARTFORD, fitted, or to shine in Courts   5
With unaffected Grace, or walk the Plain
With Innocence and Meditation join'd
In soft Assemblage, listen to my Song,
Which thy own Season paints; when Nature all
Is blooming, and benevolent, like thee.   10
 And see where surly WINTER passes off,
Far to the North, and calls his ruffian Blasts:
His Blasts obey, and quit the howling Hill,

---

5 *HARTFORD* Frances Thynne, Countess of Hertford (1699–1754), Lady of the Bedchamber to Princess, later Queen, Caroline. A poet herself, she extended patronage to several poets. Thomson wrote part of

Spring while her guest at Marlborough Castle, Wiltshire.
5–6 *or ... or* 'either ... or'.
13 *howling* 'dreary', 'desolate'.

The shatter'd Forest, and the ravag'd Vale;
While softer Gales succeed, at whose kind Touch,   15
Dissolving Snows in livid Torrents lost,
The Mountains lift their green Heads to the Sky.
    As yet the trembling Year is unconfirm'd,
And WINTER oft at Eve resumes the Breeze,
Chills the pale Morn, and bids his driving Sleets   20
Deform the Day delightless: so that scarce
The Bittern knows his Time, with Bill ingulpht,
To shake the sounding Marsh; or from the Shore
The Plovers when to scatter o'er the Heath,
And sing their wild Notes to the listening Waste.   25
    At last from *Aries* rolls the bounteous Sun,
And the bright *Bull* receives him. Then no more
Th' expansive Atmosphere is cramp'd with Cold;
But, full of Life and vivifying Soul,
Lifts the light Clouds sublime, and spreads them thin,   30
Fleecy, and white, o'er all-surrounding Heaven.
    Forth fly the tepid Airs; and unconfin'd,
Unbinding Earth, the moving Softness strays.
Joyous, th' impatient Husbandman perceives
Relenting Nature, and his lusty Steers   35
Drives from their Stalls, to where the well-us'd Plow
Lies in the Furrow, loosen'd from the Frost.
There, unrefusing to the harness'd Yoke,
They lend their Shoulder, and begin their Toil,
Chear'd by the simple Song and soaring Lark.   40
Meanwhile, incumbent o'er the shining Share,
The Master leans, removes th' obstructing Clay,
Winds the whole Work, and sidelong lays the Glebe.
    White, thro' the neighbouring Fields the Sower stalks,
With measur'd Step; and, liberal, throws the Grain   45
Into the faithful Bosom of the Ground.
The Harrow follows harsh, and shuts the Scene.
    Be gracious, HEAVEN! for now laborious Man
Has done his Part. Ye fostering Breezes, blow!
Ye softening Dews, ye tender Showers, descend!   50
And temper all, thou world-reviving Sun,
Into the perfect Year! Nor, ye, who live
In Luxury and Ease, in Pomp and Pride,
Think these lost Themes unworthy of your Ear:

16 *livid* 'leaden-grey'.
17 Cf. 'their broad bare backs upheave / Into the clouds; their tops ascend the sky' (*Paradise Lost*, 7:285–6).
22–3 *Bittern* A marsh-bird which makes a distinctive 'boom' call during the mating season. Thomson wrongly assumes it makes the noise by dipping its bill under water.
24–5 *Plovers* Short-billed wading birds who winter on the shore but return inland to breed in spring and are often seen swooping over ploughed fields.
26 *Aries* The Ram, the first sign of the zodiac, which the sun enters on 20 or 21 March.
27 *Bull* Taurus, the second sign of the zodiac, which the sun enters on 21 April.
28 *cramp'd* 'compressed'. Cold air is denser than warm air.
30 *sublime* 'aloft'.
41 *incumbent* 'leaning' (Lat. *incumbens*); *Share* 'ploughshare'.
42 The clay sticking to the plough prevents clean furrows.
43 *Winds* 'turns'; *Glebe* 'earth'.
44 Sambrook suggests that the sower looks white either because he is using a bed-sheet as a seed-hopper, or because he has become covered with the powdered lime used to coat seeds to protect them from pests.

Such Themes as these the *rural* MARO sung   55
To wide-imperial *Rome*, in the full Height
Of Elegance and Taste, by *Greece* refin'd.
In antient Times, the sacred Plow employ'd
The Kings, and awful Fathers of Mankind:
And Some, with whom compar'd, your Insect-Tribes   60
Are but the Beings of a Summer's Day,
Have held the Scale of Empire, rul'd the Storm
Of mighty War; then, with victorious Hand,
Disdaining little Delicacies, seiz'd
The Plow, and greatly independant scorn'd   65
All the vile Stores Corruption can bestow.
　　Ye generous BRITONS, venerate the Plow!
And o'er your Hills, and long withdrawing Vales,
Let Autumn spread his Treasures to the Sun,
Luxuriant, and unbounded! As the Sea,   70
Far thro' his azure turbulent Domain,
Your Empire owns, and from a thousand Shores
Wafts all the Pomp of Life into your Ports;
So with superior Boon may your rich Soil,
Exuberant, Nature's better Blessings pour   75
O'er every Land, the naked Nations cloath,
And be th' exhaustless Granary of a World!
　　Nor only thro' the lenient Air this Change,
Delicious, breathes; the penetrative Sun,
His Force deep-darting to the dark Retreat   80
Of Vegetation, sets the steaming Power
At large, to wander o'er the vernant Earth,
In various Hues; but chiefly thee, gay *Green!*
Thou smiling Nature's universal Robe!
United Light and Shade! where the Sight dwells   85
With growing Strength, and ever-new Delight.
　　From the moist Meadow to the wither'd Hill,
Led by the Breeze, the vivid Verdure runs,
And swells, and deepens, to the cherish'd Eye.

---

55 *rural MARO* Virgil, author of the rustic *Georgics*. Cf. 456.

58–66 Thomson here alludes to early Roman farmer-statesmen admired for their incorruptible civic virtue. Most famous was Cincinnatus, called from the plough to be dictator in 458 BC. After sixteen days in which he defeated Rome's enemies he resigned office and returned to his farm.

60 *Insect-Tribes* A satirical periphrasis for modern politicians.

66 In 1744 Thomson added this reference to 'Corruption' – a key term in the Patriot propaganda directed at Walpole's government.

74 *Boon* 'blessing', 'gift'.

76–7 Britain had exported wool since the Middle Ages. During the first half of the eighteenth century Britain also exported large quantities of grain.

78 *lenient* 'softening', 'soothing'.

79–89 The first of many scientific explanations for the natural world in *The Seasons*. These lines on sap flow and colouring of plants draw primarily on Stephen Hales's *Vegetable Staticks* (1727), and Richard Bradley's *New Improvements of Planting and Gardening* (1717–18), which also supplied the information on crop blights in 114–36. Hales describes how the sun's heat brings moisture to the roots and raises sap by transpiration. Bradley thought that the movement of this fluid caused variety of colour in plants.

81 *steaming Power* 'sap'.

82 *vernant* 'green and flourishing'.

84 *smiling* The English equivalent of Lat. *laetus* ('cheerful', 'abundant'), a term Virgil often uses for the appearance of crops.

The Hawthorn whitens; and the juicy Groves 90
Put forth their Buds, unfolding by Degrees,
Till the whole leafy Forest stands display'd,
In full Luxuriance, to the sighing Gales;
Where the Deer rustle thro' the twining Brake,
And the Birds sing conceal'd. At once, array'd 95
In all the Colours of the flushing Year,
By Nature's swift and secret-working Hand,
The Garden glows, and fills the liberal Air
With lavish Fragrance; while the promis'd Fruit
Lies yet a little Embryo, unperceiv'd, 100
Within its crimson Folds. Now from the Town
Buried in Smoke, and Sleep, and noisom Damps,
Oft let me wander o'er the dewy Fields,
Where Freshness breathes, and dash the trembling Drops
From the bent Bush, as thro' the verdant Maze 105
Of Sweet-briar Hedges I pursue my Walk;
Or taste the Smell of Dairy; or ascend
Some Eminence, AUGUSTA, in thy Plains,
And see the Country, far-diffus'd around,
One boundless Blush, one white-empurpled Shower 110
Of mingled Blossoms; where the raptur'd Eye
Hurries from Joy to Joy, and, hid beneath
The fair Profusion, yellow Autumn spies.
    If, brush'd from *Russian* Wilds, a cutting Gale
Rise not, and scatter from his humid Wings 115
The clammy Mildew; or, dry-blowing, breathe
Untimely Frost; before whose baleful Blast
The full-blown Spring thro' all her Foliage shrinks,
Joyless, and dead, a wide-dejected Waste.
For oft, engender'd by the hazy North, 120
Myriads on Myriads, Insect-Armies waft
Keen in the poison'd Breeze; and wasteful eat,
Thro' Buds and Bark, into the blacken'd Core,
Their eager Way. A feeble Race! yet oft
The sacred Sons of Vengeance! on whose Course 125
Corrosive Famine waits, and kills the Year.
To check this Plague the skilful Farmer Chaff,
And blazing Straw, before his Orchard burns;
Till, all involv'd in Smoke, the latent Foe
From every Cranny suffocated falls: 130
Or scatters o'er the Blooms the pungent Dust
Of Pepper, fatal to the frosty Tribe:

101–2 By the time Thomson wrote *Spring* London was already suffering serious coal-smoke pollution; *noisom Damps* 'offensive vapours'.
107 *taste the Smell* 'Taste' or 'tast' was a northern dialect word for 'to smell': but Thomson also evokes synaesthesia (the mingling of sense-impressions). Cf. 475–9.
108 *Eminence* 'hill'; *AUGUSTA* The title given to Roman London during the fourth century, often used by Restoration and eighteenth-century poets to evoke a sense of imperial power. Cf. Pope, *Windsor-Forest*, 334, 375.
110 *empurpled* 'brightly coloured'.
111–13 Thomson requires the 'eye' of the imagination or intellect to 'see' beyond the limitations of the physical eye. Cf. 183–5; 459; 495–6.
127 *Chaff* 'corn husks'.
129 *involv'd* 'wrapped in' (Lat. *involvo*); *latent* 'hidden' (Lat. *latens*).
132 *frosty Tribe* Biting insects from the north.

Or, when th' envenom'd Leaf begins to curl,
With sprinkled Water drowns them in their Nest:
Nor, while they pick them up with busy Bill,   135
The little trooping Birds unwisely scares.
        Be patient, Swains; these cruel-seeming Winds
Blow not in vain. Far hence they keep, repress'd,
Those deepening Clouds on Clouds, surcharg'd with Rain,
That o'er the vast *Atlantic* hither borne,   140
In endless Train, would quench the Summer-Blaze,
And, chearless, drown the crude unripen'd Year.
        The North-East spends his Rage, and now, shut up
Within his iron Caves, th' effusive South
Warms the wide Air, and o'er the Void of Heaven   145
Breathes the big Clouds with vernal Showers distent.
At first a dusky Wreath they seem to rise,
Scarce staining Ether; but by fast Degrees,
In Heaps on Heaps, the doubling Vapour sails
Along the loaded Sky, and mingling deep   150
Sits on th' Horizon round a settled Gloom.
Not such as wintry Storms on Mortals shed,
Oppressing Life, but lovely, gentle, kind,
And full of every Hope and every Joy,
The Wish of Nature. Gradual, sinks the Breeze,   155
Into a perfect Calm; that not a Breath
Is heard to quiver thro' the closing Woods,
Or rustling turn the many-twinkling Leaves
Of Aspin tall. Th' uncurling Floods, diffus'd
In glassy Breadth, seem thro' delusive Lapse   160
Forgetful of their Course. 'Tis Silence all,
And pleasing Expectation. Herds and Flocks
Drop the dry Sprig, and mute-imploring eye
The falling Verdure. Hush'd in short Suspense,
The plumy People streak their Wings with Oil,   165
To throw the lucid Moisture trickling off;
And wait th' approaching Sign to strike, at once,
Into the general Choir. Even Mountains, Vales,
And Forests seem, impatient, to demand
The promis'd Sweetness. Man superior walks   170
Amid the glad Creation, musing Praise,
And looking lively Gratitude. At last,
The Clouds consign their Treasures to the Fields,
And, softly shaking on the dimpled Pool
Prelusive Drops, let all their Moisture flow,   175
In large Effusion o'er the freshen'd World.
The stealing Shower is scarce to patter heard,
By such as wander thro' the Forest-Walks,
Beneath th' umbrageous Multitude of Leaves.

---

144 *effusive* 'outpouring' (Lat. *effusio*).
146 *vernal* 'spring' (adj.); *distent* 'swollen' (Lat. *distentus*).
148 *Ether* The medium lighter and more fluid than air
    which was thought to fill the upper regions of space.
159 *uncurling* 'without ripples'.

160 *delusive* 'undiscernible'; *Lapse* 'falling' (Lat. *lapsus*).
165 *plumy People* Birds.
175 *Prelusive* 'preliminary'.
179 *umbrageous* 'shady'.

But who can hold the Shade, while Heaven descends   180
In universal Bounty, shedding Herbs,
And Fruits, and Flowers, on Nature's ample Lap?
Swift Fancy fir'd anticipates their Growth;
And, while the milky Nutriment distills,
Beholds the kindling Country colour round.   185
    Thus all day long the full-distended Clouds
Indulge their genial Stores, and well-shower'd Earth
Is deep enrich'd with vegetable Life;
Till, in the western Sky, the downward Sun
Looks out, effulgent, from amid the Flush   190
Of broken Clouds, gay-shifting to his Beam.
The rapid Radiance instantaneous strikes
Th' illumin'd Mountain, thro' the Forest streams,
Shakes on the Floods, and in a yellow Mist,
Far smoking o'er th' interminable Plain,   195
In twinkling Myriads lights the dewy Gems.
Moist, bright, and green, the Landskip laughs around.
Full swell the Woods; their every Musick wakes,
Mix'd in wild Concert with the warbling Brooks
Increas'd, the distant Bleatings of the Hills,   200
The hollow Lows responsive from the Vales,
Whence blending all the sweeten'd Zephyr springs.
Meantime refracted from yon eastern Cloud,
Bestriding Earth, the grand ethereal Bow
Shoots up immense; and every Hue unfolds,   205
In fair Proportion running from the Red,
To where the Violet fades into the Sky.
Here, awful NEWTON, the dissolving Clouds
Form, fronting on the Sun, thy showery Prism;
And to the sage-instructed Eye unfold   210
The various Twine of Light, by thee disclos'd
From the white mingling Maze. Not so the Swain,
He wondering views the bright Enchantment bend,
Delightful, o'er the radiant Fields, and runs
To catch the falling Glory; but amaz'd   215
Beholds th' amusive Arch before him fly,
Then vanish quite away. Still Night succeeds,
A soften'd Shade, and saturated Earth
Awaits the Morning-Beam, to give to Light,
Rais'd thro' ten thousand different Plastic Tubes,   220
The balmy Treasures of the former Day.

180 *hold* 'keep to'.
183 *Fancy* 'imagination' (the term used here in the first edition of *Spring*). See 455n.
184 *milky Nutriment* 'sap'.
196 *dewy Gems* The buds, sparkling with sunlight, look like gems. (Lat. *gemma* can mean either 'bud' or 'jewel'.)
202 *Zephyr* The mild west wind.
208 *NEWTON* Sir Isaac Newton (1642–1727), the great mathematician and natural philosopher who developed ground-breaking theories of gravitation and of colour.

His *Philosophiae Naturalis Principia Mathematica* appeared in 1687; his *Opticks* (from which Thomson draws this account of the rainbow) in 1704. Thomson wrote a moving poem on his death in 1727.
209 *Prism* Newton arrived at his theory of colour after producing a spectrum of colours by passing a ray of sunlight through a glass prism.
216 *amusive* 'deceptive'.
220 *Plastic Tubes* 'pliant sap vessels'.

Then spring the living Herbs, profusely wild,
O'er all the deep-green Earth, beyond the Power
Of Botanist to number up their Tribes:
Whether he steals along the lonely Dale,   225
In silent Search; or thro' the Forest, rank
With what the dull Incurious Weeds account,
Bursts his blind Way; or climbs the Mountain-Rock,
Fir'd by the nodding Verdure of its Brow.
With such a liberal Hand has Nature flung   230
Their Seeds abroad, blown them about in Winds,
Innumerous mix'd them with the nursing Mold,
The moistening Current, and prolifick Rain.
    But who their Virtues can declare? Who pierce
With Vision pure, into these secret Stores   235
Of Health, and Life, and Joy? The Food of Man,
While yet he liv'd in Innocence, and told
A Length of golden Years, unflesh'd in Blood,
A Stranger to the savage Arts of Life,
Death, Rapine, Carnage, Surfeit, and Disease,   240
The Lord, and not the Tyrant of the World.
    The first fresh Dawn then wak'd the gladden'd Race
Of uncorrupted Man, nor blush'd to see
The Sluggard sleep beneath its sacred Beam.
For their light Slumbers gently fum'd away;   245
And up they rose as vigorous as the Sun,
Or to the Culture of the willing Glebe,
Or to the chearful Tendance of the Flock.
Meantime the Song went round; and Dance and Sport
Wisdom and friendly Talk, successive stole   250
Their Hours away. While in the rosy Vale
Love breath'd his infant Sighs, from Anguish free,
And full replete with Bliss; save the sweet Pain,
That, inly thrilling, but exalts it more.
Nor yet injurious Act, nor surly Deed,   255
Was known among these happy Sons of HEAVEN;
For Reason and Benevolence were Law.
Harmonious Nature too look'd smiling on.
Clear shone the Skies, cool'd with eternal Gales,
And balmy Spirit all. The youthful Sun   260
Shot his best Rays, and still the gracious Clouds
Drop'd Fatness down; as, o'er the swelling Mead,
The Herds and Flocks, commixing, play'd secure.
This when, emergent from the gloomy Wood,

226–7 *rank … account* Sambrook glosses: 'with plants
    which dull and incurious people reckon to be weeds'.
236–71 Thomson follows classical precedent in describing a
    mythic innocent 'Golden Age' ruled by Saturn,
    gradually deteriorating through the Silver, Bronze and
    Iron Ages. Modern man lives in the last. The myth has
    close parallels with the Biblical story of the Garden of
    Eden and mankind's loss of his paradisal state.

Thomson's main sources are Ovid, *Metamorphoses*,
    1:89–112; Virgil, *Eclogues*, 4; and Isaiah, 11:6–8, with
    echoes of *Paradise Lost*.
238 *unflesh'd in* 'unstimulated by the taste of'.
242–6 Cf. *Paradise Lost*, 5:1–7.
245 *fum'd* 'evaporated'.
247–8 *Or … Or* 'Either … Or'.
262 *Fatness* 'fruitfulness'.

The glaring Lion saw, his horrid Heart 265
Was meeken'd, and he join'd his sullen Joy.
For Music held the whole in perfect Peace:
Soft sigh'd the Flute; the tender Voice was heard,
Warbling the vary'd Heart; the Woodlands round
Apply'd their Quire; and Winds and Waters flow'd 270
In Consonance. Such were those Prime of Days.
    But now those white unblemish'd Minutes, whence
The fabling Poets took their golden Age,
Are found no more amid these iron Times,
These Dregs of Life! Now the distemper'd Mind 275
Has lost that Concord of harmonious Powers,
Which forms the Soul of Happiness; and all
Is off the Poise within: the Passions all
Have burst their Bounds; and Reason half extinct,
Or impotent, or else approving, sees 280
The foul Disorder. Senseless, and deform'd,
Convulsive Anger storms at large; or pale,
And silent, settles into fell Revenge.
Base Envy withers at another's Joy,
And hates that Excellence it cannot reach. 285
Desponding Fear, of feeble Fancies full,
Weak, and unmanly, loosens every Power.
Even Love itself is Bitterness of Soul,
A pensive Anguish pining at the Heart:
Or, sunk to sordid Interest, feels no more 290
That noble Wish, that never-cloy'd Desire,
Which, selfish Joy disdaining, seeks, alone,
To bless the dearer Object of its Flame.
Hope sickens with Extravagance; and Grief,
Of Life impatient, into Madness swells; 295
Or in dead Silence wastes the weeping Hours.
These, and a thousand mix'd Emotions more,
From ever-changing Views of Good and Ill,
Form'd infinitely various, vex the Mind
With endless Storm. Whence, deeply rankling, grows 300
The partial Thought, a listless Unconcern,
Cold, and averting from our Neighbour's Good;
Then dark Disgust, and Hatred, winding Wiles,
Coward Deceit, and ruffian Violence.
At last, extinct each social Feeling, fell 305
And joyless Inhumanity pervades,
And petrifies the Heart. Nature disturb'd
Is deem'd, vindictive, to have chang'd her Course.
    Hence, in old dusky Time, a Deluge came:

265 *horrid* 'savage'.
266 *sullen* 'deep-voiced'.
270 *Quire* 'choir'.
275–308 Cf. *Paradise Lost*, 9:1121–89.
275 *distemper'd* 'unbalanced'.
305 *fell* 'cruel'.
309–22 Thomson's source here is Thomas Burnet's influential *The Theory of the Earth* (translated from Latin 1684–9), a cosmogony inspired by his voyage across the Alps. Burnet claimed that before the Flood the world was a smooth sphere where constant spring reigned. Water was contained inside the sphere, and the Flood occurred when the earth's surface fractured, throwing up a deluge that engulfed the world, leaving mountains and oceans in its wake. Simultaneously the various seasonal changes commenced. Thomson follows Milton in attributing the seasons to the Fall. Lines 317–22 echo *Paradise Lost*, 10:651–6 and 4:147–8.

When the deep-cleft disparting Orb, that arch'd   310
The central Waters round, impetuous rush'd,
With universal Burst, into the Gulph,
And o'er the high-pil'd Hills of fractur'd Earth
Wide-dash'd the Waves, in Undulation vast;
Till, from the Center to the streaming Clouds,   315
A shoreless Ocean tumbled round the Globe.
    The Seasons since have, with severer Sway,
Oppress'd a broken World: the Winter keen
Shook forth his Waste of Snows; and Summer shot
His pestilential Heats. Great Spring, before,   320
Green'd all the Year; and Fruits and Blossoms blush'd,
In social Sweetness, on the self-same Bough.
Pure was the temperate Air; an even Calm
Perpetual reign'd, save what the Zephyrs bland
Breath'd o'er the blue Expanse: for then nor Storms   325
Were taught to blow, nor Hurricanes to rage;
Sound slept the Waters; no sulphureous Glooms
Swell'd in the Sky, and sent the Lightning forth;
While sickly Damps, and cold autumnal Fogs,
Hung not, relaxing, on the Springs of Life.   330
But now, of turbid Elements the Sport,
From Clear to Cloudy tost, from Hot to Cold,
And Dry to Moist, with inward-eating Change,
Our drooping Days are dwindled down to Nought,
Their Period finish'd ere 'tis well begun.   335
    And yet the wholesome Herb neglected dies;
Tho' with the pure exhilarating Soul
Of Nutriment and Health, and vital Powers,
Beyond the Search of Art, 'tis copious blest.
For, with hot Ravine fir'd, ensanguin'd Man   340
Is now become the Lion of the Plain,
And worse. The Wolf, who from the nightly Fold
Fierce-drags the bleating Prey, ne'er drunk her Milk,
Nor wore her warming Fleece: nor has the Steer,
At whose strong Chest the deadly Tyger hangs,   345
E'er plow'd for him. They too are temper'd high,
With Hunger stung, and wild Necessity,
Nor lodges Pity in their shaggy Breast.
But *Man*, whom Nature form'd of milder Clay,
With every kind Emotion in his Heart,   350
And taught alone to weep; while from her Lap
She pours ten thousand Delicacies, Herbs,
And Fruits, as numerous as the Drops of Rain
Or Beams that gave them Birth: shall he, fair Form!

329–35 Burnet asserted that seasonal changes caused the human body to age by repeatedly relaxing and contracting its tissues.

336–73 Thomson's argument for vegetarianism is based on Ovid, *Metamorphoses*, 15:75–142. George Cheyne's influential *Essay on Health and Long Life* (1724) recommended a vegetarian diet for health reasons. Thomson may also have been inspired by Gay's *Trivia*, 2:231–42.

340 *Ravine* The appetite to kill and devour; *ensanguin'd* 'blood-stained'.

346 *temper'd high* 'hot-tempered'.

Who wears sweet Smiles, and looks erect on Heaven,   355
E'er stoop to mingle with the prowling Herd,
And dip his Tongue in Gore? The Beast of Prey,
Blood-stain'd deserves to bleed: but you, ye Flocks,
What have you done; ye peaceful People, What,
To merit Death? You, who have given us Milk   360
In luscious Streams, and lent us your own Coat
Against the Winter's Cold? And the plain Ox,
That harmless, honest, guileless Animal,
In What has he offended? He, whose Toil,
Patient and ever-ready, clothes the Land   365
With all the Pomp of Harvest; shall he bleed,
And struggling groan beneath the cruel Hands
Even of the Clowns he feeds? And That perhaps,
To swell the Riot of th' autumnal Feast,
Won by his Labour? This the feeling Heart   370
Would tenderly suggest: but 'tis enough,
In this late Age, adventurous, to have touch'd
Light on the Numbers of the *Samian* Sage.
High HEAVEN forbids the bold presumptuous Strain,
Whose wisest Will has fix'd us in a State   375
That must not yet to pure Perfection rise.
Besides, who knows, how *rais'd* to higher Life,
From Stage to Stage, the *Vital Scale ascends?*
    Now when the first foul Torrent of the Brooks,
Swell'd with the vernal Rains, is ebb'd away;   380
And, whitening, down their mossy-tinctur'd Stream
Descends the billowy Foam: now is the Time,
While yet the dark-brown Water aids the Guile,
To tempt the Trout. The well-dissembled Fly,
The Rod fine-tapering with elastic Spring,   385
Snatch'd from the hoary Steed the floating Line,
And all thy slender watry Stores prepare.
But let not on thy Hook the tortur'd Worm,
Convulsive, twist in agonizing Folds;
Which, by rapacious Hunger swallow'd deep,   390
Gives, as you tear it from the bleeding Breast
Of the weak helpless uncomplaining Wretch,
Harsh Pain and Horror to the tender Hand.
    When, with his lively Ray, the potent Sun
Has pierc'd the Streams, and rous'd the finny Race,   395
Then, issuing chearful, to thy Sport repair;
Chief should the Western Breezes curling play,

368 *Clowns* 'rural labourers'.

373 *Samian Sage* Pythagoras, the Greek philosopher born at Samos *c.*580 BC, urged vegetarianism because he believed in metempsychosis, the transmigration of souls between human and animal bodies. See Gay, *Trivia*, 2:237.

377–8 Thomson seems to believe that souls ascend through the great chain of being ('*Vital Scale*') to greater purity.

381 *mossy-tinctur'd* 'coloured by peat'.

386 Fishing lines were made from horse-hair.

388–93 Whereas the 'Fly' (384) lodges in the tough cartilage of the fish's mouth, the worm is swallowed, making it impossible to remove the hook without ripping the fish's intestines. The worm, the fish and the angler's hand all suffer.

396 *issuing* 'sallying forth'. The verbs *repair, pursue* (401) and *throw* (408) are in the imperative mood – the poet is instructing the reader.

And light o'er Ether bear the shadowy Clouds.
High to their Fount, this Day, amid the Hills,
And Woodlands warbling round, trace up the Brooks;   400
The Next, pursue their rocky-channel'd Maze,
Down to the River, in whose ample Wave
Their little Naiads love to sport at large.
Just in the dubious Point, where with the Pool
Is mix'd the trembling Stream, or where it boils   405
Around the Stone, or from the hollow'd Bank,
Reverted, plays in undulating Flow,
There throw, nice-judging, the delusive Fly;
And, as you lead it round in artful Curve,
With Eye attentive mark the springing Game.   410
Strait as above the Surface of the Flood
They wanton rise, or urg'd by Hunger leap,
Then fix, with gentle Twitch, the barbed Hook:
Some lightly tossing to the grassy Bank,
And to the shelving Shore, slow-dragging some,   415
With various Hand proportion'd to their Force.
If yet too young, and easily deceiv'd,
A worthless Prey scarce bends your pliant Rod,
Him, piteous of his Youth, and the short Space
He has enjoy'd the vital Light of Heaven,   420
Soft disengage, and back into the Stream
The speckled Infant throw. But should you lure
From his dark Haunt, beneath the tangled Roots
Of pendant Trees, the Monarch of the Brook,
Behoves you then to ply your finest Art.   425
Long time he, following cautious, scans the Fly;
And oft attempts to seize it, but as oft
The dimpled Water speaks his jealous Fear.
At last, while haply o'er the shaded Sun
Passes a Cloud, he desperate takes the Death,   430
With sullen Plunge. At once he darts along,
Deep-struck, and runs out all the lengthen'd Line;
Then seeks the farthest Ooze, the sheltering Weed,
The cavern'd Bank, his old secure Abode;
And flies aloft, and flounces round the Pool,   435
Indignant of the Guile. With yielding Hand,
That feels him still, yet to his furious Course
Gives way, you, now retiring, following now
Across the Stream, exhaust his idle Rage:
Till floating broad upon his breathless Side,   440
And to his Fate abandon'd, to the Shore
You gaily drag your unresisting Prize.
    Thus pass the temperate Hours: but when the Sun
Shakes from his Noon-day Throne the scattering Clouds,
Even shooting listless Languor thro' the Deeps;   445
Then seek the Bank where flowering Elders croud,

---

403 *Naiads* Water-nymphs.
408 *nice-judging* 'with precise judgement'.
412 *wanton* 'playful'.
416 *With various Hand* 'with differing degrees of strength'.

424 *Monarch* Either the salmon or the adult trout.
428 *jealous* 'suspicious'.
446 *Elders* The red elder tree, found in Scotland and the
    north-east, flowers in spring.

Where scatter'd wild the Lily of the Vale
Its balmy Essence breathes, where Cowslips hang
The dewy Head, where purple Violets lurk,
With all the lowly Children of the Shade: 450
Or lie reclin'd beneath yon spreading Ash,
Hung o'er the Steep; whence, borne on liquid Wing,
The sounding Culver shoots; or where the Hawk,
High, in the beetling Cliff, his Airy builds.
There let the Classic Page thy Fancy lead 455
Thro' rural Scenes; such as the *Mantuan* Swain
Paints in the matchless Harmony of Song.
Or catch thy self the Landskip, gliding swift
Athwart Imagination's vivid Eye:
Or by the vocal Woods and Waters lull'd, 460
And lost in lonely Musing, in a Dream,
Confus'd, of careless Solitude, where mix
Ten thousand wandering Images of Things,
Soothe every Gust of Passion into Peace,
All but the Swellings of the soften'd Heart, 465
That waken, not disturb the tranquil Mind.
　　Behold yon breathing Prospect bids the Muse
Throw all her Beauty forth. But who can paint
Like Nature? Can Imagination boast,
Amid its gay Creation, Hues like hers? 470
Or can it mix them with that matchless Skill,
And lose them in each other, as appears
In every Bud that blows? If Fancy then
Unequal fails beneath the pleasing Task;
Ah what shall Language do? Ah where find Words 475
Ting'd with so many Colours; and whose Power,
To Life approaching, may perfume my Lays
With that fine Oil, those aromatic Gales,
That inexhaustive flow continual round?
　　Yet tho' successless, will the Toil delight. 480
Come then, ye Virgins, and ye Youths, whose Hearts
Have felt the Raptures of refining Love;
And thou, AMANDA, come, Pride of my Song!
Form'd by the Graces, Loveliness itself!
Come with those downcast Eyes, sedate and sweet, 485
Those Looks demure, that deeply pierce the Soul;
Where with the Light of thoughtful Reason mix'd,
Shines lively Fancy and the feeling Heart:
Oh come! and while the rosy-footed May
Steals blushing on, together let us tread 490
The Morning-Dews, and gather in their Prime
Fresh-blooming Flowers, to grace thy braided Hair,

452 *liquid* 'bright' (Lat. *liquidus*).
453 *Culver* 'wood-pigeon'.
454 *beetling* 'overhanging'; *Airy* 'eyrie', 'eagle's nest'.
455 *Fancy* Synonymous with 'Imagination' (459), the power to create images in the mind (cf. 469, 473). See Akenside, *The Pleasures of Imagination*, 1:10n.

456 *Mantuan Swain* Virgil, born near Mantua, here as author of the pastoral *Eclogues*.
478 *Oil* The oil which gives scent to plants.
483 *AMANDA* Elizabeth Young. See biographical headnote.
484 *Graces* The three classical goddesses who embody loveliness and grace.

And thy lov'd Bosom that improves their Sweets.
   See, where the winding Vale its lavish Stores,
Irriguous, spreads. See, how the Lily drinks   495
The latent Rill, scarce oozing thro' the Grass,
Of Growth luxuriant; or the humid Bank,
In fair Profusion, decks. Long let us walk,
Where the Breeze blows from yon extended Field
Of blossom'd Beans. *Arabia* cannot boast   500
A fuller Gale of Joy than, liberal, thence
Breathes thro' the Sense, and takes the ravish'd Soul.
Nor is the Mead unworthy of thy Foot,
Full of fresh Verdure, and unnumber'd Flowers,
The Negligence of *Nature*, wide, and wild;   505
Where, undisguis'd by mimic *Art*, she spreads
Unbounded Beauty to the roving Eye.
Here their delicious Task the fervent Bees,
In swarming Millions, tend. Around, athwart,
Thro' the soft Air, the busy Nations fly,   510
Cling to the Bud, and, with inserted Tube,
Suck its pure Essence, its ethereal Soul.
And oft, with bolder Wing, they soaring dare
The purple Heath, or where the Wild-thyme grows,
And yellow load them with the luscious Spoil.   515
   At length the finish'd Garden to the View
Its Vistas opens, and its Alleys green.
Snatch'd thro' the verdant Maze, the hurried Eye
Distracted wanders; now the bowery Walk
Of Covert close, where scarce a speck of Day   520
Falls on the lengthen'd Gloom, protracted sweeps;
Now meets the bending Sky, the River now
Dimpling along, the breezy-ruffled Lake,
The Forest darkening round, the glittering Spire,
Th' etherial Mountain, and the distant Main.   525
But why so far excursive? when at Hand,
Along these blushing Borders, bright with Dew,
And in yon mingled Wilderness of Flowers,
Fair-handed Spring unbosoms every Grace:
Throws out the Snow-drop, and the Crocus first;   530
The Daisy, Primrose, Violet darkly blue,
And Polyanthus of unnumber'd Dyes;
The yellow Wall-Flower, stain'd with iron Brown;
And lavish Stock that scents the Garden round.
From the soft Wing of vernal Breezes shed,   535
Anemonies; Auriculas, enrich'd

---

493 *Sweets* 'fragrance'.

495 *Irriguous* 'irrigating'; *Lily* The lent-lily or daffodil.

500 *Beans* Beams (*1746*); Arabian spices could apparently be smelt far out to sea. Cf. 'the spicy shore / Of Araby the blest' (*Paradise Lost*, 4:162–3).

505 *Negligence* 'careless abundance'.

506 *mimic Art* i.e. landscape gardening.

519–22 The subject of the whole sentence is 'the hurried Eye' (518) which 'sweeps' the bowery walk, 'meets' the bending sky and the river, lake, mountain and main ('sea').

520 *Covert close* 'enclosed thicket'.

530–54 Cf. Milton, *Lycidas*, 142–51.

532 *Polyanthus* A bright multi-coloured strain of primula.

534 *lavish* i.e. of its fragrance.

536–7 *Auricula* A type of primula also called Bear's ear, the inner petals ('velvet Leaves') of which are powdered with white or grey ('shining Meal').

With shining Meal o'er all their velvet Leaves;
And full Renunculas, of glowing Red.
Then comes the Tulip-Race, where Beauty plays
Her idle Freaks: from Family diffus'd   540
To Family, as flies the Father Dust,
The varied Colours run; and, while they *break*
On the charm'd Eye, th' exulting Florist marks,
With secret Pride the Wonders of his Hand.
No gradual Bloom is wanting; from the Bud,   545
First-born of Spring, to Summer's musky Tribes:
Nor Hyacinths, of purest virgin White,
Low-bent, and blushing inward; nor Jonquils,
Of potent Fragrance; nor Narcissus fair,
As o'er the fabled Fountain hanging still;   550
Nor broad Carnations; nor gay-spotted Pinks;
Nor, shower'd from every Bush, the Damask-rose.
Infinite Numbers, Delicacies, Smells,
With Hues on Hues Expression cannot paint,
The Breath of Nature, and her endless Bloom.   555
　　　Hail, SOURCE OF BEINGS! UNIVERSAL SOUL
Of Heaven and Earth! ESSENTIAL PRESENCE, hail!
To THEE I bend the Knee; to THEE my Thoughts,
Continual, climb; who, with a Master-hand,
Hast the great Whole into Perfection touch'd.   560
By THEE the various vegetative Tribes,
Wrapt in a filmy Net, and clad with Leaves,
Draw the live Ether, and imbibe the Dew.
By THEE dispos'd into congenial Soils,
Stands each attractive Plant, and sucks, and swells   565
The juicy Tide; a twining Mass of Tubes.
At THY Command the vernal Sun awakes
The torpid Sap, detruded to the Root
By wintry Winds, that now in fluent Dance,
And lively Fermentation, mounting, spreads   570
All this innumerous-colour'd Scene of things.
　　　As rising from the vegetable World
My Theme ascends, with equal Wing ascend,
My panting Muse; and hark, how loud the Woods
Invite you forth in all your gayest Trim.   575
Lend me your Song, ye Nightingales! oh pour
The mazy-running Soul of Melody
Into my varied Verse! while I deduce,

---

538 *Renuncula* A plant from the buttercup family with
vibrantly coloured bowl-shaped flowers.
540 *idle Freaks* Whimsical flecks or streaks of colour.
541 *Father Dust* 'pollen'.
542 *break* 'burst into colour'.
546 *musky Tribes* Heavily scented flowers.
548 *Jonquils* A type of daffodil.
549–50 In Greek myth Narcissus, a handsome youth, fell in
love with his own reflection in a pool and died in
despair. The gods transformed him into the flower that
bears his name.

557 *ESSENTIAL PRESENCE* God as absolute being.
562 *filmy Net* A network of fine sap vessels.
563 *live Ether* The ether, or upper air, was thought to
contain an acid which created salt-petre or nitre,
essential to sustain plant life.
565 *attractive* Drawing moisture from the earth.
568 *detruded* 'forced down' (Lat. *detrudo*).
577 *mazy-running* Cf. 'The melting voice through mazes
running' (Milton, *L'Allegro*, 142).
578 *deduce* 'trace the course of' (Lat. *deduco*).

From the first Note the hollow Cuckoo sings,
The Symphony of Spring, and touch a Theme   580
Unknown to Fame, *the Passion of the Groves.*
      When first the Soul of Love is sent abroad,
Warm thro' the vital Air, and on the Heart
Harmonious seizes, the gay Troops begin,
In gallant Thought, to plume the painted Wing;   585
And try again the long-forgotten Strain,
At first faint-warbled. But no sooner grows
The soft Infusion prevalent, and wide,
Than, all alive, at once their Joy o'erflows
In Musick unconfin'd. Up-springs the Lark,   590
Shrill-voic'd, and loud, the Messenger of Morn;
Ere yet the Shadows fly, he mounted sings
Amid the dawning Clouds, and from their Haunts
Calls up the tuneful Nations. Every Copse
Deep-tangled, Tree irregular, and Bush   595
Bending with dewy Moisture, o'er the Heads
Of the coy Quiristers that lodge within,
Are prodigal of Harmony. The Thrush
And Wood-lark, o'er the kind contending Throng
Superior heard, run thro' the sweetest Length   600
Of Notes; when listening *Philomela* deigns
To let them joy, and purposes, in Thought
Elate, to make her Night excel their Day.
The Black-bird whistles from the thorny Brake;
The mellow Bullfinch answers from the Grove: 605
Nor are the Linnets, o'er the flowering Furze
Pour'd out profusely, silent. Join'd to These,
Innumerous Songsters, in the freshening Shade
Of new-sprung Leaves, their Modulations mix
Mellifluous. The Jay, the Rook, the Daw,   610
And each harsh Pipe discordant heard alone,
Aid the full Concert: while the Stock-dove breathes
A melancholy Murmur thro' the Whole.
      'Tis Love creates their Melody, and all
This Waste of Music is the Voice of Love;   615
That even to Birds, and Beasts, the tender Arts
Of pleasing teaches. Hence the glossy kind
Try every winning way inventive Love
Can dictate, and in Courtship to their Mates
Pour forth their little Souls. First, wide around,   620
With distant Awe, in airy Rings they rove,
Endeavouring by a thousand Tricks to catch

---

584 *gay Troops* Brightly coloured birds.
585 *gallant* 'amorous'.
588 *Infusion* i.e. love.
597 *Quiristers* 'choristers'.
599 *kind* 'of their species'.
601 *Philomela* The nightingale. In Greek myth Philomela, daughter of the King of Athens, was raped and had her tongue cut out by her brother-in-law Tereus, King of Thrace. The gods turned her into a nightingale.

606 *Furze* A wild thorny yellow-flowering shrub.
607 *These,* These (*1746*).
610 *Daw* 'jackdaw'.
615 *Waste* 'profusion'.
617 *glossy kind* Birds, whose glossy plumage is important for mating rituals.

The cunning, conscious, half-averted Glance
Of their regardless Charmer. Should she seem
Softening the least Approvance to bestow, 625
Their Colours burnish, and by Hope inspir'd,
They brisk advance; then, on a sudden struck,
Retire disorder'd; then again approach;
In fond rotation spread the spotted Wing,
And shiver every Feather with Desire. 630
    Connubial Leagues agreed, to the deep Woods
They haste away, all as their Fancy leads,
Pleasure, or Food, or secret Safety prompts;
That NATURE's *great Command* may be obey'd,
Nor all the sweet Sensations they perceive 635
Indulg'd in vain. Some to the Holly-Hedge
Nestling repair, and to the Thicket some;
Some to the rude Protection of the Thorn
Commit their feeble Offspring. The cleft Tree
Offers its kind Concealment to a Few, 640
Their Food its Insects, and its Moss their Nests.
Others apart far in the grassy Dale,
Or roughening Waste, their humble Texture weave.
But most in woodland Solitudes delight,
In unfrequented Glooms, or shaggy Banks, 645
Steep, and divided by a babbling Brook,
Whose Murmurs soothe them all the live-long Day,
When by kind Duty fix'd. Among the Roots
Of Hazel, pendant o'er the plaintive Stream,
They frame the first Foundation of their Domes; 650
Dry Sprigs of Trees, in artful Fabrick laid,
And bound with Clay together. Now 'tis nought
But restless Hurry thro' the busy Air,
Beat by unnumber'd Wings. The Swallow sweeps
The slimy Pool, to build his hanging House 655
Intent. And often, from the careless Back
Of Herds and Flocks, a thousand tugging Bills
Pluck Hair and Wool; and oft, when unobserv'd,
Steal from the Barn a Straw: till soft and warm,
Clean, and compleat, their Habitation grows. 660
    As thus the patient Dam assiduous sits,
Not to be tempted from her tender Task,
Or by sharp Hunger, or by smooth Delight,
Tho' the whole loosen'd Spring around Her blows,
Her sympathizing Lover takes his Stand 665
High on th' opponent Bank, and ceaseless sings
The tedious Time away; or else supplies
Her place a moment, while she sudden flits
To pick the scanty Meal. Th' appointed Time
With pious Toil fulfill'd, the callow Young, 670
Warm'd and expanded into perfect Life,
Their brittle Bondage break, and come to Light,

---

624 *regardless* 'indifferent'.
631 *Connubial Leagues* 'marriage partnerships'.
650 *Domes* 'homes' (Lat. *domus*).
651 *Fabrick* 'construction'.
661 *Dam* 'mother'.

A helpless Family, demanding Food
With constant Clamour. O what Passions then,
What melting Sentiments of kindly Care,   675
On the new Parents seize! Away they fly
Affectionate, and undesiring bear
The most delicious Morsel to their Young,
Which equally distributed, again
The Search begins. Even so a gentle Pair,   680
By Fortune sunk, but form'd of generous Mold,
And charm'd with Cares beyond the vulgar Breast,
In some lone Cott amid the distant Woods,
Sustain'd alone by providential HEAVEN,
Oft, as they weeping eye their infant Train,   685
Check their own Appetites and give them all.
    Nor Toil alone they scorn: exalting Love,
By the great FATHER OF THE SPRING inspir'd,
Gives instant Courage to the *fearful* Race,
And to the *simple* Art. With stealthy Wing,   690
Should some rude Foot their woody Haunts molest,
Amid a neighbouring Bush they silent drop,
And whirring thence, as if alarm'd, deceive
Th' unfeeling School-Boy. Hence, around the Head
Of wandering Swain, the white-wing'd Plover wheels   695
Her sounding Flight, and then directly on
In long Excursion skims the level Lawn,
To tempt him from her Nest. The Wild-Duck, hence,
O'er the rough Moss, and o'er the trackless Waste
The Heath-Hen flutters, (pious Fraud!) to lead   700
The hot pursuing Spaniel far astray.
    Be not the Muse asham'd, here to bemoan
Her Brothers of the Grove, by tyrant Man
Inhuman caught, and in the narrow Cage
From Liberty confin'd, and boundless Air.   705
Dull are the pretty Slaves, their Plumage dull,
Ragged, and all its brightening Lustre lost;
Nor is that sprightly Wildness in their Notes,
Which, clear and vigorous, warbles from the Beech.
Oh then, ye Friends of Love and Love-taught Song,   710
Spare the soft Tribes, this barbarous Art forbear!
If on your Bosom Innocence can win,
Music engage, or Piety persuade.
    But let not chief the Nightingale lament
Her ruin'd Care, too delicately fram'd   715
To brook the harsh Confinement of the Cage.

---

680 *gentle Pair* of human beings.
682 *charm'd with Cares* 'tenderly concerned for the objects
    in their care', i.e. children. An earlier version read
    'pierc'd with Cares', or afflicted with anxieties.
683 *Cott* 'cottage'.
690 *Art* 'cunning'.
696 *sounding* 'diving'. The plover dips and dives when
    trying to distract predators from its nest.

700 *Heath-Hen* The black grouse.
702–3 The Muses were often depicted with wings.
    Thomson imagines a kinship between his winged Muse
    and the birds.
715 *ruin'd Care* 'lost offspring'.
716 *brook* 'tolerate'.

Oft when, returning with her loaded Bill,
Th' astonish'd Mother finds a vacant Nest,
By the hard Hand of unrelenting Clowns
Robb'd, to the Ground the vain Provision falls;　　　　720
Her Pinions ruffle, and low-drooping scarce
Can bear the Mourner to the poplar Shade;
Where, all abandon'd to Despair, she sings
Her Sorrows thro' the Night; and, on the Bough,
Sole-sitting, still at every dying Fall　　　　725
Takes up again her lamentable Strain
Of winding Woe; till wide around the Woods
Sigh to her Song, and with her Wail resound.
　　But now the feather'd Youth their former Bounds,
Ardent, disdain; and, weighing oft their Wings,　　　　730
Demand the free Possession of the Sky.
This one glad Office more, and then dissolves
Parental Love at once, now needless grown.
Unlavish *Wisdom* never works in vain.
'Tis on some Evening, sunny, grateful, mild,　　　　735
When nought but Balm is breathing thro' the Woods,
With yellow Lustre bright, that the new Tribes
Visit the spacious Heavens, and look abroad
On Nature's Common, far as they can see,
Or wing, their Range, and Pasture. O'er the Boughs　　　　740
Dancing about, still at the giddy Verge
Their Resolution fails; their Pinions still,
In loose Libration stretch'd, to trust the Void
Trembling refuse: till down before them fly
The Parent-Guides, and chide, exhort, command,　　　　745
Or push them off. The surging Air receives
The plumy Burden; and their self-taught Wings
Winnow the waving Element. On Ground
Alighted, bolder up again they lead,
Farther and farther on, the lengthening Flight;　　　　750
Till vanish'd every Fear, and every Power
Rouz'd into Life and Action, light in Air
Th' acquitted Parents see their soaring Race,
And once rejoicing never know them more.
　　High from the Summit of a craggy Cliff,　　　　755
Hung o'er the Deep, such as amazing frowns
On utmost *Kilda*'s Shore, whose lonely Race
Resign the setting Sun to *Indian* Worlds,
The royal Eagle draws his vigorous Young,
Strong-pounc'd, and ardent with paternal Fire.　　　　760
Now fit to raise a Kingdom of their own,

725 *dying Fall* A sinking note or gradually lowering
　cadence. Cf. 'That strain again, it had a dying fall'
　(*Twelfth Night*, I.i.4).
732 *glad Office* 'willing duty'.
736 *Balm* A soothing atmosphere.
743 *Libration* 'balance'.
748 *Winnow* 'thresh', 'beat'; *waving Element* 'undulating
　air'.

757 *Kilda's Shore* St Kilda, the most westerly inhabited
　island in the Outer Hebrides, in north-west Scotland.
758 St Kilda is still in daylight when the sun has set in the
　rest of Britain; *Indian Worlds* The Americas.
760 *pounc'd* 'clawed'.

He drives them from his Fort, the towering Seat,
For Ages, of his Empire; which, in Peace,
Unstain'd he holds, while many a League to sea
He wings his Course, and preys in distant Isles.   765
    Should I my Steps turn to the rural Seat,
Whose lofty Elms, and venerable Oaks,
Invite the Rook, who high amid the Boughs,
In early Spring, his airy City builds,
And ceaseless caws amusive; there, well-pleas'd,   770
I might the various Polity survey
Of the mixt Houshold-Kind. The careful Hen
Calls all her chirping Family around,
Fed, and defended by the fearless Cock,
Whose Breast with ardour flames, as on he walks,   775
Graceful, and crows Defiance. In the Pond,
The finely-checker'd Duck, before her Train,
Rows garrulous. The stately-sailing Swan
Gives out his snowy Plumage to the Gale;
And, arching proud his Neck, with oary Feet   780
Bears forward fierce, and guards his Osier-Isle,
Protective of his Young. The Turkey nigh,
Loud-threatning, reddens; while the Peacock spreads
His every-colour'd Glory to the Sun,
And swims in radiant Majesty along.   785
O'er the whole homely Scene, the cooing Dove
Flies thick in amorous Chace, and wanton rolls
The glancing Eye, and turns the changeful Neck.
    While thus the gentle Tenants of the Shade
Indulge their purer Loves, the rougher World   790
Of Brutes, below, rush furious into Flame,
And fierce Desire. Thro' all his lusty Veins
The Bull, deep-scorch'd, the raging Passion feels.
Of Pasture sick, and negligent of Food,
Scarce seen, he wades among the yellow Broom,   795
While o'er his ample Sides the rambling Sprays
Luxuriant shoot; or thro' the mazy Wood
Dejected wanders, nor th' inticing Bud
Crops, tho' it presses on his careless Sense.
And oft, in jealous madning Fancy wrapt,   800
He seeks the Fight; and, idly-butting, feigns
His Rival gor'd in every knotty Trunk.
Him should he meet, the bellowing War begins;
Their Eyes flash Fury; to the hollow'd Earth,
Whence the Sand flies, they mutter bloody Deeds,   805
And groaning deep th' impetuous Battle mix:
While the fair Heifer, balmy-breathing, near,
Stands kindling up their Rage. The trembling Steed,
With this hot Impulse seiz'd in every Nerve,
Nor hears the Rein, nor heeds the sounding Thong;   810

---

764 *Unstain'd* 'with unblemished reputation'.
770 *amusive* 'engagingly'.
771 *various Polity* 'different communities'.
772 *Houshold-Kind* i.e. domestic fowl.

789–830 This mock-heroic account of the 'loves of the
    beasts' is modelled on Virgil's *Georgics*, 3:212–54.
810 *hears* 'obeys'.

Blows are not felt; but tossing high his Head,
And by the well-known Joy to distant Plains
Attracted strong, all wild he bursts away;
O'er Rocks, and Woods, and craggy Mountains flies;
And, neighing, on the aërial Summit takes   815
Th' exciting Gale; then, steep-descending, cleaves
The headlong Torrents foaming down the Hills,
Even where the Madness of the straiten'd Stream
Turns in black Eddies round: such is the force
With which his frantick Heart and Sinews swell.   820
   Nor undelighted, by the boundless Spring,
Are the broad Monsters of the foaming Deep:
From the deep Ooze and gelid Cavern rous'd,
They flounce and tumble in unwieldy Joy.
Dire were the Strain, and dissonant, to sing   825
The cruel Raptures of the Savage Kind:
How by this Flame their native Wrath sublim'd,
They roam, amid the Fury of their Heart,
The far-resounding Waste in fiercer Bands,
And growl their horrid Loves. But this the Theme   830
I sing, enraptur'd, to the BRITISH FAIR,
Forbids, and leads me to the Mountain-brow,
Where sits the Shepherd on the grassy Turf,
Inhaling, healthful, the descending Sun.
Around him feeds his many-bleating Flock,   835
Of various Cadence; and his sportive Lambs,
This way and that convolv'd, in friskful glee,
Their Frolicks play. And now the sprightly Race
Invites them forth; when swift, the Signal given,
They start away, and sweep the massy Mound   840
That runs around the Hill; the Rampart once
Of iron War, in ancient barbarous Times,
When disunited BRITAIN ever bled,
Lost in eternal Broil: ere yet she grew
To this deep-laid indissoluble State,   845
Where *Wealth* and *Commerce* lift the golden Head;
And, o'er our Labours, *Liberty* and *Law*,
Impartial, watch, the Wonder of a World!
   What is this *mighty Breath*, ye Curious, say,
That, in a powerful Language, felt not heard,   850
Instructs the Fowls of Heaven; and thro' their Breast
These Arts of Love diffuses? What, but GOD?
Inspiring GOD! who boundless Spirit all,
And unremitting Energy, pervades,

---

826 *Kind* 'species', but with a pun on 'kind' as 'sexually
   yielding'.
827 *sublim'd* 'refined'.
830 *horrid* 'rough'.
830–2 Thomson's respect for his women readers prevents
   him from expanding this account of savage sex.
837 *convolv'd* rolled around together (Lat. *convolvo*).
840–2 Sambrook suggests this recalls the Celtic Early Iron
   Age fort on Southdean Law where Thomson grew up.

843–5 A reference to the long history of border warfare
   before the 1707 Act of Union which united England
   and Scotland in 'indissoluble State'.
844 *Broil* 'conflict'.
853 *Inspiring* In the stronger sense of 'breathing into' (Lat.
   inspiro).

Adjusts, sustains, and agitates the Whole.   855
He ceaseless works *alone*, and yet *alone*
Seems not to work; with such perfection fram'd
Is this complex stupendous Scheme of Things.
But, tho' conceal'd, to every purer Eye
Th' informing Author in his Works appears: 860
Chief, lovely Spring, in thee, and thy soft Scenes,
The SMILING GOD is seen; while Water, Earth,
And Air attest his Bounty; which exalts
The Brute-Creation to this finer Thought,
And annual melts their undesigning Hearts   865
Profusely thus in Tenderness and Joy.
   Still let my Song a nobler Note assume,
And sing th' infusive Force of Spring on Man;
When Heaven and Earth, as if contending, vye
To raise his Being, and serene his Soul.   870
Can he forbear to join the general Smile
Of Nature? Can fierce Passions vex his Breast,
While every Gale is Peace, and every Grove
Is Melody? Hence! from the bounteous Walks
Of flowing Spring, ye sordid Sons of Earth,   875
Hard, and unfeeling of another's Woe,
Or only lavish to yourselves; away!
But come, ye generous Minds, in whose wide Thought,
Of all his Works, CREATIVE BOUNTY burns,
With warmest Beam; and on your open Front,   880
And liberal Eye, sits, from his dark Retreat,
Inviting modest Want. Nor, till invok'd,
Can restless Goodness wait; your active Search
Leaves no cold wintry Corner unexplor'd;
Like silent-working HEAVEN, surprizing oft   885
The lonely Heart with unexpected Good.
For you the roving Spirit of the Wind
Blows Spring abroad; for you the teaming Clouds
Descend in gladsome Plenty o'er the World;
And the Sun sheds his kindest Rays for you,   890
Ye Flower of human Race! — In these green Days,
Reviving Sickness lifts her languid Head;
Life flows afresh; and young-ey'd Health exalts
The whole Creation round. Contentment walks
The sunny Glade, and feels an inward Bliss   895
Spring o'er his Mind, beyond the Power of Kings
To purchase. Pure Serenity apace
Induces Thought, and Contemplation still.
By swift degrees the Love of Nature works,

860 *informing* 'animating'.
862 *SMILING* See 84n.
864 *finer Thought* i.e. love.
870 *serene* 'to make serene'.
875 *sordid Sons of Earth* 'selfish materialists'.
878–903 Throughout *The Seasons* Thomson emphasizes the

importance of benevolence and social love. Like Shaftesbury, Thomson believed that they stemmed from an innate moral sense and were not merely an aspect of self-love.
880 *Front* 'forehead'.
891 *green Days* 'spring'.

And warms the Bosom; till at last sublim'd   900
To Rapture, and enthusiastic Heat,
We feel the present DEITY, and taste
The Joy of GOD to see a happy World!
  These are the Sacred Feelings of thy Heart,
Thy Heart inform'd by Reason's purer Ray,   905
O LYTTELTON, the Friend! thy Passions thus
And Meditations vary, as at large,
Courting the Muse, thro' HAGLEY-PARK you stray,
Thy *British Tempe!* There along the Dale,
With Woods o'er-hung, and shag'd with mossy Rocks,   910
Whence on each Hand the gushing Waters play,
And down the rough Cascade white-dashing fall,
Or gleam in lengthen'd Vista thro' the Trees,
You silent steal; or sit beneath the Shade
Of solemn Oaks, that tuft the swelling Mounts   915
Thrown graceful round by Nature's careless Hand,
And pensive listen to the various Voice
Of rural Peace: the Herds, the Flocks, the Birds,
The hollow-whispering Breeze, the Plaint of Rills,
That, purling down amid the twisted Roots   920
Which creep around, their dewy Murmurs shake
On the sooth'd Ear. From these abstracted oft,
You wander thro' the Philosophic World;
Where in bright Train continual Wonders rise,
Or to the curious or the pious Eye.   925
And oft, conducted by Historic Truth,
You tread the long Extent of backward Time:
Planning, with warm Benevolence of Mind,
And honest Zeal unwarp'd by Party-Rage,
BRITANNIA's Weal; how from the venal Gulph   930
To raise her Virtue, and her Arts revive.
Or, turning thence thy View, these graver Thoughts
The Muses charm: while, with sure Taste refin'd,
You draw th' inspiring Breath of antient Song;
Till nobly rises, emulous, thy own.   935
Perhaps thy lov'd LUCINDA shares thy Walk,
With Soul to thine attun'd. Then Nature all
Wears to the Lover's Eye a Look of Love;
And all the Tumult of a guilty World,
Tost by ungenerous Passions, sinks away.   940
The tender Heart is animated Peace;
And as it pours its copious Treasures forth,
In vary'd Converse, softening every Theme,
You, frequent-pausing, turn, and from her Eyes,

---

906 *LYTTELTON* See headnote.
908 Hagley Park was Lyttelton's country estate near
  Stourbridge in Worcestershire. During the 1740s he
  transformed the gardens into a much-admired
  landscape.
909 *Tempe* A beautiful valley in Thessaly, Greece, celebrated
  by classical poets.

910 *shag'd* 'made rough'. Cf. Pope, *Eloisa to Abelard*, 20.
919 *Plaint* 'mournful sound'.
926–31 Thomson describes Lyttelton's Patriot agenda – to
  rescue Britain from party faction and corruption and to
  restore her national integrity and culture.
936 *LUCINDA* Lucy Fortescue married Lyttelton in 1742.
  She died in 1747 aged twenty-nine.

Where meeken'd Sense, and amiable Grace,   945
And lively Sweetness dwell, enraptur'd, drink
That nameless Spirit of etherial Joy,
Inimitable Happiness! which Love,
Alone, bestows, and on a *favour'd Few*.
Meantime you gain the Height, from whose fair Brow   950
The bursting Prospect spreads immense around;
And snatch'd o'er Hill and Dale, and Wood and Lawn,
And verdant Field, and darkening Heath between,
And Villages embosom'd soft in Trees,
And spiry Towns by surging Columns mark'd   955
Of houshold Smoak, your Eye excursive roams:
Wide-stretching from the *Hall*, in whose kind Haunt
The *Hospitable Genius* lingers still,
To Where the broken Landskip, by Degrees,
Ascending, roughens into rigid Hills;   960
O'er which the *Cambrian* Mountains, like far Clouds
That skirt the blue Horizon, dusky, rise.
   Flush'd by the Spirit of the genial Year,
Now from the Virgin's Cheek a fresher Bloom
Shoots, less and less, the live Carnation round;   965
Her Lips blush deeper Sweets; she breathes of Youth;
The shining Moisture swells into her Eyes,
In brighter Flow; her wishing Bosom heaves,
With Palpitations wild; kind Tumults seize
Her Veins, and all her yielding Soul is Love.   970
From the keen Gaze her Lover turns away,
Full of the dear exstatic Power, and sick
With sighing Languishment. Ah then, ye Fair!
Be greatly cautious of your sliding Hearts:
Dare not th' infectious Sigh; the pleading Look,   975
Down-cast, and low, in meek Submission drest,
But full of Guile. Let not the fervent Tongue,
Prompt to deceive, with Adulation smooth,
Gain on your purpos'd Will. Nor in the Bower,
Where Woodbines flaunt, and Roses shed a Couch,   980
While Evening draws her crimson Curtains round,
Trust your soft Minutes with betraying Man.
   And let th' aspiring Youth beware of Love,
Of the smooth Glance beware; for 'tis too late,
When on his Heart the Torrent-Softness pours.   985
Then Wisdom prostrate lies, and fading Fame
Dissolves in Air away; while the fond Soul,
Wrapt in gay Visions of unreal Bliss,
Still paints th' illusive Form; the kindling Grace;
Th' inticing Smile; the modest-seeming Eye,   990
Beneath whose beauteous Beams, belying Heaven,
Lurk searchless Cunning, Cruelty, and Death:

961 *Cambrian Mountains* Welsh mountains which could be
seen in the distance from Hagley.
965 *Carnation* 'pinkness'.

975 *Dare not* 'do not trust'.
991 *belying* 'counterfeiting'.
992 *searchless* 'inscrutable'.

And still, false-warbling in his cheated Ear,
Her syren Voice, enchanting, draws him on,
To guileful Shores, and Meads of fatal Joy.   995
    Even present, in the very Lap of Love
Inglorious laid; while Musick flows around,
Perfumes, and Oils, and Wine, and wanton Hours;
Amid the Roses fierce Repentance rears
Her snaky Crest: a quick-returning Pang   1000
Shoots thro' the conscious Heart; where Honour still,
And great Design, against th' oppressive Load
Of Luxury, by Fits, impatient heave.
    But absent, what fantastic Woes, arrous'd,
Rage in each Thought, by restless Musing fed,   1005
Chill the warm Cheek, and blast the Bloom of Life?
Neglected Fortune flies; and sliding swift,
Prone into Ruin, fall his scorn'd Affairs.
'Tis nought but Gloom around. The darken'd Sun
Loses his Light. The rosy-bosom'd Spring   1010
To weeping Fancy pines; and yon bright Arch,
Contracted, bends into a dusky Vault.
All Nature fades extinct; and she alone
Heard, felt, and seen, possesses every Thought,
Fills every Sense, and pants in every Vein.   1015
Books are but formal Dulness, tedious Friends;
And sad amid the social Band he sits,
Lonely, and unattentive. From the Tongue
Th' unfinish'd Period falls: while borne away,
On swelling Thought, his wafted Spirit flies   1020
To the vain Bosom of his distant Fair;
And leaves the Semblance of a Lover, fix'd
In melancholy Site, with Head declin'd,
And love-dejected Eyes. Sudden he starts,
Shook from his tender Trance, and restless runs   1025
To glimmering Shades, and sympathetic Glooms;
Where the dun Umbrage o'er the falling Stream,
Romantic, hangs; there thro' the pensive Dusk
Strays, in heart-thrilling Meditation lost,
Indulging all to Love: or on the Bank   1030
Thrown, amid drooping Lilies, swells the Breeze
With Sighs unceasing, and the Brook with Tears.
Thus in soft Anguish he consumes the Day,
Nor quits his deep Retirement, till the Moon
Peeps thro' the Chambers of the fleecy East,   1035
Enlighten'd by degrees, and in her Train

994 *syren* Sirens in Greek myth were beautiful female
  creatures, sometimes shown as half-woman, half-bird,
  whose enchanting song lured men to their deaths.
1000 *snaky Crest* The snake-haired female Furies of Greek
  and Roman myth were sometimes used to represent a
  guilty conscience.
1002 *great Design* 'noble purpose'.

1011 *Arch* 'sky'.
1019 *Period* 'sentence'.
1021 *vain* 'empty'.
1023 *Site* 'posture'.
1027 *dun Umbrage* 'dusky shade'.
1028 *Romantic* 'Fanciful, full of wild scenery' (Dr Johnson,
  citing these lines).

Leads on the gentle Hours; then forth he walks,
Beneath the trembling Languish of her Beam,
With soften'd Soul, and wooes the Bird of Eve
To mingle Woes with his: or while the World   1040
And all the Sons of Care lie hush'd in Sleep,
Associates with the midnight Shadows drear;
And, sighing to the lonely Taper, pours
His idly-tortur'd Heart into the Page,
Meant for the moving Messenger of Love;   1045
Where Rapture burns on Rapture, every Line
With rising Frenzy fir'd. But if on Bed
Delirious flung, Sleep from his Pillow flies.
All Night he tosses, nor the balmy Power
In any Posture finds; till the grey Morn   1050
Lifts her pale Lustre on the paler Wretch,
Exanimate by Love: and then perhaps
Exhausted Nature sinks a while to Rest,
Still interrupted by distracted Dreams,
That o'er the sick Imagination rise,   1055
And in black Colours paint the mimick Scene.
Oft with th' Enchantress of his Soul he talks;
Sometimes in Crouds distress'd; or if retir'd
To secret-winding flower-enwoven Bowers,
Far from the dull Impertinence of Man,   1060
Just as he, credulous, his endless Cares
Begins to lose in blind oblivious Love,
Snatch'd from her yielded Hand, he knows not how,
Thro' Forests huge, and long untravel'd Heaths
With Desolation brown, he wanders waste,   1065
In Night and Tempest wrapt; or shrinks aghast,
Back, from the bending Precipice; or wades
The turbid Stream below, and strives to reach
The farther Shore; where succourless, and sad,
She with extended Arms his Aid implores,   1070
But strives in vain; borne by th' outragious Flood
To distance down, he rides the ridgy Wave,
Or whelm'd beneath the boiling Eddy sinks.
These are the charming Agonies of Love,
Whose Misery delights. But thro' the Heart   1075
Should Jealousy its Venom once diffuse,
'Tis then delightful Misery no more,
But Agony unmix'd, incessant Gall,
Corroding every Thought, and blasting all
Love's Paradise. Ye fairy Prospects, then,   1080
Ye Beds of Roses, and ye Bowers of Joy,
Farewel! Ye Gleamings of departed Peace,
Shine out your last! the yellow-tinging Plague

1037 *Hours* In Greek myth, goddesses who preside over the seasons and hours and who usher in the dawn.
1038 *Languish* 'tender gaze'.
1039 *Bird of Eve* The nightingale.
1052 *Exanimate* 'deprived of life and spirit' (Lat. *exanimis*).
1056 *mimick* 'imagined'.

1060 *Impertinence* 'unwelcome intrusiveness'.
1065 *waste* 'aimlessly'.
1067–73 A fantasy inspired by the classical myth of Leander, who swam the Hellespont to visit his mistress Hero but was finally drowned.
1083 *yellow-tinging Plague* 'jealousy'.

Internal Vision taints, and in a Night
Of livid Gloom Imagination wraps.   1085
Ah then instead of love-enliven'd Cheeks,
Of sunny Features, and of ardent Eyes
With flowing Rapture bright, dark Looks succeed,
Suffus'd, and glaring with untender Fire,
A clouded Aspect, and a burning Cheek,   1090
Where the whole poison'd Soul, malignant, sits,
And frightens Love away. Ten thousand Fears
Invented wild, ten thousand frantic Views
Of horrid Rivals, hanging on the Charms
For which he melts in Fondness, eat him up   1095
With fervent Anguish, and consuming Rage.
In vain Reproaches lend their idle Aid,
Deceitful Pride, and Resolution frail,
Giving false Peace a Moment. Fancy pours,
Afresh, her Beauties on his busy Thought,   1100
Her first Endearments, twining round the Soul,
With all the Witchcraft of ensnaring Love.
Strait the fierce Storm involves his Mind anew,
Flames thro' the Nerves, and boils along the Veins:
While anxious Doubt distracts the tortur'd Heart;   1105
For even the sad Assurance of his Fears
Were Peace to what he feels. Thus the warm Youth,
Whom Love deludes into his thorny Wilds,
Thro' flowery-tempting Paths, or leads a Life
Of fever'd Rapture, or of cruel Care;   1110
His brightest Aims extinguish'd all, and all
His lively Moments running down to waste.
    But happy they! the happiest of their Kind!
Whom gentler Stars unite, and in one Fate
Their Hearts, their Fortunes, and their Beings blend.   1115
'Tis not the coarser Tie of human Laws,
Unnatural oft, and foreign to the Mind,
That binds their Peace, but Harmony itself,
Attuning all their Passions into Love;
Where Friendship full-exerts her softest Power,   1120
Perfect Esteem enliven'd by Desire
Ineffable, and Sympathy of Soul;
Thought meeting Thought, and Will preventing Will,
With boundless Confidence: for nought but Love
Can answer Love, and render Bliss secure.   1125
Let him, ungenerous, who, alone intent
To bless himself, from sordid Parents buys
The loathing Virgin, in eternal Care,
Well-merited, consume his Nights and Days:
Let barbarous Nations, whose inhuman Love   1130
Is wild Desire, fierce as the Suns they feel;
Let Eastern Tyrants from the Light of Heaven
Seclude their Bosom-slaves, meanly possess'd

1107 *warm* 'amorous'.   1123 *preventing* 'anticipating'.
1113–76 Thomson's description of ideal love derives in part
    from *Paradise Lost*, 4:750–70.

Of a meer, lifeless, violated Form:
While Those whom Love cements in holy Faith,   1135
And equal Transport, free as Nature live,
Disdaining Fear. What is the World to them,
Its Pomp, its Pleasure, and its Nonsense all!
Who in each other clasp whatever fair
High Fancy forms, and lavish Hearts can wish;   1140
Something than Beauty dearer, should they look
Or on the Mind, or mind-illumin'd Face,
Truth, Goodness, Honour, Harmony, and Love,
The richest Bounty of indulgent HEAVEN.
Mean-time a smiling Offspring rises round,   1145
And mingles both their Graces. By degrees,
The human Blossom blows; and every Day,
Soft as it rolls along, shews some new Charm,
The Father's Lustre, and the Mother's Bloom.
Then infant Reason grows apace, and calls   1150
For the kind Hand of an assiduous Care.
Delightful Task! to rear the tender Thought,
To teach the young Idea how to shoot,
To pour the fresh Instruction o'er the Mind,
To breathe th' enlivening Spirit, and to fix   1155
The generous Purpose in the glowing Breast.
Oh speak the Joy! ye, whom the sudden Tear
Surprizes often, while you look around,
And nothing strikes your Eye but Sights of Bliss,
All various Nature pressing on the Heart: 1160
An elegant Sufficiency, Content,
Retirement, rural Quiet, Friendship, Books,
Ease and alternate Labour, useful Life,
Progressive Virtue, and approving HEAVEN.
These are the matchless Joys of virtuous Love;   1165
And thus their Moments fly. The Seasons thus,
As ceaseless round a jarring World they roll,
Still find them happy; and consenting SPRING
Sheds her own rosy Garland on their Heads:
Till Evening comes at last, serene and mild;   1170
When after the long vernal Day of Life,
Enamour'd more, as more Remembrance swells
With many a Proof of recollected Love,
Together down they sink in social Sleep;
Together freed, their gentle Spirits fly   1175
To Scenes where Love and Bliss immortal reign.

1139 *fair* 'beauty'.   1174 They die together.
1153 *shoot* 'grow', 'flourish'.

Richard Savage (*c*.1697–1743)

Even in his own time, Savage was better known for his sensational life than for his poetry. He emerged from obscurity in 1715. Arrested for writing seditious Jacobite ballads, he claimed to be the unacknowledged bastard son of Anne Brett, Countess of Macclesfield, and the late Richard Savage, fourth Earl Rivers. The key to Savage's true identity will never be known. He certainly believed himself to be blue-blooded and convinced many that his mother had perversely disowned him. In 1726 the literary patron Aaron Hill published a 'benefit' anthology of poems for Savage, whose circle of literary friends also included the young Samuel Johnson. Johnson's moving biography (1744) shows the intensity of feeling this charming, erratic and dangerous personality inspired. Savage was the archetypal indigent poet: a talker, drinker and gambler who could throw away a year's wages in one night and be left next day with no shoes on his feet, forced to sleep in London shop doors. His intimate knowledge of Grub Street supplied Pope with details for *The Dunciad*. In 1727 Savage stabbed a man to death in a pub brawl and was found guilty of murder, but was granted a pardon by Queen Caroline. He assumed the role of 'volunteer laureate' for the Queen and other Hanoverian royals, producing a series of insincere birthday odes (his true sympathies were almost certainly Jacobite) and a panegyric on Walpole. His friends persuaded him to escape debt by retiring to Wales, but London lured him back and he died in penury in Newgate gaol.

Savage's best-known poem is the brazenly self-advertising *The Bastard*. He spent over eight years writing *The Wanderer*, his longest work. It went through several versions and titles, from 'The Enthusiast' to 'The Misfortunes of Life' and by 1729 had expanded to five cantos and just under 2,000 lines. Savage sold the poem for ten guineas but his obsessive concern with the details of its publication shows he saw it as his masterpiece. *The Wanderer* bears the stamp of Savage's literary friendship with Thomson and the poets of Aaron Hill's circle in the mid-1720s, all of whom were producing long, meditative, sublime poems of natural description. None of these poems is distinguished for its organization and coherence, but the disjointedness of *The Wanderer* is of a different order from the 'want of method' in *The Seasons*. Composed of a series of episodes around the central, idealized figure of a Hermit-poet, the poem moves from the world of external description to a psychologically charged dream-like landscape in which even the most innocent of natural episodes ends in violence, depredation and loss. In Canto 4 the images succeed each other in a kaleidoscopic way, as Johnson noted – strange and beautiful in themselves, but disturbingly 'without Order'. The giant colossus and ruined colonnades paced by huge allegorical abstractions seem to prefigure Coleridge's visionary landscapes. The following text is that of the 1729 first edition.

The Wanderer

Canto IV

STILL o'er my Mind wild *Fancy* holds her Sway,
Still on strange, visionary Land I stray.
Now Scenes crowd thick! Now indistinct appear!
Swift glide the *Months*, and turn the varying Year!
   Near the *Bull*'s Horn Light's rising Monarch draws;   5
Now on it's Back the *Pleiades* he thaws!
From vernal Heat pale *Winter* forc'd to flie,
Northward retires, yet turns a watry Eye;
Then with an aguish Breath nips infant Blooms,
Deprives unfolding Spring of rich Perfumes,   10
Shakes the slow-circling Blood of human Race,
And in sharp, livid Looks contracts the Face.

---

5 *Bull's Horn* The constellation of Taurus, second sign of the zodiac, which the sun enters on 21 April.

6 *Pleiades* A cluster of seven stars named after the daughters of the Titan Atlas and Pleione. They had special significance for marking the seasons, especially the time for sowing and planting.

7 *vernal* 'spring'.

12 *livid* 'leaden', 'bluish grey'.

Now o'er *Norwegian* Hills he strides away:
Such slipp'ry Paths *Ambition*'s Steps betray.
Turning with Sighs, far, spiral Firs he sees,   15
Which bow obedient to the Southern Breeze.
Now from yon *Zemblan* Rock his Crest he shrouds,
Like *Fame*'s, obscur'd amid the whitening Clouds;
Thence his lost Empire is with Tears deplor'd:
Such Tyrants shed o'er Liberty restor'd.   20
Beneath his Eye (that throws malignant Light
Ten Times the measur'd Round of mortal Sight)
A waste, pale-glimmering, like a Moon, that wanes,
A wild Expanse of frozen Sea contains.
It cracks! vast, floating Mountains beat the Shore!   25
Far off he hears those icy Ruins roar,
And from the hideous Crash distracted flies,
Like One, who feels his dying Infant's Cries.
Near, and more near the rushing Torrents sound,
And one great Rift runs thro' the vast Profound,   30
Swift as a shooting Meteor; groaning loud,
Like deep-roll'd Thunder thro' a rending Cloud.
The late-dark *Pole* now feels unsetting Day:
In Hurricanes of Wrath he whirls his Way;
O'er many a polar *Alp* to *Frost* he goes,   35
O'er crackling Vales, embrown'd with melting Snows;
Here Bears stalk Tenants of the barren Space,
Few Men, unsocial Those! — a barb'rous Race!
At length the Cave appears! the Race is run:
Now he recounts vast Conquests lost, and won,   40
And taleful in th'Embrace of *Frost* remains,
Barr'd from our Climes, and bound in icy Chains.
    Mean while the Sun his Beams on *Cancer* throws,
Which now beneath his warmest Influence glows.
From glowing *Cancer* fall'n the King of Day,   45
Red thro' the kindling *Lyon*, shoots his Ray.
The tawny Harvest pays the earlier Plough,
And mellowing Fruitage loads the bending Bough.
'Tis Day-spring. Now green Lab'rinths I frequent,
Where *Wisdom* oft retires to meet *Content*.   50
    The mounting Lark her warbling Anthem lends,
From Note to Note the ravish'd Soul ascends;
As thus it wou'd the Patriarch's Ladder climb,
By some good Angel led to Worlds sublime:
Oft (Legends say) the Snake, with waken'd Ire,   55
Like *Envy* rears in many a scaly Spire;

14–26 Winter retreats northwards through Norway to the island of Nova Zembla, which marks the eastern boundary of the White Sea to the north of Russia. Nova Zembla's mountains are always covered in ice and snow.

43 *Cancer* The Crab, fourth sign of the zodiac, which the sun enters at the summer solstice on 21 or 22 June.

45 *King of Day* The sun.

46 *Lyon* Leo, fifth sign of the zodiac, which the sun enters on 22 July.

47 *pays* 'repays'.

49 *Day-spring* 'daybreak'.

53 *Patriarch's Ladder* Jacob dreamt that he saw a ladder which stretched into heaven with ascending and descending angels (Genesis, 28:10–12).

56 *Spire* 'coil'.

Then Songsters drop, then yield their vital Gore,
And Innocence, and Musick are no more.
   Mild rides the Morn in orient Beauty drest,
An azure Mantle, and a purple Vest,   60
Which blown by Gales her gemmy Feet display,
Her amber Tresses negligently gay.
Collected now her rosy Hand they fill,
And, gently wrung, the pearly Dews distill.
The songful Zephyrs, and the laughing Hours   65
Breathe sweet; and strew her opening Way with Flowers.
   The chatt'ring Swallows leave their nested Care,
Each promising Return with plenteous Fare.
So the fond Swain, who to the Market hies,
Stills with big Hopes his Infant's tender Cries.   70
   Yonder two Turtles, o'er their callow Brood,
Hang hov'ring, ere they seek their guiltless Food.
Fondly they bill. Now to their morning Care,
Like our first Parents part the am'rous Pair:
But ah! — a Pair no more! — with spreading Wings,   75
From the high, sounding Cliff a Vultur springs;
Steady he sails along th'aerial Grey,
Swoops down, and bears yon tim'rous Dove away.
Start we, who, worse than Vulturs, *Nymrods* find,
Men meditating Prey on human Kind?   80
   Wild Beasts to gloomy Dens re-pace their Way,
Where their couch'd Young demand the slaughter'd Prey.
Rooks from their nodding Nests black-swarming fly,
And in hoarse Uproar tell the fowler nigh.
   Now in his Tabernacle rouz'd, the Sun   85
Is warn'd the blue, aetherial Steep to run:
While on his Couch of floating Jasper laid,
From his bright Eye *Sleep* calls the dewy Shade.
The crystal Dome transparent Pillars raise,
Whence beam'd from Saphirs living Azure plays: 90
The liquid Floor, in-wrought with Pearls divine,
Where all his Labours in Mosaic shine.
His Coronet, a Cloud of Silver-white;
His Robe with unconsuming Crimson bright,
Varied with Gems, all Heaven's collected Store;   95
While his loose Locks descend, a golden Shower.
If to his Steps compar'd, we tardy find
The *Grecian* Racers, who outstript the Wind.

---

57 *vital Gore* 'life-blood'.
61 *gemmy* 'glistening like gems'.
63 'they' refers to the 'pearly Dews' (64).
64 *distill* 'trickle in tiny drops'.
65 *Zephyrs* Mild breezes; *Hours* See Thomson, *Spring*, 1037n.
67 *Care* 'offspring'.
71 *Turtles* 'turtle-doves'; *callow* 'unfledged'.
79 *Start we* 'are we surprised'; *Nymrods* Genesis, 10:9 describes Nimrod, the great grandson of Noah, as 'a

mighty hunter before the Lord'. Biblical commentary depicted him as the archetypal despot who hunted men for sport (cf. Pope, *Windsor-Forest*, 61–2).
85 *Tabernacle* A curtained tent, with Biblical associations of a shrine. The strangely artificial description of the sky (85–92) draws loosely on Revelation 21, in which the heavenly city of Jerusalem is made of crystal and precious stones. The sun in his 'Crimson' robe (94) recalls a Christ-figure.
86 *Steep* 'sky'.

Fleet to the glowing Race behold him start!
His quick'ning Eyes a quiv'ring Radiance dart,   100
And, while the last, nocturnal Flag is furl'd,
Swift into Life and Motion look the World.
The Sun-flow'r now averts her blooming Cheek
From West, to view his Eastern Lustre break.
What gay, creative Pow'r his Presence brings?   105
Hills, Lawns, Lakes, Villages! — the Face of Things,
All Night beneath successive Shadows miss'd,
Instant begins in Colours to exist:
But absent these from Sons of Riot keep,
Lost in impure, unmeditating Sleep.   110
    T'unlock his Fence, the new-ris'n Swain prepares,
And ere forth-driv'n recounts his fleecy Cares;
When, lo! an ambush'd Wolf, with Hunger bold,
Springs at the Prey, and fierce invades the Fold!
But by the Pastor not in vain defied,   115
Like our arch Foe by some coelestial Guide.
    Spread on yon Rock the Sea-Calf I survey,
Bask'd in the Sun his Skin reflects the Day:
He sees yon tow'r-like Ship the Waves divide,
And slips again beneath the glassy Tide.   120
    The watry Herbs, and Shrubs, and Vines, and Flowers
Rear their bent Heads, o'ercharg'd with nightly Showers.
    Hail glorious Sun! to whose attractive Fires,
The waken'd, vegetative Life aspires!
The Juices, wrought by thy directive Force,   125
Thro' Plants, and Trees, perform their Genial Course,
Extend in Root, with Bark unyielding bind
The hearted Trunk; or weave the branching Rind;
Expand in Leaves, in flow'ry Blossoms shoot,
Bleed in rich Gums, and swell the ripen'd Fruit.   130
From thee, bright, universal Pow'r! began
Instinct in Brute, and gen'rous Love in Man.
    Talk'd I of Love? — Yon Swain, with am'rous Air,
Soft swells his Pipe, to charm the rural Fair.
She milks the Flocks; then, list'ning as he plays,   135
Steals in the running Brook a conscious Gaze.
    The Trout, that deep, in Winter, ooz'd remains,
Up-springs, and sunward turns its crimson Stains.
    The Tenants of the Warren, vainly chac'd,
Now lur'd to ambient Fields for green Repast,   140
Seek their small, vaulted Labyrinths in vain;
Entangling Nets betray the skipping Train;
Red Massacres thro' their Republic fly,
And Heaps on Heaps by ruthless Spaniels dye.
    The Fisher, who the lonely Beech has stray'd,   145
And all the live-long Night his Net-work spread,

99 *Fleet* 'swift'.
112 *fleecy Cares* 'sheep'.
116 *arch Foe* Satan.
117 *Sea-Calf* 'seal'.
123 *attractive* 'attracting'.

134 *Fair* 'fair one'.
137 *ooz'd* 'buried in mud'.
139 *Warren* Rabbit colony.
140 *ambient* 'surrounding'.
145 *who the lonely* 'who to the lonely'.

Drags *in*, and bears the loaded Snare away;
Where flounce deceiv'd th'expiring, finny Prey.
   Near *Neptune*'s Temple, (*Neptune*'s now no more)
Whose Statue plants a Trident on the Shore,   150
In sportive Rings the gen'rous Dolphins wind,
And eye, and think the Image human-Kind:
Dear, pleasing Friendship! — See! the Pile commands
The Vale, and grim as *Superstition* stands!
Time's Hand there leaves its Print of mossy green,   155
With Hollows, carv'd for Snakes, and Birds obscene.
   O *Gibbs*, whose Art the solemn Fane can raise,
Where *God* delights to dwell, and *Man* to praise;
When moulder'd thus the Column falls away,
Like some great Prince, majestic in Decay;   160
When *Ignorance*, and *Scorn* the Ground shall tread,
Where *Wisdom* tutor'd, and *Devotion* pray'd;
Where shall thy pompous Work our Wonder claim?
What, but the Muse alone, preserve thy Name?
   The Sun shines, broken, through yon Arch, that rears   165
This once-round Fabric, half-depriv'd by Years,
Which rose a stately Colonade, and crown'd
Encircling Pillars, now unfaithful found;
In Fragments, these the Fall of those forebode,
Which, nodding, just up-heave their crumbling Load.   170
High, on yon Column, which has batter'd stood,
Like some stripp'd Oak, the Grandeur of the Wood,
The Stork inhabits her aerial Nest;
By her are Liberty and Peace carest;
She flies the Realms, that own despotick Kings,   175
And only spreads o'er free-born States her Wings.
The Roof is now the Daw's, or Raven's Haunt,
And loathsome Toads in the dark Entrance pant;
Or Snakes, that lurk to snap the heedless Fly,
And fated Bird, that oft comes flutt'ring by.   180
   An Aqueduct across yon Vale is laid,
Its Channel thro' a ruin'd Arch betray'd;
Whirl'd down a Steep, it flies with torrent-Force,
Flashes, and roars, and plows a devious Course.

149–84 The connecting motif here is a sequence of
  (imaginary?) architectural ruins – a pervasive theme in
  eighteenth-century poetry that permits a meditation on
  the universality of death, the transience of power etc.,
  as well as a Gothic frisson. Cf. Dyer, *Grongar Hill*,
  70–93; Pope, *Windsor-Forest*, 66–72.
149 *Neptune's Temple* Neptune, god of the sea, was usually
  depicted with a trident. Savage may not have a specific
  temple in mind, though part of a large temple to
  Poseidon still stands on the promontory of Sunium in
  Attica, Greece.
153 A startling mid-line transition from seascape to inland.
  The 'Friendship' may refer back to the man-friendly
  dolphins; the 'Pile' which dominates the valley is
  presumably a great house fallen into decay.

156 *obscene* 'ill-omened'. Cf. Pope, *Windsor-Forest*, 71.
157 *Gibbs* James Gibbs (1682–1754), distinguished architect
  whose public buildings include St Martin-in-the-
  Fields, London, and the Radcliffe Camera, Oxford. His
  work drew on both vernacular and neoclassical styles;
  Fane 'temple'.
163 *pompous* 'magnificent'.
164 Savage ambitiously claims that poems like his will
  outlast Gibbs's buildings.
173–6 According to Dutch myth, storks would live only in
  liberty-loving republics. Cf. Collins, *Ode to Liberty*, 57.
175 *own* 'acknowledge'.
177 *Daw* 'jackdaw'.

Attracted Mists a golden Cloud commence,   185
While through high-colour'd Air strike Rays intense.
Betwixt two Points, which yon steep Mountains show,
Lies a mild Bay, to which kind Breezes flow.
Beneath a Grotto, arch'd for calm Retreat,
Leads length'ning in the Rock — Be this my Seat.   190
Heat never enters here; but *Coolness* reigns
O'er Zephyrs, and distilling, watry Veins.
Secluded now I trace th'instructive Page,
And live o'er Scenes of many a backward Age;
Thro' Days, Months, Years, thro' Time's whole Course I run,   195
And present stand where Time it self begun.
   Ye mighty *Dead* of just, distinguish'd Fame,
Your thoughts, (ye bright Instructers!) here I claim.
Here ancient Knowledge opens Nature's Springs;
Here Truths historic give the Hearts of Kings.   200
Hence Contemplation learns white Hours to find,
And labours Virtue on th'attentive Mind.
O lov'd Retreat! thy Joys Content bestow,
Nor Guilt, nor Shame, nor sharp Repentance know.
What the fifth *Charles* long aim'd in Power to see,   205
That Happiness he found reserv'd in Thee.
   Now let me change the Page — Here *Tully* weeps
While in Death's icy Arms his *Tullia* sleeps,
His Daughter dear! — Retir'd I see him mourn,
By all the Frenzy now of Anguish torn.   210
Wild his Complaint! Nor sweeter *Sorrow*'s Strains,
When *Singer* for *Alexis* lost complains.
Each Friend condoles, expostulates, reproves:
More than a Father raving *Tully* loves;
Or *Sallust* censures thus! — Unheeding Blame,   215
He schemes a Temple to his *Tullia*'s Name.
Thus o'er my *Hermit* once did Grief prevail,
Thus rose *Olympia*'s Tomb, his moving Tale,
The Sighs, Tears, frantic Starts, that banish Rest,
And all the bursting Sorrows of his Breast.   220
   But hark! a sudden Pow'r attunes the Air!
Th'inchanting Sound enamour'd Breezes bear;
Now low, now high, they sink, or lift the Song,
Which the Cave echoes sweet, and sweet the Creeks prolong.

---

192 *watry Veins* 'rivulets'.

194 *backward* 'past'.

200 *give* 'reveal'.

201 *white* 'auspicious, happy'.

202 *labours* 'urges'.

205–6 Charles V (1500–58), Holy Roman Emperor and King of Spain, abdicated in 1555 and retired to a small house attached to a Spanish monastery.

207 *Tully* Marcus Tullius Cicero (106–43 BC), Roman orator and statesman. The death of his daughter Tullia (79–45 BC) threw him into despair. He wrote a treatise, *De Consolatione*, in her memory.

212 *Singer* The devout poetess Elizabeth Singer Rowe (1674–1734) wrote a well-known poem in 1719 on her husband's death in which she addresses him as Alexis.

215 *Sallust* Sallust was a Roman historian (86–35 BC). But Savage is referring to the pseudo-Sallustian *In M. Tullium Ciceronem Oratorio*, which accuses Cicero of excessive or unnatural love for his daughter.

217–20 In the first three cantos of *The Wanderer* the poet meets a Hermit living in a cave who recounts the story of his life. Formerly wealthy and successful, he has been driven to solitude and despair by the death of his young wife, Olympia.

I listen'd, gaz'd, when, wondrous to behold!   225
From Ocean steam'd a Vapour gath'ring roll'd:
A blue, round Spot on the Mid-roof it came,
Spread broad, and redden'd into dazzling Flame.
Full-orb'd it shone, and dimm'd the swimming Sight,
While doubling Objects danc'd with darkling Light.   230
Amaz'd I stood! — amaz'd I still remain!
What earthly Pow'r this Wonder can explain?
Gradual at length the Lustre dies away:
My Eyes restor'd a mortal Form survey.
My Hermit-Friend? 'Tis He. — All hail! (he cries.)   235
I see, and wou'd alleviate thy Surprize.
The vanish'd Meteor was Heaven's Message meant,
To warn thee hence; I knew the high Intent.
Hear then! In this sequester'd Cave retir'd,
Departed Saints converse with Men inspir'd.   240
'Tis sacred Ground; nor can thy Mind endure,
Yet unprepar'd, an Intercourse so pure.
Quick let us hence — And now extend thy Views
O'er yonder Lawn; there find the heav'n-born *Muse*!
Or seek her, where she trusts her tuneful Tale   245
To the mid, silent Wood, or vocal Vale;
Where Trees half check the Light with trembling Shades,
Close in deep Glooms, or open clear in Glades:
Or where surrounding Vistas far descend,
The Landscape varied at each less'ning End!   250
She, only *She* can mortal Thought refine,
And raise thy Voice to Visitants divine.

230 *darkling* 'obscure', 'shaded'. Almost oxymoronic.   242 *Intercourse* 'communion with the spiritual'.
239–40 Cf. the cave in Thomson's *Summer*, 524–6, where
   'antient Bards th'inspiring Breath, / Extatic, felt; and,
   from this World retir'd, / Convers'd with Angels'.

John Dyer (1699–1757)

A tension between the practical and the aesthetic pervades Dyer's life and writing. His father, a Welsh attorney, planned a professional career for his second son and had little sympathy with his passion for painting and poetry. Dyer left Westminster School early and returned home to Wales to work in his father's office. But Robert Dyer's sudden death in 1720 liberated him from paternal expectations and gave him a degree of financial independence. He abandoned the law and headed for London to study painting with Jonathan Richardson. In the capital Dyer enjoyed a bohemian lifestyle as a member of Aaron Hill's literary coterie, along with fellow-poets James Thomson, David Mallet, Richard Savage and the scandalous Martha Fowke Sansom. Six of Dyer's early poems featured in Savage's *Miscellany* (1726), a showcase for the 'Hillarian' circle's verse. These early pieces, which included *Grongar Hill*, were influenced by his childhood memories of the romantic Welsh mountain landscape near Aberglasney in Carmarthenshire. In 1724 the aspiring artist travelled to Italy, and in Florence and Rome he deepened his knowledge of Italian art and antiquities. The visit also gave him a more melancholy vision of the precariousness of civilization. In *The Ruins of Rome* (finally published in 1740), the romantic descriptiveness of *Grongar Hill* is sharpened by a political message as the classical ruins offer a warning to a Britain that is poised between commercial prosperity and moral collapse. The speaker's exhortation to hard work and commercial activity is a further departure from the pensive scene-painting of Dyer's early poems. The shift reflects a change in Dyer's life which occurred in his thirtieth year, when he moved from literary London to rural Herefordshire. In 1734, after four years as an itinerant artist, he took up residence at Mapleton, a rundown farm he was due to inherit and which he rapidly restored to economic profitability. It was the first of a series of farms Dyer managed over the next six years, and the practical expertise he gained is evident in his long poem on the wool industry, *The Fleece*. During this period he married Sarah Ensor Hawkins, a young widow, with whom he had several children, and he also produced plans for a 'Commercial Map of England'. In 1741 Dyer rather unexpectedly took holy orders and moved to Catthorpe in Leicestershire to start life as a country parson, and it was here he began writing *The Fleece*. On a visit to London in 1751 he showed parts of the poem to Philip Yorke, later Earl of Hardwicke, who became Dyer's patron and supplied him with a series of lucrative livings in Lincolnshire. *The Fleece* was finally published in March 1757. Dyer's health declined rapidly in the following months and he died in December of that year.

Grongar Hill

The poem first appeared in Savage's *Miscellaneous Poems and Translations* (1726) in the form of an irregular Pindaric ode. But it was in this tighter octosyllabic couplet version, also published in 1726, that *Grongar Hill* achieved fame. Dyer grew up close to the foot of Grongar Hill on the River Towy in Carmarthenshire, Wales. The hill was already noted as a site of ancient British earthworks and ruined fortifications, and the region as a whole was rich in literary associations. Although the poem's title echoes *Cooper's Hill*, Dyer departs from the Denham/Pope tradition of topographical poetry by describing a landscape shaped by memory and personal meaning rather than one constructed to yield a consistent political reading. Dyer's recent training as a painter influenced his attempt to convey the colours and perspective of the landscape: hence the emphasis on the visual imagination and the use of terms such as 'vistoe' and 'landskip'. Yet the poem is informed by a moral as well as an aesthetic sensibility. The description of the ruined castle in 71–92 prompts a meditation on the vanity of human wishes and a sequence of reflections on human life which invite comparison with Gray's *Elegy*. The 'perspective' afforded by the hill-top view indicates the relative scale of human endeavours and achievements. *Grongar Hill* was enormously popular: Dr Johnson claimed that 'when it is once read, it will be read again'. The poem draws on Horace's celebration of rural retirement exemplified by Pomfret's *The Choice* and on Milton's *L'Allegro* and *Il Penseroso*. But the ecstatic sensory experience of nature celebrated in 137–45 also links it to the work of Dyer's close friend Thomson. The text is that of David Lewis's *Miscellaneous Poems, by Several Hands* (1726), the form in which the poem first became widely known. Line 147, inadvertently omitted from that edition, has been supplied from Dyer's *Poems* (1761).

Silent Nymph, with curious Eye!
Who, the purple Ev'ning, lye
On the Mountain's lonely Van,
Beyond the Noise of busy Man,
Painting fair the form of Things,   5
While the yellow Linnet sings;
Or the tuneful Nightingale
Charms the Forest with her Tale;
Come with all thy various Hues,
Come, and aid thy Sister Muse;   10
Now while *Phœbus* riding high
Gives Lustre to the Land and Sky!
Grongar Hill invites my Song,
Draw the Landskip bright and strong;
Grongar, in whose Mossie Cells   15
Sweetly-musing Quiet dwells:
Grongar, in whose silent Shade,
For the modest Muses made,
So oft I have, the Even still,
At the Fountain of a Rill,   20
Sate upon a flow'ry Bed,
With my Hand beneath my Head;
And stray'd my Eyes o'er *Towy*'s Flood,
Over Mead, and over Wood,
From House to House, from Hill to Hill,   25
'Till Contemplation had her fill.
   About his chequer'd Sides I wind,
And leave his Brooks and Meads behind,
And Groves, and Grottoes where I lay,
And Vistoes shooting Beams of Day: 30
Wider and wider spreads the Vale;
As Circles on a smooth Canal:
The Mountains round, unhappy Fate,
Sooner or later, of all Height!
Withdraw their Summits from the Skies,   35
And lessen as the others rise:
Still the Prospect wider spreads,
Adds a thousand Woods and Meads,
Still it widens, widens still,
And sinks the newly-risen Hill.   40
   Now, I gain the Mountain's Brow,
What a Landskip lies below!

---

1 *Silent Nymph* Dyer here seems to be invoking the 'Sister Muse' (10) of Painting to assist his poetic Muse. The Pindaric version opens with an appeal to Imagination ('*Fancy!* Nymph that loves to lie / On the lonely Eminence').

2–3 The puzzling syntax of these lines is clarified by adding 'does' after 'Who'.

3 *Van* 'summit'.

6 *yellow Linnet* Here the Shropshire name for the goldfinch.

11 *Phœbus* Apollo, Greek god of sun and poetry.

15 *Cells* 'caves'.

20 *Fountain of a Rill* 'source of a stream'.

23 *Towy* See headnote.

30 *Vistoes* 'vistas'.

33–40 As the poet ascends, the surrounding hills seem to grow smaller and smaller.

No Clouds, no Vapours intervene,
But the gay, the open Scene
Does the Face of Nature show,   45
In all the Hues of Heaven's Bow!
And, swelling to embrace the Light,
Spreads around beyond the Sight.
  Old Castles on the Cliffs arise,
Proudly tow'ring in the Skies!   50
Rushing from the Woods, the Spires
Seem from hence ascending Fires!
Half his Beams *Apollo* sheds,
On the yellow Mountain-Heads!
Gilds the Fleeces of the Flocks;   55
And glitters on the broken Rocks!
  Below me Trees unnumber'd rise,
Beautiful in various Dies:
The gloomy Pine, the Poplar blue,
The yellow Beech, the sable Yew,   60
The slender Firr, that taper grows,
The sturdy Oak with broad-spread Boughs.
And beyond the purple Grove,
Haunt of *Phillis*, Queen of Love!
Gawdy as the op'ning Dawn,   65
Lies a long and level Lawn,
On which a dark Hill, steep and high,
Holds and charms the wand'ring Eye!
Deep are his Feet in *Towy*'s Flood,
His Sides are cloath'd with waving Wood,   70
And antient Towers crown his Brow,
That cast an awful Look below;
Whose ragged Walls the Ivy creeps,
And with her Arms from falling keeps;
So both a Safety from the Wind   75
On mutual Dependance find.
  'Tis now the Raven's bleak Abode;
'Tis now th'Apartment of the Toad;
And there the Fox securely feeds;
And there the pois'nous Adder breeds,   80
Conceal'd in Ruins, Moss and Weeds:
While, ever and anon, there falls,
Huge heaps of hoary moulder'd Walls.
Yet Time has seen, that lifts the low,
And level lays the lofty Brow,   85
Has seen this broken Pile compleat,
Big with the Vanity of State;
But transient is the Smile of Fate!
A little Rule, a little Sway,
A Sun-beam in a Winter's Day   90
Is all the Proud and Mighty have,

---

63 *purple* 'richly coloured'.
64 *Phillis* A conventional pastoral name. Virgil, *Eclogue* 7,
   which praises 'Phillis', features a catalogue of trees.
65 *Gawdy* 'brilliant'.

71–87 Dyer may be describing either Dynevor Castle or
   Dryslwyn Castle, both visible from Grongar Hill.
77–81 Cf. Pope, *Windsor-Forest*, 67–72.

Between the Cradle and the Grave.
   And see the Rivers how they run,
Thro' Woods and Meads, in Shade and Sun,
Sometimes swift, and sometimes slow,   95
Wave succeeding Wave they go
A various Journey to the Deep,
Like human Life to endless Sleep!
Thus is Nature's Vesture wrought,
To instruct our wand'ring Thought;   100
Thus she dresses green and gay,
To disperse our Cares away.
   Ever charming, ever new,
When will the Landskip tire the View!
The Fountain's Fall, the River's Flow,   105
The woody Vallies, warm and low;
The windy Summit, wild and high,
Roughly rushing on the Sky!
The pleasent Seat, the ruin'd Tow'r,
The naked Rock, the shady Bow'r;   110
The Town and Village, Dome and Farm,
Each give each a double Charm,
As Pearls upon an *Æthiop's* Arm.
   See on the Mountain's southern side,
Where the Prospect opens wide,   115
Where the Ev'ning gilds the Tide;
How close and small the Hedges lie!
What streaks of Meadows cross the Eye!
A Step methinks may pass the Stream,
So little distant Dangers seem;   120
So we mistake the Future's face,
Ey'd thro' Hope's deluding Glass;
As yon Summits soft and fair,
Clad in Colours of the Air,
Which, to those who journey near,   125
Barren, and brown, and rough appear;
Still we tread tir'd the same coarse Way.
The Present's still a cloudy Day.
   O may I with my self agree,
And never covet what I see: 130
Content me with an humble Shade,
My Passions tam'd, my Wishes laid;
For while our Wishes wildly roll,
We banish Quiet from the Soul:
'Tis thus the Busy beat the Air;   135
And Misers gather Wealth and Care.
   Now, ev'n now, my Joy runs high,
As on the Mountain-turf I lie;
While the wanton *Zephir* sings,
And in the Vale perfumes his Wings;   140
While the Waters murmur deep;
While the Shepherd charms his Sheep;

---

99 *Vesture* 'clothing'.   139 *Zephir* Mild breeze.
111 *Dome* 'mansion'.

While the Birds unbounded fly,
And with Musick fill the Sky.
Now, ev'n now, my Joy runs high.   145
    Be full, ye Courts, be great who will;
Search for Peace with all your skill:
Open wide the lofty Door,
Seek her on the marble Floor,
In vain ye search, she is not there;   150
In vain ye search the Domes of Care!
Grass and Flowers Quiet treads,
On the Meads, and Mountain-heads,
Along with Pleasure, close ally'd,
Ever by each other's Side: 155
And often, by the murm'ring Rill,
Hears the Thrush, while all is still,
Within the Groves of *Grongar Hill*.

The Fleece

The Fleece marks the culmination of one of the eighteenth century's most popular and versatile literary forms, the georgic. Dyer's poem differs from notable earlier examples such as Gay's *Trivia* or Thomson's *The Seasons* in restoring to the form the practical didactic element of Virgil's original *Georgics*. At the start of the first book Dyer proclaims his theme, 'The care of sheep, the labours of the loom, / And arts of trade', and it is to these three components of the British woollen industry that the poem is devoted. The georgic, which is concerned with the fallen world of human toil, offered a more appropriate genre for Dyer's treatment of shepherds and sheep than the pastoral idyll. The Miltonic invocation which opens Book 3 declares the poem's epic 'high style' and announces Dyer's poetic ambition. *The Fleece*, which he regarded as his greatest work, was designed to celebrate the commercial energies of Britain and to depict her social classes as working harmoniously together in a shared national purpose. But even in its own time *The Fleece* failed to win a wide audience. Dyer's adherence to the factual details of sheep-dip, dye-vats and spinning machines already seemed inherently prosaic to a mid-century readership accustomed to Akenside, Collins and the Wartons' celebration of the poetic imagination. Later readers have been alienated by Dyer's enthusiasm for the fruits of progress: urban development of the countryside,

northern chimneys belching smoke, the wonders of industrial technology. Two of the 'improvements' Dyer celebrates (enclosure in Book 2 and the workhouse in Book 3) would supply the focus for moral indignation in Goldsmith's *The Deserted Village* (1770) and Crabbe's *The Village* (1783). But such hindsight may distort the picture. *The Fleece* can be viewed as an alternative, even corrective, to the poetic introspection of the mid-eighteenth century. Dyer is committed not to an exploration of his own emotions but to the construction of a broader social vision unified by the virtues of labour and trade. In this respect the poem picks up from the closing passage of Pope's *Windsor-Forest* (1713). Dyer's nation, mapped out in loving detail through its rivers and waterways, combines a continuity with the past (note the Roman place-names) and an exciting future of growth and change. In *The Fleece* patriotism only occasionally lapses into xenophobia. In fact Book 3's warm account of Britain as a great melting pot that has welcomed and absorbed thousands of French and Belgian Huguenots, immigrant victims of political oppression, offers striking historical parallels to our own age.

The Fleece was published on 15 March 1757 after it had undergone scrutiny and revision by a board of critics, including Mark Akenside. The text reproduced below is that of the first edition. We are grateful to Dr John Goodridge for his help with the annotation.

BOOK III

The Argument

Introduction. Recommendation of labor. The several methods of spinning. Description of the loom, and of weaving. Variety of looms. The fulling-mill described, and the progress of the manufacture. Dying of cloth, and the excellence of the French in that art. Frequent negligence of our artificers. The ill consequences of idleness. County-workhouses proposed; with a description of one. Good effects of industry exemplified in the prospect of Burstal and Leeds; and the cloth-market there described.

Preference of the labors of the loom to other manufactures, illustrated by some comparisons. History of the art of weaving: its removal from the Netherlands, and settlement in several parts of England. Censure of those, who would reject the persecuted and the stranger. Our trade and prosperity owing to them. Of the manufacture of tapestry, taught us by the Saracens. Tapestries of Blenheim described. Different arts, procuring wealth to different countries. Numerous inhabitants, and their industry, the surest source of it. Hence a wish, that our country were open to all men. View of the roads and rivers, through which our manufactures are conveyed. Our navigations not far from the seats of our manufactures: other countries less happy. The difficult work of Egypt in joining the Nile to the Red Sea; and of France in attempting, by canals, a communication between the ocean and the Mediterranean. Such junctions may more easily be performed in England, and the Trent and Severn united to the Thames. Description of the Thames, and the port of London.

> Proceed, Arcadian muse, resume the pipe
> Of Hermes, long disus'd, tho' sweet the tone,
> And to the songs of nature's choristers
> Harmonious. Audience pure be thy delight,
> Though few: for every note which virtue wounds,   5
> However pleasing to the vulgar herd,
> To the purg'd ear is discord. Yet too oft
> Has false dissembling vice to am'rous airs
> The reed apply'd, and heedless youth allur'd:
> Too oft, with bolder sound, enflam'd the rage   10
> Of horrid war. Let now the fleecy looms
> Direct our rural numbers, as of old,
> When plains and sheepfolds were the muses' haunts.
>   So thou, the friend of ev'ry virtuous deed
> And aim, though feeble, shalt these rural lays   15
> Approve, O HEATHCOTE, whose benevolence
> Visits our vallies; where the pasture spreads,
> And where the bramble; and would justly act
> True charity, by teaching idle want
> And vice the inclination to do good,   20
> Good to themselves, and in themselves to all,
> Through grateful toil. Ev'n nature lives by toil:
> Beast, bird, air, fire, the heav'ns, and rolling worlds,
> All live by action: nothing lies at rest,
> But death and ruin: man is born to care;   25
> Fashion'd, improv'd, by labor. This of old,
> Wise states observing, gave that happy law,
> Which doom'd the rich and needy, ev'ry rank,
> To manual occupation; and oft call'd
> Their chieftains from the spade, or furrowing plough,   30
> Or bleating sheepfold. Hence utility
> Through all conditions; hence the joys of health;

1 *Arcadian* 'pastoral' (Arcadia is the idealized setting for Virgil's *Eclogues*).

2 *Hermes* Greek god of herdsmen, merchants and travellers.

4–5 *Audience pure ... Though few* Cf. 'fit audience find, though few' (*Paradise Lost,* 7:31).

17 *HEATHCOTE* Sir John Heathcote, MP (*c.*1689–1759), Dyer's patron. He was a keen supporter of enclosure and agricultural improvement.

24 Cf. Cowper, *The Task*, 1:367.

27 *that happy law* One of the laws established in Athens by the reformer Solon (*c.*640–after 561 BC) required all citizens to maintain themselves by work to prevent idleness.

29–30 See Thomson, *Spring*, 58–66n.

Hence strength of arm, and clear judicious thought;
Hence corn, and wine, and oil, and all in life
Delectable. What simple nature yields   35
(And nature does her part) are only rude
Materials, cumbers on the thorny ground;
'Tis toil that makes them wealth; that makes the fleece,
(Yet useless, rising in unshapen heaps)
Anon, in curious woofs of beauteous hue,   40
A vesture usefully succinct and warm,
Or, trailing in the length of graceful folds,
A royal mantle. Come, ye village nymphs,
The scatter'd mists reveal the dusky hills;
Grey dawn appears; the golden morn ascends,   45
And paints the glitt'ring rocks, and purple woods,
And flaming spires; arise, begin your toils;
Behold the fleece beneath the spiky comb
Drop its long locks, or, from the mingling card,
Spread in soft flakes, and swell the whiten'd floor.   50
    Come, village nymphs, ye matrons, and ye maids,
Receive the soft material: with light step
Whether ye turn-around the spacious wheel,
Or, patient sitting, that revolve, which forms
A narrower circle. On the brittle work   55
Point your quick eye; and let the hand assist
To guide and stretch the gently-less'ning thread:
Even, unknotted twine will praise your skill.
    A diff'rent spinning ev'ry diff'rent web
Asks from your glowing fingers: some require   60
The more compact, and some the looser wreath;
The last for softness, to delight the touch
Of chamber'd delicacy: scarce the cirque
Need turn-around, or twine the length'ning flake.
    There are, to speed their labor, who prefer   65
Wheels double-spol'd, which yield to either hand
A sev'ral line: and many yet adhere
To th'ancient distaff, at the bosom fix'd,
Casting the whirling spindle as they walk:
At home, or in the sheepfold, or the mart,   70
Alike the work proceeds. This method still

37 *cumbers* 'obstacles'.

40 *curious woofs* 'intricate woven cloths'.

41 *vesture* 'garment'; *succinct* 'girdled'.

48–9 *spiky comb … mingling card* The two chief tools in preparing wool for spinning. Heated iron combs were used to straighten and smooth the fibres of long wools intended for worsted manufacture. Short wool for the manufacture of woollens was brushed between two 'cards' (flat paddles set with metal pins, like hairbrushes) to create an interlocking body of fibres whose finished yarn would have a woolly texture.

53–5 Dyer describes larger spinning wheels that had to be worked while standing, and smaller wheels at which the spinner could sit.

58 *unknotted twine* The skilful hand-spinner could produce an even, smooth twine.

59 *web* The whole piece of cloth.

61 *wreath* Yarn of a specified texture and twist.

63 *chamber'd delicacy* i.e. housebound invalids.

63–4 *scarce the cirque … or twine* The yarn is so fine that the spinner scarcely need turn the wheel ('cirque') or spin the hand-spindle to make it.

66 *Wheels double-spol'd* Wheels that could feed two spools at once, known as double-flyer wheels.

67 *sev'ral* 'separate'; *many yet* many, yet (*1757*).

68 *distaff* The ancient hand-held spindle and distaff method of spinning wool was still widely used by women.

Norvicum favours, and the Icenian towns:
It yields their airy stuffs an apter thread.
This was of old, in no inglorious days,
The mode of spinning, when th'Egyptian prince   75
A golden distaff gave that beauteous nymph,
Too beauteous HELEN: no uncourtly gift
Then, when each gay diversion of the fair
Led to ingenious use. But patient art,
That on experience works, from hour to hour,   80
Sagacious, has a spiral engine form'd,
Which, on an hundred spoles, an hundred threads,
With one huge wheel, by lapse of water, twines,
Few hands requiring; easy-tended work,
That copiously supplies the greedy loom.   85
    Nor hence, ye nymphs, let anger cloud your brows;
The more is wrought, the more is still requir'd:
Blithe o'er your toils, with wonted song, proceed:
Fear not surcharge; your hands will ever find
Ample employment. In the strife of trade,   90
These curious instruments of speed obtain
Various advantage, and the diligent
Supply with exercise, as fountains sure,
Which, ever-gliding, feed the flow'ry lawn.
Nor, should the careful State, severely kind,   95
In ev'ry province, to the house of toil
Compel the vagrant, and each implement
Of ruder art, the comb, the card, the wheel,
Teach their unwilling hands, nor yet complain.
Yours, with the public good, shall ever rise,   100
Ever, while o'er the lawns, and airy downs,
The bleating sheep and shepherd's pipe are heard;
While in the brook ye blanch the glist'ning fleece,
And th' am'rous youth, delighted with your toils,
Quavers the choicest of his sonnets, warm'd   105
By growing traffick, friend to wedded love.
    The am'rous youth with various hopes inflam'd,
Now on the busy stage see him step forth,
With beating breast: high-honour'd he beholds
Rich industry. First, he bespeaks a loom: 110
From some thick wood the carpenter selects

---

72 *Norvicum* Norwich (Lat.); *Icenian towns* 'The Iceni were the inhabitants of Suffolk' (Dyer).

75–7 Helen of Troy was given a golden distaff as a gift by Alkandre, wife of Polybus.

81 *spiral engine* 'Paul's engine for cotton and fine wool' (Dyer). Lewis Paul (d. 1759), of Birmingham, patented his roller spinning machine in 1738, and a modified version in 1758. See 292–302.

82 *spoles* 'spools'.

83 *lapse* 'fall' (the engine is powered by a water-wheel).

86 *anger* An allusion to weavers' protests against mass production. In 1719 the Spitalfields weavers rioted against the import of cheap finished textiles, and in 1739 Wiltshire weavers rioted against falling wage-rates.

88 *wonted* 'accustomed'.

89 *surcharge* A surcharge on the wool supply as demand rose with industrialization.

95 *severely kind* Cf. Pope, *Eloisa to Abelard*, 249.

96 *house of toil* Parish workhouse.

99 *nor yet complain* Female wool-workers complained that such conscripted poor-labour undercut their rates and affected market prices.

103 *blanch* 'wash'.

106 *traffick* 'trade'.

110 *bespeaks* 'orders'.

A slender oak, or beech of glossy trunk,
Or saplin ash: he shapes the sturdy beam,
The posts, and treadles; and the frame combines.
The smith, with iron screws, and plated hoops,   115
Confirms the strong machine, and gives the bolt
That strains the roll. To these the turner's lathe,
And graver's knife, the hollow shuttle add.
Various professions in the work unite;
For each on each depends. Thus he acquires   120
The curious engine, work of subtle skill;
Howe'er, in vulgar use around the globe
Frequent observ'd, of high antiquity
No doubtful mark: th' advent'rous voyager,
Toss'd over ocean to remotest shores,   125
Hears on remotest shores the murm'ring loom;
See the deep-furrowing plough, and harrow'd field,
The wheel-mov'd waggon, and the discipline
Of strong-yok'd steers. What needful art is new?
  Next, the industrious youth employs his care   130
To store soft yarn; and now he strains the warp
Along the garden-walk, or highway side,
Smoothing each thread; now fits it to the loom,
And sits before the work: from hand to hand
The thready shuttle glides along the lines,   135
Which open to the woof, and shut, altern:
And ever and anon, to firm the work,
Against the web is driv'n the noisy frame,
That o'er the level rushes, like a surge,
Which, often dashing on the sandy beach,   140
Compacts the trav'ller's road: from hand to hand
Again, across the lines oft op'ning, glides
The thready shuttle, while the web apace
Increases, as the light of eastern skies,
Spread by the rosy fingers of the morn;   145
And all the fair expanse with beauty glows.
  Or, if the broader mantle be the task,
He chuses some companion to his toil.
From side to side, with amicable aim,
Each to the other darts the nimble bolt,   150
While friendly converse, prompted by the work,
Kindles improvement in the op'ning mind.
  What need we name the sev'ral kinds of looms?
Those delicate, to whose fair-colour'd threads
Hang figur'd weights, whose various numbers guide   155
The artist's hand: he, unseen flow'rs, and trees,

116 *Confirms* 'strengthens'.
118 *graver* 'engraver'.
131 *strains the warp* The weaver begins by stretching and
    smoothing the woollen threads that go lengthwise in
    the loom. The process takes place outdoors.
136 *woof* Cross-threads; *altern* 'in turn'.
145 *rosy fingers of the morn* 'Rosy-fingered' is Homer's
    repeated epithet for the dawn.

147 *broader mantle* A woollen cloth used for blankets, made
    on a broad loom where two weavers pass the shuttle
    back and forth between them.
155 *figur'd weights* Used to give tension, with different
    weights for different kinds of cloth.

And vales, and azure hills, unerring works.
Or that, whose num'rous needles, glitt'ring bright,
Weave the warm hose to cover tender limbs:
Modern invention: modern is the want.   160
    Next, from the slacken'd beam the woof unroll'd,
Near some clear-sliding river, Aire or Stroud,
Is by the noisy fulling-mill receiv'd;
Where tumbling waters turn enormous wheels,
And hammers, rising and descending, learn   165
To imitate the industry of man.
    Oft the wet web is steep'd, and often rais'd,
Fast-dripping, to the river's grassy bank;
And sinewy arms of men, with full-strain'd strength,
Wring out the latent water: then, up-hung   170
On rugged tenters, to the fervid sun
Its level surface, reeking, it expands;
Still bright'ning in each rigid discipline,
And gath'ring worth; as human life, in pains,
Conflicts, and troubles. Soon the clothier's shears,   175
And burler's thistle, skim the surface sheen.
The round of work goes on, from day to day,
Season to season. So the husbandman
Pursues his cares; his plough divides the glebe;
The seed is sown; rough rattle o'er the clods   180
The harrow's teeth; quick weeds his hoe subdues;
The sickle labors, and the slow team strains;
Till grateful harvest-home rewards his toils.
    Th'ingenious artist, learn'd in drugs, bestows
The last improvement; for th'unlabour'd fleece   185
Rare is permitted to imbibe the dye.
In penetrating waves of boiling vats
The snowy web is steep'd, with grain of weld,
Fustic, or logwood, mix'd, or cochineal,
Or the dark purple pulp of Pictish woad,   190
Of stain tenacious, deep as summer skies,
Like those, that canopy the bow'rs of Stow
After soft rains, when birds their notes attune,
Ere the melodious nightingale begins.

159 *hose* 'stockings'.
161 *woof unroll'd* i.e. the finished cloth is removed from the loom.
162 *Aire or Stroud* Rivers in West Yorkshire and Gloucestershire.
163 *fulling-mill* A mill for cleaning and thickening cloth.
167 *steep'd* 'soaked'.
171 *tenters* Hooks or pegs on which the cloth was stretched.
172 *reeking* 'steaming'.
176 *burler's thistle* The teasel, a thistle-like plant, was used by the cloth dresser ('burler') to raise a nap on the surface of the cloth.
179 *glebe* 'soil'.
184 *Th'ingenious artist* The skilful dyer. Before dyeing could

take place, the fleece had to be prepared by washing out dirt and natural oils.
188 *weld* Yellow dye made from the plant Reseda Luteola.
189 *Fustic* Yellow dye from the wood of the American fustic tree; *logwood* A blue-black dye from the central American tree Haematoxylon Campechianum; *cochineal* A bright red dye made from the dried bodies of the Mexican insect Coccus Cacti.
190 *woad* An historic blue dye made from the leaves of Isatis Tinctoria. The Picts, an ancient northern British tribe, had used it to paint and tattoo their bodies.
192 *Stow* Lord Cobham's gardens. See Pope, *Epistle to Burlington*, 70n.

From yon broad vase behold the saffron woofs   195
Beauteous emerge; from these the azure rise;
This glows with crimson; that the auburn holds;
These shall the prince with purple robes adorn;
And those the warrior mark, and those the priest.
    Few are the primal colours of the art;   200
Five only; black, and yellow, blue, brown, red;
Yet hence innumerable hues arise.
    That stain alone is good, which bears unchang'd
Dissolving water's, and calcining sun's,
And thieving air's attacks. How great the need,   205
With utmost caution to prepare the woof,
To seek the best-adapted dyes, and salts,
And purest gums! since your whole skill consists
In op'ning well the fibres of the woof,
For the reception of the beauteous dye,   210
And wedging ev'ry grain in ev'ry pore,
Firm as a diamond in gold enchas'd.
    But what the pow'rs, which lock them in the web;
Whether incrusting salts, or weight of air,
Or fountain-water's cold contracting wave,   215
Or all combin'd, it well befits to know.
Ah! wherefore have we lost our old repute?
And who enquires the cause, why Gallia's sons
In depth and brilliancy of hues excel?
Yet yield not, Britons; grasp in ev'ry art   220
The foremost name. Let others tamely view,
On crouded Smyrna's and Byzantium's strand,
The haughty Turk despise their proffer'd bales.
    Now see, o'er vales, and peopled mountain-tops,
The welcome traders, gath'ring ev'ry web   225
Industrious, ev'ry web too few. Alas!
Successless oft their industry, when cease
The loom and shuttle in the troubled streets;
Their motion stopt by wild intemperance,
Toil's scoffing foe, who lures the giddy rout   230
To scorn their task-work, and to vagrant life
Turns their rude steps; while misery, among
The cries of infants, haunts their mould'ring huts.
    O when, through ev'ry province, shall be rais'd
Houses of labor, seats of kind constraint,   235
For those, who now delight in fruitless sports,
More than in chearful works of virtuous trade,
Which honest wealth would yield, and portion due
Of public welfare? Ho, ye poor, who seek,
Among the dwellings of the diligent,   240
For sustenance unearn'd; who stroll abroad
From house to house, with mischievous intent,
Feigning misfortune: Ho, ye lame, ye blind;
Ye languid limbs, with real want oppress'd,

195 *saffron woofs* 'orange-yellow cloths'.
197 *auburn* 'reddish-brown'.
204 *calcining* 'oxidizing'.
218 *Gallia's sons* The French cloth-finishers.

221–3 The French exported fine cloth to the eastern
Mediterranean. There is no evidence for Dyer's
assertion that it was rejected by the Turkish merchants
of Smyrna and Istanbul.

Who tread the rough highways, and mountains wild,   245
Through storms, and rains, and bitterness of heart;
Ye children of affliction, be compell'd
To happiness: the long-wish'd day-light dawns,
When charitable rigor shall detain
Your step-bruis'd feet. Ev'n now the sons of trade,   250
Where-e'er their cultivated hamlets smile,
Erect the mansion: here soft fleeces shine;
The card awaits you, and the comb, and wheel:
Here shroud you from the thunder of the storm;
No rain shall wet your pillow: here abounds   255
Pure bevrage; here your viands are prepar'd;
To heal each sickness the physician waits,
And priest entreats to give your MAKER praise.
    Behold, in Calder's vale, where wide around
Unnumber'd villa's creep the shrubby hills,   260
A spacious dome for this fair purpose rise.
High o'er the open gates, with gracious air,
ELIZA's image stands. By gentle steps
Up-rais'd, from room to room we slowly walk,
And view with wonder, and with silent joy,   265
The sprightly scene; where many a busy hand,
Where spoles, cards, wheels, and looms, with motion quick,
And ever-murm'ring sound, th'unwonted sense
Wrap in surprise. To see them all employ'd,
All blithe, it gives the spreading heart delight,   270
As neither meats, nor drinks, nor aught of joy
Corporeal, can bestow. Nor less they gain
Virtue than wealth, while, on their useful works
From day to day intent, in their full minds
Evil no place can find. With equal scale   275
Some deal abroad the well-assorted fleece;
These card the short, those comb the longer flake;
Others the harsh and clotted lock receive,
Yet sever and refine with patient toil,
And bring to proper use. Flax too, and hemp,   280
Excite their diligence. The younger hands
Ply at the easy work of winding yarn
On swiftly-circling engines, and their notes
Warble together, as a choir of larks:
Such joy arises in the mind employ'd.   285
Another scene displays the more robust,
Rasping or grinding tough Brasilian woods,

252 *Erect the mansion* 'This alludes to the workhouses at Bristol, Birmingham, &c' (Dyer). Parish workhouses were usually contracted out to manufacturers who fed and clothed the inmates in return for their labour.
256 *viands* 'food'.
259 *Calder* 'A river in Yorkshire, which runs below Halifax, and passes by Wakefield' (Dyer).
261–302 This is probably a description of the Halifax workhouse established by Nathaniel Waterhouse

(1586–1642), which was incorporated in 1635. The workhouse regime was far harsher and more brutal than Dyer's idealized picture.
263 *ELIZA* Queen Elizabeth I, whose portrait was set into the stonework above the gates.
278 *lock* Poor-quality short wool, from the legs and belly of the sheep.
287 *Brasilian woods* Brazil wood or 'bahia', a tropical hardwood which supplied a red or purple dye.

And what Campeachy's disputable shore
Copious affords to tinge the thirsty web;
And the Caribbee isles, whose dulcet canes   290
Equal the honey-comb. We next are shown
A circular machine, of new design,
In conic shape: it draws and spins a thread
Without the tedious toil of needless hands.
A wheel, invisible, beneath the floor,   295
To ev'ry member of th'harmonious frame
Gives necessary motion. One, intent,
O'erlooks the work: the carded wool, he says,
Is smoothly lapp'd around those cylinders,
Which, gently turning, yield it to yon cirque   300
Of upright spindles, which, with rapid whirl,
Spin out, in long extent, an even twine.
　　From this delightful mansion (if we seek
Still more to view the gifts which honest toil
Distributes) take we now our eastward course,   305
To the rich fields of Burstal. Wide around
Hillock and valley, farm and village, smile:
And ruddy roofs, and chimney-tops, appear,
Of busy Leeds, up-wafting to the clouds
The incense of thanksgiving: all is joy;   310
And trade and business guide the living scene,
Roll the full cars, adown the winding Aire
Load the slow-sailing barges, pile the pack
On the long tinkling train of slow-pac'd steeds.
As when a sunny day invites abroad   315
The sedulous ants, they issue from their cells
In bands unnumber'd, eager for their work;
O'er high, o'er low, they lift, they draw, they haste
With warm affection to each other's aid;
Repeat their virtuous efforts, and succeed.   320
Thus all is here in motion, all is life:
The creaking wain brings copious store of corn:
The grazier's sleeky kine obstruct the roads;
The neat-dress'd housewives, for the festal board
Crown'd with full baskets, in the field-way paths   325
Come tripping on; th'echoing hills repeat
The stroke of ax and hammer; scaffolds rise,
And growing edifices; heaps of stone,
Beneath the chissel, beauteous shapes assume

288 *Campeachy* Campeche, a Mexican seaport, was taken by
　the English in 1659 and subsequently much fought
　over. It supplied logwood (see 189n).
290 *Caribbee isles* A number of dyewoods were imported
　from the Spanish West Indies as part of the slave trade;
　dulcet canes i.e. sugar-cane.
291–302 'A circular machine – a most curious machine,
　invented by Mr. Paul. It is at present contrived to spin
　cotton; but it may be made to spin fine carded wool'
　(Dyer). This is a fuller account of the machine
　mentioned in 3:81.

306 *Burstal* Birstall, seven miles south-west of Leeds.
308–37 Leeds, Yorkshire, England's main clothmaking and
　marketing centre since the seventeenth century, was at
　this time enjoying rapid commercial expansion.
312 *cars* 'carts'; *Aire* Navigation of the River Aire, on which
　Leeds stands, had recently been improved.
322 *wain* 'wagon'.
323 *kine* 'cows'.

Of frize and column. Some, with even line,   330
New streets are marking in the neighb'ring fields,
And sacred domes of worship. Industry,
Which dignifies the artist, lifts the swain,
And the straw cottage to a palace turns,
Over the work presides. Such was the scene   335
Of hurrying Carthage, when the Trojan chief
First view'd her growing turrets. So appear
Th'increasing walls of busy Manchester,
Sheffield, and Birmingham, whose redd'ning fields
Rise and enlarge their suburbs. Lo, in throngs,   340
For ev'ry realm, the careful factors meet,
Whisp'ring each other. In long ranks the bales,
Like war's bright files, beyond the sight extend.
Straight, ere the sounding bell the signal strikes,
Which ends the hour of traffick, they conclude   345
The speedy compact; and, well-pleas'd, transfer,
With mutual benefit, superior wealth
To many a kingdom's rent, or tyrant's hoard.
    Whate'er is excellent in art proceeds
From labor and endurance: deep the oak   350
Must sink in stubborn earth its roots obscure,
That hopes to lift its branches to the skies:
Gold cannot gold appear, until man's toil
Discloses wide the mountain's hidden ribs,
And digs the dusky ore, and breaks and grinds   355
Its gritty parts, and laves in limpid streams,
With oft-repeated toil, and oft in fire
The metal purifies: with the fatigue,
And tedious process of its painful works,
The lusty sicken, and the feeble die.   360
    But chearful are the labors of the loom,
By health and ease accompany'd: they bring
Superior treasures speedier to the state,
Than those of deep Peruvian mines, where slaves
(Wretched requital) drink, with trembling hand,   365
Pale palsy's baneful cup. Our happy swains
Behold arising, in their fatt'ning flocks,
A double wealth; more rich than Belgium's boast,
Who tends the culture of the flaxen reed;
Or the Cathayan's, whose ignobler care   370

335–7 *Carthage* The ancient city on the Tunisian coast of North Africa was the most important trading power of the western Mediterranean until destroyed by the Romans in 149 BC; *Trojan chief* Aeneas. Dyer alludes to Virgil, *Aeneid*, 1:421–2.

339 *redd'ning* i.e. from the colour of bricks. Cf. Anna Seward, *Colebrooke Dale*, 67–73.

340–8 The Leeds open-air cloth market operated from 7 to 8 a.m. ('the hour of traffick'). Dyer's account resembles the description in Daniel Defoe's *Tour* (1724).

341 *factors* 'merchants'.

342 *Whisp'ring* 'you cannot hear a word spoken in the whole market … 'tis all done in a whisper' (Defoe).

350–2 Cf. Cowper, *The Task*, 1:377–84.

364 *Peruvian mines* Spain made great profits from the silver mines of Peru, which exploited slave labour.

366 *palsy's baneful cup* Probably a mixture of chemicals, including mercury, used in the silver-extraction process. Mercury poisoning causes tremors ('palsy').

368 *double wealth* i.e. the value of the sheep and the wool.

370 *Cathayan* Chinese; *ignobler care* The silk-making process involves destroying the silkworm.

Nurses the silkworm; or of India's sons,
Who plant the cotton-grove by Ganges' stream.
Nor do their toils and products furnish more,
Than gauds and dresses, of fantastic web,
To the luxurious: but our kinder toils   375
Give cloathing to necessity; keep warm
Th'unhappy wand'rer, on the mountain wild
Benighted, while the tempest beats around.
    No, ye soft sons of Ganges, and of Ind,
Ye feebly delicate, life little needs   380
Your fem'nine toys, nor asks your nerveless arm
To cast the strong-slung shuttle, or the spear.
Can ye defend your country from the storm
Of strong Invasion? Can ye want endure,
In the besieged fort, with courage firm?   385
Can ye the weather beaten vessel steer,
Climb the tall mast, direct the stubborn helm,
Mid wild discordant waves, with steady course?
Can ye lead out, to distant colonies,
Th'o'erflowings of a people, or your wrong'd   390
Brethren, by impious persecution driv'n,
And arm their breasts with fortitude to try
New regions; climes, though barren, yet beyond
The baneful pow'r of tyrants? These are deeds
To which their hardy labors well prepare   395
The sinewy arm of Albion's sons. Pursue,
Ye sons of Albion, with unyielding heart,
Your hardy labors: let the sounding loom
Mix with the melody of ev'ry vale;
The loom, that long-renown'd, wide-envy'd gift   400
Of wealthy Flandria, who the boon receiv'd
From fair Venetia; she the Grecian nymphs;
They from Phenicé, who obtain'd the dole
From old Ægyptus. Thus, around the globe,
The golden-footed sciences their path   405
Mark, like the sun, enkindling life and joy;
And, follow'd close by ignorance and pride,
Lead day and night o'er realms. Our day arose
When ALVA's tyranny the weaving arts
Drove from the fertile vallies of the Scheld.   410
With speedy wing, and scatter'd course, they fled,
Like a community of bees, disturb'd
By some relentless swain's rapacious hand;

---

374 *gauds* 'showy finery'.
379–81 A vogue for Indian garments threatened the British
    textile industry.
396 *Albion* Britain.
400–4 Dyer traces the history of the loom from the
    Egyptians, through the Phoenicians, the Greeks, and
    the Venetian Empire, to Flanders (Belgium–Holland).
403 *dole* 'gift'.
408–69 An account of the geographical distribution and

economic activities of Huguenot refugees who fled
    from Flanders during Elizabeth I's reign, bringing new
    textile skills to England.
409 *ALVA* Ferdinand, Duke of Alva (1507–82), Governor of
    the Spanish Netherlands from 1567, whose draconian
    persecution of Protestants drove 100,000 of them into
    exile.
410 *Scheld* The river Scheldt in Flanders.

While good ELIZA, to the fugitives
Gave gracious welcome; as wise Ægypt erst 415
To troubled Nilus, whose nutritious flood
With annual gratitude enrich'd her meads.
Then, from fair Antwerp, an industrious train
Cross'd the smooth channel of our smiling seas;
And in the vales of Cantium, on the banks 420
Of Stour alighted, and the naval wave
Of spacious Medway: some on gentle Yare,
And fertile Waveney, pitch'd; and made their seats
Pleasant Norvicum, and Colcestria's tow'rs:
Some to the Darent sped their happy way: 425
Berghem, and Sluys, and elder Bruges, chose
Antona's chalky plains, and stretch'd their tents
Down to Clausentum, and that bay supine
Beneath the shade of Vecta's cliffy isle.
Soon o'er the hospitable realm they spread, 430
With cheer reviv'd; and in Sabrina's flood,
And the Silurian Tame, their textures blanch'd:
Not undelighted with Vigornia's spires,
Nor those, by Vaga's stream, from ruins rais'd
Of ancient Ariconium: nor less pleas'd 435
With Salop's various scenes; and that soft tract
Of Cambria, deep-embay'd, Dimetian land,
By green hills fenc'd, by ocean's murmur lull'd;
Nurse of the rustic bard, who now resounds
The fortunes of the fleece; whose ancestors 440
Were fugitives from superstition's rage,
And erst, from Devon, thither brought the loom;
Where ivy'd walls of old Kidwelly's tow'rs,

---

414 *ELIZA* During the eighteenth century Queen Elizabeth was viewed as a champion of trade and commerce.

415–17 Lower Egypt's soil is enriched by the annual flooding of the Nile.

420 *Cantium* Kent (Dyer gives Latin place-names).

421–5 *Stour ... Medway ... Yare ... Waveney ... Darent* Five rivers of southeastern England important for the textile industry. The Stour flows through Canterbury; the Medway is home to the Royal Naval Dockyards at Chatham; the Yare flows near Norwich, the Waveney along the Norfolk/Suffolk border, and the Darent through west Kent into the Thames.

424 *Norvicum* Norwich; *Colcestria* Colchester.

426 Towns in Flanders.

427 *Antona* The River Test in Hampshire, which enters the sea at Southampton Water (the Anton is a tributary).

428 *Clausentum* A Roman site at Southampton.

429 *Vecta* The Isle of Wight.

431 *Sabrina's flood* The River Severn, which flows along the Welsh borders. Sabrina, the Severn's mythical river-nymph, is celebrated by Spenser (*The Faerie Queene*) and Milton (*Masque*).

432 *Tame* The River Teme joins the Severn at Worcester on the borders of Siluria (south-east Wales).

433 *Vigornia* Worcester.

434 *Vaga* The River Wye.

435 *Ariconium* An ancient British settlement in Herefordshire. See John Philips, *The Splendid Shilling*, 32.

436 *Salop* Shropshire.

436–45 An affectionate account of Carmarthenshire, south-west Wales (the 'Dimetian land') where Dyer ('the rustic bard') grew up. The sixteenth-century historian Camden lists the 'Dimetae' counties as Carmarthenshire, Pembrokeshire and Cardiganshire.

443 *Kidwelly* Cydwelli in Carmarthenshire, home of Dyer's family.

Nodding, still on their gloomy brows project
Lancastria's arms, emboss'd in mould'ring stone.   445
     Thus then, on Albion's coast, the exil'd band,
From rich Menapian towns, and the green banks
Of Scheld alighted; and, alighting, sang
Grateful thanksgiving. Yet, at times, they shift
Their habitations, when the hand of pride,   450
Restraint, or southern luxury, disturbs
Their industry, and urges them to vales
Of the Brigantes; where, with happier care
Inspirited, their art improves the fleece,
Which occupation erst, and wealth immense,   455
Gave Brabant's swarming habitants, what time
We were their shepherds only; from which state,
With friendly arm, they rais'd us; nathless some
Among our old and stubborn swains misdeem'd,
And envy'd, who enrich'd them; envy'd those,   460
Whose virtues taught the varletry of towns
To useful toil to turn the pilf'ring hand.
     And still, when bigotry's black clouds arise
(For oft they sudden rise in papal realms),
They from their isle, as from some ark secure,   465
Careless, unpitying, view the fiery bolts
Of superstition, and tyrannic rage,
And all the fury of the rolling storm,
Which fierce pursues the suff'rers in their flight.
Shall not our gates, shall not Britannia's arms   470
Spread ever open to receive their flight?
A virtuous people, by distresses oft
(Distresses for the sake of truth endur'd)
Corrected, dignify'd; creating good
Where-ever they inhabit: this, our isle   475
Has oft experienc'd; witness all ye realms
Of either hemisphere, where commerce flows:
Th'important truth is stampt on ev'ry bale;
Each glossy cloth, and drape of mantle warm,
Receives th'impression, ev'ry airy woof,   480
Cheyney, and bayse, and serge, and alepine,
Tammy, and crape, and the long countless list
Of woollen webs; and ev'ry work of steel;
And that crystalline metal, blown or fus'd,

445 *Lancastria's arms* In 1298 Matilda, the niece of Pain de
    Cadurcis, original builder of Kidwelly Castle, married
    Henry of Lancaster, who completed the building work
    incorporating his coat of arms. The lands became
    merged in the Duchy of Lancaster when their
    granddaughter Blanche married John of Gaunt.
447 *Menapian* Belgian.
452–3 *vales / Of the Brigantes* The Yorkshire Dales
    (inhabited by the ancient British tribe of Brigantes).
456 *Brabant* A region of Flanders situated between the
    Meuse and Scheldt rivers.

461 *varletry* 'riff-raff'.
481–2 Some of the main types of woollen cloth: *Cheyney*
    was a type of worsted fabric; *bayse* (modern baize), a
    light cloth; *serge*, a cheap and durable woollen clothing
    fabric; *alepine* or alapeen was made from a mixture of
    wool and silk or mohair and cotton; *Tammy* was a good
    quality worsted with a glazed finish; *crape*, a fine
    worsted used for clergymen's dress and for mourning
    apparel.
484–6 The tradition of fine glassmaking, introduced into
    England by Huguenot refugees.

Limpid as water dropping from the clefts 485
Of mossy marble: not to name the aids
Their wit has giv'n the fleece, now taught to link
With flax, or cotton, or the silk-worm's thread,
And gain the graces of variety:
Whether to form the matron's decent robe, 490
Or the thin-shading trail for Agra's nymphs;
Or solemn curtains, whose long gloomy folds
Surround the soft pavilions of the rich.
    They too the many-colour'd Arras taught
To mimic nature, and the airy shapes 495
Of sportive fancy: such as oft appear
In old Mosaic pavements, when the plough
Up-turns the crumbling glebe of Weldon field;
Or that, o'ershaded erst by Woodstock's bow'r,
Now grac'd by Blenheim, in whose stately rooms 500
Rise glowing tapestries, that lure the eye
With MARLB'ROUH'S wars: here Schellenbergh exults,
Behind surrounding hills of ramparts steep,
And vales of trenches dark; each hideous pass
Armies defend; yet on the hero leads 505
His Britons, like a torrent, o'er the mounds.
Another scene is Blenheim's glorious field,
And the red Danube. Here, the rescu'd states
Crouding beneath his shield: there, Ramillies'
Important battle: next, the tenfold chain 510
Of Arleux burst, and th'adamantine gates
Of Gaul flung open to the tyrant's throne.
A shade obscures the rest — Ah, then what pow'r
Invidious from the lifted sickle snatch'd
The harvest of the plain? So lively glows 515
The fair delusion, that our passions rise
In the beholding, and the glories share
Of visionary battle. This bright art
Did zealous Europe learn of pagan hands,
While she assay'd with rage of holy war 520
To desolate their fields: but old the skill:

491 'There is woven at Manchester, for the East Indies, a very thin stuff, of thread and cotton; which is cooler than the manufactures of that country, where the material is only cotton' (Dyer). Agra was the Moghul capital of northern India.

494 *Arras* A tapestry wall-hanging. The art of making illustrated tapestries derived from Flanders, though it was introduced into England before the Huguenot immigrants.

497 *Mosaic pavements* Dyer alludes to Roman villas discovered at Great Weldon, Northamptonshire (1738), and Stonesfield, near Woodstock, Oxfordshire (1712).

500 *Blenheim* The palace at Woodstock built 1705–24 for John Churchill, Duke of Marlborough (1650–1722).

501 De Vost's celebrated tapestries at Blenheim depict the Duke's military victories.

502 *Schellenbergh* A hill overlooking the Danube where Marlborough defeated the French and Bavarian forces on 2 July 1704.

507 *Blenheim* A Bavarian village, site of Marlborough's overwhelming victory on 13 August 1704.

509 *Ramillies* A Belgian village, scene of Marlborough's victory over the French on 23 May 1706.

510–11 *tenfold chain / Of Arleux* The line of French fortifications which Marlborough overran.

513 *A shade obscures the rest* Dyer hints that Britain negotiated a dishonourable peace with France in 1713. Pope celebrated the treaty in *Windsor-Forest*.

Long were the Phrygians' pict'ring looms renown'd;
Tyre also, wealthy seat of arts, excell'd,
And elder Sidon, in th'historic web.
　　Far-distant Tibet in her gloomy woods   525
Rears the gay tent, of blended wool unwov'n,
And glutinous materials: the Chinese
Their porcelain, Japan its varnish boasts.
Some fair peculiar graces ev'ry realm,
And each from each a share of wealth acquires.   530
　　But chief by numbers of industrious hands
A nation's wealth is counted: numbers raise
Warm emulation: where that virtue dwells,
There will be traffick's seat; there will she build
Her rich emporium. Hence, ye happy swains,   535
With hospitality inflame your breast,
And emulation: the whole world receive,
And with their arts, their virtues, deck your isle.
Each clime, each sea, the spacious orb of each,
Shall join their various stores, and amply feed   540
The mighty brotherhood; while ye proceed,
Active and enterprising, or to teach
The stream a naval course, or till the wild,
Or drain the fen, or stretch the long canal,
Or plough the fertile billows of the deep.   545
Why to the narrow circle of our coast
Should we submit our limits, while each wind
Assists the stream and sail, and the wide main
Wooes us in ev'ry port? See Belgium build,
Upon the foodful brine, her envy'd pow'r;   550
And, half her people floating on the wave,
Expand her fishy regions. Thus our isle,
Thus only may Britannia be enlarg'd. —
But whither, by the visions of the theme
Smit with sublime delight, but whither strays   555
The raptur'd muse, forgetful of her task?
　　No common pleasure warms the gen'rous mind,
When it beholds the labors of the loom;
How widely round the globe they are dispers'd,
From little tenements by wood or croft,   560
Through many a slender path, how sedulous,
As rills to rivers broad, they speed their way
To public roads, to Fosse, or Watling-street,
Or Armine, ancient works; and thence explore,

---

522 *Phrygians* The inhabitants of Phrygia (now western
　　Turkey).
523–4 *Tyre … Sidon* Phoenician ports in the eastern
　　Mediterranean.
525–7 The Tibetan yak-hair tent is woven, but Dyer may
　　be describing an earlier form.
548 *main* 'ocean'.
549–52 During the eighteenth century Belgium witnessed
　　an expansion of its fishing industry and a newly
　　prominent role in international trade.

557–80 Dyer's catalogue of British rivers important to
　　textile manufacture is indebted to several literary
　　sources, notably Spenser's *Faerie Queene*, IV.xi.24–72,
　　and Michael Drayton's topographical poem *Poly-
　　Olbion* (1622). See also Pope, *Windsor-Forest*, 335–46.
563–4 Fosse Way, Watling Street and Ermine Street were
　　the chief roads in Roman Britain.

Through ev'ry navigable wave, the sea, 565
That laps the green earth round: thro' Tyne, and Tees,
Through Weare, and Lune, and merchandizing Hull,
And Swale, and Aire whose crystal waves reflect
The various colours of the tinctur'd web;
Through Ken, swift rolling down his rocky dale, 570
Like giddy youth impetuous, then at Wick
Curbing his train, and, with the sober pace
Of cautious eld, meand'ring to the deep;
Through Dart, and sullen Exe, whose murm'ring wave
Envies the Dune and Rother, who have won 575
The serge and kersie to their blanching streams;
Through Towy, winding under Merlin's tow'rs,
And Usk, that frequent, among hoary rocks,
On her deep waters paints th'impending scene,
Wild torrents, craggs, and woods, and mountain snows. 580
The northern Cambrians, an industrious tribe,
Carry their labors on pigmean steeds,
Of size exceeding not Leicestrian sheep,
Yet strong and sprightly: over hill and dale
They travel unfatigued, and lay their bales 585
In Salop's streets, beneath whose lofty walls
Pearly Sabrina waits them with her barks,
And spreads the swelling sheet. For no-where far
From some transparent river's naval course
Arise, and fall, our various hills and vales, 590
No-where far distant from the masted wharf.
We need not vex the strong laborious hand
With toil enormous, as th'Egyptian king,
Who join'd the sable waters of the Nile,
From Memphis' tow'rs, to th'Erythræan gulph: 595
Or as the monarch of enfeebled Gaul,
Whose will imperious forc'd an hundred streams,
Through many a forest, many a spacious wild,
To stretch their scanty trains from sea to sea,

566 *Tyne, and Tees* Major rivers of north-east England flowing into the North Sea.

567 *Weare, and Lune, and merchandizing Hull* Rivers flowing into the North Sea, Irish Sea and Humber estuary, respectively.

568 *Swale, and Aire* Rivers of the Yorkshire Dales, north-west of Leeds.

570 *Ken* The river Kent ('Ken' or 'Can' in the eighteenth century) rises in the Westmoreland fells and flows through Kendal to Morecambe Bay.

571 *Wick* The village of Sedgwick, 4 miles south of Kendal.

573 *eld* 'old age'.

574 *Dart, and … Exe* Rivers in Devon flowing into the English Channel.

575 *Dune and Rother* The Rivers Don and Rother meet at Rotherham, Yorkshire.

576 *serge and kersie* Types of hardwearing cloth used for work clothes.

577 *Towy* See *Grongar Hill*, headnote. The area was the legendary home of the magician Merlin.

578 *Usk* Welsh river entering the Severn estuary at Newport.

581 *Cambrians* Welshmen.

582 *pigmean steeds* Welsh ponies were small, though not as small as Leicester sheep.

586 *Salop* The walled town of Shrewsbury, on the River Severn.

587 *pearly Sabrina* See 431n.

593–5 According to Herodotus, the Egyptian King Necos began constructing a canal across the Suez Isthmus to join the Nile with the Red Sea. The project was completed by King Darius I of Persia (521–486 BC).

596 *monarch of enfeebled Gaul* Louis XIV (1638–1715) improved the navigability of many French rivers. The construction of the Canal du Midi linking the Atlantic and the Mediterranean proved ruinously expensive.

That some unprofitable skiff might float   600
Across irriguous dales, and hollow'd rocks.
   Far easier pains may swell our gentler floods,
And through the centre of the isle conduct
To naval union. Trent and Severn's wave,
By plains alone disparted, woo to join   605
Majestic Thamis. With their silver urns
The nimble-footed Naiads of the springs
Await, upon the dewy lawn, to speed
And celebrate the union; and the light
Wood-nymphs; and those, who o'er the grots preside,   610
Whose stores bituminous, with sparkling fires,
In summer's tedious absence, chear the swains,
Long sitting at the loom; and those besides,
Who crown, with yellow sheaves, the farmer's hopes;
And all the genii of commercial toil: 615
These on the dewy lawns await, to speed
And celebrate the union, that the fleece,
And glossy web, to ev'ry port around
May lightly glide along. Ev'n now behold,
Adown a thousand floods, the burden'd barks,   620
With white sails glist'ning, through the gloomy woods
Haste to their harbours. See the silver maze
Of stately Thamis, ever chequer'd o'er
With deeply-laden barges, gliding smooth
And constant as his stream: in growing pomp,   625
By Neptune still attended, slow he rolls
To great Augusta's mart, where lofty trade,
Amid a thousand golden spires enthron'd,
Gives audience to the world: the strand around
Close swarms with busy crouds of many a realm.   630
What bales, what wealth, what industry, what fleets!
Lo, from the simple fleece how much proceeds.

604–6 Dyer had first described his proposal to link the three principal navigable rivers of England, the Trent, Severn and Thames, in his unpublished 'Commercial Map of England', begun in 1737.

607 *Naiads* River-nymphs.

610–13 Dyer imagines cave-nymphs watching over coal mines ('stores bituminous'). Coal was then used as a light source in Scotland and northern England.

626 *Neptune* God of the Sea. The Thames is a tidal river.

627 *Augusta* The Roman name for London during the fourth century, used by poets to evoke imperial power. Cf. Pope, *Windsor-Forest*, 334.

Stephen Duck (1705?–1756)

When the Thresher Poet was 'discovered' in 1730 he was widely fêted as a literary prodigy – a humble farm labourer who wrote verses superior, some said, to Pope's. The truth was more complex; but the mythologizing of Stephen Duck is an early instance of the eighteenth century's interest in untutored genius. Duck was born in Charlton St Peter, Wiltshire, to parents of upper labouring status. He attended a local charity school until fourteen, then worked with his parents on a farm they briefly rented before becoming a hired labourer. The demands of domestic life (marriage at nineteen and the rapid production of three children) hardened his determination to 'improve' himself. He studied late at night or during work-breaks, first arithmetic, then poetry, building up with a friend a small library of several dozen volumes including *The Spectator*, Milton's *Paradise Lost*, some Shakespeare, and Dryden's translation of Virgil. By 1729 Duck was writing his own poetry. The local clergy and gentry commissioned pieces from the rhyming thresher, the most ambitious of which, *The Shunamite* (a paraphrase of Kings 2:4), was written for the wife of Duck's most important local patron, the Reverend Stanley, recorder of Pewsey. She also requested from him the autobiographical poem which became Duck's signature piece, *The Thresher's Labour*. Duck's early poems were pirated under the title *Poems on Several Subjects*, a volume which went through seven printings in 1730 alone. In September of that year Queen Caroline herself summoned Duck to an audience, for which his new mentors Dr Clarke, Prebendary of Winchester, and Charlotte Clayton, the Queen's lady-in-waiting, carefully prepared him.

The death of Duck's wife Anne in October 1730 marked a decisive break between his old and new lives. Installed in a small house in Richmond with a royal pension of £30 per annum, Duck was required to master social and literary protocol. Royal patronage promoted Duck's popularity yet also emasculated his verse. His *Poems on Several Occasions* (1736), the first authorized edition of his works, boasted an enviable subscription list, yet the self-abasing tone of its dedication to the Queen resounds through the proficient but dutiful poems which fill the volume. Duck 'ascended' through a series of symbolic occupations, from a Yeoman of the Guard in 1733 (when he married the Queen's housekeeper Sarah Big) to master of Duck Island in St James's Park and keeper, in 1735, of Queen Caroline's Merlin's Cave, a new 'gothick' building in Richmond gardens allegorically glorifying the Hanoverian dynasty.

Inevitably, Duck became a butt for opposition satirists bent on ridiculing Caroline's cultural pretensions. Her death in 1737 was for him both a loss and a liberation. In 1746 Duck took holy orders, becoming a chaplain in the dragoons, then a preacher at Kew Chapel, then finally the successful and popular Rector of Byfleet, Surrey. It was here he wrote his last major poem, the historical-descriptive *Caesar's Camp* (posthumously published in 1757). In 1756 Duck drowned himself in a pond behind a Reading tavern: a suicide which it is tempting, but probably wrong, to ascribe to the labouring-class poet's alienation from his roots and community.

The strength of *The Thresher's Labour* lies in its graphic account, edged with resentment, of the working year from the labourer's perspective – an unremitting cycle of toil. The festive harvest supper supplies only the illusion of an ending: it is a 'cheat' belied by the unceasing demands of the next day's work. Threshing, a noisy, monotonous, backbreaking indoor job performed during winter and the spare hours in other seasons, forms the consistent motif in the labourer's year – an anti-pastoral inversion of the literary shepherd's ease among fields, fountains and lambkins. Yet Duck also takes a certain professional pride and even pleasure in his work, both in the rhythmic precision of the threshing and especially in the carefully choreographed reaping scenes. Although critics have long praised Duck for his rural 'realism', *The Thresher's Labour*, even in its original form, is a self-consciously literary work containing allusions and episodes (such as the sudden rain-storm or the extended simile comparing chattering women with birds) modelled on classical sources. Duck's patronizing dismissal of women workers provoked Mary Collier's trenchant riposte, *The Woman's Labour* (1739). Duck's success inspired a series of 'working' poets to make their voices heard (see Ann Yearsley) as well as anticipating the work of later rural poets such as John Clare and Robert Bloomfield.

The text printed here is that of the first edition of 1730. In 1734 Duck claimed that the poem had never been published with his approval: the first edition he authorized is that of the 1736 *Poems on Several Subjects*. But by this date Duck had acquired a more self-consciously classical and correct manner, and had revised his original poem accordingly. While not necessarily inferior, it is certainly different from the 1730 text. We have recorded the most significant variants in the footnotes.

The Thresher's Labour

THE grateful Tribute of these rural Lays,
Which to her Patron's Hand the Muse conveys,
Deign to accept; 'tis just She Tribute bring
To Him whose Bounty gives her Life to sing:
To Him whose generous Favours tune her Voice,   5
And bid her 'midst her Poverty rejoice.
Inspir'd by These, she dares her self prepare,
To sing the Toils of each revolving Year:
Those endless Toils, which always grow anew,
And the poor *Thresher*'s destin'd to pursue;   10
Ev'n these with pleasure can the Muse rehearse,
When You, and Gratitude, command the Verse.
    Soon as the Harvest hath laid bare the Plains,
And Barns well-fill'd reward the Farmer's Pains;
What Corn each Sheaf will yield, intent to hear,   15
And guess from thence the Profits of the Year;
Or else impending Ruin to prevent,
By paying, timely, threat'ning Landlord's Rent,
He calls his Threshers forth: Around we stand,
With deep Attention waiting his Command.   20
To each our Tasks he readily divides,
And pointing, to our different Stations guides.
As he directs, to different Barns we go;
Here two for Wheat, and there for Barley two.
But first, to shew what he expects to find,   25
These Words, or Words like these, disclose his Mind:
So dry the Corn was carried from the Field,
So easily 'twill Thresh, so well 'twill Yield;
Sure large Day's Work I well may hope for now;
Come, strip, and try, let's see what you can do.   30
Divested of our Cloaths, with Flail in Hand,
At a just Distance, Front to Front we stand;
And first the Threshall's gently swung, to prove,
Whether with just Exactness it will move:
That once secure, more quick we whirl them round,   35
From the strong Planks our Crab-Tree Staves rebound,
And echoing Barns return the rattling Sound.
Now in the Air our knotty Weapons fly;
And now with equal Force descend from high:
Down one, one up, so well they keep the Time,   40
The *Cyclops* Hammers could not truer chime;
Nor with more heavy Strokes could *Ætna* groan,

---

2 *Patron* The Reverend Mr Stanley. See headnote.
13–19 Soon as the golden Harvest quits the Plain,
    And CERES' Gifts reward the Farmer's Pain;
    What Corn each Sheaf will yield, intent to hear,
    And guess from thence the Profits of the Year,
    He calls his Reapers forth ... (*1736*)
31 *Flail* A tool for threshing corn by hand consisting of a

short wooden club known as a 'swingle' or 'swipple',
which swings freely from a wooden staff or handle.
33 *Threshall* 'flail'.
35 *secure* 'established'.
36 *Crab-Tree* The wild apple tree, characterized by its
crooked form and knotted branches.

When *Vulcan* forg'd the Arms for *Thetis'* Son.
In briny Streams our Sweat descends apace,
Drops from our Locks, or trickles down our Face.   45
No intermission in our Works we know;
The noisy Threshall must for ever go.
Their Master absent, others safely play;
The sleeping Threshall doth it self betray.
Nor yet the tedious Labour to beguile,   50
And make the passing Minutes sweetly smile.
Can we, like Shepherds, tell a merry Tale?
The Voice is lost, drown'd by the noisy Flail.
But we may think — Alas! what pleasing thing
Here to the Mind can the dull Fancy bring?   55
The Eye beholds no pleasant Object here:
No chearful Sound diverts the list'ning Ear.
The Shepherd well may tune his Voice to sing,
Inspir'd by all the Beauties of the Spring:
No Fountains murmur here, no Lambkins play,   60
No Linets warble, and no Fields look gay;
'Tis all a dull and melancholy Scene,
Fit only to provoke the Muses Spleen.
When sooty Pease we thresh, you scarce can know
Our native Colour, as from Work we go;   65
The Sweat, and Dust, and suffocating Smoke,
Make us so much like *Ethiopians* look:
We scare our Wives, when Evening brings us home;
And frighted Infants think the Bug-bear come.
Week after Week we this dull Task pursue,   70
Unless when winnowing Days produce a new;
A new indeed, but frequently a worse,
The Threshall yields but to the Master's Curse:
He counts the Bushels, counts how much a Day,
Then swears we've idled half our Time away.   75
Why look ye, Rogues! D'ye think that this will do?
Your Neighbours thresh as much again as you.
Now in our Hands we wish our noisy Tools,
To drown the hated Names of Rogues and Fools;

41–3 These lines are heavily influenced by Dryden's translation of Virgil's *Georgics*, 4: 245–6, 251–3: 'As when the *Cyclops*, at th'Almighty Nod, / New Thunder hasten for their angry God ... / With lifted Arms they order ev'ry Blow, / And chime their sounding Hammers in a Row; / With labour'd Anvils *Aetna* groans below.'

41 *Cyclops* In Hesiod, the three Cyclopes, sons of heaven and earth, made the thunderbolts of Zeus. They were often depicted as the workmen of Hephaestus, Greek god of fire and crafts.

42 *Aetna* Europe's highest active volcano in Sicily, sometimes described as Vulcan's workshop.

43 *Vulcan* The Roman god of fire and the smithy, identified with Hephaestus; *Thetis' Son* The Greek hero Achilles, son of King Peleus and the sea-nymph Thetis. Homer's *Iliad*, 18:546–719 describes how Hephaestus forged the great shield of Achilles.

55 *Fancy* 'imagination'.

64 *sooty Pease* Pea-plants were threshed to release the dried peas. It was a messy business: 'With peas and beans, it is well to thresh in the open on account of the clouds of black dust which are knocked out of them' (Thomas Hennell, *The Old Farm* (1984); first published in 1934 as *Change on the Farm*).

69 *Bug-bear* 'bogeyman'; an imaginary monster used by parents to frighten children into good behaviour.

71 *winnowing* The process of separating grain from chaff by tossing the threshed corn in the air.

74 *Bushel* A measure used to weigh corn.

But wanting those, we just like School-boys look,   80
When th' angry Master views the blotted Book:
They cry their Ink was faulty, and their Pen;
We, The Corn threshes bad, 'twas cut too green.
But now the Winter hides his hoary Head,
And Nature's Face is with new Beauty spread;   85
The Spring appears, and kind Refreshing Showers
New clothe the Field with Grass, and deck with Flowers.
Next her, the ripening Summer presses on,
And *Sol* begins his longest Stage to run:
Before the Door our welcome Master stands,   90
And tells us the ripe Grass requires our Hands.
The long much-wish'd Intelligence imparts
Life to our Looks, and Spirit to our Hearts:
We wish the happy Season may be fair,
And joyful, long to breathe in opener Air.   95
This Change of Labour seems to give much Ease;
With Thoughts of Happiness our Joy's complete,
There's always Bitter mingled with the Sweet.
When Morn does thro' the Eastern Windows peep,
Strait from our Beds we start, and shake off Sleep;   100
This new Employ with eager haste to prove,
This new Employ becomes so much our Love:
Alas! that human Joys shou'd change so soon,
Even this may bear another Face at Noon!
The Birds salute us as to Work we go,   105
And a new Life seems in our Breasts to glow.
A-cross one's Shoulder hangs a Scythe well steel'd,
The Weapon destin'd to unclothe the Field:
T'other supports the Whetstone, Scrip, and Beer;
That for our Scythes, and These ourselves to chear.   110
And now the Field design'd our Strength to try
Appears, and meets at last our longing Eye;
The Grass and Ground each chearfully surveys,
Willing to see which way th'Advantage lays.
As the best Man, each claims the foremost Place,   115
And our first Work seems but a sportive Race:
With rapid Force our well-whet Blades we drive,
Strain every Nerve, and Blow for Blow we give:
Tho' but this Eminence the Foremost gains,
Only t'excel the rest in Toil and Pains.   120
But when the scorching Sun is mounted high,
And no kind Barns with friendly Shades are nigh,
Our weary Scythes entangle in the Grass,
And Streams of Sweat run trickling down a-pace;

---

89 *Sol* The sun.
91 *ripe Grass* The haymaking (to line 204).
92 *Intelligence* 'information'.
96 An unrhymed line.
99–100 When first the Lark sings Prologue to the Day, /
    We rise, admonish'd by his early Lay (*1736*).
109 *Whetstone* Stone used to sharpen blades; *Scrip* 'satchel'.

115–20 And, Hero–like, each claims the foremost Place.
    At first our Labour seems a sportive Race:
    With rapid Force our sharpen'd Blades we drive,
    Strain ev'ry Nerve, and Blow for Blow we give.
    All strive to vanquish, tho' the Victor gains
    No other Glory, but the greatest Pains. (*1736*)
119 *Eminence* 'distinction'.

Our sportive Labour we too late lament, 125
And wish that Strength again, we vainly spent.
Thus in the Morn a Courser I have seen,
With headlong Fury scour the level Green,
Or mount the Hills, if Hills are in his way,
As if no Labour could his Fire allay, 130
Till the meridian Sun with sultry Heat,
And piercing Beams hath bath'd his Sides in Sweat;
The lengthen'd Chace scarce able to sustain,
He measures back the Hills and Dales with pain.
With Heat and Labour tir'd, our Scythes we quit, 135
Search out a shady Tree, and down we sit;
From Scrip and Bottle hope new Strength to gain;
But Scrip and Bottle too are try'd in vain.
Down our parch'd Throats we scarce the Bread can get,
And quite o'er-spent with Toil, but faintly eat; 140
Nor can the Bottle only answer all,
Alas! the Bottle and the Beer's too small.
Our Time slides on, we move from off the Grass,
And each again betakes him to his Place.
Not eager now, as late, our Strength to prove, 145
But all contented regular to move:
Often we whet, as often view the Sun,
To see how near his tedious Race is run;
At length he vails his radiant Face from sight,
And bids the weary Traveller good-night: 150
Homewards we move, but so much spent with Toil,
We walk but slow, and rest at every Stile.
Our good expecting Wives, who think we stay,
Got to the Door, soon eye us in the way;
Then from the Pot the Dumpling's catch'd in haste, 155
And homely by its side the Bacon's plac'd.
Supper and Sleep by Morn new Strength supply,
And out we set again our Works to try:
But not so early quite, nor quite so fast,
As to our Cost we did the Morning past. 160
Soon as the rising Sun hath drank the Dew,
Another Scene is open'd to our View;
Our Master comes, and at his Heels a Throng
Of prattling Females, arm'd with Rake and Prong:
Prepar'd, whil'st he is here, to make his Hay; 165
Or, if he turns his Back, prepar'd to play.
But here, or gone, sure of this Comfort still,
Here's Company, so they may chat their fill:
And were their Hands as active as their Tongues,
How nimbly then would move their Rakes and Prongs? 170
The Grass again is spread upon the Ground,
Till not a vacant Place is to be found;
And while the piercing Sun-beams on it shine,
The Haymakers have time allow'd to dine:

127 *Courser* A swift horse.
128 *scour* 'move rapidly across'.
142 The zeugma contains a pun. 'Small beer' was the name
  for watery weak beer.

153 *stay* 'linger'.
155 *Dumpling* Left-over bread dough boiled in the pot after
  the pig-meat.
164 *Prong* 'fork'.

That soon dispatch'd, they still sit on the Ground,   175
And the brisk Chat renew'd, a-fresh goes round:
All talk at once; but seeming all to fear,
That all they speak so well, the rest won't hear;
By quick degrees so high their Notes they strain,
That Standers-by can naught distinguish plain: 180
So loud their Speech, and so confus'd their Noise,
Scarce puzzled Echo can return a Voice;
Yet spite of this, they bravely all go on,
Each scorns to be, or seem to be, outdone:
Till (unobserv'd before) a low'ring Sky,   185
Fraught with black Clouds, proclaims a Shower nigh;
The tattling Croud can scarce their Garments gain,
Before descends the thick impetuous Rain:
Their noisy Prattle all at once is done,
And to the Hedge they all for Shelter run.   190
    Thus have I seen on a bright Summer's Day,
On some green Brake a Flock of Sparrows play;
From Twig to Twig, from Bush to Bush they fly,
And with continu'd Chirping fill the Sky;
But on a sudden, if a Storm appears,   195
Their chirping Noise no longer dins your Ears;
They fly for Shelter to the thickest Bush,
There silent sit, and all at once is hush.
But better Fate succeeds this rainy Day,
And little Labour serves to make the Hay;   200
Fast as 'tis cut, so kindly shines the Sun,
Turn'd once or twice, the pleasing Work is done:
Next Day the Cocks appear in equal Rows,
Which the glad Master in safe Reeks bestows.
    But now the Field we must no longer range,   205
And yet, hard Fate! still Work for Work we change.
Back to the Barns again in haste we're sent,
Where lately so much Time we pensive spent:
Not pensive now; we bless the friendly Shade,
And to avoid the parching Sun are glad.   210
But few Days here we're destin'd to remain,
Before our Master calls us forth again:
For Harvest now, says he, yourselves prepare,
The ripen'd Harvest now demands your Care.
Early next Morn I shall disturb your Rest,   215
Get all things ready, and be quickly drest.
Strict to his Word, scarce the next Dawn appears,
Before his hasty Summons fills our Ears.
Obedient to his Call, strait up we get,
And finding soon our Company complete;   220
With him, our Guide, we to the Wheat-Field go;
He, to appoint, and we, the Work to do.
Ye Reapers, cast your Eyes around the Field,
And view the Scene its different Beauties yield:

192 *Brake* 'thicket'.   204 *Reeks* 'ricks' (haystacks).
203 *Cocks* Gathered sheaves of hay.   213 *Harvest* The wheat harvest (to line 263).

Then look again with a more tender Eye,   225
To think how soon it must in Ruin lie.
For once set in, where-e'er our Blows we deal,
There's no resisting of the well-whet Steel:
But here or there, where-e'er our Course we bend,
Sure Desolation does our Steps attend.   230
Thus when *Arabia*'s Sons, in hopes of Prey,
To some more fertile Country take their way;
How beauteous all things in the Morn appear,
There Villages, and pleasing Cots are here;
So many pleasing Objects meet the Sight,   235
The ravish'd Eye could willing gaze 'till Night:
But long e'er then, where-e'er their Troops have past,
Those pleasant Prospects lie a gloomy Waste.
    The Morning past, we sweat beneath the Sun,
And but uneasily our Work goes on.   240
Before us we perplexing Thistles find,
And Corn blown adverse with the ruffling Wind:
Behind our Backs the Female Gleaners wait,
Who sometimes stoop, and sometimes hold a Chat.
Each Morn we early rise, go late to Bed,   245
And lab'ring hard, a painful Life we lead:
For Toils, scarce ever ceasing, press us now,
Rest never does, but on the Sabbath show,
And barely that, our Master will allow.
Nor, when asleep, are we secure from Pain,   250
We then perform our Labours o'er again:
Our mimic Fancy always restless seems,
And what we act awake, she acts in Dreams.
Hard Fate! Our Labours ev'n in Sleep don't cease,
Scarce *Hercules* e'er felt such Toils as these.   255
At length in Rows stands up the well-dry'd Corn,
A grateful Scene, and ready for the Barn.
Our well-pleas'd Master views the Sight with joy,
And we for carrying all our Force employ.
Confusion soon o'er all the Field appears,   260
And stunning Clamours fill the Workmens Ears;
The Bells, and clashing Whips, alternate sound,
And rattling Waggons thunder o'er the Ground.
The Wheat got in, the Pease, and other Grain,
Share the same Fate, and soon leave bare the Plain: 265
In noisy Triumph the last Load moves on,
And loud Huzza's proclaim the Harvest done.

---

234 *Cots* 'cottages'.
241 *perplexing* 'troublesome'.
243–6 Behind our Master waits; and if he spies
    One charitable Ear, he grudging cries,
    "Ye scatter half your Wages o'er the Land."
    Then scrapes the Stubble with his greedy Hand. (*1736*)
243 *Gleaners* The practice of gleaning involved gathering up
    the ears of corn left behind by the reapers, and was
    usually granted as a favour to poorer women and
    children (see Collier, *The Woman's Labour*, 89–100).

Gleaners would not normally have followed behind the
backs of reapers, since gleaning was permitted only
after the harvest had been gathered in. Duck here
elides two distinct labour processes, but changed the
passage in 1736 (above). See Thompson and Sugden,
p. 29.
255 *Hercules* The Greek hero charged with performing
    twelve formidably difficult labours.
256–7 But soon we rise the bearded Crop again, / Soon
    PHŒBUS' Rays well dry the golden Grain (*1736*).

Our Master joyful at the welcome Sight,
Invites us all to feast with him at Night.
A Table plentifully spread we find,   270
And Jugs of humming Beer to cheer the Mind;
Which he, too generous, pushes on so fast,
We think no Toils to come, nor mind the past.
But the next Morning soon reveals the Cheat,
When the same Toils we must again repeat: 275
To the same Barns again must back return,
To labour there for room for next Year's Corn.
    Thus, as the Year's revolving Course goes round,
No respite from our Labour can be found:
Like *Sysiphus*, our Work is never done,   280
Continually rolls back the restless Stone:
Now growing Labours still succeed the past,
And growing always new, must always last.

271 *humming* 'strong', 'frothy'.
280 *Sysiphus* In Greek myth Sisyphus continually outwitted the gods by his cunning. They devised a famous punishment for him: to push up to the top of a hill a large rock which, just as it was about to reach the summit, would roll down again.

Mary Collier (1690?–c.1762)

'I who am the Author of these Poems was Born near Midhurst in Sussex of poor, but honest Parents, by whom I was taught to read when very Young, and took great delight in it; but my Mother dying, I lost my Education, Never being put to School: As I grew up, I was set to such labour as the Country afforded. My Recreation was reading, I bought and borrow'd many Books.' This is how Mary Collier opens her brief autobiographical 'Remarks' prefixed to the edition of her *Poems* (Winchester, 1762). These two pages represent almost the sum of what we know about her. A poem written in 1761 gives her age then as 71, and we do not know when or where she died. Such is the anonymity of the 'Washer-woman, at Petersfield in Hampshire', as she was described on the title page of *The Woman's Labour: An Epistle to Mr. Stephen Duck; In Answer to his late Poem, called The Thresher's Labour* (London, 1739). In her 'Remarks' she describes how this poem came about: 'after [my Father's] Death being left alone, I came to Petersfield, where my chief Employment was, Washing, Brewing and such labour, still devoting what leisure time I had to Books. After several Years thus Spent, Duck's Poems came abroad, which I soon got by heart, fancying he had been too Severe on the Female Sex in his Thresher's Labour brought me to a Strong propensity to call an Army of Amazons to vindicate the injured Sex: Therefore I answer'd him to please my own humour, little thinking to make it Public it lay by me several Years and by now and then repeating a few lines to amuse myself and entertain my Company, it got Air.' Unlike Duck, however, Collier was not drawn into the great world. *The Woman's Labour*, printed at her own charge, failed to seize the public imagination as the thresher's poems had done, and she continued to live by physical labour ('I lost nothing, neither did I gain much, others run away with the profit'). Her poem is at times plodding and repetitive, but this is not inappropriate: work for her is never transformed or justified by a wider context as it is for Duck. It remains hard labour in which the material qualities of things demand attention. Set against the social realities of the daily struggle, her brief references to the timeless world of Greek myth make a telling ironic point.

The rest of Collier's story is quickly told: 'Having continued a Washerwoman till I was Sixty-Three Years of Age, I left Petersfield to go and take care of a Farm House near Alton, and there I staid till turn'd of Seventy, And then the infirmities of Age rendered me incapable of the labour of that place. Now I have retired to a Garret (The Poor Poets Fate) in Alton where I am endeavouring to pass the Relict of my days in Piety, Purity, Peace, and an Old Maid.'

The following text is that of the 1739 first edition, with two emendations (see notes).

The Woman's Labour

Immortal Bard! thou Fav'rite of the Nine!
Enrich'd by Peers, advanc'd by CAROLINE!
Deign to look down on One that's poor and low,
Remembring you yourself was lately so;
Accept these Lines: Alas! what can you have   5
From her, who ever was, and's still a Slave?
No Learning ever was bestow'd on me;
My Life was always spent in Drudgery:
And not alone; alas! with Grief I find,
It is the Portion of poor Woman-kind.   10
Oft have I thought as on my Bed I lay,
Eas'd from the tiresome Labours of the Day,
Our first Extraction from a Mass refin'd,
Could never be for Slavery design'd;
'Till Time and Custom by degrees destroy'd   15
That happy State our Sex at first enjoy'd.
When Men had us'd their utmost Care and Toil,
Their Recompence was but a Female Smile;
When they by Arts or Arms were render'd Great,

1 *Nine* The nine Muses.   2 *CAROLINE* See Stephen Duck headnote.

They laid their Trophies at a Woman's Feet;   20
They, in those Days, unto our Sex did bring
Their Hearts, their All, a Free-will Offering;
And as from us their Being they derive,
They back again should all due Homage give.
    JOVE once descending from the Clouds, did drop   25
In Show'rs of Gold on lovely *Danae*'s Lap;
The sweet-tongu'd Poets, in those generous Days,
Unto our Shrine still offer'd up their Lays:
But now, alas! that Golden Age is past,
We are the Objects of your Scorn at last.   30
    And you, great DUCK, upon whose happy Brow
The Muses seem to fix the Garland now,
In your late *Poem* boldly did declare
Alcides' Labours can't with your's compare;
And of your annual Task have much to say,   35
Of Threshing, Reaping, Mowing Corn and Hay;
Boasting your daily Toil, and nightly Dream,
But can't conclude your never-dying Theme,
And let our hapless Sex in Silence lie
Forgotten, and in dark Oblivion die;   40
But on our abject State you throw your Scorn,
And Women wrong, your Verses to adorn.
You of Hay-making speak a Word or two,
As if our Sex but little Work could do:
This makes the honest Farmer smiling say,   45
He'll seek for Women still to make his Hay;
For if his Back be turn'd, their Work they mind
As well as Men, as far as he can find.
For my own Part, I many a *Summer*'s Day
Have spent in throwing, turning, making Hay;   50
But ne'er could see, what you have lately found,
Our Wages paid for sitting on the Ground.
'Tis true, that when our Morning's Work is done,
And all our Grass expos'd unto the Sun,
While that his scorching Beams do on it shine,   55
As well as you, we have a Time to dine:
I hope, that since we freely toil and sweat
To earn our Bread, you'll give us Time to eat.
That over, soon we must get up again,
And nimbly turn our Hay upon the Plain;   60
Nay, rake and prong it in, the Case is clear;
Or how should Cocks in equal Rows appear?
But if you'd have what you have wrote believ'd,
I find, that you to hear us talk are griev'd:

---

26 *Danae* In Greek myth, the daughter of the King of
Argos, who while imprisoned in a tower was seduced by
Jove descending on her in a shower of gold. The result
was Perseus.
34 *Alcides* Hercules. Cf. Duck, *The Thresher's Labour*, 255.
61 *prong* 'fork'. *1739* has 'prow' (not in *OED*), which

would seem to be a misprint. An emendation to 'prong'
is warranted by the reference in *The Thresher's Labour*
to which Collier is responding: 'And were their Hands
as active as their Tongues, / How nimbly then would
move their Rakes and Prongs?' (Duck, 169–70).
62 *Cocks* Cf. Duck, 203.

In this, I hope, you do not speak your Mind,   65
For none but *Turks*, that ever I could find,
Have Mutes to serve them, or did e'er deny
Their Slaves, at Work, to chat it merrily.
Since you have Liberty to speak your Mind,
And are to talk, as well as we, inclin'd,   70
Why should you thus repine, because that we,
Like you, enjoy that pleasing Liberty?
What! would you lord it quite, and take away
The only Privilege our Sex enjoy?
   When Ev'ning does approach, we homeward hie,   75
And our domestic Toils incessant ply:
Against your coming Home prepare to get
Our Work all done, our House in order set;
Bacon and *Dumpling* in the Pot we boil,
Our Beds we make, our Swine we feed the while;   80
Then wait at Door to see you coming Home,
And set the Table out against you come:
Early next Morning we on you attend;
Our Children dress and feed, their Cloaths we mend;
And in the Field our daily Task renew,   85
Soon as the rising Sun has dry'd the Dew.
   When Harvest comes, into the Field we go,
And help to reap the Wheat as well as you;
Or else we go the Ears of Corn to glean;
No Labour scorning, be it e'er so mean;   90
But in the Work we freely bear a Part,
And what we can, perform with all our Heart.
To get a Living we so willing are,
Our tender Babes into the Field we bear,
And wrap them in our Cloaths to keep them warm,   95
While round about we gather up the Corn;
And often unto them our Course do bend,
To keep them safe, that nothing them offend:
Our Children that are able, bear a Share
In gleaning Corn, such is our frugal Care.   100
When Night comes on, unto our Home we go,
Our Corn we carry, and our Infant too;
Weary, alas! but 'tis not worth our while
Once to complain, or *rest at ev'ry Stile*;
We must make haste, for when we Home are come,   105
Alas! we find our Work but just begun;
So many Things for our Attendance call,
Had we ten Hands, we could employ them all.
Our Children put to Bed, with greatest Care
We all Things for your coming Home prepare: 110
You sup, and go to Bed without delay,
And rest yourselves till the ensuing Day;
While we, alas! but little Sleep can have,
Because our froward Children cry and rave;

---

79 *Dumpling* Cf. Duck, 155–6.   **104** Cf. Duck, 152.
86 This line is almost identical to Duck, 161.   **114** *froward* 'naughty', 'ungovernable'.

Yet, without fail, soon as Day-light doth spring,   115
We in the Field again our Work begin,
And there, with all our Strength, our Toil renew,
Till *Titan*'s golden Rays have dry'd the Dew;
Then home we go unto our Children dear,
Dress, feed, and bring them to the Field with care.   120
Were this your Case, you justly might complain
That Day nor Night you are secure from Pain;
Those mighty Troubles which perplex your Mind,
(*Thistles* before, and *Females* come behind)
Would vanish soon, and quickly disappear,   125
Were you, like us, encumber'd thus with Care.
What you would have of us we do not know:
We oft' take up the Corn that you do mow;
We cut the Peas, and always ready are
In ev'ry Work to take our proper Share;   130
And from the Time that Harvest doth begin,
Until the Corn be cut and carry'd in,
Our Toil and Labour's daily so extreme,
That we have hardly ever *Time to dream*.
        The Harvest ended, Respite none we find;   135
The hardest of our Toil is still behind:
Hard Labour we most chearfully pursue,
And out, abroad, a Charing often go:
Of which I now will briefly tell in part,
What fully to declare is past my Art;   140
So many Hardships daily we go through,
I boldly say, the like *you* never knew.
        When bright *Orion* glitters in the Skies
In *Winter* Nights, then early we must rise;
The Weather ne'er so bad, Wind, Rain, or Snow,   145
Our Work appointed, we must rise and go;
While you on easy Beds may lie and sleep,
Till Light does thro' your Chamber-windows peep.
When to the House we come where we should go,
How to get in, alas! we do not know: 150
The Maid quite tir'd with Work the Day before,
O'ercome with Sleep; we standing at the Door
Oppress'd with Cold, and often call in vain,
E're to our Work we can Admittance gain:
But when from Wind and Weather we get in,   155
Briskly with Courage we our Work begin;
Heaps of fine Linen we before us view,
Whereon to lay our Strength and Patience too;
Cambricks and Muslins, which our Ladies wear,
Laces and Edgings, costly, fine, and rare,   160
Which must be wash'd with utmost Skill and Care;
With Holland Shirts, Ruffles and Fringes too,

---

118 *Titan* The sun. In Greek myth, one of the Titans (Hyperion) was father of the sun (Helios).
124 Cf. Duck, 241–3.
134 *Time to dream* Cf. Duck, 253.
138 *Charing* A 'charwoman' was hired by the day to do household jobs (chores).

159 *Cambricks* Fine white linen, originally made at Cambrai in France; *Muslins* Delicately woven cotton.
162 *Holland* A linen fabric; *Ruffles* Ornamental frills, often of lace.

Fashions which our Fore-fathers never knew.
For several Hours here we work and slave,
Before we can one Glimpse of Day-light have;   165
We labour hard before the Morning's past,
Because we fear the Time runs on too fast.
   At length bright *Sol* illuminates the Skies,
And summons drowsy Mortals to arise;
Then comes our Mistress to us without fail,   170
And in her Hand, *perhaps*, a Mug of Ale
To cheer our Hearts, and also to inform
Herself, what Work is done that very Morn;
Lays her Commands upon us, that we mind
Her Linen well, nor *leave the Dirt behind:*   175
Not this alone, but also to take care
We don't her Cambricks nor her Ruffles tear;
And *these* most strictly does of us require,
To save her Soap, and sparing be of Fire;
Tells us her Charge is great, nay furthermore,   180
Her Cloaths are fewer than the Time before.
Now we drive on, resolv'd our Strength to try,
And what we can, we do most willingly;
Until with Heat and Work, 'tis often known,
Not only Sweat, but Blood runs trickling down   185
Our Wrists and Fingers; still our Work demands
The constant Action of our lab'ring Hands.
   Now Night comes on, from whence you have Relief,
But that, alas! does but increase our Grief;
With heavy Hearts we often view the Sun,   190
Fearing he'll set before our Work is done;
For either in the Morning, or at Night,
We piece the *Summer*'s Day with Candle-light.
Tho' we all Day with Care our Work attend,
Such is our Fate, we know not when 'twill end: 195
When Ev'ning's come, you Homeward take your Way,
We, till our Work is done, are forc'd to stay;
And after all our Toil and Labour past,
Six-pence or Eight-pence pays us off at last;
For all our Pains, no Prospect can we see   200
Attend us, but *Old Age* and *Poverty*.
   The *Washing* is not all we have to do:
We oft change Work for Work as well as you.
Our Mistress of her Pewter doth complain,
And 'tis our Part to make it clean again.   205
This Work, tho' very hard and tiresome too,
Is not the worst we hapless Females do:
When Night comes on, and we quite weary are,
We scarce can count what falls unto our Share;
Pots, Kettles, Sauce-pans, Skillets, we may see,   210

---

193 *piece* 'make complete'.

199 At this period beer was twopence a quart (two pints);
   The Woman's Labour sold for sixpence. As a thresher
   Stephen Duck received a weekly wage of 'Four
   Shillings and Sixpence', which is ninepence a day.

204–5 On the technique for cleaning pewter, see Leapor,
   Crumble-Hall, 150–5.

210 *Skillet* A boiling-pan with feet and a long handle,
   placed on the fire.

Skimmers and Ladles, and such Trumpery,
Brought in to make complete our Slavery.
Tho' early in the Morning 'tis begun,
'Tis often very late before we've done;
Alas! our Labours never know an End;   215
On Brass and Iron we our Strength must spend;
Our tender Hands and Fingers scratch and tear:
All this, and more, with Patience we must bear.
Colour'd with Dirt and Filth we now appear;
Your threshing *sooty Peas* will not come near.   220
All the Perfections Woman once could boast,
Are quite obscur'd, and altogether lost.
  Once more our Mistress sends to let us know
She wants our Help, because the Beer runs low:
Then in much haste for Brewing we prepare,   225
The Vessels clean, and scald with greatest Care;
Often at Midnight from our Bed we rise;
At other Times, ev'n *that* will not suffice;
Our Work at Ev'ning oft we do begin,
And 'ere we've done, the Night comes on again.   230
Water we pump, the Copper we must fill,
Or tend the Fire; for if we e'er stand still,
Like you, when threshing, we a Watch must keep,
Our Wort boils over if we dare to sleep.
  But to rehearse all Labour is in vain,   235
Of which we very justly might complain:
For us, you see, but little Rest is found;
Our Toil increases as the Year runs round.
While you to *Sysiphus* yourselves compare,
With *Danaus' Daughters* we may claim a Share;   240
For while *he* labours hard against the Hill,
Bottomless Tubs of Water *they* must fill.
  So the industrious Bees do hourly strive
To bring their Loads of Honey to the Hive;
Their sordid Owners always reap the Gains,   245
And poorly recompense their Toil and Pains.

211 *Skimmer* A shallow, often perforated, utensil for
   skimming liquids.
220 Cf. Duck, 64.
227 *Midnight ... rise;* Midnight, ... rise (*1739*).
231 *Copper* A large copper boiling vessel used for laundry
   or cooking.
234 *Wort* A frothy infusion of malt or other grain;
   unfermented beer.

239 *Sysiphus* Cf. Duck, 280.
240 *Danaus' Daughters* Forty-nine of the fifty sisters ('the
   Danaids') were punished in the underworld by having
   to fill leaking jars with water. They had stabbed their
   forty-nine husbands to death on their wedding night.
245 *sordid* 'selfish', 'money-grubbing'.

Samuel Johnson (1709–1784)

No other eighteenth-century writer quite matches Dr Johnson's literary range and intensity of moral vision. The fact that he produced some of his best work under commercial pressure in order to earn a living challenged Pope and Swift's image of the slipshod, ignorant Grub Street hack. Few university academics were as widely read as Johnson, whose reading habits began early in his father's Lichfield bookshop. As a child, scrofula badly scarred his face and damaged his sight and hearing. He developed a shambling gait and in later years the compulsive ticks and mannerisms characteristic of Tourette's syndrome. Johnson's stubborn character overcame these physical obstacles. Lack of funds forced him to leave Pembroke College, Oxford in 1730, but the debilitating depression which at first overwhelmed him helped shape his profound compassion for human, especially mental, suffering. After briefly writing for the *Birmingham Journal*, in 1735 he married a forty-six-year-old widow, Elizabeth Porter, and established a school at Edial near Lichfield which soon proved a dismal failure. In 1737 he left for London with his pupil David Garrick, the future actor. There Johnson began work for Edward Cave, founder of the *Gentleman's Magazine*, to which he contributed essays, poems, Latin verses and a series of semi-fictional parliamentary debates. In the late 1730s the headstrong Johnson, like his friend Richard Savage, harboured opposition, possibly even Jacobite sympathies. These emerge in *London* (1738), a Juvenalian diatribe against Walpolian corruption, and also the following year the mock-prophetic *Marmor Norfolciense* and *A Compleat Vindication of the Licensers of the Stage*, an attack on Walpole's Stage Licensing Act. However, by the time Johnson wrote his *Life of Savage* (1744) he had distanced himself from his former Patriot zeal. Far more characteristic was the tragic universality of his second imitation of Juvenal, *The Vanity of Human Wishes* (1749). During these years Johnson was continually short of money. In 1749 Garrick gained him £300 for the benefit nights of his rather wooden verse tragedy *Irene*, and in 1750 he started *The Rambler*, a literary periodical written both for profit and to break the monotony of

work on his monumental *Dictionary of the English Language* (1755). If this mighty work established Johnson as a national authority on the English language, then *The Rambler* (in Boswell's words) established him as 'a majestick teacher of moral and religious wisdom'. The latter qualities permeate *The History of Rasselas, Prince of Abyssinia* (1759), an oriental tale whose humour and compassion temper its ironic exposure of the fallibility of human dreams.

In 1762 King George III granted Johnson an annual pension of £300, which relieved him from incessant toil. During the 1760s he met his future biographer Boswell, and with Sir Joshua Reynolds founded his distinguished 'Club' (whose members came to include Burke, Goldsmith, Garrick, the Wartons, Sheridan, Gibbon, Adam Smith and Charles James Fox). A memorable conversationalist, Johnson turned his trenchant wit against the newly fashionable sensibility, and as the tastes of the age moved against him his critical views aroused admiration and distaste in equal proportions. The preface to his long-awaited edition of Shakespeare (1765) attempted to put the brake on the bard-worship that was sweeping the nation, and his greatest critical work, *The Lives of the Poets* (1779–81), presented Pope's translations of Homer rather than Milton as the supreme poetic model.

Johnson is better known for his prose than his poetry, yet the habit of writing verse, which began in his mid-teens, continued unabated throughout his life. His extraordinary powers of memory are evidenced by his habit of writing verse in his head then subsequently committing it to paper, sometimes bothering to jot down only the second half of each line as an *aide-mémoire*. Johnson wrote with equal facility in Latin as in English. The detachment afforded by Latin clothed some of his most intense personal emotions. His English poetry, by contrast, tends to address objective or general themes. Aside from his many tributes to his close friends, and epilogues and prologues to many plays, Johnson's most famous poems remain *London* and *The Vanity of Human Wishes*.

The Vanity of Human Wishes

The Vanity of Human Wishes, an imitation of the tenth satire of the Roman poet Juvenal, is very different from the earlier *London*. Thales, the speaker in *London*, borrows the moral indignation and self-pity of Juvenal's Umbricius in Satire 3, and both rail against the corruptions of city life before departing for rural backwaters. Like its Juvenalian original,

London is a topical satire whose vigorous invective against specific targets mirrored the national mood of 1738. Yet Johnson, who disliked much of Swift's and Pope's satiric writing, was not by temperament a satirist. His consciousness of his own share of human folly and frailty sat uncomfortably with the required ridicule of similar faults in others. Juvenal's tenth satire on the folly of human desires – for wealth, long life, power, beauty – and the liabilities which inevitably accompany them, corresponded to a theme close to Johnson's heart, one later developed in *Rasselas*. Yet whereas Juvenal focuses on the individual and the graphically physical, Johnson's poem, avoiding Juvenal's scurrility, explores the shared psychological traits which drive a Xerxes, an Alexander or a Charles XII. The poem's famous opening lines typify the series of emotionally powerful moral abstractions which dominate Johnson's verse. The dynamic verbs and elemental images which permeate the poem – blazing fires, ebbing streams, floods, cataclysms – shape the impression that man is impelled towards self-destruction by powerful psychological forces of which he is never fully conscious. Thus the poem, elegiac rather than ironic, comes closer to tragedy than to satire. Whereas

Juvenal's poem closes with a jocular recourse to Stoic self-reliance, Johnson's poem ends with an appeal to Christian consolation. God's 'celestial Wisdom' can teach the faith, patience and love needed to enable the trapped individual to escape the confines of his own desires.

The Vanity of Human Wishes. The Tenth Satire of Juvenal, Imitated, less immediately popular than *London*, was first published in quarto on 9 January 1749 – the first work to carry Johnson's own name. Johnson later claimed 'I wrote the first seventy lines … in the course of one morning, in that small house beyond the church at Hampstead. The whole number was composed before I committed a single couplet to writing.' In 1755 Johnson made some significant changes for its appearance in Dodsley's *Collection of Poems*. The text used here is that of the first edition.

Let Observation with extensive View,
Survey Mankind, from *China* to *Peru*;
Remark each anxious Toil, each eager Strife,
And watch the busy Scenes of crouded Life;
Then say how Hope and Fear, Desire and Hate,   5
O'erspread with Snares the clouded Maze of Fate,
Where wav'ring Man, betray'd by vent'rous Pride,
To tread the dreary Paths without a Guide;
As treach'rous Phantoms in the Mist delude,
Shuns fancied Ills, or chases airy Good.   10
How rarely Reason guides the stubborn Choice,
Rules the bold Hand, or prompts the suppliant Voice,
How Nations sink, by darling Schemes oppres'd,
When Vengeance listens to the Fool's Request.
Fate wings with ev'ry Wish th' afflictive Dart,   15
Each Gift of Nature, and each Grace of Art,
With fatal Heat impetuous Courage glows,
With fatal Sweetness Elocution flows,
Impeachment stops the Speaker's pow'rful Breath,
And restless Fire precipitates on Death.   20
     But scarce observ'd the Knowing and the Bold,
Fall in the gen'ral Massacre of Gold;
Wide-wasting Pest! that rages unconfin'd,
And crouds with Crimes the Records of Mankind,
For Gold his Sword the Hireling Ruffian draws,   25
For Gold the hireling Judge distorts the Laws;
Wealth heap'd on Wealth, nor Truth nor Safety buys,
The Dangers gather as the Treasures rise.
     Let Hist'ry tell where rival Kings command,
And dubious Title shakes the madded Land,   30
When Statutes glean the Refuse of the Sword,

---

15 The arrow of suffering is driven home by every wish, gift, etc.
19 *Impeachment* Prosecution for treason or corruption.

20 *precipitates on* 'hastens'.
30 *dubious Title* 'uncertain claim to the throne'.
31 I.e. oppressive laws complete the destruction.

How much more safe the Vassal than the Lord,
Low sculks the Hind beneath the Rage of Pow'r,
And leaves the *bonny Traytor* in the *Tow'r*,
Untouch'd his Cottage, and his Slumbers sound,   35
Tho' Confiscation's Vulturs clang around.
   The needy Traveller, serene and gay,
Walks the wild Heath, and sings his Toil away.
Does Envy seize thee? crush th' upbraiding Joy,
Encrease his Riches and his Peace destroy,   40
New Fears in dire Vicissitude invade,
The rustling Brake alarms, and quiv'ring Shade,
Nor Light nor Darkness bring his Pain Relief,
One shews the Plunder, and one hides the Thief.
   Yet still the gen'ral Cry the Skies assails   45
And Gain and Grandeur load the tainted Gales;
Few know the toiling Statesman's Fear or Care,
Th'insidious Rival and the gaping Heir.
   Once more, *Democritus*, arise on Earth,
With chearful Wisdom and instructive Mirth,   50
See motley Life in modern Trappings dress'd,
And feed with varied Fools th' eternal Jest:
Thou who couldst laugh where Want enchain'd Caprice,
Toil crush'd Conceit, and Man was of a Piece;
Where Wealth unlov'd without a Mourner dy'd;   55
And scarce a Sycophant was fed by Pride;
Where ne'er was known the Form of mock Debate,
Or seen a new-made Mayor's unwieldy State;
Where change of Fav'rites made no Change of Laws,
And Senates heard before they judg'd a Cause;   60
How wouldst thou shake at *Britain*'s modish Tribe,
Dart the quick Taunt, and edge the piercing Gibe?
Attentive Truth and Nature to descry,
And pierce each Scene with Philosophic Eye.
To thee were solemn Toys or empty Shew,   65
The Robes of Pleasure and the Veils of Woe:
All aid the Farce, and all thy Mirth maintain,
Whose Joys are causeless, or whose Griefs are vain.
   Such was the Scorn that fill'd the Sage's Mind,
Renew'd at ev'ry Glance on Humankind;   70
How just that Scorn ere yet thy Voice declare,
Search every State, and canvass ev'ry Pray'r.
   Unnumber'd Suppliants croud Preferment's Gate,
Athirst for Wealth, and burning to be great;

---

33 *Hind* 'peasant'.

34 *bonny Traytor* A reference to the four Scottish lords executed in 1746–7 for their part in the Jacobite Rising of 1745. The word 'bonny' is distinctly Scottish and combines the meanings 'attractive' and 'admired'. In 1755 Johnson changed the word to 'wealthy'.

36 *clang* 'make a shrill cry'.

39 *upbraiding Joy* 'the joy (of the rich man) that makes you resentful'.

42 *Brake* 'thicket'.

46 *Gales* 'breezes'.

49 *Democritus* Greek philosopher (460–*c.*357 BC) who believed happiness derived from peace of mind. His mirth at the spectacle of human life earned him the title 'the laughing philosopher'.

56 *Sycophant* 'flatterer'.

61 *shake* i.e. with laughter.

72 *canvass* 'sift or examine' (Johnson's *Dictionary*).

Delusive Fortune hears th'incessant Call,   75
They mount, they shine, evaporate, and fall.
On ev'ry Stage the Foes of Peace attend,
Hate dogs their Flight, and Insult mocks their End.
Love ends with Hope, the sinking Statesman's Door
Pours in the Morning Worshiper no more;   80
For growing Names the weekly Scribbler lies,
To growing Wealth the Dedicator flies,
From every Room descends the painted Face,
That hung the bright *Palladium* of the Place,
And smoak'd in Kitchens, or in Auctions sold,   85
To better Features yields the Frame of Gold;
For now no more we trace in ev'ry Line
Heroic Worth, Benevolence Divine:
The Form distorted justifies the Fall,
And Detestation rids th'indignant Wall.   90
    But will not *Britain* hear the last Appeal,
Sign her Foes Doom, or guard her Fav'rites Zeal;
Through Freedom's Sons no more Remonstrance rings,
Degrading Nobles and controuling Kings;
Our supple Tribes repress their Patriot Throats,   95
And ask no Questions but the Price of Votes;
With Weekly Libels and Septennial Ale,
Their Wish is full to riot and to rail.
    In full-blown Dignity, see *Wolsey* stand,
Law in his Voice, and Fortune in his Hand: 100
To him the Church, the Realm, their Pow'rs consign,
Thro' him the Rays of regal Bounty shine,
Turn'd by his Nod the Stream of Honour flows,
His Smile alone Security bestows:
Still to new Heights his restless Wishes tow'r,   105
Claim leads to Claim, and Pow'r advances Pow'r;
Till Conquest unresisted ceas'd to please,
And Rights submitted, left him none to seize.
At length his Sov'reign frowns — the Train of State
Mark the keen Glance, and watch the Sign to hate.   110
Where-e'er he turns he meets a Stranger's Eye,
His Suppliants scorn him, and his Followers fly;
Now drops at once the Pride of aweful State,
The golden Canopy, the glitt'ring Plate,

---

80 *Morning Worshiper* Clients seeking preferment attended great men's 'levees', or morning audiences.
81 *weekly Scribbler* 'political journalist'.
82 *Dedicator* A writer who dedicates his work to a rich or influential patron in hope of reward.
83 *painted Face* i.e. family portraits.
84 *Palladium* A protective talisman, named after the image of the goddess Pallas Athena which was kept in Troy to prevent the city from being captured.
93 *Remonstrance* A reference to the Grand Remonstrance, a list of grievances which parliament presented to Charles I on 1 December 1641.
95 *supple Tribes* i.e. politicians; *Patriot* A title carried by the political opposition to Walpole's government

symbolizing disinterested high principle. After its leading members had been bought off with places or peerages by the mid-1740s, 'Patriot' was often a cynical term of abuse.
97 *Septennial Ale* After the Septennial Act of 1716, general elections were called every seven years. The candidates often supplied free beer, leading to wide-scale rioting.
99 *Wolsey* Thomas Wolsey (c.1475–1530), Cardinal and Lord Chancellor under Henry VIII. Of low birth, he rose to the height of power and wealth until he fell from royal favour. The King removed him from office in 1529 and arrested him for high treason in 1530. He died soon after. Wolsey takes the place of Sejanus in Juvenal.

The regal Palace, the luxurious Board,   115
The liv'ried Army, and the menial Lord.
With Age, with Cares, with Maladies oppress'd,
He seeks the Refuge of Monastic Rest.
Grief aids Disease, remember'd Folly stings,
And his last Sighs reproach the Faith of Kings.   120
    Speak thou, whose Thoughts at humble Peace repine,
Shall *Wolsey*'s Wealth, with *Wolsey*'s End be thine?
Or liv'st thou now, with safer Pride content,
The richest Landlord on the Banks of *Trent*?
For why did *Wolsey* by the Steps of Fate,   125
On weak Foundations raise th' enormous Weight?
Why but to sink beneath Misfortune's Blow,
With louder Ruin to the Gulphs below?
    What gave great *Villiers* to th' Assassin's Knife,
And fix'd Disease on *Harley*'s closing Life?   130
What murder'd *Wentworth*, and what exil'd *Hyde*,
By Kings protected, and to Kings ally'd?
What but their Wish indulg'd in Courts to shine,
And Pow'r too great to keep or to resign?
    When first the College Rolls receive his Name,   135
The young Enthusiast quits his Ease for Fame;
Resistless burns the Fever of Renown,
Caught from the strong Contagion of the Gown;
O'er *Bodley*'s Dome his future Labours spread,
And *Bacon*'s Mansion trembles o'er his Head;   140
Are these thy Views? proceed, illustrious Youth,
And Virtue guard thee to the Throne of Truth,
Yet should thy Soul indulge the gen'rous Heat,
Till captive Science yields her last Retreat;
Should Reason guide thee with her brightest Ray,   145
And pour on misty Doubt resistless Day;

---

116 *menial* 'subservient'.

124 *Trent* The river which runs just north of Lichfield, Johnson's home town, fifteen miles north of Birmingham. Johnson extols the peace of provincial life.

129 *Villiers* George Villiers (1592–1628), first Duke of Buckingham. A favourite of King James I, he became an object of popular hatred and was assassinated by John Felton, a discharged naval officer.

130 *Disease* 'trouble'; *Harley* Robert Harley (1661–1724), first Earl of Oxford, leader of the Tories under Queen Anne. Following George I's accession in 1714 he was imprisoned and impeached. See Swift, *Verses on the Death of Dr Swift*, 365–90n.

131 *Wentworth* Thomas Wentworth (1593–1641), first Earl of Strafford and Charles I's chief advisor. He was executed by the Long Parliament; *Hyde* Edward Hyde (1609–74), first Earl of Clarendon. Lord Chancellor in 1660, he was banished in 1667 and spent his final years in France.

132 *to Kings ally'd* Clarendon's daughter Anne married the future James II and was mother to two queens, Mary and Anne.

135–64 This passage on the idealistic scholar replaces Juvenal's portrait of a young orator. It is autobiographical and echoes themes earlier explored in Johnson's poem, *The Young Author* (1743).

138 *the Gown* Academic dress.

139 *Bodley's Dome* The Bodleian Library in Oxford, founded and endowed by Sir Thomas Bodley (1545–1613). 'Dome' (Lat. *domus*) here means 'edifice' or 'building'.

140 *Bacon's Mansion* Oxford legend said that the study of the medieval philosopher Roger Bacon in the gatehouse on Folly Bridge would fall if someone more learned than Bacon walked under it.

143–4 The lines play with sexual suggestion.

143 *gen'rous* 'fertile'.

144 *Science* 'learning'.

Should no false Kindness lure to loose Delight,
Nor Praise relax, nor Difficulty fright;
Should tempting Novelty thy Cell refrain,
And Sloth's bland Opiates shed their Fumes in vain;   150
Should Beauty blunt on Fops her fatal Dart,
Nor claim the Triumph of a letter'd Heart;
Should no Disease thy torpid Veins invade,
Nor Melancholy's Phantoms haunt thy Shade;
Yet hope not Life from Grief or Danger free,   155
Nor think the Doom of Man revers'd for thee:
Deign on the passing World to turn thine Eyes,
And pause awhile from Learning to be wise;
There mark what Ills the Scholar's Life assail,
Toil, Envy, Want, the Garret, and the Jail.   160
See Nations slowly wise, and meanly just,
To buried Merit raise the tardy Bust.
If Dreams yet flatter, once again attend,
Hear *Lydiat*'s Life, and *Galileo*'s End.
        Nor deem, when Learning her lost Prize bestows   165
The glitt'ring Eminence exempt from Foes;
See when the Vulgar 'scap'd, despis'd or aw'd,
Rebellion's vengeful Talons seize on *Laud*.
From meaner Minds, tho' smaller Fines content
The plunder'd Palace or sequester'd Rent;   170
Mark'd out by dangerous Parts he meets the Shock,
And fatal Learning leads him to the Block:
Around his Tomb let Art and Genius weep,
But hear his Death, ye Blockheads, hear and sleep.
        The festal Blazes, the triumphal Show,   175
The ravish'd Standard, and the captive Foe,
The Senate's Thanks, the Gazette's pompous Tale,
With Force resistless o'er the Brave prevail.
Such Bribes the rapid *Greek* o'er *Asia* whirl'd,
For such the steady *Romans* shook the World;   180
For such in distant Lands the *Britons* shine,
And stain with Blood the *Danube* or the *Rhine*;
This Pow'r has Praise, that Virtue scarce can warm,
Till Fame supplies the universal Charm.

147 *Kindness* 'sociable inclinations', with a sexual overtone.
149 *Cell* i.e. study; *refrain* 'spare'.
160 In 1755 Johnson famously replaced the word 'Garret' with 'Patron', a dig at Lord Chesterfield, who had failed in his promised patronage for Johnson's *Dictionary*.
164 *Lydiat* Thomas Lydiat (1572–1646), a mathematician and Biblical scholar. Although poor, he was famous in his day but forgotten after his death; *Galileo* (1564–1642), the great Italian astronomer forced by the Inquisition to deny the validity of the Copernican (sun-centred) theory of the universe. He spent his last years blind and deaf.
168 *Laud* William Laud (1573–1645), Archbishop of

Canterbury under Charles I. He was impeached and executed by the Long Parliament in 1645, not (as Johnson suggests) for his 'fatal Learning' but for his High Church policies. He was a benefactor of Oxford University.
171 *Parts* 'talents'.
177 *Gazette* The official Court newspaper.
179 *rapid Greek* Alexander the Great (356–323 BC), brilliant Greek military leader.
181–2 British troops had recently fought in continental Europe 1743–8, though without repeating the brilliance of Marlborough's campaigns, 1702–11.
183 I.e. Praise succeeds where Virtue fails.

Yet Reason frowns on War's unequal Game,   185
Where wasted Nations raise a single Name,
And mortgag'd States their Grandsires Wreaths regret
From Age to Age in everlasting Debt;
Wreaths which at last the dear-bought Right convey
To rust on Medals, or on Stones decay.   190
    On what Foundation stands the Warrior's Pride?
How just his Hopes let *Swedish Charles* decide;
A Frame of Adamant, a Soul of Fire,
No Dangers fright him, and no Labours tire;
O'er Love, o'er Force, extends his wide Domain,   195
Unconquer'd Lord of Pleasure and of Pain;
No Joys to him pacific Scepters yield,
War sounds the Trump, he rushes to the Field;
Behold surrounding Kings their Pow'r combine,
And One capitulate, and One resign;   200
Peace courts his Hand, but spread her Charms in vain;
'Think Nothing gain'd, he cries, till nought remain,
'On *Moscow*'s Walls till *Gothic* Standards fly,
'And all is Mine beneath the Polar Sky.'
The March begins in Military State,   205
And Nations on his Eye suspended wait;
Stern Famine guards the solitary Coast,
And Winter barricades the Realms of Frost;
He comes, nor Want nor Cold his Course delay;—
Hide, blushing Glory, hide *Pultowa*'s Day: 210
The vanquish'd Hero leaves his broken Bands,
And shews his Miseries in distant Lands;
Condemn'd a needy Supplicant to wait,
While Ladies interpose, and Slaves debate.
But did not Chance at length her Error mend?   215
Did no subverted Empire mark his End?
Did rival Monarchs give the fatal Wound?
Or hostile Millions press him to the Ground?
His Fall was destin'd to a barren Strand,

---

186 *a single Name* 'one man's reputation'.
187 *Wreaths* 'triumphs'.
192 *Swedish Charles* Charles XII (1682–1718), King of Sweden. A courageous military leader, he conquered Denmark, Saxony and Poland. He pursued the Russian army towards Moscow in 1707 but in 1709 was defeated by the Russians at Pultowa and fled to Turkey. Despite opposition, he returned to Sweden in 1714 and managed to raise a fresh army. In autumn 1718 he began a campaign against Norway, but was killed during the siege of Fridrikshald. His death was a severe blow to English Jacobitism, since he had been a close ally of the Old Pretender. Johnson had considered writing a play about him. This passage is Johnson's equivalent of Juvenal's portrait of Hannibal.

195 *Force* Later revised to 'fear'. Editors unnecessarily suppose 'Force' to be a misreading of Johnson's handwriting.
197 *pacific* 'peaceful'.
200 *One capitulate* Frederick IV of Denmark; *One resign* Augustus II of Poland, deposed in 1704 and replaced by Charles's favourite, Stanislas I.
203 *Gothic* The term was used at this time to describe the Nordic or Teutonic races.
214 *Ladies interpose* Perhaps a reference to Catherine, empress of Peter the Great, who supposedly caused the Turkish Grand Vizier to let the Russian army escape from disaster in 1711; or possibly to Charles's sister, who worked on his behalf to secure his return to Sweden.

A petty Fortress, and a dubious Hand;   220
He left the Name, at which the World grew pale,
To point a Moral, or adorn a Tale.
    All Times their Scenes of pompous Woes afford,
From *Persia*'s Tyrant to *Bavaria*'s Lord.
In gay Hostility, and barb'rous Pride,   225
With half Mankind embattled at his Side,
Great *Xerxes* comes to seize the certain Prey,
And starves exhausted Regions in his Way;
Attendant Flatt'ry counts his Myriads o'er,
Till counted Myriads sooth his Pride no more;   230
Fresh Praise is try'd till Madness fires his Mind,
The Waves he lashes, and enchains the Wind;
New Pow'rs are claim'd, new Pow'rs are still bestow'd,
Till rude Resistance lops the spreading God;
The daring *Greeks* deride the Martial Shew,   235
And heap their Vallies with the gaudy Foe;
Th' insulted Sea with humbler Thoughts he gains,
A single Skiff to speed his Flight remains;
Th' incumber'd Oar scarce leaves the dreaded Coast
Through purple Billows and a floating Host.   240
    The Bold *Bavarian*, in a luckless Hour,
Tries the dread Summits of *Cesarean* Pow'r,
With unexpected Legions bursts away,
And sees defenceless Realms receive his Sway;
Short Sway! fair *Austria* spreads her mournful Charms,   245
The Queen, the Beauty, sets the World in Arms;
From Hill to Hill the Beacons rousing Blaze
Spreads wide the Hope of Plunder and of Praise;
The fierce *Croatian*, and the wild *Hussar*,
And all the Sons of Ravage croud the War;   250
The baffled Prince in Honour's flatt'ring Bloom
Of hasty Greatness finds the fatal Doom,
His Foes Derision, and his Subjects Blame,
And steals to Death from Anguish and from Shame.
    Enlarge my Life with Multitude of Days,   255
In Health, in Sickness, thus the Suppliant prays;
Hides from himself his State, and shuns to know,
That Life protracted is protracted Woe.
Time hovers o'er, impatient to destroy,

---

220 *dubious Hand* Charles was thought to have been shot by his own aide-de-camp, though Voltaire contests the story in his *Histoire de Charles XII* (1732).

224 *Persia's Tyrant* Xerxes (*c.*519–465 BC), King of Persia, who embarked on a massive invasion of Greece but was defeated in the sea-battle of Salamis in 480 BC; *Bavaria's Lord* Charles Albert (1697–1745), Elector of Bavaria, became Holy Roman Emperor in 1742.

232 Xerxes ordered the sea to be whipped for wrecking his bridge of boats.

238 After the defeat at Salamis Xerxes fled in a boat towards the Hellespont, ploughing through the bodies of his own dead troops.

241–54 Charles Albert invaded the 'defenceless Realms' of Upper Austria and Bohemia only to become a puppet of his ally, Frederick the Great. He died dishonoured in 1745.

246 *The Queen* Maria Theresa (1717–80), Queen of Hungary and Bavaria, and Archduchess of Austria. An ally of Britain, she successfully defended her realm during the War of the Austrian Succession, 1740–8.

249 *Hussar* Hungarian light-horseman.

And shuts up all the Passages of Joy: 260
In vain their Gifts the bounteous Seasons pour,
The Fruit Autumnal, and the Vernal Flow'r,
With listless Eyes the Dotard views the Store,
He views, and wonders that they please no more;
Now pall the tastless Meats, and joyless Wines,   265
And Luxury with Sighs her Slave resigns.
Approach, ye Minstrels, try the soothing Strain,
And yield the tuneful Lenitives of Pain:
No Sounds alas would touch th'impervious Ear,
Though dancing Mountains witness'd *Orpheus* near;   270
Nor Lute nor Lyre his feeble Pow'rs attend,
Nor sweeter Musick of a virtuous Friend,
But everlasting Dictates croud his Tongue,
Perversely grave, or positively wrong.
The still returning Tale, and ling'ring Jest,   275
Perplex the fawning Niece and pamper'd Guest,
While growing Hopes scarce awe the gath'ring Sneer,
And scarce a Legacy can bribe to hear;
The watchful Guests still hint the last Offence,
The Daughter's Petulance, the Son's Expence,   280
Improve his heady Rage with treach'rous Skill,
And mould his Passions till they make his Will.
     Unnumber'd Maladies each Joint invade,
Lay Siege to Life and press the dire Blockade;
But unextinguish'd Av'rice still remains,   285
And dreaded Losses aggravate his Pains;
He turns, with anxious Heart and cripled Hands,
His Bonds of Debt, and Mortgages of Lands;
Or views his Coffers with suspicious Eyes,
Unlocks his Gold, and counts it till he dies.   290
     But grant, the Virtues of a temp'rate Prime
Bless with an Age exempt from Scorn or Crime;
An Age that melts in unperceiv'd Decay,
And glides in modest Innocence away;
Whose peaceful Day Benevolence endears,   295
Whose Night congratulating Conscience cheers;
The gen'ral Fav'rite as the gen'ral Friend:
Such Age there is, and who could wish its end?
     Yet ev'n on this her Load Misfortune flings,
To press the weary Minutes flagging Wings: 300
New Sorrow rises as the Day returns,
A Sister sickens, or a Daughter mourns.
Now Kindred Merit fills the sable Bier,
Now lacerated Friendship claims a Tear.
Year chases Year, Decay pursues Decay,   305
Still drops some Joy from with'ring Life away;

---

268 *Lenitives* 'soothers'.
270 *Orpheus* The legendary Greek musician and poet whose
   music could charm wild beasts and make trees and
   rocks move.
275–6 Cf. Swift, *Verses on the Death of Dr Swift*, 89–98.

279 *last* 'latest'.
281 *Improve* 'increase'.
303 *sable Bier* Coffin stand draped in black.
306 *Still* 'repeatedly'.

New Forms arise, and diff'rent Views engage,
Superfluous lags the Vet'ran on the Stage,
Till pitying Nature signs the last Release,
And bids afflicted Worth retire to Peace.   310
          But few there are whom Hours like these await,
Who set unclouded in the Gulphs of Fate.
From *Lydia*'s Monarch should the Search descend,
By *Solon* caution'd to regard his End,
In Life's last Scene what Prodigies surprise,   315
Fears of the Brave, and Follies of the Wise?
From *Marlb'rough*'s Eyes the Streams of Dotage flow,
And *Swift* expires a Driv'ler and a Show.
          The teeming Mother, anxious for her Race,
Begs for each Birth the Fortune of a Face: 320
Yet *Vane* could tell what Ills from Beauty spring;
And *Sedley* curs'd the Form that pleas'd a King.
Ye Nymphs of rosy Lips and radiant Eyes,
Whom Pleasure keeps too busy to be wise,
Whom Joys with soft Varieties invite   325
By Day the Frolick, and the Dance by Night,
Who frown with Vanity, who smile with Art,
And ask the latest Fashion of the Heart,
What Care, what Rules your heedless Charms shall save,
Each Nymph your Rival, and each Youth your Slave?   330
An envious Breast with certain Mischief glows,
And Slaves, the Maxim tells, are always Foes.
Against your Fame with Fondness Hate combines,
The Rival batters, and the Lover mines.
With distant Voice neglected Virtue calls,   335
Less heard, and less the faint Remonstrance falls;
Tir'd with Contempt, she quits the slipp'ry Reign,
And Pride and Prudence take her Seat in vain.
In croud at once, where none the Pass defend,
The harmless Freedom, and the private Friend.   340
The Guardians yield, by Force superior ply'd;
By Int'rest, Prudence; and by Flatt'ry, Pride.
Here Beauty falls betray'd, despis'd, distress'd,
And hissing Infamy proclaims the rest.

---

308 *lags* 'lingers'.
311 *But* 'only'.
312 *set … in* 'descend into'.
313 *Lydia's Monarch* Croesus, the fabulously wealthy King of Lydia in the sixth century BC. He was overthrown and put to death by Cyrus in 546 BC.
314 Solon (*c.*640–after 561 BC), the famous Greek legislator, advised Croesus that wealth alone did not bring happiness.
317 *Marlb'rough* John Churchill (1650–1722), the great Whig statesman and military commander in the War of the Spanish Succession. He was paralysed by two strokes in 1716 and died in 1722.

318 By the time Swift died, he had been senile for at least four years.
319 *teeming* 'pregnant'.
321 *Vane* Anne Vane (1705–36), mistress to Frederick, Prince of Wales. She and their illegitimate son died soon after Frederick deserted her to marry Augusta of Saxe-Gotha.
322 *Sedley* Catherine Sedley (1657–1717), mistress of the Duke of York who abandoned her when he became James II.
334 *batters* 'besieges'; *mines* Digs tunnels packed with explosive under the besieged city.

Where then shall Hope and Fear their Objects find?   345
Must dull Suspence corrupt the stagnant Mind?
Must helpless Man, in Ignorance sedate,
Swim darkling down the Current of his Fate?
Must no Dislike alarm, no Wishes rise,
No Cries attempt the Mercies of the Skies?   350
Enquirer, cease, Petitions yet remain,
Which Heav'n may hear, nor deem Religion vain.
Still raise for Good the supplicating Voice,
But leave to Heav'n the Measure and the Choice.
Safe in his Pow'r, whose Eyes discern afar   355
The secret Ambush of a specious Pray'r.
Implore his Aid, in his Decisions rest,
Secure whate'er he gives, he gives the best.
Yet with the Sense of sacred Presence prest,
When strong Devotion fills thy glowing Breast,   360
Pour forth thy Fervours for a healthful Mind,
Obedient Passions, and a Will resign'd;
For Love, which scarce collective Man can fill;
For Patience sov'reign o'er transmuted Ill;
For Faith, that panting for a happier Seat,   365
Thinks Death kind Nature's Signal of Retreat:
These Goods for Man the Laws of Heav'n ordain,
These Goods he grants, who grants the Pow'r to gain;
With these celestial Wisdom calms the Mind,
And makes the Happiness she does not find.   370

346 *Suspence* 'vacillation'.
348 In 1755 this line was altered to 'Roll darkling down the
   torrent of his fate'. The earlier reading shows mankind
   choosing not to resist fate; *darkling* 'in the dark'.

363 'For love so capacious that mankind can scarcely fill it'.
366 *Signal of Retreat* The trumpet call announcing the end
   of the day's battle.

On the Death of Dr Robert Levet

Johnson's London house was home to a strange assortment of needy individuals. Among them was Robert Levet, a lay physician of uncouth, dirty appearance and taciturn manners, who ran a large medical practice in the London slums. His sudden death on 17 January 1782, aged 76, prompted Johnson to write the following elegy, whose power derives from its muted understatement, its lexicographer's precise attention to the meaning of words such as 'officious'

and 'obscurely', and its perception of Levet's place in the larger scheme of humanity. Johnson's account of Levet's unstinting kindness to the urban poor bears comparison with Crabbe's satirical portrait of Levet's antitype, the differently 'officious' quack doctor attending the poor of *The Village*, published only three months earlier. This poem first appeared in the *Gentleman's Magazine*, 53 (August 1783), pp. 695–6, from where the following text is taken.

Condemn'd to hope's delusive mine,
   As on we toil from day to day,
By sudden blasts, or slow decline,
   Our social comforts drop away.

Well tried through many a varying year,   5
   See LEVET to the grave descend;

Officious, innocent, sincere,
 Of ev'ry friendless name the friend.

Yet still he fills affection's eye,
 Obscurely wise, and coarsely kind;   10
Nor, letter'd arrogance, deny
 Thy praise to merit unrefin'd.

When fainting nature call'd for aid,
 And hov'ring death prepar'd the blow,
His vig'rous remedy display'd   15
 The power of art without the show.

In misery's darkest caverns known,
 His useful care was ever nigh,
Where hopeless anguish pour'd his groan,
 And lonely want retir'd to die.   20

No summons mock'd by chill delay,
 No petty gain disdain'd by pride,
The modest wants of ev'ry day
 The toil of ev'ry day supplied.

His virtues walk'd their narrow round,   25
 Nor made a pause, nor left a void;
And sure th' Eternal Master found
 The single talent well employ'd.

The busy day, the peaceful night,
 Unfelt, uncounted, glided by;   30
His frame was firm, his powers were bright,
 Tho' now his eightieth year was nigh.

Then with no throbbing fiery pain,
 No cold gradations of decay,
Death broke at once the vital chain,   35
 And free'd his soul the nearest way.

---

7 Johnson exploits richer meanings in these words, from their Latin roots: *Officious* combines 'dutiful' and 'kind' (Lat. *officium* 'a kindness or service' – cf. Pope, *Epistle to Dr Arbuthnot*, 408); *innocent* is also 'upright' and 'disinterested' (Lat. *innocens*); *sincere* here means 'genuine', 'uncorrupted' (Lat. *sincerus* – cf. Cowper, *Yardley Oak*, 116n).

10 *Obscurely* 'inconspicuously'. Johnson disliked obscurity in our modern sense.

17 *caverns* cavern's (*GM*).

28 *The single talent* For the parable of the talents, see Matthew, 25:14–30.

35–6 Cf. Parnell, *A Night-Piece on Death*, 87–90.

36 *free'd* forc'd (*GM*). The sense of the previous line ('broke … chain') suggests that Johnson wrote 'free'd' but his handwriting was misread by the printer. However, 'forc'd' also occurs in early transcripts and other early printings.

Mary Jones (1707–1778)

She lived with her brother, Oliver Jones (1705–75), the Precentor of Christ Church, Oxford (leader of the singing in the cathedral). Samuel Johnson, who came to know her during his visits to Oxford, called her 'The Chantress' and would address her in the words of Milton's *Il Penseroso*: 'Thee Chantress oft the woods among, I woo ...' Thomas Warton recalled: 'She was often of our parties. She was a very ingenious poetess ... and on the whole was a most sensible, agreeable, and amiable woman.' By the early 1730s she had become a close friend of the Hon. Martha Lovelace, daughter of the fourth Baron Lovelace (d. 1709), and several of her female relatives, including Lady Bowyer and Charlot Clayton, to each of whom she began addressing poems. Her cloistered life in Oxford alternated with visits to Windsor Castle (where Martha Lovelace lived as a maid of honour to Queen Caroline) and other aristocratic houses. In her poetry she could draw on her experience of courtly manners and society speech, and on her sharp observation of the world of public affairs. Her good-humoured satire suggests she was happy to be an outsider. But her wealthy friends determined to push her into print, and the result was *Miscellanies in Prose and Verse*, published by subscription in 1750 with an extremely impressive list of some 1,400 subscribers (including a large aristocratic roll-call). The volume, which contained letters and essays as well as poetry, was dedicated to the Princess Royal, and was given a long and glowing review by Ralph Griffiths in the *Monthly Review*, 6 (1752), pp. 213–23: '[Her] name will not be less an honour to her country, and to the republic of letters, than her amiable life and manners are to her own sex ... her compositions in verse are superior to those of any other female writer since the days of Mrs. *Catherine Philips* [d. 1664]'. In her preface Mary Jones described her poems as 'the produce of pure nature only, and most of them wrote at a very early age', and her shrinking modesty took to an extreme the notion that a woman could not claim a poetic career: 'The poetry she can say nothing to; it being quite accidental, that her thoughts ever rambled into rhyme'. Although respected in her literary circle, Mary Jones appears to have written little poetry after the 1730s, and she never published a second volume. It is clear from her *Epistle to Lady Bowyer* that Jones had great admiration for Pope and felt that she and everyone else was writing in his shadow; but although her poems have many Popean echoes, their ear for the spoken word and their spirited geniality give them an individual flavour.

An Epistle to Lady Bowyer

First published in *Miscellanies* (1750), pp. 1–7, the text given here. It was apparently written not long before 28 July 1736 (see note to line 84). The poem is addressed to Anne Stonehouse (*c*.1709–85), who in 1733 married Sir William Bowyer, third Baronet, of Denham Court, Buckinghamshire (1710–67). Jones's chief model here is Pope's *Epistle to Dr Arbuthnot*, and her poem shares its theme of poetic and personal integrity (the rejection of patronage, the unwillingness of the poet to compromise with fashion and public demands, the private friendships set against worldly flattery – even the prayer for the mother). Pope's poem came to be thought of as the prologue to his satires, and Mary Jones chose hers to open the *Miscellanies*. Both Pope and Jones, however, share a model in Horace, whose praise of a life of virtuous retreat with simple food and honest friends was influential throughout the eighteenth century. Jones's poem was printed in full in Griffiths's review: '[it] exhibits such a lively picture of the author's disposition and turn of sentiments, as cannot fail of entertaining'.

> How much of paper's spoil'd! what floods of ink!
> And yet how few, how very few can think!
> The knack of writing is an easy trade;
> But to think well requires — at least a Head.
> Once in an age, *one* Genius may arise,   5
> With wit well-cultur'd, and with learning wise.
> Like some tall oak, behold his branches shoot!
> No tender scions springing at the root.
> Whilst lofty *Pope* erects his laurell'd head,
> No lays, like mine, can live beneath his shade.   10
> Nothing but weeds, and moss, and shrubs are found.

Cut, cut them down, why cumber they the ground?
　And yet you'd have me write! — For what? for whom?
To curl a Fav'rite in a dressing-room?
To mend a candle when the snuff's too short?　　　　　　15
Or save rappee for chamber-maids at Court?
Glorious ambition! noble thirst of fame! —
No, but you'd have me write — to get a name.
Alas! I'd live unknown, unenvy'd too;
'Tis more than *Pope*, with all his wit can do.　　　　　20
'Tis more than You, with wit and beauty join'd,
A pleasing form, and a discerning mind.
The world and I are no such cordial friends;
I have my purpose, they their various ends.
I say my pray'rs, and lead a sober life,　　　　　　　25
Nor laugh at *Cornus*, or at *Cornus'* wife.
What's fame to me, who pray, and pay my rent?
If my friends know me honest, I'm content.
　Well, but the joy to see my works in print!
My self too pictur'd in a Mezzo-Tint!　　　　　　　30
The Preface done, the Dedication fram'd,
With lies enough to make a Lord asham'd!
Thus I step forth; an Auth'ress in some sort.
My Patron's name? 'O choose some Lord at Court.
One that has money which he does not use,　　　　　35
One you may flatter much, that is, abuse.
For if you're nice, and cannot change your note,
Regardless of the trimm'd, or untrimm'd coat;
Believe me, friend, you'll ne'er be worth a groat'.
　Well then, to cut this mighty matter short,　　　　40
I've neither friend, nor interest at Court.
Quite from St. *James*'s to thy stairs, *Whitehall*,
I hardly know a creature, great or small,
Except one Maid of Honour, worth 'em all.
I have no bus'ness there. Let those attend　　　　　45
The courtly Levee, or the courtly Friend,
Who more than fate allows them, dare to spend.
Or those whose avarice, with much, craves more,
The pension'd Beggar, or the titled Poor.
These are the thriving Breed, the tiny Great!　　　　50
Slaves! wretched Slaves! the Journeymen of State!
Philosophers! who calmly bear disgrace,
Patriots! who sell their country for a place.
　Shall I for these disturb my brains with rhyme?
For these, like *Bavius* creep, or *Glencus* climb?　　　55
Shall I go late to rest, and early rise,
To be the very creature I despise?
With face unmov'd, my poem in my hand,
Cringe to the porter, with the footman stand?

---

14 For use as curling-papers in a lady's hair.
16 *rappee* Cheap snuff.
26 *Cornus* A cuckold (Lat. *cornu* 'horn').
30 *Mezzo-Tint* A method of engraving.

37 *nice* 'over-scrupulous'.
44 *Maid of Honour* 'Honourable Miss *Lovelace*' (Jones's note).
46 *Levee* 'formal assembly'.

Perhaps my lady's maid, if not too proud, 60
Will stoop, you'll say, to wink me from the croud,
Will entertain me, till his lordship's drest,
With what my lady eats, and how she rests:
How much she gave for such a birth-day gown,
And how she trampt to ev'ry shop in town. 65
   Sick at the news, impatient for my lord,
I'm forc'd to hear, nay smile at ev'ry word.
Tom raps at last, — 'His lordship begs to know
Your name? your bus'ness?' — Sir, I'm not a foe.
I come to charm his lordship's list'ning ears 70
With verses, soft as music of the spheres.
'Verses! — Alas! his lordship seldom reads:
Pedants indeed with learning stuff their heads;
But my good lord, as all the world can tell,
Reads not ev'n tradesmen's bills, and scorns to spell. 75
But trust your lays with me. Some things I've read,
Was born a poet, tho' no poet bred:
And if I find they'll bear my nicer view,
I'll recommend your poetry — and you'.
   Shock'd at his civil impudence, I start, 80
Pocket my poem, and in haste depart;
Resolv'd no more to offer up my wit,
Where footmen in the seat of critics sit.
   Is there a Lord whose great unspotted soul,
Not places, pensions, ribbons can control; 85
Unlac'd, unpowder'd, almost unobserv'd,
Eats not on silver, while his train are starv'd;
Who tho' to nobles, or to kings ally'd,
Dares walk on foot, while slaves in coaches ride;
With merit humble, and with greatness free, 90
Has bow'd to *Freeman*, and has din'd with Me;
Who bred in foreign courts, and early known,
Has yet to learn the cunning of his own;
To titles born, yet heir to no estate,
And, harder still, too honest to be great; 95
If such an one there be, well-bred, polite?
To Him I'll dedicate, for Him I'll write.
   Peace to the rest. I can be no man's slave;
I ask for nothing, tho' I nothing have.
By Fortune humbled, yet not sunk so low 100
To shame a friend, or fear to meet a foe.
Meanness, in ribbons or in rags, I hate;
And have not learnt to flatter, ev'n the Great.
Few friends I ask, and those who love me well;
What more remains, these artless lines shall tell. 105
   Of *honest* parents, not of *great*, I came;
Not known to fortune, quite unknown to fame.

---

84 'Right Hon. *Nevil* Lord *Lovelace*, who dy'd soon after, in the 28*th* year of his age' (Jones's note). He was Martha Lovelace's brother, and died 28 July 1736. Mary Jones's elegy on him is printed in the *Miscellanies*.

91 *Freeman* Probably intended to represent a figure of political and financial independence.

Frugal and plain, at no man's cost they eat,
Nor knew a baker's, or a butcher's debt.
O be their precepts ever in my eye!   110
For one has learnt to live, and one to die.
Long may her widow'd age by heav'n be lent
Among my blessings! and I'm well content.
I ask no more, but in some calm retreat,
To sleep in quiet, and in quiet eat.   115
No noisy slaves attending round my room;
My viands wholesome, and my waiters dumb.
No orphans cheated, and no widow's curse,
No houshold lord, for better or for worse.
No monstrous sums to tempt my soul to sin,   120
But just enough to keep me plain, and clean.
And if sometimes, to smooth the rugged way,
Charlot should smile, or You approve my lay,
Enough for me. I cannot put my trust
In lords; smile lies, eat toads, or lick the dust.   125
Fortune her favours much too dear may hold:
An honest heart is worth its weight in *gold*.

111–13 Cf. Pope, *Epistle to Dr Arbuthnot*, 408–13.
117 A dumb-waiter: a wooden tray-holder or the tray itself. *OED*'s first recorded use of the term is 1738, but this would seem to antedate it.

123 *Charlot* Mary Jones's close friend, Charlot Clayton (d. 1743). Several poems in the *Miscellanies* are addressed to her.
125 *eat toads* A 'toad-eater' was a flatterer or social parasite.

Of Desire.
An Epistle to the Hon. Miss Lovelace.

The text is that first published in *Miscellanies* (1750), pp. 26–35. The poem's shrewd intelligence and lively character-drawing effectively exposes some of life's postures and platitudes. Her tone of wise cheerfulness itself makes an argumentative point.

Whence these impetuous movements of the breast?
Why beat our hearts, unknowing where to rest?
Must we still long untasted joys to taste,
Pant for the future, yet regret the past?
Can reason, can a stoic's pride control   5
This unremitting sickness of the soul?
Reason! what's that, when lawless Passion rules?
The jest of sense, and jargon of the schools.
Some few perhaps have by its lore been taught
To think, and wish, just only what they ought: 10
Sufficient to themselves, their wants are such,
They neither ask amiss, nor wish too much.
Here freedom dwells, and revels unconfin'd,
With plenty, ease, and indolence of mind;
True greatness, wisdom, virtue, hence must rise;   15
And here that home-felt joy, Contentment, lies.
    O Thou! for whom my fancy prunes her wing,
For whom I love to tune the trembling string,

16 *home-felt* 'felt in the heart'. Cf. Milton's 'sacred and home-felt delight' (*Masque*, 261).

What would we more than wisdom, virtue, ease?
Tell, if you can, for you're content with these.   20
   Why reason some, and some why passion rules,
Is because some are wise, and some are fools;
Their reason and their passion still at strife,
Like some meek pair in wedlock yok'd for life:
In the same int'rest, tugging diff'rent ways,   25
What one commands, the other disobeys.
Blest state! where this alone is fixt and sure,
To disagree, while sun and moon endure.
Hence listless, weary, sick, chagrin'd at home,
In search of happiness abroad we roam: 30
And yet the wisest of us all have own'd,
If 'twas not there, 'twas no where to be found.
There ev'n the poor may taste felicity,
If with contentment any such there be.
   'Monstrous! (cries *Fulvia*) 'twou'd a stoic vex!   35
For what's content without a coach and six?' —
So humble, *Fulvia*! so deserving too!
Pity such worth should unregarded go —
Down on your knees again, and beg of fate,
Instead of six, to give *your* chariot eight.   40
   Elvira's passion was a china jar;
The brute, her lord, contemns such brittle ware.
No matter. — See! the glitt'ring columns rise,
Pile above pile, and emulate the skies.
Fresh cargoes come, fresh longings these create;   45
And what is twenty pieces for a plate?
Debates ensue; he brandishes his cane,
Down go the pyramids of Porcellane.
She faints, she falls, and in a sigh profound,
Yeilds her high soul, and levels with the ground.   50
'Cruel! farewel! — (were the last words she spoke)
For what is life, now all my China's broke!'
   Few can the stings of Disappointment bear!
One sends a curse to Heav'n, and one a pray'r;
The pious motive's much the same in both,   55
In him that swears, and him that fears an oath.
The fervent curse, and penitential pray'r,
Proceed alike from anguish, pride, despair.
Hence sober *Catius* lifts his hands and eyes,
And mad *Corvino* curses God, and dies.   60
   'What joy, (cries *Cotta* in his calm retreat)
Had I but such an office in the state!
That post exactly suits my active mind,
And sure my genius was for courts design'd'.
Thou hast it, friend, — for 'tis in *Fancy*'s pow'r;   65
Learn to be thankful, and teaze Heav'n no more.
See! how kind Fancy gen'rously supplies

23–4 An interesting variant on Pope's more idealistic image of marriage: 'For *Wit* and *Judgment* often are at strife, / Tho' meant each other's Aid, like *Man* and *Wife*' (*Essay on Criticism*, 82–3).

47–52 Cf. Pope, *Epistle to a Lady*, 268.
60 Cf. 'And sad Sir Balaam curses God and dies' (Pope, *Epistle to Bathurst*, 402).

What a whole thankless land thy worth denies.
See! how she paints the lovely flatt'ring scene,
With all the pleasure, and without the pain.   70
Make much of Fancy's favours, and believe
You'll hardly match the pleasures she can give.
    Of injur'd merit some aloud complain;
'My cruel angel!' — cries the love-sick swain.
Her marble heart at length to love inclin'd,   75
His cruel angel grows perversely kind.
What would he more? — One wish remains to make,
That Heav'n, in pity, would his angel take.
    Oft on events most men miscalculate,
Then call misfortune, what indeed was fate.   80
We see a little, and presume the rest,
And that is always right which pleases best.
Why supple *Courtine* miss'd of such a post,
Was not his want of conduct, or of cost,
For he brib'd high; five hundred pieces gave;   85
But ah! hard fate! his patron scorns a knave.
    'O for a husband, handsome and well-bred!'
(Was the last pray'r the chaste *Dyctinna* made.)
Kind Heav'n at length her soft petition heeds,
But one wish gain'd, a multitude succeeds —   90
She wants an heir, she wants a house in town,
She wants a title, or she wants a gown.
Poor *Cornus*! make thy will, bequeath, and give:
For if her wants continue, who would live?
    Sure to be wishing still, is still to grieve;   95
And proves the man or poor, or much a slave.
Will none the wretched crawling thing regard,
Who stoops so very low, and begs so hard?
You call this meanness, and the wretch despise;
Alas! he stoops to soar, and sinks to rise: 100
Now on the knee, now on the wing is found,
As insects spring with vigour from the ground.
    Bless me! the Doctor! — what brings him to court?
It is not want; for lo! his comely port.
The lions lack, and hunger feel, I grant;   105
But they who serve the Lord can nothing want.
Why stands he here then, elbow'd to and fro?
Has he no care of souls? No work to do?
Go home, good doctor, preach and pray, and give;
By far more blessed this, than to receive. —   110
Alas! the doctor's meek, and much resign'd;
But all his tenants pay their tithes in kind:
So that of debts, repairs, and taxes clear,
He hardly saves — two hundred pounds a year.

93 *Cornus* See *Epistle to Lady Bowyer*, 26.
96 *or ... or* 'either ... or'.
103 *Doctor* A Doctor of Divinity.
104 *comely port* 'graceful bearing'.
105 'The young lions do lack, and suffer hunger: but they
that seek the Lord shall not want any good thing'
(Psalm 34:10). In *Miscellanies* the line reads 'The lion's
lack, and hunger feel, I grant'.

112 *Tithes* Duties of one tenth of a parish's produce,
usually paid to the parson (in accord with Leviticus,
27:30). These statutory payments (often commuted to
cash) could be a source of resentment among farmers
and smallholders.

Then let him soar, 'tis on devotion's wing;   115
Who asks a bishopric, asks no bad thing:
A coach does much an holy life adorn;
Then muzzle not the ox who treads the corn.
    'Enough of these. Now tell us, if you can,
Is there that thing on earth, *a happy man?*'   120
Well then, the wondrous man I happy call,
Has but few wishes, and enjoys them all.
Blest in his fame, and in his fortune blest,
No craving void lies aching in his breast.
His passions cool, his expectations low,   125
Can he feel want, or disappointments know?
Yet if success be to his virtues giv'n,
Can relish that, and leave the rest to Heav'n.
    What, tho' for ever with our selves at strife,
None wishes to lay down his load of life.   130
The wretch who threescore suns has seen roll o'er,
His lungs with lacerating ulcers sore,
Sollicits Heav'n to add the other score.
Today, indeed, his portion's pain and sorrow;
But joy and ease are hoarded for tomorrow.   135
    Soft smiling Hope! thou anchor of the mind!
The only resting-place the wretched find;
How dost thou all our anxious cares beguile!
And make the orphan, and the friendless smile.
All fly to thee, thou gentle dawn of peace!   140
The coward's fortitude, the brave's success,
The lover's ease, the captive's liberty,
The only flatt'rer of the poor and me.
With thee, on pleasure's wings, thro' life we're born,
Without thee, wretched, friendless, and forlorn.   145
Possest of thee, the weary pilgrim strays
Thro' barren desarts, and untrodden ways:
Thirsty and faint, his nerves new vigour strings,
And full of thee he quaffs immortal springs.
The martyr'd saint, whom anguish and the rod   150
Have prov'd, thro' thee walks worthy of his God.
In vain are axes, flames, and tort'ring wheels;
He feels no torment, who no terrour feels:
Thro' thee his well-try'd spirit upward springs,
And spurns at titles, scepters, thrones, and kings.   155
    O full of thee! in quiet may I live,
The few remaining moments Heav'n shall give!
Come then, thou honest flatt'rer, to my breast!
Friend of my health, and author of my rest!
Thro' thee, the future cloudless all appears,   160
A short, but smiling train of happy years.
Pass but this instant, storms and tempests cease,
And all beyond's the promis'd land of peace.
No passion's mists, by no false joys misled,

118 'Thou shalt not muzzle the ox when he treadeth out the
    corn' (Deuteronomy, 25:4).

No ties forgot, no duties left unpaid,   165
No lays unfinish'd, and no aching head.
    Born with a temper much inclin'd to ease,
Whatever gives me that, is sure to please.
I ask not riches; yet alike would fly
The friendless state of want and penury.   170
This wish howe'er be mine: to live unknown,
In some serene retreat, my time my own,
To all obliging, yet a slave to none.
Content, my riches; silence be my fame;
My pleasures, ease; my honours, *your* esteem.   175
    And *you*, blest maid! who all you want possess,
Already to your self your happiness,
This modest wish methinks you now let fall,
'O give me *Wisdom*, Heav'n! and I have all'.

After the Small Pox

First published in *Miscellanies* (1750), pp. 79–80 (the text given here). The poem's pragmatic message on the superiority of heart and mind over mere beauty can be compared with Clarissa's in Pope's *The Rape of the Lock* (5:9–34), and the style here is similarly epigrammatic and brisk, but without Pope's hint of pathos. Jones's model seems to be Swift's *Stella's Birthday, 1721*, which likewise develops the image of woman as a commodity and her beauty a commercial sign. On the smallpox theme Lady Mary Wortley Montagu's *Saturday. The Small-Pox* employs more drama and emotion in giving the victim's own viewpoint.

When skillful traders first set up,
To draw the people to their shop,
They strait hang out some gaudy sign,
Expressive of the goods within.
The Vintner has his boy and grapes,   5
The Haberdasher thread and tapes,
The Shoemaker exposes boots,
And Monmouth Street old tatter'd suits.
    So fares it with the nymph divine;
For what is Beauty but a Sign?   10
A face hung out, thro' which is seen
The nature of the goods within.
    Thus the coquet her beau ensnares
With study'd smiles, and forward airs;
The graver prude hangs out a frown   15
To strike th'audacious gazer down;
But she alone, whose temp'rate wit
Each nicer medium can hit,
Is still adorn'd with ev'ry grace,
And wears a sample in her face.   20
    What tho' some envious folks have said,
That *Stella* now must hide her head,
That all her stock of beauty's gone,
And ev'n the very sign took down:

8 *Monmouth Street* A famous second-hand clothes market.

18 *nicer* 'finer', 'more delicate'; *hit* 'capture'.
19 *Is still* 'continues to be'.

Yet grieve not at the fatal blow;   25
For if you break a while, we know,
'Tis bankrupt like, more rich to grow.
A fairer sign you'll soon hang up,
And with fresh credit open shop:
For nature's pencil soon shall trace,   30
And once more finish off your face,
Which all your neighbours shall out-shine,
And of your Mind remain the Sign.

26–9 I.e. after failing commercially ('breaking') her debts can be cancelled and she can set up a new business.

30 *pencil* 'artist's paint-brush'.

Mary Leapor (1722–1746)

The whole of Leapor's life was spent in the environs of Brackley, Northamptonshire, where her father was a gardener and nurseryman. Having attended the local free school (it must be assumed), she went into service at Weston Hall where she was employed by Susanna Jennens, herself a writer of poems, and the library at Weston may have given Leapor opportunities to widen her reading. It has recently been established that she moved on to work as a kitchen maid at Edgcote House, eight miles north-west of Brackley (see headnote to *Crumble-Hall*), but after being dismissed she returned to keep house for her father. She wrote voluminously in her spare time, describing herself as having 'a restless Mind, rack'd with unprofitable Invention'. In about September 1745 she gained the friendship and admiration of Bridget Freemantle (the 'Artemisia' of her poems), who encouraged her to publish, but, like Mary Jones, she was dismissive of her own work and rather alarmed at coming to public notice. Her death from measles on 12 November 1746 meant that her *Poems upon Several Occasions* appeared posthumously (1748) for the benefit of her father. It had some six hundred subscribers. An account of Leapor's appearance describes her as 'extremely swarthy, and quite emaciated, with a long crane-neck, and a short body, much resembling, in shape, a bass-viol' (a letter from 'W', *Gentleman's Magazine*, 54 (1784), p. 807), and the preface to the 1748 *Poems* records that she was 'courteous and obliging to all, chearful, good-natured,

and contented in the Station of Life in which Providence had placed her'; it notes that 'the Author she most admired was Mr. *Pope*, whom she chiefly endeavoured to imitate'. A further volume of her work was printed by subscription in 1751, and this included several letters as well as Bridget Freemantle's memoir of her. According to this Leapor destroyed many of her early poems, but she was a fluent writer and on one occasion 'Artemisia' watched her at work, 'her Thoughts seeming to flow as fast as she could put them upon Paper'. The immediacy and liveliness of *An Epistle to Artemisia* catches something of the easy intimacy between them, and Leapor's shrewd observation of life around her. She had a small library of her own books, 'of about sixteen or seventeen single Volumes, among which were Part of Mr. *Pope*'s Works, *Dryden*'s Fables, some Volumes of Plays, &c.', and it is clear that she knew Pope especially well. The 1748 preface remarks that 'had she lived to correct and finish these first Productions of a young unassisted Genius, certainly they would have been greatly improved'. But a modern reader need not be so sure: Leapor's poetry avoids the smoothness and predictability that could once be mistaken for 'finish', and in spite of the echoes of her admired model it would be misleading to think of her as a failed Pope. On the contrary, it is in her discomposure – her unexpected juxtapositions, her ear for lively rhythms, and her off-centre angles of vision – that much of her power lies.

Dorinda at her Glass

In this poem we seem to be revisiting Pope's Belinda thirty-six years on. Leapor's sensitive development of the 'ageing beauty' motif can be compared with Pope's *Epistle to a Lady*, 219–56. Another related text is Flavia's lament for her lost looks in Lady Mary Wortley Montagu's *Saturday. The Small-Pox*. In

Leapor's poem the older woman is given her own voice to register a considerable range of emotions from sympathy to disgust. The text given here is that of its first publication, in *Poems upon Several Occasions* (1748), pp. 1–8.

> *Dorinda*, once the fairest of the Train,
> Toast of the Town, and Triumph of the Plain;
> Whose shining Eyes a thousand Hearts alarm'd,
> Whose Wit inspired, and whose Follies charm'd:
> Who, with Invention, rack'd her careful Breast   5
> To find new Graces to insult the rest,
> Now sees her Temples take a swarthy Hue,
> And the dark Veins resign their beauteous Blue;
> While on her Cheeks the fading Roses die,
> And the last Sparkles tremble in her Eye.   10
>   Bright Sol had drove the sable Clouds away,
> And chear'd the Heavens with a Stream of Day,

The woodland Choir their little Throats prepare,
To chant new Carols to the Morning Air:
In Silence wrap'd, and curtain'd from the Day,   15
On her sad Pillow lost *Dorinda* lay;
To Mirth a Stranger, and the like to Ease,
No Pleasures charm her, nor no Slumbers please.
For if to close her weary Lids she tries,
Detested Wrinkles swim before her Eyes;   20
At length the Mourner rais'd her aking Head,
And discontented left her hated Bed.
But sighing shun'd the Relicks of her Pride,
And left the Toilet for the Chimney Side:
Her careless Locks upon her Shoulders lay   25
Uncurl'd, alas! because they half were Gray;
No magick Baths employ her skilful Hand,
But useless Phials on her Table stand:
She slights her Form, no more by Youth inspir'd,
And loaths that Idol which she once admir'd.   30
At length all trembling, of herself afraid,
To her lov'd Glass repair'd the weeping Maid,
And with a Sigh address'd the alter'd Shade.
Say, what art thou, that wear'st a gloomy Form,
With low'ring Forehead, like a northern Storm;   35
Cheeks pale and hollow, as the Face of Woe,
And Lips that with no gay Vermilion glow?
Where is that Form which this false Mirror told
Bloom'd like the Morn, and shou'd for Ages hold;
But now a Spectre in its room appears,   40
All scar'd with Furrows, and defac'd with Tears;
Say, com'st thou from the Regions of Despair,
To shake my Senses with a meagre Stare?
Some stragg'ling Horror may thy Phantom be,
But surely not the mimick Shape of me.   45
Ah! yes — the Shade its mourning Visage rears,
Pants when I sigh, and answers to my Tears:
Now who shall bow before this wither'd Shrine,
This Mortal Image, that was late Divine?
What Victim now will praise these faded Eyes,   50
Once the gay Basis for a thousand Lyes?
   Deceitful Beauty — false as thou art gay,
And is it thus thy Vot'ries find their Pay;
This the Reward of many careful Years,
Of Morning Labours, and of Noon-day Fears,   55
The Gloves anointed, and the bathing-Hour,
And soft Cosmetick's more prevailing Pow'r;
Yet to thy Worship still the fair Ones run,
And hail thy Temples with the rising Sun;
Still the brown Damsels to thy Altars pay   60

---

26 Cf. Pope, *The Rape of the Lock*, 5:26.
28 *Phials* 'small bottles'.
46–7 Cf. Milton's Eve admiring her own reflection:

'Pleased it returned as soon with answering looks / Of sympathy and love' (*Paradise Lost*, 4:464–5).
53 *Vot'ries* 'devoted worshippers'.

Sweet-scented Unguents, and the Dews of *May*;
Sempronia smooths her wrinkled Brows with Care,
And *Isabella* curls her grisled Hair:
See poor *Augusta* of her Glass afraid,
Who even trembles at the Name of Maid,   65
Spreads the fine *Mechlin* on her shaking Head,
While her thin Cheeks disown the mimick Red.
Soft *Silvia*, who no Lover's Breast alarms,
Yet simpers out the Ev'ning of her Charms,
And tho' her Cheek can boast no rosy Dye,   70
Her gay Brocades allure the gazing Eye.
    But hear, my Sisters — Hear an ancient Maid,
Too long by Folly, and her Arts betray'd;
From these light Trifles turn your partial Eyes,
'Tis sad *Dorinda* prays you to be wise;   75
And thou *Celinda*, thou must shortly feel
The sad Effect of Time's revolving Wheel;
Thy Spring is past, thy Summer Sun declin'd,
See Autumn next, and Winter stalks behind:
But let not Reason with thy Beauties fly,   80
Nor place thy Merit in a brilliant Eye;
'Tis thine to charm us by sublimer ways,
And make thy Temper, like thy Features, please:
And thou, *Sempronia*, trudge to Morning Pray'r,
Nor trim thy Eye-brows with so nice a Care;   85
Dear Nymph believe — 'tis true, as you're alive,
Those Temples show the Marks of Fifty-five.
Let *Isabel* unload her aking Head
Of twisted Papers, and of binding Lead;
Let sage *Augusta* now, without a Frown,   90
Strip those gay Ribbands from her aged Crown;
Change the lac'd Slipper of delicious Hue
For a warm Stocking, and an easy Shoe;
Guard her swell'd Ancles from Rheumatick Pain,
And from her Cheek expunge the guilty Stain.   95
    Wou'd smiling *Silvia* lay that Hoop aside,
'Twou'd show her Prudence, not betray her Pride;
She, like the rest, had once her fragrant Day,
But now she twinkles in a fainter Ray.
Those youthful Airs set off their Mistress now,   100
Just as the Patch adorns her Autumn Brow:
In vain her Feet in sparkling Laces glow,
Since none regard her Forehead, nor her Toe.
Who would not burst with Laughter, or with Spleen,
At *Prudo*, once a Beauty, as I ween?   105
But now her Features wear a dusky Hue,
The little Loves have bid her Eyes adieu:
Yet she pursues the Pleasures of her Prime,
And vain Desires, not subdu'd by Time;

61 *Unguents* 'ointments'.
63 *grisled* 'grey'.
66 *Mechlin* Lace produced at Mechlin, Belgium.
88–9 Cf. Pope, *The Rape of the Lock*, 4:99–102.

96 *Hoop* A circle of whalebone worn beneath a skirt, usually as a hoop-petticoat.
105 *as I ween* 'as I understand' (deliberately archaic – it was so long ago).

Thrusts in amongst the Frolick and the Gay,   110
But shuts her Daughter from the Beams of Day:
The Child, she says, is indolent and grave,
And tells the World *Ophelia* can't behave:
But while *Ophelia* is forbid the Room,
Her Mother hobbles in a Rigadoon;   115
Or to the Sound of melting Musick dies,
And in their Sockets rolls her blinking Eyes;
Or stuns the Audience with her hideous Squal,
While Scorn and Satire whisper through the Hall.
    Hear this, ye fair Ones, that survive your Charms,   120
Nor reach at Folly with your aged Arms;
Thus *Pope* has sung, thus let *Dorinda* sing;
'Virtue, brave Boys, — 'tis Virtue makes a King':
Why not a Queen? fair Virtue is the same
In the rough Hero, and the smiling Dame: 125
Dorinda's Soul her Beauties shall pursue,
Tho' late I see her, and embrace her too:
Come, ye blest Graces, that are sure to please,
The Smile of Friendship, and the careless Ease;
The Breast of Candour, the relenting Ear,   130
The Hand of Bounty, and the Heart sincere:
May these the Twilight of my Days attend,
And may that Ev'ning never want a Friend
To smooth my Passage to the silent Gloom,
And give a Tear to grace the mournful Tomb.   135

115 *Rigadoon* A lively dance (French *rigaudon*).
118 *Squal* 'loud and discordant voice'.

123 Pope, *Imitation of Horace*, Epistle I.i (1738), 92.
130 *Candour* 'kindly openness of mind'.

An Epistle to a Lady

The letter combines the lighter conversational tone of Pope's epistolary style with, towards the end, some of the gestures and rhythms of his *Eloisa to Abelard*, perhaps appropriately for a poem that pictures life's rigours and frustrations. 'Mira' is Leapor's own *nom de plume* in much of her work. The text that follows is that of the first printing, *Poems upon Several Occasions* (1748), pp. 38–41.

In vain, dear Madam, yes in vain you strive,
Alas! to make your luckless *Mira* thrive.
For *Tycho* and *Copernicus* agree,
No golden Planet bent its Rays on me.
    'Tis twenty Winters, if it is no more;   5
To speak the Truth, it may be Twenty four.
As many Springs their 'pointed Space have run,
Since *Mira*'s Eyes first open'd on the Sun.
'Twas when the Flocks on slabby Hillocks lye,
And the cold Fishes rule the watry Sky: 10
But tho' these Eyes the learned Page explore,

1 *strive,* strive; (*1748*).
3 Tycho Brahe (1546–1601), the Danish astronomer who
  calculated the positions of hundreds of stars; and
  Nicolas Copernicus (1473–1543), the Polish founder of
  modern astronomy whose *De Revolutionibus* proved the
  sun, not the earth, to be the centre of the universe.

7 *'pointed* 'appointed'.
9 *slabby* 'muddy'.
10 *Fishes* Pisces, the twelfth sign of the zodiac, which the
   sun enters on 21 February. Leapor was born on the
   26th.

And turn the pond'rous Volumes o'er and o'er,
I find no Comfort from their Systems flow,
But am dejected more as more I know.
Hope shines a while, but like a Vapour flies,   15
(The Fate of all the Curious and the Wise)
For, Ah! cold *Saturn* triumph'd on that Day,
And frowning *Sol* deny'd his golden Ray.
    You see I'm learned, and I shew't the more,
That none may wonder when they find me poor.   20
Yet *Mira* dreams, as slumbring Poets may,
And rolls in Treasures till the breaking Day:
While Books and Pictures in bright Order rise,
And painted Parlours swim before her Eyes:
Till the shrill Clock impertinently rings,   25
And the soft Visions move their shining Wings:
Then *Mira* wakes, — her Pictures are no more,
And through her Fingers slides the vanish'd Ore.
Convinc'd too soon, her Eye unwilling falls
On the blue Curtains and the dusty Walls: 30
She wakes, alas! to Business and to Woes,
To sweep her Kitchen, and to mend her Clothes.
    But see pale Sickness with her languid Eyes,
At whose Appearance all Delusion flies:
The World recedes, its Vanities decline,   35
Clorinda's Features seem as faint as mine:
Gay Robes no more the aking Sight admires,
Wit grates the Ear, and melting Musick tires:
Its wonted Pleasures with each Sense decay,
Books please no more, and Paintings fade away: 40
The sliding Joys in misty Vapours end:
Yet let me still, Ah! let me grasp a Friend:
And when each Joy, when each lov'd Object flies,
Be you the last that leaves my closing Eyes.
    But how will this dismantl'd Soul appear,   45
When strip'd of all it lately held so dear,
Forc'd from its Prison of expiring Clay,
Afraid and shiv'ring at the doubtful Way.
    Yet did these Eyes a dying Parent see,
Loos'd from all Cares except a Thought for me,   50
Without a Tear resign her short'ning Breath,
And dauntless meet the ling'ring Stroke of Death.
Then at th'Almighty's Sentence shall I mourn:
'Of Dust thou art, to Dust shalt thou return'.
Or shall I wish to stretch the Line of Fate,   55
That the dull Years may bear a longer Date,
To share the Follies of succeeding Times
With more Vexations and with deeper Crimes:
Ah no — tho' Heav'n brings near the final Day,

17 *Saturn* The traditional bringer of melancholy.
18 *Sol* The sun.
23 *bright Order* Cf. Pope, *The Rape of the Lock*, 3:168.

45 *dismantl'd* 'unclothed', its bodily covering removed.
54 God's words to the fallen Adam, Genesis, 3:19.
56 *Date* 'duration'.

For such a Life I will not, dare not pray;   60
But let the Tear for future Mercy flow,
And fall resign'd beneath the mighty Blow.
Nor I alone — for through the spacious Ball,
With me will Numbers of all Ages fall:
And the same Day that *Mira* yields her Breath,   65
Thousands may enter through the Gates of Death.

63 *Ball* The earth's globe.

The Enquiry

Partly an imaginative response to the first epistle of Pope's *Essay on Man* and its concept of the 'vast chain of being' (1:189–246), the poem also shares some of the excitement of Joseph Addison's *Spectator*, 420 (2 July 1712), which moves from the infinite spaces of the galaxy to the minute worlds visible only through the newly developed microscope ('we might … discover in the smallest Particle of this little World, a new inexhausted Fund of Matter, capable of being spun out into another Universe'). Leapor's witty imagination delights in such incongruities of scale ('With each plump Fruit we swallow down a Tree'). An interesting poem for comparison is Anna Barbauld's *A Summer Evening's Meditation* (1773), which conducts a more mystical and sublime survey of creation. *The Enquiry* was first printed in *Poems upon Several Occasions* (1748), pp. 196–200, the text given here.

In vain, alas! (do lazy Mortals cry)
In vain wou'd Wisdom trace the boundless Sky,
Where doubled Wonders upon Wonders rise,
And Worlds on Worlds confound our dazzl'd Eyes:
Better be still — Let Nature rest, say they,   5
Than err by Guess and with Opinion stray:
Then tell me, why our Eyes were made to view
Those Orbs that glister in the fluid Blue?
Why in our Sight those shining Wonders roll?
Or why to Man was giv'n a thinking Soul?   10
May I not ask how moves the radiant Sun?
How the bright Stars their pointed Circuits run?
What warms those Worlds that so remotely shine?
And what can temper *Saturn*'s frozen Clime?
Who that beholds the full-orb'd Moon arise,   15
That chearful Empress of the nightly Skies;
Who wou'd not ask (cou'd learned Sages tell)
What kind of People on her Surface dwell?
But there we pause — Not *Newton*'s Art can show
A Truth, perhaps, not fit for us to know.   20
    How great the Pow'r, who gave those Worlds to roll;
The Thought strikes inward, and confounds the Soul;
Fall down, O Man — Ah fall before the Rod
Of this Almighty, All-creating God:
But hark — from Heav'n there came a chearing Sound;   25
Now Man revives, and smile the Worlds around:
'Tis Mercy — lo a golden Ray descends,
And Hope and Comfort in the Lustre blends.
    When from the Stars we turn our aking Eyes,

12 *pointed* 'appointed'.
19–20 In Milton's *Paradise Lost* the angel Raphael warns Adam against such enquiries: 'Think only what concerns thee and thy being; / Dream not of other worlds, what creatures there / Live' (8:174–6).

To Earth we bend them where new Wonders rise;   30
Where Life and Death the equal Scale suspend,
New Beings rising as the former end.
Who not surpris'd can trace each just Degree
From the swift Eagle to the peevish Bee;
From the fierce Lion that will yield to none,   35
To the weak Mouse that hides her from the Sun!
　　How near one Species to the next is join'd,
The due Gradations please a thinking Mind;
And there are Creatures which no Eye can see,
That for a Moment live and breathe like me: 40
Whom a small Fly in bulk as far exceeds,
As yon tall Cedar does the waving Reeds:
These we can reach — and may we not suppose
There still are Creatures more minute than those.
　　Wou'd Heav'n permit, and might our Organs bear   45
To pierce where Comets wave their blazing Hair:
Where other Suns alternate set and rise,
And other Moons light up the chearful Skies:
The ravish'd Soul might still her Search pursue,
Still find new Wonders op'ning on her view: 50
From thence to Worlds in Miniature descend,
And still press forward, but shou'd find no End:
Where little Forests on a Leaf appear,
And Drops of Dew are mighty Oceans there:
These may have Whales that in their Waters play,   55
And wanton out their Age of half a Day:
In those small Groves the smaller Birds may sing,
And share like us their Winter and their Spring.
　　Pluck off yon Acorn from its Parent Bough,
Divide that Acorn in the midst — and now   60
In its firm Kernel a fair Oak is seen
With spreading Branches of a sprightly Green:
From this young Tree a Kernel might we rend,
There wou'd another its small Boughs extend.
　　All Matter lives, and shews its Maker's Power;   65
There's not a Seed but what contains a Flower:
Tho' unobserv'd its secret Beauty lies,
Till we are blest with Microscopick Eyes.
When for blue Plumbs our longing Palate calls,
Or scarlet Cherries that adorn the Walls;   70
With each plump Fruit we swallow down a Tree,
And so destroy whole Groves that else wou'd be
As large and perfect as those Shades we see.
　　Behold yon Monster that unwieldy laves
Beneath the Surface of the briny Waves: 75
Still as he turns, the troubl'd Sea divides;
And rolls in Eddies from his slimy Sides.
　　Less huge the Dolphin to the Sun displays
His Scales, and in the smoother Ocean plays:

37–8 The theory of the *plenum* or continuity of creation from highest to lowest forms. See Pope, *Essay on Man*, 1:43–8, 207–46.

68 Cf. 'Why has not Man a microscopic eye? / For this plain reason, Man is not a Fly' (*Essay on Man*, 1:193–4).

Still less the Herring and round Mackrel sweep   80
The shallow Tide, nor trust the roaring Deep:
How far by gradual numberless Degrees,
The senseless Oyster is remov'd from these.
  Who follows Nature through her mazy Way,
From the mute Insect to the Fount of Day,   85
(Where now she rises, now her Steps decline)
Has need of Judgment better taught than mine:
But on this Subject we have talk'd too long,
Where grave-fac'd Wisdom may itself be wrong.

Man the Monarch

Leapor's reworking of the Biblical Creation story offers a challenge to the patriarchal account of Adam's creation in the Book of Genesis. Alongside this she sets the activity of a benign (or at least well-intentioned) female 'Nature' shaping the identity of woman, and in her poem the word of God has to compete with the gossip of 'A tattling Dame' (50) who has her own account to give. First printed in *Poems* (1751), pp. 7–10, the text given here.

Amaz'd we read of Nature's early Throes:
How the fair Heav'ns and pond'rous Earth arose:
How blooming Trees unplanted first began;
And Beasts submissive to their Tyrant, Man:
To Man, invested with despotic Sway,   5
While his mute Brethren tremble and obey;
Till Heav'n beheld him insolently vain,
And check'd the Limits of his haughty Reign.
Then from their Lord the rude Deserters fly,
And, grinning back, his fruitless Rage defy;   10
Pards, Tygers, Wolves, to gloomy Shades retire,
And Mountain-Goats in purer Gales respire.
To humble Valleys, where soft Flowers blow,
And fatt'ning Streams in crystal Mazes flow,
Full of new Life, the untam'd Coursers run,   15
And roll, and wanton, in the chearful Sun;
Round their gay Hearts the dancing Spirits rise,
And rouse the Lightnings in their rolling Eyes:
To cragged Rocks destructive Serpents glide,
Whose mossy Crannies hide their speckled Pride: 20
And monstrous Whales on foamy Billows ride.
Then joyful Birds ascend their native Sky:
But where! ah! where, shall helpless Woman fly?
  Here smiling Nature brought her choicest Stores,
And roseat Beauty on her Fav'rite pours: 25
Pleas'd with her Labour, the officious Dame
With-held no Grace would deck the rising Frame.
Then view'd her Work, and view'd, and smil'd again,
And kindly whisper'd, Daughter, live, and reign.

4–6 'And God said, Let us make man in our image, after our likeness: and let them have dominion over the fish of the sea, and over the fowl of the air, and over the cattle, and over all the earth' (Genesis, 1:26).
8 Cf. Gray, *Ode on a Distant Prospect of Eton College*, 36.

12 *respire* 'breathe more freely'.
15 *Coursers* 'racing horses'. Cf. Thomson, *Spring*, 808–20.
26 *officious* 'kindly attentive'.
27 *rising Frame* 'developing body'.

But now the Matron mourns her latest Care,   30
And sees the Sorrows of her darling Fair;
Beholds a *Wretch*, whom she design'd a *Queen*,
And weeps that e'er she form'd the weak Machine.
In vain she boasts her Lip of scarlet Dyes,
Cheeks like the Morning, and far-beaming Eyes;   35
Her Neck refulgent — fair and feeble Arms,
A Set of useless and neglected Charms.
She suffers Hardship with afflictive Moans:
Small Tasks of Labour suit her slender Bones.
Beneath a Load her weary Shoulders yield,   40
Nor can her Fingers grasp the sounding Shield;
She sees and trembles at approaching Harms,
And Fear and Grief destroy her fading Charms.
Then her pale Lips no pearly Teeth disclose,
And Time's rude Sickle cuts the yielding Rose.   45
Thus wretched Woman's short-liv'd Merit dies:
In vain to Wisdom's sacred Help she flies;
Or sparkling Wit but lends a feeble Aid:
'Tis all Delirium from a wrinkled Maid.
    A tattling Dame, no matter where, or who;   50
Me it concerns not — and it need not you;
Once told this Story to the listening Muse,
Which we, as now it serves our Turn, shall use.
    When our Grandsire nam'd the feather'd Kind,
Pond'ring their Natures in his careful Mind,   55
'Twas then, if on our Author we rely,
He view'd his Consort with an envious Eye;
Greedy of Pow'r, he hugg'd the tott'ring Throne;
Pleased with the Homage, and would reign alone;
And, better to secure his doubtful Rule,   60
Roll'd his wise Eye-balls, and pronounc'd her *Fool*.
The regal Blood to distant Ages runs:
Sires, Brothers, Husbands, and commanding Sons,
The Sceptre claim; and ev'ry Cottage brings
A long Succession of Domestic Kings.   65

33 *Machine* The human body as formed of co-ordinating parts.
36 *refulgent* 'radiating beauty'.
54 *Grandsire* 'Mrs. Leapor frequently writes the Words *Sire*, *Fire*, *Spire*, *Hour*, &c. each as if two Syllables' (note in *1751*).

54–5 'And Adam gave names to all cattle, and to the fowl of the air, and to every beast of the field' (Genesis, 2:20).
59 *with the* with (*1751*).

An Epistle to Artemisia. On Fame

In the last fourteen months of Leapor's life Bridget Freemantle ('Artemisia') was her closest friend. She lived in the nearby village of Hinton where her father had been Rector, and was keenly interested in Leapor's work: 'I indulg'd my Curiosity in calling upon her often ... My expressing some Fear of being troublesome in coming so frequently, occasion'd a great Variety of Invitations, both in Verse and Prose; which I could seldom resist. . . . From this Time to that of her Death, few Days pass'd in which I did not either see or hear from her; for she gave me the Pleasure of seeing all her Poems as soon as they were finish'd' (*1751*, pp. xx–xxi). Freemantle edited Leapor's posthumous *Poems*, adding a memoir and some of Leapor's letters to her, and she was anxious to nurture her dead friend's reputation. As the addressee of this poem she plays a role equivalent to John Arbuthnot in Pope's *Epistle*, a confidante to whom the poet can speak freely about her hopes and exasperations. Leapor had a considerable local reputation, and extra amusement comes from the picture of her village-Twickenham where, like Pope, she is besieged by demanding callers (Cf. *Epistle to Dr Arbuthnot*, 1–68). In the poem's rich characterization and lively conversation Leapor shows her mastery of using verse rhythms for humorous effect, and the epistle has the ebullience and confidence of a mature poetic voice. The text is that of the first printing, *Poems* (1751), pp. 43–54. We have standardized the positioning of quotation marks, which in *1751* are erratically placed and sometimes left unclosed.

> Say, *Artemisia*, do the Slaves of Fame
> Deserve our Pity, or provoke our Blame?
> Whose airy Hopes, like some new-kindled Fire,
> A Moment blaze, and then in Smoke expire;
> Or like a Babe i'th'midst of Plenty cry,   5
> And leave their Supper for a painted Fly.
>   Bold *Maro* paints her of gigantic Size,
> And makes her Forehead prop the lofty Skies;
> With Eyes and Ears he hung the Lady round,
> And her shrill Clarion shook the Heavens around: 10
> Then worthy Names the trembling Notes prolong,
> And Actions blazing in immortal Song;
> But, weary now, and grown an antient Maid,
> Her Strength exhausted, and her Lungs decay'd;
> Her unspread Wings resign their plumy Pride,   15
> And her hoarse Trumpet dangles by her Side.
> A Handmaid leads the purblind Dame along,
> Black *Slander* call'd, with never-ceasing Tongue;
> And when this Servant whispers in her Ears,
> She to her Mouth the heavy Trumpet rears: 20
> The rattling Concave sends a horrid Cry,
> And smoking Scandals hiss along the Sky;
> Yet round her still the supple Vot'ries croud,
> And pay Devotion to a painted Cloud:
> The fond *Ixions* spread their longing Arms,   25
> And grasp a Vapour for a *Juno*'s Charms.
>   The Hero brave, that never knew to shun
> The pointed Cannon, or the bursting Gun,
> Of Bruises vain, and prodigal of Scars,
> Returns from Pillage, and successful Wars.   30
> But if the sullen Rout refuse to pay
> The vulgar Triumphs of a noisy Day,
> To his sad Bosom pale Despondence creeps,
> And the stern Soldier like an Infant weeps:

6 *painted Fly* 'butterfly'.

7 *Maro* Virgil. His allegorical description of *Fama* or 'Rumour' (*Aeneid*, 4:173–97) represents the spread of gossip in Carthage about Dido and Aeneas. Leapor's choice of words is close to Dryden's translation where the goddess is called 'Fame': 'Soon grows the Pygmee to Gigantic size; / Her Feet on Earth, her Forehead in the Skies ... / ... As many Plumes as raise her lofty flight, / So many piercing Eyes inlarge her sight ... / ... And round with listning Ears the flying Plague is hung. / She fills the peaceful Universe with Cries'.

11 *worthy Names* i.e. Dido and Aeneas.

17 *purblind* 'dim-sighted'.

20 *Trumpet* Fourdrinier's engraving for Dryden's *Virgil* pictures 'Fame' blowing a long trumpet, not part of Virgil's description.

21 *rattling Concave* The mouth of the trumpet.

23 *supple Vot'ries* 'compliant worshippers'.

25 *Ixion* In Greek myth the ruler of the Lapiths who tried to seduce Zeus's wife, Hera. To frustrate him Zeus formed a cloud in Hera's shape. (Juno, wife of Jupiter, is her Roman equivalent.)

29 *prodigal* 'lavish'.

31 *Rout* 'company'.

Caballing Sceptics shake the frighted Gown,   35
And Poets tremble at an Idiot's Frown:
The Scorn of Fools can pierce a noble Heart,
And wound an Author in the tend'rest Part.
    Rich *Merrio* thought, like Eastern Kings, to raise
By lofty Columns everlasting Praise;   40
His broad Foundations half the Field surround,
And Piles of Timber load the sinking Ground.
This Heav'n beheld, and smil'd at seeing Man,
Whose Joy is Vapour, and whose Life a Span,
Who Death's black Warrant ev'ry Moment fears,   45
Still building Castles for a thousand Years.
On this grand Wretch was pass'd an early Doom;
And *Merrio*, summon'd to the silent Gloom,
Feels, ere his Eyes behold the glowing Spires,
The Stroke of Fate, and with a Sigh expires.   50
All reas'ning Creatures, tho' by diff'rent Ways,
Would prove their Title to a Share of Praise.
Cornelia's Praise consists in plaiting well;
Pastora's Fingers at a Knot excel:
Her gaudy Ribbands gay *Sabina* furls;   55
But looks with Envy on *Aurelia*'s Curls.
    Unhappy *Delia* thought, a shining Gown
Would gain Respect, and win the gazing Town;
But *Envy* rose, to clip her rising Wings;
And, grinning ghastly (as the Poet sings),   60
In *Claudia*'s Shape dissolv'd the Lady's Pride,
And slily whisper'd, *Delia*'s Gown is dy'd.
    Ev'n *Mira*'s Self, presuming on the Bays,
Appears among the Candidates for Praise:
Has watch'd Applause, as from the Lips it fell;   65
With what Success? — Why, that the Muse shall tell.
May *Artemisia* not refuse to hear!
For Praise could ne'er offend her gentle Ear.
I count the Patrons of my early Song,
And pay the Tribute to their Shares belong: 70
What Sorrows too oppress'd the Muse's Wing,
Till your Good-nature gave her Strength to sing!
    Once *Delpho* read — Sage *Delpho*, learn'd and wise,
O'er the scrawl'd Paper cast his judging Eyes,
Whose lifted Brows confess'd a Critic's Pride,   75
While his broad Thumb mov'd nimbly down the Side.
His Form was like some Oracle profound:
The list'ning Audience form'd a Circle round:
But *Mira*, fixing her presuming Eyes

35 *Caballing* 'conspiratorial'; *Gown* 'clergy'.

44 *Span* The distance measured by the outstretched hand, from thumb to little finger. Cf. Cowper, *Yardley Oak*, 147–51.

46 *building Castles* The meaning includes the metaphorical sense of 'indulging in wishful fantasies'. Leapor's poem, *Mopsus; or, The Castle Builder*, develops this idea.

52 *Would* 'wish to'.

53–6 Women dressing their hair.

63 *Bays* Laurels of poetic fame.

73 *Delpho* The critic as oracle, particularly the oracle of Apollo at Delphi.

On the stern Image, thus impatient cries: 80
Sir, will they prosper? — Speak your Judgment, pray.
Replies the Statue — Why, perhaps they may.
For further Answers we in vain implore:
The Charm was over, and it spoke no more.
    Cressida comes, the next unbidden Guest; 85
Small was her Top-knot, and her Judgment less:
A decent Virgin, blest with idle Time,
Now gingles Bobbins; and now ponders Rhime:
Not ponders — reads — Not reads — but looks 'em o'er
To little Purpose, like a thousand more. 90
    "Your Servant, *Molly*."
                  "I am yours the same."
"I pay this Visit, *Molly*, to your Fame:
'Twas That that brought me here; or let me die."
"My Fame's oblig'd: And truly so am I."
"Then fetch me something; for I must not stay 95
Above four Hours."
              "But you'll drink some Tea?"
We sip, and read; we laugh, and chat between.
"The Air is pleasant, and the Fields are green.
Well, *Molly*, sure, there never was thy Fellow.
But don't my Ruffles look exceeding yellow? 100
My Apron's dirty — *Mira*, well, I vow,
That Thought of yours was very pretty now.
I've read the like, tho' I forget the Place:
But, Mrs. *Mira*, How-d'ye like my Lace?"
    Afflicted *Mira*, with a languid Eye, 105
Now views the Clock, and now the Western Sky.
"The Sun grows lower: Will you please to walk?"
"No; read some more."
            "But I had rather talk."
"Perhaps you're tired."
            "Truly that may be."
"Or think me weak."
           "Why, *Cressy*, Thoughts are free." 110
At last we part, with Congees at the Door:
"I'd thank you, *Mira*; but my Thanks are poor.
I wish, alas! But Wishes are in vain.
I like your Garden; and I'll come again.
Dear, how I wish! — I do, or let me die, 115
That we liv'd near"
        — Thinks *Mira*, "So don't I."
    This Nymph, perhaps, as some had done before,
Found the cold Welcome, and return'd no more.
    Then *Vido* next to *Mira*'s Cott appears,
And with soft Praise salutes her list'ning Ears; 120
Whose Maxim was, with Truth not to offend,
And, right or wrong, his Bus'ness to commend.
Look here, cries *Mira*; pray peruse this Song:
Ev'n I, its Parent, see there's something wrong.

---

88 *Bobbin* 'A small pin of wood, with a notch, to wind the thread about when women weave lace' (Johnson).

100 *Ruffles* Ornamental frills, often of lace.
111 *Congees* Formal leave-takings.

"But you mistake: 'Tis excellent indeed."   125
"Then I'll correct it."
                              "No, there is no Need."
"Pray, *Vido*, look on these: Methinks they smell
Too much of *Grub-street*: That myself can tell."
"Not so indeed, they're easy and polite."
"And can you bear 'em?"
                              "I could read till Night."   130
But *Mira*, tho' too partial to the Bays,
And, like her Brethren, not averse to Praise;
Had learn'd this Lesson: Praise, if planted wrong,
Is more destructive than a spiteful Tongue.
      Comes *Codrus* next, with Talents to offend;   135
A simple Tutor, and a saucy Friend,
Who pour'd thick Sonnets like a troubled Spring,
And such as *Butler*'s wide-mouth'd Mortals sing:
In shocking *Rhimes* a Nymph's Perfections tells,
Like the harsh Ting-Tong of some Village-Bells.   140
Then a rude Quarrel sings thro' either Ear,
And *Mira*'s Levee once again is clear.
      Now the dull Muses took their usual Rest;
The Babes slept soundly in their tiny Chest.
Not so their Parent: Fortune still would send   145
Some proud Director, or ill-meaning Friend:
At least we thought their sowre Meanings ill,
Whose Lectures strove to cross a stubborn Will.
      Parthenia cries, "Why, *Mira*, you are dull,
And ever musing, till you crack your Skull;   150
Still poking o'er your What-d'ye-call — your Muse:
But pr'ythee, *Mira*, when dost clean thy Shoes?"
      Then comes *Sophronia*, like a barb'rous *Turk*:
"You thoughtless Baggage, when d'ye mind your Work?
Still o'er a Table leans your bending Neck: 155
Your Head will grow prepost'rous, like a Peck.
Go, ply your Needle: You might earn your Bread;
Or who must feed you when your Father's dead?"
She sobbing answers, "Sure, I need not come
To you for Lectures; I have store at home.   160
What can I do?"
                  " — Not scribble."
                                          " — But I will."
"Then get thee packing — and be aukward still."
      Thus wrapp'd in Sorrow, wretched *Mira* lay,
Till *Artemisia* swept the Gloom away:

---

128 *Grub-street* 'hack-work'. Cf. Pope, *The Dunciad*, 1:44.
129 *polite* Includes the sense of 'polished' (Lat. *politus*).
136 *saucy* 'presumptuous'.
137–8 Lonsdale (*Women Poets*, p. 526) notes that Leapor's reference is to Samuel Butler's satiric portrait of Whachum the versifier: 'His *Sonnets* charm'd th'attentive Crowd, / By wide-mouth'd Mortal trol'd aloud' (*Hudibras*, II.iii.383–4).
142 *Levee* 'reception' (as held by royalty); *clear* 'emptied'.
144 *Babes* 'Her Poems' (*1751* note). 'She brought a little Box, where her Papers lay in a careless confus'd manner, and allow'd me to look them all over' (Freemantle's Memoir of Leapor, *1751*, p. xix).
153 *Sophronia* The name recurs in Leapor's poems. She is probably to be identified with the housekeeper or head cook at Edgcote House (Cf. *Crumble-Hall*, 113–20 and headnote). See Greene, *Mary Leapor*, p. 15.
156 *Peck* A dry measure of two gallons.
160 *store* 'plenty'.

The laughing Muse, by her Example led,   165
Shakes her glad Wings, and quits the drowsy Bed.
    Yet some Impertinence pursues me still;
And so I fear it ever must, and will.
So soft *Pappilia* o'er the Table bends
With her small Circle of insipid Friends;   170
Who wink, and stretch, and rub their drowsy Eyes,
While o'er their Heads Imperial Dulness flies.
"What can we do? We cannot stir for Show'rs:
Or what invent, to kill the irksome Hours?
Why, run to *Leapor*'s, fetch that idle Play: 175
'Twill serve to laugh at all the live-long Day."
    Preferment great! To beat one's weary Brains,
To find Diversion only when it rains!
    Methinks I feel this coward Bosom glow:
Say, *Artemisia*, shall I speak, or no?   180
The Muse shall give herself no saucy Airs,
But only bid 'em softly — Read their Pray'rs.

177 *Preferment* 'privilege'.

Crumble-Hall

Leapor's version of the traditional country-house poem has a fascinating mix of ingredients. Its celebration of old-fashioned plenty and hospitality recalls Ben Jonson's *To Penshurst* (1616), but a satiric element emerges that reminds the reader of Timon's villa in Pope's *Epistle to Burlington*. In the Old England of Crumble-Hall the taste and status of its owners are represented by the carvings and paintings; those truly at home, along with the spiders and mice, seem to be the 'menial Train' in the kitchen and parlour, which Leapor knew well. Her observant 'below stairs' view moves from the 'good old *English Fare*' of its Gothic past to the modern improvements that threaten the estate. It has recently been shown (*A Northamptonshire Garland: An Anthology of Northamptonshire Poets with Biographical Notes*, ed. Trevor Hold (Northampton: Northamptonshire Libraries, 1989), p. 103n; Greene, *Mary Leapor*, pp. 15–17) that the original for Crumble-Hall was Edgcote House, where Leapor worked as a kitchen maid until *c.* summer 1745. Edgcote was a large medieval house with a rich history, having been owned by Henry V when Prince of Wales, and in the next century by Thomas Cromwell and Anne of Cleves, before coming into the Chauncy family. Leapor's sense of impending destruction was all too justified: between 1747 and 1752 Richard Chauncy (*c.*1690–1760) pulled the old building down and built the present house on the site. The poem was first printed in *Poems* (1751), pp. 111–22, the text given here.

When Friends or Fortune frown on *Mira*'s Lay,
Or gloomy Vapours hide the Lamp of Day;
With low'ring Forehead, and with aching Limbs,
Oppress'd with Head-ach, and eternal Whims,
Sad *Mira* vows to quit the darling Crime: 5
Yet takes her Farewel, and repents, in Rhyme.
    But see (more charming than *Armida*'s Wiles)
The Sun returns, and *Artemisia* smiles:
Then in a trice the Resolutions fly;
And who so frolick as the Muse and I?   10
We sing once more, obedient to her Call;
Once more we sing; and 'tis of *Crumble-Hall*;
That *Crumble-Hall*, whose hospitable Door

7 *Armida* The enchantress in Tasso's *Gerusalemme Liberata* who lured Christian knights into her magic garden.

Has fed the Stranger, and reliev'd the Poor;
Whose *Gothic* Towers, and whose rusty Spires,   15
Were known of old to Knights, and hungry Squires.
There powder'd Beef, and Warden-Pies, were found;
And Pudden dwelt within her spacious Bound:
Pork, Peas, and Bacon (good old *English* Fare!),
With tainted Ven'son, and with hunted Hare: 20
With humming Beer her Vats were wont to flow,
And ruddy *Nectar* in her Vaults to glow.
Here came the Wights, who battled for Renown,
The sable Frier, and the russet Clown:
The loaded Tables sent a sav'ry Gale,   25
And the brown Bowls were crown'd with simp'ring Ale;
While the Guests ravag'd on the smoking Store,
Till their stretch'd Girdles would contain no more.
    Of this rude Palace might a Poet sing
From cold *December* to returning Spring;   30
Tell how the Building spreads on either Hand,
And two grim Giants o'er the Portals stand;
Whose grisled Beards are neither comb'd nor shorn,
But look severe, and horribly adorn.
    Then step within — there stands a goodly Row   35
Of oaken Pillars — where a gallant Show
Of mimic Pears and carv'd Pomgranates twine,
With the plump Clusters of the spreading Vine.
Strange Forms above, present themselves to View;
Some Mouths that grin, some smile, and some that spew.   40
Here a soft Maid or Infant seems to cry:
Here stares a Tyrant, with distorted Eye:
The Roof — no *Cyclops* e'er could reach so high:
Not *Polypheme*, tho' form'd for dreadful Harms,
The Top could measure with extended Arms.   45
Here the pleas'd Spider plants her peaceful Loom:
Here weaves secure, nor dreads the hated Broom.
But at the Head (and furbish'd once a Year)
The Heralds mystic Compliments appear:
Round the fierce Dragon *Honi Soit* entwines,   50
And Royal *Edward* o'er the Chimney shines.
    Safely the Mice through yon dark Passage run,
Where the dim Windows ne'er admit the Sun.
Along each Wall the Stranger blindly feels;

---

17 *powder'd* 'salted'; *Warden-Pies* Pies made with warden
    pears, an old variety of baking fruit; served at the
    sheep-shearing in *The Winter's Tale* (IV.iii.45).
20 *tainted* 'well hung'.
21 *humming* 'really strong'. Cf. Duck, *The Thresher's
    Labour*, 271.
22 *Nectar* 'sweet wine'.
23 *Wights* 'people' (an archaism).
24 *Clown* 'peasant'. Cf. 'But all come in, the farmer, and
    the clown' (Jonson, *To Penshurst*, 48).
26 *simp'ring* 'simmering'.

33 *grisled* 'grey'.
34 *adorn* 'ornate'.
43 *Cyclops* One-eyed giants of Greek myth, credited with
    feats of wall-building. Polyphemus imprisoned Ulysses
    and his men (*Odyssey*, 9).
49 *Heralds mystic Compliments* The family coat of arms.
50 *entwines* twines (*1751*).
50–1 'Honi soit qui mal y pense' ('Evil be to him who evil
    thinks'), the motto of the Order of the Garter, the
    highest order of English knighthood, instituted by
    Edward III *c.*1344.

And (trembling) dreads a Spectre at his Heels.   55
   The sav'ry Kitchen much Attention calls:
Westphalia Hams adorn the sable Walls:
The Fires blaze; the greasy Pavements fry;
And steaming Odours from the Kettles fly.
   See! yon brown Parlour on the Left appears,   60
For nothing famous, but its leathern Chairs,
Whose shining Nails like polish'd Armour glow,
And the dull Clock beats audible and slow.
But on the Right we spy a Room more fair:
The Form — 'tis neither long, nor round, nor square;   65
The Walls how lofty, and the Floor how wide,
We leave for learned *Quadrus* to decide.
Gay *China* Bowls o'er the broad Chimney shine,
Whose long Description would be too sublime:
And much might of the Tapestry be sung: 70
But we're content to say, The Parlour's hung.
   We count the Stairs, and to the Right ascend,
Where on the Walls the gorgeous Colours blend.
There doughty *George* bestrides the goodly Steed;
The Dragon's slaughter'd, and the Virgin freed: 75
And there (but lately rescu'd from their Fears)
The Nymph and serious *Ptolemy* appears:
Their aukward Limbs unwieldy are display'd;
And, like a Milk-wench, glares the royal Maid.
   From hence we turn to more familiar Rooms;   80
Whose Hangings ne'er were wrought in *Grecian* Looms:
Yet the soft Stools, and eke the lazy Chair,
To Sleep invite the Weary, and the Fair.
   Shall we proceed? — Yes, if you'll break the Wall:
If not, return, and tread once more the Hall.   85
Up ten Stone Steps now please to drag your Toes,
And a brick Passage will succeed to those.
Here the strong Doors were aptly fram'd to hold
Sir *Wary*'s Person, and Sir *Wary*'s Gold.
Here *Biron* sleeps, with Books encircled round;   90
And him you'd guess a Student most profound.
Not so — in Form the dusty Volumes stand:
There's few that wear the Mark of *Biron*'s Hand.
   Would you go farther? — Stay a little then:
Back thro' the Passage — down the Steps again;   95
Thro' yon dark Room — Be careful how you tread
Up these steep Stairs — or you may break your Head.
These Rooms are furnish'd amiably, and full:
Old Shoes, and Sheep-ticks bred in Stacks of Wool;

57 *Westphalia* The province in western Germany, source of the best ham and bacon.

70–1 Leapor jokingly refrains from giving a detailed description of the wall-hangings, a staple of romance-writing (Cf. Spenser's House of Busyrane, *Faerie Queene*, III.xi.28–46).

74 *George* The dragon-slaying patron saint of England.

77–9 'Presumably the tapestry showed Ptolemy and Cleopatra's relief at being rescued by Julius Caesar from the enemies who had deposed them' (Valerie Rumbold, *British Journal for 18C Studies*, 19 (1996), p. 75).

82–3 Cf. Pope, *Epistle to Burlington*, 149.

86 Cf. *Epistle to Burlington*, 131.

Grey *Dobbin*'s Gears, and Drenching-Horns enow;   100
Wheel-spokes — the Irons of a tatter'd Plough.
   No farther — Yes, a little higher, pray:
At yon small Door you'll find the Beams of Day,
While the hot Leads return the scorching Ray.
Here a gay Prospect meets the ravish'd Eye: 105
Meads, Fields, and Groves, in beauteous Order lie.
From hence the Muse precipitant is hurl'd,
And drags down *Mira* to the nether World.
   Thus far the Palace — Yet there still remain
Unsung the Gardens, and the menial Train.   110
Its Groves anon — its People first we sing:
Hear, *Artemisia*, hear the Song we bring.
Sophronia first in Verse shall learn to chime,
And keep her Station, tho' in *Mira*'s Rhyme;
Sophronia sage! whose learned Knuckles know   115
To form round Cheese-cakes of the pliant Dough;
To bruise the Curd, and thro' her Fingers squeeze
Ambrosial Butter with the temper'd Cheese:
Sweet Tarts and Pudden, too, her Skill declare;
And the soft Jellies, hid from baneful Air.   120
   O'er the warm Kettles, and the sav'ry Steams,
Grave *Colinettus* of his Oxen dreams:
Then, starting, anxious for his new-mown Hay,
Runs headlong out to view the doubtful Day:
But Dinner calls with more prevailing Charms;   125
And surly *Gruffo* in his aukward Arms
Bears the tall Jugg, and turns a glaring Eye,
As tho' he fear'd some Insurrection nigh
From the fierce Crew, that gaping stand a-dry.
   O'er-stuffed with Beef; with Cabbage much too full,   130
And Dumpling too (fit Emblem of his Skull!)
With Mouth wide open, but with closing Eyes
Unwieldy *Roger* on the Table lies.
His able Lungs discharge a rattling Sound:
Prince barks, *Spot* howls, and the tall Roofs rebound.   135
Him *Urs'la* views; and, with dejected Eyes,
"Ah! *Roger*, Ah!" the mournful Maiden cries:
"Is wretched *Urs'la* then your Care no more,
That, while I sigh, thus you can sleep and snore?
Ingrateful *Roger*! wilt thou leave me now?   140
For you these Furrows mark my fading Brow:
For you my Pigs resign their Morning Due:
My hungry Chickens lose their Meat for you:
And, was it not, Ah! was it not for thee,
No goodly Pottage would be dress'd by me.   145
For thee these Hands wind up the whirling Jack,
Or place the Spit across the sloping Rack.
I baste the Mutton with a chearful Heart,

---

100 *Gears* 'harness'; *Drenching-Horns* Contraptions for
conveying a potion into a horse's mouth.
104 *Leads* Of the roof.
146 *Jack* A mechanism for turning the roasting meat. 'W'

describes Leapor in the kitchen (at Edgcote?)
'sometimes taking up her pen while the jack was
standing still, and the meat scorching' (*Gentleman's
Magazine* (1784), p. 807).

Because I know my *Roger* will have Part."
    Thus she — But now her Dish-kettle began   150
To boil and blubber with the foaming Bran.
The greasy Apron round her Hips she ties,
And to each Plate the scalding Clout applies:
The purging Bath each glowing Dish refines,
And once again the polish'd Pewter shines.   155
    Now to those Meads let frolick Fancy rove,
Where o'er yon Waters nods a pendent Grove;
In whose clear Waves the pictur'd Boughs are seen,
With fairer Blossoms, and a brighter Green.
Soft flow'ry Banks the spreading Lakes divide: 160
Sharp-pointed Flags adorn each tender Side.
See! the pleas'd Swans along the Surface play;
Where yon cool Willows meet the scorching Ray,
When fierce *Orion* gives too warm a Day.
    But, hark! what Scream the wond'ring Ear invades!   165
The *Dryads* howling for their threaten'd Shades:
Round the dear Grove each Nymph distracted flies
(Tho' not discover'd but with Poet's Eyes):
And shall those Shades, where *Philomela*'s Strain
Has oft to Slumber lull'd the hapless Swain;   170
Where Turtles us'd to clap their silken Wings;
Whose rev'rend Oaks have known a hundred Springs;
Shall these ignobly from their Roots be torn,
And perish shameful, as the abject Thorn;
While the slow Carr bears off their aged Limbs,   175
To clear the Way for Slopes, and modern Whims;
Where banish'd Nature leaves a barren Gloom,
And aukward Art supplies the vacant Room?
Yet (or the Muse for Vengeance calls in vain)
The injur'd Nymphs shall haunt the ravag'd Plain: 180
Strange Sounds and Forms shall teaze the gloomy Green;
And Fairy-Elves by *Urs'la* shall be seen:
Their new-built Parlour shall with Echoes ring:
And in their Hall shall doleful Crickets sing.
    Then cease, *Diracto*, stay thy desp'rate Hand;   185
And let the Grove, if not the Parlour, stand.

150–5 Boiling bran-water, traditionally used as a stain-remover.
153 *Clout* 'piece of cloth'.
161 *Flags* 'water-reeds'.
164 *Orion* The constellation containing Sirius, the dog-star ('Orion's hound').
166 *Dryads* Tree-nymphs, who were believed to die with their particular tree.

168 Cf. Pope, *The Rape of the Lock*, 5:124.
169 *Philomela* The nightingale.
171 *Turtles* 'turtle-doves'.
175 *Carr* 'cart'.
176–8 Cf. Robert Lloyd, *The Cit's Country Box*, 67–82, 99–110.

Mira's Picture

As Leapor notes at the end of the poem, this amusing portrait of herself as a literary rustic is an exercise in caricature. In 1712, *Spectator*, 537 had described that style of art: 'those burlesque Pictures, which the *Italians* call *Caracatura*'s; where the Art consists in preserving, amidst distorted and aggravated Features, some distinguishing Likeness of the Person; but in such a Manner as to transform the most agreeable Beauty into the most odious Monster'. Underlying the comedy is the idealized shepherdess of conventional pastoral. The text given here is that of the first printing, in *Poems on Several Occasions* (1751), pp. 294–8.

CORYDON. PHILLARIO.

Or, MIRA's Picture.

A PASTORAL.

Within the Bounds of yonder fruitful Plain
Liv'd *Corydon*, a harmless Shepherd Swain;
Whose Care was chiefly to his Flock confin'd,
Whose smiling Features spoke a chearful Mind.
Behind his Dwelling stood a friendly Hill;   5
Before it, Pastures, and a purling Rill.
  From the great Mart of Business, and of Fame,
To this Retreat, the gay *Phillario* came:
He came — But how he spent the ling'ring Hours,
Amid still Meadows, and ambrosial Bow'rs;   10
Whether he liv'd on Blackberries and Whey,
Or if he sigh'd for Ombre and Bohea;
Whether he thought a Summer's Day too long;
To tell, is not the Purpose of my Song:
'Tis their Discourse alone that fills our Tale.   15
Begin — One Morning, in a flow'ry Vale,
This Couple walk'd, to hear the Linnet sing,
And share the Beauties of the dawning Spring:
Phillario thus — What Nymph, O Shepherd! reigns
The rural Toast of these delightful Plains?   20
For much I fear th'*Arcadian* Nymphs outshine
The shiv'ring Beauties of this Northern Clime.

CORYDON.

Young *Daphne* some, and some *Amynta* praise;
Some doat on *Delia* for her graceful Ease:
Some wond'ring Swain bright *Cynthia*'s Eye inspires;   25
Another *Claudia*'s charming Voice admires:
Some like no Face but *Phillada*'s the fair;
And some *Cymene*'s, with the raven Hair.

PHILLARIO.

But who is she that walks from yonder Hill,
With studious Brows, and Night-cap Dishabille?   30
That looks a Stranger to the Beams of Day;
And counts her Steps, and mutters all the Way?

---

7 *Mart* 'commercial centre'.
10 *ambrosial* 'divinely fragrant'.
11 *Whey* Watery milk, the by-product of country cheese-
   making.
12 *Ombre* The card game. See Pope, *The Rape of the Lock*,
   3:27n. *Bohea* The finest black tea (pronounced
   'Bo-háy').

20 *Toast* 'beauty'.
21 *Arcadian* Belonging to the idealized world of classical
   pastoral.
30 *Dishabille* 'informal negligence of dress'.
32 *mutters* So does the poet in Gray, *Elegy Written in a
   Country Church Yard*, 106.

CORYDON.

'Tis *Mira*, Daughter to a Friend of mine;
'Tis she that makes your what-d'ye-call — your Rhyme.
I own the Girl is something out o'th'way: 35
But how d'ye like her? Good *Phillario*, say!

PHILLARIO.

Like her! — I'd rather beg the friendly Rains
To sweep that Nuisance from thy loaded Plains;
That ——

CORYDON.

— Hold, *Phillario!* She's a Neighbour's Child:
'Tis true, her Linen may be something soil'd.   40

PHILLARIO.

Her Linen, *Corydon!* — Herself, you mean.
Are such the Dryads of thy smiling Plain?
Why, I could swear it, if it were no Sin,
That yon lean Rook can shew a fairer Skin.

CORYDON.

What tho' some Freckles in her Face appear?   45
That's only owing to the time o'th'Year.
Her Eyes are dim, you'll say: Why, that is true:
I've heard the Reason, and I'll tell it you.
By a Rush-Candle (as her Father says)
She sits whole Ev'nings, reading wicked Plays.   50

PHILLARIO.

She read! — She'd better milk her brindled Cows:
I wish the Candle does not singe her Brows,
So like a dry Furze-faggot; and, beside,
Not quite so even as a Mouse's Hide.

CORYDON.

Come, come; you view her with malicious Eyes: 55
Her Shape ——

PHILLARIO.

—— Where Mountains upon Mountains rise!
And, as they fear'd some Treachery at hand,
Behind her Ears her list'ning Shoulders stand.

CORYDON.

But she has Teeth ——

42 *Dryads* Tree-nymphs.
51 *brindled* 'tawny brown'.
53 *Furze-faggot* 'bundle of gorse for firewood'.
54 *Mouse's Hide* Cf. Swift, *A Beautiful Young Nymph Going to Bed*, 13.

56 Cf. Pope on the struggles of poetic ambition: 'Hills peep o'er Hills, and *Alps* on *Alps* arise!' (*An Essay on Criticism*, 232).

PHILLARIO.
—— Consid'ring how they grow,
'Tis no great matter if she has or no: 60
They look decay'd with Posset, and with Plumbs,
And seem prepar'd to quit her swelling Gums.

CORYDON.
No more, my Friend! for see, the Sun grows high,
And I must send the Weeders to my Rye:
Those spurious Plants must from the Soil be torn,   65
Lest the rude Brambles over-top the Corn.

Note, *This Description of her Person is a Caracature.*

61 *Posset* Hot milk curdled with wine or ale, sweetened   **65** *spurious* 'false', 'illegitimate' (i.e. the weeds).
with spices and honey or sugar. *Plumbs* 'plums'.

Mark Akenside (1721–1770)

Poetry formed only a part of Akenside's upwardly mobile career. His father had a butcher's shop in Newcastle-upon-Tyne, and after attending the Grammar School he moved to the nonconformist academy run by William Wilson, a minister attached to the local Unitarian chapel which his family attended. Akenside's religious enthusiasm, political convictions and literary talents were all precocious, and during 1737–8 he had four poems printed in the *Gentleman's Magazine*, including a blistering attack on Walpole's Spanish policy. Carrying the hopes and financial support of his dissenting congregation he entered Edinburgh University in 1739 with a view to becoming a minister of the church, but within a year he moved to the study of medicine. By 1742 he had returned to Newcastle where he worked hard on *The Pleasures of Imagination*, and in 1743 he submitted the manuscript to Robert Dodsley (the leading publisher of poetry during the 1740s and 1750s), asking the substantial sum of £120. Dodsley later told how he himself 'carried the work to Pope, who, having looked into it, advised him not to make a niggardly offer, for "this was no everyday writer"' (Samuel Johnson, 'Life of Akenside'). It was published anonymously in January 1744 and by November had reached a fourth edition. With his poem a popular success Akenside went over to the University of Leiden in Holland during April–May, where he took the degree of M.D. and published his doctoral thesis, 'On the Origin and Growth of the Human Foetus'. Back in England he tried to establish himself as a physician at Northampton, but with little success – perhaps the local residents were made uneasy by his vanity and overbearing manner, or by his unconcealed political fervour (Dr Johnson said he 'deafened the place with clamours for liberty'). This was evident in his *Epistle to Curio* (1744), a satiric attack on William Pulteney, Earl of Bath, for deserting the opposition cause. Akenside, remarked Johnson with a shudder, was 'no friend to anything established'.

The publication of his *Odes on Several Subjects* (1745), an exercise in classical correctness, disappointed the literary public (the Wartons thought they had 'a vast deal of the *frigid*') and Akenside was destined never to repeat his early poetic success. But his role in the literary 'establishment' was confirmed when Dodsley made him editor of his new literary fortnightly, *The Museum* (1746–7), a magazine which gave opportunities to young writers of the Dodsley stable. Akenside was also well represented in the sixth volume of Dodsley's *Collection of Poems* (1758). During the 1750s his professional ambitions began to be fulfilled, and his medical career took over. His lifelong friend, Jeremiah Dyson, with whom he lived in Hampstead for a time, fitted up a house for him in Bloomsbury Square in London and gave him a chariot and £300 a year. His private practice became distinctly fashionable, and his rise to eminence was marked by his becoming fellow of the Royal Society (1753), fellow of the Royal College of Physicians (1754), Principal Physician at St Thomas's Hospital (1759), and in 1761 one of the Queen's physicians (by this time he himself had switched political allegiance).

Thomas Pettigrew's *Memoirs of Lettsom* (1817) records that Akenside 'had a pale strumous countenance, but was always very neat and elegant in his dress. He wore a large white wig, and carried a long sword … he would order some of the [servants], on his visiting-days, to precede him with brooms to clear the way, and prevent the patients from too nearly approaching him' (1:22–3). In 1761 a friend made him a present of Milton's bed, but sleeping in this does not seem to have given him fresh poetic ambitions. He did not leave poetry entirely, but the last decade of his life was largely spent revising earlier work. Most notably he embarked on a thorough rewriting and extension to five books of *The Pleasures of the Imagination* (as it was renamed), left incomplete at his death.

The Pleasures of Imagination

BOOK ONE

This philosophical poem in three books was published on 16 January 1744 when its author was twenty-two, and it is full of the idealism, exuberance and, above all, the confidence of youth. It combines the 'delightful teaching' of Horatian didactic poetry with the lofty ambitions of Miltonic epic, rising to the height of its own great argument to tell of the universe of the human mind ('bear witness, earth and heav'n!', 481). Imagination for Akenside is the mediator between the internal and external worlds, between the aesthetic order (beauty) and the moral order (truth and virtue), and it is thus crucial to human life. The following extracts from the lengthy 'Design' prefixed to the poem will give some idea of Akenside's aims:

There are certain powers in human nature which seem to hold a middle place between the organs of bodily sense and the faculties of moral perception: They have been call'd by a very general name, THE POWERS OF IMAGINATION. Like the external senses, they relate to matter and motion; and at the same time, give the mind ideas analogous to those of moral approbation and dislike. … The Design of the following poem is to give a view of *these*, in the largest acceptation of the term; *so that whatever our imagination feels from the agreeable appearances of nature, and all the various entertainment we meet with either in poetry, painting, music, or any of the elegant arts, might be deducible from one or other of those principles in the constitution of the human mind, which are here establish'd and explain'd.* … [T]he subject before us tending almost constantly to admiration and enthusiasm, seem'd rather to demand a more open, pathetic and figur'd stile. This too appear'd more natural, as the author's aim was not so much to give formal precepts, or enter into the way of direct argumentation, as by exhibiting the most ingaging prospects of nature, to enlarge and harmonize the imagination, and by that means insensibly dispose the minds of men to the same dignity of taste in religion, morals, and civil life. 'Tis on this account that he is so careful to point out the benevolent intention of the author of nature in every principle of the human constitution here insisted on; and also to unite the moral excellencies of life in the same point of view with the meer external objects of good taste; thus recommending them in common to our natural propensity for admiring what is beautiful and lovely. ('The Design', pp. v–xi)

Akenside's poem is deeply imbued with his reading of Greek philosophy and the work of more recent moralist-aestheticians, notably the Earl of Shaftesbury (the various texts gathered into his *Characteristicks*, 1711), Joseph Addison (his essay on 'The Pleasures of the Imagination' published over eleven consecutive issues of *The Spectator* in June and July 1712), and Francis Hutcheson (*An Inquiry into the Original of our Ideas of Beauty and Virtue*, 1725). In each of these works aesthetics (beauty) combines with morality (goodness and virtue), in a fusion that ultimately looks back to Plato's form of the Good/Beautiful (*to kalon*). The most neoplatonic is Shaftesbury, with his concept of a universal ideal of Nature-as-system, being in harmony with which is 'virtue', i.e. the state of being fully attuned: regular, good and beautiful at the same time. Addison's more democratic aesthetics are empirical, concerned with the visual and affective aspects of the arts, especially poetry, and they engage with questions of why we all respond to colours, landscapes, emotions, etc., and how the mind combines images and creates new ones, loving to range beyond the merely material. Hutcheson works between absolute and relative beauty, between ideal and empirical, but is indebted to his teacher Shaftesbury in asserting the beauty of virtue; Hutcheson stresses the power of Mind, by which aesthetic issues are raised from sensual to intellectual/moral. Each of these writers exerted an influence on Akenside, and the notes try to give some sense of how he used them.

The blank verse of the poem is deceptively fluent: there are many successive run-on lines, and the argument often builds up through lengthy sentences and paragraphs. The reader can be swept on by the images and the musicality of the verse while missing the intensity of argument that some passages have. It is necessary to pause over certain phrases to catch the compressed and specific meaning. Simple words like 'consent', 'quarry', 'sincere', 'genial' or 'luxury' can be misinterpreted by us modern readers for whom they have lost the rich nuances they used to have, and phrases like 'fabric of the sphere' and 'weigh the moment' (86, 89) can seem vague at first reading, whereas Akenside is working to make precise, almost technical, points. Some attempt has been made in the notes to indicate the richness of the poem's vocabulary.

The Pleasures of Imagination made its mark on the poetry of the Romantics: Coleridge's *Eolian Harp*, Wordsworth's *Prelude* and Keats's *Ode on a Grecian Urn* are each indebted to different aspects of the poem: to its concept of organic responsiveness, its verse cadences, its coalescing of beauty and truth.

In Book Two Akenside goes on to consider the nature of the passions (positive and negative) and the active power of virtue, and Book Three explores the imagination's tendencies towards deception and vice, and the role of ridicule in exposing them, before moving on to a joyful evocation of the power of nature and the human mind. Here in Book One Akenside celebrates the universal mind, develops Addison's three categories of greatness, novelty and beauty, and moves the latter into a neoplatonic Trinity with truth and goodness. The stress is on energy and exploration, and on the importance of finding links between internal vision and external action, 'private life' (507) and 'publick pow'r' (565).

From the beginning the poem was published with Akenside's notes (reduced through successive editions), some of which are useful, others wordy and obscure. They are only selectively quoted here. The text of *The Pleasures of Imagination* can never be said to have stabilized: Akenside took several opportunities to revise the poem before deciding finally to rewrite it. The text of Book One given here is that which he revised for the first octavo edition (the third) of May 1744, four months after the first of the quarto editions. Further revisions were made for the 1754 edition, but the text which follows is that of the twenty-two-year-old poet who has had the chance to take a second and third look at his work.

With what attractive charms this goodly frame
Of nature touches the consenting hearts
Of mortal men; and what the pleasing stores
Which beauteous imitation thence derives
To deck the poet's, or the painter's toil;   5
My verse unfolds. Attend, ye gentle POW'RS
OF MUSICAL DELIGHT! and while I sing
Your gifts, your honours, dance around my strain.
Thou, smiling queen of every tuneful breast,
Indulgent FANCY! from the fruitful banks   10
Of Avon, whence thy rosy fingers cull
Fresh flow'rs and dews to sprinkle on the turf
Where *Shakespeare* lies, be present: and with thee
Let FICTION come, upon her vagrant wings
Wafting ten thousand colours thro' the air,   15
And, by the glances of her magic eye,
Combining each in endless, fairy forms,
Her wild creation. Goddess of the lyre
Which rules the accents of the moving sphere,
Wilt thou, eternal HARMONY! descend,   20
And join this festive train? for with thee comes
The guide, the guardian of their lovely sports,
Majestic TRUTH; and where TRUTH deigns to come,
Her sister LIBERTY will not be far.
Be present all ye GENII who conduct   25
The wand'ring footsteps of the youthful bard,
New to your springs and shades: who touch his ear
With finer sounds: who heighten to his eye
The bloom of nature, and before him turn
The gayest, happiest attitudes of things.   30

    Oft have the laws of each poetic strain
The critic-verse imploy'd; yet still unsung
Lay this prime subject, tho' importing most
A poet's name: for fruitless is th'attempt

1–2 *goodly frame / Of nature* 'Frame of nature' is Shaftesbury's phrase for the universe as a single articulate system (*An Enquiry Concerning Virtue*, I.2.i). Cf. Hamlet's 'this goodly frame, the earth' (II.ii.298), and Adam's 'this goodly frame' (*Paradise Lost*, 8:15). The system is 'attractive' (line 1) because it naturally draws everything together.

2 *consenting* includes the meaning 'in harmony with'. Cf. 112 and 465.

6–8 Recalls the celebration of divine harmonies in *Paradise Lost*, where angels 'with songs / And choral symphonies … Circle his throne rejoicing' (5:161–3).

10 *FANCY* Until the end of the eighteenth century the terms 'imagination' and 'fancy' were interchangeable, the former from the Lat. *imaginatio*, the latter from the Gk. *phantasia*. In his first 'Pleasures of the Imagination'

essay (*Spectator*, 411), Addison speaks of 'the Imagination or Fancy (which I shall use promiscuously)'.

13 Shakespeare as 'fancy's child' (Milton, *L'Allegro*, 133), an idea also picked up by Joseph Warton, *The Enthusiast*, 170–2.

14–18 Akenside hints at the dangers of 'Fiction' by associating her with those figures in Pope who exemplify the instability and self-indulgence of the imagination: the sylphs (*The Rape of the Lock*, 2:59–68) and the goddess Dulness (*The Dunciad*, 1:82). Hence the need for Truth as a guide (22–3). Fiction without Truth would be delightful but false.

19 *sphere* Alludes to the Pythagorean concept of cosmic harmony (the music of the spheres) described in Plato, *Republic*, 10.

By dull obedience and the curb of rules,   35
For creeping toil to climb the hard ascent
Of high Parnassus. Nature's kindling breath
Must fire the chosen genius; nature's hand
Must point the path, and imp his eagle-wings
Exulting o'er the painful steep to soar   40
High as the summit: there to breathe at large
Æthereal air; with bards and sages old,
Immortal sons of praise. These flatt'ring scenes
To this neglected labour court my song;
Yet not unconscious what a doubtful task   45
To paint the finest features of the mind,
And to most subtile and mysterious things
Give colour, strength and motion. But the love
Of nature and the muses bids explore,
Thro' secret paths erewhile untrod by man,   50
The fair poetic region, to detect
Untasted springs, to drink inspiring draughts;
And shade my temples with unfading flow'rs
Cull'd from the laureate vale's profound recess,
Where never poet gain'd a wreath before.   55

　　From heav'n my strains begin; from heav'n descends
The flame of genius to the human breast,
And love and beauty, and poetic joy
And inspiration. Ere the radiant sun
Sprung from the east, or 'mid the vault of night   60
The moon suspended her serener lamp;
Ere mountains, woods, or streams adorn'd the globe;
Or wisdom taught the sons of men her lore;
Then liv'd th'eternal ONE: then deep-retir'd
In his unfathom'd essence, view'd at large   65
The uncreated images of things;
The radiant sun, the moon's nocturnal lamp,
The mountains, woods and streams, the rolling globe,
And wisdom's form cœlestial. From the first
Of days, on them his love divine he fix'd,   70
His admiration: till in time compleat,
What he admir'd and lov'd, his vital smile
Unfolded into being. Hence the breath
Of life informing each organic frame,

37 *Parnassus* The mountain sacred to Apollo and the
　　Muses, symbol of poetic ambition.
39–43 *imp* 'engraft feathers onto'. Longinus's treatise on
　　the Sublime, *Peri Hypsous*, means literally 'On
　　Soaring'. The flight of poetic imagination became
　　proverbial (cf. 'flight of fancy').
45–55 Akenside's version of Milton's invocation to
　　Paradise Lost (1:12–16).

53–5 The laurel wreath awarded by Apollo, token of poetic
　　fame.
64–6 The Platonic essential ideas of everything ('forms')
　　existing in the divine mind. They are unchanging,
　　unlike their earthly counterparts. The 'ONE' is the
　　Monad, the deity as first cause, one and the same
　　throughout all space and time.
72 *vital* 'life-giving'.

Hence the green earth, and wild resounding waves;   75
Hence light and shade alternate; warmth and cold;
And clear autumnal skies and vernal show'rs,
And all the fair variety of things.

But not alike to every mortal eye
Is this great scene unveil'd. For since the claims   80
Of social life, to diff'rent labours urge
The active pow'rs of man; with wise intent
The hand of nature on peculiar minds
Imprints a diff'rent byass, and to each
Decrees its province in the common toil.   85
To some she taught the fabric of the sphere,
The changeful moon, the circuit of the stars,
The golden zones of heav'n: to some she gave
To weigh the moment of eternal things,
Of time, and space, and fate's unbroken chain,   90
And will's quick impulse: others by the hand
She led o'er vales and mountains, to explore
What healing virtue swells the tender veins
Of herbs and flow'rs; or what the beams of morn
Draw forth, distilling from the clifted rind   95
In balmy tears. But some, to higher hopes
Were destin'd; some within a finer mould
She wrought, and temper'd with a purer flame.
To these the sire omnipotent unfolds
The world's harmonious volume, there to read   100
The transcript of himself. On every part
They trace the bright impressions of his hand:
In earth or air, the meadow's purple stores,
The moon's mild radiance, or the virgin's form
Blooming with rosy smiles, they see portray'd   105
That uncreated beauty, which delights
The mind supreme. *They* also feel her charms,
Enamour'd; *they* partake th'eternal joy.

As Memnon's marble harp, renown'd of old
By fabling Nilus, to the quivering touch   110
Of Titan's ray, with each repulsive string
Consenting, sounded thro' the warbling air
Unbidden strains; ev'n so did nature's hand
To certain species of external things,

---

78 *variety* An important aesthetic principle in the eighteenth century. For Hutcheson, 'Unity amidst Variety' is an essential element of beauty. Cf Pope, *Windsor-Forest*, 15–16.

86 *fabric of the sphere* 'formation of the heavens'. Cf. *Paradise Lost*, 8:76 ('fabric of the heavens').

89 *weigh the moment* 'assess the significance'.

95 *clifted rind* 'split bark' (of a tree or plant ready for grafting).

103 *purple stores* 'colourful abundance'.

106 *uncreated beauty* The platonic form of the beautiful. Cf. 66.

109–24 A giant statue supposedly of Memnon, son of the dawn in Greek myth, which stood before a temple in Egyptian Thebes, was thought to sing at dawn when struck by the sun's rays. This passage on the interfusing of the mind and nature proved influential for Romantic theories of organic unity. Cf. Coleridge's *The Eolian Harp*.

111 *repulsive* 'returning a sound'.

Attune the finer organs of the mind: 115
So the glad impulse of congenial pow'rs,
Or of sweet sound, or fair-proportion'd form,
The grace of motion, or the bloom of light,
Thrills thro' imagination's tender frame,
From nerve to nerve: all naked and alive   120
They catch the spreading rays: till now the soul
At length discloses every tuneful spring,
To that harmonious movement from without,
Responsive. Then the inexpressive strain
Diffuses its inchantment: fancy dreams   125
Of sacred fountains and Elysian groves,
And vales of bliss: the intellectual pow'r
Bends from his awful throne a wond'ring ear,
And smiles: the passions gently sooth'd away,
Sink to divine repose, and love and joy   130
Alone are waking; love and joy, serene
As airs that fan the summer. O! attend,
Whoe'er thou art whom these delights can touch,
Whose candid bosom the refining love
Of nature warms, O! listen to my song;   135
And I will guide thee to her fav'rite walks,
And teach thy solitude her voice to hear,
And point her loveliest features to thy view.

Know then, whate'er of nature's pregnant stores,
Whate'er of mimic art's reflected forms   140
With love and admiration thus inflame
The pow'rs of fancy, her delighted sons
To three illustrious orders have referr'd;
Three sister-graces, whom the painter's hand,
The poet's tongue confesses; the *sublime*,   145
The *wonderful*, the *fair*. I see them dawn!
I see the radiant visions, where they rise,
More lovely than when Lucifer displays
His beaming forehead thro' the gates of morn,
To lead the train of Phœbus and the spring.   150

Say, why was man so eminently rais'd
Amid the vast creation; why ordain'd
Thro' life and death to dart his piercing eye,
With thoughts beyond the limit of his frame;

---

119 *tender frame* 'sensitized fabric'.
123–4 Akenside develops this idea in Book Three: 'th'attentive mind, / By this harmonious action on her pow'rs, / Becomes herself harmonious: wont so long / In outward things to meditate the charm / Of sacred order, soon she seeks at home / To find a kindred order' (3:599–604).
140 The mimetic (imitative) as opposed to the creative. Here (144) he links poetry to painting, regarded as the most mimetic of the arts.
145–6 Akenside develops Addison's categories of the great,

uncommon and beautiful (*Spectator*, 412), themselves indebted to Longinus's distinction between the great, extraordinary and beautiful (*On the Sublime*, 35). Akenside goes on to consider in turn the sublime (151–221), the wonderful (232–70) and the beautiful (271–437).
148 *Lucifer* The morning star.
150 *Phœbus* The sun.
151–221 This passage is a reworking of Longinus's chapter 35, as Akenside points out in a note.

But that th'Omnipotent might send him forth   155
In sight of mortal and immortal pow'rs,
As on a boundless theatre, to run
The great career of justice; to exalt
His gen'rous aim to all diviner deeds;
To shake each partial purpose from his breast;   160
And thro' the mists of passion and of sense,
And thro' the tossing tide of chance and pain
To hold his course unfalt'ring, while the voice
Of truth and virtue, up the steep ascent
Of nature, calls him to his high reward,   165
Th'applauding smile of heav'n? Else wherefore burns
In mortal bosoms this unquenched hope,
That breathes from day to day sublimer things,
And mocks possession? wherefore darts the mind,
With such resistless ardor to embrace   170
Majestic forms? impatient to be free,
Spurning the gross controul of wilful might;
Proud of the strong contention of her toils;
Proud to be daring? Who but rather turns
To heav'n's broad fire his unconstrained view,   175
Than to the glimm'ring of a waxen flame?
Who that, from Alpine heights, his lab'ring eye
Shoots round the wide horizon, to survey
The Nile or Ganges rowl his wasteful tide
Thro' mountains, plains, thro' empires black with shade,   180
And continents of sand; will turn his gaze
To mark the windings of a scanty rill
That murmurs at his feet? The high-born soul
Disdains to rest her heav'n-aspiring wing
Beneath its native quarry. Tir'd of earth   185
And this diurnal scene, she springs aloft
Thro' fields of air; pursues the flying storm;
Rides on the volley'd lightning thro' the heav'ns;
Or yok'd with whirlwinds and the northern blast,
Sweeps the long tract of day. Then high she soars   190
The blue profound, and hovering o'er the sun
Beholds him pouring the redundant stream
Of light; beholds his unrelenting sway
Bend the reluctant planets to absolve

157–8 *theatre* 'public stage'; *run* 'follow'; *career* 'course'.

161 According to neoplatonic thought, bodily distractions clouded the mind's vision: 'yielding to the senses, phantasy ... afflicts the body and beclouds the mind' (Pico della Mirandola, *De Imaginatione*, 1501).

177–83 'Thus by the very propensity of nature we are led to admire, not little springs or shallow rivulets, however clear and delicious, but the Nile, the Rhine, the Danube, and much more than all, the Ocean' (Longinus, 35). (Akenside's note.)

185 *quarry* 'place of origin'. The divine soul yearns to escape its material confinement.

185–221 The neoplatonic ascent of mind. The pattern for such cosmic flights was set by Philo Judæus, first century AD: '[the mind] is borne yet higher to the ether and the circuit of heaven, and is whirled round with the dances of planets and fixed stars ... carrying its gaze beyond the confines of all substance discernible by sense, it comes to a point at which it reaches out after the intelligible world, and on descrying in that world sights of surpassing loveliness ... it is seized by a sober intoxication' (*On the Creation*, 69–71).

192 *redundant* 'superabundant'.

194 *absolve* 'complete' (Lat. *absolvo*).

The fated rounds of time. Thence far effus'd   195
She darts her swiftness up the long career
Of devious comets; thro' its burning signs
Exulting circles the perennial wheel
Of nature, and looks back on all the stars,
Whose blended light, as with a milky zone,   200
Invests the orient. Now amaz'd she views
Th'empyreal waste, where happy spirits hold,
Beyond this concave heav'n, their calm abode;
And fields of radiance, whose unfading light
Has travell'd the profound six thousand years,   205
Nor yet arrives in sight of mortal things.
Ev'n on the barriers of the world untir'd
She meditates th'eternal depth below;
Till, half recoiling, down the headlong steep
She plunges; soon o'erwhelm'd and swallow'd up   210
In that immense of being. There her hopes
Rest at the fated goal. For from the birth
Of mortal man, the sov'reign Maker said,
That not in humble or in brief delight,
Not in the fading echoes of renown,   215
Pow'rs purple robes, or pleasure's flow'ry lap,
The soul should find injoyment: but from these
Turning disdainful to an equal good,
Thro' all th'ascent of things inlarge her view,
Till every bound at length should disappear,   220
And infinite perfection close the scene.

    Call now to mind what high, capacious pow'rs
Lie folded up in man; how far beyond
The praise of mortals, may th'eternal growth
Of nature to perfection half divine,   225
Expand the blooming soul? What pity then
Should sloth's unkindly fogs depress to earth
Her tender blossom; choak the streams of life,
And blast her spring! Far otherwise design'd
Almighty wisdom; nature's happy cares   230
Th'obedient heart far otherwise incline.
Witness the sprightly joy when aught unknown
Strikes the quick sense, and wakes each active pow'r
To brisker measures: witness the neglect
Of all familiar prospects, tho' beheld   235
With transport once; the fond, attentive gaze
Of young astonishment; the sober zeal
Of age, commenting on prodigious things.
For such the bounteous providence of heav'n,

197 *signs* Of the zodiac.
200 *zone* 'girdle'.
202 *empyreal* 'celestial'.
206 'It was a notion of the great Mr. *Huygens* [1629–93, Dutch physicist], that there may be fix'd stars at such a distance from our solar system, as that their light should not have had time to reach us, even from the creation of the world to this day' (Akenside's note).

222–9 An organic image of human potential. On the poem's links with Akenside's work on embryology, see Robin Dix, 'Organic Theories of Art: The Importance of Embryology', *Notes and Queries*, 230 (1985), pp. 215–18.
232–4 'Every thing that is *new* or *uncommon* raises a Pleasure in the Imagination, because it fills the Soul with an agreeable Surprise' (Addison, *Spectator*, 412).

In every breast implanting this desire   240
Of objects new and strange, to urge us on
With unremitted labour to pursue
Those sacred stores that wait the ripening soul,
In truth's exhaustless bosom. What need words
To paint its pow'r? For this, the daring youth   245
Breaks from his weeping mother's anxious arms,
In foreign climes to rove: the pensive sage
Heedless of sleep, or midnight's harmful damp,
Hangs o'er the sickly taper; and untir'd
The virgin follows, with inchanted step,   250
The mazes of some wild and wond'rous tale,
From morn to eve; unmindful of her form,
Unmindful of the happy dress that stole
The wishes of the youth, when every maid
With envy pin'd. Hence finally, by night   255
The village-matron, round the blazing hearth,
Suspends the infant-audience with her tales,
Breathing astonishment! of witching rhymes,
And evil spirits; of the death-bed call
To him who robb'd the widow, and devour'd   260
The orphan's portion; of unquiet souls
Ris'n from the grave to ease the heavy guilt
Of deeds in life conceal'd; of shapes that walk
At dead of night, and clank their chains, and wave
The torch of hell around the murd'rer's bed.   265
At every solemn pause the croud recoil
Gazing each other speechless, and congeal'd
With shiv'ring sighs: till eager for th'event,
Around the beldame all arrect they hang,
Each trembling heart with grateful terrors quell'd.   270

But lo! disclos'd in all her smiling pomp,
Where BEAUTY onward moving claims the verse
Her charms inspire: the freely-flowing verse
In thy immortal praise, O form divine,
Smooths her mellifluent stream. Thee, BEAUTY, thee   275
The regal dome, and thy enlivening ray
The mossy roofs adore: thou, better sun!
For ever beamest on th'enchanted heart
Love, and harmonious wonder, and delight
Poetic. Brightest progeny of heav'n!   280
How shall I trace thy features? where select
The roseate hues to emulate thy bloom?
Haste then, my song, thro' nature's wide expanse,
Haste then, and gather all her comeliest wealth,
Whate'er bright spoils the florid earth contains,   285
Whate'er the waters, or the liquid air,
To deck thy lovely labour. Wilt thou fly

255–70 Imagination as superstition ('old wives' tales').

269 *arrect* 'alert and attentive' (Lat. *arrectus*, '[ears] pricked up').

270 *grateful* 'pleasing'.

286 *liquid* 'clear'.

287–91 The fabled Gardens of the Hesperides beyond the western ocean, where Zeus's golden apples were guarded by the dragon, Ladon.

With laughing Autumn to th'Atlantic isles,
And range with him th'Hesperian field, and see,
Where'er his fingers touch the fruitful grove,   290
The branches shoot with gold; where'er his step
Marks the glad soil, the tender clusters glow
With purple ripeness, and invest each hill
As with the blushes of an evening sky?
Or wilt thou rather stoop thy vagrant plume,   295
Where, gliding thro' his daughter's honour'd shades,
The smooth Penéus from his glassy flood
Reflects purpureal Tempe's pleasant scene?
Fair Tempe! haunt belov'd of sylvan pow'rs,
Of nymphs and fauns; where in the golden age   300
They play'd in secret on the shady brink
With ancient Pan: while round their choral steps
Young hours and genial gales with constant hand
Show'r'd blossoms, odours, show'r'd ambrosial dews,
And spring's Elysian bloom. Her flow'ry store   305
To thee nor Tempe shall refuse; nor watch
Of winged Hydra guard Hesperian fruits
From thy free spoil. O bear then, unreprov'd,
Thy smiling treasures to the green recess
Where young Dione stays. With sweetest airs   310
Intice her forth to lend her angel-form
For beauty's honour'd image. Hither turn
Thy graceful footsteps; hither, gentle maid,
Incline thy polish'd forehead: let thy eyes
Effuse the mildness of their azure dawn;   315
And may the fanning breezes waft aside
Thy radiant locks, disclosing, as it bends
With airy softness from the marble neck,
The cheek fair-blooming, and the rosy lip
Where winning smiles and pleasure sweet as love,   320
With sanctity and wisdom, temp'ring blend
Their soft allurement. Then the pleasing force
Of nature, and her kind parental care,
Worthier I'd sing: then all th'enamour'd youth,
With each admiring virgin to my lyre   325
Should throng attentive, while I point on high
Where beauty's living image, like the morn

---

295 *stoop* 'swoop'; *vagrant plume* 'roving wings' (more
    positive than 14).
296 The river-god Peneus, to save his daughter Daphne
    from Apollo's embraces, turned her into a laurel tree
    (Ovid, *Metamorphoses*, 1:452–567). She is now
    sheltering her father as he flows.
298 *Tempe* The valley of the River Peneus near Mt
    Olympus, celebrated in classical writings for its beauty
    and shade.
302 *Pan* Greek god of shepherds and flocks.

303 *hours* Cf. Gray, *Ode on the Spring*, 1–2.
307 *Hydra* 'dragon'. See 287–91n.
310 *Dione* According to Homer, the mother of Aphrodite,
    and in that regard the origin of beauty. She was
    sometimes identified with her daughter, as here.
314 *polish'd* 'smooth'.
314–22 Akenside seems to be recalling the face of the
    goddess in Botticelli's *Birth of Venus*, now in the Uffizi,
    Florence. See 329–35.

That wakes in Zephyr's arms the blushing May,
Moves onward; or as Venus, when she stood
Effulgent on the pearly car, and smil'd,   330
Fresh from the deep, and conscious of her form,
To see the Tritons tune their vocal shells,
And each cœrulean sister of the flood
With fond acclaim attend her o'er the waves,
To seek th'Idalian bow'r. Ye smiling band   335
Of youths and virgins, who thro' all the maze
Of young desire with rival-steps pursue
This charm of beauty; if the pleasing toil
Can yield a moment's respite, hither turn
Your favourable ear, and trust my words.   340
I do not mean to wake the gloomy form
Of superstition drest in wisdom's garb,
To damp your tender hopes; I do not mean
To bid the jealous thund'rer fire the heav'ns,
Or shapes infernal rend the groaning earth   345
To fright you from your joys: my chearful song
With better omens calls you to the field,
Pleas'd with your gen'rous ardour in the chace,
And warm as you. Then tell me, for you know,
Does beauty ever deign to dwell where health   350
And active use are strangers? Is her charm
Confess'd in aught, whose most peculiar ends
Are lame and fruitless? Or did nature mean
This awful stamp the herald of a lye;
To hide the shame of discord and disease,   355
And catch with fair hypocrisy the heart
Of idle faith? O no! with better cares,
Th'indulgent mother, conscious how infirm
Her offspring tread the paths of good and ill,
By this illustrious image, in each kind   360
Still most illustrious where the object holds
Its native pow'rs most perfect, she by this
Illumes the headlong impulse of desire,
And sanctifies his choice. The generous glebe
Whose bosom smiles with verdure, the clear tract   365
Of streams delicious to the thirsty soul,
The bloom of nectar'd fruitage ripe to sense,
And every charm of animated things,
Are only pledges of a state sincere,
Th'integrity and order of their frame,   370
When all is well within, and every end

---

328 *Zephyr* The west wind.
330 *pearly car* Oyster shell. According to tradition
   Aphrodite sprang from the foam (Gk. *aphros*) of the
   sea.
332 *Tritons* Sea-gods, commonly shown blowing on conch-
   shells.
333 *cœrulean* 'dark blue'.
335 *Idalian bow'r* Venus's sacred grove in Cyprus.

344 *thund'rer* Zeus.
350–1 'Natural health is the just proportion, truth, and
   regular course of things in a constitution. 'Tis the
   inward beauty of the body' (Shaftesbury, *Miscellaneous
   Reflections*, III.2).
352 *peculiar* 'particular'.
364 *generous glebe* 'fertile soil'.
369 *pledges* 'tokens'; *sincere* 'pure' (Lat. *sincerus*).

Accomplish'd. Thus was beauty sent from heav'n,
The lovely ministress of truth and good
In this dark world: for truth and good are one,
And beauty dwells in them, and they in her,   375
With like participation. Wherefore then,
O sons of earth! would you dissolve the tye?
O wherefore, with a rash, imperfect aim,
Seek you those flow'ry joys with which the hand
Of lavish fancy paints each flatt'ring scene   380
Where beauty seems to dwell, nor once inquire
Where is the sanction of eternal truth,
Or where the seal of undeceitful good,
To save your search from folly? Wanting these,
Lo! beauty withers in your void imbrace,   385
And with the glitt'ring of an idiot's toy
Did fancy mock your vows. Nor let the gleam
Of youthful hope that shines upon your hearts,
Be chill'd or clouded at this awful task,
To learn the lore of undeceitful good,   390
And truth eternal. Tho' the pois'nous charms
Of baleful superstition, guide the feet
Of servile numbers, thro' a dreary way
To their abode, thro' desarts, thorns and mire;
And leave the wretched pilgrim all forlorn   395
To muse at last, amid the ghostly gloom
Of graves, and hoary vaults, and cloister'd cells;
To walk with spectres thro' the midnight shade,
And to the screaming owl's accursed song
Attune the dreadful workings of his heart;   400
Yet be not you dismay'd. A gentler star
Your lovely search illumines. From the grove
Where wisdom talk'd with her Athenian sons,
Could my ambitious hand intwine a wreath
Of PLATO's olive with the Mantuan bay,   405
Then should my pow'rful voice at once dispell
These monkish horrors: then in light divine
Disclose th'Elysian prospect, where the steps
Of those whom nature charms, thro' blooming walks,

372–7 In a long note to this passage Akenside quotes
Xenophon's *Memorabilia*: 'Do you imagine, says
Socrates … that what is good is not also beautiful?
Have you not observed that these appearances always
co-incide? Virtue, for instance, in the same respect as to
which we call it good, is ever acknowledg'd to be
beautiful also … The beauty of human bodies
corresponds, in like manner, with that œconomy of
parts which constitutes them good'. Shaftesbury
reworked this: 'what is beautiful is harmonious and
proportionable; what is harmonious and proportionable
is true; and what is at once both beautiful and true is,
of consequence, agreeable and good' (*Miscellaneous
Reflections*, III.2). See also Plato, *Symposium*,
210A–212B. Cf. Keats, *Ode on a Grecian Urn*, 49.

380 *fancy* Here imagination as mere superficial and
temporary appearance.
391–400 'this Poetry … owes its Original to the Darkness
and Superstition of later Ages, when pious Frauds were
made use of to amuse Mankind, and frighten them into
a Sense of their Duty. Our Forefathers … loved to
astonish themselves with the Apprehensions of
Witchcraft, Prodigies, Charms and Enchantments'
(Addison, *Spectator*, 419).
402 *grove* The Akademia, a sacred olive grove near Athens,
where Plato founded his Academy.
405 *Mantuan* Virgil, born near Mantua. The crown of bay-
laurel was a symbol of poetic honours. The lines voice
Akenside's ambitions as a philosopher-poet.

Thro' fragrant mountains and poetic streams,   410
Amid the train of sages, heroes, bards,
Led by their winged Genius and the choir
Of laurell'd science and harmonious art,
Proceed exulting to th'eternal shrine,
Where truth inthron'd with her cœlestial twins,   415
The undivided part'ners of her sway,
With good and beauty reigns. O let not us,
Lull'd by luxurious pleasure's languid strain,
Or crouching to the frowns of bigot-rage,
O let not us a moment pause to join   420
The god-like band. And if the gracious pow'r
That first awaken'd my untutor'd song,
Will to my invocation breathe anew
The tuneful spirit; then thro' all our paths,
Ne'er shall the sound of this devoted lyre   425
Be wanting; whether on the rosy mead,
When summer smiles, to warn the melting heart
Of luxury's allurement; whether firm
Against the torrent and the stubborn hill
To urge bold virtue's unremitted nerve,   430
And wake the strong divinity of soul
That conquers chance and fate; or whether struck
For sounds of triumph, to proclaim her toils
Upon the lofty summit, round her brow
To twine the wreathe of incoruptive praise;   435
To trace her hallow'd light thro' future worlds,
And bless heav'n's image in the heart of man.

Thus with a faithful aim have we presum'd,
Advent'rous, to delineate nature's form;
Whether in vast, majestic pomp array'd,   440
Or drest for pleasing wonder, or serene
In beauty's rosy smile. It now remains,
Thro' various being's fair-proportion'd scale,
To trace the rising lustre of her charms,
From their first twilight, shining forth at length   445
To full meridian splendour. Of degree
The least and lowliest, in th'effusive warmth
Of colours mingling with a random blaze,
Doth beauty dwell. Then higher in the line
And variation of determin'd shape,   450
Where truth's eternal measures mark the bound
Of circle, cube, or sphere. The third ascent

---

419 *crouching* 'cowering'.

428 *luxury* 'self-indulgence'.

435 *incoruptive* 'incorruptible'.

438–9 *presum'd,* / *Advent'rous* Cf. 'Bold deed thou hast presumed, adventurous Eve' (*Paradise Lost*, 9:921).

440–2 A rhetorical *collectio* or gathering together of the three categories just considered: sublime, wonderful, beautiful.

442–86 Evoking the 'scale of beauty', Akenside considers in

ascending order: colour, shape, 'natural concretes' (colour and shape combined), vegetables, animals, minds. Here he is drawing on Plato, Addison, Shaftesbury and Hutcheson. See Alfred O. Aldridge, 'Akenside and the Hierarchy of Beauty', *MLQ*, 8 (1947), pp. 65–7.

451–2 For Hutcheson, 'artificial Forms, Figures, Theorems' constituted 'absolute' beauty (*Inquiry* (1729 edn), p. 15).

Unites this varied symmetry of parts
With colour's bland allurement; as the pearl
Shines in the concave of its azure bed,   455
And painted shells indent their speckled wreathe.
Then more attractive rise the blooming forms
Thro' which the breath of nature has infus'd
Her genial pow'r to draw with pregnant veins
Nutritious moisture from the bounteous earth,   460
In fruit and seed prolific: thus the flow'rs
Their purple honours with the spring resume;
And such the stately tree which autumn bends
With blushing treasures. But more lovely still
Is nature's charm, where to the full consent   465
Of complicated members, to the bloom
Of colour, and the vital change of growth,
Life's holy flame and piercing sense are giv'n,
And active motion speaks the temper'd soul:
So moves the bird of Juno; so the steed   470
With rival ardour beats the dusty plain,
And faithful dogs with eager airs of joy
Salute their fellows. Thus doth beauty dwell
There most conspicuous, ev'n in outward shape,
Where dawns the high expression of a mind: 475
By steps conducting our inraptur'd search
To that eternal origin, whose pow'r,
Thro' all th'unbounded symmetry of things,
Like rays effulging from the parent sun,
This endless mixture of her charms diffus'd.   480
MIND, MIND alone, bear witness, earth and heav'n!
The living fountains in itself contains
Of beauteous and sublime: here hand in hand,
Sit paramount the Graces; here inthron'd,
Cœlestial Venus, with divinest airs,   485
Invites the soul to never-fading joy.
Look then abroad thro' nature, to the range
Of planets, suns, and adamantine spheres
Wheeling unshaken thro' the void immense;
And speak, O man! does this capacious scene   490
With half that kindling majesty dilate
Thy strong conception, as when Brutus rose
Refulgent from the stroke of Cæsar's fate,
Amid the croud of patriots; and his arm

---

459 *genial* 'life-giving'.
462 *purple* 'brightly coloured'.
469 *temper'd* 'the elements harmoniously mixed'.
470 *bird of Juno* The peacock.
473–5 'Beauty has always relation to the *Sense* of some Mind' (Hutcheson, *Inquiry*, Section I.i.1).
481–3 Shaftesbury, following Plato, held that the mind immediately recognizes beauty by reference to an idea of perfection existing within itself: 'Does not the beautiful form … speak the beauty of the design whenever it strikes you? What is it but the design which

strikes? What is it you admire but mind, or the effect of mind?' (*The Moralists*, III.2).
491 *dilate* 'expand'.
492–500 Akenside's note refers to Cicero, *Philippics*, 2:28: 'The moment Caesar was killed … Brutus raised his bloodstained dagger high, called on Cicero [Tully] by name, and congratulated him on the recovery of freedom'. On Akenside's zeal for political liberty, see biographical headnote.
493 *Refulgent* 'radiant'.

Aloft extending, like eternal Jove   495
When guilt brings down the thunder, call'd aloud
On Tully's name, and shook his crimson steel,
And bade the father of his country, hail!
For lo! the tyrant prostrate on the dust,
And Rome again is free? — Is aught so fair   500
In all the dewy landscapes of the spring,
In the bright eye of Hesper or the morn,
In nature's fairest forms, is aught so fair
As virtuous friendship? as the candid blush
Of him who strives with fortune to be just?   505
The graceful tear that streams from other's woes?
Or the mild majesty of private life,
Where peace with ever-blooming olive crowns
The gate; where honour's liberal hands effuse
Unenvy'd treasures, and the snowy wings   510
Of innocence and love protect the scene?
Once more search, undismay'd, the dark profound
Where nature works in secret; view the beds
Of min'ral treasure, and th'eternal vault
That bounds the hoary ocean; trace the forms   515
Of atoms moving with incessant change
Their elemental round; behold the seeds
Of being, and the energy of life
Kindling the mass with ever-active flame:
Then to the secrets of the working mind   520
Attentive turn; from dim oblivion call
Her fleet, ideal band; and bid them, go!
Break thro' time's barrier, and o'ertake the hour
That saw the heav'ns created: then declare
If aught were found in those external scenes   525
To move thy wonder now. For what are all
The forms which brute, unconscious matter wears;
Greatness of bulk, or symmetry of parts?
Not reaching to the heart, soon feeble grows
The superficial impulse; dull their charms,   530
And satiate soon, and pall the languid eye.
Not so the moral species, or the pow'rs
Of genius and design; th'ambitious mind
There sees herself: by these congenial forms
Touch'd and awaken'd; with intenser act   535
She bends each nerve, and meditates well-pleas'd
Her features in the mirror. For of all
Th'inhabitants of earth, to man alone
Creative wisdom gave to lift his eye

---

502 *Hesper* The evening star (Venus).

506 *graceful* Includes the more spiritual sense.

508 *olive* Emblem of peace ('olive branch').

509 *effuse* 'pour out' (Lat. *effundo – effusus*).

512–21 The chaotic seed-bed of nature, the primal stage in the creative process (Ovid, *Metamorphoses*, 1:5–20), was often reworked in terms of literary creativity. Cf. Pope, *The Dunciad*, 1:55–70.

532 *moral species* Akenside now turns from the species (category) of natural philosophy to that of moral philosophy, i.e. the realm of mind and intention. In this, human capacities mirror the divine (533–7).

534 *congenial* 'kindred'.

535 *act* This presupposes volition or 'will' (541) as distinguished from mere 'impulse' (116). Akenside has now moved to mental *activity* rather than *responsiveness*.

To truth's eternal measures; thence to frame   540
The sacred laws of action and of will,
Discerning justice from unequal deeds,
And temperance from folly. But beyond
This energy of truth, whose dictates bind
Assenting reason, the benignant sire,   545
To deck the honour'd paths of just and good,
Has added bright imagination's rays:
Where virtue rising from the awful depth
Of truth's mysterious bosom, doth forsake
The unadorn'd condition of her birth;   550
And dress'd by fancy in ten thousand hues,
Assumes a various feature, to attract,
With charms responsive to each gazer's eye,
The hearts of men. Amid his rural walk,
Th'ingenuous youth whom solitude inspires   555
With purest wishes, from the pensive shade
Beholds her moving, like a virgin-muse
That wakes her lyre to some indulgent theme
Of harmony and wonder: while among
The herd of servile minds, her strenuous form   560
Indignant flashes on the patriot's eye,
And thro' the rolls of memory appeals
To ancient honour; or in act serene,
Yet watchful, raises the majestic sword
Of publick pow'r, from dark ambition's reach   565
To guard the sacred volume of the laws.

    Genius of ancient Greece! whose faithful steps
Well-pleas'd I follow thro' the sacred paths
Of nature and of science; nurse divine
Of all heroic deeds and fair desires!   570
O! let the breath of thy extended praise
Inspire my kindling bosom to the height
Of this untemper'd theme. Nor be my thoughts
Presumptuous counted, if, amid the calm
That sooths this vernal evening into smiles,   575
I steal impatient from the sordid haunts
Of strife and low ambition, to attend
Thy sacred presence in the sylvan shade,
By their malignant footsteps ne'er profan'd.

---

540 *measures* 'criteria', 'standards of judgement'.

542 *unequal* 'unjust'.

548–9 'According to the opinion of those who assert *moral obligation* to be founded on an immutable and universal law, and that pathetic feeling which is usually call'd the moral sense, to be determin'd by the peculiar temper of the imagination and the earliest associations of ideas' (Akenside's note).

551 An idea treated more negatively by Pope in *Epistle to Cobham*: 'All Manners take a tincture from our own, / Or come discolour'd thro' our Passions shown. / Or Fancy's beam enlarges, multiplies, / Contracts, inverts, and gives ten thousand dyes' (25–8).

557 *her* i.e. virtue (548). Milton invokes the natural beauty of virtue when Satan longs for Eve: 'abashed the devil stood, / And felt how awful goodness is, and saw / Virtue in her shape how lovely, saw, and pined / His loss' (*Paradise Lost*, 4:846–9).

560 *strenuous* 'vigorous'.

573 *untemper'd* 'immoderate'.

Descend, propitious! to my favour'd eye;   580
Such in thy mien, thy warm, exalted air,
As when the Persian tyrant, foil'd and stung
With shame and desperation, gnash'd his teeth
To see thee rend the pageants of his throne;
And at the lightning of thy lifted spear   585
Crouch'd like a slave. Bring all thy martial spoils,
Thy palms, thy laurels, thy triumphal songs,
Thy smiling band of arts, thy godlike sires
Of civil wisdom, thy heroic youth
Warm from the schools of glory. Guide my way   590
Thro' fair Lycéum's walk, the green retreats
Of Academus, and the thymy vale,
Where oft inchanted with Socratic sounds,
Ilissus pure devolv'd his tuneful stream
In gentler murmurs. From the blooming store   595
Of these auspicious fields, may I unblam'd
Transplant some living blossoms to adorn
My native clime: while far above the flight
Of fancy's plume aspiring, I unlock
The springs of ancient wisdom; while I join   600
Thy name, thrice honour'd! with th'immortal praise
Of nature; while to my compatriot youth
I point the high example of thy sons,
And tune to Attic themes the British lyre.

582 *Persian tyrant* Xerxes, defeated by the Greeks at Salamis in 480 BC.

591 *Lycéum* The sacred grove and gymnasium near Athens where Aristotle taught.

592 *Academus* See 402–3.

594 *Ilissus* 'One of the rivers on which *Athens* was situated. *Plato*, in some of the finest dialogues, lays the scene of the conversation with *Socrates* on its banks' (Akenside's note).

Thomas Gray (1716–1771)

In the decades after 1750 Gray's reputation as a poet soared, and the author of the *Elegy* and the *Odes* ranked for many second only to Milton. Yet during years when the reading public were rediscovering the *furor poeticus* this shy scholar, disconcerted by his fame, refused to be the natural genius or wild visionary. A bookish youth at Eton, and an elegant Latinist at Peterhouse, Cambridge (1734–8), Gray intended to study the law; but in 1739 his horizons suddenly expanded when his friend Horace Walpole sought his company on the Grand Tour to Italy. Gray was deeply stirred by the landscape, history and art, and was swept, sometimes awkwardly, into the social whirl that surrounded the Prime Minister's son. After two happy years, chiefly spent in Florence and Rome, there was a sudden quarrel and in late summer 1741 Gray made his way home alone. Within a short time his father died, and his mother and her two sisters settled together in the village of Stoke Poges, Buckinghamshire. During the long summer vacations of the 1740s and 1750s this village with its old churchyard and surrounding beech woods was Gray's second home. Now back in England he found a soul-mate in Richard West (at school Gray, West, Walpole and Thomas Ashton had formed 'The Quadruple Alliance') and he began sending him Latin poetry. West's death in June 1742 affected Gray deeply. He returned that autumn to Cambridge as a Fellow-Commoner, and for most of his remaining life he made the university his home. He graduated Bachelor of Laws in 1743 and thereafter lived the life of a don, but without the teaching and administrative commitments of a formal fellowship. Gray had also been writing poetry in English, but with little thought of publication. Like many other younger poets of the 1740s he was brought into the limelight by the bookseller Robert Dodsley, who published the *Eton Ode* (1747) and included some of Gray's work in his *Collection of Poems* (1748). However, it was the *Elegy* in 1751 that brought Gray instant national fame. Dodsley continued to lavish care on his star author with *Designs by Mr. R. Bentley for Six Poems by Mr. T. Gray* (1753), a volume that treats Gray as a 'classic' text, spaciously printed and with the most handsome engravings. This status was confirmed by the *Odes* (1757), poems in the lofty Pindaric style which few understood but many admired, and Gray seemed to be

confirming himself as the second Milton. But such a role was not for him, and at this point his creative urges ceased. At the age of forty he turned his back on a poetic career. In the same year he declined the offer of the Poet Laureateship.

In 1756 Gray moved from Peterhouse to Pembroke College and became absorbed in his researches for a history of poetry, but the project eventually lapsed. Three of the ten items that make up his collected poems of 1768 were pioneering verse translations from Old Icelandic and Welsh: *The Fatal Sisters*, *The Descent of Odin* and *The Triumphs of Owen*. Gray's manuscripts, especially his extensive commonplace book still at Pembroke, testify to the thoroughness and obsessive precision of his studies, which as well as the classical, Welsh and Northern languages, included music, natural science and botany, English antiquities, and architectural history. None of this scholarly work was published. In 1768 he was appointed Regius Professor of Modern History, but never gave any lectures. By his death in 1771 only fourteen short poems of his had appeared in print.

Gray was a learned and shy man who spent much of his life in academic circles, and this image seems to have dominated criticism of his poetry. But other images of him need to be allowed to register. He had a rich sense of humour, a delight in gossip, in music and the theatre; he was deeply stirred by mountain landscapes and fascinated by the minute life he observed under his microscope; he enjoyed travelling around Britain to explore new places, and had devoted friends to whom he wrote some of the finest letters in the language: witty, hilarious, enraptured, satirical, moving. A criticism of Gray's poetry that cannot draw on such complexities and connect up his fastidiousness and deep feeling, precision and verbal energy, will fall short. Locating Gray's place in literary history has caused problems for critics; those who see him as a staging post between the 'Augustan' Pope and the 'Romantic' Wordsworth tend to neuroticize his work as being the product of uncertainty and frustration. An alternative is to see him as a figure linking those great classical poets of passionate purity, Milton and Keats. Neither is the 'correct' view, but each illuminates a different side of Gray's work.

Ode on the Spring

The transcript in Gray's commonplace book is headed 'Noon-Tide, An Ode'. Under the title 'Ode' it was first printed in Dodsley's *Collection of Poems* (1748),

2:265–7. The poem was written at the height of Gray's revived friendship with Richard West ('Favonius') in response to a poem regretting the lateness of the spring which West had sent him on 5 May 1742: 'Dear Gray, that always in my heart / Possessest far the better part, … / … O join with mine thy tuneful lay, / And invocate the tardy May' (*Correspondence*, 1:201). The transcript, however, carries Gray's poignant note: 'at Stoke, the beginning of June, 1742. sent to Fav: not knowing he was then Dead'. On its completion Gray had sent the poem to West, but it was returned to him unopened, West having died on 1 June, aged twenty-five. The ironies of the ode are lighter and more sportive, and Gray's self-consciousness at playing the rustic moralist adds an extra dimension. Text from *Designs by Mr. R. Bentley* (1753), where the poem is entitled simply 'Ode'.

Lo! where the rosy-bosom'd Hours,
Fair VENUS' train appear,
Disclose the long-expecting flowers,
And wake the purple year!
The Attic warbler pours her throat,   5
Responsive to the cuckow's note,
The untaught harmony of spring:
While whisp'ring pleasure as they fly,
Cool Zephyrs thro' the clear blue sky
Their gather'd fragrance fling.   10

Where'er the oak's thick branches stretch
A broader browner shade;
Where'er the rude and moss-grown beech
O'er-canopies the glade;
Beside some water's rushy brink   15
With me the Muse shall sit, and think
(At ease reclin'd in rustic state)
How vain the ardour of the Crowd,
How low, how little are the Proud,
How indigent the Great!   20

Still is the toiling hand of Care:
The panting herds repose:
Yet hark, how thro' the peopled air
The busy murmur glows!
The insect youth are on the wing,   25
Eager to taste the honied spring,
And float amid the liquid noon:
Some lightly o'er the current skim,
Some shew their gayly-gilded trim
Quick-glancing to the sun.   30

1 *Hours* The 'horai', Greek goddesses of the seasons, who attended Aphrodite (Venus).
2 *VENUS* Here 'Venus Genetrix', the universal mother, goddess of the earth's fertility, richness and variety. She is celebrated at the opening of Lucretius's *De Rerum Natura*.
4 *purple* 'richly coloured'.
5 *Attic warbler* Nightingale.
9 *Zephyrs* The west winds.
11–16 The traditional setting for a poetic meditation. The stanza particularly recalls the melancholy Jaques in *As You Like It*, II.i (see Myrddin Jones, 'Gray, Jaques, and the Man of Feeling', *Review of English Studies*, 25

(1974), pp. 39–48). Cf. *Elegy Written in a Country Church Yard*, 101–4.
20 *indigent* 'lacking'.
23 *peopled* Cf. 'the green myriads in the peopled grass' (Pope, *Essay on Man*, 1:210).
25 Cf. 'And fair-fac'd youth is ever on the wing' (Richard West, *Ad Amicos*, 56). See headnote to *Sonnet on the Death of Richard West*.
27 *liquid* 'bright and clear' (Lat. *liquidus*).
30 Cf. 'sporting with quick glance / Show to the sun their waved coats dropped with gold' (*Paradise Lost*, 7:405–6).

To Contemplation's sober eye
Such is the race of Man:
And they that creep, and they that fly,
Shall end where they began.
Alike the Busy and the Gay   35
But flutter thro' life's little day,
In fortune's varying colours drest:
Brush'd by the hand of rough Mischance,
Or chill'd by age, their airy dance
They leave, in dust to rest.   40

Methinks I hear in accents low
The sportive kind reply:
Poor moralist! and what art thou?
A solitary fly!
Thy Joys no glittering female meets,   45
No hive hast thou of hoarded sweets,
No painted plumage to display:
On hasty wings thy youth is flown;
Thy sun is set, thy spring is gone —
We frolick, while 'tis May.   50

Sonnet on the Death of Richard West

See previous headnote. Gray's transcript in his commonplace book carries the note: 'at Stoke, Aug: 1742'. The poem was first printed after Gray's death in his *Poems* (1775). On 4 July 1737 West had sent Gray an English poem, *Ad Amicos* ('to my friends'), picturing his own death: 'The world will pass as chearful as before, / Bright as before the day-star will appear, / The fields as verdant, and the skies as clear … Unknown and silent will depart my breath, / Nor Nature e'er take notice of my death' (*Correspondence*, 1:63). Gray makes this indifference the theme of his sonnet. It plays against the intensity of his own feelings, the search for an object amid the endless cycle of the natural world. The rising of the blushing young god has an especial irony. Text from commonplace book, p. 284, where it is entitled 'Sonnet'.

In vain to me the smileing Mornings shine,
And redning Phœbus lifts his golden Fire:
The Birds in vain their amorous Descant joyn;
Or chearful Fields resume their green Attire:
These Ears, alas! for other Notes repine,   5
A different Object do these Eyes require.
My lonely Anguish melts no Heart, but mine;
And in my Breast the imperfect Joys expire.
Yet Morning smiles the busy Race to chear,
And new-born Pleasure brings to happier Men: 10
The Fields to all their wonted Tribute bear:
To warm their little Loves the Birds complain:
I fruitless mourn to him, that cannot hear,
And weep the more, because I weep in vain.

2 *Phœbus* As the youthful God of Light associated with the sun, Apollo was named 'Phœbus' ('the bright one').
3 *Descant* 'soaring accompaniment'. Cf. *Paradise Lost*, 4:603.

6 *require* Both 'need' and 'search for' (Lat. *requiro*).
11 *wonted* 'customary'.

Ode on a Distant Prospect of Eton College

In Gray's commonplace book the poem follows *Ode on the Spring* and precedes the West sonnet. Like the sonnet it is dated 'at Stoke, Aug: 1742', but it would seem to have been completed first. There it is entitled: 'Ode. on a distant Prospect of Windsor, & the adjacent Country'. It was published by Dodsley in 1747 as an anonymous folio pamphlet (the earliest of Gray's English poems to be printed), and then included under Gray's name in *Collection of Poems* (1748), 2:261–4. In the commonplace book it is accompanied by a rueful Greek quotation from Menander ('I am a man – sufficient reason to be sad'), and this became the poem's motto in the 1768 edition. A contemporary of Gray's at Eton recalled in 1798: 'both Mr. Gray and his friend [Walpole] were looked upon as too delicate, upon which account they had few associates, and never engaged in any exercise, nor partook of any boyish amusement' (*Gentleman's Magazine*, NS 25 (1846), p. 141). The ode makes an interesting pairing with the West sonnet. In this poem external Nature is supplanted by a tortured projection of the inner world; objectless cycle is now fatalistic progress. A *Paradise Lost* in miniature, the poem moves between Eden and Hell, exploring the interplay of innocence and ignorance, and with knowledge once more holding the key. Text from *1753*.

Ye distant spires, ye antique towers,
That crown the watry glade,
Where grateful Science still adores
Her HENRY's holy Shade;
And ye, that from the stately brow   5
Of WINDSOR's heights th'expanse below
Of grove, of lawn, of mead survey,
Whose turf, whose shade, whose flowers among
Wanders the hoary Thames along
His silver-winding way.   10

Ah happy hills, ah pleasing shade,
Ah fields belov'd in vain,
Where once my careless childhood stray'd,
A stranger yet to pain!
I feel the gales, that from ye blow,   15
A momentary bliss bestow,
As waving fresh their gladsome wing,
My weary soul they seem to sooth,
And, redolent of joy and youth,
To breath a second spring.   20

Say, Father THAMES, for thou hast seen
Full many a sprightly race
Disporting on thy margent green
The paths of pleasure trace,
Who foremost now delight to cleave   25
With pliant arm thy glassy wave?
The captive linnet which enthrall?
What idle progeny succeed

2 *watry glade* Cf. Pope, *Windsor-Forest*, 128.
3 *Science* 'Knowledge'.
4 King Henry VI (1421–71) founded Eton in 1440. Cf. *Windsor-Forest*, 311–13.
6 Windsor Castle, the royal residence overlooking the Thames opposite Eton.

9 *hoary* 'ancient'.
15 *gales* 'gentle breezes'.
23 *margent* 'bank'. Cf. 'By slow Meander's margent green' (Milton, *Masque*, 231).
26 *glassy wave* Cf. 'the glassy, cool, translucent wave' (*Masque*, 860).

To chase the rolling circle's speed,
Or urge the flying ball?   30

While some on earnest business bent
Their murm'ring labours ply
'Gainst graver hours, that bring constraint
To sweeten liberty:
Some bold adventurers disdain   35
The limits of their little reign,
And unknown regions dare descry:
Still as they run they look behind,
They hear a voice in every wind,
And snatch a fearful joy.   40

Gay hope is theirs by fancy fed,
Less pleasing when possest;
The tear forgot as soon as shed,
The sunshine of the breast:
Theirs buxom health of rosy hue,   45
Wild wit, invention ever-new,
And lively chear of vigour born;
The thoughtless day, the easy night,
The spirits pure, the slumbers light,
That fly th'approach of morn.   50

Alas, regardless of their doom,
The little victims play!
No sense have they of ills to come,
Nor care beyond to-day:
Yet see how all around 'em wait   55
The Ministers of human fate,
And black Misfortune's baleful train!
Ah, shew them where in ambush stand
To seize their prey the murth'rous band!
Ah, tell them, they are men!   60

These shall the fury Passions tear,
The vulturs of the mind,
Disdainful Anger, pallid Fear,
And Shame that sculks behind;

---

29 *rolling circle* Child's hoop.
32 *murm'ring labours* They repeat passages from memory, in preparation for class.
38–9 Cf. Aeneas escaping from Troy: 'I was frightened by every breeze and startled by every sound ... nor did I look back for my lost one, nor cast a thought behind' (*Aeneid*, 2:728, 740–1).
41 *fancy* 'imagination'.
45 *buxom* 'vigorous'.
47 *lively chear* Cf. 'In either cheek depeincten lively cheer' (Spenser, *Shepherd's Calendar*, 'April', 69).

55–80 The emotional torments that come with maturity.
57 *baleful* 'pernicious'.
61–90 Gray's vision recalls the grisly figures that Aeneas encounters in Hades (*Aeneid*, 6:273–81), also Spenser's imitation of the passage for his Cave of Mammon (*Faerie Queene*, II.vii.21–3). Cf. Thomson on the destructive passions, *Spring*, 278–308.
61 *fury Passions* Cf. 'The Fury-passions from that blood began' (Pope, *Essay on Man*, 3:167).

Or pineing Love shall waste their youth, 65
Or Jealousy with rankling tooth,
That inly gnaws the secret heart,
And Envy wan, and faded Care,
Grim-visag'd comfortless Despair,
And Sorrow's piercing dart. 70

Ambition this shall tempt to rise,
Then whirl the wretch from high,
To bitter Scorn a sacrifice,
And grinning Infamy.
The stings of Falshood those shall try, 75
And hard Unkindness' alter'd eye,
That mocks the tear it forc'd to flow;
And keen Remorse with blood defil'd,
And moody Madness laughing wild
Amid severest woe. 80

Lo, in the vale of years beneath
A griesly troop are seen,
The painful family of Death,
More hideous than their Queen:
This racks the joints, this fires the veins, 85
That every labouring sinew strains,
Those in the deeper vitals rage:
Lo, Poverty, to fill the band,
That numbs the soul with icy hand,
And slow-consuming Age. 90

To each his suff'rings: all are men,
Condemn'd alike to groan,
The tender for another's pain;
Th'unfeeling for his own.
Yet ah! why should they know their fate? 95
Since sorrow never comes too late,
And happiness too swiftly flies.
Thought would destroy their paradise.
No more; where ignorance is bliss,
'Tis folly to be wise. 100

---

80 *Amid* (*1747, 1748*) Amidst (*1753*).
81–3 Cf. the 'valley of the shadow of death' (Psalm 23).
The emphasis now shifts to physical pains.
81 Cf. 'I am declin'd / Into the vale of years' (*Othello*,
III.iii.265–6).
98–100 Gray recalls the scene in which Ajax says farewell

to his infant son: 'I may well envy you, for you have no
sense of these evils. Indeed, life is sweetest before the
feelings are awakened (it is pleasantest to be without
thought) and one learns to know joy and pain …
Meanwhile, feed on the light breezes and nurse your
tender life' (Sophocles, *Ajax*, 552–9).

Ode on the Death of a Favourite Cat, Drowned in a Tub of Gold Fishes

The tragic feline belonged to Horace Walpole. Promising his friend a poem of 'condolence', Gray was anxious to get things right: 'it would be a sensible satisfaction to me … to know for certain, who it is I lament. I knew Zara and Selima, (Selima, was it? or Fatima) or rather I knew them both together; for I cannot justly say which was which … one's handsome cat is always the cat one likes best; or, if one be alive and the other dead, it is usually the latter that is the handsomest' (*Correspondence*, 1:271). This combination of levity and sententiousness (being a 'Favourite' is precarious) found its way into the poem. It was completed between *c.*22 February (the date of this letter) and 1 March, when Gray sent it to Walpole. The heroicomical note is struck from the outset, and Selima is Helen of Troy, Eve in Paradise and Pope's Belinda, emblems of pride and beauty awaiting their fall. Roger Lonsdale compares her with Virgil's reckless Camilla (*Aeneid*, 11:759–804), the Volscian queen killed while she is distracted by a warrior's glittering armour – the episode had been moralized by Addison in *Spectator*, 15 as showing woman's love for 'everything that is showy and superficial'. Gray's poem was first printed in Dodsley's *Collection of Poems* (1748), 2:267–9, and was lightly revised for *1753*, the text given here. Substantive variants from *1748* are recorded in the notes.

'Twas on a lofty vase's side,
Where China's gayest art had dy'd
   The azure flowers, that blow;
Demurest of the tabby kind,
The pensive Selima reclin'd,   5
   Gazed on the lake below.

Her conscious tail her joy declar'd;
The fair round face, the snowy beard,
   The velvet of her paws,
Her coat, that with the tortoise vies,   10
Her ears of jet, and emerald eyes,
   She saw; and purr'd applause.

Still had she gaz'd: but 'midst the tide
Two angel forms were seen to glide,
   The Genii of the stream: 15
Their scaly armour's Tyrian hue
Thro' richest purple to the view
   Betray'd a golden gleam.

The hapless Nymph with wonder saw:
A whisker first and then a claw,   20
   With many an ardent wish,
She stretch'd in vain to reach the prize.
What female heart can gold despise?
   What Cat's averse to fish?

Presumptuous Maid! with looks intent   25
Again she stretch'd, again she bent,
   Nor knew the gulf between.
(Malignant Fate sat by, and smil'd)
The slipp'ry verge her feet beguil'd,
   She tumbled headlong in.   30

3 *blow* 'bloom'.
4–5 Cf. Helen on the walls of Troy: 'Meantime the brightest of the Female Kind, / The matchless *Helen* o'er the Walls reclin'd' (Pope, *Iliad*, 3:473–4). Lines 4–5 are transposed in *1748*.
5 *Selima* The heroine of *Tamerlane* (1702), a tragedy by Nicholas Rowe.

6–18 Recalls the narcissism of Eve gazing at her image in the lake, *Paradise Lost*, 4:460–6.
10 *Her* The (*1748*).
14 *angel* beauteous (*1748*).
16 *Tyrian hue* Cf. Pope, *Windsor-Forest*, 142.
24 *averse to* a foe to (*1748*).

Eight times emerging from the flood
She mew'd to ev'ry watry God,
   Some speedy aid to send.
No Dolphin came, no Nereid stirr'd:
Nor cruel *Tom*, nor *Susan* heard.   35
   A Fav'rite has no friend!

From hence, ye Beauties, undeceiv'd,
Know, one false step is ne'er retriev'd,
   And be with caution bold.
Not all that tempts your wand'ring eyes   40
And heedless hearts, is lawful prize;
   Nor all, that glisters, gold.

31 For the proverbial 'Thrice …' Gray substitutes a playful allusion to the cat's nine lives.
32 Cf. the cries of Lodona, *Windsor-Forest*, 197–8.
34 *Dolphin* Arion the semi-mythical Greek poet was rescued from drowning by a dolphin which had been charmed by his singing; *Nereid* a sea-maiden, the daughters of the sea god Nereus.

35 *nor* or (*1753*); *Susan* Harry (*1748*).
36 What fav'rite has a friend! (*1748*).
42 Proverbial. Cf. 'All that glisters is not gold' (*The Merchant of Venice*, II.vii.65).

Elegy Written in a Country Church Yard

When first published as a seven-page pamphlet on 15 February 1751, Gray's *Elegy* achieved immediate fame. It was reprinted in newspapers, magazines and miscellanies, and ran through eight editions by 1753. It is not possible to date Gray's work on the poem with certainty, but Lonsdale (*The Poems of Gray, Collins, and Goldsmith* (1969), pp. 103–10) has made a cogent case for placing its first writing in 1746–7: it seems to be recalling phrases and passages in the verse of Akenside, Collins, the Wartons and others, published during 1743–7. The similarities to Joseph Warton's *Ode to Evening* (see headnote to that poem) would support a date after 4 December 1746. The surviving Eton College MS represents the earliest known version before a major reworking took place, and it was not until 12 June 1750 that Gray sent a copy of the completed poem to Walpole, 'having put an end to a thing, whose beginning you have seen long ago' (*Correspondence*, 1:326). Gray made some corrections and further minor revisions to the *Elegy* for its

inclusion in *Designs by Mr. R. Bentley* (1753), and it is this text that is given here. In extending the *Elegy* beyond the ending he originally envisaged (see note to line 72), Gray added an extra layer of irony. As in *Ode on the Spring* he executes a self-scrutinizing turn, which here places the poet in his own grave, with an illiterate rustic remembering him.

Gray's poem is intensely allusive. In this respect it can be seen as continuing the tradition of pastoral elegy, a genre which as part of its mourning tribute interweaves earlier voices into a garland of allusion. The text of Gray's *Elegy* is in itself an 'ample page / Rich with the spoils of time'. Only a limited number of parallel passages and echoed phrases can be noted here. Lonsdale's 1969 Longman edition (see above) is invaluable in helping the reader appreciate the full tapestry of Gray's poem, and anyone wishing to explore this aspect further should consult his annotations.

The Curfew tolls the knell of parting day,
The lowing herd wind slowly o'er the lea,
The plowman homeward plods his weary way,
And leaves the world to darkness and to me.

Now fades the glimmering landscape on the sight,   5
And all the air a solemn stillness holds,

1 In *1768* Gray acknowledged his source in Dante: 'from afar he hears the bell that seems to mourn the dying

day' (*Purgatorio*, 8:5–6). Gray originally wrote 'dying day'.

Save where the beetle wheels his droning flight,
And drowsy tinklings lull the distant folds;

Save that from yonder ivy-mantled tow'r
The mopeing owl does to the moon complain   10
Of such, as wand'ring near her secret bow'r,
Molest her ancient solitary reign.

Beneath those rugged elms, that yew-tree's shade,
Where heaves the turf in many a mould'ring heap,
Each in his narrow cell for ever laid,   15
The rude Forefathers of the hamlet sleep.

The breezy call of incense-breathing Morn,
The swallow twitt'ring from the straw-built shed,
The cock's shrill clarion, or the ecchoing horn,
No more shall rouse them from their lowly bed.   20

For them no more the blazing hearth shall burn,
Or busy houswife ply her evening care:
No children run to lisp their sire's return,
Or climb his knees the envied kiss to share.

Oft did the harvest to their sickle yield,   25
Their furrow oft the stubborn glebe has broke;
How jocund did they drive their team afield!
How bow'd the woods beneath their sturdy stroke!

Let not Ambition mock their useful toil,
Their homely joys, and destiny obscure;   30
Nor Grandeur hear with a disdainful smile,
The short and simple annals of the poor.

The boast of heraldry, the pomp of pow'r,
And all that beauty, all that wealth e'er gave,
Awaits alike th'inevitable hour.   35
The paths of glory lead but to the grave.

Nor you, ye Proud, impute to These the fault,
If Mem'ry o'er their Tomb no Trophies raise,
Where thro' the long-drawn isle and fretted vault
The pealing anthem swells the note of praise.   40

9–12 Cf. Thomas Warton, *The Pleasures of Melancholy*,
    32–7.
14 Cf. Parnell, *A Night-Piece on Death*, 29–30.
26 *glebe* 'soil'.
33–5 There has been much discussion suggesting that
    'hour' is the subject of the sentence (the hour

awaits …). But Gray seems to be treating 'all' as a
cumulative and powerful singular: everything awaits the
inevitable hour of death.
38 *Trophies* 'carved symbols'.
39 *fretted vault* 'elaborately carved roof'.

Can storied urn or animated bust
Back to its mansion call the fleeting breath?
Can Honour's voice provoke the silent dust,
Or Flatt'ry sooth the dull cold ear of Death?

Perhaps in this neglected spot is laid   45
Some heart once pregnant with celestial fire,
Hands, that the rod of empire might have sway'd,
Or wak'd to extasy the living lyre.

But Knowledge to their eyes her ample page
Rich with the spoils of time did ne'er unroll;   50
Chill Penury repress'd their noble rage,
And froze the genial current of the soul.

Full many a gem of purest ray serene,
The dark unfathom'd caves of ocean bear:
Full many a flower is born to blush unseen,   55
And waste its sweetness on the desert air.

Some village-Hampden, that with dauntless breast
The little Tyrant of his fields withstood;
Some mute inglorious Milton here may rest,
Some Cromwell guiltless of his country's blood.   60

Th'applause of list'ning senates to command,
The threats of pain and ruin to despise,
To scatter plenty o'er a smiling land,
And read their hist'ry in a nation's eyes

Their lot forbad: nor circumscrib'd alone   65
Their growing virtues, but their crimes confin'd;
Forbad to wade through slaughter to a throne,
And shut the gates of mercy on mankind,

The struggling pangs of conscious truth to hide,
To quench the blushes of ingenuous shame,   70
Or heap the shrine of Luxury and Pride
With incense kindled at the Muse's flame.

---

41 *storied* 'telling a story'. Cf. 'storied windows' (Milton, *Il Penseroso*, 159).

43 *provoke* 'call forth' (Lat. *provoco*), as well as the modern sense.

44 *Death?* Death! (*1753*).

46 Cf. 'pregnant with infernal flame' (*Paradise Lost*, 6:483).

52 Cf. *Ode on a Distant Prospect of Eton College*, 89; *genial* 'creative'.

55–6 Cf. Pope, *The Rape of the Lock*, 4:157–8.

57 *Hampden* John Hampden, MP (1594–1643), leading Parliamentary opponent of King Charles I.

60 *Cromwell* Oliver Cromwell (1599–1658), general of the Parliamentary forces during the Civil War and Lord Protector 1653–8. For Hampden, Milton and Cromwell, Gray originally wrote Cato, Tully (Cicero) and Caesar.

67 The image recalls Shakespeare's Richard III and Macbeth.

68 Cf. 'The gates of mercy shall be all shut up' (*Henry V*, III.iii.10).

70 *ingenuous* 'innocent and open'.

71–2 I.e. indulge in poetic flattery of the rich and powerful.

Far from the madding crowd's ignoble strife,
Their sober wishes never learn'd to stray;
Along the cool sequester'd vale of life   75
They kept the noiseless tenor of their way.

Yet ev'n these bones from insult to protect
Some frail memorial still erected nigh,
With uncouth rhimes and shapeless sculpture deck'd,
Implores the passing tribute of a sigh.   80

Their name, their years, spelt by th'unletter'd muse,
The place of fame and elegy supply:
And many a holy text around she strews,
That teach the rustic moralist to dye.

For who to dumb Forgetfulness a prey,   85
This pleasing anxious being e'er resign'd,
Left the warm precincts of the chearful day,
Nor cast one longing ling'ring look behind?

On some fond breast the parting soul relies,
Some pious drops the closing eye requires;   90
Ev'n from the tomb the voice of Nature cries,
Ev'n in our Ashes live their wonted Fires.

For thee, who mindful of th'unhonour'd Dead
Dost in these lines their artless tale relate;
If chance, by lonely contemplation led,   95
Some kindred Spirit shall inquire thy fate,

Haply some hoary-headed Swain may say,
'Oft have we seen him at the peep of dawn
'Brushing with hasty steps the dews away
'To meet the sun upon the upland lawn.   100

72 Here Gray's original version concluded with the
following four stanzas:

The thoughtless World to Majesty may bow
Exalt the brave, & idolize Success
But more to Innocence their Safety owe
Than Power & Genius e'er conspired to bless

And thou, who mindful of the unhonour'd Dead
Dost in these Notes their artless Tale relate
By Night & lonely Contemplation led
To linger in the gloomy Walks of Fate

Hark how the sacred Calm, that broods around
Bids ev'ry fierce tumultuous Passion cease
In still small Accents whisp'ring from the Ground
A grateful Earnest of eternal Peace

No more with Reason & thyself at Strife
Give anxious Cares & endless Wishes room
But thro' the cool sequester'd Vale of Life
Pursue the silent Tenour of thy Doom.
                        (Eton College MS)

73 *madding* 'frenzied'.
85–6 Cf. 'for who would lose, / Though full of pain, this
  intellectual being' (*Paradise Lost*, 2:146–7).
88 Cf. *Ode on a Distant Prospect of Eton College*, 38–9, and
  note.
90 Cf. *Sonnet on the Death of Richard West*, 6.
92 Cf. Lucretius, *De Rerum Natura*, 4:923–8: 'for then the
  Body would lie in the cold Arms of eternal Death; then
  no Part of the Soul would lie retired within the Limbs,
  as a Fire remains covered under a Heap of Ashes; from
  whence the Senses might be kindled again through the
  Body, as a Flame is soon raised from hidden Fire' (1743
  transl.). *wonted* 'accustomed'.
93 The speaker addresses himself. Cf. note to line 72
  (second stanza).
95 *chance* 'perchance'.
97 *hoary-headed* 'grey-haired'.
99 Cf. Thomson, *Spring*, 103–5.

'There at the foot of yonder nodding beech
'That wreathes its old fantastic roots so high,
'His listless length at noontide wou'd he stretch,
'And pore upon the brook that babbles by.

'Hard by yon wood, now smiling as in scorn,   105
'Mutt'ring his wayward fancies he wou'd rove,
'Now drooping, woeful wan, like one forlorn,
'Or craz'd with care, or cross'd in hopeless love.

'One morn I miss'd him on the custom'd hill,
'Along the heath and near his fav'rite tree;   110
'Another came; nor yet beside the rill,
'Nor up the lawn, nor at the wood was he;

'The next with dirges due in sad array
'Slow thro' the church-way path we saw him born.
'Approach and read (for thou can'st read) the lay,   115
'Grav'd on the stone beneath yon aged thorn.'

The EPITAPH.

Here rests his head upon the lap of Earth
A Youth to Fortune and to Fame unknown,
Fair Science frown'd not on his humble birth,
And Melancholy mark'd him for her own.   120

Large was his bounty, and his soul sincere,
Heav'n did a recompence as largely send:
He gave to Mis'ry all he had, a tear,
He gain'd from Heav'n ('twas all he wish'd) a friend.

No farther seek his merits to disclose,   125
Or draw his frailties from their dread abode,
(There they alike in trembling hope repose)
The bosom of his Father and his God.

101–4 Cf. Shakespeare's melancholy Jaques: 'he lay along / Under an oak, whose antique root peeps out / Upon the brook that bawls along this wood' (*As You Like It*, II.i.30–2). See *Ode on the Spring*, 11–16, and note.
112 *he;* he, (*1753*).
116 A further stanza followed, omitted in *1753*: 'There scatter'd oft, the earliest of the Year, / By Hands unseen, are Show'rs of Violets found: / The Red-breast loves to build, & warble there, / And little Footsteps lightly print the Ground.'
117 *lap of Earth* Virgil, *Aeneid*, 3:509 (*gremio telluris*).
119 *Science* 'Knowledge'.
120 *Melancholy* Heightened sensibility. Cf. Thomas Warton, *The Pleasures of Melancholy*, 92–4.

The Progress of Poesy. A Pindaric Ode

The Progress of Poesy and *The Bard* were first published by Horace Walpole at his Strawberry Hill Press as *Odes, by Mr. Gray* (1757). They soon became enormously admired by a baffled reading public ('nobody understands me, & I am perfectly satisfied', Gray wrote to William Mason, 7 September 1757). But the odes' obscurity led to embarrassing mistakes by reviewers and critics, and Gray eventually bowed to pressure by adding footnotes to them for his 1768 *Poems*. Difficulty and daring were thought appropriate for a 'Pindaric', a genre which invited comparison with the most dazzling of Greek lyric writers, Pindar (518–438 BC), whose odes were metrically adventurous (no two used the same metre) and were praised as challenging, fervid and inspired. For his own celebration of poetic power, Gray focuses his *Progress* on the continued inheritance of Ancient Greece, and his debt to Pindar is made explicit; but

Gray also invokes the inspired word of the Hebrew Bible, and the voice of that other great lyricist, King David. The ode to some extent explores its own genealogy as a modern representative of a twin Hellenistic–Hebraic tradition. In its emphasis on voice, it is also able to accommodate the 'primitive' oral poetry of other nations. The poem carries the imprint of Gray's researches into the history of English, or rather British, poetry, an aborted project he worked on between 1753 and 1762.

In his commonplace book Gray entitles the poem *Ode in the Greek Manner*. He adopts the triadic structure of Greek lyric, in which two symmetrical stanzas (the 'strophe' and 'antistrophe' – so called from the chorus dancing to right and left in turn as

they sang) are followed by the 'epode' in a different though related metrical form. Gray marked these in his commonplace book transcript. His ode has three such triads, making nine stanzas in all, and like Pindar's odes it is regular, in that each triad is identical in rhyme and metre.

Annotating Gray's odes poses problems of scope and detail. Once again, Lonsdale's exhaustive commentary would repay study. Here we have tried to be as full as possible within the constraints of space. Gray's own notes are given in italics; some of the more obvious glosses have been omitted, and a few cuts have been made in his notes, indicated by ellipses. Both text and notes are those of *Poems* (1768).

φωνᾶντα συνετοῖσιν ·ἐζ
δὲ τὸ πᾶν ἑρμηνέων χατίζει

I.1

Awake, Æolian lyre, awake,
And give to rapture all thy trembling strings.
From Helicon's harmonious springs
A thousand rills their mazy progress take:
The laughing flowers, that round them blow,   5
Drink life and fragrance as they flow.
Now the rich stream of music winds along
Deep, majestic, smooth, and strong,
Thro' verdant vales, and Ceres' golden reign:
Now rowling down the steep amain,   10
Headlong, impetuous, see it pour:
The rocks, and nodding groves rebellow to the roar.

I.2

Oh! Sovereign of the willing soul,
Parent of sweet and solemn-breathing airs,
Enchanting shell! the sullen Cares,   15
And frantic Passions hear thy soft controul.
On Thracia's hills the Lord of War,
Has curb'd the fury of his car,

Motto Pindar, *Olympian Odes*, 2:85–6 ('vocal to the intelligent alone – for the rest they need interpreters').

1 *Awake, my glory: awake, lute and harp. David's Psalms.* [Psalm 57:8] *Pindar styles his own poetry with its musical accompanyments ... Æolian song. The subject and simile, as usual with Pindar, are united.* (Gray). The 'Aeolian' was a Greek musical scale.

3–12 *The various sources of poetry, which gives life and lustre to all it touches, are here described; its quiet majestic progress ... and its more rapid and irresistible course ...* (Gray).

3 *Helicon* The mountain haunt of the Muses.

5 *blow* 'bloom'.

9 *Ceres* Goddess of the earth's fertility.

10–12 Horace compares Pindar with 'a rushing mountain river which rains have swollen above its banks' (*Odes*, IV.ii.5–6).

10 *amain* 'violently'.

13–24 *Power of harmony to calm the turbulent sallies of the soul* (Gray). Gray gives his source as Pindar, *Pythian Odes*, 1:5–12.

14 Cf. 'a soft and solemn-breathing sound' (Milton, *Masque*, 554).

15–16 Cf. Collins, *The Passions*, 3–4.

17 *Thracia* Thrace was the most northerly part of Greece, considered barbarous by Athenians. *Lord of War* Mars.

18 *car* 'chariot'.

And drop'd his thirsty lance at thy command.
Perching on the scept'red hand   20
Of Jove, thy magic lulls the feather'd king
With ruffled plumes, and flagging wing:
Quench'd in dark clouds of slumber lie
The terror of his beak, and light'nings of his eye.

I.3

Thee the voice, the dance, obey,   25
Temper'd to thy warbled lay.
O'er Idalia's velvet-green
The rosy-crowned Loves are seen
On Cytherea's day
With antic Sports, and blue-eyed Pleasures,   30
Frisking light in frolic measures;
Now pursuing, now retreating,
Now in circling troops they meet:
To brisk notes in cadence beating
Glance their many-twinkling feet.   35
Slow melting strains their Queen's approach declare:
Where'er she turns the Graces homage pay.
With arms sublime, that float upon the air,
In gliding state she wins her easy way:
O'er her warm cheek, and rising bosom, move   40
The bloom of young Desire, and purple light of Love.

II.1

Man's feeble race what Ills await,
Labour, and Penury, the racks of Pain,
Disease, and Sorrow's weeping train,
And Death, sad refuge from the storms of Fate!   45
The fond complaint, my Song, disprove,
And justify the laws of Jove.
Say, has he giv'n in vain the heav'nly Muse?
Night, and all her sickly dews,
Her Spectres wan, and Birds of boding cry,   50
He gives to range the dreary sky:
Till down the eastern cliffs afar
Hyperion's march they spy, and glitt'ring shafts of war.

---

21 *Jove* Jupiter (Gk. *Zeus*); *feather'd king* Cf. 'the eagle, feath'red king' (Shakespeare, *The Phoenix and Turtle*, 11).

25 *Power of harmony to produce all the graces of motion in the body* (Gray). Gray moves on to poetic rhythm.

26 *Temper'd* 'attuned'.

27–9 Aphrodite (Venus) is frequently called 'Idalian' or 'Cytherean' after places associated with her. She reputedly came ashore on the island of Cythera off the southern tip of the Greek mainland.

35 Gray compares *Odyssey*, 8:265 ('with feet that seemed to twinkle as they moved').

37 The three Graces who personify life's grace and beauty, and become symbols of gratitude; they particularly accompany the Muses and Aphrodite.

42–5 Cf. *Ode on a Distant Prospect of Eton College*, 61–90.

42–53 *To compensate the real and imaginary ills of life, the Muse was given to Mankind by the same Providence that sends the Day by its chearful presence to dispel the gloom and terrors of the Night* (Gray).

46 *fond* 'foolish'.

48 *heav'nly Muse* Urania, Muse of Astronomy; as divine vision she is invoked at the opening of Milton's *Paradise Lost*.

53 *Hyperion* The sun.

II.2

In climes beyond the solar road,
Where shaggy forms o'er ice-built mountains roam,   55
The Muse has broke the twilight-gloom
To chear the shiv'ring Native's dull abode.
And oft, beneath the od'rous shade
Of Chili's boundless forests laid,
She deigns to hear the savage Youth repeat   60
In loose numbers wildly sweet
Their feather-cinctured Chiefs, and dusky Loves.
Her track, where'er the Goddess roves,
Glory pursue, and generous Shame,
Th' unconquerable Mind, and Freedom's holy flame.   65

II.3

Woods, that wave o'er Delphi's steep,
Isles, that crown th'Egæan deep,
Fields, that cool Ilissus laves,
Or where Mæander's amber waves
In lingering Lab'rinths creep,   70
How do your tuneful Echoes languish,
Mute, but to the voice of Anguish?
Where each old poetic Mountain
Inspiration breath'd around:
Ev'ry shade and hallow'd Fountain   75
Murmur'd deep a solemn sound:
Till the sad Nine in Greece's evil hour
Left their Parnassus for the Latian plains.
Alike they scorn the pomp of tyrant-Power,
And coward Vice, that revels in her chains.   80
When Latium had her lofty spirit lost,
They sought, oh Albion! next thy sea-encircled coast.

III.1

Far from the sun and summer-gale,
In thy green lap was Nature's Darling laid,
What time, where lucid Avon stray'd,   85

54–65 *Extensive influence of poetic Genius over the remotest and most uncivilized nations: its connection with liberty, and the virtues that naturally attend on it (See the Erse, Norwegian, and Welch Fragments, the Lapland and American songs.)* (Gray). By the Erse fragments Gray means *Fragments of Ancient Poetry* (1760) – see headnote to James Macpherson.

60 *repeat* 'celebrate'.

62 *cinctured* 'belted'. Cf. 'the American so girt / With feathered cincture, naked else and wild' (*Paradise Lost*, 9:1116–17). Cf. also Pope, *Windsor-Forest*, 404, 410.

63 *Goddess* The Muse.

63–5 *Her track … pursue* Gray's Latinate word-order reverses object and verb.

65 Cf. 'the unconquerable will' (*Paradise Lost*, 1:106).

66–82 *Progress of Poetry from Greece to Italy, and from Italy to England. Chaucer was not unacquainted with the writings of Dante or of Petrarch. The Earl of Surrey and Sir Tho. Wyatt had travelled to Italy, and formed their taste there; Spenser imitated the Italian writers; Milton improved on them: but this School expired soon after the Restoration, and a new one arose on the French model, which has subsisted ever since* (Gray).

66–70 Lonsdale notes that these are Greek poetic landscapes associated with lyric (the Aegean islands), tragedy (Athens) and epic (Asia Minor). *Mæander* A river in Turkey noted for its winding course.

77 *Nine* The Muses.

78 *Parnassus* Apollo's mountain overlooking Delphi. *Latian* 'Roman'.

82 *Albion* Britain.

83–8 Shakespeare as a child of nature. Cf. Joseph Warton, *The Enthusiast*, 169–79.

To Him the mighty Mother did unveil
Her aweful face: The dauntless Child
Stretch'd forth his little arms, and smiled.
This pencil take (she said) whose colours clear
Richly paint the vernal year: 90
Thine too these golden keys, immortal Boy!
This can unlock the gates of Joy;
Of Horrour that, and thrilling Fears,
Or ope the sacred source of sympathetic Tears.

III.2

Nor second He, that rode sublime   95
Upon the seraph-wings of Extasy,
The secrets of th'Abyss to spy.
He pass'd the flaming bounds of Place and Time:
The living Throne, the saphire-blaze,
Where Angels tremble, while they gaze,   100
He saw; but blasted with excess of light,
Closed his eyes in endless night.
Behold, where Dryden's less presumptuous car,
Wide o'er the fields of Glory bear
Two Coursers of ethereal race,   105
With necks in thunder cloath'd, and long-resounding pace.

III.3

Hark, his hands the lyre explore!
Bright-eyed Fancy hovering o'er
Scatters from her pictur'd urn
Thoughts, that breath, and words, that burn.   110
But ah! 'tis heard no more —
Oh! Lyre divine, what daring Spirit
Wakes thee now? tho' he inherit
Nor the pride, nor ample pinion,

---

86 *mighty Mother* Cybele, the Roman 'magna mater', goddess of untamed nature. Cf. Pope, *The Dunciad*, 1:1.

89 *pencil* 'artist's paintbrush'.

90 *vernal year* Springtime.

95–102 Milton as poet of the Sublime. Cf. Isaac Watts, *The Adventurous Muse*, 35–55.

97 Cf. Satan's flight, 'To wing the desolate abyss, and spy / This new created world' (*Paradise Lost*, 4:936–7).

99 Gray compares the sapphire throne of Ezekiel, 1:26. Cf. Collins, *Ode on the Poetical Character*, 32.

102 Cf. Dryden's description of the dying Dido, who 'closed her Lids at last, in endless Night' (*Aeneid*, 4:993). Milton was completely blind from the age of forty-four.

105–6 *Meant to express the stately march and sounding energy of Dryden's rhimes* (Gray). *Coursers* Horses bred for speed.

106 Gray compares 'Hast thou given the horse strength? hast thou clothed his neck with thunder?' (Job, 39:19). Pope praised Dryden's 'full resounding line' (*Imitations of Horace, Epistle* II.i.268).

108 *Fancy* 'Imagination'.

111 *We have had in our language no other odes of the sublime kind, than that of Dryden on St. Cecilia's day: for Cowley (who had his merit) yet wanted judgment, style, and harmony, for such a task. That of Pope is not worthy of so great a man. Mr. Mason [Gray's friend William Mason] indeed of late days has touched the true chords, and with a masterly hand, in some of his Choruses …* (Gray).

112–13 A similar question is asked by Collins, *Ode on the Poetical Character*, 51–4.

113 *he* Gray himself.

114 *pinion* 'wing'.

That the Theban Eagle bear   115
Sailing with supreme dominion
Thro' the azure deep of air:
Yet oft before his infant eyes would run
Such forms, as glitter in the Muse's ray
With orient hues, unborrow'd of the Sun: 120
Yet shall he mount, and keep his distant way
Beyond the limits of a vulgar fate,
Beneath the Good how far — but far above the Great.

115 *Pindar compares himself to that bird, and his enemies to*
ravens that croak and clamour in vain below, while it
pursues its flight, regardless of their noise (Gray).

The Bard. A Pindaric Ode

See previous headnote. During his researches into literary history Gray became engrossed in early British poetry and made extensive notes on the Welsh bards and the old Celtic language. His imagination was caught by the native oral tradition that existed before Wales was conquered by the English King, Edward I (1239–1307). In an Advertisement prefixed to *The Bard* he notes: 'The following Ode is founded on a Tradition current in Wales, that EDWARD THE FIRST, when he compleated the conquest of that country, ordered all the Bards, that fell into his hands, to be put to death'. (In fact, as Gray later discovered, Edward had merely imposed restrictions on their movement round the country and their asking for money from the people.) Gray's widely admired ode offered its early readers an image of the poet as prophet and persecuted outsider, and it recaptured qualities of sound and vision associated with the pre-literary. As the bard arouses the dead poets who had given Wales its independent identity it is clear that the ode also laments a lost tradition and a dispersed community. Gray's sole remaining voice plunges to

his death, but within a few years other writers, notably Macpherson and Chatterton, would be stirred by the possibilities such figures offered, and would attempt to reconstruct, as authentically as possible, the voices and communities of the past.

Gray began work on the ode early in 1755, but by October he had broken off after completing only a few lines of the third strophe (i.e. to line 100 or 104) and nothing further was done for eighteen months. But in the spring of 1757 he was galvanized into action by an encounter with the genuine bardic tradition. The blind Welsh harper, John Parry (d. 1782), visited Cambridge and 'scratch'd out such ravishing blind Harmony, such tunes of a thousand year old with names enough to choak you, as have set all this learned body a'dancing' (Gray–Mason, [24/31] May 1757). Within a month *The Bard* was completed, and it was published later that year along with *The Progress of Poesy*.

Both text and notes given here are those of *Poems* (1768). A few of Gray's notes have been shortened where indicated.

I.1

'Ruin seize thee, ruthless King!
'Confusion on thy banners wait,
'Tho' fann'd by Conquest's crimson wing
'They mock the air with idle state.
'Helm, nor Hauberk's twisted mail,   5
'Nor even thy virtues, Tyrant, shall avail
'To save thy secret soul from nightly fears,
'From Cambria's curse, from Cambria's tears!'
Such were the sounds, that o'er the crested pride

4 In a note Gray compares 'Mocking the air with colors idlely spread' (Shakespeare, *King John*, V.i.72).
5 *The Hauberk was a texture of steel ringlets, or rings*

interwoven, forming a coat of mail, that sate close to the body, and adapted itself to every motion (Gray).
8 *Cambria* Wales.

Of the first Edward scatter'd wild dismay, 10
As down the steep of Snowdon's shaggy side
He wound with toilsome march his long array.
Stout Glo'ster stood aghast in speechless trance:
To arms! cried Mortimer, and couch'd his quiv'ring lance.

I.2

On a rock, whose haughty brow 15
Frowns o'er old Conway's foaming flood,
Robed in the sable garb of woe,
With haggard eyes the Poet stood;
(Loose his beard, and hoary hair
Stream'd, like a meteor, to the troubled air) 20
And with a Master's hand, and Prophet's fire,
Struck the deep sorrows of his lyre.
'Hark, how each giant-oak, and desert cave,
'Sighs to the torrent's aweful voice beneath!
'O'er thee, oh King! their hundred arms they wave, 25
'Revenge on thee in hoarser murmurs breath;
'Vocal no more, since Cambria's fatal day,
'To high-born Hoël's harp, or soft Llewellyn's lay.

I.3

'Cold is Cadwallo's tongue,
'That hush'd the stormy main: 30
'Brave Urien sleeps upon his craggy bed:
'Mountains, ye mourn in vain
'Modred, whose magic song
'Made huge Plinlimmon bow his cloud-top'd head.
'On dreary Arvon's shore they lie, 35
'Smear'd with gore, and ghastly pale:
'Far, far aloof th'affrighted ravens sail;
'The famish'd Eagle screams, and passes by.
'Dear lost companions of my tuneful art,

---

11 Snowdon *was a name given by the Saxons to that mountainous tract, which the Welch themselves call* Craigian-eryri: *it included all the highlands of Caernarvonshire and Merionethshire, as far east as the river Conway* (Gray).

13 *Gilbert de Clare* [1243–95], *surnamed the Red, Earl of Gloucester and Hertford, son-in-law to King Edward* (Gray).

14 *Edmond de Mortimer, Lord of Wigmore. They both were Lords-Marchers, whose lands lay on the borders of Wales, and probably accompanied the King in this expedition* (Gray). Gray actually means Roger de Mortimer (?1231–82), sixth Baron Wigmore. *couch'd* 'lowered into an attacking position'.

18 *haggard* 'A metaphor taken from an unreclaim'd Hawk, wch is call'd a *Haggard*, & looks wild & *farouche* & jealous of its liberty' (Gray–Wharton, 21 August 1755).

19–20 *The image was taken from a well-known picture of Raphaël, representing the Supreme Being in the vision of Ezekiel* ... (Gray). It is now in the Pitti, Florence. *hoary* 'grey'.

20 Gray compares: 'Shone like a meteor streaming to the wind' (*Paradise Lost*, 1:537).

28–34 The bard's roll-call of the other slaughtered bards is fictitious, but Gray uses genuine names.

34 *Plinlimmon* A mountain in central Wales.

35 *The shores of Caernarvonshire opposite to the isle of Anglesey* (Gray).

38 *Cambden and others observe, that eagles used annually to build their aerie among the rocks of Snowdon, which from thence (as some think) were named by the Welch Craigian-eryri, or the crags of the eagles. At this day (I am told) the highest point of Snowdon is called* the eagle's nest ... (Gray).

'Dear, as the light that visits these sad eyes,   40
'Dear, as the ruddy drops that warm my heart,
'Ye died amidst your dying country's cries —
'No more I weep. They do not sleep.
'On yonder cliffs, a griesly band,
'I see them sit, they linger yet,   45
'Avengers of their native land:
'With me in dreadful harmony they join,
'And weave with bloody hands the tissue of thy line.'

II.1
"Weave the warp, and weave the woof,
"The winding-sheet of Edward's race.   50
"Give ample room, and verge enough
"The characters of hell to trace.
"Mark the year, and mark the night,
"When Severn shall re-eccho with affright
"The shrieks of death, thro' Berkley's roofs that ring,   55
"Shrieks of an agonizing King!
"She-Wolf of France, with unrelenting fangs,
"That tear'st the bowels of thy mangled Mate,
"From thee be born, who o'er thy country hangs
"The scourge of Heav'n. What Terrors round him wait!   60
"Amazement in his van, with Flight combined,
"And Sorrow's faded form, and Solitude behind.

II.2
"Mighty Victor, mighty Lord,
"Low on his funeral couch he lies!
"No pitying heart, no eye, afford   65
"A tear to grace his obsequies.
"Is the sable Warriour fled?
"Thy son is gone. He rests among the Dead.
"The Swarm, that in thy noon-tide beam were born?
"Gone to salute the rising Morn.   70
"Fair laughs the Morn, and soft the Zephyr blows,

40–1 Gray compares: 'As dear to me as are the ruddy drops / That visit my sad heart' (*Julius Caesar*, II.i.289–90). Cf. also 'thou / Revisit'st not these eyes' (*Paradise Lost*, 3:22–3).

43 In his copy of *Odes* Gray notes this 'double cadence' as an imitation of a Welsh metre, but also as intending to lend 'a wild spirit and variety to the Epode'. There are other examples in the poem. See Lonsdale, p. 188.

47–8 Gray also notes: 'The image is taken from an ancient Scaldic Ode, written in the old-Norwegian tongue about A:D:1029'. This was translated by him as *The Fatal Sisters* (1761). See Lonsdale, pp. 189, 210–20.

48 *tissue* 'richly interwoven cloth'.

49 The dead bards join in chorus, and in lines 49–100 prophesy the calamities that await England and Edward I's descendants. *warp* The fixed thread; *woof* The cross thread.

54–5 *Edward the Second, cruelly butchered in Berkley-Castle*

(Gray). Berkeley is near the River Severn. The King was murdered there in 1327.

57 *Isabel of France, Edward the Second's adulterous Queen* (Gray). Isabella (1292–1358) procured her husband's murder and with Roger Mortimer virtually ruled England during her son's minority, 1327–30.

59 *Triumphs of Edward the Third in France* (Gray).

61 *in his van* 'going before him'.

64 *Death of that King* [1377], *abandoned by his Children, and even robbed in his last moments by his Courtiers and his Mistress* (Gray).

66 *obsequies* 'funeral'.

67 *Edward, the Black Prince* [1330–76], *dead some time before his Father* (Gray).

71 *Magnificence of Richard the Second's reign* [1377–99]. *See Froissart, and other contemporary Writers* (Gray). *Zephyr* West wind.

"While proudly riding o'er the azure realm
"In gallant trim the gilded Vessel goes;
"Youth on the prow, and Pleasure at the helm;
"Regardless of the sweeping Whirlwind's sway,   75
"That, hush'd in grim repose, expects his evening-prey.

II.3

"Fill high the sparkling bowl,
"The rich repast prepare,
"Reft of a crown, he yet may share the feast:
"Close by the regal chair   80
"Fell Thirst and Famine scowl
"A baleful smile upon their baffled Guest.
"Heard ye the din of battle bray,
"Lance to lance, and horse to horse?
"Long Years of havock urge their destined course,   85
"And thro' the kindred squadrons mow their way.
"Ye Towers of Julius, London's lasting shame,
"With many a foul and midnight murther fed,
"Revere his Consort's faith, his Father's fame,
"And spare the meek Usurper's holy head.   90
"Above, below, the rose of snow,
"Twined with her blushing foe, we spread:
"The bristled Boar in infant-gore
"Wallows beneath the thorny shade.
"Now, Brothers, bending o'er th'accursed loom   95
"Stamp we our vengeance deep, and ratify his doom.

III.1

"Edward, lo! to sudden fate
"(Weave we the woof. The thread is spun)
"Half of thy heart we consecrate.
"(The web is wove. The work is done.)"   100
'Stay, oh stay! nor thus forlorn

77 *Richard the Second, (as we are told by Archbishop Scroop
and the confederate Lords in their manifesto, by Thomas of
Walsingham, and all the older Writers,) was starved to
death. The story of his assassination by Sir Piers of
Ex[t]on is of much later date* (Gray).
81 *Fell* 'fierce'.
82 *baleful* 'malignant'.
86 *kindred squadrons* The descendants of the two brothers,
Dukes of York and Lancaster, sons of Edward III. The
Wars of the Roses were a prolonged power struggle
between the two houses, 1455–85.
87 *Henry the Sixth, George Duke of Clarence, Edward the
Fifth, Richard Duke of York, &c. believed to be murthered
secretly in the Tower of London. The oldest part of that
structure is vulgarly attributed to Julius Caesar* (Gray).
89 *Consort* Queen (here Margaret, King Henry VI's wife).
Father King Henry V (d. 1422). *Margaret of Anjou, a
woman of heroic spirit, who struggled hard to save her
Husband and her Crown* (Gray).

90 *Henry the Sixth very near being canonized. The line of
Lancaster had no right of inheritance to the Crown*
(Gray). Cf. *Ode on a Distant Prospect of Eton College*, 4.
91 *The white and red roses, devices of York and Lancaster*
(Gray).
93 *The silver Boar was the badge of Richard the Third;
whence he was usually known in his own time by the name
of* the Boar (Gray). *infant-gore* Richard's supposed
responsibility for the murder of the princes in the
Tower.
99 *Eleanor of Castile died a few years after the conquest of
Wales. The heroic proof she gave of her affection for her
Lord is well known* … (Gray). Eleanor (d. 1290), queen
of Edward I, is said to have saved his life by sucking
poison from a wound.
101 The bard now addresses the chorus. He looks forward
to the time (1485) when the Welsh house of Tudor will
restore the 'Briton-line', and poetry will reach its
consummation in Spenser, Shakespeare and Milton.

'Leave me unbless'd, unpitied, here to mourn:
'In yon bright track, that fires the western skies,
'They melt, they vanish from my eyes.
'But oh! what solemn scenes on Snowdon's height　　　　105
'Descending slow their glitt'ring skirts unroll?
'Visions of glory, spare my aching sight,
'Ye unborn Ages, crowd not on my soul!
'No more our long-lost Arthur we bewail.
'All-hail, ye genuine Kings, Britannia's Issue, hail!　　　110

III.2

'Girt with many a Baron bold
'Sublime their starry fronts they rear;
'And gorgeous Dames, and Statesmen old
'In bearded majesty, appear.
'In the midst a Form divine!　　　　115
'Her eye proclaims her of the Briton-Line;
'Her lyon-port, her awe-commanding face,
'Attemper'd sweet to virgin-grace.
'What strings symphonious tremble in the air,
'What strains of vocal transport round her play!　　　　120
'Hear from the grave, great Taliessin, hear;
'They breathe a soul to animate thy clay.
'Bright Rapture calls, and soaring, as she sings,
'Waves in the eye of Heav'n her many-colour'd wings.

III.3

'The verse adorn again　　　　125
'Fierce War, and faithful Love,
'And Truth severe, by fairy Fiction drest.
'In buskin'd measures move
'Pale Grief, and pleasing Pain,
'With Horrour, Tyrant of the throbbing breast.　　　　130
'A Voice, as of the Cherub-Choir,
'Gales from blooming Eden bear;
'And distant warblings lessen on my ear,

109　*It was the common belief of the Welch nation, that King Arthur was still alive in Fairy-Land, and should return again to reign over Britain* (Gray).

110　*Both Merlin and Taliessin had prophesied, that the Welch should regain their sovereignty over this island; which seemed to be accomplished in the House of Tudor* (Gray). *All-hail* Recalls the greeting of the witches in *Macbeth*: 'All hail, hail to thee …' (*Macbeth*, I.iii.48). In IV.i they show Macbeth a pageant of eight future kings, descendents of Banquo.

112　*fronts* 'foreheads'. Cf. Christ's 'starry front' in Milton, *The Passion*, 18.

117　Gray's note here quotes a historian describing the 'lion-like' dignity of the Tudor Queen, Elizabeth I (1533–1603).

121　*Taliessin, chief of the Bards, flourished in the VIth*

Century. His works are still preserved, and his memory held in high veneration among his Countrymen (Gray). The manuscript 'Book of Taliesin' is a thirteenth-century collection of poems by various authors and from different periods.

125–7　The subject and object of the sentence are inverted. Gray alludes to Spenser and the opening stanza of his *Faerie Queene*: 'Fierce warres and faithful loves shall moralize my song'.

128　*Shakespear* (Gray); *buskin* The high boot worn by tragic actors on the Athenian stage. Cf. 'the buskined stage' (Milton, *Il Penseroso*, 102).

131　*Milton* (Gray). Cf. 'choirs of cherubim' (*Paradise Lost*, 3:666).

133　*The succession of Poets after Milton's time* (Gray).

'That lost in long futurity expire.
'Fond impious Man, think'st thou, yon sanguine cloud,   135
'Rais'd by thy breath, has quench'd the Orb of day?
'To-morrow he repairs the golden flood,
'And warms the nations with redoubled ray.
'Enough for me: With joy I see
'The different doom our Fates assign.   140
'Be thine Despair, and scept'red Care,
'To triumph, and to die, are mine.'
He spoke, and headlong from the mountain's height
Deep in the roaring tide he plung'd to endless night.

134 'why you would alter *lost* in long futurity I do not see, unless becáuse you think *lost* & *expire* are tautologous, or because it looks as if the end of the prophecy were disappointed by it, & that people may think Poetry in Britain was some time or other really to expire: whereas the meaning is only, that it was lost to his ear from the immense distance. I can not give up *lost*, for it begins with an L' (Gray–Mason, 11 June 1757).

135 *sanguine* 'blood-red'.

137 *repairs* 'renews'.

William Collins (1721–1759)

Among the young poets of the 1740s William Collins's voice is the most elusive and difficult. The earlier critical obsession with his madness and instability has thankfully subsided, and the emphasis has shifted from the visual to the aural dimension of his work. The wild visionary can now be more subtly appreciated as a voice steeped in the tradition of the Greek lyric singer. Born in Chichester, Sussex, the son of a prosperous hatter and Mayor of the town, Collins was sent to Winchester College in 1734, where he became a close friend of Joseph Warton. Poems by the two schoolboys were jointly published in the *Gentleman's Magazine* in October 1739, and the following year both went up to Oxford. Like the Warton brothers Collins published his first volume while an undergraduate: his anonymous *Persian Eclogues* (1742) are a set of exotic pastorals written in a 'rich and figurative style' and intended (according to the preface) to challenge the coolness of English taste. After graduating in 1743, Collins settled in London as a 'literary adventurer, with many projects in his head, and very little money in his pocket' (Johnson). He made proposals for a 'History of the Revival of Learning', undertook a translation of Aristotle's *Poetics*, and planned a tragedy for Drury Lane, but none of these ambitions materialized. By May 1746 Collins and Warton were planning a joint volume of odes, but Collins's *Odes on Several Descriptive and Allegoric Subjects* came out separately on 20 December (with '1747' on the title page). One of the earliest readers was Thomas Gray, who wrote to a friend on 27 December: 'Have you seen the Works of two young Authors, a Mr Warton & a Mr Collins, both Writers of Odes? it is odd enough, but each is the half of a considerable Man, & one the Counter-Part of the other. the first has but little Invention, very poetical choice of Expression, & a good Ear. the second [Collins], a fine Fancy, model'd upon the Antique, a bad Ear, great Variety of Words, & Images with no Choice at all. they both deserve to last some Years, but will not.' Unlike Warton's, Collins's *Odes* did not reach a second edition (indeed, he later destroyed all the unsold copies which he had generously bought from the publisher). In 1749 financial pressures were lifted by a bequest of £2,000 from his uncle, but this does not seem to have brought his major projects any nearer completion. Some further poetry was however being written in which Collins developed his sense of an animated, mystical Nature: his *Ode Occasion'd by the Death of Mr Thomson* (1749) evokes the poet's spirit now absorbed into the natural scene; and his longest poem (not printed until 1788), *Ode on the Popular Superstitions of the Highlands*, offers a weird and enchanted Scottish landscape stalked by the ghosts of history. At this point Collins's literary career petered out. Almost nothing is known of him during the period 1751–3, except that he became seriously ill and travelled in France to restore his health. By 1754 the picture has suddenly darkened. He spent a month in Oxford, but according to Thomas Warton was 'so weak and low, that he could not bear conversation'. Another friend recalled seeing him 'in a very affecting situation, struggling, and conveyed by force, in the arms of two or three men'. After a period at a madhouse in Chelsea, he moved to live with his sister in the cathedral cloisters at Chichester. Here he would occasionally 'rave much & make great Moanings', but in his calm and lucid intervals would have the Bible read to him. He died on 12 June 1759.

Three of Collins's odes were printed in Dodsley's *Collection* (2nd edn, 1748), but generally his work remained ignored until John Langhorne's edition of his *Poetical Works* in 1765. Langhorne's book, with its rapturous commentary on the poet's sublime imagination, went through further editions, and by the 1780s Collins's odes were highly esteemed. Anna Laetitia Barbauld brought out a further edition in 1797. The intense visionary lyricism won admirers among the Romantics: the young Coleridge preferred Collins's odes to those of Gray, and in 1818 Hazlitt declared: 'He leaves stings in the minds of his readers, certain traces of thought and feelings which never wear out'.

Ode on the Poetical Character

Like Gray's *The Progress of Poesy* (1757), Collins's ode engages with questions of poetic continuity and inheritance. It is driven by a conviction that poetry has lost touch with its true nature as an inspired, imaginative and prophetic power; Collins therefore attempts to return to the native visionary tradition of Spenser and Milton. Crucial to this is his rejection of Waller (69), whom many saw as the inaugurator of a 'French School' of correctness and wit (Dryden, Addison, Prior and Pope) which had held sway since the Restoration of 1660. But Collins's myth of poetic power as an imaginative gift of divine origin makes his own position ambiguous. His rapt and eagle-eyed vision would seem to claim the magic belt for himself, yet the dramatic 'In vain' (72) declares such ambitions to be no longer attainable. The ode offers an interesting comparison with Gray's view of his poetic inheritance in the final stanza of the *Progress*. The text is that of *Odes* (1747), pp. 14–18, the first and only printing in Collins's lifetime. Unfortunately the printer overlooked the fact that sections 1 and 3 of the poem (strophe and antistrophe) are metrically identical. In our text some minor adjustments in layout have been made to bring them into line with each other. Placed either side of a simple middle section of sixteen octosyllabic (four-stress) couplets, each consists of four octosyllabic couplets followed by fourteen intricately rhymed lines patterned in four and five stresses with a final alexandrine (six stresses).

> As once, if not with light Regard,
> I read aright that gifted Bard,
> (Him whose School above the rest
> His Loveliest *Elfin* Queen has blest.)
> One, only One, unrival'd Fair,   5
> Might hope the magic Girdle wear,
> At solemn Turney hung on high,
> The Wish of each love-darting Eye;
>
> Lo! to each other Nymph in turn applied,
> As if, in Air unseen, some hov'ring Hand,   10
> Some chaste and Angel-Friend to Virgin-Fame,
> With whisper'd Spell had burst the starting Band,
> It left unblest her loath'd dishonour'd Side;
>   Happier hopeless Fair, if never
>   Her baffled Hand with vain Endeavour   15
> Had touch'd that fatal Zone to her denied!
> Young *Fancy* thus, to me Divinest Name,
>   To whom, prepar'd and bath'd in Heav'n,
>   The Cest of amplest Pow'r is giv'n:
> To few the God-like Gift assigns,   20
> To gird their blest prophetic Loins,
> And gaze her Visions wild, and feel unmix'd her Flame!
>
>   2
> The Band, as Fairy Legends say,
> Was wove on that creating Day,
> When He, who call'd with Thought to Birth   25
> Yon tented Sky, this laughing Earth,
> And drest with Springs, and Forests tall,
> And pour'd the Main engirting all,
> Long by the lov'd *Enthusiast* woo'd,

1–22 An extended reference to the episode of the belt, or 'Cestus', of Venus in Spenser's *Faerie Queene*. The belt represents 'chaste love' (IV.v.3), so that 'whosoever contrarie doth prove, / Might not the same about her middle weare'. Many of the most beautiful women compete for it, but only Amoret is able to fix it round her waist. In Spenser's story the belt is finally returned to its rightful owner, Florimell, the type of chaste and virtuous love (V.iii.27–8). Collins uses it here to symbolize poetic power: in his myth the 'Cest' is entrusted to 'Fancy' (Imagination) who grants the divine gift to very few.

7 *Turney* 'tournament'.
16 *Zone* 'belt'.
22 *gaze* 'gaze on'.
24 *creating Day* The fourth day of Creation (Genesis 1:14–19).
26 *tented* 'stretched like a canopy'.
28 *Main* 'ocean'.
29 *Enthusiast* 'one divinely inspired or possessed', i.e. Fancy. Joseph Warton addresses her as 'O warm, enthusiastic maid' in *Ode to Fancy*, 117.

Himself in some Diviner Mood,   30
Retiring, sate with her alone,
And plac'd her on his Saphire Throne,
The whiles, the vaulted Shrine around,
Seraphic Wires were heard to sound,
Now sublimest Triumph swelling,   35
Now on Love and Mercy dwelling;
And she, from out the veiling Cloud,
Breath'd her magic Notes aloud:
And Thou, Thou rich-hair'd Youth of Morn,
And all thy subject Life was born!   40
The dang'rous Passions kept aloof,
Far from the sainted growing Woof:
But near it sate Ecstatic *Wonder*,
List'ning the deep applauding Thunder:
And *Truth*, in sunny Vest array'd,   45
By whose the Tarsel's Eyes were made;
All the shad'wy Tribes of *Mind*,
In braided Dance their Murmurs join'd,
And all the bright uncounted *Pow'rs*,
Who feed on Heav'n's ambrosial Flow'rs.   50
Where is the Bard, whose Soul can now
Its high presuming Hopes avow?
Where He who thinks, with Rapture blind,
This hallow'd Work for Him design'd?

3

High on some Cliff, to Heav'n up-pil'd,   55
Of rude Access, of Prospect wild,
Where, tangled round the jealous Steep,
Strange Shades o'erbrow the Valleys deep,
And holy *Genii* guard the Rock,
Its Gloomes embrown, its Springs unlock,   60
While on its rich ambitious Head,
An *Eden*, like his own, lies spread.

I view that Oak, the fancied Glades among,
By which as *Milton* lay, His Ev'ning Ear,
From many a Cloud that drop'd Ethereal Dew,   65

---

32 *Saphire Throne* Alludes to Ezekiel's vision of 'the glory of the Lord' when he received his prophecy (Ezekiel, 1:26). Cf. Gray, *The Progress of Poesy*, 99.

34 *Wires* 'harp strings'.

39 *Youth of Morn* A figure who recalls the Greek god Apollo, embodiment of youth, beauty, poetry, prophecy and (as Phoebus Apollo) the sun (Cf. Gray, *Sonnet on the Death of Richard West*, 2). Collins's ode draws on each of these attributes. This power, with all his 'subject Life' (everything over which he presides), is the offspring of the divinely inspired Fancy.

42 *sainted growing Woof* The sacred fabric of the belt, which is being woven on this day.

44 *List'ning* 'listening to'.

45–6 Truth as the companion of Imagination, not its enemy. Cf. Akenside, *The Pleasures of Imagination*, 1:21–3.

46 *Tarsel* Tercel, or male hawk.

48 *braided* 'intricate'.

50 *ambrosial* 'divinely scented'.

52 *avow* 'affirm' or 'maintain' (with something of the older sense of 'consecrate').

54 *hallow'd Work* Belt.

55–62 Cf. Milton's Garden of Eden, *Paradise Lost*, 4:132–45. This passage answers the 'where?' of line 51.

57 *jealous* 'protective'.

63 *Oak* At Dodona, a sanctuary of Zeus, the oracle's prophecies came from a sacred oak.

Nigh spher'd in Heav'n its native Strains could hear:
On which that ancient Trump he reach'd was hung;
   Thither oft his Glory greeting,
   From *Waller*'s Myrtle Shades retreating,
With many a Vow from Hope's aspiring Tongue,   70
My trembling Feet his guiding Steps pursue;
   In vain — Such Bliss to One alone,
   Of all the Sons of Soul was known,
   And Heav'n, and *Fancy*, kindred Pow'rs,
   Have now o'erturn'd th'inspiring Bow'rs,   75
Or curtain'd close such Scene from ev'ry future View.

66 *its native Strains* Milton's immortal soul recognizes the celestial harmonies of its divine birthplace.

67 The trumpet hanging from an oak suggests an instrument of prophecy.

69 *Waller's Myrtle Shades* Edmund Waller (1606–87), admired for his smooth love poetry (the myrtle was sacred to Venus). The phrase recalls Milton's refusal to 'sport with Amaryllis in the shade' (*Lycidas*, 68), i.e. indulge in amorous verses.

75 Cf. Sir Guyon's destruction of the Bower of Bliss, an artificial paradise of self-indulgence (*Faerie Queene*, II.xii.83).

Ode to Evening

Although Collins and Joseph Warton intended to publish their odes jointly, their voices are markedly different, as a comparison of their respective odes to evening will reveal. Where Warton composes a harmonious mood-picture, Collins's sinuous syntax conducts us on a more wide-ranging quest for an elusive goddess. For his poem Collins adopts the metre invented by Milton for a translation of Horace's 'Pyrrha' ode (*Odes*, 1:5), alternating pairs of five- and three-stress lines ('without rhyme according to the Latin measure' as Milton noted). Collins's poem was first printed in *Odes* (1747), pp. 36–8, and was then revised for inclusion in Robert Dodsley's *Collection of Poems*, 2nd edn (1748), 1:331–2 (the text given here). Readers will note the more selective capitalization, compared with the *Odes* text of the other Collins items. The trend during the century was increasingly towards modern practice, and the house style of Dodsley's *Collection* was influential. This was the text in which the poem first reached a wide public. The earlier 1747 readings are listed in the separate Textual Notes.

If ought of oaten stop, or pastoral song,
May hope, chaste EVE, to sooth thy modest ear,
   Like thy own solemn springs,
   Thy springs, and dying gales,
O NYMPH reserv'd, while now the bright-hair'd sun   5
Sits in yon western tent, whose cloudy skirts,
   With brede ethereal wove,
   O'erhang his wavy bed:
Now air is hush'd, save where the weak-ey'd bat,
With short shrill shriek flits by on leathern wing,   10

1 *oaten stop* Finger-holes in the reed pipe of the shepherd-poet. Cf. 'sound of pastoral reed with oaten stops' (Milton, *Masque*, 344).

4 *dying gales* Cf. Pope, *Eloisa to Abelard*, 159.

5–8 Cf. 'the sun in bed, / Curtained with cloudy red' (Milton, *Nativity Ode*, 229–30).

7 *brede* 'embroidery' (of sunset colours). Cf. *Ode to Liberty*, 103–4.

10 Cf. 'the lether-winged Batt' (Spenser, *Faerie Queene*, II.xii.36).

Or where the Beetle winds
His small but sullen horn,
As oft he rises 'midst the twilight path,
Against the pilgrim born in heedless hum:
    Now teach me, Maid compos'd,   15
    To breathe some soften'd strain,
Whose numbers stealing thro' thy darkning vale,
May not unseemly with its stillness suit,
    As musing slow, I hail
    Thy genial lov'd return!   20
For when thy folding star arising shews
His paly circlet, at his warning lamp
    The fragrant Hours, and Elves
    Who slept in flow'rs the day,
And many a Nymph who wreaths her brows with sedge,   25
And sheds the fresh'ning dew, and lovelier still,
    The PENSIVE PLEASURES sweet
    Prepare thy shadowy car.
Then lead, calm Vot'ress, where some sheety lake
Cheers the lone heath, or some time-hallow'd pile,   30
    Or up-land fallows grey
    Reflect its last cool gleam.
But when chill blust'ring winds, or driving rain,
Forbid my willing feet, be mine the hut,
    That from the mountain's side,   35
    Views wilds, and swelling floods,
And hamlets brown, and dim-discover'd spires,
And hears their simple bell, and marks o'er all
    Thy dewy fingers draw
    The gradual dusky veil.   40
While Spring shall pour his show'rs, as oft he wont,
And bathe thy breathing tresses, meekest Eve!
    While Summer loves to sport,
    Beneath thy ling'ring light;
While sallow Autumn fills thy lap with leaves;   45
Or Winter yelling thro' the troublous air,
    Affrights thy shrinking train,
    And rudely rends thy robes;

11–14 Cf. Gray, *Elegy*, 7; also Milton, *Lycidas*, 28 ('the grey-fly winds her sultry horn').

14 *pilgrim* 'traveller'.

17 *numbers* 'notes' (also used for poetic metre).

21 *folding star* The Evening Star signalling the shepherd to pen his sheep. Cf. 'The star that bids the shepherd fold' (*Masque*, 93).

23 *Hours* Here miniaturized. Cf. Gray, *Ode on the Spring*, 1.

29 *Vot'ress* A woman leading a life of dedication or religious observance.

30 *pile* 'building'.

31 *fallows* Ploughed land left to lie fallow. Cf. 'fallows grey' (Milton, *L'Allegro*, 71).

32 The word *its* has aroused critical debate, and an emendation to *thy* has been suggested. But this is unnecessary. Collins does seem to be recording the last glimmer of the evening light, and if so, then *its* can be taken (as Lonsdale suggests) to refer back to Evening's 'shadowy car' (i.e. the shadows moving across the scene).

41 *as oft he wont* 'as his custom often is'.

45 *sallow* 'brownish yellow'.

48 Cf. 'Her looser golden lockes he rudely rent' (*Faerie Queene*, II.i.11).

So long, sure-found beneath the Sylvan shed,
Shall FANCY, FRIENDSHIP, SCIENCE, rose-lip'd HEALTH,　　　　50
Thy gentlest influence own,
And hymn thy fav'rite name!

49 *Sylvan* 'woodland' (after Silvanus, god of the woods).
50 *SCIENCE* 'Learning'.

TEXTUAL NOTES
　　The substantive variants with *1747* are as follows: **2**
May hope, O pensive *Eve*, to sooth thine Ear (*1747*); **3**
solemn (*1748*) brawling (*1747*); **24** flow'rs (*1748*) Buds
(*1747*); **29–32** Then let me rove some wild and heathy

Scene, / Or find some Ruin 'midst its dreary Dells, /
Whose Walls more awful nod / By thy religious
Gleams. (*1747*) [NB 'it's' (*1748*) has been corrected to
'its']; **33** But when (*1748*) Or if (*1747*); **34** Forbid
(*1748*) Prevent (*1747*); **49** So long regardful of thy quiet
Rule, (*1747*); **50** rose-lip'd HEALTH (*1748*) smiling *Peace*
(*1747*); **52** hymn (*1748*) love (*1747*).

Ode to Liberty

Collins's invocation of Liberty exploits the potential
of the ode form to make a public political statement. It
combines a sweep across history with a focused
concern for an immediate national issue. It was
evidently written during the autumn of 1746 shortly
after the capture of Genoa (see lines 46–9), when
preliminary peace negotiations held out hope for an
end to the European war that had begun in 1740. (The
'War of the Austrian Succession' was finally
concluded by the Treaty of Aix-La-Chapelle, 1748.)
The ode opens with warlike notes but ends on a vision
of peace: the amorous British youths (139) form a
vivid contrast to the warlike young Spartans (3), yet
both are preoccupied with beautiful hair. In the
course of the poem Liberty is invited to accommodate
another more pleasing figure, Concord, as the classical
tradition reconciles itself to the native Gothic.
Influential on the shape of this ode was James

Thomson's *Liberty, A Poem* (five parts, 1735–6),
which traced Liberty 'from the first Ages [in Greece
and Rome] down to her excellent Establishment in
Great Britain', but also stressed how easily national
freedoms might be lost and civilized values decay. The
Jacobite uprising of 1745 with its terrible aftermath at
Culloden (April 1746) was raising urgent questions
about British nationhood, and in autumn 1746 young
men who had followed the *Tartan* (not Spartan) Fife
were being publicly executed across the land. This
difficult and allusive ode has not been highly regarded
by critics; but its intricate dynamics are fascinating.
The poem negotiates between idealism and
pragmatism, continuity and separation, legend and
fact, and it does not merely celebrate its goddess, but
also tests and challenges her. The text is that of the
first printing, *Odes* (1747), pp. 22–31.

STROPHE
Who shall awake the *Spartan* Fife,
And call in solemn Sounds to Life,
The Youths, whose Locks divinely spreading,
　　Like vernal Hyacinths in sullen Hue,
At once the Breath of Fear and Virtue shedding,　　　　5
　　Applauding *Freedom* lov'd of old to view?

1–6 The Greek city state of Sparta, 'the sober, hard, /
And Man-subduing City; which no Shape / Of Pain
could conquer, nor of Pleasure charm' (Thomson,
Liberty, 2:111–13). Spartan youths were dedicated to
the military life until the age of thirty. Their soldiers
went into battle to the sound of flutes (here 'fife') after

the ritual combing of their hair (Herodotus, 7:208–9).
Sparta was admired in the eighteenth century for its
system of government: 'Each Power so checking, and
supporting, Each / That firm for Ages, and unmov'd, it
stood' (*Liberty*, 2:117–18).
　4 *vernal* 'spring'.

What New *Alcæus*, Fancy-blest,
Shall sing the Sword, in Myrtles drest,
    At *Wisdom*'s Shrine a-while its Flame concealing,
(What Place so fit to seal a Deed renown'd?)   10
    Till she her brightest Lightnings round revealing,
It leap'd in Glory forth, and dealt her prompted Wound!
    O Goddess, in that feeling Hour,
    When most its Sounds would court thy Ears,
        Let not my Shell's misguided Pow'r,   15
    E'er draw thy sad, thy mindful Tears.
No, *Freedom*, no, I will not tell,
How *Rome*, before thy weeping Face,
With heaviest Sound, a Giant-statue, fell,
Push'd by a wild and artless Race,   20
From off its wide ambitious Base,
When Time his Northern Sons of Spoil awoke,
    And all the blended Work of Strength and Grace,
    With many a rude repeated Stroke,
And many a barb'rous Yell, to thousand Fragments broke.   25

EPODE
2.

Yet ev'n, where'er the least appear'd,
Th'admiring World thy Hand rever'd;
Still 'midst the scatter'd States around,
Some Remnants of Her Strength were found;
They saw by what escap'd the Storm,   30
How wond'rous rose her perfect Form;
How in the great the labour'd Whole,
Each mighty Master pour'd his Soul!
For sunny *Florence*, Seat of Art,
Beneath her Vines preserv'd a part,   35
Till They, whom Science lov'd to name,
(O who could fear it?) quench'd her Flame.
And lo, an humbler Relick laid
In jealous *Pisa*'s Olive Shade!
See small *Marino* joins the Theme,   40
Tho' least, not last in thy Esteem:
Strike, louder strike th'ennobling Strings

7–12 The first move to overthrow tyranny in Athens was made by two lovers, Harmodius and Aristogeiton, who in 514 BC tried to assassinate the tyrant brothers, Hipparchus and Hippias, at the Panathenaea (the festival in honour of Athena, patron goddess of Athens and the personification of Wisdom). Hipparchus was killed, but Hippias survived and Harmodius and Aristogeiton were put to death. The pair became celebrated as Athens' own freedom-fighters. A song praising their exploits survives (Athenaeus, *Deipnosophistæ*, 15:695), beginning 'In a myrtle-branch I will carry my sword'. In the eighteenth century the song was wrongly attributed to Alcaeus.
13–25 The sack of Rome by the Goths in 410 AD.

15 *Shell* 'lyre'. See *The Passions*, 3.
26–33 Fragments of classical culture remained scattered over Europe.
36 *They* 'The Family of the *Medici*' (Collins). Patrons of learning ('Science'), the Medici were the ruling family of Florence and later Dukes of Tuscany, from 1434 to 1737.
39 Pisa briefly recovered its independence from Florence, 1494–1509. It had been annexed in 1406.
40 *Marino* 'The little Republic of *San Marino*' (Collins). It had survived a threat to its independence, 1739–40.
42–5 The Venetian Republic. At the annual wedding ceremony between Venice and the sea, the Doge (chief magistrate) cast a gold ring into the Adriatic.

To those, whose Merchant Sons were Kings;
To Him, who deck'd with pearly Pride,
In *Adria* weds his green-hair'd Bride;   45
Hail Port of Glory, Wealth, and Pleasure,
Ne'er let me change this *Lydian* Measure:
Nor e'er her former Pride relate,
To sad *Liguria*'s bleeding State.
Ah no! more pleas'd thy Haunts I seek,   50
On wild *Helvetia*'s Mountains bleak:
(Where, when the favor'd of thy Choice,
The daring Archer heard thy Voice;
Forth from his Eyrie rous'd in Dread,
The rav'ning *Eagle* northward fled.)   55
Or dwell in willow'd Meads more near,
With Those to whom thy Stork is dear:
Those whom the Rod of *Alva* bruis'd,
Whose Crown a *British* Queen refus'd!
The Magic works, Thou feel'st the Strains,   60
One holier Name alone remains;
The perfect Spell shall then avail,
Hail Nymph, ador'd by *Britain*, Hail!

ANTISTROPHE

Beyond the Measure vast of Thought,
The Works, the Wizzard *Time* has wrought!   65
   The *Gaul*, 'tis held of antique Story,
Saw *Britain* link'd to his now adverse Strand,
   No Sea between, nor Cliff sublime and hoary,
He pass'd with unwet Feet thro' all our Land.

46–9 The city state of Genoa ('Liguria') had been captured by Britain's ally, Austria, on 6 September 1746. The Genoese expelled the Austrians with considerable slaughter on 5 December. Collins's ode was evidently completed by then.

47 *Lydian Measure* The Lydian mode in Greek music was conducive to softness and relaxation; it was condemned by Plato for being effeminate, but valued by Aristotle and others for delightful recreation. There appears to be a contradiction with 'ennobling' (42), which was the tendency of the Dorian mode, of which Plato approved. Cf. Joseph Warton, *The Enthusiast*, 86 and note.

50–5 Switzerland ('Helvetia') fought for its independence from Austria (whose emblem is the eagle) in the fourteenth century, with the help of the legendary archer William Tell. Those in Britain who wished to continue the European war did so on the grounds of supporting Austria, so Collins's instances of Austrian aggression (cf. Genoa above) make a political point.

56–9 The United Provinces, or 'Spanish Netherlands'. The Duke of Alva (1508–82) suppressed Dutch

independence in 1567, driving thousands of Protestant Huguenots to England. Queen Elizabeth I supported the Provinces, but diplomatically turned down their offer of the crown.

57 'The *Dutch*, amongst whom there are very severe Penalties for those who are convicted of killing this Bird. They are kept tame in almost all their Towns, and particularly at the *Hague*, of the Arms of which they make a Part. The common People of *Holland* are said to entertain a superstitious Sentiment, That if the whole Species of them should become extinct, they should lose their Liberties' (Collins). Cf. Savage, *The Wanderer*, 4:173–6.

67 'This Tradition [that Britain and France were originally joined] is mention'd by several of our old Historians. Some Naturalists too have endeavour'd to support the Probability of the Fact, by Arguments drawn from the correspondent Disposition of the two opposite Coasts. I don't remember that any Poetical Use has been hitherto made of it' (Collins).

68 *hoary* Here 'white'.

To the blown *Baltic* then, they say,   70
The wild Waves found another way,
Where *Orcas* howls, his wolfish Mountains rounding;
Till all the banded West at once 'gan rise,
A wide wild Storm ev'n Nature's self confounding,
With'ring her Giant Sons with strange uncouth Surprise.   75
This pillar'd Earth so firm and wide,
By Winds and inward Labors torn,
In Thunders dread was push'd aside,
And down the should'ring Billows born.
And see, like Gems, her laughing Train,   80
The little Isles on ev'ry side,
Mona, once hid from those who search the Main,
Where thousand Elfin Shapes abide,
And *Wight* who checks the west'ring Tide,
For Thee consenting Heav'n has each bestow'd,   85
A fair Attendant on her sov'reign Pride:
To Thee this blest Divorce she ow'd,
For thou hast made her Vales thy lov'd, thy last Abode!

SECOND EPODE

Then too, 'tis said, an hoary Pile,
'Midst the green Navel of our Isle,   90
Thy Shrine in some religious Wood,
O Soul-enforcing Goddess stood!
There oft the painted Native's Feet,
Were wont thy Form celestial meet:
Tho' now with hopeless Toil we trace   95
Time's backward Rolls, to find its place;
Whether the fiery-tressed *Dane*,
Or *Roman*'s self o'erturn'd the Fane,
Or in what Heav'n-left Age it fell,
'Twere hard for modern Song to tell.   100
Yet still, if Truth those Beams infuse,
Which guide at once, and charm the Muse,
Beyond yon braided Clouds that lie,
Paving the light-embroider'd Sky:
Amidst the bright pavilion'd Plains,   105
The beauteous *Model* still remains.

---

70 *Baltic* The sea between Germany and Scandinavia.
72 *Orcas* The northern tip of Scotland; the Orcades were the adjacent Orkney Islands.
75 *Giant Sons* The mythical first inhabitants of Britain.
82 *Mona* 'There is a Tradition in the Isle of *Man* [in the Irish Sea], that a Mermaid becoming enamour'd of a young Man of extraordinary Beauty, took an Opportunity of meeting him one day as he walked on the Shore, and open'd her Passion to him, but was receiv'd with a Coldness, occasion'd by his Horror and Surprize at her Appearance. This however was so misconstrued by the Sea-Lady, that in revenge for his Treatment of her, she punish'd the whole Island, by

covering it with a Mist, so that all who attempted to carry on any Commerce with it, either never arriv'd at it, but wander'd up and down the Sea, or were on a sudden wreck'd upon its Cliffs' (Collins).
84 *Wight* The Isle of Wight, off the coast of southern England.
89 *hoary Pile* 'ancient building'.
90 *Navel* 'centre'. Cf. 'Within the navel of this hideous wood' (Milton, *Masque*, 519).
98 *Fane* 'temple'.
103–4 Cf. *Ode to Evening*, 6–7.
106 *Model* 'prototype'.

There happier than in Islands blest,
Or Bow'rs by Spring or *Hebe* drest,
The Chiefs who fill our *Albion*'s Story,
In warlike Weeds, retir'd in Glory,   110
Hear their consorted *Druids* sing
Their Triumphs to th'immortal String.
    How may the Poet now unfold,
What never Tongue or Numbers told?
How learn delighted, and amaz'd,   115
What Hands unknown that Fabric rais'd?
Ev'n now before his favor'd Eyes,
In *Gothic* Pride it seems to rise!
Yet *Græcia*'s graceful Orders join,
Majestic thro' the mix'd Design;   120
The secret Builder knew to chuse,
Each sphere-found Gem of richest Hues:
Whate'er Heav'n's purer Mold contains,
When nearer Suns emblaze its Veins;
There on the Walls the *Patriot*'s Sight,   125
May ever hang with fresh Delight,
And, grav'd with some Prophetic Rage,
Read *Albion*'s Fame thro' ev'ry Age.
    Ye Forms Divine, ye Laureate Band,
That near her inmost Altar stand!   130
Now sooth Her, to her blissful Train
Blithe *Concord*'s social Form to gain:
Concord, whose Myrtle Wand can steep
Ev'n *Anger*'s blood-shot Eyes in Sleep:
Before whose breathing Bosom's Balm,   135
Rage drops his Steel, and Storms grow calm;
Her let our Sires and Matrons hoar
Welcome to *Britain*'s ravag'd Shore,
Our Youths, enamour'd of the Fair,
Play with the Tangles of her Hair,   140
Till in one loud applauding Sound,
The Nations shout to Her around,
O how supremely art thou blest,
Thou, Lady, Thou shalt rule the West!

---

107 *Islands blest* Some historians identified Britain with the 'Islands of the Blest', or Hesperides, of classical myth.

108 *Hebe* Greek goddess of youth.

111 *Druids* See Thomas Warton, *The Pleasures of Melancholy*, 307.

114 *Tongue or Numbers* Oral or written poetry.

117–28 British liberties envisaged as a Druid temple; its assimilation of Gothic and classical styles perhaps symbolizes for Collins a 'mix'd' British Constitution that unites the native British tradition to the best of Ancient Greece.

122–4 The belief that precious minerals were formed by the sun's rays penetrating deep into the earth. Cf. Smart, *A Song to David*, 151–6.

127 *grav'd* 'engraved'.

129–32 These lines are enigmatic. One interpretation may be as follows: Liberty's ideal representatives, crowned with her laurels and presiding at 'her inmost Altar', are asked to reconcile the goddess (and themselves?) to an acceptance of a 'social' (practical), not merely 'divine' (ideal), form: i.e. to give Freedom a tangible existence through peace and reconciliation ('Concord'). In the autumn of 1746 abortive peace negotiations were being held at Breda. The British cabinet was divided, with First Minister Henry Pelham seeking peace while the King and Secretary of State (the Duke of Newcastle) wished to press on with the war. Collins hopes that 'Concord' might become the 'social Form' of Liberty.

139–40 Cf. 'To sport with Amaryllis in the shade, / Or with the tangles of Neaera's hair' (Milton, *Lycidas*, 69–70).

The Passions. An Ode for Music

The Passions was performed on 2 July 1750 in the Sheldonian Theatre, Oxford, during the annual Encænia celebrations (the setting by the Professor of Music, William Hayes, for orchestra, chorus and soloists, survives in the Bodleian Library). The ancient Greek lyric, including the odes of Pindar, had been sung at festivals and games, with words and music (usually a single lyre) regarded as of equal importance, and Collins celebrates these classical roots. An English tradition of ode performance had been established since the reign of Charles II, and Dryden's odes, *Alexander's Feast* and *A Song for St Cecilia's Day* (both models for Collins), were well known in Handel's settings. The Oxford Ode was the climax of the university's annual commemoration of benefactors, and one listener recalled of *The Passions* that 'the choruses were very full and majestic, and the airs [i.e. solos] gave completely the spirit of the Passions which they were intended to imitate'. Collins himself was not present, so we do not know what he thought of the fact that his own ending (from line 93) was replaced by one written by the university's Chancellor, the Earl of Litchfield. Collins's *Passions* became popular, and there were further performances at Winchester and Gloucester, and other musical settings in the 1780s. The poem was a frequent recitation-piece (see Mr Wopsle's performance in Dickens's *Great Expectations*, chapter 7).

Collins's poem acknowledges the rich variety of music's claims and powers: it is the friend of both wisdom and pleasure (96), a divine maiden and a playful mimic. Each of his competing passions, taking the stage in turn, seems to exploit it differently. Text from the first publication in *Odes* (1747), pp. 46–52.

> When Music, Heav'nly Maid, was young,
> While yet in early *Greece* she sung,
> The Passions oft to hear her Shell,
> Throng'd around her magic Cell,
> Exulting, trembling, raging, fainting,   5
> Possest beyond the Muse's Painting;
> By turns they felt the glowing Mind,
> Disturb'd, delighted, rais'd, refin'd.
> Till once, 'tis said, when all were fir'd,
> Fill'd with Fury, rapt, inspir'd,   10
> From the supporting Myrtles round,
> They snatch'd her Instruments of Sound,
> And as they oft had heard a–part
> Sweet Lessons of her forceful Art,
> Each, for Madness rul'd the Hour,   15
> Would prove his own expressive Pow'r.
>
> First *Fear* his Hand, its Skill to try,
>   Amid the Chords bewilder'd laid,
> And back recoil'd he knew not why,
>   Ev'n at the Sound himself had made.   20
>
> Next *Anger* rush'd, his Eyes on fire,
>   In Lightnings own'd his secret Stings,
> In one rude Clash he struck the Lyre,
>   And swept with hurried Hand the Strings.

3 *Shell* The ancient Greek lyre used a tortoise shell as a sound-box.
9–10 Cf. Pope, *Eloisa to Abelard*, 201–2; *fury* 'divinely inspired frenzy'.
11 *Myrtles* Sacred to Venus, goddess of love.
13 *a–part* 'individually'.

16 *expressive Pow'r* The 'expressive' aspect of music becomes increasingly emphasized during the eighteenth century in a move away from an earlier stress on the 'imitative'. Influential in this trend was Charles Avison's *Essay on Musical Expression* (1752).

With woful Measures wan *Despair*   25
   Low sullen Sounds his Grief beguil'd,
A solemn, strange, and mingled Air,
   'Twas sad by Fits, by Starts 'twas wild.

But Thou, O *Hope*, with Eyes so fair,
   What was thy delightful Measure?   30
Still it whisper'd promis'd Pleasure,
   And bad the lovely Scenes at distance hail!
Still would Her Touch the Strain prolong,
   And from the Rocks, the Woods, the Vale,
She call'd on Echo still thro' all the Song;   35
   And where Her sweetest Theme She chose,
   A soft responsive Voice was heard at ev'ry Close,
And *Hope* enchanted smil'd, and wav'd Her golden Hair.

And longer had She sung, — but with a Frown,
   Revenge impatient rose,   40
He threw his blood-stain'd Sword in Thunder down,
     And with a with'ring Look,
   The War-denouncing Trumpet took,
And blew a Blast so loud and dread,
Were ne'er Prophetic Sounds so full of Woe.   45
     And ever and anon he beat
     The doubling Drum with furious Heat;
   And tho' sometimes each dreary Pause between,
     Dejected *Pity* at his Side,
     Her Soul-subduing Voice applied,   50
   Yet still He kept his wild unalter'd Mien,
While each strain'd Ball of Sight seem'd bursting from his Head.

   Thy Numbers, *Jealousy*, to nought were fix'd,
     Sad Proof of thy distressful State,
   Of diff'ring Themes the veering Song was mix'd,   55
     And now it courted *Love*, now raving call'd on *Hate*.

With Eyes up-rais'd, as one inspir'd,
Pale *Melancholy* sate retir'd,
And from her wild sequester'd Seat,
In Notes by Distance made more sweet,   60
Pour'd thro' the mellow *Horn* her pensive Soul:
   And dashing soft from Rocks around,
   Bubbling Runnels join'd the Sound;
Thro' Glades and Glooms the mingled Measure stole,
   Or o'er some haunted Stream with fond Delay,   65
     Round an holy Calm diffusing,

---

26 *beguil'd* 'diverted', 'charmed away'.

35 *Echo* A nymph, rejected by Narcissus, whose body
   wasted away leaving only an echoing voice. Ovid,
   Metamorphoses, 3:339–510.

43 *denouncing* 'proclaiming'.

51 *Mien* 'appearance'.

53 *Numbers* 'notes'.

57–8 *Eyes up-rais'd* Cf. Milton's 'divinest Melancholy', her
   'looks commercing with the skies' (*Il Penseroso*, 12, 39).

65 *haunted Stream* Cf. 'On summer eves by haunted
   stream' (*L'Allegro*, 130).

Love of Peace, and lonely Musing,
In hollow Murmurs died away.

But O how alter'd was its sprightlier Tone!
When *Chearfulness*, a Nymph of healthiest Hue,   70
   Her Bow a-cross her Shoulder flung,
   Her Buskins gem'd with Morning Dew,
Blew an inspiring Air, that Dale and Thicket rung,
   The Hunter's Call to *Faun* and *Dryad* known!
   The Oak-crown'd *Sisters*, and their chast-eye'd *Queen*,   75
   Satyrs and sylvan Boys were seen,
   Peeping from forth their Alleys green;
Brown *Exercise* rejoic'd to hear,
And *Sport* leapt up, and seiz'd his Beechen Spear.

Last came *Joy*'s Ecstatic Trial,   80
He with viny Crown advancing,
   First to the lively Pipe his Hand addrest,
But soon he saw the brisk awak'ning Viol,
   Whose sweet entrancing Voice he lov'd the best.
      They would have thought who heard the Strain,   85
      They saw in *Tempe*'s Vale her native Maids,
      Amidst the festal sounding Shades,
To some unwearied Minstrel dancing,
   While as his flying Fingers kiss'd the Strings,
   LOVE fram'd with *Mirth*, a gay fantastic Round,   90
   Loose were Her Tresses seen, her Zone unbound,
   And HE amidst his frolic Play,
As if he would the charming Air repay,
Shook thousand Odours from his dewy Wings.

O *Music*, Sphere-descended Maid,   95
Friend of Pleasure, *Wisdom*'s Aid,
Why, Goddess, why to us deny'd?
Lay'st Thou thy antient Lyre aside?
As in that lov'd *Athenian* Bow'r,
You learn'd an all-commanding Pow'r,   100
Thy mimic Soul, O Nymph endear'd,
Can well recall what then it heard.
Where is thy native simple Heart,
Devote to Virtue, Fancy, Art?
Arise as in that elder Time,   105
Warm, Energic, Chaste, Sublime!

69–79 A hunting scene, with Chearfulness as Diana, the virgin goddess of the chase.
72 *Buskins* Calf-length boots.
74 *Dryad* 'tree-nymph'.
76 *sylvan* 'woodland'.
78 *Brown* 'sun-tanned'.
86 *Tempe* See Akenside, *The Pleasures of Imagination*, 1:296–305.
89 Cf. 'With flying Fingers touch'd the Lyre' (Dryden, *Alexander's Feast*, 22).

90 Cf. 'in a light fantastic round' (Milton, *Masque*, 144).
91 *Zone* 'belt'.
95 *Sphere-descended* i.e. having come down to us mortals from heaven, recalling the music of the spheres.
101 *mimic* Music's imitative capacity, which Collins's own ode exploits.
104 *Devote* 'Dedicated'.
106 *Energic* 'vigorous'.

Thy Wonders in that God–like Age,
Fill thy recording *Sister*'s Page —
'Tis said, and I believe the Tale,
Thy humblest *Reed* could more prevail,   110
Had more of Strength, diviner Rage,
Than all which charms this laggard Age,
Ev'n all at once together found,
Cæcilia's mingled World of Sound —
O bid our vain Endeavors cease,   115
Revive the just Designs of *Greece*,
Return in all thy simple State!
Confirm the Tales Her Sons relate!

108 *recording Sister* Clio, the Muse of History.
110 *Reed* The simple reed pipe.

112 *laggard* 'backward'.
114 *Cæcilia* St Cecilia, patron saint of music.

Joseph Warton (1722–1800)

The Wartons were the sons of Thomas Warton the Elder (1688–1745), friend of Pope and Prior, Professor of Poetry at Oxford 1718–28, and later Vicar of Basingstoke, Hampshire. Often regarded as a single literary phenomenon, Joseph and his brother Thomas were devoted friends, and as poet-critics they shared an ambition to redirect public taste away from wit and didacticism towards poetry's creative and imaginative aspects. Joseph states this aim in the bold Advertisement to his *Odes on Various Subjects* (1746): 'The Public has been so much accustom'd of late to didactic Poetry alone, and Essays on moral Subjects, that any work where the imagination is much indulged, will perhaps not be relished or regarded. The author therefore of these pieces is in some pain least certain austere critics should think them too fanciful and descriptive. But as he is convinced that the fashion of moralizing in verse has been carried too far, and as he looks upon Invention and Imagination to be the chief faculties of a Poet, so he will be happy if the following Odes may be look'd upon as an attempt to bring back Poetry into its right channel.' Warton's words catch the confidence and ambition of younger poets in the 1740s who felt that poetry was about to take a new direction and that they might shape it.

As a student at Oriel College, Oxford, 1740–4, Warton had already completed two longer poems, as if experimenting with the old and new modes: *Fashion* (1742) is a heroic-couplet satire in the witty style of Pope and Young, whereas *The Enthusiast* (1744) celebrates in blank verse the power of nature and imagination. Both texts, however, are linked by their attacks on superficiality and artifice, on the tyrannies of current fashion.

It was as a critic and editor that Warton achieved fame. He contributed literary papers to *The Adventurer* (1752–4) and edited the *Works of Virgil* in four volumes (1753), with his own critical essays and translations of the *Eclogues* and *Georgics*. His best-known and most controversial work, *An Essay on the Writings and Genius of Pope* (1756), caused a stir in the literary world by demoting the poet to the 'second class' of moral and ethical writers, and maintaining that Pope lacked imaginative power. The second volume did not appear until 1782, and in the intervening years Warton's duties as an educator took priority. In 1755 he was appointed second master of Winchester, the school where he had been a pupil, and he became its Headmaster in 1766. In this role he proved to be a popular father figure (by this time he had a large family of his own): he neglected discipline and preferred to encourage his boys' poetic talents. Warton had a wide circle of literary friends, and he and his brother made regular Christmas visits to London for the theatre and literary salons. After his retirement in 1793 he published a nine-volume edition of Pope (1797) and began a four-volume edition of Dryden, completed by his son John in 1811.

Warton's taste was for the sublime and pathetic, for powerful sentiments and striking images. Fanny Burney described him in his later years as a 'rapturist', a man of warm feelings and animated conversation, who would hug his acquaintances as he enthused over a poem or a prospect. The reader of his youthful poetry can have much the same experience. Warton the poet really belongs to the 1740s, when a new generation was seeking to expand poetry's range and imaginative potential. His work during that decade, along with the *Essay on Pope*, makes him a crucial figure at a time of aesthetic reassessment and the development of a new poetic sensibility.

The Enthusiast: Or The Lover of Nature

In the youthful work during the 1740s of Akenside, Collins and the Warton brothers, the reader is aware of a new confidence in the aesthetic aspects of poetry – in the primacy of beauty, imagination and pleasure, and the conviction that Truth can be found through aesthetic experience. Joseph Warton's *The Enthusiast* (originally written in 1740 and published four years later) is direct and unashamed in celebrating a shift away from the poet's social responsibilities. The naiveté of its enthusiasm is all part of the poem's strategy for turning the poet back to what Warton called 'pure poetry': 'a clear head, and acute understanding are not sufficient, alone, to make a POET ... the most solid observations on human life, expressed with the utmost elegance and brevity, are MORALITY, and not POETRY ...

it is a creative and glowing IMAGINATION, and that alone, that can stamp a writer with this exalted and very uncommon character' (*Essay on Pope* (1756), pp. iv–v). As in the *Essay*, so in this poem, Warton's rebellion against the poetry of wit and sense makes Pope its chief target. Here the *Epistle to Burlington*, with its picture of a collaboration between Art and Nature, is the focus for Warton's argument. *The Enthusiast* stages a return to the primal and the primitive, but also a poetic return to the poetry of Milton and Shakespeare, a tradition that the Warton brothers felt had been broken by an age of poetical correctness and moralizing. Warton's image of the infant Shakespeare cradled in imagination's lap becomes an emblem for the poet's authentic 'natural' voice.

The poem became well known through its inclusion in Robert Dodsley's *Collection of Poems* (3 vols, 1748), a popular anthology that was extended and reprinted throughout the century. For this Warton took the opportunity to extend and rework his 1744 text, and it is this revised 1748 version (3:68–78) that is given here.

> *Rure vero barbaroque lætatur*   MARTIAL
>
> —— *Ut! mihi devio*
> *Rupes, & vacuum nemus*
> *Mirari libet!* ——   HORACE

Ye green-rob'd Dryads, oft' at dusky eve
By wondering shepherds seen, to forests brown,
To unfrequented meads, and pathless wilds,
Lead me from gardens deck'd with art's vain pomps.
Can gilt alcoves, can marble-mimick gods,   5
Parterres embroider'd, obelisks, and urns
Of high relief; can the long, spreading lake,
Or vista lessening to the sight; can Stow
With all her Attick fanes, such raptures raise,
As the thrush-haunted copse, where lightly leaps   10
The fearful fawn the rustling leaves along,
And the brisk squirrel sports from bough to bough,
While from an hollow oak, whose naked roots
O'erhang a pensive rill, the busy bees
Hum drowsy lullabies? The bards of old,   15
Fair nature's friends, sought such retreats, to charm
Sweet Echo with their songs; oft' too they met
In summer evenings, near sequester'd bow'rs,
Or mountain-nymph, or muse, and eager learn'd
The moral strains she taught to mend mankind.   20
As to a secret grot Ægeria stole
With patriot Numa, and in silent night
Whisper'd him sacred laws, he list'ning sat
Rapt with her virtuous voice, old Tyber lean'd
Attentive on his urn, and hush'd his waves.   25
    Rich in her weeping country's spoils Versailles
May boast a thousand fountains, that can cast
The tortur'd waters to the distant heav'ns;
Yet let me choose some pine-top'd precipice
Abrupt and shaggy, whence a foamy stream,   30
Like Anio, tumbling roars; or some bleak heath,
Where straggling stand the mournful juniper,
Or yew-tree scath'd; while in clear prospect round,
From the grove's bosom spires emerge, and smoak

Mottos Martial, *Epigrams*, 3:58 ('rejoices in the true, rough landscape'); Horace, *Odes*, 3:25 ('How I love to wander and gaze in awe at empty woods and cliffs!').

6 *Parterres* Formal flower-beds.

8 *Stow* Lord Cobham's estate at Stowe, Buckinghamshire, celebrated by Pope, *Epistle to Burlington*, 70.

9 *Attick fanes* 'classical temples'.

21–3 In Roman tradition the reign of Numa (seventh century BC) was a Golden Age when religious institutions were founded. The historian Livy (I.21.3) tells how at night the king received advice from the nymph Egeria at her sacred spring.

26 *Versailles* Louis XIV's palace had in England become a byword for empty grandeur. Cf. *Epistle to Burlington*, 71.

31 *Anio* A tributary of the Tiber, famed for its spectacular cascades.

34–5 Cf. Thomson, *Spring*, 954–6.

In bluish wreaths ascends, ripe harvests wave,   35
Low, lonely cottages, and ruin'd tops
Of Gothick battlements appear, and streams
Beneath the sun-beams twinkle — the shrill lark,
That wakes the wood-man to his early task,
Or love-sick Philomel, whose luscious lays   40
Sooth lone night-wanderers, the moaning dove
Pitied by listening milk-maid, far excell
The deep-mouth'd viol, the soul-lulling lute,
And battle-breathing trumpet. Artful sounds!
That please not like the choristers of air,   45
When first they hail th'approach of laughing May.
   Can Kent design like nature? Mark where Thames
Plenty and pleasure pours thro' Lincoln's meads;
Can the great artist, tho' with taste supreme
Endu'd, one beauty to this Eden add?   50
Tho' he, by rules unfetter'd, boldly scorns
Formality and method, round and square
Disdaining, plans irregularly great.
   Creative Titian, can thy vivid strokes,
Or thine, O graceful Raphael, dare to vie   55
With the rich tints that paint the breathing mead?
The thousand-colour'd tulip, violet's bell
Snow-clad and meek, the vermil-tinctur'd rose,
And golden crocus? — Yet with these the maid,
Phillis or Phoebe, at a feast or wake,   60
Her jetty locks enamels; fairer she,
In innocence and home-spun vestments dress'd,
Than if coerulean saphires at her ears
Shone pendent, or a precious diamond-cross
Heav'd gently on her panting bosom white.   65
   Yon' shepherd idly stretch'd on the rude rock,
Listening to dashing waves, and sea-mews clang
High-hovering o'er his head, who views beneath
The dolphin dancing o'er the level brine,
Feels more true bliss than the proud admiral,   70
Amid his vessels bright with burnish'd gold
And silken streamers, tho' his lordly nod
Ten thousand war-worn mariners revere.
And great Æneas gaz'd with more delight
On the rough mountain shagg'd with horrid shades,   75

40 *Philomel* Nightingale.

47–53 Paragraph added in *1748*.

47 William Kent (1684–1748), architect and designer, friend of Pope and Burlington. He popularized the 'natural' style of gardening at Stowe and elsewhere. Horace Walpole considered him 'the inventor of an art that … improves nature'.

48 *Lincoln's meads* 'The earl of Lincoln's terrace at Weybridge in Surry, one of the finest spots in Europe' (Warton's note).

54–5 The Italian painters Titian (*c.*1488–1576) and

Raphael (1483–1520) were in contrasting ways both masters of colour.

60 *wake* A local parish festival.

61 *jetty* 'jet-black'; *enamels* 'decorates'.

63 *coerulean* 'dark blue' (Lat. *caeruleus*).

64–5 Cf. Pope, *The Rape of the Lock*, 2:7; *pendent* 'hanging' (another Latinate word).

67 *sea-mews clang* 'the harsh call of seagulls'. Cf. *Paradise Lost*, 11:835.

75 Cf. 'shagged with horrid shades' (Milton, *Masque*, 428); also Pope, *Eloisa to Abelard*, 20.

(Where cloud-compelling Jove, as fancy dream'd,
Descending shook his direful Ægis black)
Than if he enter'd the high Capitol
On golden columns rear'd, a conquer'd world
Exhausted to enrich its stately head.   80
More pleas'd he slept in poor Evander's cott
On shaggy skins, lull'd by sweet nightingales,
Than if a Nero, in an age refin'd,
Beneath a gorgeous canopy had plac'd
His royal guest, and bade his minstrels sound   85
Soft slumb'rous Lydian airs, to sooth his rest.
   Happy the first of men, ere yet confin'd
To smoaky cities; who in sheltering groves,
Warm caves, and deep-sunk vallies liv'd and lov'd,
By cares unwounded; what the sun and showers,   90
And genial earth untillag'd could produce,
They gather'd grateful, or the acorn brown,
Or blushing berry; by the liquid lapse
Of murm'ring waters call'd to slake their thirst,
Or with fair nymphs their sun-brown limbs to bathe;   95
With nymphs who fondly clasp their fav'rite youths,
Unaw'd by shame, beneath the beechen shade,
Nor wiles, nor artificial coyness knew.
Then doors and walls were not; the melting maid
Nor frowns of parents fear'd, nor husband's threats;   100
Nor had curs'd gold their tender hearts allur'd;
Then beauty was not venal. Injur'd love,
O whither, God of raptures, art thou fled?
While avarice waves his golden wand around,
Abhorr'd magician, and his costly cup   105
Prepares with baneful drugs, t'enchant the souls
Of each low-thoughted fair to wed for gain.
   In earth's first infancy (as sung the bard,
Who strongly painted what he boldly thought)
Tho' the fierce north oft smote with iron whip   110
Their shiv'ring limbs, tho' oft the bristly boar
Or hungry lion 'woke them with their howls,
And scar'd them from their moss-grown caves to rove
Houseless and cold in dark tempestuous nights;

---

77 *Ægis* Zeus's goat-skin shield, fringed with snakes and the Medusa's head. Thunder resulted from its shaking.

81 *Evander* Aeneas's host on his reaching the site of Rome. He advised the hero to scorn riches (*Aeneid*, 8:359–69).

83 *Nero* (37–68), Roman emperor famed for art and excess.

86 *Lydian airs* In *Republic* Plato condemned the Lydian mode in music as effeminate. Cf. 'Lap me in soft Lydian airs' (Milton, *L'Allegro*, 136). Cf. Collins, *Ode to Liberty*, 47 and note.

87 'See Lucretius, lib. V.' (Warton's note). Most of the details in lines 87–129 are drawn from Lucretius, *De Rerum Natura*, 5:925–1010.

91 *genial* 'fertile'.

93–4 Cf. 'liquid lapse of murmuring streams' (*Paradise Lost*, 8:263).

102 *venal* 'corrupt'.

104–6 Recalls the wand and cup of the enchanter Comus in Milton's *Masque*.

108 *the bard* 'Lucretius' (Warton's note). 'They would flee from their rocky shelters when a foaming boar or mighty lion appeared ... and fill the woods with their cries ... But thousands were not sent to destruction in a single day's battle, and sailors were not dashed on the rocks by the billowing sea' (*De Rerum Natura*, 5:984–1001).

Yet were not myriads in embattel'd fields   115
Swept off at once, nor had the raging seas
O'erwhelm'd the found'ring bark and shrieking crew;
In vain the glassy ocean smil'd to tempt
The jolly sailor unsuspecting harm,
For commerce ne'er had spread her swelling sails,   120
Nor had the wond'ring Nereids ever heard
The dashing oar: then famine, want, and pine,
Sunk to the grave their fainting limbs; but us
Diseaseful dainties, riot and excess,
And feverish luxury destroy. In brakes   125
Or marshes wild unknowingly they crop'd
Herbs of malignant juice, to realms remote
While we for powerful poisons madly roam,
From every noxious herb collecting death.
What tho' unknown to those primæval sires,   130
The well-arch'd dome, peopled with breathing forms
By fair Italia's skilful hand, unknown
The shapely column, and the crumbling busts
Of awful ancestors in long descent?
Yet why should man mistaken deem it nobler   135
To dwell in palaces, and high-roof'd halls,
Than in God's forests, architect supreme!
Say, is the Persian carpet, than the field's
Or meadow's mantle gay, more richly wov'n;
Or softer to the votaries of ease   140
Than bladed grass, perfum'd with dew-drop'd flow'rs?
O taste corrupt! that luxury and pomp
In specious names of polish'd manners veil'd,
Should proudly banish nature's simple charms!
All-beauteous nature! by thy boundless charms   145
Oppress'd, O where shall I begin thy praise,
Where turn th'ecstatick eye, how ease my breast
That pants with wild astonishment and love!
Dark forests, and the opening lawn, refresh'd
With ever-gushing brooks, hill, meadow, dale,   150
The balmy bean-field, the gay-clover'd close,
So sweetly interchang'd, the lowing ox,
The playful lamb, the distant water-fall
Now faintly heard, now swelling with the breeze,
The sound of pastoral reed from hazel-bower,   155
The choral birds, the neighing steed, that snuffs
His dappled mate, stung with intense desire,
The ripen'd orchard when the ruddy orbs
Betwixt the green leaves blush, the azure skies,
The chearful sun that thro' earth's vitals pours   160
Delight and health and heat; all, all conspire
To raise, to sooth, to harmonize the mind,
To lift on wings of praise, to the great sire
Of being and of beauty, at whose nod

---

121 *Nereids* Sea-maidens, daughters of Nereus the sea-god.
122 *pine* 'suffering'.

145–67 Passage added in *1748*.
157 Cf. Thomson, *Spring*, 791–2.

Creation started from the gloomy vault   165
Of dreary Chaos, while the griesly king
Murmur'd to feel his boisterous power confin'd.
   What are the lays of artful Addison,
Coldly correct, to Shakespear's warblings wild?
Whom on the winding Avon's willow'd banks   170
Fair fancy found, and bore the smiling babe
To a close cavern: (still the shepherds shew
The sacred place, whence with religious awe
They hear, returning from the field at eve,
Strange whisp'ring of sweet musick thro' the air)   175
Here, as with honey gather'd from the rock,
She fed the little prattler, and with songs
Oft' sooth'd his wondering ears, with deep delight
On her soft lap he sat, and caught the sounds.
   Oft' near some crouded city would I walk,   180
Listening the far-off noises, rattling cars,
Loud shouts of joy, sad shrieks of sorrow, knells
Full slowly tolling, instruments of trade,
Striking mine ears with one deep-swelling hum.
Or wand'ring near the sea, attend the sounds   185
Of hollow winds, and ever-beating waves.
Ev'n when wild tempests swallow up the plains,
And Boreas' blasts, big hail, and rains combine
To shake the groves and mountains, would I sit,
Pensively musing on th'outragious crimes   190
That wake heav'n's vengeance: at such solemn hours,
Dæmons and goblins thro' the dark air shriek,
While Hecat, with her black-brow'd sisters nine,
Rides o'er the earth, and scatters woes and death.
Then too, they say, in drear Ægyptian wilds   195
The lion and the tiger prowl for prey
With roarings loud! the list'ning traveller
Starts fear-struck, while the hollow-echoing vaults
Of pyramids encrease the deathful sounds.
   But let me never fail in cloudless nights,   200
When silent Cynthia in her silver car
Thro' the blue concave slides, when shine the hills,
Twinkle the streams, and woods look tip'd with gold,
To seek some level mead, and there invoke
Old midnight's sister Contemplation sage,   205
(Queen of the rugged brow, and stern-fix'd eye)
To lift my soul above this little earth,
This folly-fetter'd world; to purge my ears,
That I may hear the rolling planet's song,

---

168 Joseph Addison (1672–1719), arbiter of literary taste and (with Sir Richard Steele) proprietor of *The Spectator*. He was Pope's 'Atticus' (*Epistle to Dr Arbuthnot*, 193–214; cf. 192n).

169 *warblings wild* Cf. 'If … sweetest Shakespeare fancy's child, / Warble his native wood-notes wild' (Milton, *L'Allegro*, 132–4).

171 *fancy* 'imagination'. Cf. the mythic infancy of

Contemplation in Thomas Warton, *The Pleasures of Melancholy*, 306–15.

188 *Boreas* The north wind.

193 *Hecat* Hecate, the triple-formed Greek goddess who sent ghosts and demons into the world. Her nine sisters would seem to be Warton's invention.

201 *Cynthia* The moon.

And tuneful turning spheres: if this be barr'd,   210
The little Fayes that dance in neighbouring dales,
Sipping the night-dew, while they laugh and love,
Shall charm me with aërial notes. — As thus
I wander musing, lo, what awful forms
Yonder appear! sharp-ey'd Philosophy   215
Clad in dun robes, an eagle on his wrist,
First meets my eye; next, virgin Solitude
Serene, who blushes at each gazer's sight;
Then Wisdom's hoary head, with crutch in hand,
Trembling, and bent with age; last Virtue's self   220
Smiling, in white array'd, who with her leads
Sweet Innocence, that prattles by her side,
A naked boy! — Harrass'd with fear I stop,
I gaze, when Virtue thus — 'Whoe'er thou art,
Mortal, by whom I deign to be beheld   225
In these my midnight-walks; depart, and say
That henceforth I and my immortal train
Forsake Britannia's isle; who fondly stoops
To Vice, her favourite paramour.' — She spoke,
And as she turn'd, her round and rosy neck,   230
Her flowing train, and long ambrosial hair,
Breathing rich odours, I enamour'd view.
    O who will bear me then to western climes,
(Since Virtue leaves our wretched land) to fields
Yet unpolluted with Iberian swords;   235
To isles of innocence, from mortal view
Deeply retir'd, beneath a plantane's shade,
Where Happiness and Quiet sit enthron'd;
With simple Indian swains, that I may hunt
The boar and tiger thro' Savannah's wild,   240
Thro' fragrant desarts, and thro' citron-groves.
There fed on dates and herbs, would I despise
The far-fetch'd cates of Luxury, and hoards
Of narrow-hearted Avarice; nor heed
The distant din of the tumultuous world.   245
So when rude whirlwinds rouze the roaring main,
Beneath fair Thetis sits, in coral caves,
Serenely gay, nor sinking sailors cries
Disturb her sportive nymphs, who round her form
The light fantastick dance, or for her hair   250
Weave rosy crowns, or with according lutes
Grace the soft warbles of her honied voice.

---

216 *eagle* Symbolic of heavenward flight and vision.

229–32 Virtually a translation of Virgil's description of Venus, who has just appeared to Aeneas: 'She spoke, and as she turned away, her rosy neck shone brightly. From her head her ambrosial tresses breathed celestial fragrance' (*Aeneid*, 1:402–4). See David B. Morris, 'Joseph Warton's Figure of Virtue: Poetic Indirection in "The Enthusiast"', *Philological Quarterly*, 50 (1971), pp. 378–83.

231 *ambrosial* 'divinely fragrant'.

235 *Iberian* Spanish.

237 *plantane* 'plane-tree'.

243 *cates* 'delicacies'.

247 *Thetis* One of the Nereids (see 121 above), and the mother of Achilles.

Ode to Evening

Warton's poem may have influenced Gray's *Elegy Written in a Country Church Yard*. The atmospherics of this evening mood-picture, the woodman 'homeward bent' in the first stanza, the kissing of the children on his return, the harmonizing of distant sounds, and the subsiding of the passions in a 'holy calm', are all features of Gray's twilight scene, and stanza six seems to be echoed in two lines of Gray's earliest version of his poem: 'Hark how the sacred Calm, that broods around / Bids ev'ry fierce tumultuous Passion cease'. When Gray read Warton's *Odes* he commented that their author had 'but little Invention, very poetical choice of Expression, & a good Ear' (Gray–Wharton, 27 December 1746), and indeed the sound of Warton's evening quatrains, with their judicious use of assonance and alliteration, may also have lodged in his mind. However, in line with Warton's 'Advertisement' to his *Odes* (see biographical headnote), there is no moralizing on his landscape; the ploughmen meet to wrestle on the village green, and other figures are there whistling and singing. It is a timeless scene where ancient Greece and rural England meet. The poem was first printed in *Odes on Various Subjects* (1746). The following text is that of the slightly revised second edition (1747), pp. 30–1.

> Hail meek-ey'd maiden, clad in sober grey,
> Whose soft approach the weary woodman loves,
> As homeward bent to kiss his prattling babes,
> He jocund whistles thro' the twilight groves.
>
> When PHOEBUS sinks behind the gilded hills,   5
> You lightly o'er the misty meadows walk,
> The drooping daisies bathe in dulcet dews,
> And nurse the nodding violet's slender stalk:
>
> The panting Dryads, that in day's fierce heat
> To inmost bowers and cooling caverns ran,   10
> Return to trip in wanton evening-dance,
> Old SYLVAN too returns, and laughing PAN.
>
> To the deep wood the clamorous rooks repair,
> Light skims the swallow o'er the wat'ry scene,
> And from the sheep-cotes, and fresh-furrow'd field,   15
> Stout plowmen meet to wrestle on the green.
>
> The swain that artless sings on yonder rock,
> His nibbling sheep and lengthening shadow spies,
> Pleas'd with the cool, the calm, refreshful hour,
> And with hoarse hummings of unnumber'd flies.   20
>
> Now every passion sleeps; desponding Love,
> And pining Envy, ever-restless Pride;
> An holy calm creeps o'er my peaceful soul,
> Anger and mad Ambition's storms subside.
>
> O modest EVENING, oft' let me appear   25
> A wandering votary in thy pensive train,
> List'ning to every wildly-warbling throat
> That fills with farewell notes the dark'ning plain.

9 *Dryads* Tree-nymphs.
12 The gods Silvanus (Lat. 'of the woods') and Pan were both associated with wild places.
13 Cf. Thomas Warton, *The Pleasures of Melancholy*, 144–5.

The Dying Indian

Warton had a taste for the primitive and exotic, and he viewed the Spanish 'civilizing' of America with indignation. In his companion poem *The Revenge of America* the Genius of 'Old India' sits on the highest peak of the Andes and curses the plunderers of Peru ('What woes, he cry'd, hath lust of gold / O'er my poor country widely roll'd ... / ... I see all Europe's children curst / With lucre's universal thirst'). *The Dying Indian* shows a similar interest in the voice of the noble savage, in which violence and superstition are paired with honour and integrity. But Warton's exotic picture of America is also a confused one. He seems to have read Voltaire's *Essai sur les Mœurs* (published in English translation 1754) with its description of the bloody sacrifices to 'Visiliputsli' (by 1755 Warton was planning to write 'An Account of all

the Works of Voltaire'), and so his doomed Inca warrior finds himself invoking the war-god of the Aztecs. In the 1766 edition Warton changed 'Vitzipultzi's statue' (13) to 'Pachacamac's altar', Pachacamac being the Peruvians' name for 'the Divine Majesty', according to Garcilaso de la Vega (*The Royal Commentaries of Peru*, 2:2). Warton seems to have known Garcilaso's moving account of the Inca civilization and its overthrow by Spanish forces under Francisco Pizarro, 1532–3.

Warton's poem is judged to be the earliest dramatic monologue (see P. Hobsbaum, 'The Rise of the Dramatic Monologue', *Hudson Review*, 28 (1975), pp. 227–45). The text below is from the first printing, Dodsley's *A Collection of Poems*, IV (1755), pp. 209–10.

The dart of Izdabel prevails! 'twas dipt
In double poison — I shall soon arrive
At the blest island, where no tigers spring
On heedless hunters; where anana's bloom
Thrice in each moon; where rivers smoothly glide,   5
Nor thundering torrents whirl the light canoe
Down to the sea; where my forefathers feast
Daily on hearts of Spaniards! — O my son,
I feel the venom busy in my breast,
Approach, and bring my crown, deck'd with the teeth   10
Of that bold christian who first dar'd deflour
The virgins of the sun; and, dire to tell!
Robb'd Vitzipultzi's statue of its gems!
I mark'd the spot where they interr'd this traitor,
And once at midnight stole I to his tomb,   15
And tore his carcass from the earth, and left it
A prey to poisonous flies. Preserve this crown
With sacred secrecy: if e'er returns
Thy much-lov'd mother from the desart woods
Where, as I hunted late, I hapless lost her,   20
Cherish her age. Tell her I ne'er have worship'd
With those that eat their God. And when disease
Preys on her languid limbs, then kindly stab her
With thine own hands, nor suffer her to linger,
Like christian cowards, in a life of pain.   25
I go! great COPAC beckons me! farewell!

2–8 Cf. Pope's 'poor Indian', *Essay on Man*, 1:99–108. See *Notes and Queries*, 229 (1984), pp. 403–4.
4 *anana* 'pineapple'.
12 The 'Virgins of the Sun' were housed in a convent at Cuzco, and were never allowed to see a man, not even the Inca himself. They spent their time offering sacrifices to the sun and spinning garments for the monarch. A detailed account is given in Garcilaso de la Vega, *The Royal Commentaries of Peru* (1609–17), tr. Sir Paul Rycaut (1688), 4:1.

13 *Vitzipultzi* The Aztec war-god, Huitzilopochtli, before whose statue human sacrifices were made. It is described and illustrated in Antonio de Solis, *Histoire De La Conquête du Mexique* (1692), one of Voltaire's sources. De Solis has 'Viztzilipuztli', and Voltaire 'Visiliputsli'.
26 *great COPAC* The Peruvians attributed all their laws and religious observances to Manco Capac, their first Inca, or ruler (Garcilaso, *Commentaries*, 2:4).

Thomas Warton (1728–1790)

From the age of sixteen Thomas Warton's home was Trinity College, Oxford, of which he became a fellow in 1752. By then he had made his name with several volumes of verse, including *The Pleasures of Melancholy* (1747) and *The Triumph of Isis* (1750), in which he defended the university after an attack by William Mason of Cambridge. Like his father before him he was elected Oxford's Professor of Poetry, 1756–66, and he delivered regular lectures on the literature of ancient Greece. He was respected both as a classical scholar (with his edition of Theocritus, 1770) and as a literary historian. His *Observations on the Faerie Queene* (1754; enlarged 1762) was the first attempt to explore Spenser's medieval sources, and his *History of English Poetry* (3 vols, 1774–81) was a pioneer work that narrated the history of English literature from the Norman Conquest to the early seventeenth century, being left unfinished at his death. A lifelong admirer of Milton, Warton edited the early poems in 1785, and his own verse sometimes consciously echoes them. Along with his brother Joseph he worked to supplant the 'School of Pope' with a 'School of Milton' (these are Warton's terms) which would re-establish the native line of poetry running from Chaucer and Spenser to Shakespeare and Milton. Warton's taste for romance and imagination placed him in direct opposition to his friend Samuel Johnson, who disliked the early Milton and regarded Pope's Homer as the ultimate poetic achievement. When Warton's *Poems* were published in 1777 Johnson described them as 'Phrase that Time has flung away, / Uncouth Words in Disarray: / Trickt in Antique Ruff and Bonnet, / Ode and Elegy and Sonnet'.

Warton was an enthusiast for the genuine Gothic, and he spent much time on rambles across England and Wales exploring what remained of the medieval past, sketching and describing buildings for his projected 'History of Gothic Architecture'. He became Poet Laureate to George III in 1785, and in the same year was elected Camden Professor of History. In Oxford and Winchester (where he passed the vacations with his brother) he was much loved as a good-natured humorist and punster, whose eccentricities of slovenly dress, a love of tavern company, and a delight in hunting and military reviews, were unusual for a member of the academic establishment. His sensitive and thoughtful retrospection, juxtaposing past and present, imagination and reason, the solitary and the social, was a direct influence on the younger generation of poets in the 1780s, including William Lisle Bowles, Charlotte Smith and Thomas Russell, and on the early verse of Southey, Coleridge and Wordsworth.

The Pleasures of Melancholy

This youthful poem was written in 1745 when Warton was seventeen. Like his brother's *The Enthusiast* (1744), it is part contemplation, part polemic, and it sets the authentic against the artificial, romantic description alongside satiric cameo. During 1745 Warton was also making sketches for a poetic diptych, 'Summer' and 'Winter', modelled on Milton's *L'Allegro* and *Il Penseroso*. The project was never completed, but we can detect in *The Pleasures of Melancholy* the imprint of Milton's twin poems. Like the *Penseroso*, Warton's melancholy speaker invokes a visionary goddess to lead him through a series of sublime and intense situations. He finds a doppelgänger in Milton's divinely inspired melancholic who banishes the blithe sociability of his companion 'L'Allegro' and welcomes in his place the dark, tragic and essentially private experience. Like Joseph's *The Enthusiast*, Thomas's poem sees imagination as the key to unlock this world, so that even malicious enchanters (Busirane, Archimago, Comus, Hecate) serve its purpose. The values of *The Dunciad* have been reversed: Pope's universal nightmare has become a private fantasy, and Pope's own Eloisa finds a home here.

The poem was published as *The Pleasures of Melancholy. A Poem*, 1747. It was extensively revised for Dodsley's *Collection of Poems*, IV (1755), pp. 214–25, the text given here. Some of Warton's major changes are noted.

————*Præcipe lugubres*
Cantus, Melpomene! —— HOR.

Mother of musings, Contemplation sage,
Whose grotto stands upon the topmost rock
Of Teneriff; 'mid the tempestuous night,
On which, in calmest meditation held,
Thou hear'st with howling winds the beating rain   5
And drifting hail descend; or if the skies
Unclouded shine, and thro' the blue serene
Pale Cynthia rolls her silver-axled car,
Whence gazing stedfast on the spangled vault
Raptur'd thou sit'st, while murmurs indistinct   10
Of distant billows sooth thy pensive ear
With hoarse and hollow sounds; secure, self-blest,
There oft thou listen'st to the wild uproar
Of fleets encount'ring, that in whispers low
Ascends the rocky summit, where thou dwell'st   15
Remote from man, conversing with the spheres!
O lead me, queen sublime, to solemn glooms
Congenial with my soul; to chearless shades,
To ruin'd seats, to twilight cells and bow'rs,
Where thoughtful Melancholy loves to muse,   20
Her fav'rite midnight haunts. The laughing scenes
Of purple Spring, where all the wanton train
Of Smiles and Graces seem to lead the dance
In sportive round, while from their hands they show'r
Ambrosial blooms and flow'rs, no longer charm;   25
Tempe, no more I court thy balmy breeze,
Adieu green vales! ye broider'd meads, adieu!
  Beneath yon' ruin'd abbey's moss-grown piles
Oft let me sit, at twilight hour of eve,
Where thro' some western window the pale moon   30
Pours her long-levell'd rule of streaming light;
While sullen sacred silence reigns around,
Save the lone screech-owl's note, who builds his bow'r
Amid the mould'ring caverns dark and damp,
Or the calm breeze, that rustles in the leaves   35
Of flaunting ivy, that with mantle green
Invests some wasted tow'r. Or let me tread
Its neighb'ring walk of pines, where mus'd of old
The cloyster'd brothers: thro' the gloomy void
That far extends beneath their ample arch   40
As on I pace, religious horror wraps
My soul in dread repose. But when the world
Is clad in Midnight's raven-colour'd robe,
'Mid hollow charnel let me watch the flame

Motto On title page of *1747*. 'Teach me a song of
  mourning, O Melpomene' (Horace, *Odes*, 1:24). Cf. 213
  below.
  3 *Teneriff* Largest of the Canary Islands. The peak of El
  Piton (12,000 ft) was once thought to be the highest
  point in the world. Cf. *Paradise Lost*, 4:987.
22 *purple* 'colourful'.

25 *Ambrosial* 'divinely scented'.
26 *Tempe* Cf. Akenside, *The Pleasures of Imagination*,
  1:298–305.
31 Cf. 'With thy long levelled rule of streaming light'
  (Milton, *Masque*, 339).
32–7 Cf. Gray, *Elegy*, 9–12.
44 *charnel* Mortuary chapel.

Of taper dim, shedding a livid glare 45
O'er the wan heaps; while airy voices talk
Along the glimm'ring walls; or ghostly shape
At distance seen, invites with beck'ning hand
My lonesome steps, thro' the far-winding vaults.
Nor undelightful is the solemn noon 50
Of night, when haply wakeful from my couch
I start: lo, all is motionless around!
Roars not the rushing wind; the sons of men
And every beast in mute oblivion lie;
All nature's hush'd in silence and in sleep. 55
O then how fearful is it to reflect,
That thro' the still globe's aweful solitude,
No being wakes but me! 'till stealing sleep
My drooping temples bathes in opiate dews.
Nor then let dreams, of wanton folly born, 60
My senses lead thro' flowery paths of joy;
But let the sacred Genius of the night
Such mystic visions send, as Spenser saw,
When thro' bewild'ring Fancy's magic maze,
To the fell house of Busyrane, he led 65
Th'unshaken Britomart; or Milton knew,
When in abstracted thought he first conceiv'd
All heav'n in tumult, and the Seraphim
Come tow'ring, arm'd in adamant and gold.
  Let others love soft summer's ev'ning smiles, 70
As, list'ning to the distant water-fall,
They mark the blushes of the streaky west;
I choose the pale December's foggy glooms.
Then, when the sullen shades of ev'ning close,
Where thro' the room a blindly-glimm'ring gleam 75
The dying embers scatter, far remote
From Mirth's mad shouts, that thro' th'illumin'd roof
Resound with festive echo, let me sit,
Blest with the lowly cricket's drowsy dirge.
Then let my thought contemplative explore 80
This fleeting state of things, the vain delights,
The fruitless toils, that still our search elude,
As thro' the wilderness of life we rove.
This sober hour of silence will unmask
False Folly's smile, that like the dazzling spells 85
Of wily Comus cheat th'unweeting eye
With blear illusion, and persuade to drink
That charmed cup, which Reason's mintage fair
Unmoulds, and stamps the monster on the man.

46–7 Cf. Pope, *Eloisa to Abelard*, 306.

63–6 *The Faerie Queene*, III.xi–xii. The house of the 'vile enchanter' Busirane, symbolizing false love and imaginative excess.

69 Cf. Milton's description of Satan: 'Came towering, armed in adamant and gold' (*Paradise Lost*, 6:110).

75–6 Cf. 'Where glowing embers through the room / Teach light to counterfeit a gloom' (Milton, *Il Penseroso*, 79–80).

86 *Comus* The enchanter in Milton's *Masque*; *unweeting* 'unwitting'.

Eager we taste, but in the luscious draught   90
Forget the pois'nous dregs that lurk beneath.
    Few know that elegance of soul refin'd,
Whose soft sensation feels a quicker joy
From Melancholy's scenes, than the dull pride
Of tasteless splendor and magnificence   95
Can e'er afford. Thus Eloise, whose mind
Had languish'd to the pangs of melting love,
More genuine transport found, as on some tomb
Reclin'd, she watch'd the tapers of the dead;
Or thro' the pillar'd iles, amid pale shrines   100
Of imag'd saints, and intermingled graves,
Mus'd a veil'd votaress; than Flavia feels,
As thro' the mazes of the festive ball
Proud of her conquering charms, and beauty's blaze,
She floats amid the silken sons of dress,   105
And shines the fairest of th'assembled fair.
    When azure noon-tide chears the dædal globe,
And the blest regent of the golden day
Rejoices in his bright meridian bow'r,
How oft my wishes ask the night's return,   110
That best befriends the melancholy mind!
Hail, sacred Night! thou too shalt share my song!
Sister of ebon-scepter'd Hecat, hail!
Whether in congregated clouds thou wrap'st
Thy viewless chariot, or with silver crown   115
Thy beaming head encirclest, ever hail!
What tho' beneath thy gloom the sorceress-train,
Far in obscured haunt of Lapland-moors,
With rhymes uncouth the bloody cauldron bless;
Tho' Murder wan, beneath thy shrouding shade   120
Summons her slow-ey'd vot'ries to devise
Of secret slaughter, while by one blue lamp
In hideous conf'rence sits the list'ning band,
And start at each low wind, or wakeful sound:
What tho' thy stay the pilgrim curseth oft,   125
As all benighted in Arabian wastes
He hears the wilderness around him howl
With roaming monsters, while on his hoar head
The black-descending tempest ceaseless beats;
Yet more delightful to my pensive mind   130
Is thy return, than bloomy morn's approach,
Ev'n then, in youthful pride of opening May,
When from the portals of the saffron east
She sheds fresh roses, and ambrosial dews.
Yet not ungrateful is the morn's approach,   135
When dropping wet she comes, and clad in clouds,
While thro' the damp air scowls the louring south,
Blackening the landscape's face, that grove and hill
In formless vapours undistinguish'd swim:

96–9 Cf. *Eloisa to Abelard*, 305–6.
107 *dædal* 'cunningly fashioned'.
109 Cf. 'the full-blazing sun, / Which now sat high in his
    meridian tower' (*Paradise Lost*, 4:29–30).

113–24 Warton is recalling the witch scenes in *Macbeth*,
    notably III.v where Hecat addresses the weird sisters.
    Cf. Joseph Warton, *The Enthusiast*, 193.
133 *saffron* Orange-yellow.

Th'afflicted songsters of the sadden'd groves 140
Hail not the sullen gloom; the waving elms
That hoar thro' time, and rang'd in thick array,
Enclose with stately row some rural hall,
Are mute, nor echo with the clamors hoarse
Of rooks rejoicing on their airy boughs; 145
While to the shed the dripping poultry croud,
A mournful train: secure the village-hind
Hangs o'er the crackling blaze, nor tempts the storm;
Fix'd in th'unfinish'd furrow rests the plough:
Rings not the high wood with enliv'ning shouts 150
Of early hunter: all is silence drear;
And deepest sadness wraps the face of things.
   Thro' POPE's soft song tho' all the Graces breathe,
And happiest art adorn his Attic page;
Yet does my mind with sweeter transport glow, 155
As at the root of mossy trunk reclin'd,
In magic SPENSER's wildly-warbled song
I see deserted Una wander wide
Thro' wasteful solitudes, and lurid heaths,
Weary, forlorn; than when the fated fair, 160
Upon the bosom bright of silver Thames,
Launches in all the lustre of brocade,
Amid the splendors of the laughing Sun.
The gay description palls upon the sense,
And coldly strikes the mind with feeble bliss. 165
   Ye Youths of Albion's beauty-blooming isle,
Whose brows have worn the wreath of luckless love,
Is there a pleasure like the pensive mood,
Whose magic wont to sooth your soften'd souls?
O tell how rapturous the joy, to melt 170
To Melody's assuasive voice; to bend
Th'uncertain step along the midnight mead,
And pour your sorrows to the pitying moon,
By many a slow trill from the bird of woe
Oft interrupted; in embowering woods 175
By darksome brook to muse, and there forget
The solemn dulness of the tedious world,
While Fancy grasps the visionary fair:
And now no more th'abstracted ear attends
The water's murm'ring lapse, th'entranced eye 180
Pierces no longer thro' th'extended rows
Of thick-rang'd trees; 'till haply from the depth
The woodman's stroke, or distant-tinkling team,
Or heifer rustling thro' the brake, alarms

154 *Attic* 'classical'.
158 *Una* The heroine of *Faerie Queene*, Book One, separated from her lover the Red Cross Knight by the enchanter Archimago.
160 *fated fair* Pope's Belinda. Cf. *The Rape of the Lock*, 2:4.
165 *1747* continued with the following paragraph, omitted from *1755*: 'O wrap me then in shades of darksom pine, / Bear me to caves by desolation brown, / To dusky vales, and hermit-haunted rocks! / And hark, methinks

resounding from the gloom / The voice of Melancholy strikes mine ear; / "Come, leave the busy trifles of vain life, / And let these twilight mansions teach thy mind / The Joys of Musing, and of solemn Thought."'
166 *Albion* Britain.
171 *assuasive* 'soothing'.
174 *bird of woe* 'The owle ... That prophete is of wo' (Chaucer).

Th'illuded sense, and mars the golden dream.   185
These are delights that absence drear has made
Familiar to my soul, e'er since the form
Of young Sapphira, beauteous as the Spring,
When from her vi'let-woven couch awak'd
By frolic Zephyr's hand, her tender cheek   190
Graceful she lifts, and blushing from her bow'r,
Issues to cloath in gladsome-glist'ring green
The genial globe, first met my dazzled sight:
These are delights unknown to minds profane,
And which alone the pensive soul can taste.   195
    The taper'd choir, at the late hour of pray'r,
Oft let me tread, while to th'according voice
The many-sounding organ peals on high,
The clear slow-dittied chaunt, or varied hymn,
'Till all my soul is bath'd in ecstasies,   200
And lap'd in Paradise. Or let me sit
Far in sequester'd iles of the deep dome,
There lonesome listen to the sacred sounds,
Which, as they lengthen thro' the Gothic vaults,
In hollow murmurs reach my ravish'd ear.   205
Nor when the lamps expiring yield to night,
And solitude returns, would I forsake
The solemn mansion, but attentive mark
The due clock swinging slow with sweepy sway,
Measuring Time's flight with momentary sound.   210
    Nor let me fail to cultivate my mind
With the soft thrillings of the tragic muse,
Divine Melpomene, sweet Pity's nurse,
Queen of the stately step, and flowing pall.
Now let Monimia mourn with streaming eyes   215
Her joys incestuous, and polluted love:
Now let soft Juliet in the gaping tomb
Print the last kiss on her true Romeo's lips,
His lips yet reeking from the deadly draught.
Or Jaffeir kneel for one forgiving look.   220
Nor seldom let the Moor on Desdemone
Pour the misguided threats of jealous rage.
By soft degrees the manly torrent steals
From my swoln eyes; and at a brother's woe
My big heart melts in sympathizing tears.   225
    What are the splendors of the gaudy court,
Its tinsel trappings, and its pageant pomps?
To me far happier seems the banish'd Lord
Amid Siberia's unrejoycing wilds
Who pines all lonesome, in the chambers hoar   230
Of some high castle shut, whose windows dim
In distant ken discover trackless plains,

190 *Zephyr* The mild west wind.
196 *taper'd* 'candle-lit'.
198–201 Cf. *Il Penseroso*, 161–6.
206–10 These lines added *1755*.
213 *Melpomene* The Muse of Tragedy.

215 *Monimia* The heroine of Otway's *The Orphan* (1680),
    tricked into bed by her husband's twin brother.
220 *Jaffeir* In Otway's *Venice Preserv'd* (1682).
221 *Moor* Othello.

Where Winter ever whirls his icy car;
While still repeated objects of his view,
The gloomy battlements, and ivied spires   235
That crown the solitary dome, arise;
While from the topmost turret the slow clock,
Far heard along th'inhospitable wastes,
With sad-returning chime awakes new grief;
Ev'n he far happier seems than is the proud,   240
The potent Satrap, whom he left behind
'Mid Moscow's golden palaces, to drown
In ease and luxury the laughing hours.
   Illustrious objects strike the gazer's mind
With feeble bliss, and but allure the sight,   245
Nor rouze with impulse quick th'unfeeling heart.
Thus seen by shepherd from Hymettus' brow,
What dædal landscapes smile! here palmy groves,
Resounding once with Plato's voice, arise,
Amid whose umbrage green her silver head   250
Th'unfading olive lifts; here vine-clad hills
Lay forth their purple store, and sunny vales
In prospect vast their level laps expand,
Amid whose beauties glistering Athens tow'rs.
Tho' thro' the blissful scenes Ilissus roll   255
His sage-inspiring flood, whose winding marge
The thick-wove laurel shades; tho' roseate Morn
Pour all her splendors on th'empurpled scene;
Yet feels the hoary Hermit truer joys,
As from the cliff that o'er his cavern hangs,   260
He views the piles of fall'n Persepolis
In deep arrangement hide the darksome plain.
Unbounded waste! the mould'ring obelisc
Here, like a blasted oak, ascends the clouds;
Here Parian domes their vaulted halls disclose   265
Horrid with thorn, where lurks th'unpitying thief,
Whence flits the twilight-loving bat at eve,
And the deaf adder wreathes her spotted train,
The dwellings once of elegance and art.
Here temples rise, amid whose hallow'd bounds   270
Spires the black pine, while thro' the naked street,
Once haunt of tradeful merchants, springs the grass:
Here columns heap'd on prostrate columns, torn
From their firm base, encrease the mould'ring mass.
Far as the sight can pierce, appear the spoils   275
Of sunk magnificence! a blended scene
Of moles, fanes, arches, domes, and palaces,
Where, with his brother Horror, Ruin sits.
   O come then, Melancholy, queen of thought!

247 *Hymettus* The mountain overlooking Athens.
255 *Ilissus* Cf. Akenside, *The Pleasures of Imagination*, 1:594 and note.
258 *empurpled* 'reddened'.
261 *Persepolis* Capital of the Persian empire looted by Alexander the Great.
262 *In deep arrangement* 'piled thickly'.
265 *Parian* White marble.
266 *Horrid* 'bristling'. Cf. *Eloisa to Abelard*, 20.
277 *moles* 'sea walls'; *fanes* 'temples'.

O come with saintly look, and stedfast step,   280
From forth thy cave embower'd with mournful yew,
Where ever to the curfeu's solemn sound
List'ning thou sitt'st, and with thy cypress bind
Thy votary's hair, and seal him for thy son.
But never let Euphrosyne beguile   285
With toys of wanton mirth my fixed mind,
Nor in my path her primrose-garland cast.
Tho' 'mid her train the dimpled Hebe bare
Her rosy bosom to th'enamour'd view;
Tho' Venus, mother of the Smiles and Loves,   290
And Bacchus, ivy-crown'd, in citron-bow'r
With her on nectar-streaming fruitage feast:
What tho' 'tis her's to calm the low'ring skies,
And at her presence mild th'embattel'd clouds
Disperse in air, and o'er the face of heav'n   295
New day diffusive gleam at her approach;
Yet are these joys that Melancholy gives,
Than all her witless revels happier far;
These deep-felt joys, by Contemplation taught.
      Then ever, beauteous Contemplation, hail!   300
From thee began, auspicious maid, my song,
With thee shall end: for thou art fairer far
Than are the nymphs of Cirrha's mossy grot;
To loftier rapture thou canst wake the thought,
Than all the fabling Poet's boasted pow'rs.   305
Hail, queen divine! whom, as tradition tells,
Once, in his ev'ning walk, a Druid found,
Far in a hollow glade of Mona's woods;
And piteous bore with hospitable hand
To the close shelter of his oaken bow'r.   310
There soon the sage admiring mark'd the dawn
Of solemn musing in your pensive thought;
For when a smiling babe, you lov'd to lie
Oft deeply list'ning to the rapid roar
Of wood-hung Meinai, stream of Druids old.   315

285 *Euphrosyne* Mirth, one of the Three Graces, invoked in
   Milton's *L'Allegro*.
288 *Hebe* Embodiment of Youth (Gk. *hebe*), and the gods'
   cup-bearer. Cf. *L'Allegro*, 29–30.
303 *Cirrha's mossy grot* The Castalian Spring at Delphi,
   sacred to Apollo and the Muses.
307 *Druid* Priests of the old British religion, viewed as the

original bards. 'The children of the nobility they
retired withal into caves, or the most desolate parts of
forests; and kept them there, sometimes for 20 years,
under their discipline' (Chambers, *Cyclopædia*, 1738
edn).
308 *Mona* Anglesey (Lat. *Mona*), an island separated from
   the north coast of Wales by the Menai Strait (315).

Ode written at Vale-Royal Abbey in Cheshire

Warton's 'History of Gothic Architecture' has been
lost, but there still survive his 'Observations Critical
and Historical, on Castles, Churches, Monasteries,
and other Monuments of Antiquity in Various Parts of
England', which he compiled during his summer
rambles. He loved exploring medieval ruins, and
'Note-book in hand, he would mark, and measure,
and speculate, and admire' (so his great-nephew

recalled). This fascination is evident throughout his
poetry. In the Vale Royal ode Warton adopts the stanza
of Gray's *Elegy* for his contemplation on monastic
ruins, and there is a similar brooding sense of
mortality and a Gray-like self-consciousness about the
poet's own voice. But the ironies in Warton's ode are
more open and dramatic: while its alternating scenes
of vivid animation and gloomy decay stress the

activity of the imagination ('fancy'), the poem ends with Reason's sublime vision bursting through the cold half-light. First published in Warton's *Poems. A New Edition, with Additions* (1777). Text from the revised second edition of the same year.

As Evening slowly spreads his mantle hoar,
No ruder sounds the bounded valley fill,
Than the faint din, from yonder sedgy shore,
Of rushing waters, and the murmuring mill.

How sunk the scene, where cloyster'd Leisure mus'd!   5
Where war-worn Edward paid his aweful vow;
And, lavish of magnificence, diffus'd
His crouded spires o'er the broad mountain's brow!

The golden fans, that o'er the turrets strown,
Quick-glancing to the sun, quaint music made,   10
Are reft, and every battlement o'ergrown
With knotted thorns, and the tall sapling's shade.

The prickly thistle sheds its plumy crest,
And matted nettles shade the crumbling mass,
Where shone the pavement's surface smooth, imprest   15
With rich reflection of the storied glass.

Here hardy chieftains slept in proud repose,
Sublimely shrin'd in gorgeous imagery;
And through the lessening iles, in radiant rows,
Their consecrated banners hung on high.   20

There oxen browze, and there the sable yew
Through the dun void displays its baleful glooms;
And sheds in lingering drops ungenial dew
O'er the forgotten graves and scatter'd tombs.

By the slow clock, in duly-measur'd chime,   25
That from its airy spire full deeply toll'd,
No more the plowman counts the tedious time,
Nor distant shepherd pens his twilight fold.

High o'er the trackless heath at midnight seen,
No more the windows, rang'd in long array,   30
Where the tall shaft and fretted nook between
Thick ivy twines, the taper'd rites betray.

Title 'Founded by king Edward the first, about the year 1300 [actually 1270], in consequence of a vow which he made when in danger of being shipwrecked, during his return from a crusade' (Warton's note). The building of the Cistercian abbey of Vale Royal began in 1277. Much of the structure was dismantled after its dissolution in 1538, though the last remnants of the ancient walls and gates were not removed until the mid-nineteenth century.

1 *mantle hoar* 'grey cloak'.

10 *Quick-glancing to the sun* Cf. Gray, *Ode on the Spring*, 30 and note; *quaint* 'unusual and ingenious' (changed in later editions to *wild*).

11 *reft* 'stolen', as in 'bereft'.

16 *storied* 'telling a story'. Warton is recalling the 'storied windows' in Milton's *Il Penseroso*, 159, as much as line 41 of Gray's *Elegy*.

22 *dun* 'dusky'; *baleful* 'malignant'.

25–8 Cf. Gray, *Elegy*, 1–8.

32 *taper'd rites* 'candle-lit rituals'.

Ev'n now, amid the wavering ivy-wreaths,
(While kindred thoughts the pensive sounds inspire)
As the weak breeze in many a whisper breathes,   35
I seem to listen to the chanting quire. —

As o'er these shatter'd towers intent I muse,
Though rear'd by Charity's misguided zeal,
Yet can my breast soft Pity's sigh refuse,
Or conscious Candour's modest plea conceal?   40

For though the sorceress, Superstition blind,
Amid the pomp of dreadful sacrifice,
O'er the dim roofs, to cheat the tranced mind,
Oft bade her visionary gleams arise:

Though the vain hours unsocial Sloth beguil'd,   45
While the still cloister cold Oblivion lock'd;
And through the chambers pale, to slumbers mild
Wan Indolence her drowsy cradle rock'd:

Yet hence, enthron'd in venerable state,
Proud Hospitality dispens'd her store: 50
Ah! see, beneath yon tower's unvaulted gate,
Forlorn she sits upon the brambled floor.

Her ponderous vase, with gothic pourtraiture
Emboss'd, no more with balmy moisture flows:
Mid the mix'd shards, o'erwhelm'd in dust obscure,   55
No more, as erst, the golden goblet glows.

Sore beat by storms in Glory's arduous way,
Here might Ambition muse, a pilgrim sage;
Here raptur'd see, Religion's evening ray
Gild the calm walks of his reposing age.   60

Here antient Art her dedal fancies play'd
In the quaint mazes of the crisped roof;
In mellow glooms the speaking pane array'd,
And rang'd the cluster'd column, massy-proof.

Here Learning, guarded from a barbarous age,   65
Hover'd awhile, nor dar'd attempt the day;
And patient trac'd upon the pictur'd page
The holy legend, or heroic lay.

Hither the solitary minstrel came
An honour'd guest, while the grim evening sky   70
Hung lowering, and around the social flame
Tun'd his bold harp to tales of chivalry.

---

40 *Candour* 'kindly openness of mind'.
42 *the pomp of dreadful sacrifice* Cf. Pope, *Eloisa to Abelard*,
356.
54 *balmy* 'soothing'.
55 *shards* 'broken fragments'.

61 *dedal* (or 'dædal') 'inventive and intricate' (after
Dædalus, the mythical Greek builder of King Minos's
labyrinth).
64 *massy-proof* 'weighty and impenetrable'. Cf. 'antique
pillars massy proof' (*Il Penseroso*, 158).

Thus sings the Muse, all pensive and alone;
Nor scorns, within the deep fane's inmost cell,
To pluck the grey moss from the mantled stone,   75
Some holy founder's mouldering name to spell.

Thus sings the Muse: — yet partial as she sings,
With fond regret surveys these ruin'd piles:
And with fair images of antient things
The captive bard's obsequious mind beguiles.   80

But much we pardon to th'ingenuous Muse;
Her fairy shapes are trick'd by Fancy's pen:
Severer Reason forms far other views,
And scans the scene with philosophic ken.

From these deserted domes, new glories rise;   85
More useful institutes, adorning man,
Manners enlarg'd, and new civilities,
On fresh foundations build the social plan.

Science, on ampler plume, a bolder flight
Essays, escap'd from Superstition's shrine: 90
While freed Religion, like primeval light
Bursting from chaos, spreads her warmth divine.

74 *fane* 'temple'.
80 *obsequious* 'dutiful towards the dead' (obsequy = 'funeral rites'), but with the added suggestion of 'compliant'.
81 *ingenuous* 'without guile, candid'. Cf. 40.
84 *ken* 'vision'.

89 *Science* 'Acquired knowledge'.
91 *freed Religion* In the 1530s the dissolution of the monasteries followed the declaration of Henry VIII as supreme head of the English Church.

Sonnet: To the River Lodon

Perhaps the most influential sonnet of the century, Warton's poem created a vogue for the revisiting of river banks, in which the tracings of memory allow a measuring of present against past. Bowles, Coleridge and Wordsworth absorbed its influence, and the latter's *Tintern Abbey* expands the characteristic structure ('Since first ... interval between ... Yet still') to produce a masterpiece out of this minor genre. The Loddon, a tributary of the Thames, rises near Basingstoke. It was also Pope's 'native stream' for which he created his Lodona myth (cf. *Windsor-Forest*, 171–208). First published in Warton's *Poems. A New Edition, with Additions* (1777). Text from the revised second edition of the same year.

Ah! what a weary race my feet have run,
    Since first I trod thy banks with alders crown'd,
    And thought my way was all through fairy ground,
    Beneath thy azure sky, and golden sun:
Where first my muse to lisp her notes begun!   5
    While pensive memory traces back the round,
    Which fills the varied interval between;
    Much pleasure, more of sorrow, marks the scene.
Sweet native stream! those skies and suns so pure

1–3 Cf. 'The wayes through which my weary steppes I guyde / In this delightful land of Faerie' (Spenser, *Faerie Queene*, VI.i.1), quoted by Warton as the closing words of his *Observations on the Faerie Queene* (1754).

No more return, to chear my evening road!   10
  Yet still one joy remains, that not obscure,
Nor useless, all my vacant days have flow'd,
  From youth's gay dawn to manhood's prime mature;
  Nor with the Muse's laurel unbestow'd.

14 *Muse's laurel* Poetic honours. Warton was to become
Poet Laureate in 1785.

Verses on Sir Joshua Reynolds's Painted Window at New-College Oxford

Reynolds (1723–92) was President of the Royal Academy from its inception in 1768 and a figure of great authority over the culture of his day, both artistic and literary. His annual addresses to the Academy (published as *Discourses on Art*) were admired for their forceful endorsement of the classical tradition, but also for their stylistic clarity and polish. With his friend Dr Johnson, Reynolds was at the centre of the London literary circle focused on 'The Club', which he had founded in 1764 and of which Warton became a member on 5 March 1782. The *Verses* were published two months later. The poem takes for its subject Reynolds's controversial west window designed 1777–9 for the late-fourteenth-century chapel of New College and featuring a set of elegant allegorical ladies representing the Virtues. This intrusion of the classical style into one of Warton's beloved Gothic buildings (see headnote to *Ode written at Vale-Royal Abbey*) sets the scene for a typically Wartonian struggle between imagination and reason, heart and head. Warton stages a recantation of his Gothic tastes, and the victory is won by a universalized 'truth', one of the fundamental principles of the *Discourses*, especially the recently published seventh. The poem is really Warton's affectionate compliment to his friend and patron. Reynolds responded with good-humoured scepticism: 'I owe you great obligations for the Sacrifice which you have made, or pretend to have made, to modern Art, I say pretend, for tho' it be allowed that you have like a true Poet feigned marvellously well, and have opposed the two different stiles with the skill of a Connoisseur, yet I may be allowed to entertain some doubts of the sincerity of your conversion, I have no great confidence in the recantation of such an old offender' (Reynolds–Warton, 13 May 1782). Warton was widely respected as an authority on Gothic architecture, and in his *Observations on the Faerie Queene* (2nd edn, 1762) he was the first to differentiate its various styles. He collected and preserved medieval glass and fitted up the windows of Trinity College library with pieces he had rescued. The poem's final note of reconciliation is perhaps an uneasy one. The text is that of the 'Second Edition, Corrected' of 1783.

Ah, stay thy treacherous hand, forbear to trace
Those faultless forms of elegance and grace!
Ah, cease to spread the bright transparent mass,
With Titian's pencil, o'er the speaking glass!
Nor steal, by strokes of art with truth combin'd,   5
The fond illusions of my wayward mind!
For long, enamour'd of a barbarous age,
A faithless truant to the classic page;
Long have I lov'd to catch the simple chime
Of minstrel-harps, and spell the fabling rime;   10
To view the festive rites, the knightly play,
That deck'd heroic Albion's elder day;
To mark the mouldering halls of Barons bold,
And the rough castle, cast in giant mould;
With Gothic manners Gothic arts explore,   15
And muse on the magnificence of yore.

4 *Titian* (c.1488–1576), Venetian painter; *pencil* Artist's brush.

12 *Albion* Britain.

16 *yore* 'long ago'.

But chief, enraptur'd have I lov'd to roam,
A lingering votary, the vaulted dome,
Where the tall shafts, that mount in massy pride,
Their mingling branches shoot from side to side;   20
Where elfin sculptors, with fantastic clew,
Oer the long roof their wild embroidery drew;
Where SUPERSTITION, with capricious hand
In many a maze the wreathed window plann'd,
With hues romantic ting'd the gorgeous pane,   25
To fill with holy light the wondrous fane;
To aid the builder's model, richly rude,
By no Vitruvian symmetry subdued;
To suit the genius of the mystic pile:
Whilst as around the far-retiring ile,   30
And fretted shrines with hoary trophies hung,
Her dark illumination wide she flung,
With new solemnity, the nooks profound,
The caves of death, and the dim arches frown'd.
From bliss long felt unwillingly we part: 35
Ah, spare the weakness of a lover's heart!
Chase not the phantoms of my fairy dream,
Phantoms that shrink at Reason's painful gleam!
That softer touch, insidious artist, stay,
Nor to new joys my struggling breast betray!   40
     Such was a pensive bard's mistaken strain. —
But, oh, of ravish'd pleasures why complain?
No more the matchless skill I call unkind
That strives to disenchant my cheated mind.
For when again I view thy chaste Design,   45
The just proportion, and the genuin line;
Those native pourtraitures of Attic art,
That from the lucid surface seem to start;
Those tints, that steal no glories from the day,
Nor ask the sun to lend his streaming ray;   50
The doubtful radiance of contending dies,
That faintly mingle, yet distinctly rise;
Twixt light and shade the transitory strife;
The feature blooming with immortal life:
The stole in casual foldings taught to flow,   55
Not with ambitious ornaments to glow;
The tread majestic, and the beaming eye

18 *votary* 'devoted worshipper'.

21 *clew* 'thread'.

22 Cf. Warton's description of the roof of the choir at Gloucester Cathedral: 'the most delicate fretwork is expressed in stone ... where it is thrown, like a web of embroidery over the old vaulting' (*Observations on the Faerie Queene*, 2:191).

25–6 Medieval glass was formed of individual translucent pieces of coloured glass made by the old 'pot-metal technique' in which oxides were used to colour the molten glass. The technique had been largely forgotten by the eighteenth century.

26 *fane* 'temple'.

28 *Vitruvian* Cf. Montagu, *An Epistle to Lord Bathurst*, 7 and note.

31 *fretted* 'elaborately carved'; *hoary* 'venerable'.

47 *Attic* The purest form of classicism. Attica was the country around Athens.

49–50 The colours were not responsive to the sunlight. Cf. 93–100n.

55–6 Reynolds recommended painting simple drapery, 'without those whimsical capricious forms by which all other dresses are embarrassed' (*Discourse* 7, 1776).

That lifted speaks its commerce with the sky;
Heaven's golden emanation, gleaming mild
Oer the mean cradle of the virgin's child: 60
Sudden, the sombrous imagery is fled,
Which late my visionary rapture fed:
Thy powerful hand has broke the Gothic chain,
And brought my bosom back to truth again:
To truth, by no peculiar taste confin'd,   65
Whose universal pattern strikes mankind;
To truth, whose bold and unresisted aim
Checks frail caprice, and fashion's fickle claim;
To truth, whose Charms deception's magic quell,
And bind coy Fancy in a stronger spell.   70
   Ye brawny Prophets, that in robes so rich,
At distance due, possess the crisped nich;
Ye Rows of Patriarchs, that sublimely rear'd
Diffuse a proud primeval length of beard:
Ye Saints, who clad in crimson's bright array,   75
More pride than humble poverty display:
Ye Virgins meek, that wear the palmy crown
Of patient faith, and yet so fiercely frown:
Ye Angels, that from clouds of gold recline,
But boast no semblance to a race divine: 80
Ye tragic Tales of legendary lore,
That draw devotion's ready tear no more:
Ye Martyrdoms of unenlighten'd days,
Ye Miracles, that now no wonder raise:
Shapes, that with one broad glare the gazer strike,   85
Kings, Bishops, Nuns, Apostles, all alike!
Ye Colours, that th'unwary sight amaze,
And only dazzle in the noontide blaze!
No more the Sacred Window's round disgrace,
But yield to Grecian groupes the shining space.   90
Lo, from the canvas Beauty shifts her throne,
Lo, Picture's powers a new formation own!
Behold she prints upon the crystal plain,
With her own energy, th'expressive stain!
The mighty Master spreads his mimic toil   95
More wide, nor only blends the breathing oil;
But calls the lineaments of life compleat
From genial alchymy's creative heat;

59–60 Couplet added *1783*. The Nativity scene in the window's central panel was not placed in the chapel until summer 1783, having been exhibited in London in a darkened room, where according to Horace Walpole it made a 'glorious' effect. He was very disappointed when he saw it in the chapel itself that September: 'Sir Joshua's washy Virtues make the Nativity a dark spot … which happened, as I knew it would, from most of Jarvis's colours not being transparent' (Walpole–Conway, 6 October 1785).

63–70 'The natural appetite or taste of the human mind is for *Truth* … / … In the midst of the highest flights of fancy or imagination, reason ought to preside from first to last' (*Discourse* 7).

72 *crisped* 'curled'.

93–100 Reynolds's window was made by the eighteenth-century 'enamel technique' in which the design was painted onto transparent glass using a palette of coloured enamels. It was then fired after painting. The 'fusion' was however less permanent than with medieval techniques – and less translucent.

98 *genial* 'life-giving'; *alchymy* The mystical chemistry of the Middle Ages which sought to transform base metals to gold.

Obedient forms to the bright fusion gives,
While in the warm enamel Nature lives.   100
   REYNOLDS, tis thine, from the broad window's height,
To add new lustre to religious light:
Not of it's pomp to strip this ancient shrine,
But bid that pomp with purer radiance shine:
With arts unknown before, to reconcile   105
The willing Graces to the Gothic pile.

101 *REYNOLDS* Altered from 'Artist' (*1782*) at Reynolds's request ('if the title page should be lost it will appear to be addressd to Mr Jervais'). Thomas Jervais (d. 1799) was the glass painter who had executed Reynolds's design.

103 *strip* Warton is thinking of the Calvinist reformers who 'strip[ped] religion of its superstitious and ostensible pageantries ... of every simple ornament, every significant symbol, and decent ceremony' (*History of English Poetry* (1781), 3:165).

Robert Lloyd (1733–1764)

After a classical education at Westminster School (where his father was second master) and Trinity College, Cambridge, Lloyd turned his back on the traditional professions and lived from hand to mouth in London as a journalist, poet, dramatist, editor and translator, earning what money he could from the booksellers. A lapse into debt and despair was the fate of many 'hacks' of his time, and accounts of Lloyd speak of his 'idleness and intemperance' and 'reckless dissipation'. Along with six other Old Westminsters (who included Charles Churchill, William Cowper, George Colman and Bonnell Thornton) he formed the Nonsense Club, which dined every Thursday and specialized in satirical humour and parody. His best-known satire, *The Actor* (1760), reached a fourth edition by 1764, and his *Poems* were published by subscription in 1762. The following year he was arrested for debt, and he died in the Fleet prison on 15 December 1764, a fortnight after the production of his comic opera *The Capricious Lovers* at Drury Lane.

The Cit's Country Box was first published in the *Connoisseur*, 135 (26 August 1756), a humorous weekly established by Colman and Thornton, and personified by its fashionable social critic, 'Mr Town'. Throughout the century, the leisured and wealthy 'Town' in the western parts of London defined itself against the 'City', the dynamo of trade and money-making to the east. The 'Cit' was a wealthy tradesman-citizen, here a common-council-man of one of the London City wards, with enough money to buy himself a rural lifestyle a few miles out in the suburbs, to which he could commute with the family at weekends. These beginnings of suburban Englishness, now at the heart of the nation's character, are here mocked for their off-the-peg vulgarity as a tasteless repro of a genuine country life. Such invaders into the landscape were importing their sham 'style' where it did not belong. Lloyd's poem catches the Thriftys' cockney vulgarity (*warm, snug, in clover, countrified*) and associates it with the popular Chinese-Gothic styles being picked up by the new suburbanites. A prose equivalent of Lloyd's satire, perhaps by Lloyd himself, had appeared two years earlier as *Connoisseur, 33* ('Letter, on the Villas of our Tradesmen'): 'In these dusty retreats, where the want of *London* smoke is supplied by the smoke of *Virginia* tobacco, our chief citizens are accustomed to pass the end and the beginning of every week. Their Boxes, (as they are modestly called) … which stand single, and at a distance from the road, have always a summer-house at the end of a small garden; which being erected upon a wall adjoining to the highway, commands a view of every carriage, and gives the owner an opportunity of displaying his best wig to every one that passes by …' (17 September 1754). Lloyd's scorn for modern lapses in taste can be compared with Pope's aristocratic satire in *Epistle to Burlington*. What follows is the slightly revised text in Lloyd's *Poems* (1762), pp. 43–9.

The Cit's Country Box

Vos sapere & solos aio bene vivere, quorum,
Conspicitur nitidis fundata pecunia villis.
HOR.

The wealthy Cit, grown old in trade,
Now wishes for the rural shade,
And buckles to his one-horse chair,
Old *Dobbin*, or the founder'd mare;
While wedg'd in closely by his side,   5
Sits Madam, his unwieldy bride,
With *Jacky* on a stool before 'em,
And out they jog in due decorum.
Scarce past the turnpike half a mile,
How all the country seems to smile!   10
And as they slowly jog together,
The Cit commends the road and weather;

Motto 'Only men like you, I maintain, are wise and live well, whose invested wealth is displayed in handsome villas' (Horace, *Epistles*, 1:15). The *Connoisseur*'s translation is: 'O Cit thrice happy, that canst range / To *Bow* or *Clapham* from the *'Change*; / In whose spruce *Villa* is display'd / The plumb, thou hast acquir'd by trade!' (a 'plum' was £100,000).
4 *founder'd* 'lame'.

While Madam doats upon the trees,
And longs for ev'ry house she sees,
Admires its views, its situation,   15
And thus she opens her oration.
  What signify the loads of wealth,
Without that richest jewel, health?
Excuse the fondness of a wife,
Who doats upon your precious life!   20
Such easeless toil, such constant care,
Is more than human strength can bear.
One may observe it in your face —
Indeed, my dear, you break apace:
And nothing can your health repair,   25
But exercise, and country air.
Sir Traffic has a house, you know,
About a mile from *Cheney-Row:*
He's a *good* man, indeed 'tis true,
But not so *warm*, my dear, as you: 30
And folks are always apt to sneer —
One would not be out-done, my dear!
  Sir Traffic's name so well apply'd
Awak'd his brother merchant's pride;
And Thrifty, who had all his life   35
Paid utmost deference to his wife,
Confess'd her arguments had reason,
And by th'approaching summer season,
Draws a few hundreds from the stocks,
And purchases his Country Box.   40
  Some three or four mile out of town,
(An hour's ride will bring you down,)
He fixes on his choice abode,
Not half a furlong from the road:
And so convenient does it lay,   45
The stages pass it ev'ry day:
And then so snug, so mighty pretty,
To have an house so near the city!
Take but your places at the Boar
You're set down at the very door.   50
  Well then, suppose them fix'd at last,
White-washing, painting, scrubbing past,
Hugging themselves in ease and clover,
With all the fuss of moving over;
Lo, a new heap of whims are bred!   55
And wanton in my lady's head.
  Well to be sure, it must be own'd,
It is a charming spot of ground;
So sweet a distance for a ride,
And all about so *countrified!*   60
'Twould come to but a trifling price
To make it quite a paradise;

28 *Cheney-Row* By the Thames at Chelsea, then on the
  western edge of London.
30 *warm* 'comfortably off'.

39 *stocks* Investments in the City stock-market.
44 *not half a furlong* About a hundred yards.
49 *the Boar* A coaching inn.

I cannot bear those nasty rails,
Those ugly broken mouldy pales:
Suppose, my dear, instead of these,   65
We build a railing, all Chinese.
Although one hates to be expos'd,
'Tis dismal to be thus inclos'd;
One hardly any object sees —
I wish you'd fell those odious trees.   70
Objects continual passing by
Were something to amuse the eye,
But to be pent within the walls —
One might as well be at St. Paul's.
Our house beholders would adore,   75
Was there a level lawn before,
Nothing its views to incommode,
But quite laid open to the road;
While ev'ry trav'ler in amaze,
Should on our little mansion gaze,   80
And pointing to the choice retreat,
Cry, that's Sir Thrifty's Country Seat.
    No doubt her arguments prevail,
For Madam's TASTE can never fail.
    Blest age! when all men may procure,   85
The title of a Connoisseur;
When noble and ignoble herd,
Are govern'd by a single word;
Though, like the royal German dames,
It bears an hundred Christian names;   90
As Genius, Fancy, Judgment, Goût,
Whim, Caprice, Je-ne-scai-quoi, Virtù:
Which appellations all describe
TASTE, and the modern *tasteful* tribe.
    Now bricklay'rs, carpenters, and joiners,   95
With Chinese artists, and designers,
Produce their schemes of alteration,
To work this wond'rous reformation.
The useful dome, which secret stood,
Embosom'd in the yew-tree's wood,   100
The trav'ler with amazement sees
A temple, Gothic, or Chinese,
With many a bell, and tawdry rag on,
And crested with a sprawling dragon;
A wooden arch is bent astride   105
A ditch of water, four foot wide,
With angles, curves, and zigzag lines,
From Halfpenny's exact designs.

---

70 Cf. Pope, *Epistle to a Lady*, 37–40.

84–94 *'Taste* is at present the darling idol of the polite
world … The fine ladies and gentlemen dress with
Taste; the architects, whether *Gothic* or *Chinese*, build
with Taste; the painters paint with Taste; the poets
write with Taste; critics read with Taste; and, in short,
fidlers, players, singers, dancers, and mechanics
themselves, are all the sons and daughters of Taste'

(*Connoisseur*, 120). Cf. Pope, *Epistle to Burlington*,
13–18.

108 *Halfpenny* Little is known of 'William Halfpenny'
(alternatively 'Michael Hoare'), who published ready-
made designs in Gothic or Chinese tastes. The items in
the poem could have been chosen from his *New Designs
for Chinese Temples* (1750–2).

In front, a level lawn is seen,
Without a shrub upon the green,   110
Where Taste would want its first great law,
But for the skulking, sly *ha-ha*,
By whose miraculous assistance,
You gain a prospect two fields distance.
And now from Hyde-Park Corner come   115
The Gods of Athens, and of Rome.
Here squabby Cupids take their places,
With Venus, and the clumsy Graces:
Apollo there, with aim so clever,
Stretches his leaden bow for ever;   120
And there, without the pow'r to fly,
Stands fix'd a tip-toe Mercury.
   The Villa thus completely grac'd,
All own, that Thrifty has a Taste;
And Madam's female friends, and cousins,   125
With common-council-men, by dozens,
Flock ev'ry Sunday to the Seat,
To stare about them, and to eat.

111 *want* 'lack'.
112 *ha-ha* A boundary-ditch sunk instead of a fence so as to
   give an unbroken prospect.

Christopher Smart (1722–1771)

When the young Frances Burney met Smart in September 1768, she recorded in her diary: 'How great a pity so clever, so ingenious a man should be reduced to such shocking circumstances. He is extremely grave, & has still great wildness in his manner, looks & voice – 'tis impossible to *see* him & to *think* of his words, without feeling the utmost pity & concern for him.' The trajectory of Smart's life from Cambridge College to the madhouse and the prison speaks of decline and fall, and yet what was perhaps the most original voice in eighteenth-century poetry grew out of that failure and adversity.

Smart went up to Pembroke College, Cambridge in 1739 supported by an annuity from the Vane family (his father, who had died in 1733, had been Lord Vane's estate manager). He soon distinguished himself as a classical scholar and was elected to a fellowship in 1745, teaching philosophy, classical literature, logic and the Greek New Testament. But Smart felt increasingly restricted by academic life, and in 1749 he moved to London, where he immersed himself in the musical, theatrical and literary life of the capital. In 1750 he began working as a journalist for the publisher John Newbery, editing his periodicals the *Student* (1750–1) and the *Midwife* (1751–3), and producing what must have been a large quantity of anonymous literary hack-work. It seemed that Smart could turn his hand to anything. He wrote songs for the entertainments at Vauxhall Gardens, produced verse for the magazines, and devised and performed the title role in *Mrs Midnight's Oratory*, a comic variety show that was a hit at the Haymarket Theatre and other less salubrious venues from 1751 onwards. During these years he retained his Cambridge fellowship and maintained his poetic reputation there by winning the university's Seatonian Prize (for a poem celebrating the attributes of the Deity) for five of its first six years, 1750–5. In 1752 Smart married Newbery's step-daughter, Anna Maria Carnan, an intelligent and talented woman who went on to edit Newbery's newspaper, the *Reading Mercury*, and he and his new wife took rooms in Canonbury House, Islington. Since dons could not marry, this meant the loss of Smart's Cambridge fellowship, and with it a steady income. The life of tavern and pleasure garden began to take its toll: Smart was a heavy drinker and his debts mounted with his excesses. His *Poems on Several Occasions* (1752) did not reach a second edition, and his health was evidently breaking down. His last Seatonian Poem, *Hymn to the Supreme Being, on Recovery from a dangerous Fit of Illness* (1756), was dedicated to Dr Robert James, who, Smart recorded, had three times

'rescued me from the grave'. The crisis had arrived, and by the end of the year Smart was placed under restraint. On 6 May 1757 he was admitted to St Luke's Hospital for the Insane, but was released uncured a year later. The nature of his mental problems cannot be diagnosed with certainty, but there may have been violent mood swings ('For I have a greater compass both of mirth and melancholy than another', he says in *Jubilate Agno*, B132); one unstable element was a religious fervour that caused him to pray loudly in public places whenever the need took him. 'He insisted on people praying with him', recalled Samuel Johnson, 'and I'd as lief pray with Kit Smart as any one else.' Smart's family could take the strain no longer, and early in 1759 he was moved to George Potter's private madhouse at Bethnal Green, and from that time on he was severed from his wife and two daughters. At Potter's house Smart could dig in the garden and was supplied with pen and ink, and during his confinement he worked methodically day by day on his manuscript of *Jubilate Agno*. When friends helped secure his release at the end of January 1763, he moved into a house overlooking St James's Park. There followed an intensely productive period. His most sustained and brilliant poem, *A Song to David*, was followed by *Poems by Mr Smart* and *Poems on Several Occasions* (all three published in 1763), and the following year his oratorio *Hannah* was performed and printed, as well as *Ode to … the Earl of Northumberland, … With some other Pieces*. In 1765 Smart's prominence as a religious poet was confirmed with *A Translation of the Psalms of David* and *Hymns and Spiritual Songs for the Fasts and Festivals of the Church of England*. The list of subscribers included the poets Akenside, Cowper, Gray, the Wartons and many other cultural celebrities. In 1767 he published a four-volume verse translation of the works of Horace. But in spite of this productivity his finances remained desperate. On 26 April 1770 he was yet again arrested for debt and was placed in the King's Bench prison. He died there of a liver disorder on 20 May 1771.

Contemporary responses to Smart's religious poetry tended to be coloured by his reputation for mental instability, and his work, though quite well received, had a small readership. *A Song to David* was taken to be an uneven lyric outburst rather than the controlled and intellectually focused text we appreciate today. *Jubilate Agno* remained unknown until the twentieth century. It is now possible to see Smart's two greatest poems in terms of a wider mid-century search for authentic voices and primal experiences exemplified in the work of Chatterton and

Macpherson. We can recognize him as a modern psalmist making 'a joyful noise unto God' (Psalm 66:1) who wished to bring adoration and gratitude back to religion, and for whom all life exists in praise of its creator. Like his Victorian admirer, Robert Browning, we can value Smart's intense vision and disconcerting immediacy, as a poet who 'pierced the screen / 'Twixt thing and word, lit language straight from soul'.

'my Cat Jeoffry'

(from *Jubilate Agno*)

Smart's *Jubilate Agno* ('Rejoice in the Lamb') exists in a unique fragmentary manuscript now at Harvard University. It was compiled at the rate of up to three lines a day (often just a single one) during his confinement in the madhouse, and Smart seems to have begun some time between June 1758 and April 1759, and to have worked on it until his release in January 1763. Thirty-two folio pages survive from what must have been more than twice that number, filled with his small neat hand, and divided into separate 'Let' and 'For' sheets. The manuscript was discovered and printed by W. F. Stead in 1939, but it was not until W. H. Bond's edition in 1954 that the antiphonal nature of some of the material was recognized. In the earlier stages 'Let' and 'For' sections on separate sheets were evidently intended to be delivered antiphonally by two separate voices (e.g. 'Let Eliada rejoice with the Gier-eagle who is swift and of great penetration / For I bless the Lord Jesus for the memory of GAY, POPE and SWIFT' B84). The 'For' verses tend throughout to be more personal in character, invoking blessings on people Smart admired or who had helped him, and in the 'Let' verses figures from the Bible are associated with animals, birds, fish, etc. Interest in the nature and techniques of Hebrew poetry had been aroused by the Oxford lectures of Smart's friend Robert Lowth, 1741–50, published as *De sacra poesi Hebraeorum* (1753), and Lowth's discussion of antiphonal performance may have influenced what Smart called his 'MAGNIFICAT', or song of praise (B43). During his confinement Smart had plenty of time to observe the activities of his cat, Jeoffry, and in the 'For' lines devoted to him (there are no corresponding 'Let' lines) he is lovingly celebrated as a creature full of the spirit of life, of divine electricity. He becomes an exemplary Christian who watches for the Lord and is in His hands. The lines on Jeoffry given here are from the Harvard manuscript as transcribed and edited by Karina Williamson (*The Poetical Works of Christopher Smart*, vol. 1 (Oxford, 1980)). They consist of lines 695–768 of Fragment B, which ends at that point. Earlier in Fragment B Smart wrote: 'For my talent is to give an impression upon words by punching, that when the reader casts his eye upon 'em, he takes up the image from the mould which I have made' (B404), and this catches very well the vividness of our picture of Jeoffry.

> For I will consider my Cat Jeoffry.
> For he is the servant of the Living God duly and daily serving him.
> For at the first glance of the glory of God in the East he worships in his way.
> For is this done by wreathing his body seven times round with elegant quickness.
> For then he leaps up to catch the musk, which is the blessing of God upon his prayer.　5
> For he rolls upon prank to work it in.
> For having done duty and received blessing he begins to consider himself.
> For this he performs in ten degrees.
> For first he looks upon his fore-paws to see if they are clean.
> For secondly he kicks up behind to clear away there.　10
> For thirdly he works it upon stretch with the fore paws extended.
> For fourthly he sharpens his paws by wood.
> For fifthly he washes himself.
> For Sixthly he rolls upon wash.
> For Seventhly he fleas himself, that he may not be interrupted upon the beat.　15
> For Eighthly he rubs himself against a post.

5 *musk* '[Musked Crane's-bill] is preserved in many gardens, for the sweet Scent its Leaves afford when rubb'd between the Fingers, which occasion'd its being called Musk, or Muscovy' (Philip Miller, *The Gardeners Dictionary* (1759), s.v. 'Geranium').

6 *upon prank* 'for a frolic'.

15 *upon the beat* 'on his rounds'.

For Ninthly he looks up for his instructions.
For Tenthly he goes in quest of food.
For having consider'd God and himself he will consider his neighbour.
For if he meets another cat he will kiss her in kindness. 20
For when he takes his prey he plays with it to give it chance.
For one mouse in seven escapes by his dallying.
For when his day's work is done his business more properly begins.
For he keeps the Lord's watch in the night against the adversary.
For he counteracts the powers of darkness by his electrical skin and glaring eyes. 25
For he counteracts the Devil, who is death, by brisking about the life.
For in his morning orisons he loves the sun and the sun loves him.
For he is of the tribe of Tiger.
For the Cherub Cat is a term of the Angel Tiger.
For he has the subtlety and hissing of a serpent, which in goodness he suppresses. 30
For he will not do destruction, if he is well-fed, neither will he spit without
    provocation.
For he purrs in thankfulness, when God tells him he's a good Cat.
For he is an instrument for the children to learn benevolence upon.
For every house is incompleat without him and a blessing is lacking in the spirit.
For the Lord commanded Moses concerning the cats at the departure of the Children
    of Israel from Egypt. 35
For every family had one cat at least in the bag.
For the English Cats are the best in Europe.
For he is the cleanest in the use of his fore-paws of any quadrupede.
For the dexterity of his defence is an instance of the love of God to him exceedingly.
For he is the quickest to his mark of any creature. 40
For he is tenacious of his point.
For he is a mixture of gravity and waggery.
For he knows that God is his Saviour.
For there is nothing sweeter than his peace when at rest.
For there is nothing brisker than his life when in motion. 45
For he is of the Lord's poor and so indeed is he called by benevolence perpetually —
    Poor Jeoffry! poor Jeoffry! the rat has bit thy throat.
For I bless the name of the Lord Jesus that Jeoffry is better.
For the divine spirit comes about his body to sustain it in compleat cat.
For his tongue is exceeding pure so that it has in purity what it wants in musick.
For he is docile and can learn certain things. 50
For he can set up with gravity which is patience upon approbation.

24 *the Lord's watch* 'Blessed are those servants, whom the lord when he cometh shall find watching' (Luke, 12:37); *the adversary* 'Be sober, be vigilant; because your adversary the devil, as a roaring lion, walketh about, seeking whom he may devour' (1 Peter, 5:8).

25 *electrical skin* 'Cats have this property ['natural electricity'] in the greatest degree of any animal ... It appears to me of singular use to animals destin'd to catch their prey in the dark; they give a sudden and quick erection to their furr, which raises the electrical fire, and this, by its quickness rushing along the long pointed hairs over their eyes, and illuminating the pupils enables them to perceive and seize their prey' (*Gentleman's Magazine*, 24 (1754), p. 113).

27 *orisons* 'prayers'.

29 *Cherub Cat* Cf. 'cherub Contemplation' (Milton, *Il Penseroso*, 54). In the celestial hierarchy the *cherubim* had the capacity to see God and excelled in knowledge of Him.

35 'And a mixed multitude went up also with them; and flocks, and herds, even very much cattle' (Exodus, 12:38). At this date the term 'cattle' could include any creature reared or bred. Cats are mentioned nowhere in the Bible.

36 *cat ... in the bag* 'secret' (Cf. the proverbial 'Let the cat out of the bag').

46 *the Lord's poor* 'Blessed are the poor in spirit: for theirs is the kingdom of heaven' (Matthew, 5:3).

51 *set up* 'sit up (late at night)' (*OED* 'set' 154kk); *upon approbation* 'put to the test'.

For he can fetch and carry, which is patience in employment.
For he can jump over a stick which is patience upon proof positive.
For he can spraggle upon waggle at the word of command.
For he can jump from an eminence into his master's bosom. 55
For he can catch the cork and toss it again.
For he is hated by the hypocrite and miser.
For the former is affraid of detection.
For the latter refuses the charge.
For he camels his back to bear the first notion of business. 60
For he is good to think on, if a man would express himself neatly.
For he made a great figure in Egypt for his signal services.
For he killed the Ichneumon-rat very pernicious by land.
For his ears are so acute that they sting again.
For from this proceeds the passing quickness of his attention. 65
For by stroaking of him I have found out electricity.
For I perceived God's light about him both wax and fire.
For the Electrical fire is the spiritual substance, which God sends from heaven to
    sustain the bodies both of man and beast.
For God has blessed him in the variety of his movements.
For, tho he cannot fly, he is an excellent clamberer. 70
For his motions upon the face of the earth are more than any other quadrupede.
For he can tread to all the measures upon the musick.
For he can swim for life.
For he can creep.

53 *positive* 'absolute'.
54 *spraggle* 'sprawl' (*OED* 'sprackle'); *upon waggle* 'while shaking about'.
62 The ancient Egyptians domesticated cats and mummified them after death.

63 *Ichneumon* A close relative of the mongoose, venerated by ancient Egyptians for destroying crocodile eggs.
64 *again* 'in response' (*OED* 'again' 3).

A Song to David

The poem was printed as a handsome quarto pamphlet on 6 April 1763, Smart's first publication after his confinement ended in January. According to his nephew it was written along with the translation of the Psalms in a burst of creative activity on his release. However, one of the first reviewers, John Langhorne, remarked that he had been informed that it was composed in the madhouse 'when the Author was denied the use of pen, ink, and paper, and was obliged to indent his lines, with the need of a key, upon the wainscot' (*Monthly Review*, 28 (1763), p. 321). This image has the deep truth of myth (and is therefore almost certainly spurious). It expresses something about the poem's character: the disciplined intensity of the vision incised into the wooden panelling by a man holding a key (to the door, or the poem?), meaning compressed, no word wasted, the work built up line by line, stanza by stanza, to completion. The poem's symmetry is indeed striking. Forming the keystone of the eighty-six stanzas is a central block of ten (nos *39–48*) which is an 'exercise' (a word combining the idea of a spiritual meditation with a disciplined task) on the Ten Commandments or

'decalogue'. Placed either side of it are two direct invocations (*38*: O *DAVID, scholar of the Lord!* and *49*: O *DAVID, highest in the list*). The opening thirty-seven stanzas begin with a triad addressing David (*1–3*), a set of thirteen stanzas celebrating David's virtues as a group (*4*) and individually (*5–16*), a set of thirteen itemizing the effects and the subjects of David's songs (*17–29*), and a meditation on the Seven Pillars of Wisdom in terms of the week of Creation (*30–7*). After the central block is a thirty-seven-stanza song of praise (*50–86*). This is initiated by the word 'PRAISE' (line 295), and it comprises a set of thirteen stanzas of 'ADORATION' evoking the four seasons (*51–63*) (with the key word moving line by line twice through the stanza), a set celebrating the five senses (*64–70*), and a final section (*71–86*) in which Smart mounts to his climax through 'five degrees' (from *Sweet* to *Glorious*), ending with the triadic declaration: 'DETERMIN'D, DAR'D, and DONE'.

To modern readers the most appealing aspect of the poem is its celebration of the plenitude of nature. As with his cat Jeoffry, Smart delights in the energy and potential of each created thing, whether vegetable, animal or mineral. Here the world itself is a text, the natural equivalent of the temple at Jerusalem planned by David (line 38), and everything finds a place, however humble. Smart's vision throughout is sharp in its detail, his intellectual grasp firm, his ironies ingenious, his choice of word exact and telling.

Considered as the author of the Biblical Psalms, King David represents for Smart the supreme poet, the original lyric celebrator of the living world, but also a man chosen to fulfil God's purposes on earth. As a pattern of perfection he becomes a fusion of divine and human, a type of Christ ('Bright effluence of exceeding grace', 22), just as Christ himself is invoked when Smart re-envisages the Old Testament commandments and translates them into more Christ-like terms ('Turn from old Adam to the New', 280). But Smart is also defending a figure whose character had recently become the focus of controversy. In 1760 Samuel Chandler published a sermon praising King George II as a modern King David, and this provoked an anonymous reply, *The*

History of the Man after God's Own Heart, an uncompromising assault on David's character as cruel, vindictive, lascivious and hypocritical. During 1761–2 various writers were springing to David's defence, and Smart's idealized picture of David owes something to these. As might be expected, the poem is packed with Biblical allusion. Readers wishing to explore this aspect further are recommended to consult the commentary in *The Poetical Works of Christopher Smart*, vol. 2, ed. Marcus Walsh and Karina Williamson (Oxford, 1983), pp. 429–47, to which our own notes are considerably indebted.

After the first edition of 1763 the poem was included in Smart's *Poems on Several Occasions* later that year, and there was one more printing of the poem in Smart's lifetime when it was included, with a few minor corrections, in *A Translation of the Psalms of David* (1765). The latter text is given here. Material from Smart's prefatory summary of the poem (headed *Contents*) is italicized in our footnotes. His few annotations appear in normal type.

1

O THOU, that sit'st upon a throne,
With harp of high majestic tone,
 To praise the King of kings;
And voice of heav'n-ascending swell,
Which, while its deeper notes excell,
 Clear, as a clarion, rings: 5

2

To bless each valley, grove and coast,
And charm the cherubs to the post
 Of gratitude in throngs;
To keep the days on Zion's mount,   10
And send the year to his account,
 With dances and with songs:

3

O Servant of God's holiest charge,
The minister of praise at large,
 Which thou may'st now receive;   15
From thy blest mansion hail and hear,
From topmost eminence appear
 To this the wreath I weave.

4

Great, valiant, pious, good, and clean,
Sublime, contemplative, serene,   20
 Strong, constant, pleasant, wise!
Bright effluence of exceeding grace;

10 *keep* 'celebrate', 'record'. *Zion's mount* The city of David built on one of Jerusalem's hills (1 Kings, 8:1), also the Heavenly City.
18 *wreath* 'garland'.

19 *The excellence and lustre of David's character in twelve points of view* (Smart).
22 Cf. 'Bright effluence of bright essence increate' (Milton, *Paradise Lost*, 3:6).

Best man! — the swiftness and the race,
The peril, and the prize!

5

Great — from the lustre of his crown,   25
From Samuel's horn and God's renown,
   Which is the people's voice;
For all the host, from rear to van,
Applauded and embrac'd the man —
   The man of God's own choice.   30

6

Valiant — the word, and up he rose —
The fight — he triumph'd o'er the foes,
   Whom God's just laws abhor;
And arm'd in gallant faith he took
Against the boaster, from the brook,   35
   The weapons of the war.

7

Pious — magnificent and grand;
'Twas he the famous temple plann'd:
   (The seraph in his soul)
Foremost to give the Lord his dues,   40
Foremost to bless the welcome news,
   And foremost to condole.

8

Good — from Jehudah's genuine vein,
From God's best nature good in grain,
   His aspect and his heart;   45
To pity, to forgive, to save,
Witness En-gedi's conscious cave,
   And Shimei's blunted dart.

9

Clean — if perpetual prayer be pure,
And love, which could itself innure   50
   To fasting and to fear —
Clean in his gestures, hands, and feet,
To smite the lyre, the dance compleat,
   To play the sword and spear.

25–96 *proved from the history of his life* (Smart). David's twelve virtues are individually presented.

26 Samuel anointed David with oil (1 Samuel, 16:13).

35 *boaster* Goliath. David's weapons were 'five smooth stones out of the brook' (1 Samuel, 17:40).

38 David gave his son Solomon the divinely inspired plans for the temple at Jerusalem (1 Chronicles, 28:11–21).

41 E.g. of Nathan's prophecy of David's royal house (2 Samuel, 7:16).

42 *condole* 'lament'. Cf. David's laments for Jonathan (2 Samuel, 1:19–27) and Absalom (2 Samuel, 18:33).

43 *Jehudah* David was from the tribe of Judah, or Jehudah.

44 *in grain* 'inherently'.

45 *aspect* 'appearance'.

47 *conscious* 'sharing the secret'. David spared Saul's life in the cave at En-gedi (1 Samuel, 24).

48 David pardoned Shimei who had cursed and stoned him (2 Samuel, 19:21–3).

50 *innure* 'accustom'.

10

Sublime — invention ever young,   55
Of vast conception, tow'ring tongue
   To God th'eternal theme;
Notes from yon exaltations caught,
Unrival'd royalty of thought,
   O'er meaner strains supreme.   60

11

Contemplative — on God to fix
His musings, and above the six
   The sabbath-day he blest;
'Twas then his thoughts self-conquest prun'd,
And heavenly melancholy tun'd,   65
   To bless and bear the rest.

12

Serene — to sow the seeds of peace,
Rememb'ring, when he watch'd the fleece,
   How sweetly Kidron purl'd —
To further knowledge, silence vice,   70
And plant perpetual paradise
   When God had calm'd the world.

13

Strong — in the Lord, who could defy
Satan, and all his powers that lie
   In sempiternal night;   75
And hell, and horror, and despair
Were as the lion and the bear
   To his undaunted might.

14

Constant — in love to God THE TRUTH,
Age, manhood, infancy, and youth —   80
   To Jonathan his friend
Constant, beyond the verge of death;
And Ziba, and Mephibosheth,
   His endless fame attend.

15

Pleasant — and various as the year;   85
Man, soul, and angel, without peer,
   Priest, champion, sage and boy;
In armour, or in ephod clad,

---

64 Self-control disciplined his mind.
69 *Kidron* A brook near Jerusalem, site of David's boyhood as a shepherd.
77 The young David killed a lion and bear (1 Samuel, 17:34–7).
81–2 'Then Jonathan and David made a covenant, because he loved him as his own soul' (1 Samuel, 18:3). See 42n.

83 When David handed over Saul's seven sons to death, he spared Mephibosheth (Saul's grandson and Jonathan's son); Saul's servant Ziba was given stewardship of Saul's possessions.
88–90 *ephod* 'priestly vestment'.

His pomp, his piety was glad;
    Majestic was his joy.   90

16

Wise — in recovery from his fall,
Whence rose his eminence o'er all,
    Of all the most revil'd;
The light of Israel in his ways,
Wise are his precepts, prayer and praise,   95
    And counsel to his child.

17

His muse, bright angel of his verse,
Gives balm for all the thorns that pierce,
    For all the pangs that rage;
Blest light, still gaining on the gloom,   100
The more than Michal of his bloom,
    Th'Abishag of his age.

18

He sung of God — the mighty source
Of all things — the stupendous force
    On which all strength depends;   105
From whose right arm, beneath whose eyes,
All period, pow'r, and enterprize
    Commences, reigns, and ends.

19

Angels — their ministry and meed,
Which to and fro with blessings speed,   110
    Or with their citterns wait;
Where Michael with his millions bows,
Where dwells the seraph and his spouse,
    The cherub and her mate.

20

Of man — the semblance and effect   115
Of God and Love — the Saint elect
    For infinite applause —
To rule the land, and briny broad,

---

91 *fall* David's adultery with Bath-sheba and killing of her husband Uriah (2 Samuel, 11–12). He later repented after being threatened by God. This is the crux of the dispute over David's character.

95–6 The books of Psalms and Proverbs, supposedly written by David for the young Solomon.

97 *He consecrates his genius for consolation and edification* (Smart).

101 *Michal* David's first wife (Saul's daughter).

102 *Abishag* In old age David was brought a young virgin, Abishag, to lie with him and keep him warm (1 Kings, 1:1–4).

103–56 *The subjects he made choice of – the Supreme Being – angels; men of renown; the works of nature in all directions, either particularly or collectively considered* (Smart).

109 *meed* 'giving of proper rewards'.

111 *cittern* A stringed instrument.

112 The angelic legions.

113–14 'For spirits when they please / Can either sex assume, or both' (*Paradise Lost*, 1:423–4).

115–16 'And God said, Let us make man in our image' (Genesis, 1:26).

118 *briny broad* 'salty expanse'.

To be laborious in his laud,
And heroes in his cause.   120

21

The world — the clustring spheres he made,
The glorious light, the soothing shade,
   Dale, champaign, grove, and hill;
The multitudinous abyss,
Where secrecy remains in bliss,   125
   And wisdom hides her skill.

22

Trees, plants, and flow'rs — of virtuous root;
Gem yielding blossom, yielding fruit,
   Choice gums and precious balm;
Bless ye the nosegay in the vale,   130
And with the sweetners of the gale
   Enrich the thankful psalm.

23

Of fowl — e'en ev'ry beak and wing
Which chear the winter, hail the spring,
   That live in peace or prey;   135
They that make music, or that mock,
The quail, the brave domestic cock,
   The raven, swan, and jay.

24

Of fishes — ev'ry size and shape,
Which nature frames of light escape,   140
   Devouring man to shun:
The shells are in the wealthy deep,
The shoals upon the surface leap,
   And love the glancing sun.

25

Of beasts — the beaver plods his task;   145
While the sleek tygers roll and bask,
   Nor yet the shades arouse:
Her cave the mining coney scoops;
Where o'er the mead the mountain stoops,
   The kids exult and brouse.   150

26

Of gems — their virtue and their price,
Which hid in earth from man's device,

---

119 *laud* 'praise'.
123 *champaign* 'treeless plain'.
124–6 'My substance was not hid from thee, when I was made in secret, and curiously wrought in the lowest parts of the earth' (Psalm 139:15).
127 *virtuous* 'effective in healing'.

128 Cf. 'blossoms and fruit at once' (*Paradise Lost*, 4:148); *Gem* 'bud'.
140 *of light escape* 'nimbly elusive'.
148 *coney* The damon, or Syrian rock-badger.
150 *exult* 'frisk' (Lat. *exsulto*).
151–6 Cf. Collins, *Ode to Liberty*, 122–4.

Their darts of lustre sheathe;
The jasper of the master's stamp,
The topaz blazing like a lamp   155
    Among the mines beneath.

27

Blest was the tenderness he felt
When to his graceful harp he knelt,
    And did for audience call;
When satan with his hand he quell'd,   160
And in serene suspence he held
    The frantic throes of Saul.

28

His furious foes no more malign'd
As he such melody divin'd,
    And sense and soul detain'd;   165
Now striking strong, now soothing soft,
He sent the godly sounds aloft,
    Or in delight refrain'd.

29

When up to heav'n his thoughts he pil'd,
From fervent lips fair Michal smil'd,   170
    As blush to blush she stood;
And chose herself the queen, and gave
Her utmost from her heart, 'so brave,
    And plays his hymns so good'.

30

The pillars of the Lord are sev'n,   175
Which stand from earth to topmost heav'n;
    His wisdom drew the plan;
His WORD accomplish'd the design,
From brightest gem to deepest mine,
    From CHRIST enthron'd to man.   180

31

Alpha, the cause of causes, first
In station, fountain, whence the burst
    Of light, and blaze of day;
Whence bold attempt, and brave advance,
Have motion, life, and ordinance,   185
    And heav'n itself its stay.

157–74 *He obtains power over infernal spirits, and the malignity of his enemies; wins the heart of Michal* (Smart).

161–2 David's harp-playing banished the 'evil spirit' from Saul (1 Samuel, 16:23).

164 *divin'd* 'created by divine means'.

175–222 *[He] shews that the pillars of knowledge are the monuments of God's works in the first week* (Smart). The Seven Pillars of Wisdom (Proverbs, 9:1) were traditionally associated with the temple (cf. 38), and Smart extends this analogy to the seven days of Creation (Genesis, 1), with the world taking shape like a massive church. Smart assigns to each day a letter of the Greek alphabet.

178 *WORD* The creating Word, or *logos*: 'In the beginning was the Word, and the Word was with God, and the Word was God' (John, 1:1).

181–6 Day One: 'And God said, Let there be light: and there was light'.

185 *ordinance* 'arrangement'.

32

Gamma supports the glorious arch
On which angelic legions march,
    And is with sapphires pav'd;
Thence the fleet clouds are sent adrift,   190
And thence the painted folds, that lift
    The crimson veil, are wav'd.

33

Eta with living sculpture breathes,
With verdant carvings, flow'ry wreathes
    Of never-wasting bloom;   195
In strong relief his goodly base
All instruments of labour grace,
    The trowel, spade, and loom.

34

Next Theta stands to the Supreme —
Who form'd, in number, sign, and scheme,   200
    Th'illustrious lights that are;
And one address'd his saffron robe,
And one, clad in a silver globe,
    Held rule with ev'ry star.

35

Iota's tun'd to choral hymns   205
Of those that fly, while he that swims
    In thankful safety lurks;
And foot, and chapitre, and niche,
The various histories enrich
    Of God's recorded works.   210

36

Sigma presents the social droves,
With him that solitary roves,
    And man of all the chief;
Fair on whose face, and stately frame,
Did God impress his hallow'd name,   215
    For ocular belief.

37

OMEGA! GREATEST and the BEST,
Stands sacred to the day of rest,

187–92 Day Two: 'And God made the firmament [the vault of Heaven]'.

191–2 Cf. 'thou … who stretchest out the heavens like a curtain' (Psalm 104:2).

193–8 Day Three: 'And God said, Let the earth bring forth grass, the herb yielding seed, and the fruit tree yielding fruit'.

199–204 Day Four: And God made two great lights; the greater light to rule the day, and the lesser light to rule the night: he made the stars also'.

202 *address'd* 'attired himself in'; *saffron* 'orange-yellow'.

205–10 Day Five: 'And God said, Let the waters bring forth abundantly the moving creature that hath life, and fowl that may fly above the earth'.

208 *chapitre* 'capital' (of a pillar).

211–16 Day Six: 'And God said, Let the earth bring forth the living creature … Let us make man in our image'.

217–22 Day Seven: 'Thus the heavens and the earth were finished … and he rested on the seventh day'. OMEGA 'And he said unto me, It is done. I am Alpha and Omega, the beginning and the end' (Revelation, 21:6).

For gratitude and thought;
Which bless'd the world upon his pole,   220
And gave the universe his goal,
    And clos'd th'infernal draught.

38
O DAVID, scholar of the Lord!
Such is thy science, whence reward,
    And infinite degree;   225
O strength, O sweetness, lasting ripe!
God's harp thy symbol, and thy type
    The lion and the bee!

39
There is but One who ne'er rebell'd,
But One by passion unimpell'd,   230
    By pleasures unintic't;
He from himself his semblance sent,
Grand object of his own content,
    And saw the God in CHRIST.

40
Tell them I am, JEHOVA said   235
To MOSES; while earth heard in dread,
    And smitten to the heart,
At once above, beneath, around,
All nature, without voice or sound,
    Replied, O Lord, THOU ART.   240

41
Thou art — to give and to confirm,
For each his talent and his term;
    All flesh thy bounties share:
Thou shalt not call thy brother fool;
The porches of the Christian school   245
    Are meekness, peace, and pray'r.

42
Open, and naked of offence,
Man's made of mercy, soul, and sense;

222 *draught* 'catch': 'the kingdom of heaven is like unto a net, that was cast into the sea, and gathered of every kind' (Matthew, 13:47).

225 *degree* A pun: David's learning ('science') has achieved the supreme qualification.

227 *type* 'emblem' (an image expressing his qualities).

228 '[A]nd, behold, there was a swarm of bees and honey in the carcase of the lion' (Judges, 14:8); hence Samson's riddle, 'out of the strong came forth sweetness' (14:14).

229–88 *An exercise upon the decalogue* (Smart). The Ten Commandments of Exodus, 20:1–17, are here interpreted in more positive terms.

229–34 One: 'I am the Lord thy God ... Thou shalt have no other gods before me'.

235–40 Two: 'Thou shalt not make unto thee any graven image, or any likeness of any thing that is in heaven above, or that is in the earth beneath, or that is in the water under the earth'.

235–6 'And God said unto Moses, I AM THAT I AM: and he said, Thus shalt thou say unto the children of Israel, I AM hath sent me unto you' (Exodus, 3:14).

241–6 Three: 'Thou shalt not take the name of the Lord thy God in vain'.

245 Smart's contrast is with the porch or 'painted stoa' at Athens where philosophical discussion took place (hence 'Stoic'). See Acts, 17:16–34.

247–52 Four: 'Remember the sabbath day, to keep it holy'.

God arm'd the snail and wilk;
Be good to him that pulls thy plough;   250
Due food and care, due rest, allow
    For her that yields thee milk.

43

Rise up before the hoary head,
And God's benign commandment dread,
    Which says thou shalt not die: 255
'Not as I will, but as thou wilt,'
Pray'd He whose conscience knew no guilt;
    With whose bless'd pattern vie.

44

Use all thy passions! — love is thine,
And joy, and jealousy divine;   260
    Thine hope's eternal fort,
And care thy leisure to disturb,
With fear concupiscence to curb,
    And rapture to transport.

45

Act simply, as occasion asks;   265
Put mellow wine in season'd casks;
    Till not with ass and bull:
Remember thy baptismal bond;
Keep from commixtures foul and fond,
    Nor work thy flax with wool.   270

46

Distribute: pay the Lord his tithe,
And make the widow's heart-strings blithe;
    Resort with those that weep:
As you from all and each expect,
For all and each thy love direct,   275
    And render as you reap.

47

The slander and its bearer spurn,
And propagating praise sojourn
    To make thy welcome last;

249 *wilk* 'whelk' (shellfish).
253–8 Five: 'Honour thy father and thy mother'; *hoary* 'grey'.
256 Christ's prayer to his father in the garden of Gethsemane (Mark, 14:36).
258 *vie with* 'emulate'.
259–64 Six: 'Thou shalt not kill'.
260 *jealousy* 'zeal'.
265–70 Seven: 'Thou shalt not commit adultery'.
266 'Neither do men put new wine into old bottles: else the bottles break' (Matthew, 9:17).
267 'Thou shalt not plow with an ox and an ass together' (Deuteronomy, 22:10).

268 To 'renounce … the carnal desires of the flesh'.
269 'Thou shalt not lie with mankind, as with womankind: it is abomination' (Leviticus, 18:22).
270 'neither shall a garment mingled of linen and woollen come upon thee' (Leviticus, 19:19).
271–6 Eight: 'Thou shalt not steal'.
271 *tithe* 'share', literally one tenth. See Deuteronomy, 14:28–9.
277–82 Nine: 'Thou shalt not bear false witness against thy neighbour'.
278 *sojourn* 'linger'.

Turn from old Adam to the New;   280
By hope futurity pursue;
   Look upwards to the past.

48

Controul thine eye, salute success,
Honour the wiser, happier bless,
   And for thy neighbour feel;   285
Grutch not of mammon and his leaven,
Work emulation up to heaven
   By knowledge and by zeal.

49

O DAVID, highest in the list
Of worthies, on God's ways insist,   290
   The genuine word repeat:
Vain are the documents of men,
And vain the flourish of the pen
   That keeps the fool's conceit.

50

PRAISE above all — for praise prevails;   295
Heap up the measure, load the scales,
   And good to goodness add:
The gen'rous soul her Saviour aids,
But peevish obloquy degrades;
   The Lord is great and glad.   300

51

For ADORATION all the ranks
Of angels yield eternal thanks,
   And DAVID in the midst;
With God's good poor, which, last and least
In man's esteem, thou to thy feast,   305
   O blessed bride-groom, bidst.

52

For ADORATION seasons change,
And order, truth, and beauty range,
   Adjust, attract, and fill:
The grass the polyanthus cheques;   310

280 *New* Christ, the second Adam.

283–8 Ten: 'Thou shalt not covet thy neighbour's house ... nor his ox, nor his ass, nor any thing that is thy neighbour's'.

286 I.e. 'Do not envy the rich man his surplus'. With a nice irony, the 'leaven' is also the unregenerate element of a person: 'Purge out therefore the old leaven, that ye may be a new lump' (1 Corinthians, 5:7).

287–8 The true leavening or transforming qualities.

289–90 The traditional 'Nine Worthies' included (besides David) Julius Caesar, Hector and Alexander.

291 *Psalm 119* (Smart).

295–306 *The transcendent virtue of praise and adoration* (Smart).

299 *obloquy* 'slander'.

301 Smart claimed: 'I am the Reviver of ADORATION amongst ENGLISH-MEN' (*Jubilate Agno*, B332).

304–6 The parable of the man who invited the poor to dinner (Luke, 14:16–21).

306 Christ as bridegroom (Matthew, 9:15; John, 3:29).

307–78 *An exercise upon the seasons, and the right use of them* (Smart). Three stanzas on each of the four seasons.

307–24 Spring.

310 *polyanthus* A colourful primula.

And polish'd porphyry reflects,
   By the descending rill.

53

Rich almonds colour to the prime
For ADORATION; tendrils climb,
   And fruit-trees pledge their gems;   315
And Ivis with her gorgeous vest
Builds for her eggs her cunning nest,
   And bell-flowers bow their stems.

54

With vinous syrup cedars spout;
From rocks pure honey gushing out,   320
   For ADORATION springs:
All scenes of painting croud the map
Of nature; to the mermaid's pap
   The scaled infant clings.

55

The spotted ounce and playsome cubs   325
Run rustling 'mongst the flow'ring shrubs,
   And lizards feed the moss;
For ADORATION beasts embark,
While waves upholding halcyon's ark
   No longer roar and toss.   330

56

While Israel sits beneath his fig,
With coral root and amber sprig
   The wean'd advent'rer sports;
Where to the palm the jasmin cleaves,
For ADORATION 'mong the leaves   335
   The gale his peace reports.

57

Increasing days their reign exalt,
Nor in the pink and mottled vault
   Th'opposing spirits tilt;
And, by the coasting reader spy'd,   340

---

313 *almonds* Aaron's rod blossomed and yielded almonds (Numbers, 17:8).

316 *Ivis* 'Humming-bird' (Smart).

320 '[W]ith honey out of the rock should I have satisfied thee' (Psalm 81:16).

325–42 Summer.

325 *ounce* The cheetah, or possibly lynx.

327 *feed* 'feed on'.

328 'There is a large quadruped that preys upon fish, and provides himself with a piece of timber for that purpose, with which he is very handy' (Smart).

329–30 *halcyon's ark* The floating nest of the kingfisher.

The ancients believed that calm days around the winter solstice marked their nesting time. For Milton the image symbolized Christ's birth into a peaceful world 'While birds of calm sit brooding on the charmèd wave' (*Nativity Ode*, 68).

331 'But they shall sit every man under his vine and under his fig tree; and none shall make them afraid' (Micah, 4:4).

333 *wean'd advent'rer* Child. Coral and amber were used for teething-rings and toys respectively.

338 An angry sky?

340 *coasting* 'travelling by a river or lake'.

The silverlings and crusions glide
    For ADORATION gilt.

58

For ADORATION rip'ning canes
And cocoa's purest milk detains
    The western pilgrim's staff;   345
Where rain in clasping boughs inclos'd,
And vines with oranges dispos'd,
    Embow'r the social laugh.

59

Now labour his reward receives,
For ADORATION counts his sheaves   350
    To peace, her bounteous prince;
The nectarine his strong tint imbibes,
And apples of ten thousand tribes,
    And quick peculiar quince.

60

The wealthy crops of whit'ning rice,   355
'Mongst thyine woods and groves of spice,
    For ADORATION grow;
And, marshall'd in the fenced land,
The peaches and pomegranates stand,
    Where wild carnations blow.   360

61

The laurels with the winter strive;
The crocus burnishes alive
    Upon the snow-clad earth:
For ADORATION myrtles stay
To keep the garden from dismay,   365
    And bless the sight from dearth.

62

The pheasant shows his pompous neck;
And ermine, jealous of a speck
    With fear eludes offence:
The sable, with his glossy pride,   370
For ADORATION is descried,
    Where frosts the wave condense.

63

The chearful holly, pensive yew,
And holy thorn, their trim renew;

---

341 Silver and gold fishes. Smart puns on 'crucian' (a carp) and 'chrusion' (Gk.), a gold coin. A silverling was a shekel, the chief silver coin of the Hebrews (Isaiah, 7:23).
343–60 Autumn.
344 *cocoa* 'coconut'.
345 *western pilgrim* 'traveller to the Americas'.

354 *quick* 'sharp tasting'.
356 *thyine* A gum-yielding tree, part of the rich merchandise of Babylon (Revelation, 18:12).
361–78 Winter.
368 *speck* The black spot (of the tail) characteristic of the rich white fur of the ermine, worn by the nobility.
374 *holy thorn* 'hawthorn'.

The squirrel hoards his nuts: 375
All creatures batten o'er their stores,
And careful nature all her doors
    For ADORATION shuts.

64

For ADORATION, DAVID's psalms
Lift up the heart to deeds of alms;   380
    And he, who kneels and chants,
Prevails his passions to controul,
Finds meat and med'cine to the soul,
    Which for translation pants.

65

For ADORATION, beyond match,   385
The scholar bulfinch aims to catch
    The soft flute's iv'ry touch;
And, careless on the hazle spray,
The daring redbreast keeps at bay
    The damsel's greedy clutch.   390

66

For ADORATION, in the skies,
The Lord's philosopher espies
    The Dog, the Ram, and Rose;
The planets ring, Orion's sword;
Nor is his greatness less ador'd   395
    In the vile worm that glows.

67

For ADORATION on the strings
The western breezes work their wings,
    The captive ear to sooth. —
Hark! 'tis a voice — how still, and small —   400
That makes the cataracts to fall,
    Or bids the sea be smooth.

68

For ADORATION, incense comes
From bezoar, and Arabian gums;
    And from the civet's furr.   405

376 *batten* 'grow fat'.
377–8 Like a good housewife?
380 *deed of alms* A pun.
383 '[B]ehold, at the bank of the river were very many trees
    … Then said he unto me … the fruit thereof shall be
    for meat, and the leaf thereof for medicine' (Ezekiel,
    47:7–8, 12).
384 *translation* 'crossing to heaven'.
385–420 *An exercise upon the senses, and how to subdue them*
    (Smart).
385–90 Touch.
386 *scholar* Pet bullfinches were admired for their ability to
    memorize tunes.

391–6 Sight.
393 Constellations.
397–402 Hearing.
397–9 The Aeolian (or wind) harp.
400 God's 'still small voice' called to Elijah (1 Kings,
    19:12).
403–8 Smell.
404 *bezoar* A medicinal stone found in ruminant animals.
405 *civet* The civet-cat, whose musky secretions were prized
    in perfumery.

But as for prayer, or ere it faints,
Far better is the breath of saints
    Than galbanum and myrrh.

69

For ADORATION from the down
Of dam'sins to th'anana's crown,   410
    God sends to tempt the taste;
And while the luscious zest invites
The sense, that in the scene delights,
    Commands desire be chaste.

70

For ADORATION, all the paths   415
Of grace are open, all the baths
    Of purity refresh;
And all the rays of glory beam
To deck the man of God's esteem,
    Who triumphs o'er the flesh.   420

71

For ADORATION, in the dome
Of Christ the sparrows find an home;
    And on his olives perch:
The swallow also dwells with thee,
O man of God's humility,   425
    Within his Saviour's CHURCH.

72

Sweet is the dew that falls betimes,
And drops upon the leafy limes;
    Sweet Hermon's fragrant air:
Sweet is the lilly's silver bell,   430
And sweet the wakeful tapers smell
    That watch for early pray'r.

73

Sweet the young nurse with love intense,
Which smiles o'er sleeping innocence;
    Sweet when the lost arrive: 435
Sweet the musician's ardour beats,
While his vague mind's in quest of sweets,
    The choicest flow'rs to hive.

408 Spices used in incense.
409–14 Taste.
410 *dam'sins* 'damson-plums'; *anana* 'pineapple'.
421–516 *An amplification in five degrees* [sweet, strong, beauteous, precious, glorious], *which is wrought up to this conclusion, That the best poet which ever lived was thought worthy of the highest honour which possibly can be conceived, as* the Saviour of the world was ascribed to his house, and called his son in the body (Smart).

422 'Yea, the sparrow hath found an house, and the swallow a nest for herself' (Psalm 84:3).
423 'I am like a green olive tree in the house of God: I trust in the mercy of God for ever and ever' (Psalm 52:8).
429 The image is one of divine blessing, 'As the dew of Hermon, and as the dew that descended upon the mountains of Zion' (Psalm 133:3).
437 *vague* 'wandering'.

74

Sweeter in all the strains of love,
The language of thy turtle dove,   440
   Pair'd to thy swelling chord;
Sweeter with ev'ry grace endu'd,
The glory of thy gratitude,
   Respir'd unto the Lord.

75

Strong is the horse upon his speed;   445
Strong in pursuit the rapid glede,
   Which makes at once his game:
Strong the tall ostrich on the ground;
Strong thro' the turbulent profound
   Shoots xiphias to his aim.   450

76

Strong is the lion — like a coal
His eye-ball — like a bastion's mole
   His chest against the foes:
Strong, the gier-eagle on his sail,
Strong against tide, th'enormous whale   455
   Emerges, as he goes.

77

But stronger still, in earth and air,
And in the sea, the man of pray'r;
   And far beneath the tide;
And in the seat to faith assign'd,   460
Where ask is have, where seek is find,
   Where knock is open wide.

78

Beauteous the fleet before the gale;
Beauteous the multitudes in mail,
   Rank'd arms and crested heads: 465
Beauteous the garden's umbrage mild,
Walk, water, meditated wild,
   And all the bloomy beds.

79

Beauteous the moon full on the lawn;
And beauteous, when the veil's withdrawn,   470
   The virgin to her spouse:
Beauteous the temple deck'd and fill'd,
When to the heav'n of heav'ns they build
   Their heart-directed vows.

---

444 *Respir'd* 'breathed' (Lat. *respiro*).
446 *glede* 'hawk'.
450 *xiphias* 'The sword-fish' (Smart).
452 *bastion's mole* 'massive projecting fortification'.
454 *gier-eagle* 'vulture'.

461–2 'Ask, and it shall be given you; seek, and ye shall find; knock, and it shall be opened unto you' (Matthew, 7:7).
467 *meditated wild* A garden wilderness, conducive to contemplation.

80

Beauteous, yea beauteous more than these,   475
The shepherd king upon his knees,
   For his momentous trust;
With wish of infinite conceit,
For man, beast, mute, the small and great,
   And prostrate dust to dust.   480

81

Precious the bounteous widow's mite;
And precious, for extreme delight,
   The largess from the churl:
Precious the ruby's blushing blaze,
And alba's blest imperial rays,   485
   And pure cerulean pearl.

82

Precious the penitential tear;
And precious is the sigh sincere,
   Acceptable to God:
And precious are the winning flow'rs,   490
In gladsome Israel's feast of bow'rs,
   Bound on the hallow'd sod.

83

More precious that diviner part
Of David, ev'n the Lord's own heart,
   Great, beautiful, and new: 495
In all things where it was intent,
In all extreams, in each event,
   Proof — answ'ring true to true.

84

Glorious the sun in mid career;
Glorious th'assembled fires appear;   500
   Glorious the comet's train:
Glorious the trumpet and alarm;
Glorious th'almighty stretch'd-out arm;
   Glorious th'enraptur'd main:

---

476 *shepherd king* David.

478 *conceit* 'conception'.

479 *mute* Cf. Akenside's celebration of God's creation, 'From the mute shell-fish gasping on the shore, / To men, to angels' (*The Pleasures of Imagination*, 2:343–5). Cf. 249 above.

481 Mark, 12:41–4.

483 '2 Samuel, 25:18' (Smart). Abigail's gifts of provisions to David against the will of her 'churlish' husband. Later she became one of David's wives.

485 *alba* 'Revelation, 2:17' (Smart). '[I] will give him a white stone, and in the stone a new name written, which no man knoweth saving he that receiveth it.'

486 *cerulean* Here 'sky-blue'.

491 *feast of bow'rs* The Feast of Tabernacles, the autumn festival giving thanks for the bounty of nature, and for God's guidance through the wilderness (Leviticus, 23:39–43).

494 'I have found David ... a man after mine own heart' (Acts, 13:22).

495 Addison's three distinctive aesthetic categories (*Spectator*, 412). Cf. Akenside, *The Pleasures of Imagination*, 1:145–6 and note.

503–4 God dividing the Red Sea (Psalm 136:12–13).

85

Glorious the northern lights astream;   505
Glorious the song, when God's the theme;
   Glorious the thunder's roar:
Glorious hosanna from the den;
Glorious the catholic amen;
   Glorious the martyr's gore: 510

86

Glorious — more glorious is the crown
Of Him that brought salvation down
   By meekness, call'd thy Son;
Thou at stupendous truth believ'd,
And now the matchless deed's atchiev'd,   515
   DETERMIN'D, DAR'D, and DONE.

FINIS

505 *northern lights* The aurora borealis.
508 *den* 'prison' (Acts, 16:25).
509 *catholic* 'universal'.
513 'Jesus Christ, the son of David' (Matthew, 1:1).
516 '[T]hat that is determined shall be done' (Daniel, 11:36).

TEXTUAL NOTES
Three changes have been made to the 1765 copytext:
409 *down* down, (*1765*); **412** *invites* invites, (*1765*); **439** *strains* Strains (*1765*).

On a Bed of Guernsey Lilies
Written in September 1763

'For the flower glorifies God and the root parries the adversary ... / ... For the warp and woof of flowers are worked by perpetual moving spirits ... / ... For flowers are peculiarly the poetry of Christ' (*Jubilate Agno*, B499–506). Moira Dearnley (*The Poetry of Christopher Smart* (1967), pp. 210–11) has drawn attention to the links between this poem and an article, 'Some Account of the Guernsey Lilly, with Animadversions thereon', in the *Christian's Magazine* (1760), which used the flower for a meditation on hope and fortitude: 'Be not disheartened at your lot, O Christian, when God seems to have withdrawn his holy assistance from you; contemplate on the various changes which this flower undergoes; submit and support yourself with Christian fortitude and resignation; and rely on this, that God will not utterly forsake you'. The poem was published in *Ode to the Right Honourable the Earl of Northumberland ... With some other Pieces* (1764), pp. 17–18, the text given here.

I

Ye beauties! O how great the sum
   Of sweetness that ye bring;
On what a charity ye come
   To bless the latter spring!
How kind the visit that ye pay,   5
Like strangers on a rainy day,
   When heartiness despair'd of guests:
No neighbour's praise your pride alarms,
No rival flow'r surveys your charms,
   Or heightens, or contests!   10

Title The autumn-flowering Guernsey lily (*Nerine Sarniensis*) is said to have first grown in Guernsey (the Channel Islands) from bulbs washed ashore from the wreck of a ship from Japan, about 1659. It has sparkling rosy-red flowers.

II

Lo, thro' her works gay nature grieves
  How brief she is and frail,
As ever o'er the falling leaves
  Autumnal winds prevail.
Yet still the philosophic mind   15
Consolatory food can find,
  And hope her anchorage maintain:
We never are deserted quite;
'Tis by succession of delight
  That love supports his reign.   20

James Macpherson (1736–1796)

In the decades that followed the final defeat of the Stuart cause at Culloden (1746) some prominent Scottish writers and scholars became concerned with recovering what remnants there were of a native Highland culture, and although there was very little manuscript material (and none earlier than 1512), a tradition of oral poetry lived on in the communities of the north-west. Old ballads and fragments of heroic tales handed down through generations were still being sung in the strong rhythms of the native Gaelic. James Macpherson was entrusted with discovering and translating whatever he could of this material. What he made out of it became a crucial text of European romanticism and the subject of a controversy that still reverberates today.

In October 1759, as a young tutor fresh from his studies at the University of Aberdeen, Macpherson was persuaded by John Home, the Edinburgh playwright, to translate one of the Gaelic pieces he had collected, and the result was 'the Death of Oscur' (fragment 7, below). It immediately aroused excitement in the literary circles of Aberdeen and Edinburgh, and Macpherson was sponsored to travel along the west coast to find more. He presented a selection of material as *Fragments of Ancient Poetry* (June 1760). Thomas Gray, who had been sent specimens in manuscript, was '*extasié* with their infinite beauty', and though he had doubts about the genuineness of the pieces, he considered their creator to be 'the very Demon of Poetry'. Some of the volume's first readers were thrilled, but also tantalized by the suggestion in the preface that the great national epic of Scotland was waiting to be recovered. Such a find was Macpherson's immediate priority, and after a further journey gathering Gaelic materials he delivered *Fingal: An Ancient Epic Poem in Six Books* (December 1761) and *Temora: An Ancient Epic Poem in Eight Books* (March 1763), both 'translated' by himself. In 1765 they were published together, along with some shorter episodes, as *The Works of Ossian.*

Macpherson and his third-century bard achieved immediate fame. But many (including notably Dr Johnson) were sceptical, and it soon became clear that Macpherson's role had been a remarkably creative one. The 'translations' in his own brand of rhythmical prose are part invention, part imaginative reconstruction, but they are infused with what he heard from the old Gaelic singers and storytellers. Ossian ('Oscian' in fragment 8 below) is Oisin mac Fhinn, the legendary Gaelic bard and warrior, to whom many oral ballads were attributed, and whose mythical history features in Irish manuscripts from the twelfth century onwards. Unlike other collectors, Macpherson was not a scholar, and the genuine old ballads that he heard disappointed him with their crudeness and inelegance. It is no surprise therefore that the *Fragments of Ancient Poetry* appear well attuned to the sensibility of their mid-eighteenth-century readers. As Thomas Warton remarked in his *History of English Poetry* (1774), the Ossian poems 'frequently give place to a gentler set of manners, to the social sensibilities of polished life, and a more civilised and elegant species of imagination', and he detected 'instances of an elevated strain of friendship, of love, and other sentimental feelings'. Macpherson can be viewed as constructing a feminized heroism that is as much indebted to contemporary stage tragedies (like Home's *Douglas*, 1756) and recent sentimental fiction as it is to the heroic Highland past. Readers responded ecstatically to Macpherson's interweaving of the primal with the polite, the blood struggle with the moral conscience, to scenes in which father, son, lover and friend confront each other in a succession of sublime, eerily disconnected landscapes. For the next sixty years and more Ossianic noble doom seized the European romantic imagination. The two pieces given here are from the lightly revised second edition of *Fragments of Ancient Poetry* which appeared later in 1760, pp. 31–40.

Fragment 7

This is the first fragment Macpherson 'translated' for Home, and is modelled on the traditional Gaelic ballad. The speaker is the aged Ossian himself, and the three characters are Oscur his son, Oscur's friend Dermid (son of Morny), and the beautiful daughter of Dargo, the warrior they have both killed.

Why openest thou afresh the spring of my grief, O son of Alpin, inquiring how Oscur fell? My eyes are blind with tears; but memory beams on my heart. How can I relate the mournful death of the head of the people! Prince of the warriors, Oscur my son, shall I see thee no more!

He fell as the moon in a storm; as the sun from the midst of his 5
course, when clouds rise from the waste of the waves, when the blackness of the storm inwraps the rocks of Ardannider. I, like an ancient oak on Morven, I moulder alone in my place. The blast hath lopped my branches away; and I tremble at the wings of the north. Prince of the warriors, Oscur my son! shall I see thee no more! 10

Dermid and Oscur were one: They reaped the battle together. Their friendship was strong as their steel; and death walked between them to the field. They came on the foe like two rocks falling from the brows of Ardven. Their swords were stained with the blood of the valiant: warriors fainted at their names. Who was a match for Oscur, but Dermid? and who 15
for Dermid, but Oscur?

They killed mighty Dargo in the field; Dargo before invincible. His daughter was fair as the morn; mild as the beam of night. Her eyes, like two stars in a shower: her breath, the gale of spring: her breasts, as the new-fallen snow floating on the moving heath. The warriors saw her, and loved; their 20
souls were fixed on the maid. Each loved her, as his fame; each must possess her or die. But her soul was fixed on Oscur; my son was the youth of her love. She forgot the blood of her father; and loved the hand that slew him.

Son of Oscian, said Dermid, I love; O Oscur, I love this maid. But her soul cleaveth unto thee; and nothing can heal Dermid. Here, pierce this 25
bosom, Oscur; relieve me, my friend, with thy sword.

My sword, son of Morny, shall never be stained with the blood of Dermid.

Who then is worthy to slay me, O Oscur son of Oscian? Let not my life pass away unknown. Let none but Oscur slay me. Send me with honour to 30
the grave, and let my death be renowned.

Dermid, make use of thy sword; son of Morny, wield thy steel. Would that I fell with thee! that my death came from the hand of Dermid!

They fought by the brook of the mountain; by the streams of Branno. Blood tinged the silvery stream, and crudled round the mossy stones. 35
Dermid the graceful fell; fell, and smiled in death.

And fallest thou, son of Morny; fallest thou by Oscur's hand! Dermid invincible in war, thus do I see thee fall! — He went, and returned to the maid whom he loved; returned, but she perceived his grief.

Why that gloom, son of Oscian? what shades thy mighty soul? 40

Though once renowned for the bow, O maid, I have lost my fame. Fixed on a tree by the brook of the hill, is the shield of Gormur the brave, whom in battle I slew. I have wasted the day in vain, nor could my arrow pierce it.

Let me try, son of Oscian, the skill of Dargo's daughter. My hands 45
were taught the bow: my father delighted in my skill.

---

2 *Oscur* Here he is the son of Ossian. Macpherson later makes him the son of Caruth so as to avoid contradicting the traditional account of the death of Ossian's son after a quarrel. The latter story is told in Book 1 of *Temora*.

8 *Morven* 'All the North-west coast of Scotland probably went of old under the name of Morven, which signifies a ridge of very high hills' (Macpherson's note to *Fingal*, Book 3). In Gaelic 'Morven' is literally 'great mountain'.

35 *crudled* 'curdled'.

She went. He stood behind the shield. Her arrow flew and pierced his breast.

Blessed be that hand of snow; and blessed thy bow of yew! I fall resolved on death: and who but the daughter of Dargo was worthy to slay   50
me? Lay me in the earth, my fair-one; lay me by the side of Dermid.

Oscur! I have the blood, the soul of the mighty Dargo. Well pleased I can meet death. My sorrow I can end thus. — She pierced her white bosom with steel. She fell; she trembled; and died.

By the brook of the hill their graves are laid; a birch's unequal shade   55
covers their tomb. Often on their green earthen tombs the branchy sons of the mountain feed, when mid-day is all in flames, and silence is over all the hills.

47–8 'Nothing was held by the ancient Highlanders more essential to their glory, than to die by the hand of some person worthy or renowned. This was the occasion of Oscur's contriving to be slain by his mistress, now that he was weary of life. In those early times suicide was utterly unknown among that people, and no traces of it are found in the old poetry. Whence the translator suspects the account that follows of the daughter of Dargo killing herself, to be the interpolation of some later Bard' (Macpherson's note, 1760).
53 *thus* Reminiscent of Othello's suicide: 'And smote him – thus' [he stabs himself] (*Othello*, V.ii.356).
56 *branchy* 'antlered'.

Fragment 8

In this fragment the blind Ossian remembers the day he fought alongside his father Fingal (Son of Corval) and his own son Oscur, three generations together. On that day heroism was succeeded by mercy. The influence of Gray's *The Bard* (1757) can be detected in this figure, the last of his race, lamenting the dead.

By the side of a rock on the hill, beneath the aged trees, old Oscian sat on the moss; the last of the race of Fingal. Sightless are his aged eyes; his beard is waving in the wind. Dull through the leafless trees he heard the voice of the north. Sorrow revived in his soul: he began and lamented the dead.

How hast thou fallen like an oak, with all thy branches round thee!   5
Where is Fingal the King? where is Oscur my son? where are all my race? Alas! in the earth they lie. I feel their tombs with my hands. I hear the river below murmuring hoarsely over the stones. What dost thou, O river, to me? Thou bringest back the memory of the past.

The race of Fingal stood on thy banks, like a wood in a fertile soil.   10
Keen were their spears of steel. Hardy was he who dared to encounter their rage. Fillan the great was there. Thou Oscur wert there, my son! Fingal himself was there, strong in the grey locks of years. Full rose his sinewy limbs; and wide his shoulders spread. The unhappy met with his arm, when the pride of his wrath arose.   15

The son of Morny came; Gaul, the tallest of men. He stood on the hill like an oak; his voice was like the streams of the hill. Why reigneth alone, he cries, the son of the mighty Corval? Fingal is not strong to save: he is no support for the people. I am strong as a storm in the ocean; as a whirlwind on the hill. Yield, son of Corval; Fingal, yield to me. He came like a rock   20
from the hill, resounding in his arms.

2–3 Cf. 'Loose his beard, and hoary hair / Stream'd, like a meteor, to the troubled air' (Gray, *The Bard* (1757), 19–20).
12 *Fillan* Ossian's half-brother.
16 *Gaul* An authentic hero (Goll mac Morna). In *Fingal* and *Temora* he takes command of Fingal's army.
20–1 *He came ... arms* Added for 2nd edn (1760).

Oscur stood forth to meet him; my son would meet the foe. But
Fingal came in his strength, and smiled at the vaunter's boast. They threw
their arms round each other; they struggled on the plain. The earth is
ploughed with their heels. Their bones crack as the boat on the ocean,   25
when it leaps from wave to wave. Long did they toil; with night, they fell on
the sounding plain; as two oaks, with their branches mingled, fall crashing
from the hill. The tall son of Morny is bound; the aged overcame.

Fair with her locks of gold, her smooth neck, and her breasts of
snow; fair, as the spirits of the hill when at silent noon they glide along   30
the heath; fair, as the rain-bow of heaven; came Minvane the maid. Fingal!
she softly saith, loose me my brother Gaul. Loose me the hope of my race,
the terror of all but Fingal. Can I, replies the King, can I deny the lovely
daughter of the hill? take thy brother, O Minvane, thou fairer than the snow
of the north!   35

Such, Fingal! were thy words; but thy words I hear no more.
Sightless I sit by thy tomb. I hear the wind in the wood; but no more I hear
my friends. The cry of the hunter is over. The voice of war is ceased.

Thomas Chatterton (1752–1770)

The young man who died in a London garret at the age of seventeen was certainly a precocious talent. Today's standard edition of his works (ed. Donald S. Taylor (Oxford, 1971)) runs to 1,200 pages in two volumes. Within a decade he had become the boy genius of Romantic myth who had been led into suicide by society's neglect. But in reality Chatterton was a mature, ambitious, independent and politically committed individual, and also much cleverer than most of his elders. Born in Bristol, the son of a poor schoolmaster who died before he was born, he attended Colston's charity school, and at the age of fourteen was bound apprentice to an attorney, spending most of his time copying legal documents. The youth was a voracious reader and grew fascinated with some old parchments that his father had taken from a chest in the muniment room of St Mary Redcliffe (this medieval church with which the Chatterton family had been connected since Elizabethan times remains one of the finest in England). He began creating various old documents that included heraldries, architectural drawings, eyewitness accounts, rolls, inscriptions and maps. With the help of his own specially compiled glossary of medieval English he also began writing poems in the guise of Thomas Rowley. Around the 'secular priest' Rowley and his friend and patron William Canynge (an actual fifteenth-century Mayor of Bristol) Chatterton created a fully imagined medieval world, in which Rowley and Canynge offered a model of an enlightened culture that no longer existed. Chatterton set out to fill the gaps in history and establish continuities with Anglo-Saxon England, to give Bristol a proud pre-Conquest history, and to create a brilliant flowering of fifteenth-century poetry

which would rewrite the story of literature's long decline after Chaucer. This ambitious project went hand in hand with Chatterton's aims as a political writer. While Rowley was creating an idealized civic culture, Chatterton the anonymous satirist was attacking the corruptions of government and Court in a stream of anonymous poems and essays in the newspapers.

In 1770 he gave up his apprenticeship and moved to London. Rowleian documents and poems had begun to appear in print and were causing a stir in Bristol, but Chatterton's attempts to interest London publishers and patrons in his medieval 'discoveries' (notably James Dodsley and Horace Walpole) proved futile. Those frustrations were however counterbalanced by hopes that he would find a role in John Wilkes's circle as a radical writer. When he died of an overdose of arsenic (which may have been medicinal) he was on the brink of establishing himself as an anti-government journalist. But Romantic myth soon took over and he slipped into the role of delicate suicidal child whose faery visions had been mocked by the literary establishment.

Among the English Romantics the young Coleridge identified himself with the tragic genius and became famous as the author of the *Monody on the Death of Chatterton*. But it was Keats who saw most clearly the poet's genuine contribution to the English language. In 1819 he wrote: 'Chatterton … is the purest writer in the English Language. He has no French idiom, or particles like Chaucer – 'tis genuine English Idiom in English Words.' Beneath the Chatterton myth is a real poet who found freshness in what was old, and who helped keep English poetry in touch with its medieval roots.

Mynstrelles Songe

The tragedy of *Ælla* was one of Chatterton's most ambitious works. It gave Bristol its own Saxon hero, Ælla, the keeper of Bristol Castle who fought against the Danish invaders. In this 'Tragycal Enterlude' Chatterton was supplying England's earliest known heroic verse drama, while showing that Bristol's Rowley had been a significant influence on Stratford's Shakespeare a century later. The wedding celebrations of Ælla and Birtha are interrupted when he is called away to fight the Danes (echoes here of Act One of

Othello). Birtha remains at Bristol anxiously awaiting news. In order to raise her spirits her companion Egwina asks the minstrels to sing ('Perchaunce the swotie sounde maie chase your wiere [*grief*] awaie'), but not surprisingly their song of tragic love leaves Birtha just as apprehensive and melancholy as before. The text is that of the first edition of the posthumous *Poems, supposed to have been written at Bristol, by Thomas Rowley, and others* (1777), pp. 136–9. Chatterton's own glosses are given (C).

O! synge untoe mie roundelaie,
O! droppe the brynie teare wythe mee,
Daunce ne moe atte hallie daie,
Lycke a reynynge ryver bee;
　Mie love ys dedde,　　　　　　　　　　　5
　Gon to hys death-bedde,
　Al under the wyllowe tree.

Blacke hys cryne as the wyntere nyghte,
Whyte hys rode as the sommer snowe,
Rodde hys face as the mornynge lyghte,　　　10
Cale he lyes ynne the grave belowe;
　Mie love ys dedde,
　Gon to hys deathe-bedde,
　Al under the wyllowe tree.

Swote hys tyngue as the throstles note,　　　15
Quycke ynn daunce as thoughte canne bee,
Defte hys taboure, codgelle stote,
O! hee lyes bie the wyllowe tree:
　Mie love ys dedde,
　Gonne to hys deathe-bedde,　　　　　　　20
　Alle underre the wyllowe tree.

Harke! the ravenne flappes hys wynge,
In the briered delle belowe;
Harke! the dethe-owle loude dothe synge,
To the nyghte-mares as heie goe;　　　　　　25
　Mie love ys dedde,
　Gonne to hys deathe-bedde,
　Al under the wyllowe tree.

See! the whyte moone sheenes onne hie;
Whyterre ys mie true loves shroude;　　　　　30
Whyterre yanne the mornynge skie,
Whyterre yanne the evenynge cloude;
　Mie love ys dedde,
　Gon to hys deathe-bedde,
　Al under the wyllowe tree.　　　　　　　　35

Heere, uponne mie true loves grave,
Schalle the baren fleurs be layde,
Nee one hallie Seyncte to save
Al the celness of a mayde.

---

4 *reynynge* 'running' (C).
5–6 Cf. one of Ophelia's mad songs: 'No, no, he is dead, / Go to thy death-bed, / He never will come again' (*Hamlet*, IV.v.192–4).
7 *wyllowe* Symbolic of disappointed love. Cf. Desdemona's willow song: 'The fresh streams ran by her, and murmur'd her moans, / Sing willow, willow, willow' (*Othello*, IV.iii.44–5).

8 *cryne* 'hair' (C).
9 *rode* 'complexion' (C).
11 *Cale* 'cold'.
15 *Swote* 'sweet'.
17 *taboure* A small drum.
25 *heie* 'they'.
39 *celness* 'coldness'.

Mie love ys dedde, 40
Gonne to hys death-bedde,
Alle under the wyllowe tree.

Wythe mie hondes I'lle dente the brieres
Rounde his hallie corse to gre,
Ouphante fairie, lyghte youre fyres, 45
Heere mie boddie stylle schalle bee.
   Mie love ys dedde,
   Gon to hys death-bedde,
   Al under the wyllowe tree.

Comme, wythe acorne-coppe and thorne, 50
Drayne mie hartys blodde awaie;
Lyfe and all yttes goode I scorne,
Daunce bie nete, or feaste by daie.
   Mie love ys dedde,
   Gon to hys death-bedde, 55
   Al under the wyllowe tree.

Waterre wytches, crownede wythe reytes,
Bere mee to yer leathalle tyde.
I die; I comme; mie true love waytes.
Thos the damselle spake, and dyed. 60

43 *dente* 'set'.
45 *Ouphante* 'elfin'.
50–6 This stanza was Keats's favourite, as his friend Benjamin Bailey recalled: 'Methinks I now hear him recite, or *chant*, in his peculiar manner, the following stanza … The first line to his ear possessed the great

charm. Indeed his sense of melody was quite exquisite'.
57 *reytes* 'water-flags' (C), i.e. wild irises.

TEXTUAL NOTE
In lines 50 and 52 '&' has been replaced by 'and'.

'Stay, curyous traveller'

A Discorse on Brystowe is one of Chatterton's most ingenious manuscripts, fabricated in order to give Bristol an extensive pre-Norman history and to create a thousand-year Christian tradition centred on his beloved church of St Mary Redcliffe. The text combines supposed eleventh-century material with Rowley's fifteenth-century additions, and Chatterton intersperses these with drawings of several lost buildings, including previous churches on the Redcliffe site. The *Discorse* offers documentation to prove that William Canynge (d. 1474) had built the present church from first stone to last. Making St Mary Redcliffe Canynge's creation was vital for Chatterton's imagined world. Sadly, the tradition on which Chatterton relied was mistaken: the church had been largely completed by 1380, and Canynge's role was that of repairer and improver. In the *Discorse* Rowley celebrates the newly completed church, and breaks into poetry as he does so: 'This worke now fynished is a true Pycture of the Buylder Greete and Noble, the Glorie and delyght of Bristowe … of which take yee my Lynes for lack of better'. These three stanzas then follow. Both Gothic church and poem are characterized by a simple strength that joins literal and metaphorical, stone and breath, earth and heaven. The poem was extracted and printed in the first edition of *Poems* (1777), pp. 276–7, the text given here.

Stay, curyous traveller, and pass not bye,
Until this fetive pile astounde thine eye.
Whole rocks on rocks with yron joynd surveie,
And okes with okes entremed disponed lie.

2 *fetive pile* 'elegant building'.

4 *entremed* 'intermingled'; *disponed* 'disposed'.

This mightie pile, that keeps the wyndes at baie,   5
Fyre-levyn and the mokie storme defie,
That shootes aloofe into the reaulmes of daie,
Shall be the record of the Buylders fame for aie.

Thou seest this maystrie of a human hand,
The pride of Brystowe and the Westerne lande,   10
Yet is the Buylders vertues much moe greete,
Greeter than can bie Rowlies pen be scande.
Thou seest the saynctes and kynges in stonen state,
That seemd with breath and human soule dispande,
As payrde to us enseem these men of state,   15
Such is greete Canynge's mynde when payrd to God elate.

Well maiest thou be astound, but view it well;
Go not from hence before thou see thy fill,
And learn the Builder's vertues and his name;
Of this tall spyre in every countye telle,   20
And with thy tale the lazing rych men shame;
Showe howe the glorious Canynge did excelle;
How hee good man a friend for kynges became,
And gloryous paved at once the way to heaven and fame.

6 *Fyre-levyn* 'lightening'; *mokie* 'murky'.   15 *payrde* 'compared'; *enseem* 'seem'.
14 *dispande* 'expanded'.

An Excelente Balade of Charitie:
As wroten bie the gode Prieste Thomas Rowley, 1464.

Chatterton submitted the poem to the *Town and Country Magazine* in the summer of 1770, only to have it rejected as unsuitable. It has traditionally been read as a personal accusation levelled at the failure of London's charity system. But Chatterton's parable (based on Jesus's story of the Good Samaritan, Luke, 10:30–7) also has wider issues in its sights, including religious hypocrisy and social inequality. The strong echoes of Chaucer, in which details like the Abbot's gold button (51) are used to make satiric points, implies that things have not improved since the fourteenth century. The *Balade*, which soon became Chatterton's most admired poem, was printed in the first edition of *Poems* (1777), pp. 203–9, 'from a single sheet in Chatterton's hand-writing' (now lost), and that text is given here. Chatterton supplied his own glosses and notes to help his readers, and we record these in the annotation (C).

In Virgyne the sweltrie sun gan sheene,
And hotte upon the mees did caste his raie;
The apple rodded from its palie greene,
And the mole peare did bende the leafy spraie;
The peede chelandri sunge the livelong daie;   5
'Twas nowe the pride, the manhode of the yeare,
And eke the grounde was dighte in its mose defte aumere.

Title 'Thomas Rowley, the author, was born at Norton Mal-reward in Somersetshire, educated at the Convent of St. Kenna at Keynesham, and died at Westbury in Gloucestershire' (C).
1 *Virgyne* 'Virgo'.
2 *mees* 'meads' (C), i.e. 'meadows'.

3 *rodded* 'reddened, ripened' (C).
4 *mole* 'soft' (C).
5 *peede chelandri* 'pied goldfinch' (C).
7 *dighte* 'drest, arrayed' (C); *defte* 'neat, ornamental' (C); *aumere* 'a loose robe or mantle' (C).

The sun was glemeing in the midde of daie,
Deadde still the aire, and eke the welken blue,
When from the sea arist in drear arraie   10
A hepe of cloudes of sable sullen hue,
The which full fast unto the woodlande drewe,
Hiltring attenes the sunnis fetive face,
And the blacke tempeste swolne and gatherd up apace.

Beneathe an holme, faste by a pathwaie side,   15
Which dide unto Seyncte Godwine's covent lede,
A hapless pilgrim moneynge did abide,
Pore in his viewe, ungentle in his weede,
Longe bretful of the miseries of neede,
Where from the hail-stone coulde the almer flie?   20
He had no housen theere, ne anie covent nie.

Look in his glommed face, his sprighte there scanne;
Howe woe-be-gone, how withered, forwynd, deade!
Haste to thie church-glebe-house, asshrewed manne!
Haste to thie kiste, thie onlie dortoure bedde.   25
Cale, as the claie whiche will gre on thie hedde,
Is Charitie and Love aminge highe elves;
Knightis and Barons live for pleasure and themselves.

The gatherd storme is rype; the bigge drops falle;
The forswat meadowes smethe, and drenche the raine;   30
The comyng ghastness do the cattle pall,
And the full flockes are drivynge ore the plaine;
Dashde from the cloudes the waters flott againe;
The welkin opes; the yellow levynne flies;
And the hot fierie smothe in the wide lowings dies.   35

Liste! now the thunder's rattling clymmynge sound
Cheves slowlie on, and then embollen clangs,
Shakes the hie spyre, and losst, dispended, drown'd,

9 *welken* 'the sky, the atmosphere' (C).
10 *arist* 'arose' (C).
13 *Hiltring* 'hiding, shrouding' (C); *attenes* 'at once' (C); *fetive* 'beauteous' (C).
15 *holme* 'holly-tree'.
16 'It would have been *charitable*, if the author had not pointed at personal characters in this Ballad of Charity. The Abbot of St. Godwin's at the time of the writing of this was Ralph de Bellomont, a great stickler for the Lancastrian family. Rowley was a Yorkist' (C). This convent is evidently fictional.
18 *ungentle* 'beggarly' (C).
19 *bretful* 'filled with' (C).
20 *almer* 'beggar' (C).
22 *glommed* 'clouded, dejected. A person of some note in the literary world is of opinion, that *glum* and *glom* are modern cant words; and from this circumstance doubts the authenticity of Rowley's Manuscripts. Glum-mong in the Saxon signifies twilight, a dark or dubious light;

and the modern word *gloomy* is derived from the Saxon *glum*' (C).
23 *forwynd* 'dry, sapless' (C).
24 *church-glebe-house* 'the grave' (C); *asshrewed* 'accursed, unfortunate' (C).
25 *kiste* 'coffin' (C); *dortoure* 'a sleeping-room' (C).
26 *Cale* 'cold'.
27 *elves* 'creatures'.
30 *forswat* 'sun-burnt' (C); *smethe* 'smoke' (C); *drenche* 'drink' (C).
31 *ghastness* 'terror'; *pall* 'a contraction from *appall*, to fright' (C).
33 *flott* 'fly' (C).
34 *levynne* 'lightning' (C).
35 *smothe* 'steam, or vapours' (C); *lowings* 'flames' (C).
36 *clymmynge* 'noisy' (C).
37 *Cheves* 'moves' (C); *embollen* 'swelled, strengthened' (C).
38 *dispended* 'spent'.

Still on the gallard eare of terroure hanges;
The windes are up; the lofty elmen swanges;   40
Again the levynne and the thunder poures,
And the full cloudes are braste attenes in stonen showers.

Spurreynge his palfrie oere the watrie plaine,
The Abbote of Seyncte Godwynes convente came;
His chapournette was drented with the reine,   45
And his pencte gyrdle met with mickle shame;
He aynewarde tolde his bederoll at the same;
The storme encreasen, and he drew aside,
With the mist almes craver neere to the holme to bide.

His cope was all of Lyncolne clothe so fyne,   50
With a gold button fasten'd neere his chynne;
His autremete was edged with golden twynne,
And his shoone pyke a loverds mighte have binne;
Full well it shewn he thoughten coste no sinne:
The trammels of the palfrye pleasde his sighte,   55
For the horse-millanare his head with roses dighte.

An almes, sir prieste! the droppynge pilgrim saide,
O! let me waite within your covente dore,
Till the sunne sheneth hie above our heade,
And the loude tempeste of the aire is oer;   60
Helpless and ould am I alas! and poor;
No house, ne friend, ne moneie in my pouche;
All yatte I call my owne is this my silver crouche.

Varlet, replyd the Abbatte, cease your dinne;
This is no season almes and prayers to give;   65
Mie porter never lets a faitour in;
None touch mie rynge who not in honour live.
And now the sonne with the blacke cloudes did stryve,
And shettynge on the grounde his glairie raie,
The Abbatte spurrde his steede, and eftsoones roadde awaie.   70

Once moe the skie was blacke, the thounder rolde;
Faste reyneynge oer the plaine a prieste was seen;
Ne dighte full proude, ne buttoned up in golde;
His cope and jape were graie, and eke were clene;

---

39 *gallard* 'frighted' (C).

40 *elmen* 'elm'.

42 *braste* 'burst' (C).

45 *chapournette* 'A small round hat, not unlike the shapournette in heraldry, formerly worn by Ecclesiastics and Lawyers' (C).

46 *pencte* 'painted' (C); *mickle* 'great'.

47 *He aynewarde tolde his bederoll* 'He told his beads backwards; a figurative expression to signify cursing' (C).

49 *mist* 'poor, needy' (C).

50 *cope* 'a cloke' (C).

52 *autremete* 'a loose white robe, worn by Priests' (C).

53 *shoone pyke* 'shoe-points' (laces); *loverds* 'A lord' (C).

55 *trammels* Restraining straps.

56 *horse-millanare* 'I believe this trade is still in being, though but seldom employed' (C). A horse milliner dealt in decorative trappings. *dighte* 'adorned'.

63 *crouche* 'cross'.

66 *faitour* 'a beggar, or vagabond' (C).

74 *jape* 'A short surplice, worn by Friars of an inferior class, and secular priests' (C).

A Limitoure he was of order seene;   75
And from the pathwaie side then turned hee,
Where the pore almer laie binethe the holmen tree.

An almes, sir priest! the droppynge pilgrim sayde,
For sweete Seyncte Marie and your order sake.
The Limitoure then loosen'd his pouche threade,   80
And did thereoute a groate of silver take;
The mister pilgrim dyd for halline shake.
Here take this silver, it maie eathe thie care;
We are Goddes stewards all, nete of oure owne we bare.

But ah! unhailie pilgrim, lerne of me,   85
Scathe anie give a rentrolle to their Lorde.
Here take my semecope, thou arte bare I see;
Tis thyne; the Seynctes will give me mie rewarde.
He left the pilgrim, and his waie aborde.
Virgynne and hallie Seyncte, who sitte yn gloure,   90
Or give the mittee will, or give the gode man power.

75 *Limitoure* A limiter was a friar licensed to beg within   86 *Scathe* 'scarce'.
   certain limits. Chaucer's Friar is one.   87 *semecope* 'a short under-cloke' (C).
82 *halline* 'joy' (C).   89 *aborde* 'continued'.
83 *eathe* 'ease' (C).   90 *gloure* 'Glory' (C).
84 *nete* 'nought' (C).   91 *Or give* 'Either give'; *mittee* 'mighty, rich' (C).
85 *unhailie* 'unhappy' (C).

Oliver Goldsmith (?1730–1774)

The versatility which enabled the mature Goldsmith to produce masterpieces in three different genres – the novel, poetry and drama – manifested itself in his early years as capriciousness and irresolution. A clergyman's son, Goldsmith enjoyed an idyllic rural childhood in Lissoy, County Westmeath, Ireland. But even as a boy he began to adopt loud clothes and manners to divert attention from his extreme physical ugliness. At Trinity College, Dublin, Goldsmith distinguished himself primarily in flute-playing, storytelling, drinking, gambling and rioting. After finally gaining his degree in 1750 he dallied with holy orders, worked as a tutor, left home for America, missed his ship and returned home after five weeks, then gambled away money his uncle had given him to study law in London. In 1752 he took up medicine. After a year studying at Edinburgh he went to Leiden, Holland, ostensibly to attend medical lectures, then in 1755 spent a year wandering through Switzerland, Italy and France. Back in England in 1756, the unsettled Goldsmith worked as an apothecary's assistant before establishing himself, unsuccessfully, as a physician in Southwark. He then taught briefly and unhappily at a Presbyterian boys' school in Peckham while trying to secure a post as a physician with the East India Company.

A chance meeting with Ralph Griffiths, editor of the *Monthly Review*, pointed him towards a literary career. Goldsmith revealed his talents as a reviewer first for Griffiths, then for Smollett's *Critical Review*. In 1759 he became editor of a new weekly journal, *The Bee*. Over the next fifteen years Goldsmith was extraordinarily prolific, producing numerous popular histories and journal articles as well as such notable works as *The Citizen of the World* (1762), a fictional Chinese visitor's commentary on English manners and mores; *The Traveller* (1764), a couplet poem examining the influence of climate on national character; *The Vicar of Wakefield* (1766), an enduringly popular novel of English rural life; the elegiac *Deserted Village* (1770); and two highly successful stage comedies, *The Good Natur'd Man* (1768) and *She Stoops to Conquer* (1773). Goldsmith's readable style and gift for entertaining audiences ensured his literary popularity, yet his spendthrift habits coupled with a complete inability to handle his finances led to a *Dunciad*-type lifestyle and a deathbed debt of over £2,000. Goldsmith was fortunate in the friendship of Dr Johnson, long experienced in the vagaries of indigent authors, who purportedly saved him from debtors' prison by finding a publisher willing to advance him £60 for the manuscript of *The Vicar of Wakefield*. Goldsmith also became a valued member of Johnson's 'Club', the distinguished literary circle which included Edward Gibbon, Sir Joshua Reynolds, Edmund Burke and James Boswell, Johnson's biographer. Boswell criticized Goldsmith's habitual boasting in conversation and described him disparagingly as a quick yet shallow writer, but Johnson recognized in Goldsmith, for all his moral failings, a breadth of vision, tolerance and humanity akin to his own. Goldsmith died from a kidney infection at the age of forty-four. Johnson's epitaph engraved on his tomb claimed that he 'touched almost every kind of writing, and touched none that he did not adorn'.

The Deserted Village

The Deserted Village voices the same indignation about rural depopulation which some eight years earlier had prompted Goldsmith's newspaper article, 'The Revolution in Low Life' (1762). By purchasing large estates and enclosing common grazing land, wealthy merchants were forcing villagers from their homes, often to emigrate to America. Their extravagance had eroded Britain's moral backbone, her sturdy yeoman class. In his dedication to Sir Joshua Reynolds Goldsmith comments: 'I have taken all possible pains, in my country excursions, for these four or five years past, to be certain of what I alledge ... I expect the shout of modern politicians against me. For twenty or thirty years past, it has been the fashion to consider luxury as one of the greatest national advantages; and all the wisdom of antiquity in that particular, as erroneous. Still however, I must remain a professed ancient on that head, and continue to think those luxuries prejudicial to states, by which so many vices are introduced, and so many kingdoms have been undone.'

Goldsmith was well aware that in linking commercial prosperity with moral corruption he was out of step with the mood of national confidence following the victorious Seven Years' War (1756–63). His perception of national decline, his attack on luxury, and his celebration of the liberty-loving yeomanry, have more in common with Pope and Bolingbroke's Country attacks on Walpole's Whig administration in the 1720s and 1730s than with the political realities of his own time. Goldsmith's diatribe against luxury and corruption sits somewhat uneasily with the personal, elegiac and meditative qualities of his poetic inspiration. The poem is at once old-fashioned in its political polemic and proleptically Romantic in its literary sensibility. Yet if the village of Auburn is an ominous symbol of national ruin, its decay, wrought in part by the simple passage of time, stimulates the poet into a lyrical and nostalgic evocation of childhood memories. *The Deserted Village*, like many pastoral elegies, derives its power from the poet's exploration of his own sense of loss and alienation. The poem with which it is often fruitfully compared, Crabbe's *The Village*, is an ironic response to Goldsmith's rosy picture of rural life; but *The Deserted Village* also deploys its sentiment satirically, and some critics have seen it as the more radical poem of the two.

The Deserted Village was published on 26 May 1770 and was instantly popular, reaching a sixth edition by 4 October. The text we have used here is that of the first edition.

<blockquote>

Sweet Auburn, loveliest village of the plain,
Where health and plenty cheared the labouring swain,
Where smiling spring its earliest visit paid,
And parting summer's lingering blooms delayed,
Dear lovely bowers of innocence and ease,   5
Seats of my youth, when every sport could please,
How often have I loitered o'er thy green,
Where humble happiness endeared each scene;
How often have I paused on every charm,
The sheltered cot, the cultivated farm,   10
The never failing brook, the busy mill,
The decent church that topt the neighbouring hill,
The hawthorn bush, with seats beneath the shade,
For talking age and whispering lovers made.
How often have I blest the coming day,   15
When toil remitting lent its turn to play,
And all the village train from labour free
Led up their sports beneath the spreading tree,
While many a pastime circled in the shade,
The young contending as the old surveyed;   20
And many a gambol frolicked o'er the ground,
And slights of art and feats of strength went round.
And still as each repeated pleasure tired,
Succeeding sports the mirthful band inspired;
The dancing pair that simply sought renown   25
By holding out to tire each other down,
The swain mistrustless of his smutted face,
While secret laughter tittered round the place,
The bashful virgin's side-long looks of love,
The matron's glance that would those looks reprove.   30
These were thy charms, sweet village; sports like these,
With sweet succession, taught even toil to please;
These round thy bowers their chearful influence shed,
These were thy charms — But all these charms are fled.
    Sweet smiling village, loveliest of the lawn,   35
Thy sports are fled, and all thy charms withdrawn;
Amidst thy bowers the tyrant's hand is seen,

</blockquote>

1 *Auburn* Although there are real villages in England with a similar name, Goldsmith's 'Auburn' is an idealized imaginary village, probably modelled on childhood memories of Lissoy in Ireland, where he grew up.
10 *cot* 'cottage'.
15 *coming day* Sunday, the sabbath.

18 *led up* 'started off'.
25 *simply* 'naively'.
27 *mistrustless* 'unsuspecting'. The game is one in which the victim unknowingly transfers soot or grime to his face.

And desolation saddens all thy green:
One only master grasps thy whole domain,
And half a tillage stints thy smiling plain;   40
No more thy glassy brook reflects the day,
But choaked with sedges, works its weedy way.
Along thy glades, a solitary guest,
The hollow sounding bittern guards its nest;
Amidst thy desert walks the lapwing flies,   45
And tires their ecchoes with unvaried cries.
Sunk are thy bowers in shapeless ruin all,
And the long grass o'ertops the mouldering wall,
And trembling, shrinking from the spoiler's hand,
Far, far away thy children leave the land.   50
    Ill fares the land, to hastening ills a prey,
Where wealth accumulates, and men decay;
Princes and lords may flourish, or may fade;
A breath can make them, as a breath has made.
But a bold peasantry, their country's pride,   55
When once destroyed, can never be supplied.
    A time there was, ere England's griefs began,
When every rood of ground maintained its man;
For him light labour spread her wholesome store,
Just gave what life required, but gave no more.   60
His best companions, innocence and health;
And his best riches, ignorance of wealth.
    But times are altered; trade's unfeeling train
Usurp the land and dispossess the swain;
Along the lawn, where scattered hamlets rose,   65
Unwieldy wealth, and cumbrous pomp repose;
And every want to luxury allied,
And every pang that folly pays to pride.
These gentle hours that plenty bade to bloom,
Those calm desires that asked but little room,   70
Those healthful sports that graced the peaceful scene,
Lived in each look, and brightened all the green;
These far departing seek a kinder shore,
And rural mirth and manners are no more.
    Sweet AUBURN! parent of the blissful hour,   75
Thy glades forlorn confess the tyrant's power.
Here as I take my solitary rounds,
Amidst thy tangling walks, and ruined grounds,
And, many a year elapsed, return to view
Where once the cottage stood, the hawthorn grew,   80
Here, as with doubtful, pensive steps I range,
Trace every scene, and wonder at the change,

---

40 *half a tillage* Only half the former amount of land is now tilled; *stints* 'supplies grudgingly'.
44 *bittern* See Thomson, *Spring*, 22–3n. In his *History of the Earth* (1774) Goldsmith recalled: 'I remember in the place where I was a boy with what terror this bird's note affected the whole village; they considered it as the presage of some sad event'.

45 *lapwing* A bird of the plover family with a striking crest and plangent call. See Thomson, *Spring*, 24–5n.
58 *rood* A quarter of an acre.
74 *manners* 'customs'.
81–2 Goldsmith omitted this couplet from the fourth and later editions.

Remembrance wakes with all her busy train,
Swells at my breast, and turns the past to pain.
　In all my wanderings round this world of care,　　　　　85
In all my griefs — and GOD has given my share —
I still had hopes my latest hours to crown,
Amidst these humble bowers to lay me down;
My anxious day to husband near the close,
And keep life's flame from wasting by repose.　　　　　90
I still had hopes, for pride attends us still,
Amidst the swains to shew my book-learned skill,
Around my fire an evening groupe to draw,
And tell of all I felt, and all I saw;
And, as an hare whom hounds and horns pursue,　　　　95
Pants to the place from whence at first she flew,
I still had hopes, my long vexations past,
Here to return — and die at home at last.
　O blest retirement, friend to life's decline,
Retreats from care that never must be mine,　　　　　100
How blest is he who crowns in shades like these,
A youth of labour with an age of ease;
Who quits a world where strong temptations try,
And, since 'tis hard to combat, learns to fly.
For him no wretches, born to work and weep,　　　　　105
Explore the mine, or tempt the dangerous deep;
No surly porter stands in guilty state
To spurn imploring famine from his gate,
But on he moves to meet his latter end,
Angels around befriending virtue's friend;　　　　　110
Sinks to the grave with unperceived decay,
While resignation gently slopes the way;
And all his prospects brightening to the last,
His Heaven commences ere the world be past!
　Sweet was the sound when oft at evening's close,　　115
Up yonder hill the village murmur rose;
There as I past with careless steps and slow,
The mingling notes came softened from below;
The swain responsive as the milk-maid sung,
The sober herd that lowed to meet their young;　　　120
The noisy geese that gabbled o'er the pool,
The playful children just let loose from school;
The watch-dog's voice that bayed the whispering wind,
And the loud laugh that spoke the vacant mind,
These all in soft confusion sought the shade,　　　　125
And filled each pause the nightingale had made.
But now the sounds of population fail,
No chearful murmurs fluctuate in the gale,
No busy steps the grass-grown foot-way tread,
But all the bloomy flush of life is fled.　　　　　130
All but yon widowed, solitary thing
That feebly bends beside the plashy spring;

---

106 *tempt* 'venture upon'.　　　　　124 *vacant* 'carefree'.
111–12 Cf. Johnson, *The Vanity of Human Wishes*, 293–4.　　132 *plashy* 'marshy'.

She, wretched matron, forced, in age, for bread,
To strip the brook with mantling cresses spread,
To pick her wintry faggot from the thorn,　　　　　　　　　135
To seek her nightly shed, and weep till morn;
She only left of all the harmless train,
The sad historian of the pensive plain.
　Near yonder copse, where once the garden smil'd,
And still where many a garden flower grows wild;　　　140
There, where a few torn shrubs the place disclose,
The village preacher's modest mansion rose.
A man he was, to all the country dear,
And passing rich with forty pounds a year;
Remote from towns he ran his godly race,　　　　　　　145
Nor ere had changed, nor wish'd to change his place;
Unpractised he to fawn, or seek for power,
By doctrines fashioned to the varying hour;
Far other aims his heart had learned to prize,
More bent to raise the wretched than to rise.　　　　　150
His house was known to all the vagrant train,
He chid their wanderings, but relieved their pain;
The long remembered beggar was his guest,
Whose beard descending swept his aged breast;
The ruined spendthrift, now no longer proud,　　　　155
Claimed kindred there, and had his claims allowed;
The broken soldier, kindly bade to stay,
Sate by his fire, and talked the night away;
Wept o'er his wounds, or tales of sorrow done,
Shouldered his crutch, and shewed how fields were won.　160
Pleased with his guests, the good man learned to glow,
And quite forgot their vices in their woe;
Careless their merits, or their faults to scan,
His pity gave ere charity began.
　Thus to relieve the wretched was his pride,　　　　　165
And even his failings leaned to Virtue's side;
But in his duty prompt at every call,
He watched and wept, he prayed and felt, for all.
And, as a bird each fond endearment tries,
To tempt its new fledged offspring to the skies;　　　170
He tried each art, reproved each dull delay,
Allured to brighter worlds, and led the way.
　Beside the bed where parting life was layed,
And sorrow, guilt, and pain, by turns dismayed,
The reverend champion stood. At his control,　　　　175
Despair and anguish fled the struggling soul;
Comfort came down the trembling wretch to raise,
And his last faultering accents whispered praise.
　At church, with meek and unaffected grace,
His looks adorned the venerable place;　　　　　　　　180
Truth from his lips prevailed with double sway,
And fools, who came to scoff, remained to pray.

134 *cresses* Pungent but edible.
135 *faggot* A bundle of sticks for firewood.
144 *passing* 'extremely'.

146 *place* Means both 'location' and 'rank in the social
　　scale' (he was not a place-seeker).
150 *bent* 'inclined'.

The service past, around the pious man,
With ready zeal each honest rustic ran;
Even children followed with endearing wile,   185
And plucked his gown, to share the good man's smile.
His ready smile a parent's warmth exprest,
Their welfare pleased him, and their cares distrest;
To them his heart, his love, his griefs were given,
But all his serious thought had rest in Heaven.   190
As some tall cliff that lifts its awful form
Swells from the vale, and midway leaves the storm,
Tho' round its breast the rolling clouds are spread,
Eternal sunshine settles on its head.
    Beside yon straggling fence that skirts the way,   195
With blossomed furze unprofitably gay,
There, in his noisy mansion, skill'd to rule,
The village master taught his little school;
A man severe he was, and stern to view,
I knew him well, and every truant knew;   200
Well had the boding tremblers learned to trace
The day's disasters in his morning face;
Full well they laugh'd with counterfeited glee,
At all his jokes, for many a joke had he;
Full well the busy whisper circling round,   205
Conveyed the dismal tidings when he frowned;
Yet he was kind, or if severe in aught,
The love he bore to learning was in fault;
The village all declared how much he knew;
'Twas certain he could write, and cypher too;   210
Lands he could measure, terms and tides presage,
And even the story ran that he could gauge.
In arguing too, the parson owned his skill,
For e'en tho' vanquished, he could argue still;
While words of learned length, and thundering sound,   215
Amazed the gazing rustics ranged around,
And still they gazed, and still the wonder grew,
That one small head could carry all he knew.
    But past is all his fame. The very spot
Where many a time he triumphed, is forgot.   220
Near yonder thorn, that lifts its head on high,
Where once the sign-post caught the passing eye,
Low lies that house where nut-brown draughts inspired,
Where grey-beard mirth and smiling toil retired,
Where village statesmen talked with looks profound,   225
And news much older than their ale went round.
Imagination fondly stoops to trace
The parlour splendours of that festive place;
The white-washed wall, the nicely sanded floor,

---

196 *furze* Gorse, a thorny wild shrub with bright yellow
flowers.
201 *boding* 'apprehensive'.
210 *cypher* 'practise arithmetic'.
211 *terms* Calendar dates for the payment of rent, wages,
etc.; *tides* Annual festivals and holidays.

212 *gauge* Calculate the capacity of barrels and other
vessels.
223 *nut-brown draughts* i.e. ale.

The varnished clock that clicked behind the door;   230
The chest contrived a double debt to pay,
A bed by night, a chest of drawers by day;
The pictures placed for ornament and use,
The twelve good rules, the royal game of goose;
The hearth, except when winter chill'd the day,   235
With aspen boughs, and flowers, and fennel gay,
While broken tea-cups, wisely kept for shew,
Ranged o'er the chimney, glistened in a row.
   Vain transitory splendours! Could not all
Reprieve the tottering mansion from its fall!   240
Obscure it sinks, nor shall it more impart
An hour's importance to the poor man's heart;
Thither no more the peasant shall repair
To sweet oblivion of his daily care;
No more the farmer's news, the barber's tale,   245
No more the wood-man's ballad shall prevail;
No more the smith his dusky brow shall clear,
Relax his ponderous strength, and lean to hear;
The host himself no longer shall be found
Careful to see the mantling bliss go round;   250
Nor the coy maid, half willing to be prest,
Shall kiss the cup to pass it to the rest.
   Yes! let the rich deride, the proud disdain,
These simple blessings of the lowly train,
To me more dear, congenial to my heart,   255
One native charm, than all the gloss of art;
Spontaneous joys, where Nature has its play,
The soul adopts, and owns their first born sway,
Lightly they frolic o'er the vacant mind,
Unenvied, unmolested, unconfined.   260
But the long pomp, the midnight masquerade,
With all the freaks of wanton wealth arrayed,
In these, ere trifflers half their wish obtain,
The toiling pleasure sickens into pain;
And, even while fashion's brightest arts decoy,   265
The heart distrusting asks, if this be joy.
   Ye friends to truth, ye statesmen who survey
The rich man's joys encrease, the poor's decay,
'Tis yours to judge, how wide the limits stand
Between a splendid and an happy land.   270
Proud swells the tide with loads of freighted ore,
And shouting Folly hails them from her shore;
Hoards, even beyond the miser's wish abound,
And rich men flock from all the world around.

234 *twelve good rules* A board of homely instructions ('Reveal no secrets', 'Pick no quarrels' etc.) hung on the walls of many eighteenth-century homes and inns. They were supposedly found in King Charles I's study after his death; *royal game of goose* A popular board game similar to snakes and ladders.

250 *mantling* 'foaming'.
253–4 Cf. Gray, *Elegy*, 29–32.
258 *sway* 'power'.
259 *vacant* See 124n.

Yet count our gains. This wealth is but a name   275
That leaves our useful products still the same.
Not so the loss. The man of wealth and pride,
Takes up a space that many poor supplied;
Space for his lake, his park's extended bounds,
Space for his horses, equipage, and hounds;   280
The robe that wraps his limbs in silken sloth,
Has robbed the neighbouring fields of half their growth;
His seat, where solitary sports are seen,
Indignant spurns the cottage from the green;
Around the world each needful product flies,   285
For all the luxuries the world supplies.
While thus the land adorned for pleasure all
In barren splendour feebly waits the fall.
    As some fair female unadorned and plain,
Secure to please while youth confirms her reign,   290
Slights every borrowed charm that dress supplies,
Nor shares with art the triumph of her eyes.
But when those charms are past, for charms are frail,
When time advances, and when lovers fail,
She then shines forth sollicitous to bless,   295
In all the glaring impotence of dress.
Thus fares the land, by luxury betrayed,
In nature's simplest charms at first arrayed,
But verging to decline, its splendours rise,
Its vistas strike, its palaces surprize;   300
While scourged by famine from the smiling land,
The mournful peasant leads his humble band;
And while he sinks without one arm to save,
The country blooms — a garden, and a grave.
    Where then, ah, where shall poverty reside,   305
To scape the pressure of contiguous pride;
If to some common's fenceless limits strayed,
He drives his flock to pick the scanty blade,
Those fenceless fields the sons of wealth divide,
And even the bare-worn common is denied.   310
    If to the city sped — What waits him there?
To see profusion that he must not share;
To see ten thousand baneful arts combined
To pamper luxury, and thin mankind;
To see each joy the sons of pleasure know,   315
Extorted from his fellow-creature's woe.
Here, while the courtier glitters in brocade,
There the pale artist plies the sickly trade;
Here, while the proud their long drawn pomps display,

277–88 For a different view see Pope, *Epistle to Burlington*, 169–76.
280 *equipage* A coach and horses with attendant servants.
297–8 Cf. Joseph Warton, *The Enthusiast*, 142–4.
306 *contiguous* 'neighbouring'.
307–10 A diatribe against enclosure, whereby wealthy landowners purchased and fenced off for private use the common land formerly used to graze sheep and cattle.
313 *baneful* 'ruinous'.
318 *artist* 'craftsman'.

There the black gibbet glooms beside the way. 320
The dome where pleasure holds her midnight reign,
Here richly deckt admits the gorgeous train,
Tumultuous grandeur crowds the blazing square,
The rattling chariots clash, the torches glare;
Sure scenes like these no troubles ere annoy! 325
Sure these denote one universal joy!
Are these thy serious thoughts — Ah, turn thine eyes
Where the poor houseless shivering female lies.
She once, perhaps, in village plenty blest,
Has wept at tales of innocence distrest; 330
Her modest looks the cottage might adorn,
Sweet as the primrose peeps beneath the thorn;
Now lost to all; her friends, her virtue fled,
Near her betrayer's door she lays her head,
And pinch'd with cold, and shrinking from the shower, 335
With heavy heart deplores that luckless hour,
When idly first, ambitious of the town,
She left her wheel and robes of country brown.
    Do thine, sweet AUBURN, thine, the loveliest train,
Do thy fair tribes participate her pain? 340
Even now, perhaps, by cold and hunger led,
At proud men's doors they ask a little bread!
    Ah, no. To distant climes, a dreary scene,
Where half the convex world intrudes between,
Through torrid tracts with fainting steps they go, 345
Where wild Altama murmurs to their woe.
Far different there from all that charm'd before,
The various terrors of that horrid shore.
Those blazing suns that dart a downward ray,
And fiercely shed intolerable day; 350
Those matted woods where birds forget to sing,
But silent bats in drowsy clusters cling,
Those poisonous fields with rank luxuriance crowned
Where the dark scorpion gathers death around;
Where at each step the stranger fears to wake 355
The rattling terrors of the vengeful snake;
Where crouching tigers wait their hapless prey,
And savage men more murderous still than they;
While oft in whirls the mad tornado flies,
Mingling the ravaged landschape with the skies. 360
Far different these from every former scene,
The cooling brook, the grassy vested green,
The breezy covert of the warbling grove,
That only sheltered thefts of harmless love.
    Good Heaven! what sorrows gloom'd that parting day, 365
That called them from their native walks away;

320 *gibbet* 'gallows', often located at crossroads.
321 *dome* The pleasure garden at Ranelagh had a famous
    domed rotunda. But Goldsmith may just mean
    'building' (Lat. *domus*).
321–8 Cf. Mary Robinson, *The Birth-day*.
338 *wheel* 'spinning wheel'.

346 *Altama* The Altamaha river in south-east Georgia,
    North America. The trustees of the original Georgia
    colony attracted impoverished British settlers with
    misleading accounts of the climate and landscape.
357 *tigers* Here, the 'red tiger' or cougar. Naturalists of the
    day used 'tiger' for several American animals.

When the poor exiles, every pleasure past,
Hung round their bowers, and fondly looked their last,
And took a long farewell, and wished in vain
For seats like these beyond the western main;   370
And shuddering still to face the distant deep,
Returned and wept, and still returned to weep.
The good old sire, the first prepared to go
To new found worlds, and wept for others woe.
But for himself, in conscious virtue brave,   375
He only wished for worlds beyond the grave.
His lovely daughter, lovelier in her tears,
The fond companion of his helpless years,
Silent went next, neglectful of her charms,
And left a lover's for her father's arms.   380
With louder plaints the mother spoke her woes,
And blest the cot where every pleasure rose;
And kist her thoughtless babes with many a tear,
And claspt them close in sorrow doubly dear;
Whilst her fond husband strove to lend relief   385
In all the decent manliness of grief.
    O luxury! Thou curst by heaven's decree,
How ill exchanged are things like these for thee!
How do thy potions with insidious joy,
Diffuse their pleasures only to destroy!   390
Kingdoms by thee, to sickly greatness grown,
Boast of a florid vigour not their own.
At every draught more large and large they grow,
A bloated mass of rank unwieldy woe;
Till sapped their strength, and every part unsound,   395
Down, down they sink, and spread a ruin round.
    Even now the devastation is begun,
And half the business of destruction done;
Even now, methinks, as pondering here I stand,
I see the rural virtues leave the land.   400
Down where yon anchoring vessel spreads the sail
That idly waiting flaps with every gale,
Downward they move a melancholy band,
Pass from the shore, and darken all the strand.
Contented toil, and hospitable care,   405
And kind connubial tenderness, are there;
And piety with wishes placed above,
And steady loyalty, and faithful love.
And thou, sweet Poetry, thou loveliest maid,
Still first to fly where sensual joys invade;   410
Unfit in these degenerate times of shame,
To catch the heart, or strike for honest fame;
Dear charming nymph, neglected and decried,
My shame in crowds my solitary pride.

370 *seats* 'homes'; *main* 'ocean'.
409–18 Poetry was thought to flourish in a healthy nation but to decline at the onset of luxury and corruption and depart to other lands. Cf. Collins, *Ode to Liberty*; Gray, *The Progress of Poesy*.

Thou source of all my bliss, and all my woe,   415
That found'st me poor at first, and keep'st me so;
Thou guide by which the nobler arts excell,
Thou nurse of every virtue, fare thee well.
Farewell, and O where'er thy voice be tried,
On Torno's cliffs, or Pambamarca's side,   420
Whether where equinoctial fervours glow,
Or winter wraps the polar world in snow,
Still let thy voice prevailing over time,
Redress the rigours of the inclement clime;
Aid slighted truth, with thy persuasive strain   425
Teach erring man to spurn the rage of gain;
Teach him that states of native strength possest,
Tho' very poor, may still be very blest;
That trade's proud empire hastes to swift decay,
As ocean sweeps the labour'd mole away;   430
While self dependent power can time defy,
As rocks resist the billows and the sky.

---

420 *Torno* The Tornea river in northeastern Sweden; *Pambamarca* A mountain near Quito, Ecuador (on the Equator). The two locations represent extremes of cold and heat.

421 *equinoctial fervours* The burning heat at the Equator.

429–32 These lines, written by Dr Johnson, express a stoic sublimity uncharacteristic of Goldsmith.

430 *mole* A sea wall or breakwater.

George Crabbe (1754–1832)

George Crabbe, raised on the fringes of rural poverty in Aldeburgh on the Suffolk coast, harboured few illusions about 'the simple life that Nature yields'. The son of a minor customs officer, Crabbe worked as a dock hand and an apothecary's apprentice, but lack of funds thwarted his ambition to gain a medical training in London. In 1780, encouraged by the favourable local reception of his poetry, Crabbe gave up his failing apothecary's practice in Aldeburgh for a literary career in the capital. His writing was ignored until Edmund Burke, impressed by the verses Crabbe had enclosed in a begging letter, took charge of his affairs. Burke arranged for the publication of *The Library*, an early poem, and assisted Crabbe in becoming a clergyman. In 1782 he was ordained and became chaplain to Charles Manners, Duke of Rutland, at Belvoir Castle in Leicestershire. It was here that he wrote *The Village* (1783), a bleak portrait of village life which earned the praise of Dr Johnson and a wider reading public. Crabbe's success enabled him finally to marry his fiancée of eleven years' standing, Sarah Elmy, when he took on the post of curate at Stathern in Leicestershire, the first of many rural livings. In 1785 he published *The News-paper*, a Popian satire on the popular press – the last piece he was to publish for twenty-two years. During this time he unaccountably burnt nearly all he wrote until he broke silence in 1807 with *Poems by the Rev. George Crabbe LL.B.* The best of these, *The Parish Register*,

contained Crabbe's first experiments in fictional case histories of individual parishioners, a form he developed in *The Borough* (1810), notably in the story of Peter Grimes, and perfected in his *Tales* (1812) and *Tales of the Hall* (1819). Although critics have described Crabbe as a 'novelist manqué', the short verse narrative was a form uniquely suited to develop his close insights into human motivation and the consequences of major moral choices.

Crabbe's preference for the heroic couplet, his stern commitment to 'truth', and his professed contempt for visionary, imaginative poetry, seem at odds with the poetic concerns of his age: yet many of his poems share the Romantic fascination with marginal states of mind – psychosis, paranoia and hallucination. Crabbe had experienced these both professionally and personally. His wife, traumatized by the deaths of four of their six children, suffered serious mental illness between 1796 and her death in 1813; and Crabbe himself, prone to depression, had also begun to take opium in 1790 for a stomach condition. Soon after his wife's death he moved to Trowbridge in Wiltshire, where he became briefly engaged to, but failed to marry, a twenty-six-year-old admirer, Charlotte Ridout. In his later years Crabbe became a distinguished figure in London literary society, enjoying an especially close friendship with Sir Walter Scott.

The Village

The Village, first published in two books in 1783, has remained Crabbe's most famous work. Its stark description of the parish workhouse, reprinted in *The Elegant Extracts*, was familiar to generations of schoolchildren. Crabbe's provocation for *The Village*, a work based largely on his bitter memories of Aldeburgh, was the falsely sentimental account of rural life found in pastoral poetry in general and most recently in Goldsmith's portrait of the vanished 'Auburn' in *The Deserted Village* (1770). Like Goldsmith's poem, *The Village* contains angry passages of social polemic directed at a complacent establishment indifferent to the suffering of the rural poor. Yet whereas Goldsmith participates in the pastoral myth by evoking a lost world of rustic bliss, Crabbe denies that such a world ever existed. His villagers may be poor and oppressed, but they are also innately lazy, drunken and dishonest. Crabbe replaces Goldsmith's vignettes of country innocence with scenes of theft and violence. Whereas Goldsmith

idealizes the labouring poor at the expense of the bloated rich, Crabbe sees in rich and poor a mirror image of each other's vices (the venereal disease which passes from lord to swain via the country wench in Book 2 is a telling image of universal depravity). Previous poems such as Gay's *Shepherd's Week* and Duck's *Thesher's Labour* had exploited the gap between pastoral convention and rural reality, but none with the grim irony of *The Village*. The labouring poet John Clare complained that 'Crabbe writes about the peasantry as much like the Magistrate as the Poet. He is determined to show you their worst side: and as to their simple pleasures, he knows little or nothing about them.' Yet the poem, for all its 'ugly realism', memorably evokes the strange eery beauty of the Suffolk coast.

The text is that of the first edition of 1783. Crabbe lightly revised the poem in 1807, and the most significant of these changes are recorded in the editorial annotation.

BOOK I

The village life, and every care that reigns
O'er youthful peasants and declining swains;
What labour yields, and what, that labour past,
Age, in its hour of languor, finds at last;
What forms the real picture of the poor,   5
Demands a song — The Muse can give no more.
    Fled are those times, if e'er such times were seen,
When rustic poets prais'd their native green;
No shepherds now in smooth alternate verse,
Their country's beauty or their nymphs' rehearse;   10
Yet still for these we frame the tender strain,
Still in our lays fond Corydons complain,
And shepherds' boys their amorous pains reveal,
The only pains, alas! they never feel.
    On Mincio's banks, in Caesar's bounteous reign,   15
If TITYRUS found the golden age again,
Must sleepy bards the flattering dream prolong,
Mechanic echo's of the Mantuan song?
From truth and nature shall we widely stray,
Where VIRGIL, not where fancy leads the way?   20
    Yes, thus the Muses sing of happy swains,
Because the Muses never knew their pains:
They boast their peasants' pipes, but peasants now
Resign their pipes and plod behind the plough;
And few amid the rural tribe have time   25
To number syllables and play with rhyme;
Save honest DUCK, what son of verse could share
The poet's rapture and the peasant's care?
Or the great labours of the field degrade
With the new peril of a poorer trade?   30
    From one chief cause these idle praises spring,
That, themes so easy, few forbear to sing;
They ask no thought, require no deep design,
But swell the song, and liquefy the line;

7–8 'Fled are those times, when, in harmonious strains, / The rustic poet prais'd his native plains' (*1807*).

9 *alternate verse* Verses sung in turn by two shepherds (cf. Gay, *Friday; or, The Dirge*). The source is Virgil, *Eclogues*, 7:18 ('alternis versibus').

10 *country* The local countryside.

12 *Corydon* A shepherd in Virgil's seventh eclogue. Since then a conventional literary name for a shepherd-poet.

15–20 These lines were revised by Dr Johnson. The original version, according to Boswell, read:

In fairer scenes, where peaceful pleasures spring,
Tityrus, the pride of Mantuan swains might sing:
But charm'd by him, or smitten with his views,
Shall modern poets court the Mantuan muse?
From Truth and Nature shall we widely stray,
Where Fancy leads, or Virgil led the way?

15 *Mincio* A river which flows through Mantua, Italy, birthplace of the poet Virgil (70–19 BC).

16 *TITYRUS* A shepherd in Virgil's first eclogue, possibly representing the author himself.

20 *fancy* The meaning appears to shift from Crabbe's original to Johnson's emended version. Johnson here uses 'fancy' in a positive sense, placing it on the side of 'truth' and 'nature' as opposed to the slavish imitation of Virgil. Crabbe, conversely, seems to identify 'fancy' with escapist fantasy as a further type of deviation.

27 *DUCK* See Stephen Duck, headnote.

30 *poorer trade* i.e. poetry.

33–5 'For no deep thought, the trifling subjects ask, / To sing of shepherds is an easy task; / The happy youth assumes the common strain ...' (*1807*).

The gentle lover takes the rural strain,   35
A nymph his mistress and himself a swain;
With no sad scenes he clouds his tuneful prayer,
But all, to look like her, is painted fair.
    I grant indeed that fields and flocks have charms,
For him that gazes or for him that farms;   40
But when amid such pleasing scenes I trace
The poor laborious natives of the place,
And see the mid-day sun, with fervid ray,
On their bare heads and dewy temples play;
While some, with feebler hands and fainter hearts,   45
Deplore their fortune, yet sustain their parts,
Then shall I dare these real ills to hide,
In tinsel trappings of poetic pride?
    No, cast by Fortune on a frowning coast,
Which can no groves nor happy vallies boast;   50
Where other cares than those the Muse relates,
And other shepherds dwell with other mates;
By such examples taught, I paint the cot,
As truth will paint it, and as bards will not:
Nor you, ye poor, of letter'd scorn complain,   55
To you the smoothest song is smooth in vain;
O'ercome by labour and bow'd down by time,
Feel you the barren flattery of a rhyme?
Can poets sooth you, when you pine for bread,
By winding myrtles round your ruin'd shed?   60
Can their light tales your weighty griefs o'erpower,
Or glad with airy mirth the toilsome hour?
    Lo! where the heath, with withering brake grown o'er,
Lends the light turf that warms the neighbouring poor;
From thence a length of burning sand appears,   65
Where the thin harvest waves its wither'd ears;
Rank weeds, that every art and care defy,
Reign o'er the land and rob the blighted rye:
There thistles stretch their prickly arms afar,
And to the ragged infant threaten war;   70
There poppies nodding, mock the hope of toil,
There the blue bugloss paints the sterile soil;
Hardy and high, above the slender sheaf,
The slimy mallow waves her silky leaf;
O'er the young shoot the charlock throws a shade,   75
And the wild tare clings round the sickly blade;
With mingled tints the rocky coasts abound,
And a sad splendor vainly shines around.
    So looks the nymph whom wretched arts adorn,
Betray'd by man, then left for man to scorn;   80

---

53 *cot* 'cottage'.
55 Cf. Johnson, *On the Death of Dr Robert Levet*, 11–12.
63 *brake* 'bracken'.
72 *bugloss* A prickly-haired wild plant with bright blue flowers.
74 *mallow* A common wild plant with slimy hairy stems and leaves.

75 *charlock* The common name for the thick-bristled wild mustard plant.
76 *tare* Vetch, an invasive weed which grows among cultivated crops.
77–84 Cf. Goldsmith, *The Deserted Village*, 287–96.

Whose cheek in vain assumes the mimic rose,
While her sad eyes the troubled breast disclose;
Whose outward splendor is but Folly's dress,
Exposing most, when most it gilds distress.
  Here joyless roam a wild amphibious race,   85
With sullen woe display'd in every face;
Who, far from civil arts and social fly,
And scowl at strangers with suspicious eye.
  Here too the lawless vagrant of the main
Draws from his plough th'intoxicated swain;   90
Want only claim'd the labour of the day,
But vice now steals his nightly rest away.
  Where are the swains, who, daily labour done,
With rural games play'd down the setting sun;
Who struck with matchless force the bounding ball,   95
Or made the pond'rous quoit obliquely fall;
While some huge Ajax, terrible and strong,
Engag'd some artful stripling of the throng,
And foil'd beneath the young Ulysses fell;
When peals of praise the merry mischief tell?   100
Where now are these? Beneath yon cliff they stand,
To show the freighted pinnace where to land;
To load the ready steed with guilty haste,
To fly in terror o'er the pathless waste,
Or when detected in their straggling course,   105
To foil their foes by cunning or by force;
Or yielding part (when equal knaves contest)
To gain a lawless passport for the rest.
  Here wand'ring long amid these frowning fields,
I sought the simple life that Nature yields;   110
Rapine and Wrong and Fear usurp'd her place,
And a bold, artful, surly, savage race;
Who, only skill'd to take the finny tribe,
The yearly dinner, or septennial bribe,
Wait on the shore, and as the waves run high,   115
On the tost vessel bend their eager eye;
Which to their coast directs its vent'rous way,
Their's, or the ocean's miserable prey.
  As on their neighbouring beach yon swallows stand,
And wait for favouring winds to leave the land;   120

85 *amphibious* Suffolk fishermen, at home on land and
  water.
89 *vagrant* 'merchant' (*1807*); *main* 'ocean'.
96 *quoit* A heavy flat iron ring used in throwing
  competitions.
97 *Ajax* Greek hero famous for his bulk and dogged
  courage. In Homer's *Iliad*, 23 his wrestling contest
  with the smaller, more wily Odysseus (Ulysses) ends in
  a tie.
99–100 'And fell beneath him, foil'd, while far around, /
  Hoarse triumph rose and rocks return'd the sound?'
  (*1807*).
101–8 Stretches of the East Anglian coast were havens for
  local smugglers who evaded heavy import duties on
  continental liquor.

102 *pinnace* A small sailing ship.
108 *passport* Authorization to import goods without paying
  the usual duty.
113 *finny tribe* Fish.
114 *yearly dinner* An annual dinner was held after parish
  officers had been elected; *septennial bribe* After the
  Septennial Act (1716) general elections had to be held
  every seven years. Cf. Johnson, *The Vanity of Human
  Wishes*, 97.
115–18 Villagers wait to scavenge from a shipwreck.
  Wreckers would deliberately light a ship onto the rocks.
119–24 An autobiographical account of Crabbe's decision
  to leave Aldeburgh for London in 1780.

While still for flight the ready wing is spread:
So waited I the favouring hour, and fled;
Fled from these shores where guilt and famine reign,
And cry'd, Ah! hapless they who still remain;
Who still remain to hear the ocean roar,   125
Whose greedy waves devour the lessening shore;
Till some fierce tide, with more imperious sway,
Sweeps the low hut and all it holds away;
When the sad tenant weeps from door to door,
And begs a poor protection from the poor.   130
    But these are scenes where Nature's niggard hand
Gave a spare portion to the famish'd land;
Her's is the fault if here mankind complain
Of fruitless toil and labour spent in vain;
But yet in other scenes more fair in view,   135
Where Plenty smiles — alas! she smiles for few,
And those who taste not, yet behold her store,
Are as the slaves that dig the golden ore,
The wealth around them makes them doubly poor:
Or will you deem them amply paid in health,   140
Labour's fair child, that languishes with Wealth?
Go then! and see them rising with the sun,
Through a long course of daily toil to run;
Like him to make the plenteous harvest grow,
And yet not share the plenty they bestow;   145
See them beneath the dog-star's raging heat,
When the knees tremble and the temples beat;
Behold them leaning on their scythes, look o'er
The labour past, and toils to come explore;
See them alternate suns and showers engage,   150
And hoard up aches and anguish for their age;
Thro' fens and marshy moors their steps pursue,
When their warm pores imbibe the evening dew;
Then own that labour may as fatal be
To these thy slaves, as luxury to thee.   155
    Amid this tribe too oft a manly pride
Strives in strong toil the fainting heart to hide;
There may you see the youth of slender frame
Contend with weakness, weariness, and shame;
Yet urg'd along, and proudly loth to yield,   160
He strives to join his fellows of the field;
Till long contending nature droops at last,
Declining health rejects his poor repast,
His cheerless spouse the coming danger sees,

126–8 The high tides which periodically eroded the Suffolk coastline had in 1779 washed away eleven houses in Aldeburgh.

132 *spare* 'scanty'.

144–5 This couplet was dropped from *1807*, possibly on the grounds of political prudence.

144 *him* The sun.

146 *dog-star* Sirius, in the ascendant between July and August and associated with oppressive heat.

155 *luxury* 'thine excess' (*1807*). Crabbe's attack on luxury links *The Village* with Goldsmith's *Deserted Village*.

And mutual murmurs urge the slow disease.   165
Yet grant them health, 'tis not for us to tell,
Though the head droops not, that the heart is well;
Or will you urge their homely, plenteous fare,
Healthy and plain and still the poor man's share?
Oh! trifle not with wants you cannot feel,   170
Nor mock the misery of a stinted meal;
Homely not wholesome, plain not plenteous, such
As you who envy would disdain to touch.
   Ye gentle souls who dream of rural ease,
Whom the smooth stream and smoother sonnet please;   175
Go! if the peaceful cot your praises share,
Go look within, and ask if peace be there:
If peace be his — that drooping weary sire,
Or their's, that offspring round their feeble fire,
Or her's, that matron pale, whose trembling hand   180
Turns on the wretched hearth th'expiring brand.
Nor can yet time itself obtain for these
Life's latest comforts, due respect and ease;
For yonder see that hoary swain, whose age
Can with no cares except its own engage;   185
Who, propt on that rude staff, looks up to see
The bare arms broken from the withering tree;
On which, a boy, he climb'd the loftiest bough,
Then his first joy, but his sad emblem now.
   He once was chief in all the rustic trade;   190
His steady hand the straitest furrow made;
Full many a prize he won, and still is proud
To find the triumphs of his youth allow'd;
A transient pleasure sparkles in his eyes,
He hears and smiles, then thinks again and sighs: 195
For now he journeys to his grave in pain;
The rich disdain him; nay, the poor disdain;
Alternate masters now their slave command,
And urge the efforts of his feeble hand;
Who, when his age attempts its task in vain,   200
With ruthless taunts of lazy poor complain.
   Oft may you see him when he tends the sheep,
His winter charge, beneath the hillock weep;
Oft hear him murmur to the winds that blow
O'er his white locks, and bury them in snow;   205
When rouz'd by rage and muttering in the morn,
He mends the broken hedge with icy thorn.
   "Why do I live, when I desire to be
"At once from life and life's long labour free?
"Like leaves in spring, the young are blown away,   210
"Without the sorrow of a slow decay;
"I, like yon wither'd leaf, remain behind,

168 *homely* 'coarse'.
171 *stinted* 'niggardly'.
183 *latest* Those that come with old age.
198 *Alternate masters* 'A pauper who, being nearly past his
labour, is employed by different masters, for a length of

time proportioned to their occupations' (Crabbe, *1807*).
The parish Overseers of the Poor sent unemployed
men round from house to house to get work, for which
they were given their food plus sixpence a day.

"Nipt by the frost and shivering in the wind;
"There it abides till younger buds come on,
"As I, now all my fellow swains are gone;   215
"Then, from the rising generation thrust,
"It falls, like me, unnotic'd to the dust.
    "These fruitful fields, these numerous flocks I see,
"Are others' gain, but killing cares to me;
"To me the children of my youth are lords,   220
"Slow in their gifts but hasty in their words;
"Wants of their own demand their care, and who
"Feels his own want and succours others too?
"A lonely, wretched man, in pain I go,
"None need my help and none relieve my woe;   225
"Then let my bones beneath the turf be laid,
"And men forget the wretch they would not aid."
    Thus groan the old, till by disease opprest,
They taste a final woe, and then they rest.
Their's is yon house that holds the parish poor,   230
Whose walls of mud scarce bear the broken door;
There, where the putrid vapours flagging, play,
And the dull wheel hums doleful through the day;
There children dwell who know no parents' care,
Parents, who know no children's love, dwell there;   235
Heart-broken matrons on their joyless bed,
Forsaken wives and mothers never wed;
Dejected widows with unheeded tears,
And crippled age with more than childhood-fears;
The lame, the blind, and, far the happiest they!   240
The moping idiot and the madman gay.
    Here too the sick their final doom receive,
Here brought amid the scenes of grief, to grieve;
Where the loud groans from some sad chamber flow,
Mixt with the clamours of the croud below;   245
Here sorrowing, they each kindred sorrow scan,
And the cold charities of man to man.
Whose laws indeed for ruin'd age provide,
And strong compulsion plucks the scrap from pride;
But still that scrap is bought with many a sigh,   250
And pride embitters what it can't deny.
    Say ye, opprest by some fantastic woes,
Some jarring nerve that baffles your repose;
Who press the downy couch, while slaves advance
With timid eye, to read the distant glance;   255
Who with sad prayers the weary doctor teaze
To name the nameless ever-new disease;
Who with mock patience dire complaints endure,
Which real pain, and that alone can cure;

---

230 *yon house* The parish poorhouse. As an apothecary in
Aldeburgh Crabbe had been employed to tend the
poorhouse sick.
248–51 The poor-rate (local charges for the relief of the
poor), which some householders resented.

252 *fantastic* 'imaginary'. Cf. Anne Finch, *The Spleen*,
112–14.

How would ye bear in real pain to lie,   260
Despis'd, neglected, left alone to die?
How would ye bear to draw your latest breath,
Where all that's wretched paves the way for death?
  Such is that room which one rude beam divides,
And naked rafters form the sloping sides;   265
Where the vile bands that bind the thatch are seen,
And lath and mud is all that lie between;
Save one dull pane, that, coarsely patch'd, gives way
To the rude tempest, yet excludes the day:
Here, on a matted flock, with dust o'erspread,   270
The drooping wretch reclines his languid head;
For him no hand the cordial cup applies,
Or wipes the tear that stagnates in his eyes;
No friends with soft discourse his pain beguile,
Nor promise hope till sickness wears a smile.   275
  But soon a loud and hasty summons calls,
Shakes the thin roof, and echoes round the walls;
Anon, a figure enters, quaintly neat,
All pride and business, bustle and conceit;
With looks unalter'd by these scenes of woe,   280
With speed that entering, speaks his haste to go;
He bids the gazing throng around him fly,
And carries fate and physic in his eye;
A potent quack, long vers'd in human ills,
Who first insults the victim whom he kills;   285
Whose murd'rous hand a drowsy bench protect,
And whose most tender mercy is neglect.
  Paid by the parish for attendance here,
He wears contempt upon his sapient sneer;
In haste he seeks the bed where misery lies,   290
Impatience mark'd in his averted eyes;
And, some habitual queries hurried o'er.
Without reply, he rushes on the door;
His drooping patient, long inur'd to pain,
And long unheeded, knows remonstrance vain;   295
He ceases now the feeble help to crave
Of man, and mutely hastens to the grave.
  But ere his death some pious doubts arise,
Some simple fears which "bold bad" men despise;
Fain would he ask the parish priest to prove   300
His title certain to the joys above;
For this he sends the murmuring nurse, who calls
The holy stranger to these dismal walls;
And doth not he, the pious man, appear,

---

267 *lath and mud* An inferior building material in which clay
is plastered over a groundwork of thin sticks (laths).

270 *matted flock* A mattress stuffed with bits of old
shredded cloth.

283 *physic* 'medical knowledge'.

286 *bench* Of magistrates.

289 *sapient* 'knowing'.

297 *mutely hastens to* 'silent sinks into' (*1807*).

299 *"bold bad" men* A well-known phrase, perhaps first used
by Spenser of the 'bold bad man' Archimago in *The
Faerie Queene*, I.i.37, and subsequently used by
Shakespeare.

He, "passing rich with forty pounds a year?"   305
Ah! no, a shepherd of a different stock,
And far unlike him, feeds this little flock;
A jovial youth, who thinks his Sunday's task
As much as God or man can fairly ask;
The rest he gives to loves and labours light,   310
To fields the morning and to feasts the night;
None better skill'd, the noisy pack to guide,
To urge their chace, to cheer them or to chide;
Sure in his shot, his game he seldom mist,
And seldom fail'd to win his game at whist;   315
Then, while such honours bloom around his head,
Shall he sit sadly by the sick man's bed
To raise the hope he feels not, or with zeal
To combat fears that ev'n the pious feel?
 Now once again the gloomy scene explore,   320
Less gloomy now; the bitter hour is o'er,
The man of many sorrows sighs no more.
 Up yonder hill, behold how sadly slow
The bier moves winding from the vale below;
There lie the happy dead, from trouble free,   325
And the glad parish pays the frugal fee;
No more, oh! Death, thy victim starts to hear
Churchwarden stern, or kingly overseer;
No more the farmer gets his humble bow,
Thou art his lord, the best of tyrants thou!   330
 Now to the church behold the mourners come,
Sedately torpid and devoutly dumb;
The village children now their games suspend,
To see the bier that bears their antient friend;
For he was one in all their idle sport,   335
And like a monarch rul'd their little court;
The pliant bow he form'd, the flying ball,
The bat, the wicket, were his labours all;
Him now they follow to his grave, and stand
Silent and sad, and gazing, hand in hand;   340
While bending low, their eager eyes explore
The mingled relicks of the parish poor:
The bell tolls late, the moping owl flies round,
Fear marks the flight and magnifies the sound;
The busy priest, detain'd by weightier care,   345
Defers his duty till the day of prayer;
And waiting long, the crowd retire distrest,
To think a poor man's bones should lie unblest.

305 A reference to *The Deserted Village*,143–4, in which Goldsmith paints an idealized portrait of the village parson.

322 *man of many sorrows* 'He is despised and rejected of men; a man of sorrows, and acquainted with grief' (Isaiah, 53:3). Memorably set in Handel's *Messiah* as a prophecy of Jesus Christ.

332 *torpid* 'apathetic'.

342 *mingled relicks* The parish poor were sometimes buried in a common grave.

343 *moping owl* Cf. Gray, *Elegy*, 10.

Ann Yearsley (1753–1806)

Ann Cromartie was born into a poor family at Clifton, Bristol. In 1774 she married John Yearsley (1748–1803), owner of a modest property in the town, and during the next ten years gave birth to six children whom she helped to support by selling milk from door to door just as her mother had done. Yearsley lacked formal schooling but was taught to read by her brother, and her progress was such that by 1784 she knew Milton's *Paradise Lost*, several Shakespeare plays, Edward Young's *Night Thoughts*, and Pope's *Eloisa to Abelard*. When in the winter of 1783–4 the family sank into distress and were close to starvation, she was able to express her feelings of misery in poems of her own. The following summer Hannah More, the Bristol poet and educational writer, was shown a sample of Yearsley's verses by her cook and was impressed by the fact that 'though incorrect, they breathed the genuine spirit of Poetry'. She gave Yearsley an English grammar, spelling book and dictionary, and made the fateful decision to enlist support nationally for a subscription volume of the milkwoman's poems. The result of More's efforts was *Poems, on Several Occasions*, published in June 1785 with a list of over a thousand subscribers including an array of aristocrats and leading literary figures. The volume blatantly advertises More's role as Yearsley's benefactor: it includes several effusive poems addressed to her as 'Stella', and is prefaced by a ten-page letter from More to Elizabeth Montagu telling the milkwoman's story and introducing her work: 'You will find her, like all unlettered Poets, abounding in imagery, metaphor, and personification; her faults in this respect, being rather those of superfluity than of want. If her epithets are now and then bold and vehement, they are striking and original; and I should be sorry to see the wild vigour of her rustic muse polished into elegance, or laboured into correctness. Her ear is perfect; there is sometimes great felicity in the structure of her blank verse, and she often varies the pause with a happiness which looks like skill. She abounds in false concords, and inaccuracies of various kinds; the grossest of which have been corrected.'

The subscription brought Lactilla (as Yearsley was styled, from the Latin *lactis* = 'of milk') the substantial sum of £350, of which More and Montagu became joint trustees. After allotting money for clothes and furniture, More invested the rest to provide the family with a small regular income. The uproar that followed can be told by Montagu's editor: 'the ungrateful Lactilla turned upon poor Hannah in a fury, demanded the whole of the money, accused her of fraud, and – unkindest touch of all – told her that she had ruined her verses by her corrections and her reputation by her Preface' (*Mrs Montagu … Her Letters and Friendships*, ed. R. Blunt (London: Constable & Co. [1923]), 2:185). Yearsley had never concealed her robust character ('For mine's a stubborn and a savage will') and she felt demeaned by More's patronizing attitude. The prefatory letter gives us a hint of the problem: 'It is not intended to place her [Yearsley] in such a state of independence as might seduce her to devote her time to the idleness of Poetry. I hope she is convinced that the making of verses is not the great business of human life; and that, as a wife and mother, she has duties to fill.' Yearsley's poetic ambitions, however, were not to be thwarted, and after finally securing the money she went on to develop a literary career. Her poems were critically well received, reaching a fourth edition in 1786, and the following year she brought out a second volume, *Poems, on Various Subjects*. In 1793 Yearsley opened a circulating library in the Colonnade at the spa of Hotwells beneath Clifton Hill, and published her last subscription volume of poems, *The Rural Lyre* (1796). She extended her range with a verse drama, *Earl Goodwin* (performed at Bristol 1789 and published 1791), and a four-volume novel, *The Royal Captives* (1795). Her husband died in 1803, and suffering from ill health she moved to a peaceful retirement at Melksham in Wiltshire, where she died in 1806.

It is tempting to assume that More's revisal of the 1785 poems worked towards smoothing out Yearsley's rugged individual style, but it is impossible to be specific about this. The early items given here are nonetheless stamped with a strong poetic personality. Throughout her work Yearsley challenges expectations, particularly at moments when she is wrestling with thought and image in an almost metaphysical way. Moments of compression and entanglement perhaps represent Yearsley at her best, as a poet of struggle and difficulty. As the *Monthly Review* commented about her 1785 volume: 'these Poems present us with a very striking picture of a vigorous and aspiring genius, struggling with its own feelings'.

To Stella; on a Visit to Mrs Montagu

One of several poems in the 1785 volume addressed to Hannah More, here coupled with More's aristocratic friend Elizabeth Montagu (1720–1800), the leader of the so-called 'bluestockings' or 'learned ladies'. Since the 1750s Montagu's evening salon had been at the centre of London's literary culture. She headed the

Yearsley subscription, contributing twenty-two guineas, but was evidently cautious and uneasy about More's 'wonderful find'. For Yearsley the salon ('where Genius in familiar converse sits') was out of bounds, but in the poem she is able to articulate how the spirit can overcome restriction. Text from *Poems on Several Occasions* (1785), pp. 65–9.

Unequal, lost to the aspiring claim,
I neither ask, nor own th'immortal name
Of Friend; ah, no! its ardors are too great,
My soul too narrow, and too low my state;
STELLA! soar on, to nobler objects true,   5
Pour out your soul with your lov'd MONTAGU;
But, ah! shou'd either have a thought to spare,
Slight, trivial, neither worth a smile or tear,
Let it be mine; — when glowing raptures rise,
And each, aspiring, seeks her native skies;   10
When Fancy wakes the soul to extacy,
And the rapt mind is touch'd with Deity,
Quick let me from the hallow'd spot retire,
Where sacred Genius lights his awful fire.
    Crush'd as I am, by Fortune's adverse power,   15
I hail the joys which wait thy happier hour;
To hear the music of *her* matchless tongue,
On which the nameless sweets of wit are hung;
What bliss the friendship of the wise to share,
Of soul superior, and of virtues rare!   20
Where Genius in familiar converse sits,
Crowns real worth, and blasts pretending Wits;
Where great ideas, fed by Fancy, glow,
And soul-expanding notes in rapture flow;
Where pointed thought in polish'd diction drest,   25
With every grace assaults the yielding breast;
O, powers of Genius! even the Miser's heart,
In the sweet transport, bears a transient part;
He thrills, unconscious whence his pleasures come,
Who ne'er had dreamt of rapture but at home;   30
But, ah! the slight impression quickly dies,
Or on the noxious surface floating lies;
The momentary virtue ne'er was brought
To frame one bounteous deed, one generous thought,
His harden'd spirit only knows to shun   35
The lore of wisdom, and the genial sun
Of warm humanity; ah! joyless breast,
Which never hail'd a self-rewarding guest!
Then fly, cold wretch, to thy congenial cell,
And quit the haunts where sweet sensations dwell.   40
    How has your bounty cheer'd my humble state,
And chang'd the colour of my gloomy fate!
Still shall your image sooth my pensive soul,
When slow-pac'd moments, big with mischiefs, roll;

25 *pointed* 'witty'.
27–40 The temporary joy of the 'Miser' (one who hoards experience without communicating it) is only a self-enclosed egotism and does not result in positive thought or action.
34 Cf. Pope, *Epistle to a Lady*, 162.
36 *genial* 'life-giving'.
38 I.e. never experienced an occasion when a generous act was personally rewarding.
44 *mischiefs* 'misfortunes'.

Still shall I, eager, wait your wish'd return, 45
From that bright Fair who decks a SHAKESPEARE's urn
With deathless glories; every ardent prayer
Which gratitude can waft from souls sincere,
Each warm return to generous bounty due,
Shall warm my heart for you and MONTAGU. 50
   Blest pair! O, had not souls like your's been given,
The stupid Atheist well might doubt a Heaven;
Convinc'd, he now deserts his gloomy stand,
Owns MIND the noblest proof of a creating hand.
GALEN's conversion, by externals wrought, 55
Dropt far beneath sublimity of *Thought*;
But cou'd he those superior wonders find,
Which form and actuate your nobler mind,
How wou'd the Heathen, struck with vast surprise,
Atoms deny, while spirit fill'd his eyes. 60

46 See headnote to *On Mrs Montagu*.
55 *GALEN* Claudius Galenus (129–?199), Greek physician at the imperial court in Rome, and the great classical authority on medicine until the Renaissance. He held monotheistic views and admired Christian principles.
58 *actuate* 'rouse to activity'.
60 *Atoms deny* i.e. 'deny that humans can be reduced to their minutest physical ingredients'. So-called 'Galenic'

medicine had a resurgence in the eighteenth century and was associated with detailed material analysis: '*Galenical* medicine … is become all mechanical, and corpuscular: instead of qualities and degrees, every thing is now reduced to mechanical affections; to the figures, bulks, gravities, &c of the component particles' (Chambers, *Cyclopædia*, 1738 edn).

On Mrs Montagu

Elizabeth Montagu's high reputation as a critic rested on her *Essay on the Writings and Genius of Shakespear, compared with the Greek and French Dramatic Poets* (1769), a lively and quite aggressive defence of Shakespeare from the strictures of Voltaire. In it she accuses French neoclassical dramatists of forcing everything to conform to modern elegance, and of sacrificing individual character, variety and originality to the demands of formal principle. Yearsley's fascination with the concept of untaught genius took encouragement from this. Text from *Poems, on Several Occasions* (1785), pp. 101–6.

Why boast, O arrogant, imperious man,
Perfection so exclusive? are thy powers
Nearer approaching Deity? can'st thou solve
Questions which high Infinity propounds,
Soar nobler flights, or dare immortal deeds, 5
Unknown to woman, if she greatly dares
To use the powers assign'd her? Active strength,
The boast of animals, is clearly thine;
By this upheld, thou think'st the lesson rare
That female virtues teach; and poor the height 10
Which female wit obtains. The theme unfolds
Its ample maze, for MONTAGU befriends
The puzzled thought, and, blazing in the eye
Of boldest Opposition, strait presents
The soul's best energies, her keenest powers, 15
Clear, vigorous, enlighten'd; with firm wing
Swift she o'ertakes *his* Muse, which spread afar
Its brightest glories in the days of yore;

10 *virtues* Includes the sense of 'powers'.

Lo! where she, mounting, spurns the stedfast earth,
And, sailing on the cloud of science, bears   20
The banner of Perfection. ——
Ask GALLIA's mimic sons how strong her powers,
Whom, flush'd with plunder from her SHAKESPEARE's page,
She swift detects amid their dark retreats
(Horrid as CACUS in their thievish dens);   25
Regains the trophies, bears in triumph back
The pilfer'd glories to a wond'ring world.
So STELLA boasts, from her the tale I learn'd;
With pride she told it, I with rapture heard.
      O, MONTAGU! forgive me, if I sing   30
Thy wisdom temper'd with the milder ray
Of soft humanity, and kindness bland:
So wide its influence, that the bright beams
Reach the low vale where mists of ignorance lodge,
Strike on the innate spark which lay immers'd,   35
Thick clogg'd, and almost quench'd in total night —
On me it fell, and cheer'd my joyless heart.
      Unwelcome is the first bright dawn of light
To the dark soul; impatient, she rejects,
And fain wou'd push the heavenly stranger back;   40
She loaths the cranny which admits the day;
Confus'd, afraid of the intruding guest;
Disturb'd, unwilling to receive the beam,
Which to herself her native darkness shews.
      The effort rude to quench the cheering flame   45
Was mine, and e'en on STELLA cou'd I gaze
With sullen envy, and admiring pride,
Till, doubly rous'd by MONTAGU, the pair
Conspire to clear my dull, imprison'd sense,
And chase the mists which dimm'd my visual beam.   50
      Oft as I trod my native wilds alone,
Strong gusts of thought wou'd rise, but rise to die;
The portals of the swelling soul, ne'er op'd
By liberal converse, rude ideas strove
Awhile for vent, but found it not, and died.   55
Thus rust the Mind's best powers. Yon starry orbs,
Majestic ocean, flowery vales, gay groves,
Eye-wasting lawns, and Heaven-attempting hills,
Which bound th'horizon, and which curb the view;
All those, with beauteous imagery, awak'd   60
My ravish'd soul to extasy untaught,
To all the transport the rapt sense can bear;
But all expir'd, for want of powers to speak;
All perish'd in the mind as soon as born,

20 *science* 'knowledge'.
22 *GALLIA* France. Montagu's *Essay* contrasts the rule-bound French ('timid Imitators') with Shakespeare's 'original genius'.
25–9 *CACUS* The fire-breathing monster who stole the cattle of Geryon which Hercules (as one of his labours) was driving back to Greece. Hercules killed him in his cave. Virgil tells the story in *Aeneid*, 8:193–267.
32 *bland* 'gentle'.
54 *liberal converse* 'the free exchange of ideas'; *rude* 'primitive', 'rough'.
58 *wasting* 'idly occupying'.

Eras'd more quick than cyphers on the shore,   65
O'er which the cruel waves, unheedful, roll.
  Such timid rapture as young EDWIN seiz'd,
When his lone footsteps on the Sage obtrude,
Whose noble precept charm'd his wond'ring ear,
Such rapture fill'd LACTILLA's vacant soul,   70
When the bright Moralist, in softness drest,
Opes all the glories of the mental world,
Deigns to direct the infant thought, to prune
The budding sentiment, uprear the stalk
Of feeble fancy, bid idea live,   75
Woo the abstracted spirit from its cares,
And gently guide her to the scenes of peace.
Mine was that balm, and mine the grateful heart,
Which breathes its thanks in rough, but timid strains.

65 *cypher* The arithmetical zero: of no value in itself, it can infinitely multiply other numbers.
67–9 *EDWIN* 'See the Minstrel' (Yearsley's note). The poor villager Edwin is the hero of James Beattie's *The Minstrel* (1771–4), which traces 'the progress of a Poetical genius, born in a rude age, from the first dawning of fancy and reason' (Preface). In Book Two Edwin encounters a wise old hermit. The poem includes a tribute to Montagu, who was a close friend of Beattie's.
70 *LACTILLA* 'The Author' (Yearsley's note).
71 *Moralist* i.e. More.
73–5 Cf. Thomson, *Spring*, 1150–3.

TEXTUAL NOTES
  24 *retreats* retreats; (*1785*); **25** *dens); dens* (*1785*).

Clifton Hill

Written in January 1785

In Yearsley's hands what we might expect to be a conventional topographical poem becomes something stranger and more disturbing. John Dyer delighted in the endless variety of his views ('Ever charming, ever new, / When will the landscape tire the view!', *Grongar Hill*, 103–4) and Cowper established visual command (*The Task*, 1:288–90), but Yearsley is a rueful and more tentative observer, and the associations of her scene are discomforting. Where Pope's *Windsor-Forest* combined the sweep of history with a sense of local rootedness, *Clifton Hill* offers us a bitter personal retrospect and the fugitive Louisa. The role played by Cowper's Crazy Kate (1:534–56) makes an interesting comparison. A transcript of the poem in Hannah More's hand is in the Huntington Library, California (MS MO 6085). The text given here is that of the first printing, *Poems, on Several Occasions* (1785), pp. 107–27. Yearsley's own notes are marked (Y).

In this lone hour, when angry storms descend,
And the chill'd soul deplores her distant friend;
When all her sprightly fires inactive lie,
And gloomy objects fill the mental eye;
When hoary Winter strides the northern blast,   5
And FLORA's beauties at his feet are cast;
Earth by the grisly tyrant desert made,
The feather'd warblers quit the leafless shade;
Quit those dear scenes where life and love began,
And, cheerless, seek the savage haunt of man;   10
How mourns each tenant of the silent grove!
No soft sensation tunes the heart to love;
No fluttering pulse awakes to Rapture's call;
No strain responsive aids the water's fall.
The Swain neglects his Nymph, yet knows not why;   15
The Nymph, indifferent, mourns the freezing sky;

Alike insensible to soft desire,
She asks no warmth — but from the kitchen fire;
Love seeks a milder zone; half sunk in snow,
LACTILLA, shivering, tends her fav'rite cow;   20
The bleating flocks now ask the bounteous hand,
And chrystal streams in frozen fetters stand.
The beauteous red-brest, tender in her frame,
Whose murder marks the fool with treble shame,
Near the low cottage door, in pensive mood,   25
Complains, and mourns her brothers of the wood.
Her song oft wak'd the soul to gentle joys,
All but his ruthless soul whose gun destroys.
For this, rough clown, long pains on thee shall wait,
And freezing want avenge their hapless fate;   30
For these fell murders may'st thou change thy kind,
In outward form as savage as in mind;
Go, be a bear of Pythagorean name,
From man distinguish'd by thy hideous frame.
    Tho' slow and pensive now the moments roll,   35
Successive months shall from our torpid soul
Hurry these scenes again; the laughing hours
Advancing swift, shall strew spontaneous flowers;
The early-peeping snowdrop, crocus mild,
And modest violet, grace the secret wild;   40
Pale primrose, daisy, maypole-decking sweet,
And purple hyacinth together meet:
All Nature's sweets in joyous circle move,
And wake the frozen soul again to love.
    The ruddy swain now stalks along the vale,   45
And snuffs fresh ardour from the flying gale;
The landscape rushes on his untaught mind,
Strong raptures rise, but raptures undefin'd;
He louder whistles, stretches o'er the green,
By screaming milk-maids, not unheeded, seen;   50
The downcast look ne'er fixes on the swain,
They dread his eye, retire and gaze again.
'Tis mighty Love — Ye blooming maids, beware,
Nor the lone thicket with a lover dare.
No high romantic rules of honour bind   55
The timid virgin of the rural kind;
No conquest of the passions e'er was taught,
No meed e'er given them for the vanquish'd thought.
To sacrifice, to govern, to restrain,
Or to extinguish, or to hug the pain,   60
Was never theirs; instead, the fear of shame
Proves a strong bulwark, and secures their fame;
Shielded by this, they flout, reject, deny,
With mock disdain put the fond lover by;
Unreal scorn, stern looks, affected pride,   65

---

20 LACTILLA See biographical headnote.
29 *clown* 'uncouth rustic'.
31 *fell* 'terrible'.
33 *Pythagorean* Cf. *To Mr * * * *, an Unlettered Poet*, 29n.
36 *torpid* 'sluggish'.

37–8 Cf. Gray, *Ode on the Spring*, 1–3.
46 Cf. 'The conscious Heifer snuffs the stormy Gale'
(Thomson, *Winter*, 133).
58 *meed* 'reward'.

Awe the poor swain, and save the trembling bride.
    As o'er the upland hills I take my way,
My eyes in transport boundless scenes survey:
Here the neat dome where sacred raptures rise,
From whence the contrite groan shall pierce the skies;   70
Where sin-struck souls bend low in humble prayer,
And waft that sigh which ne'er is lost in air.
    Ah! sacred turf! here a fond Parent lies,
How my soul melts while dreadful scenes arise!
The past! Ah! shield me, Mercy! from that thought,   75
My aching brain now whirls, with horror fraught.
Dead! can it be? 'twas here we frequent stray'd,
And these sad records mournfully survey'd.
I mark'd the verse, the skulls her eye invite,
Whilst my young bosom shudder'd with affright!   80
My heart recoil'd, and shun'd the loathsome view;
"Start not, my child, each human thought subdue,
She calmly said; this fate shall once be thine,
My woes pronounce that it shall first be mine."
Abash'd, I caught the awful truths she sung,   85
And on her firm resolves one moment hung;
Vain boast — my bulwark tumbles to the deep,
Amaz'd — alone I climb the craggy steep;
My shrieking soul deserted, sullen views
The depths below, and Hope's fond strains refuse;   90
I listen'd not — She louder struck the lyre,
And love divine, and moral truths conspire.
    The proud Croesean crew, light, cruel, vain,
Whose deeds have never swell'd the Muses' strain,
Whose bosoms others sorrows ne'er assail,   95
Who hear, unheeding, Misery's bitter tale,
Here call for satire, would the verse avail.
Rest, impious race! — The Muse pursues her flight,
Breathes purer air on VINCENT's rugged height;
Here nibbling flocks of scanty herbage gain   100
A meal penurious from the barren plain;
Crop the low niggard bush; and, patient, try
The distant walk, and every hillock nigh:
Some bask, some bound, nor terrors ever know,
Save from the human form, their only foe.   105
Ye bleating innocents! dispel your fears,
My woe-struck soul in all your troubles shares;
'Tis but LACTILLA — fly not from the green:
Long have I shar'd with you this guiltless scene.

69 *dome* 'Clifton Church [the parish church of St Andrew]. In this church-yard the Author's Mother was buried' (Y).

73 *Parent* In her 'Prefatory Letter' Hannah More recalled the death of Mrs Cromartie: 'for the unhappy mother, all assistance came too late; she had the joy to see it arrive, but it was a joy she was no longer able to bear, and it was more fatal to her than famine had been'.

91 Cf. Collins, *The Passions*, 23.

93 *Croesean* 'It is supposed this word is derived, though not very legitimately, from Croesus' (Y). Croesus, King of Lydia, proverbial for his immense wealth, was disastrously defeated by the Persians in 546 BC.

'Tis mine to wander o'er the dewy lawn,   110
And mark the pallid streak of early dawn;
Lo! the grey dusk that fill'd the vacant space,
Now fleets, and infant light pursues the chace;
From the hill top it seeks the valley low;
Inflam'd, the cheeks of morn with blushes glow;   115
Behold it 'whelm'd in a bright flood of day,
It strives no more, but to the God gives way.
    Ye silent, solemn, strong, stupendous heights,
Whose terror-striking frown the school-boy frights
From the young daw; whilst in your rugged breast   120
The chattering brood, secured by Horror, rest.
Say, Muse, what arm the low'ring brothers cleft,
And the calm stream in this low cradle left?
Coëval with Creation they look down,
And, sunder'd, still retain their native frown.   125
Beneath those heights, lo! balmy springs arise,
To which pale Beauty's faded image flies;
Their kindly powers life's genial heat restore,
The tardy pulse, whose throbs were almost o'er,
Here beats a livelier tune. The breezy air,   130
To the wild hills invites the languid fair:
Fear not the western gale, thou tim'rous maid,
Nor dread its blast shall thy soft form invade;
Tho' cool and strong the quick'ning breezes blow,
And meet thy panting breath, 'twill quickly grow   135
More strong; then drink the odoriferous draught,
With unseen particles of health 'tis fraught.
Sit not within the threshold of Despair,
Nor plead a weakness fatal to the fair;
Soft term for INDOLENCE, politely given,   140
By which we win no joy from earth or heaven.
Foul Fiend! thou bane of health, fair Virtue's bane,
Death of true pleasure, source of real pain!
Keen exercise shall brace the fainting soul,
And bid her slacken'd powers more vigorous roll.   145
    Blame not my rustic lay, nor think me rude,
If I avow Conceit's the grand prelude
To dire disease and death. Your high-born maid,
Whom fashion guides, in youth's first bloom shall fade;
She seeks the cause, th'effect would fain elude,   150
By Death's o'erstretching stride too close pursu'd,
She faints within his icy grasp, yet stares,
And wonders why the Tyrant yet appears —
Abrupt — so soon — Thine, Fashion is the crime,

118 'St Vincent's rocks, between which flows the River
Avon' (Y).
120 *daw* 'jackdaw'. The rocks guard the nest from
predators.
122 *low'ring* 'threatening'.
126 'The Hot Wells' (Y). The hot springs issue from an
aperture at the foot of St Vincent's Rocks. The spa of
Hotwells had been fashionable since the reign of Queen
Anne. Cf. Bowles, *Elegy Written at the Hot-Wells*.
128 *genial* 'life-giving'.
136 *odoriferous* 'diffusing fragrance'.
146 *rude* 'naïve'.

Fell Dissipation does the work of time. 155
   How thickly cloath'd yon rock of scanty soil,
Its lovely verdure scorns the hand of Toil.
Here the deep green, and here the lively plays,
The russet birch, and ever-blooming bays;
The vengeful black-thorn, of wild beauties proud, 160
Blooms beauteous in the gloomy-chequer'd crowd:
The barren elm, the useful feeding oak,
Whose hamadryad ne'er should feel the stroke
Of axe relentless, 'till twice fifty years
Have crown'd her woodland joys, and fruitful cares. 165
   The pois'nous reptiles here their mischiefs bring,
And thro' the helpless sleeper dart the sting;
The toad envenom'd, hating human eyes,
Here springs to light, lives long, and aged dies.
The harmless snail, slow-journeying, creeps away, 170
Sucks the young dew, but shuns the bolder day.
(Alas! if transmigration should prevail,
I fear LACTILLA's soul must house in snail.)
The long-nosed mouse, the woodland rat is here,
The sightless mole, with nicely-pointed ear; 175
The timid rabbit hails th'impervious gloom,
Eludes the dog's keen scent, and shuns her doom.
   Various the tenants of this tangled wood,
Who skulk all day, all night review the flood,
Chew the wash'd weed driven by the beating wave, 180
Or feast on dreadful food, which hop'd a milder grave.
Hail, useful channel! Commerce spreads her wings,
From either pole her various treasure brings;
Wafted by thee, the mariner long stray'd,
Clasps the fond parent, and the sighing maid; 185
Joy tunes the cry; the rocks rebound the roar,
The deep vibration quivers 'long the shore;
The merchant hears, and hails the peeping mast,
The wave-drench'd sailor scorns all peril past;
Now love and joy the noisy crew invite, 190
And clumsy music crowns the rough delight.
   Yours be the vulgar dissonance, while I
Cross the low stream, and stretch the ardent eye,
O'er Nature's wilds; 'tis peace, 'tis joy serene,
The thought as pure as calm the vernal scene. 195
Ah, lovely meads! my bosom lighter grows,
Shakes off her huge oppressive weight of woes,
And swells in guiltless rapture; ever hail,
The tufted grove, and the low-winding vale!

---

156 'Leigh Wood' (Y).
156–65 Cf. the tree-passages in Dyer, *Grongar Hill*, 57–62; and Cowper, *The Task*, 1: 300–20.
163 *hamadryad* 'tree-nymph'.
172 *transmigration* Cf. *To Mr * * * * , an Unlettered Poet*, 29n.

182–3 *channel* The River Avon at Clifton, through which shipping reached the port of Bristol. The most flourishing trade was with the West Indies plantations, sugar being taken in exchange for slaves.

Low not, ye herds, your lusty Masters bring   200
The crop of Summer; and the genial Spring
Feels for your wants, and softens Winter's rage,
The hoarded hay-stack shall your woes assuage;
Woes summ'd in one alone, 'tis Nature's call,
That secret voice which fills creation all.   205
   Beneath this stack LOUISA's dwelling rose,
Here the fair Maniac bore three Winter's snows.
Here long she shiver'd, stiffening in the blast,
The lightnings round their livid horrors cast;
The thunders roar, while rushing torrents pour,   210
And add new woes to bleak affliction's hour;
The heavens lour dismal while the storm descends,
No Mother's bosom the soft maid befriends;
But, frighten'd, o'er the wilds she swiftly flies,
And drench'd with rains, the roofless hay-stack tries.   215
The morn was fair, and gentle —— sought
These lonely woodlands, friends to sober Thought;
With Solitude, the slow-pac'd maid is seen
Tread the dark grove, and unfrequented green,
Well —— knew their lurkings; PHOEBUS shone,   220
While, musing, she pursued the track alone.
O, thou kind friend! whom here I dare not name,
Who to LOUISA's shed of misery came,
Lur'd by the tale, sigh'd o'er her beauteous form,
And gently drew her from the beating storm,   225
Stand forth — defend, for well thou canst, the cause
Of Heaven, and justify its rigid laws;
Yet own that human laws are harshly given,
When they extend beyond the will of Heaven.
Say, can thy pen for that hard duty plead,   230
By which the meek and helpless maid's decreed
To dire seclusion? Snatch'd from guiltless joys,
To where corroding grief the frame destroys;
Monastic glooms, which active virtue cramp,
Where horrid silence chills the vital lamp;   235
Slowly and faint the languid pulses beat,
And the chill'd heart forgets its genial heat;
The dim sunk eye, with hopeless glance, explores
The solemn aisles, and death-denouncing doors,
Ne'er to be past again. — Now heaves the sigh,   240
Now unavailing sorrows fill the eye:
Fancy once more brings back the long-lost youth
To the fond soul, in all the charms of Truth;
She welcomes the lov'd image; busy Thought
Pourtrays the past, with guiltless pleasures fraught;   245
'Tis momentary bliss, 'tis rapture high,

---

206 *LOUISA* 'The beautiful unfortunate LOUISA, fugitive
Foreigner, lived three years in a state of distraction
under this hay-stack, without going into a house. She
once confessed, in a lucid interval, that she had escaped
from a Convent, in which she had been confined by her
father, on refusing a marriage of his proposing, her
affections being engaged to another man' (Y). Louisa

(d. 1800) was a German fugitive, for whom Hannah
More raised and administered a subscription, having
her removed to a private asylum.
220 *PHOEBUS* The sun.
246 *momentary bliss* Cf. Gray, *Ode on a Distant Prospect of
Eton College*, 16.

The heart o'erflows, and all is extacy.
MEMORY! I charge thee yet preserve the shade,
Ah! let not yet the glittering colours fade!
Forbear the cruel future yet to view,   250
When the sad soul must bid a long adieu,
E'en to its fancied bliss — Ah! turn not yet
Thou wretched bankrupt, that must soon forget
This farewel draught of joy: lo! Fancy dies,
E'en the thin phantom of past pleasure flies.   255
Thought sinks in real woe; too poor to give
Her present bliss, she bids the future live;
The spirit soon quits that fond clasp, for see,
The future offers finish'd misery.
Hope quite extinct, lo! frantic thro' the aisles   260
She raves, while SUPERSTITION grimly smiles.
Th'exhausted mourner mopes, then wildly stalks
Round the drear dome, and seeks the darkest walks.
The glance distracted each sad sister meets,
The sorrow-speaking eye in silence greets   265
Each death-devoted maid; LOUISA here
Runs thro' each various shape of sad despair;
Now swells with gusts of hope, now sick'ning dies;
Alternate thoughts of death and life arise
Within her panting soul; the firm resolve,   270
The new desire, in stronger fears dissolve.
She starts — then seiz'd the moment of her fate,
Quits the lone cloyster and the horrid grate,
Whilst wilder horrors to receive her wait;
Muffled, on Freedom's happy plains they stand,   275
And eager seize her not reluctant hand;
Too late to these mild shores the mourner came,
For now the guilt of flight o'erwhelms her frame:
Her broken vows in wild disorder roll,
And stick like serpents in her trembling soul;   280
THOUGHT, what art thou? of thee she boasts no more,
O'erwhelm'd, thou dy'st amid the wilder roar
Of lawless anarchy, which sweeps the soul,
Whilst her drown'd faculties like pebbles roll,
Unloos'd, uptorn, by whirlwinds of despair,   285
Each well-taught moral now dissolves in air;
Dishevel'd, lo! her beauteous tresses fly,
And the wild glance now fills the staring eye;
The balls, fierce glaring in their orbits move,
Bright spheres, where beam'd the sparkling fires of Love,   290
Now roam for objects which once fill'd her mind,
Ah! long-lost objects they must never find.
Ill starr'd LOUISA! Memory, 'tis a strain,
Which fills my soul with sympathetic pain.
Remembrance, hence, give thy vain struggles o'er,   295
Nor swell the line with forms that live no more.

To Mr * * * * , an Unlettered Poet, on Genius Unimproved

Yearsley's poem on the exciting possibilities open to the 'untaught' poet moves from the classical Castalian spring to the inner springs of the soul. She works between the world of substance and the freedom of idea, and is alert to the philosophical aspects of her theme. She has evidently been stimulated by Akenside's *The Pleasures of Imagination* (1744), a poem which shares her sense of mental adventure. The text below is that of the first printing, *Poems, on Various Subjects* (1787), pp. 77–82. In the preface to his début volume of *Poems* (1786), Robert Burns stressed his lack of learning and specifically disclaimed '*genius*' (to which 'even in his highest pulse of vanity, he has not the most distant pretensions'). Dr Tim Burke, however, suggests that Yearsley has in mind the self-taught poet, John Frederick Bryant (1753–91), 'Tobacco-Pipe Maker at Bristol', who published his *Verses … Together with His Life, Written by Himself* (London, 1787). The foreword notes that his volume is 'intended for the perusal of those who may be desirous of seeing the gradual progress of natural poetic genius'.

> Florus, canst thou define that innate spark
> Which blazes but for glory? Canst thou paint
> The trembling rapture in its infant dawn,
> Ere young Ideas spring; to local Thought
> Arrange the busy phantoms of the mind,   5
> And drag the distant timid shadows forth,
> Which, still retiring, glide unform'd away,
> Nor rush into expression? No; the pen,
> Tho' dipp'd in awful Wisdom's deepest tint,
> Can *never* paint the wild extatic mood.   10
>
>   Yet, when the bolder Image strikes thine eye,
> And uninvited grasps thy strongest thought,
> Resolv'd to shoot into this World of Things,
> Wide fly the gates of Fancy; all alarm'd,
> The thin ideal troop in haste advance,   15
> To usher in the substance-seeking Shade.
>
>   And what's the Shade which rushes on the world
> With pow'rful glare, but emblem of the soul?
>
>   Ne'er hail the fabled Nine, or snatch rapt Thought
> From the Castalian spring; 'tis not for *thee*,   20
> From embers, where the Pagan's light expires,
> To catch a flame divine. From one bright spark
> Of never-erring Faith, more rapture beams
> Than wild Mythology could ever boast.
>
>   Pursue the Eastern Magi through their groves,   25
> Where Zoroaster holds the mystic clue,
> Which leads to great Ormazes; there thou'lt find
> His God thy own; or bid thy Fancy chase
> Restless Pythag'ras thro' his varied forms,

14 *Fancy* 'Imagination'.
20 *Castalian spring* The spring on Mount Parnassus sacred to the Nine Muses.
25 *Magi* 'wise men'.
26 *Zoroaster* Gk. form of Zarathustra (*c.*630–*c.*553 BC), the Persian religious leader. Zoroastrianism conceives of history as a struggle between the principles of Good and Evil, i.e. between the creator Ormuzd (Ormazes) and the devil Ahriman (Ahrimanes).
29 *Pythag'ras* Pythagoras (*c.*580–*c.*500 BC), Greek philosopher and mystic whose doctrine of 'transmigration' (*metempsychosis*) held that the soul is reincarnated in a succession of human or animal bodies. Cf. *Clifton Hill*, 33.

And she shall see him sitting on a heap 30
Of poor Absurdity; where chearful Faith
Shall never rest, nor great Omniscience claim.
    What are the Muses, or Apollo's strains,
But harmony of soul? Like thee, estrang'd
From Science, and old Wisdom's classic lore, 35
I've patient trod the wild entangled path
Of unimprov'd Idea. Dauntless Thought
I eager seiz'd, no formal Rule e'er aw'd;
No Precedent controul'd; no Custom fix'd
My independent spirit: on the wing 40
She still shall guideless soar, nor shall the Fool,
Wounding her pow'rs, e'er bring her to the ground.
    Yet Florus, list! to thee I loudly call;
Dare thee, by all the transport Mind can reach,
Yea, by the boasted privilege of *Man*, 45
To stretch with me the spirit-raising wing
Of artless Rapture! Seek Earth's farthest bound,
Till Fancy panting, drops from endless space.
    Deep in the soul live ever tuneful springs,
Waiting the touch of Ecstasy, which strikes 50
Most pow'rful on defenceless, untaught Minds;
Then, in soft unison, the trembling strings
All move in one direction. Then the soul
Sails on Idea, and would eager dart
Thro' yon ethereal way; restless awhile, 55
Again she sinks to sublunary joy.
    Florus, rove on! pluck from the pathless vale
Of Fancy, all her loveliest, wildest sweets;
These best can please; but ah! beware, my Friend:
Timid Idea shrinks, when coldly thou 60
Would'st hail the tender shade; then strongly clasp
The coy, reluctant fugitive, or seize
The rover, as she flies; that breast alone
Is her's, all glowing with immortal flame;
And that be thine. 65

---

35 *Science* 'Learning'.
49–56 Cf. Akenside, *The Pleasures of Imagination*, 1:109–24, and notes.

56 *sublunary* 'earthly' (literally, 'beneath the moon'). The sublunary world is subject to time and decay.

Robert Burns (1759–1796)

The title page of Burns's *Poems, Chiefly in the Scottish Dialect* (Kilmarnock, 1786) billed him as 'The Simple Bard, unbroke by rules of Art'. In fact the 'untaught' ploughboy was quite a well-read young man with a keen sense of literary tradition. His father, a tenant farmer at Alloway, Ayrshire, was determined that his two eldest boys, Robert and Gilbert (b. 1760), should receive a decent education, and they were taught at the village school by John Murdoch, who encouraged their taste for literature. Robert went on to read the works of Pope and to study grammar, French and a little Latin. From 1777 Burns was the chief labourer on the family farm, and a practised ploughman, but he was also reading the work of Thomson, Shenstone, Shakespeare and the Scottish poet Allan Ramsay. By 1782, when he was working as a flax-dresser at Irvine, he had read Locke's *Essay Concerning Human Understanding*, and had developed a taste for the novels of Smollett, Mackenzie and Sterne. In 1784 Burns's father died, and he and Gilbert took a joint lease on Mossgiel, a hill farm near the village of Mauchline. But here Burns's sexual promiscuity began causing practical problems; the first of a range of illegitimate children was born in 1785, the mother being Betty Paton, a family servant, and the following year his attempt to marry another pregnant girlfriend, Jean Armour, brought opposition from her father. Burns took refuge in 'all kinds of dissipation and riot, Mason-meetings, drinking matches, and other mischief' and decided to emigrate to Jamaica. In order to pay for the journey he persuaded the Kilmarnock publisher, John Wilson, to bring out a subscription edition of his poems. Only 612 copies were issued, but the volume was critically acclaimed, and the young farmer's emigration was cancelled. On visiting Edinburgh the 'heaven-taught ploughman' (as an early review described him) was fêted in the cultural capital as a natural genius. A second subscription edition promptly sold 2,876 copies, and word of the new Scottish phenomenon rapidly spread to England. His poems were published in London in early November 1787.

But Burns was not able to live by his pen. On marrying Jean Armour in 1788 he accepted a commission as an exciseman (tax collector) at fifty pounds a year, which involved covering up to forty miles a day on horseback. This, along with his continuing struggles as a tenant farmer, took its toll, and Burns became ill with exhaustion, headaches and depression. In November 1791 he moved to Dumfries and a more local job in the Port Division, but his life remained unsettled. By this time much of his creative energy was being channelled into the writing of songs. In 1787 he had met James Johnson, whose *Scots Musical Museum* was intending to print the words and music of every surviving Scottish song. Burns enthusiastically joined him in the project, collecting and revising traditional songs, researching their provenance, and writing great numbers of original lyrics himself. During the last nine years of his life Burns wrote or reworked some 330 songs for the six volumes of the *Museum* (1787–1803) and for George Thomson's *Select Scottish Airs* (5 vols, 1793–1818).

In February 1793 a second Edinburgh edition of his *Poems*, now expanded to two volumes, included *Tam o' Shanter* and other recent work. Burns was hailed as a popular national poet; but with a large family to support, financial worries continued to trouble him (his songs were written for love not money). When famine and food riots struck Dumfries early in 1796 the Burnses were affected ('Many days my family & hundreds of other families, are absolutely without one grain of meal; as money cannot purchase it'). He became seriously ill with rheumatic fever, and eventually died on 21 July.

Burns felt his Scottish identity keenly. He celebrated the patriots Bruce and Wallace, and lamented the 1707 Act of Union by which Scotland had become 'North Britain'. He welcomed the American Revolution, and his letters after 1789 show that he approved of the 'glorious struggle for Freedom' in Europe. But as the holder of an official position under the Crown ('a placeman', as he called himself) Burns was forced to conform publicly. His earlier encounters with the Calvinist 'Kirk' had taught him the importance of keeping up appearances in a hypocritical society.

Burns's literary allegiances were more ambiguous. He felt a strong kinship with the native Scottish tradition of Dunbar, Lindsay, Douglas, and (in his own century) Ramsay and Fergusson, while admiring deeply English poets such as Thomson, Gray and Cowper. Some of his finest songs (*Ae Fond Kiss, A Red Red Rose*) speak English with a Scottish accent. However, it was the broad Scots dialect that liberated Burns with its rhythmic energy and vivid vocabulary, and it is his demotic works that most repay critical study – after being read aloud. With the help of a glossary, a shot of whisky and a bold spirit, the reader can gauge something of their power. But there is no substitute for hearing them declaimed by a Scot.

The Vision

One of the most significant of Burns's earlier poems, this is his meditation on what kind of poet he was destined to become. From one viewpoint it shows youthful self-belief, Burns's confidence that he has been chosen and is under special guidance from above; but at the same time the role of '*rustic* Bard' is a limited one, and he feels he cannot aspire to be a Thomson, Shenstone or Gray. The nature of the vision itself is ambiguous: Coila (a localized version of Scotia) speaks in poetic English, not the local dialect, and the poem moves into a different linguistic register with her appearance. An interesting comparison is with Ann Yearsley's *To Mr * * * *, an Unlettered Poet*. The verse-form is Burns's favourite 'Standard Habbie stanza' (named after 'The Life and Death of Habbie Simson', a popular seventeenth-century ballad by Robert Sempill). The text given here is the shortened version in the 1786 Kilmarnock edition, pp. 87–99.

Duan First

The sun had clos'd the *winter-day*,
The Curlers quat their roaring play,
And hunger'd Maukin taen her way
    To kail-yards green,
While faithless snaws ilk step betray   5
    Whare she has been.

The Thresher's weary *flingin-tree*,
The lee-lang day had tir'd me;
And when the Day had clos'd his e'e,
    Far i' the West,   10
Ben i' the *Spence*, right pensivelie,
    I gaed to rest.

There, lanely, by the ingle-cheek,
I sat and ey'd the spewing reek,
That fill'd, wi' hoast-provoking smeek,   15
    The auld, clay biggin;
And heard the restless rattons squeak
    About the riggin.

All in this mottie, misty clime,
I backward mus'd on wasted time,   20
How I had spent my *youthfu' prime*,
    An' done nae-thing,
But stringing blethers up in rhyme
    For fools to sing.

Duan 'a term of Ossian's for the different divisions of a digressive Poem. See his Cath-Loda, Vol. 2. of McPherson's Translation' (Burns's note). Macpherson's note adds: 'Since the extinction of the order of the bards, it has been a general name for all ancient compositions in verse'.
2 *Curlers* The Scottish sport of curling is a kind of bowls played on ice with heavy stones.
3 *Maukin* The hare.
4 *kail-yards* 'vegetable gardens'.

7 *flingin-tree* 'flail'.
11 *Spence* 'inner room'.
13 *ingle-cheek* 'chimney-corner'.
14 *reek* 'smoke'.
15 *hoast* 'cough'.
16 *biggin* 'cottage'.
17 *rattons* 'rats'.
18 *riggin* 'roof'.
19 *mottie* 'dusty'.
23 *blethers* 'babble'.

Had I to guid advice but harket,   25
I might, by this, hae led a market,
Or strutted in a Bank and clarket
      My *Cash-Account*;
While here, half-mad, half-fed, half-sarket,
      Is a' th' amount.   30

I started, mutt'ring blockhead! coof!
And heav'd on high my wauket loof,
To swear by a' yon starry roof,
      Or some rash aith,
That I, henceforth, would be *rhyme-proof*   35
      Till my last breath —

When click! the *string* the *snick* did draw;
And jee! the door gaed to the wa';
And by my ingle-lowe I saw,
      Now bleezan bright,   40
A tight, outlandish *Hizzie*, braw,
      Come full in sight.

Ye need na doubt, I held my whisht;
The infant aith, half-form'd, was crusht;
I glowr'd as eerie's I'd been dusht,   45
      In some wild glen;
When sweet, like *modest Worth*, she blusht,
      And stepped ben.

Green, slender, leaf-clad *Holly-boughs*
Were twisted, gracefu', round her brows,   50
I took her for some SCOTTISH MUSE,
      By that same token;
And come to stop those reckless vows,
      Would soon been broken.

A "hare-brain'd, sentimental trace"   55
Was strongly marked in her face;
A wildly-witty, rustic grace
      Shone full upon her;
Her *eye*, ev'n turn'd on empty space,
      Beam'd keen with *Honor*.   60

Down flow'd her robe, a *tartan* sheen,
Till half a leg was scrimply seen;

---

27 *clarket* 'written up'.
29 *sarket* 'dressed'.
31 *coof* 'clown'.
32 *wauket loof* 'horny hand'.
34 *aith* 'oath'.
37 *snick* 'latch'.
38 *wa'* 'wall'.
39 *lowe* 'flame'.
41 *tight* 'shapely'; *Hizzie* 'wench'; *braw* 'fine'.

43 *held my whisht* 'kept quiet'.
45 'I stared with fright as if I'd been butted'.
48 *ben* 'into the room'.
57 *wildly-witty* 'with the passion and imagination characteristic of poetry' (Kinsley).
61 *tartan* The ban on wearing tartan imposed after the 1745 Stuart rising had been repealed in 1782.
62 *scrimply* 'scarcely'.

And such a *leg!* my BESS, I ween,
   Could only peer it;
Sae straught, sae taper, tight and clean,
   Nane else came near it.   65

Her *Mantle* large, of greenish hue,
My gazing wonder chiefly drew;
Deep *lights* and *shades*, bold-mingling, threw
   A lustre grand;   70
And seem'd, to my astonish'd view,
   A *well-known* Land.

Here, rivers in the sea were lost;
There, mountains to the skies were tost:
Here, tumbling billows mark'd the coast,   75
   With surging foam;
There, distant shone, *Art's* lofty boast,
   The lordly dome.

Here, DOON pour'd down his far-fetch'd floods;
There, well-fed IRWINE stately thuds: 80
Auld, hermit AIRE staw thro' his woods,
   On to the shore;
And many a lesser torrent scuds,
   With seeming roar.

Low, in a sandy valley spread,   85
An ancient BOROUGH rear'd her head;
Still, as in *Scottish Story* read,
   She boasts a *Race*,
To ev'ry nobler virtue bred,
   And polish'd grace.   90

Duan Second

With musing-deep, astonish'd stare,
I view'd the heavenly-seeming *Fair*;
A whisp'ring *throb* did witness bear
   Of kindred sweet,
When with an elder Sister's air   95
   She did me greet.

"All hail! *my own* inspired Bard!
In me thy native Muse regard!
Nor longer mourn thy fate is hard,
   Thus poorly low!   100
I come to give thee such *reward*,
   As *we* bestow.

---

63 *BESS* Elizabeth Paton, a servant at Lochlea Farm, the Burns family home 1777–84. The line reverted to 'my bonnie Jean' in *1787* when Jean Armour had become Burns's acknowledged wife.
64 *peer* 'equal'.
65 *taper* 'slender'.

72 Burns's native Ayrshire, shown on her mantle.
79–81 The Ayrshire rivers, Doon, Irvine and Ayr.
86 Ayr.
90 At this point *1787* prints seven stanzas celebrating heroic figures with Ayrshire connections. There are twelve further stanzas in the Stair MS of the poem.

"Know, the great *Genius* of this Land,
Has many a light, aerial band,
Who, all beneath his high command,   105
          Harmoniously,
As *Arts* or *Arms* they understand,
          Their labors ply.

"They SCOTIA'S Race among them share;
Some fire the *Sodger* on to dare;   110
Some rouse the *Patriot* up to bare
          Corruption's heart:
Some teach the *Bard*, a darling care,
          The tuneful Art.

"'Mong swelling floods of reeking gore,   115
They ardent, kindling spirits pour;
Or, mid the venal Senate's roar,
          They, sightless, stand,
To mend the honest *Patriot-lore*,
          And grace the hand.   120

"Hence, FULLARTON, the brave and young;
Hence, DEMPSTER'S truth-prevailing tongue;
Hence, sweet harmonious BEATTIE sung
          His 'Minstrel lays';
Or tore, with noble ardour stung,   125
          The *Sceptic's* bays.

"To lower Orders are assign'd,
The humbler ranks of Human-kind,
The rustic Bard, the lab'ring Hind,
          The Artisan;   130
All chuse, as, various they're inclin'd,
          The various man.

"When yellow waves the heavy grain,
The threat'ning *Storm*, some, strongly, rein;
Some teach to meliorate the plain,   135
          With *tillage-skill*;
And some instruct the Shepherd-train,
          Blythe o'er the hill.

"Some hint the Lover's harmless wile;
Some grace the Maiden's artless smile;   140
Some soothe the Lab'rer's weary toil,
          For humble gains,

103–50 The passage playfully reworks Ariel's account of the spirits' activities in Pope, *The Rape of the Lock*, 1:41–104.
110 *Sodger* 'soldier'.
117 *venal* 'corrupt'.
121 Colonel William Fullarton (1754–1808) had fought successfully in India.

122 George Dempster, MP (1732–1818), Provost of St Andrews.
123 James Beattie (1735–1803), Scottish poet, author of *The Minstrel* (1771–4) and an *Essay on Truth* (1770), which attacked the sceptical philosophy of Hume and others.
135 *meliorate* 'improve'.

And make his *cottage-scenes* beguile
      His cares and pains.

"Some, bounded to a district-space,   145
Explore at large Man's *infant race*,
To mark the embryotic trace,
      Of *rustic Bard*;
And careful note each op'ning grace,
      A guide and guard.   150

"*Of these am I* — COILA my name;
And this district as mine I claim,
Where once the *Campbell's*, chiefs of fame,
      Held ruling pow'r:
I mark'd thy embryo-tuneful flame,   155
      Thy natal hour.

"With future hope, I oft would gaze,
Fond, on thy little, early ways,
Thy rudely-caroll'd, chiming phrase,
      In uncouth rhymes,   160
Fir'd at the simple, artless lays
      Of other times.

"I saw thee seek the sounding shore,
Delighted with the dashing roar;
Or when the *North* his fleecy store   165
      Drove thro' the sky,
I saw grim Nature's visage hoar,
      Struck thy young eye.

"Or when the deep-green-mantl'd Earth,
Warm-cherish'd ev'ry floweret's birth,   170
And joy and music pouring forth,
      In ev'ry grove,
I saw thee eye the gen'ral mirth
      With boundless love.

"When ripen'd fields, and azure skies,   175
Call'd forth the *Reaper's* rustling noise,
I saw thee leave their ev'ning joys,
      And lonely stalk,
To vent thy bosom's swelling rise,
      In pensive walk.   180

"When *youthful Love*, warm-blushing, strong,
Keen-shivering shot thy nerves along,
Those accents, grateful to thy tongue,
      Th'adored *Name*,
I taught thee how to pour in song,   185
      To soothe thy flame.

---

151 *COILA* The name is from 'Kyle', Burns's district of
Ayrshire.
153 *Campbell's* The Earls of Loudoun, major landowners in

Ayrshire. From 1784 Burns leased Mossgiel Farm on
the Loudoun estate.
167 *hoar* 'grey'.

"I saw thy pulse's maddening play,
Wild-send thee Pleasure's devious way,
Misled by Fancy's *meteor-ray*,
  By Passion driven;   190
But yet the *light* that led astray,
  Was *light* from Heaven.

"I taught thy manners-painting strains,
The *loves*, the *ways* of simple swains,
Till now, o'er all my wide domains,   195
  Thy fame extends;
And some, the pride of *Coila's* plains,
  Become thy friends.

"Thou canst not learn, nor I can show,
To paint with *Thomson's* landscape-glow;   200
Or wake the bosom-melting throe,
  With *Shenstone's* art;
Or pour, with *Gray*, the moving flow,
  Warm on the heart.

"Yet all beneath th'unrivall'd Rose,   205
The lowly Daisy sweetly blows;
Tho' large the forest's Monarch throws
  His army shade,
Yet green the juicy Hawthorn grows,
  Adown the glade.   210

"Then never murmur nor repine;
Strive in thy *humble sphere* to shine;
And trust me, not *Potosi's mine*,
  Nor *Kings regard*,
Can give a bliss o'ermatching thine,   215
  A *rustic Bard*.

"To give my counsels all in one,
Thy *tuneful flame* still careful fan;
Preserve *the dignity of Man*,
  With Soul erect;   220
And trust, the UNIVERSAL PLAN
  Will all protect.

"*And wear thou this*" — She solemn said,
And bound the *Holly* round my head:
The polish'd leaves, and berries red,   225
  Did rustling play;
And, like a passing thought, she fled,
  In light away.

---

202 William Shenstone (1714–63), most famous for his poem *The Schoolmistress* (1742).

213 *Potosi's mine* The South American silver mine; proverbial for fabulous wealth.

To a Mouse

On turning her up in her Nest, with the Plough, November, 1785.

The poem was said by Burns's brother Gilbert to have been composed while Burns was 'holding the plough' at Mossgiel Farm. But for all its seemingly spontaneous life, it has elements of a meditative, even philosophic, poem on mankind's place in the world and the difference/kinship between the human and animal kingdoms. It also plays with questions of economics and social justice: the mouse is evicted and robbed of the fruits of its labour. The poem was first printed in the 1786 Kilmarnock edition, pp. 138–40, the text given here.

> Wee, sleeket, cowran, tim'rous *beastie*,
> O, what a panic's in thy breastie!
> Thou need na start awa sae hasty,
>   Wi' bickering brattle!
> I wad be laith to rin an' chase thee,   5
>   Wi' murd'ring *pattle!*
>
> I'm truly sorry Man's dominion
> Has broken Nature's social union,
> An' justifies that ill opinion,
>   Which makes thee startle,   10
> At me, thy poor, earth-born companion,
>   An' *fellow-mortal!*
>
> I doubt na, whyles, but thou may *thieve*;
> What then? poor beastie, thou maun live!
> A *daimen-icker* in a *thrave*   15
>   'S a sma' request:
> I'll get a blessin wi' the lave,
>   An' never miss't!
>
> Thy wee-bit *housie*, too, in ruin!
> It's silly wa's the win's are strewin!   20
> An' naething, now, to big a new ane,
>   O' foggage green!
> An' bleak *December's winds* ensuin,
>   Baith snell an' keen!
>
> Thou saw the fields laid bare an' wast,   25
> An' weary *Winter* comin fast,

---

1 *sleeket* 'glossy'.

4 *bickering brattle* 'scurrying haste'.

6 *pattle* An implement for scraping mud off the ploughshare.

8 *Nature's social union* Cf. the 'voice of Nature' which speaks in Pope's *Essay on Man*: 'Go, from the Creatures thy instructions take: / Learn from the birds what food the thickets yield; / Learn from the beasts the physic of the field; / Thy arts of building from the bee receive; / Learn of the mole to plow, the worm to weave, … / …

Here too all forms of social union find' (3:172–9).

13 *whyles* 'sometimes'.

15 *daimen-icker* 'occasional ear of corn'; *thrave* 'measure'.

17 *lave* 'remainder'.

19 *wee-bit housie* 'tiny little house'.

20 *silly wa's* 'frail walls'.

21 *big* 'build'.

22 *foggage* the 'fog' or coarse 'after-grass', sprouting after the hay has been cut, usually left for the cattle.

24 *snell* 'bitter'.

An' cozie here, beneath the blast,
  Thou thought to dwell,
Till crash! the cruel *coulter* past
  Out thro' thy cell.   30

That wee-bit heap o' leaves an' stibble,
Has cost thee monie a weary nibble!
Now thou's turn'd out, for a' thy trouble,
  But house or hald,
To thole the Winter's *sleety dribble*,   35
  An' *cranreuch* cauld!

But Mousie, thou art no thy-lane,
In proving *foresight* may be vain:
The best laid schemes o' *Mice* an' *Men*,
  Gang aft agley,   40
An' lea'e us nought but grief an' pain,
  For promis'd joy!

Still, thou art blest, compar'd wi' *me!*
The *present* only toucheth thee:
But Och! I *backward* cast my e'e,   45
  On prospects drear!
An' *forward*, tho' I canna *see*,
  I *guess* an' *fear!*

29 *coulter* The projecting blade of the plough.
34 *But* 'without'; *hald* 'refuge'.
35 *thole* 'endure'.
36 *cranreuch* 'hoar-frost'.
37 *no thy-lane* 'not alone'.
40 *Gang aft agley* 'often go awry'.
43–8 The traditional distinction between the capacity of human discursive reason ('looking before and after' as Hamlet says) and reasonless beasts. The classic statement is by Cicero: 'the beast, with very little perception of past or future, adapts itself only to the present moment' (*De Officiis*, I:11). Burns turns this to the animal's advantage.

To a Louse
On Seeing one on a Lady's Bonnet at Church.

This complex little poem about social aspirations and public shame has many reverberations for Burns's situation in 1785 (Kinsley would date it to the end of the year). Notably, that summer he and his mistress Elizabeth Paton had been made to do public penance in church after the birth of their illegitimate daughter (this was the traditional punishment for 'fornication'). In the poem the vagrant woodlouse has a social mobility that his human equivalents lack. Burns's tone is throughout subtly ironic. The poem was first printed in the 1786 Kilmarnock edition, pp. 192–4, the text given here.

Ha! whare ye gaun, ye crowlan ferlie!
Your impudence protects you sairly:
I canna say but ye strunt rarely,
  Owre *gawze* and *lace*;
Tho' faith, I fear ye dine but sparely,   5
  On sic a place.

1 *crowlan ferlie* 'crawling marvel'.
2 *sairly* 'hardly'.

3 *strunt* 'strut'.

Ye ugly, creepan, blastet wonner,
Detested, shunn'd, by saunt an' sinner,
How daur ye set your fit upon her,
    Sae fine a *Lady!*   10
Gae somewhere else and seek your dinner,
    On some poor body.

Swith, in some beggar's haffet squattle;
There ye may creep, and sprawl, and sprattle,
Wi' ither kindred, jumping cattle,   15
    In shoals and nations;
Whare *horn* nor *bane* ne'er daur unsettle,
    Your thick plantations.

Now haud you there, ye're out o' sight,
Below the fatt'rels, snug and tight,   20
Na faith ye yet! ye'll no be right,
    Till ye've got on it,
The vera tapmost, towrin height
    O' *Miss's bonnet.*

My sooth! right bauld ye set your nose out,   25
As plump an' gray as onie grozet:
O for some rank, mercurial rozet,
    Or fell, red smeddum,
I'd gie you sic a hearty dose o't,
    Wad dress your droddum!   30

I wad na been surpriz'd to spy
You on an auld wife's *flainen toy*;
Or aiblins some bit duddie boy,
    On's *wylecoat*;
But Miss's fine *Lunardi*, fye!   35
    How daur ye do't?

O *Jenny* dinna toss your head,
An' set your beauties a' abread!
Ye little ken what cursed speed
    The blastie's makin!
Thae *winks* and *finger-ends*, I dread,   40
    Are notice takin!

7 *blastet wonner* 'damned wonder'.
9 *fit* 'foot'.
12 *body* 'person'.
13 *Swith* 'Off with you'; *haffet* 'lock of hair'; *squattle* 'nestle down'.
14 *sprattle* 'struggle'.
15 *cattle* 'vermin'.
17 *horn* nor *bane* Fine combs for the hair.
20 *fatt'rels* 'ribbon-ends'.
21 *Na faith ye yet!* 'Damn you!'; *right* 'settled'.
25 *bauld* 'boldly'; *set your nose out* 'show impudence'.
26 *grozet* 'gooseberry'.
27 *rozet* 'resin'.

28 *fell* 'pungent'; *smeddum* 'powder'.
30 *dress your droddum* 'thrash your backside'.
32 *flainen toy* 'flannel cap'.
33 *aiblins* 'perhaps'; *bit duddie boy* 'ragged little boy'.
34 *wylecoat* 'under-vest'.
35 *Lunardi* The latest fashion in female headgear, an extravagant balloon-shaped bonnet celebrating the pioneering flights of Vincenzo Lunardi (1759–1806). In 1785 he made the first balloon ascent in Scotland.
38 *abread* 'abroad'.
40 *blastie* 'blasted thing'.
41 *Thae* 'Those'.

O wad some Pow'r the giftie gie us
To see oursels as others see us!
It wad frae monie a blunder free us   45
An' foolish notion:
What airs in dress an' gait wad lea'e us,
And ev'n Devotion!

43 *giftie* 'gift'.

Holy Willie's Prayer

In 1784 William Fisher (1737–1809), a parish elder, instigated proceedings against Burns's friend Gavin Hamilton for his absences from public worship at Mauchline. The charge was rejected by the Ayr Presbytery (see 73–8) in January 1785, and later by the higher body of the Glasgow Synod. Burns's exposure of Fisher's hypocrisy centres on Calvin's doctrine that 'Every man … is predestinated to life or to death' (*Institutes*, III.xxi.5). Individual salvation or damnation was therefore predetermined, with the so-called 'elect' being considered saved and the 'reprobate' damned, irrespective of their works on earth. For Burns, such hard-line Calvinism allowed a man like 'Holy Willie' to maintain a blithe confidence in his own salvation (he knows all the predictable Biblical passages), while spreading a veil of self-righteousness over his solid vices. Burns circulated the poem locally, but omitted it from editions of his work. It appeared as an anonymous pamphlet in 1789, but was not printed under Burns's name until after his death. The text given here is from Kinsley's edition and is based on the Glenriddell MS (an additional stanza printed in 1802 has been omitted).

And send the Godly in a pet to pray —
POPE

O Thou that in the heavens does dwell!
Wha, as it pleases best thysel,
Sends ane to heaven and ten to h-ll,
A' for thy glory!
And no for ony gude or ill   5
They've done before thee. —

I bless and praise thy matchless might,
When thousands thou has left in night,
That I am here before thy sight,
For gifts and grace,   10
A burning and a shining light
To a' this place. —

What was I, or my generation,
That I should get such exaltation?
I, wha deserv'd most just damnation,   15
For broken laws
Sax thousand years ere my creation,
Thro' Adam's cause!

When from my mother's womb I fell,
Thou might hae plunged me deep in hell,   20
To gnash my gooms, and weep, and wail,

Motto Pope, *The Rape of the Lock*, 4:64.
11 'He was a burning and a shining light' (John, 5:35).
18 'Wherefore, as by one man sin entered into the world … so death passed upon all men, for that all have sinned' (Romans, 5:12).

21 '[T]he children of the kingdom shall be cast out into outer darkness: there shall be weeping and gnashing of teeth' (Matthew, 8:12).

In burning lakes,
Where damned devils roar and yell
                    Chain'd to their stakes. —

Yet I am here, a chosen sample,   25
To shew thy grace is great and ample:
I'm here, a pillar o' thy temple
                    Strong as a rock,
A guide, a ruler and example
                    To a' thy flock. —   30

But yet — O L—d — confess I must —
At times I'm fash'd wi' fleshly lust;
And sometimes too, in warldly trust
                    Vile Self gets in;
But thou remembers we are dust,   35
                    Defil'd wi' sin. —

O L—d — yestreen — thou kens — wi' Meg —
Thy pardon I sincerely beg!
O may't ne'er be a living plague,
                    To my dishonor!   40
And I'll ne'er lift a lawless leg
                    Again upon her. —

Besides, I farther maun avow,
Wi' Leezie's lass, three times — I trow —
But L—d, that friday I was fou   45
                    When I cam near her;
Or else, thou kens, thy servant true
                    Wad never steer her. —

Maybe thou lets this fleshly thorn
Buffet thy servant e'en and morn,   50
Lest he o'er proud and high should turn,
                    That he's sae gifted;
If sae, thy hand maun e'en be borne
                    Untill thou lift it. —

L—d bless thy Chosen in this place,   55
For here thou has a chosen race:
But G-d, confound their stubborn face,

22–4 Cf. Milton's Satan 'chained on the burning lake' (*Paradise Lost*, 1:210). The original source is Revelation, 20:10.

27 'Him that overcometh will I make a pillar in the temple of my God' (Revelation, 3:12).

32 *fash'd* 'afflicted'.

33 *trust* 'duties'.

35 '[F]or dust thou art, and unto dust shalt thou return' (Genesis, 3:19).

37 *yestreen* 'yesterday evening'.

45 *fou* 'drunk'.

48 *steer* 'stir'.

49 '[T]here was given to me a thorn in the flesh, the messenger of Satan to buffet me, lest I should be exalted above measure' (2 Corinthians, 12:7).

53 *maun* 'must'.

57 *confound* 'damn'.

And blast their name,
Wha bring thy rulers to disgrace
    And open shame. —   60

L—d mind Gaun Hamilton's deserts!
He drinks, and swears, and plays at cartes,
Yet has sae mony taking arts
        Wi' Great and Sma',
Frae G-d's ain priest the people's hearts   65
        He steals awa. —

And when we chasten'd him therefore,
Thou kens how he bred sic a splore,
And set the warld in a roar
        O' laughin at us: 70
Curse thou his basket and his store,
        Kail and potatoes. —

L—d hear my earnest cry and prayer
Against that Presbytry of Ayr!
Thy strong right hand, L—d, make it bare   75
        Upon their heads!
L—d visit them, and dinna spare,
        For their misdeeds!

O L—d my G-d, that glib-tongu'd Aiken!
My very heart and flesh are quaking   80
To think how I sat, sweating, shaking,
        And p-ssed wi' dread,
While Auld wi' hingin lip gaed sneaking
        And hid his head!

L—d, in thy day o' vengeance try him!   85
L—d visit him that did employ him!
And pass not in thy mercy by them,
        Nor hear their prayer;
But for thy people's sake destroy them,
        And dinna spare!   90

But L—d, remember me and mine
Wi' mercies temporal and divine!
That I for grace and gear may shine,
        Excell'd by nane!
And a' the glory shall be thine!   95
        AMEN! AMEN!

61 Gavin Hamilton (1751–1805), a liberal Mauchline
lawyer who sub-let Mossgiel Farm to the Burns
brothers. The 1786 Kilmarnock edition is dedicated to
him.
63 *taking* 'alluring'.
68 *sic a splore* 'such an uproar'.
72 *Kail* Green kale, a staple vegetable.

74 *Presbytry* The district ecclesiastical court.
77 *visit* 'punish'.
79 Robert Aitken (1739–1807) was Hamilton's counsel and
a noted orator.
83 William Auld (1709–91), Minister of Mauchline, the
church where Burns did penance in 1785.
93 *gear* 'possessions'.

Tam o' Shanter. A Tale

This tale of a Witches' Sabbath was Burns's own favourite among his poems. It was written in autumn 1790 for the antiquarian Francis Grose, to accompany an engraved plate of Alloway church in his *Antiquities of Scotland* (1791), and it was published there after first appearing in the *Edinburgh Herald* in March 1791. *Tam o' Shanter* was evidently conceived in a sudden burst of enthusiasm. Burns's wife, Jean Armour, recalled an autumn day by the river when her husband began to display poetic symptoms: 'He was busily engaged *crooning to himsel*; and Mrs Burns, perceiving that her presence was an interruption, loitered behind with her little ones ... Her attention was presently attracted by the strange and wild gesticulations of the bard, who now, at some distance, was agonized with an ungovernable access of joy. He was reciting very loud, and with the tears rolling down his cheeks, those animated verses [of *Tam*] which he had just conceived' (Lockhart, *Life of Burns*, 1828). Certainly the rhythmic impetus and the swagger of the dialect come vividly across when a Scot reads the poem aloud. But beneath the spontaneity are many subtleties of language and character. Levels of speech vary as the narrator touches notes of comedy, horror and morality, and as he responds to different females (his and Tam's wives, the 'gentle dames' in his audience, the old hags, the scantily dressed Nannie, his Muse, Maggie the mare). The tale was one of the additions for the enlarged second Edinburgh edition of Burns's *Poems* (1793), 2:195–208, the text given here.

> *Of Brownyis and of Bogillis full is this buke.*
> GAWIN DOUGLAS.

When chapmen billies leave the street,
And drouthy neebors, neebors meet,
As market-days are wearing late,
An' folk begin to tak the gate;
While we sit bousing at the nappy,   5
And getting fou and unco happy,
We think na on the lang Scots miles,
The mosses, waters, slaps, and styles,
That lie between us and our hame,
Whare sits our sulky sullen dame,   10
Gathering her brows like gathering storm,
Nursing her wrath to keep it warm.
    This truth fand honest *Tam o' Shanter*,
As he frae Ayr ae night did canter,
(Auld Ayr, wham ne'er a town surpasses,   15
For honest men and bonny lasses.)
    O *Tam!* hadst thou but been sae wise,
As ta'en thy ain wife *Kate's* advice!
She tauld thee weel thou was a skellum,
A blethering, blustering, drunken blellum;   20
That frae November till October,
Ae market-day thou was nae sober;
That ilka melder, wi' the miller,
Thou sat as lang as thou had siller;

Motto Gavin Douglas, *Eneados* [1513], 6:18 (prologue). Book Six of Virgil's *Aeneid* describes the hero's descent into the underworld. In Scottish tradition 'brownies' were benign and helpful spirits, unlike 'bogles'.

1 *chapmen billies* 'the gang of pedlars'.
2 *drouthy* 'thirsty'.
5 *bousing at the nappy* 'knocking back the ale'.

6 *fou* 'drunk'; *unco* 'uncommonly'.
8 *slaps* 'gaps in fences'.
14 *ae* 'one'.
19 *skellum* 'scoundrel'.
20 *blellum* 'babbler'.
23 *ilka melder* 'every corn-grinding'.
24 *siller* 'cash'.

That every naig was ca'd a shoe on,   25
The smith and thee gat roaring fou on;
That at the L——d's house, even on Sunday,
Thou drank wi' Kirkton Jean till Monday.
She prophesied that late or soon,
Thou would be found deep drown'd in Doon;   30
Or catch'd wi' warlocks in the mirk,
By *Alloway's* auld haunted kirk.
   Ah, gentle dames! it gars me greet,
To think how mony counsels sweet,
How mony lengthen'd sage advices,   35
The husband frae the wife despises!
   But to our tale: Ae market-night,
Tam had got planted unco right;
Fast by an ingle, bleezing finely,
Wi' reaming swats, that drank divinely;   40
And at his elbow, Souter *Johnny*,
His ancient, trusty, drouthy crony;
Tam lo'ed him like a vera brither;
They had been fou for weeks thegither.
The night drave on wi' sangs and clatter;   45
And ay the ale was growing better:
The landlady and *Tam* grew gracious,
Wi' favours, secret, sweet, and precious:
The Souter tauld his queerest stories;
The landlord's laugh was ready chorus: 50
The storm without might rair and rustle,
Tam did na mind the storm a whistle.
   Care, mad to see a man sae happy,
E'en drown'd himsel amang the nappy:
As bees flee hame wi' lades o' treasure,   55
The minutes wing'd their way wi' pleasure:
Kings may be blest, but *Tam* was glorious,
O'er a' the ills o' life victorious!
   But pleasures are like poppies spread,
You seize the flower, its bloom is shed;   60
Or like the snow falls in the river,
A moment white — then melts for ever;
Or like the borealis race,
That flit ere you can point their place;
Or like the rainbow's lovely form   65
Evanishing amid the storm. —
Nae man can tether time or tide;
The hour approaches *Tam* maun ride;
That hour, o' night's black arch the key-stane,

---

25 *naig* 'nag'; *ca'd* 'hammered'.
30 *Doon* The river at Alloway.
31 *warlocks* 'wizards'; *mirk* 'dark'.
32 Alloway church had become disused and ruinous by
   the 1780s. Burns's father was buried in the churchyard.
33 *gars me greet* 'makes me weep'.

39 *ingle* 'fire'.
40 *reaming swats* 'foaming new beer'.
41 *Souter* 'shoemaker'.
45 *clatter* 'gossip'.
47 *gracious* 'amiable'.
63 *borealis* The Northern Lights (Aurora Borealis).

That dreary hour he mounts his beast in;   70
And sic a night he taks the road in,
As ne'er poor sinner was abroad in.
    The wind blew as 'twad blawn its last;
The rattling showers rose on the blast;
The speedy gleams the darkness swallow'd;   75
Loud, deep, and lang, the thunder bellow'd:
That night, a child might understand,
The Deil had business on his hand.
    Weel mounted on his gray mare, *Meg*,
A better never lifted leg,   80
Tam skelpit on thro' dub and mire,
Despising wind, and rain, and fire;
Whiles holding fast his gude blue bonnet;
Whiles crooning o'er some auld Scots sonnet;
Whiles glowring round wi' prudent cares,   85
Lest bogles catch him unawares:
Kirk-Alloway was drawing nigh,
Whare ghaists and houlets nightly cry. —
    By this time he was cross the ford,
Whare, in the snaw, the chapman smoor'd;   90
And past the birks and meikle stane,
Whare drunken *Charlie* brak's neck-bane;
And thro' the whins, and by the cairn,
Whare hunters fand the murder'd bairn;
And near the thorn, aboon the well,   95
Whare *Mungo's* mither hang'd hersel. —
Before him *Doon* pours all his floods;
The doubling storm roars thro' the woods;
The lightnings flash from pole to pole;
Near and more near the thunders roll: 100
When, glimmering thro' the groaning trees,
Kirk-Alloway seem'd in a bleeze;
Thro' ilka bore the beams were glancing;
And loud resounded mirth and dancing. —
    Inspiring bold *John Barleycorn!*   105
What dangers thou canst make us scorn!
Wi' tippeny, we fear nae evil;
Wi' usquabae, we'll face the devil! —
The swats sae ream'd in *Tammie's* noddle,
Fair play, he car'd na deils a boddle.   110
But *Maggie* stood right sair astonish'd,
Till, by the heel and hand admonish'd,
She ventured forward on the light;
And, vow! *Tam* saw an unco sight!

70 *dreary* 'gloomy'.
81 *skelpit* 'thrashed'; *dub* 'puddle'.
84 *crooning* 'humming'; *sonnet* 'song'.
85 *glowring* 'staring'.
86 *bogles* 'goblins'.
88 *houlets* 'owlets'.
90 *smoor'd* 'was suffocated'.
91 *birks* 'birches'; *meikle* 'great'.

93 *whins* 'gorse'; *cairn* 'pile of stones'.
103 *ilka bore* 'every chink'.
105 *John Barleycorn* The chief ingredient of malt liquors.
107 *tippeny* 'twopenny ale'.
108 *usquabae* 'whisky'.
110 *Fair play* 'to do him justice'; *boddle* A tiny coin.
111 *sair* 'sorely'.

Warlocks and witches in a dance;   115
Nae cotillion brent new frae *France*,
But hornpipes, jigs, strathspeys, and reels,
Put life and mettle in their heels.
A winnock-bunker in the east,
There sat auld Nick, in shape o' beast;   120
A towzie tyke, black, grim, and large,
To gie them music was his charge:
He screw'd the pipes and gart them skirl,
Till roof and rafters a' did dirl. —
Coffins stood round, like open presses,   125
That shaw'd the dead in their last dresses;
And by some devilish cantraip slight
Each in its cauld hand held a light. —
By which heroic *Tam* was able
To note upon the haly table,   130
A murderer's banes in gibbet airns;
Twa span-lang, wee, unchristen'd bairns;
A thief, new-cutted frae a rape,
Wi' his last gasp his gab did gape;
Five tomahawks, wi' blude red-rusted;   135
Five scymitars, wi' murder crusted;
A garter, which a babe had strangled;
A knife, a father's throat had mangled,
Whom his ain son o' life bereft,
The grey hairs yet stack to the heft;   140
Wi' mair o' horrible and awefu',
Which even to name wad be unlawfu'.
    As *Tammie* glowr'd, amaz'd, and curious,
The mirth and fun grew fast and furious:
The piper loud and louder blew;   145
The dancers quick and quicker flew;
They reel'd, they set, they cross'd, they cleekit,
Till ilka carlin swat and reekit,
And coost her duddies to the wark,
And linket at it in her sark!   150
    Now, *Tam*, O *Tam!* had thae been queans,
A' plump and strapping in their teens,
Their sarks, instead o' creeshie flannen,
Been snaw-white seventeen hunder linnen!
Thir breeks o' mine, my only pair,   155
That ance were plush, o' gude blue hair,
I wad hae gi'en them off my hurdies,
For ae blink o' the bonie burdies!

116 *brent* 'brand'.	147 *cleekit* 'linked arms'.
117 *strathspey* A lively Highland dance.	148 *carlin* 'witch'.
119 *winnock-bunker* 'window-seat'.	149 *coost her duddies* 'threw off her clothes'.
121 *towzie tyke* 'shaggy dog'.	150 *linket* 'tripped'; *sark* 'under-garment'.
123 *skirl* 'shriek'.	151 *queans* 'young lasses'.
124 *dirl* 'shake'.	153 *creeshie flannen* 'greasy flannel'.
125 *presses* 'cupboards'.	154 *seventeen hunder* 'very finely woven'.
127 *cantraip slight* 'magic trickery'.	155 *Thir breeks* 'these trousers'.
131 *airns* 'fetters'.	156 *plush* 'long-napped velvet'.
132 *span* The span of a hand.	157 *hurdies* 'buttocks'.
134 *gab* 'mouth'.	158 *bonie burdies* 'pretty girls'.

But wither'd beldams, auld and droll,
Rigwoodie hags wad spean a foal,   160
Lowping and flinging on a crummock,
I wonder didna turn thy stomach.
    But *Tam* kend what was what fu' brawlie,
There was ae winsome wench and wawlie,
That night enlisted in the core,   165
(Lang after kend on *Carrick* shore;
For mony a beast to dead she shot,
And perish'd mony a bony boat,
And shook baith meikle corn and bear,
And kept the country-side in fear.)   170
Her cutty sark, o' Paisley harn,
That while a lassie she had worn,
In longitude tho' sorely scanty,
It was her best, and she was vauntie. —
Ah! little kend thy reverend grannie,   175
That sark she coft for her wee Nannie,
Wi' twa pund Scots, ('twas a' her riches),
Wad ever grac'd a dance of witches!
    But here my Muse her wing maun cour;
Sic flights are far beyond her pow'r;   180
To sing how Nannie lap and flang,
(A souple jade she was, and strang),
And how *Tam* stood, like ane bewitch'd,
And thought his very een enrich'd;
Even Satan glowr'd, and fidg'd fu' fain,   185
And hotch'd and blew wi' might and main:
Till first ae caper, syne anither,
Tam tint his reason a' thegither,
And roars out, "Weel done, Cutty-sark!"
And in an instant all was dark: 190
And scarcely had he Maggie rallied,
When out the hellish legion sallied.
    As bees bizz out wi' angry fyke,
When plundering herds assail their byke;
As open pussie's mortal foes,   195
When, pop! she starts before their nose;
As eager runs the market-crowd,
When "Catch the thief!" resounds aloud;
So Maggie runs, the witches follow,
Wi' mony an eldritch skreech and hollow.   200
    Ah, *Tam!* Ah, *Tam!* thou'll get thy fairin!

159 *droll* 'queer'.
160 *Rigwoodie* 'twisted'; *spean* 'wean'.
161 *Lowping* 'leaping'; *crummock* 'walking stick'.
163 *fu' brawlie* 'most admirably'.
164 *wawlie* 'strapping'.
165 *core* 'company'.
169 *bear* 'barley'.
171 *cutty sark* 'short undergarment'; *harn* 'linen'.
174 *vauntie* 'proud of it'.
176 *coft* 'bought'.
177 *pund Scots* About one-twelfth of a pound sterling.
179 *cour* 'draw in'.

184 *een* 'eyes'.
185 *fidg'd fu' fain* 'twitched with excitement'.
186 *hotch'd* 'jerked'.
187 *syne* 'then'.
188 *tint* 'lost'.
190 A Satanic inversion of 'And God said, Let there be light: and there was light' (Genesis, 1:3).
193 *fyke* 'commotion'.
194 *byke* 'hive'.
195 *open* 'give the cry of pursuit'; *pussie* The hare.
200 *eldritch* 'frightful'.
201 *fairin* 'reward'.

In hell they'll roast thee like a herrin!
In vain thy *Kate* awaits thy comin!
Kate soon will be a woefu' woman!
Now, do thy speedy utmost, Meg,   205
And win the key-stane of the brig;
There at them thou thy tail may toss,
A running stream they dare na cross.
But ere the key-stane she could make,
The fient a tail she had to shake!   210
For Nannie, far before the rest,
Hard upon noble Maggie prest,
And flew at *Tam* wi' furious ettle;
But little wist she Maggie's mettle —
Ae spring brought off her master hale,   215
But left behind her ain grey tail:
The carlin claught her by the rump,
And left poor Maggie scarce a stump.
     Now, wha this tale o' truth shall read,
Ilk man and mother's son, take heed: 220
Whene'er to drink you are inclin'd,
Or cutty-sarks run in your mind,
Think, ye may buy the joys o'er dear,
Remember Tam o' Shanter's mare.

206 'It is a well known fact that witches, or any evil spirits, have no power to follow a poor wight any farther than the middle of the next running stream. – It may be proper likewise to mention to the benighted traveller, that when he falls in with *bogles*, whatever danger may be in his going forward, there is much more hazard in turning back' (Burns's note).

210 *fient* 'devil' (i.e. no tail at all).
213 *ettle* 'intent'.
215 *hale* 'whole'.
217 *claught* 'grabbed'.

Anna Laetitia Barbauld (1743–1825)

She was born at Kibworth, Leicestershire, into a prominent dissenting family. In 1758 her father Dr John Aikin became a teacher of languages and literature at the new Warrington Academy in Lancashire, which between 1757 and 1786 gave dissenters (who were excluded from the English universities) an excellent education that included natural science and modern thought. Another tutor there, Dr Joseph Priestley (later the discoverer of oxygen and one of the great polymaths of the century) encouraged her literary talents. She lived in the intellectually stimulating atmosphere of Warrington for the next fifteen years, where she read widely and learned Latin and Greek (usually reserved for boys) as well as French and Italian. At the instigation of her younger brother John, tutor in divinity at the academy, she published her *Poems* (1773), which ran to four editions during the first twelvemonth, and in the same year brother and sister brought out a joint volume of essays, *Miscellaneous Pieces, in Prose*. In 1774 she married the Reverend Rochemont Barbauld, who had been a Warrington student, and the pair moved to Palgrave in north Suffolk, where he became the dissenting minister. Together they founded and ran a successful school for boys, and her teaching there gave rise to the popular *Lessons for Children* (1778) and other works for young readers. In 1786 they moved to Hampstead on the northern fringes of the capital, which gave her more opportunities for mixing with the literary world, and her productivity continued. A number of her poems appeared in the *Monthly Magazine*, of which her brother was the literary editor; she edited Akenside's *The Pleasures of Imagination* (1794) and the poems of Collins (1797); her verse *Epistle to William Wilberforce* (1791) was a significant contribution to the anti-slavery movement; and between 1790 and 1793 she published pamphlets of a radical tendency on religion, education and politics. In 1802 the Barbaulds settled near her brother in Stoke Newington, London, a notable centre of radical dissent, where Rochemont became minister. After what seems to have been a happy marriage, her husband's growing mental instability and violent behaviour caused him to be placed under restraint, and he drowned in 1808. Barbauld threw herself into miscellaneous literary work with reviews, essays and editions, including a popular anthology of verse and prose, *The Female Speaker*, and the mighty *British Novelists* in fifty volumes (1810). Several months after Barbauld's death her *Works* (2 vols, 1825) were published by her niece, Lucy Aikin.

Barbauld's Unitarian beliefs inform much of her writing. In rejecting the doctrine of the Trinity in favour of the unipersonality of God, Unitarianism stressed the abiding goodness of human nature, and saw the figure of God the Father as subsuming Jesus Christ's love and the Holy Spirit's universality, so as to become a single loving all-embracing force ('GOD is seen in all, and all in GOD ... Wrought in each flower, inscrib'd in evry tree', *Address to the Deity* (1767), 56). Christian mysteries are transformed to human experiences (*Corsica*, 142; *To a little invisible Being*, 19–20).

Barbauld's verse is remarkable for its range of subject and variety of verse-form, including (in addition to what is represented here from her pre-1800 work) hymn, song, ode, satire, mock-heroic, humorous occasional poem, classical imitation, elegy, character, prologue, ballad and riddle. Any selection can show only a part of her achievement.

Corsica

Like many people during 1768–9 Barbauld was deeply stirred by the Corsicans' struggle for independence. Since the fourteenth century the rugged Mediterranean island had been 'owned' by the city state of Genoa, who on 15 May 1768 sold it to the French. Their occupying troops met fierce resistance from nationalist forces under General Paoli. James Boswell's *An Account of Corsica, The Journal of a Tour to that Island; and Memoirs of Pascal Paoli* (February) helped rouse British public opinion, but the government resisted the mounting pressure to act against their old enemy France. A private pro-Corsica subscription was opened, but on 8 May 1769 Paoli's forces were routed at Pontenuovo, and Paoli escaped for England on 16 June.

Barbauld must have begun *Corsica* after February 1768, when Boswell's *Account* was published. The book made a strong impression on her, and the poem takes many of its details from it. The poem's completion, however, was problematic. The dramatic break after line 183 mirrors the shock when reports of the Corsicans' victory proved to be false. The French triumph took Britain by surprise. On 1 June 1769 the *London Chronicle* had reported the Corsicans' 'compleat victory' over the French, and for the next two weeks the news about the 'brave Corsicans' was generally good. On 13 June the *Chronicle* announced that 'the French have been defeated in no less than five different places', but it also printed a late express report of 'the Corsican troops having laid down their arms, and of the total reduction of the whole island'. The drama of this 13 June volte-face is enacted in Barbauld's text: the final paragraph was obviously added after that date. By then, however, her optimistic poem had already reached Priestley and his friends, and on 13 June (the irony is heavy) he wrote to her conveying their admiration for the poem and pressing her to send a corrected copy which could be given to Boswell and the other 'friends of liberty' in London and published 'for the benefit of those noble islanders'. Priestley told her: 'your poems ... may be the *coup de grace* to the French troops in that island' (Anna Letitia LeBreton, *Memoir of Mrs Barbauld* (1874), pp. 34–6). But by the time Barbauld received his letter the situation had changed dramatically and Priestley's plan was no longer feasible. At this point she took the opportunity to add her dramatic postscript.

During 1768–9 the issue of Corsican freedom helped focus opposition feeling in Britain, where the Tory government was under attack for corruption and for its tyrannical treatment of the popular hero, John Wilkes, MP (1727–97), who was excluded from parliament and imprisoned. From May 1768, when the London mob crying 'Wilkes and Liberty' was violently dispersed by the footguards, pressure for reform mounted; there were weeks of rioting and social order was precarious. In these circumstances 'Liberty' was not a mere abstraction: Barbauld's enthusiasm and warmth of tone are politically cast and establish the writer's credentials as a zealous 'friend of liberty' (see lines 15–17).

But the poem had narrowly missed its moment. It was not until 9 April 1772 that Boswell could record in his diary: 'I went to my club at the London Coffeehouse. Dr. Priestley read us *Corsica*, a poem by Miss Aikin of Warrington. We were very well'. It first appeared as the opening item in *Poems* (1773), the text given here.

> ———————— *A manly race*
> *Of unsubmitting spirit, wise and brave;*
> *Who still thro' bleeding ages struggled hard*
> *To hold a generous undiminish'd state;*
> *Too much in vain!*
>
> THOMSON.

Hail generous CORSICA! unconquer'd isle!
The fort of freedom; that amidst the waves
Stands like a rock of adamant, and dares
The wildest fury of the beating storm.
    And are there yet, in this late sickly age   5
(Unkindly to the tow'ring growths of virtue)
Such bold exalted spirits? Men whose deeds,
To the bright annals of old GREECE oppos'd,
Would throw in shades her yet unrival'd name,
And dim the lustre of her fairest page.   10
And glows the flame of LIBERTY so strong
In this lone speck of earth! this spot obscure,
Shaggy with woods, and crusted o'er with rock,
By slaves surrounded and by slaves oppress'd!
What then should BRITONS feel? should they not catch   15
The warm contagion of heroic ardour,
And kindle at a fire so like their own?
    Such were the working thoughts which swell'd the breast
Of generous BOSWEL; when with nobler aim

Motto *The Seasons, Autumn*, lines 897–9, 902–3. In a subtle compliment to Boswell, and making a political point closer to home, Barbauld quotes from James Thomson's patriotic celebration of Scottish nationhood. The two lines she omits are: '(As well unhappy Wallace can attest, / Great patriot-hero! ill requited chief!)'. In her poem General Paoli plays the equivalent role to William Wallace, who had led the fight for Scotland's independence from England in the 1290s.

3 *adamant* The hardest material known, from Gk. *adamas* ('invincible').

15–17 The *Monthly Review* remarked on the Corsicans: 'The English ... cannot but look upon them as their distressed BRETHREN, the younger offspring of our common parent – LIBERTY!' (*MR*, 40 (1769), p. 92).

19 James Boswell (1740–95), friend and biographer of Samuel Johnson (1791). In September 1769 he attended the Shakespeare Jubilee in Corsican dress.

And views beyond the narrow beaten track   20
By trivial fancy trod, he turn'd his course
From polish'd Gallia's soft delicious vales,
From the grey reliques of imperial Rome,
From her long galleries of laurel'd stone,
Her chisel'd heroes, and her marble gods,   25
Whose dumb majestic pomp yet awes the world,
To animated forms of patriot zeal,
Warm in the living majesty of virtue,
Elate with fearless spirit, firm, resolv'd,
By fortune unsubdued, unaw'd by power.   30
    How raptur'd fancy burns, while warm in thought
I trace the pictur'd landscape; while I kiss
With pilgrim lips devout the sacred soil
Stain'd with the blood of heroes. CYRNUS, hail!
Hail to thy rocky, deep indented shores,   35
And pointed cliffs, which hear the chafing deep
Incessant foaming round their shaggy sides:
Hail to thy winding bays, thy shelt'ring ports
And ample harbours, which inviting stretch
Their hospitable arms to every sail: 40
Thy numerous streams, that bursting from the cliffs
Down the steep channel'd rock impetuous pour
With grateful murmur: on the fearful edge
Of the rude precipice, thy hamlets brown
And straw-roof'd cots, which from the level vale   45
Scarce seen, amongst the craggy hanging cliffs
Seem like an eagle's nest aerial built:
Thy swelling mountains, brown with solemn shade
Of various trees, that wave their giant arms
O'er the rough sons of freedom; lofty pines,   50
And hardy fir, and ilex ever green,
And spreading chesnut, with each humbler plant,
And shrub of fragrant leaf, that clothes their sides
With living verdure; whence the clust'ring bee
Extracts her golden dews: the shining box,   55
And sweet-leav'd myrtle, aromatic thyme,
The prickly juniper, and the green leaf
Which feeds the spinning worm; while glowing bright
Beneath the various foliage, wildly spreads
The arbutus, and rears his scarlet fruit   60
Luxuriant, mantling o'er the craggy steeps;
And thy own native laurel crowns the scene.
Hail to thy savage forests, awful, deep:
Thy tangled thickets, and thy crowded woods,

---

22 *Gallia* France ('Gaul').

34 *CYRNUS* The classical name for Corsica (Gk. *Kurnos*).

51 *ilex* 'The ilex, or ever-green oak, is very common here, and gives the country a chearful look even in the depth of winter' (Boswell, *Account*, p. 45).

60 'The Corsican mountains are covered with the arbutus or strawberry tree, which gives a rich glowing appearance as far as the eye can reach' (*Account*, p. 46).

62 'We must not omit the laurel, to which Corsica has surely a very good claim' (*Account*, p. 46). Boswell's comment is picked up in Barbauld's play on 'laurel crowns', the traditional emblems of victory. In Corsica the living laurel flourishes, ready for future triumphs. Cf. Rome's 'laurel'd stone' (24), i.e. statues celebrating the triumphs of the past.

The haunt of herds untam'd; which sullen bound   65
From rock to rock with fierce unsocial air
And wilder gaze, as conscious of the power
That loves to reign amid the lonely scenes
Of unbroke nature: precipices huge,
And tumbling torrents; trackless desarts, plains   70
Fenc'd in with guardian rocks, whose quarries teem
With shining steel, that to the cultur'd fields
And sunny hills which wave with bearded grain
Defends their homely produce. LIBERTY,
The mountain goddess, loves to range at large   75
Amid such scenes, and on the iron soil
Prints her majestic step: for these she scorns
The green enamel'd vales, the velvet lap
Of smooth savannahs, where the pillow'd head
Of luxury reposes; balmy gales,   80
And bowers that breathe of bliss: for these, when first
This isle emerging like a beauteous gem
From the dark bosom of the Tyrrhene main
Rear'd its fair front, she mark'd it for her own,
And with her spirit warm'd: her genuine sons,   85
A broken remnant, from the generous stock
Of ancient Greece, from Sparta's sad remains,
True to their high descent, preserv'd unquench'd
The sacred fire thro' many a barbarous age:
Whom, nor the iron rod of cruel Carthage,   90
Nor the dread sceptre of imperial Rome,
Nor bloody Goth, nor grisly Saracen,
Nor the long galling yoke of proud Liguria,
Could crush into subjection. Still unquell'd
They rose superior, bursting from their chains   95
And claim'd man's dearest birthright, LIBERTY:
And long, thro' many a hard unequal strife
Maintain'd the glorious conflict; long withstood
With single arm, the whole collected force
Of haughty Genoa, and ambitious Gaul: 100
And shall withstand it, trust the faithful Muse.
It is not in the force of mortal arm,
Scarcely in fate, to bind the struggling soul
That gall'd by wanton power, indignant swells
Against oppression; breathing great revenge,   105
Careless of life, determin'd to be free.
And fav'ring heaven approves: for see the Man,
Born to exalt his own, and give mankind
A glimpse of higher natures: just, as great;

69 *unbroke* 'unsubdued', like a wild horse. Cf. 163.
75 Liberty was associated with mountainous regions
(Greece, Switzerland, and here Corsica). Milton made
this point in *L'Allegro*, 36 ('The mountain nymph,
sweet Liberty'). Boswell's *Account* opens with an
eloquent celebration of liberty.
83 The Tyrrhenian Sea, east of Corsica.

86–7 Boswell (*Account*, p. 61) describes how Corsica was
settled by a wandering tribe of Greeks exiled from
Sparta.
93 *Liguria* Genoa is the chief city of the Liguria region of
Italy.
107 *the Man* The ideal humane hero, as embodied in
General Paoli.

The soul of counsel, and the nerve of war;   110
Of high unshaken spirit, temper'd sweet
With soft urbanity, and polish'd grace,
And attic wit, and gay unstudied smiles:
Whom heaven in some propitious hour endow'd
With every purer virtue: gave him all   115
That lifts the hero, or adorns the man.
Gave him the eye sublime; the searching glance
Keen, scanning deep, that smites the guilty soul
As with a beam from heaven; on his brow
Serene, and spacious front, set the broad seal   120
Of dignity and rule; then smil'd benign
On this fair pattern of a God below,
High wrought, and breath'd into his swelling breast
The large ambitious wish to save his country.
Oh beauteous title to immortal fame!   125
The man devoted to the public, stands
In the bright records of superior worth
A step below the skies: if he succeed,
The first fair lot which earth affords, is his;
And if he falls, he falls above a throne.   130
When such their leader can the brave despair?
Freedom the cause and PAOLI the chief.
Success to your fair hopes! a British muse,
Tho' weak and powerless, lifts her fervent voice,
And breathes a prayer for your success. Oh could   135
She scatter blessings as the morn sheds dews,
To drop upon your heads! but patient hope
Must wait the appointed hour; secure of this,
That never with the indolent and weak
Will freedom deign to dwell; she must be seiz'd   140
By that bold arm that wrestles for the blessing:
'Tis heaven's best gift and must be bought with blood.
When the storm thickens, when the combat burns,
And pain and death in every horrid shape
That can appall the feeble, prowl around,   145
Then virtue triumphs; then her tow'ring form
Dilates with kindling majesty; her mien

117–21 Paoli is likened to Milton's Adam: 'His fair large front [forehead] and eye sublime declared / Absolute rule' (*Paradise Lost*, 4:300–1). Boswell had noted Paoli's gaze: 'In consequence of his being in continual danger from treachery and assassination, he has formed a habit of studiously observing every new face. . . . he looked at me, with a steadfast, keen and penetrating eye, as if he searched my very soul' (*Account*, p. 291).

132 Pasquale de Paoli (1725–1807), Corsican patriot. Led his nationalist forces against the Genoese. From 1769 he lived in England on a pension, but went back to Corsica as Commander-in-Chief after the French Revolution of 1789. Returned to England in 1795. Elizabeth Montagu presented Barbauld's *Poems* to him in 1774.

142 *gift ... bought* A contradiction criticized by the *Monthly Review* (49 (1773), p. 418), but it seems deliberate (it was left unchanged until the 1825 *Works*, when 'gift' was altered to 'prize', possibly by Barbauld's niece). Christian theology is similarly paradoxical: life was God's gift, but mankind's redemption had to be 'bought' by Jesus Christ's 'blood'. Barbauld extends this traditional idea to patriotic sacrifice.

146–7 *her ... her* i.e. virtue. Freedom allows virtue to grow and flourish, so that she takes on the expansive qualities of freedom itself. In the passage that follows Barbauld stresses virtue's physical manifestations.

147 *Dilates* 'expands'.

Breathes a diviner spirit, and enlarg'd
Each spreading feature, with an ampler port
And bolder tone, exulting, rides the storm,   150
And joys amidst the tempest: then she reaps
Her golden harvest; fruits of nobler growth
And higher relish than meridian suns
Can ever ripen; fair, heroic deeds,
And godlike action. 'Tis not meats, and drinks,   155
And balmy airs, and vernal suns, and showers
That feed and ripen minds; 'tis toil and danger;
And wrestling with the stubborn gripe of fate;
And war, and sharp distress, and paths obscure
And dubious. The bold swimmer joys not so   160
To feel the proud waves under him, and beat
With strong repelling arm the billowy surge;
The generous courser does not so exult
To toss his floating main against the wind,
And neigh amidst the thunder of the war,   165
As virtue to oppose her swelling breast
Like a firm shield against the darts of fate.
And when her sons in that rough school have learn'd
To smile at danger, then the hand that rais'd
Shall hush the storm, and lead the shining train   170
Of peaceful years in bright procession on.
Then shall the shepherd's pipe, the muse's lyre,
On CYRNUS' shores be heard: her grateful sons
With loud acclaim and hymns of cordial praise
Shall hail their high deliverers; every name   175
To virtue dear be from oblivion snatch'd,
And plac'd among the stars: but chiefly thine,
Thine, PAOLI, with sweetest sound shall dwell
On their applauding lips; thy sacred name,
Endear'd to long posterity, some muse,   180
More worthy of the theme, shall consecrate
To after ages, and applauding worlds
Shall bless the godlike man who sav'd his country.

* * * * * * * * * *

So vainly wish'd, so fondly hop'd the Muse:
Too fondly hop'd: The iron fates prevail,   185
And CYRNUS is no more. Her generous sons,
Less vanquish'd than o'erwhelm'd, by numbers crush'd,
Admir'd, unaided fell. So strives the moon
In dubious battle with the gathering clouds,

---

149 *an ampler port* 'a more open manner'.
163 *generous* 'spirited' (of animals); *courser* Horse bred for
speed.
174 *cordial* 'of the heart' (Lat. *cordis*).
184–201 This passage was added after 13 June 1769. See
headnote.

189 The line recalls Satan's description of his war against
God 'in dubious battle on the plains of heaven'
(*Paradise Lost*, 1:104). In both texts 'dubious' suggests
the outcome was in doubt.

And strikes a splendour thro' them: till at length 190
Storms roll'd on storms involve the face of heaven
And quench her struggling fires. Forgive the zeal
That, too presumptuous, whisper'd better things
And read the book of destiny amiss.
Not with the purple colouring of success 195
Is virtue best adorn'd: th'attempt is praise.
There yet remains a freedom, nobler far
Than kings or senates can destroy or give;
Beyond the proud oppressor's cruel grasp
Seated secure; uninjur'd; undestroy'd; 200
Worthy of Gods: The freedom of the mind.

195 *purple* The imperial colour, but also (poetically) the
colour of blood.

A Summer Evening's Meditation

In its combination of classical myth and Christian belief, imagination and astronomy, this flight through space has a Miltonic daring; but the poem is specifically Unitarian in its projection of the universe as God's text, there ultimately to reassure humanity. Barbauld's meditation can be compared with the cosmic mental journey in Akenside's *The Pleasures of Imagination*, 1:183–221; with Watts's *The Adventurous Muse*, which appropriately encounters Milton at the end of its flight; and with Finch's *Nocturnal Rêverie*, which ignores the heavens and explores her heightened sense of our natural surroundings. Blank verse was considered appropriate for imaginative contemplations, as Johnson said of Young's *Night Thoughts*: 'The wild diffusion of the sentiments, and the digressive sallies of imagination, would have been compressed and restrained by confinement to rhyme'. Barbauld's poem was widely admired. Wordsworth responded to it in two manuscripts of 1798 which present a less comforting and more recalcitrant universe. It cannot be dated, but was first published in *Poems* (1773) in the text given here.

One sun by day, by night ten thousand shine.
YOUNG.

'Tis past! The sultry tyrant of the south
Has spent his short-liv'd rage; more grateful hours
Move silent on; the skies no more repel
The dazzled sight, but with mild maiden beams
Of temper'd light, invite the cherish'd eye 5
To wander o'er their sphere; where hung aloft
DIAN's bright crescent, like a silver bow
New strung in heaven, lifts high its beamy horns
Impatient for the night, and seems to push
Her brother down the sky. Fair VENUS shines 10
Even in the eye of day; with sweetest beam
Propitious shines, and shakes a trembling flood
Of soften'd radiance from her dewy locks.
The shadows spread apace; while meeken'd Eve
Her cheek yet warm with blushes, slow retires 15
Thro' the Hesperian gardens of the west,

Motto Edward Young, *Night Thoughts*, 9:748. The
quotation continues: 'And light us deep into the DEITY,
/ How boundless in Magnificence and Might?'
4–5 Cf. Pope, *Epistle to a Lady*, 253–6.
7 Diana, the chaste moon-goddess, presided over
hunting.

16 *Hesperian gardens* See Akenside, *The Pleasures of
Imagination*, 1:287–91 and note. For Milton, the
Gardens of the Hesperides figured the Garden of Eden
(*Paradise Lost*, 4:250–1). Here lines 10–17 recall the
evening scene in Paradise (4:598–775).

And shuts the gates of day. 'Tis now the hour
When Contemplation, from her sunless haunts,
The cool damp grotto, or the lonely depth
Of unpierc'd woods, where wrapt in solid shade   20
She mused away the gaudy hours of noon,
And fed on thoughts unripen'd by the sun,
Moves forward; and with radiant finger points
To yon blue concave swell'd by breath divine,
Where, one by one, the living eyes of heaven   25
Awake, quick kindling o'er the face of ether
One boundless blaze; ten thousand trembling fires,
And dancing lustres, where th' unsteady eye
Restless, and dazzled wanders unconfin'd
O'er all this field of glories: spacious field!   30
And worthy of the master: he, whose hand
With hieroglyphics older than the Nile,
Inscrib'd the mystic tablet; hung on high
To public gaze, and said, adore, O man!
The finger of thy GOD. From what pure wells   35
Of milky light, what soft o'erflowing urn,
Are all these lamps so fill'd? these friendly lamps,
For ever streaming o'er the azure deep
To point our path, and light us to our home.
How soft they slide along their lucid spheres!   40
And silent, as the foot of time, fulfil
Their destin'd courses: Nature's self is hush'd,
And, but a scatter'd leaf, which rustles thro'
The thick-wove foliage, not a sound is heard
To break the midnight air; tho' the rais'd ear,   45
Intensely listening, drinks in every breath.
How deep the silence, yet how loud the praise!
But are they silent all? or is there not
A tongue in every star that talks with man,
And wooes him to be wise; nor wooes in vain: 50
This dead of midnight is the noon of thought,
And wisdom mounts her zenith with the stars.
At this still hour the self-collected soul
Turns inward, and beholds a stranger there
Of high descent, and more than mortal rank;   55
An embryo GOD; a spark of fire divine,
Which must burn on for ages, when the sun,
(Fair transitory creature of a day!)
Has clos'd his golden eye, and wrapt in shades
Forgets his wonted journey thro' the east.   60

---

33 *mystic tablet* The Universe, which bears the mysterious imprint of God. Cf. Akenside, *The Pleasures of Imagination*, 1:99–101.

40 *lucid spheres* 'translucent paths'.

48–9 Cf. Wordsworth: 'But they are silent. Still they roll along / Immeasurably distant' (*Night Piece*, 11–17); 'Why is the earth without a shape and why / Thus silent is the sky? … Has every star a tongue?' ('Are there no groans?'). See *Notes and Queries*, 238 (1993), pp. 40–1; 241 (1996), pp. 29–30. Barbauld is recalling Psalm 19:1–3: 'The heavens declare the glory of God … There is no speech nor language, where their voice is not heard'.

Ye citadels of light, and seats of GODS!
Perhaps my future home, from whence the soul
Revolving periods past, may oft look back
With recollected tenderness, on all
The various busy scenes she left below,   65
Its deep laid projects and its strange events,
As on some fond and doating tale that sooth'd
Her infant hours; O be it lawful now
To tread the hallow'd circles of your courts,
And with mute wonder and delighted awe   70
Approach your burning confines. Seiz'd in thought
On fancy's wild and roving wing I sail,
From the green borders of the peopled earth,
And the pale moon, her duteous fair attendant;
From solitary Mars; from the vast orb   75
Of Jupiter, whose huge gigantic bulk
Dances in ether like the lightest leaf;
To the dim verge, the suburbs of the system,
Where chearless Saturn 'midst her watry moons
Girt with a lucid zone, majestic sits   80
In gloomy grandeur; like an exil'd queen
Amongst her weeping handmaids: fearless thence
I launch into the trackless deeps of space,
Where, burning round, ten thousand suns appear,
Of elder beam; which ask no leave to shine   85
Of our terrestrial star, nor borrow light
From the proud regent of our scanty day;
Sons of the morning, first born of creation,
And only less than him who marks their track,
And guides their fiery wheels. Here must I stop,   90
Or is there aught beyond? What hand unseen
Impels me onward thro' the glowing orbs
Of habitable nature; far remote,
To the dread confines of eternal night,
To solitudes of vast unpeopled space,   95
The desarts of creation, wide and wild;
Where embryo systems and unkindled suns
Sleep in the womb of chaos; fancy droops,
And thought astonish'd stops her bold career.
But oh thou mighty mind! whose powerful word   100
Said, thus let all things be, and thus they were,
Where shall I seek thy presence? How unblam'd
Invoke thy dread perfection?
Have the broad eye-lids of the morn beheld thee?

---

78 *suburbs* 'outer reaches'.

79 *Saturn* Until Uranus was discovered in 1781, Saturn was the most distant planet known. The mythological Saturn embodied the spirit of melancholy and contemplation. After being criticized in the *Monthly Review* for making him female, Barbauld rewrote this passage for the third edition: 'Saturn midst his wat'ry moons / Girt with a lucid zone, in gloomy pomp, / Sits like an exil'd monarch. Fearless thence ...'

102–3 Cf. 'may I express thee unblamed?' (*Paradise Lost*, 3:3).

104 Cf. 'the opening eyelids of the morn' (Milton, *Lycidas*, 26).

Or does the beamy shoulder of Orion   105
Support thy throne? O look with pity down
On erring guilty man; not in thy names
Of terrour clad; not with those thunders arm'd
That conscious Sinai felt, when fear appall'd
The scatter'd tribes; thou hast a gentler voice,   110
That whispers comfort to the swelling heart,
Abash'd, yet longing to behold her maker.

But now my soul, unus'd to stretch her powers
In flight so daring, drops her weary wing,
And seeks again the known accustom'd spot,   115
Drest up with sun, and shade, and lawns, and streams,
A mansion fair and spacious for its guest,
And full replete with wonders. Let me here
Content and grateful, wait th' appointed time
And ripen for the skies: the hour will come   120
When all these splendours bursting on my sight
Shall stand unveil'd, and to my ravished sense
Unlock the glories of the world unknown.

107–10 The scene is God's delivery of the ten commandments on Mount Sinai: 'And all the people saw the thunderings, and the lightnings, and the noise of the trumpet, and the mountain smoking: and when the people saw it, they removed, and stood afar off' (Exodus, 20:18). Barbauld's 'mystic tablet' (33) offers nature's gentler alternative to this scene of terror.

To Mr Barbauld,
November 14, 1778

In 1778 the Barbaulds were running their school for boys at Palgrave in Suffolk, and in that year Anna Laetitia published her popular *Lessons for Children*. In this poem the playful intellect of the speaking voice suggests that Barbauld has absorbed Marvell as well as Waller. The informality and lightness of touch with which she handles the big themes of Time, Age and Mortality make this a poem that combines strength with grace. Text from *Works* (1825), 1:134–6, where it was first printed. Some slight adjustment has been made to the inconsistent 1825 indentation.

Come, clear thy studious looks awhile,
        'Tis arrant treason now
        To wear that moping brow,
When I, thy empress, bid thee smile.

        What though the fading year   5
        One wreath will not afford
        To grace the poet's hair,
        Or deck the festal board;

A thousand pretty ways we'll find
To mock old Winter's starving reign;   10
We'll bid the violets spring again,
Bid rich poetic roses blow,
Peeping above his heaps of snow;
We'll dress his withered cheeks in flowers,
        And on his smooth bald head   15
        Fantastic garlands bind:
        Garlands, which we will get

From the gay blooms of that immortal year,
　　Above the turning seasons set,
Where young ideas shoot in Fancy's sunny bowers.   20

A thousand pleasant arts we'll have
To add new feathers to the wings of Time,
　　And make him smoothly haste away:
　　　　We'll use him as our slave,
　　And when we please we'll bid him stay,   25
And clip his wings, and make him stop to view
　　　　Our studies, and our follies too;
How sweet our follies are, how high our fancies climb.

We'll little care what others do,
And where they go, and what they say;   30
　　Our bliss, all inward and our own,
Would only tarnished be, by being shown.
　　The talking restless world shall see,
　　Spite of the world we'll happy be;
　　　　But none shall know   35
　　　　How much we're so,
　　Save only Love, and we.

---

18 *immortal year* Eternity, but also partly the world of the poetic imagination.
20 *young ideas shoot* Cf. Thomson on the joy of rearing a child: 'Delightful task! to rear the tender Thought, /

To teach the young Idea how to shoot' (*Spring*, 1152–3). The Barbaulds had no children, but adopted Anna Laetitia's nephew.

The Rights of Woman

The poem would seem to be an ironic response to Mary Wollstonecraft's *Vindication of the Rights of Woman* (January 1792), which in chapter four had criticized Barbauld's poem *To a Lady, with some painted Flowers* for offering an 'ignoble comparison' of women with the softness and delicacy of flowers. Wollstonecraft states her own position in the introduction: 'I wish to persuade women to endeavour to acquire strength, both of mind and body, and to convince them that the soft phrases, susceptibility of heart, delicacy of sentiment, and refinement of taste, are almost synonymous with epithets of weakness'. Barbauld had ended her poem: 'Your best, your sweetest empire is – to please', and here she returns to the theme of empire, now in various militaristic guises, contrasting the tactics of 'wit and art' (17) with the 'soft maxims' (31) of Nature which will eventually assert themselves. If this poem *is* a response to Wollstonecraft it falsifies her position: she disliked 'empire' of any kind, and wanted an equality and mutuality based on strength, reason and virtue in both sexes (Barbauld's last line in fact echoes the *Vindication*). During 1792–3 the question of women's power was also brought into the political debate with Helen Maria Williams's radical *Letters from France* and Lætitia Matilda Hawkins's conservative riposte, *Letters on the Female Mind* (1793), which deplored the power of 'female republicans' to subvert domestic peace. Barbauld's poem, which cannot be precisely dated, fits interestingly into this context. It was first printed in *Works* (1825), 1:185–7, in the text given here.

Yes, injured Woman! rise, assert thy right!
Woman! too long degraded, scorned, opprest;
O born to rule in partial Law's despite,
Resume thy native empire o'er the breast!

Go forth arrayed in panoply divine;   5
That angel pureness which admits no stain;
Go, bid proud Man his boasted rule resign,
And kiss the golden sceptre of thy reign.

Go, gird thyself with grace; collect thy store
Of bright artillery glancing from afar;   10
Soft melting tones thy thundering cannon's roar,
Blushes and fears thy magazine of war.

Thy rights are empire: urge no meaner claim, —
Felt, not defined, and if debated, lost;
Like sacred mysteries, which withheld from fame,   15
Shunning discussion, are revered the most.

Try all that wit and art suggest to bend
Of thy imperial foe the stubborn knee;
Make treacherous Man thy subject, not thy friend;
Thou mayst command, but never canst be free.   20

Awe the licentious, and restrain the rude;
Soften the sullen, clear the cloudy brow:
Be, more than princes' gifts, thy favours sued; —
She hazards all, who will the least allow.

But hope not, courted idol of mankind,   25
On this proud eminence secure to stay;
Subduing and subdued, thou soon shalt find
Thy coldness soften, and thy pride give way.

Then, then, abandon each ambitious thought,
Conquest or rule thy heart shall feebly move,   30
In Nature's school, by her soft maxims taught,
That separate rights are lost in mutual love.

6 'Why are girls to be told that they resemble angels; but to sink them below women?' (*Vindication*, ch. 5).
7–8 'I love man as my fellow; but his scepter, real, or usurped, extends not to me, unless the reason of an individual demands my homage' (*Vindication*, ch. 2).
12 *magazine* A building for storing arms and explosives.
32 In chapter 2 of the *Vindication* Wollstonecraft

approvingly quotes Adam's words to God ('in the following lines Milton seems to coincide with me'): 'Among unequals what society / Can sort, what harmony or true delight? / Which must be mutual, in proportion due / Given and received' (*Paradise Lost*, 8:383–6).

To a little invisible Being
who is expected soon to become visible

The addressee of this poem to an unborn child has not been identified. A study of the potential (and potency) within human life and the natural world, it creates an interplay between subjective and objective, the empirical and the mysterious. The number of quatrains perhaps suggests the nine moons of gestation. The poem is undated (McCarthy and Kraft suggest *c*.1795) and was first printed in *Poems* (1825), 1:199–201, the text given here.

Germ of new life, whose powers expanding slow
For many a moon their full perfection wait, —
Haste, precious pledge of happy love, to go
Auspicious borne through life's mysterious gate.

What powers lie folded in thy curious frame, —   5
Senses from objects locked, and mind from thought!
How little canst thou guess the lofty claim
To grasp at all the worlds the Almighty wrought!

And see, the genial season's warmth to share,
Fresh younglings shoot, and opening roses glow!   10
Swarms of new life exulting fill the air, —
Haste, infant bud of being, haste to blow!

For thee the nurse prepares her lulling songs,
The eager matrons count the lingering day;
But far the most thy anxious parent longs   15
On thy soft cheek a mother's kiss to lay.

She only asks to lay her burden down,
That her glad arms that burden may resume;
And nature's sharpest pangs her wishes crown,
That free thee living from thy living tomb.   20

She longs to fold to her maternal breast
Part of herself, yet to herself unknown;
To see and to salute the stranger guest,
Fed with her life through many a tedious moon.

Come, reap thy rich inheritance of love!   25
Bask in the fondness of a Mother's eye!
Nor wit nor eloquence her heart shall move
Like the first accents of thy feeble cry.

Haste, little captive, burst thy prison doors!
Launch on the living world, and spring to light!   30
Nature for thee displays her various stores,
Opens her thousand inlets of delight.

If charmed verse or muttered prayers had power,
With favouring spells to speed thee on thy way,
Anxious I'd bid my beads each passing hour,   35
Till thy wished smile thy mother's pangs o'erpay.

---

5 Cf. 'what high, capacious pow'rs / Lie folded up in man' (Akenside, *The Pleasures of Imagination*, 1:222–3).

6 'I see no reason … to believe that the soul thinks before the senses have furnished it with ideas to think on … there appear not to be any ideas in the mind before the senses have conveyed any in' (Locke, *Essay Concerning Human Understanding* (1690), I.ii.20–3).

9 *genial season* The spring (genial = 'conducive to growth').

10 *younglings* Young plants or saplings (Cf. 'April's tender younglings', Keats, *Endymion*, 1:138).

11 Cf. Gray, *Ode on the Spring*, 23–6.

12 *blow* 'burst into flower'.

14 *matrons* Married women who helped at or after childbirth.

19–20 Hints at Jesus Christ's suffering and resurrection.

29 *prison doors* The image of the immortal soul imprisoned in the body and freed at the moment of death was an essential neoplatonic idea. Here Barbauld uses the image for birth into the physical world.

35 *bid my beads* 'offer a prayer' (a traditional phrase which need not imply the use of a rosary).

To Mr Coleridge

'The more I see of Mrs Barbauld the more I admire her – that wonderful *Propriety* of Mind! – She has great *acuteness*, very great – yet how steadily she keeps it within the bounds of practical Reason. This I almost envy as well as admire – My own Subtleties too often lead me into strange (tho' God be praised) transient Out-of-the-waynesses' (Coleridge to Estlin, 1 March 1800). The poem, with its sympathetic admonition of Coleridge's mental 'Subtleties', was evidently written in response to their meeting in Bristol in August 1797 (a manuscript copy is dated September of that year). By 1805, however, Coleridge's admiration had turned to distaste, and he characterized her rational Unitarianism as a sweet dry stick of liquorice with no roots or buds, 'nothing before and nothing behind' (*Notebooks*, 2509). For her allegorical scene Barbauld takes Bunyan's *Pilgrim's Progress* (the arbour halfway up the Hill of Difficulty, where Christian falls asleep) and combines it with the dreamscape of Ovid's Cave of Sleep (*Metamorphoses*, 11:592–615) and the allurements of James Thomson's *Castle of Indolence* (1748). As 'To Mr C——GE' the poem was first printed in the *Monthly Magazine*, 7 (April 1799), pp. 231–3, the text given here.

Midway the hill of science, after steep
And rugged paths that tire the unpractised feet,
A *grove* extends; in tangled mazes wrought,
And filled with strange enchantment:–dubious shapes
Flit through dim glades, and lure the eager foot   5
Of youthful ardour to eternal chase.
Dreams hang on every leaf: unearthly forms
Glide through the gloom; and mystic visions swim
Before the cheated sense. Athwart the mists,
Far into vacant space, huge shadows stretch   10
And seem realities; while things of life,
Obvious to sight and touch, all glowing round,
Fade to the hue of shadows — *Scruples* here,
With filmy net, most like the autumnal webs
Of floating gossamer, arrest the foot   15
Of generous enterprise; and palsy hope
And fair ambition with the chilling touch
Of sickly hesitation and blank fear.
Nor seldom *Indolence*, these lawns among,
Fixes her turf-built seat; and wears the garb   20
Of deep philosophy, and museful sits,
In dreamy twilight of the vacant mind,
Soothed by the whispering shade; for soothing soft
The shades; and vistas lengthening into air,
With moon-beam rainbows tinted — Here each mind   25
Of finer mould, acute and delicate,
In its high progress to eternal truth
Rests for a space, in fairy bowers entranced;
And loves the softened light and tender gloom;
And, pampered with most unsubstantial food,   30
Looks down indignant on the grosser world,

1 *science* 'knowledge'. Barbauld's essay, 'The Hill of Science, a Vision' (*Miscellaneous Pieces* (1773), pp. 27–38), allegorizes the distractions awaiting those who wish to ascend. The most insidious and dangerous is Indolence (cf. 19–23): 'of all the unhappy deserters from the paths of Science, none seemed less able to return than the followers of Indolence'.
5 *dim* Coleridge came to associate dimness with emotional depth and intellectual growth. 'By deep feelings we make our *Ideas dim*' (*Notebooks*, 921, February/March 1801), and he attacked the optimistic certainties of 'Barbauldian' belief as 'mock-knowledge' lacking 'feelings of dimness from *growth*' (*Notebooks*, 2509, March 1805).
13 *Scruples* 'intellectual uncertainties and hesitations'.

And matter's cumbrous shapings. Youth beloved
Of science — of the muse beloved, not here,
Not in the maze of metaphysic lore,
Build thou thy place of resting! lightly tread   35
The dangerous ground, on noble aims intent;
And be this Circe of the studious cell
Enjoyed, but still subservient. Active scenes
Shall soon with healthful spirit brace thy mind:
And fair exertion, for bright fame sustained,   40
For friends, for country, chase each spleen-fed fog
That blots the wide creation —
Now heaven conduct thee with a parent's love!

37 *Circe* The enchantress of *Odyssey*, 10.

William Cowper (1731–1800)

In his *Works of the English Poets* (1810) Alexander Chalmers declared that Cowper 'has become the universal favourite of his nation' (18:602). Writers as diverse as Coleridge, Blake and Jane Austen admired him, and during the Romantic period Cowper's verse was seen to have been forward looking, and to have brought new subjects within poetry's reach. The critic Francis Jeffrey wrote in 1803: 'Our poets had become timid and fastidious, and circumscribed ... by the observance of a limited number of models ... [Cowper] reclaimed the natural liberty, and walked abroad in the open field of observation as freely as those by whom it was originally trodden. He passed from the imitation of poets to the imitation of nature.' It is helpful to be reminded of Jeffrey's praise for Cowper's boldness, variety and originality when we encounter the man himself and his odd combination of shyness and vigour.

Son of the Rector of Berkhamsted, Hertfordshire, William Cowper (commonly pronounced 'Cooper') attended Westminster School 1742–9, and after pursuing the law in a desultory way he found that a barrister's life held less appeal than the world of the coffee-house wits. In company with his literary schoolfellows Robert Lloyd (q.v.), Bonnell Thornton, George Colman and Charles Churchill (the Nonsense Club), Cowper found he had a knack at humorous light verse (his *Epistle to Robert Lloyd, Esqr.* is the best example of this early work), and in 1756 he contributed five satirical essays to the *Connoisseur*, which Colman and Thornton were editing. But his metropolitan life ended suddenly in 1763 when he was summoned to appear before the House of Lords as nominee for the post of Clerk of the Journals. Frantic with apprehension, he attempted to kill himself by drowning, stabbing, poisoning and hanging (the garter broke as he was blacking out). At a house for the insane in St Albans a slow recovery was followed by a sudden rebirth to evangelical religion ('Immediately the full beams of the sun of righteousness shone upon me'). He lodged at Huntingdon with the Unwin family, where Mary Unwin (1724–96) found herself supplying the place of Cowper's mother, who had died when he was five, and their walks became part of an intensive daily pattern of religious devotion. In 1767 Cowper and the now widowed Mrs Unwin moved to Olney, Buckinghamshire, as neighbours of the Reverend John Newton, and there Cowper began writing hymns for their weekly prayer meetings. In January 1773, however, a further severe breakdown occurred, and having failed to kill himself in response to what he thought was God's direct command, he became convinced that he was eternally damned. For the rest of his life he lived under that sentence. He ceased to attend church or to pray, since both were futile.

Against this terrible background Cowper's life settled into a quiet routine at Olney. He kept hares, worked in his walled garden, did carpentry, wrote delightful letters, and walked out with Mary Unwin. An hour or two of poetry each day proved a healing diversion. *Olney Hymns* (1779) included sixty-six of Cowper's, and his first collection of *Poems* (1782) was well received. But it was *The Task* (1785) that brought him national popularity. In 1786 he was invited by the Throckmorton family to move into the Lodge at Weston Underwood, whose park formed one of his favourite walks (see *The Task*, Book 1), and it was there that he completed his blank-verse translation of Homer (1791) in direct competition with Pope. Cowper's severe depression periodically returned, and by 1794 it had become permanent. In 1795 his cousin John Johnson took him and Mary Unwin to live with him in Norfolk, and it was here during 1797–9 that Cowper revised his Homer and wrote his last pieces in English and Latin. He died on 25 April 1800.

Our selection includes two great poems of despair; but these stand out from the bulk of Cowper's work. What strikes the reader forcibly is the sense and sanity of his poetry, its alertness to variety, and commitment to the strenuous moral life. Cowper is a man with strong convictions and a sharp tongue. We remember that it was Cowper's energy and boldness that struck readers of the next generation. His reaction against Pope was a resistance to the polish of smooth versification, which he associated with the fashionable witty world he had left behind. Cowper was his own man, and his politics had libertarian tendencies (he welcomed the fall of the Bastille and attacked the slave trade). His embrace in *The Task* of a sinewy and rhythmically varied blank verse was clearly linked to the strength of character that underlay his timidity. As he wrote to his publisher in 1791: 'Give me a manly, rough line, with a deal of meaning in it, rather than a whole poem full of musical periods, that have nothing but their oily smoothness to recommend them.'

'Hatred and vengeance'

In the lost Croft MSS of Cowper these lines were written on the same sheet as a poem dated 31 December 1774 (see Baird and Ryskamp, 1:489), and such a dating would appropriately link them to

Cowper's conviction of his own damnation following his 1773 breakdown. The poem was first printed in *Memoirs ... of the Life of William Cowper* (1816), pp. 91–2, the text given here. The verse form is a variant of the Greek Sapphic stanza, four lines culminating in

– ^ ^ – –. Sambrook (p. 239) notes that Cowper's immediate model seems to be Isaac Watts's *The Day of Judgment. An Ode. Attempted in English Sapphick*, with its terrible vision of the fate of the damned (see lines 16–18n).

Hatred and vengeance! my eternal portion,
Scarce can endure delay of execution,
Wait, with impatient readiness, to seize my
    Soul in a moment.

Damn'd below Judas: more abhorr'd than he was,   5
Who for a few pence sold his holy Master.
Twice betray'd Jesus me, the last delinquent,
    Deems the profanest.

Man disavows, and Deity disowns me.
Hell might afford my miseries a shelter;   10
Therefore hell keeps her ever-hungry mouths all
    Bolted against me.

Hard lot! encompassed with a thousand dangers;
Weary, faint, trembling with a thousand terrors;
I'm call'd, if vanquish'd, to receive a sentence   15
    Worse than Abiram's.

Him, the vindictive rod of angry justice
Sent quick, and howling to the centre headlong;
I, fed with judgments, in a fleshly tomb, am
    Buried above ground.   20

6 *few pence* Thirty pieces of silver. See Matthew, 26:14–16.

7 *Twice betray'd* By Judas and Cowper himself.

16–18 Abiram and others were punished by God for challenging the authority of Moses: 'And the earth opened her mouth, and swallowed them up ... They, and all that appertained to them, went down alive into the pit, and the earth closed upon them' (Numbers, 16:32–3). Cf. Watts's *The Day of Judgment* (1709 edn):

'Hopeless Immortals! how they scream and shiver / While Devils push them to the Pit wide yawning / Hideous and gloomy, to receive them headlong / Down to the Centre' (25–8).

18 *quick* 'alive'.

19 'I will feed my flock ... saith the Lord God ... but I will destroy the fat and the strong; I will feed them with judgment' (Ezekiel, 34:15–16).

The Task
BOOK 1: THE SOFA

Cowper's longest original poem draws from a wide range of genres: topographical poetry, Miltonic epic, Georgic, familiar epistle, devotional verse, political and moral satire, parody, and occasional or 'album' poetry. The six books of blank verse began as an occasional poem, and *The Task* illustrates Cowper's ability to turn an exercise of the wit and fancy into a more extensive exercise of the sensory, spiritual and moral faculties. His witty and sophisticated friend Lady Austen was the poem's instigator: 'This lady happened, as an admirer of Milton, to be partial to

blank verse, and often solicited her poetical friend to try his powers in that species of composition. After repeated solicitation, he promised her, if she would furnish the subject, to comply with her request. – "O" she replied, "you can never be in want of a subject: – you can write upon any: – write upon this Sofa!" The Poet obeyed her command, and from the lively repartee of familiar conversation arose a Poem of many thousand verses, unexampled perhaps both in its origin, and its excellence' (William Hayley, *The Life, and Posthumous Writings, of William Cowper, Esqr*

(1803–4), 1:135). A vital idea here is that of 'familiar conversation'. Just as good talk holds the interest of the listener through a range of subjects and shifts in the tone of voice, so Cowper's 'divine chit-chat', as Coleridge called it, articulates the varied topics of *The Task*. (Not surprisingly, Cowper strongly influenced Coleridge's own 'conversation poems'.) Cowper appended to *The Task* the Latin motto *Fit surculus arbor* ('The shoot becomes the tree'), and this image is appropriate for the poem's whimsical origin, but also for its Cowperian concern with how things grow and are sustained, whether a plant, a kingdom, an empire, or the human spirit. Cowper began writing his 'Sofa' (as he called it) in the autumn of 1783, and by the following August he had finished the six books and was revising the whole: 'I find it severe exercise to mould it and fashion it to my mind' (Cowper–Bull, [3 August 1784]). It was published in 1785 as *The Task, A Poem in Six Books*, and it is the first edition text of Book 1 that is given here.

Cowper's opening history of the sofa raises themes that recur throughout Book 1: the ambivalence of human progress; the relationship between nature and art, simplicity and sophistication, principles and fashions; the results of luxury, wealth, indolence and stagnation; the positive and negative aspects of human energy and ingenuity. These themes continue to be developed in the succeeding books of *The Task*, in which Cowper once more articulates a wide range of tones and topics. To summarize very briefly: Book 2 (*The Time-Piece*) opens with an attack on slavery and goes on to survey the moral, political and religious decline of England; Book 3 (*The Garden*) focuses on Cowper's own simple country life and domestic happiness as a gardener; Book 4 (*The Winter Evening*) celebrates snug domesticity and reflects on poverty and the loss of rural simplicity and innocence; Book 5 (*The Winter Morning Walk*) raises thoughts on war, liberty and tyranny, and the limitations of patriotism; and Book 6 (*The Winter Walk at Noon*) moves from Cowper's love of animals to a climactic vision of the heavenly kingdom, before drawing back to the poet himself, 'My share of duties decently fulfill'd'.

Argument of the First Book

Historical deduction of seats, from the stool to the Sofa. — A School-boys ramble. — A walk in the country. — The scene described. — Rural sounds as well as sights delightful. — Another walk. — Mistake concerning the charms of solitude, corrected. — Colonnades commended. — Alcove and the view from it. — The Wilderness. — The Grove. — The Thresher. — The necessity and the benefits of exercise. — The works of nature superior to and in some instances inimitable by art. — The wearisomeness of what is commonly called a life of pleasure. — Change of scene sometimes expedient. — A common described, and the character of crazy Kate introduced upon it. — Gipsies. — The blessings of civilized life. — That state most favourable to virtue. — The South Sea Islanders compassionated, but chiefly Omai. — His present state of mind supposed. — Civilized life friendly to virtue, but not great cities. — Great cities, and London in particular, allowed their due praise, but censured. — Fete Champetre. — The book concludes with a reflection on the fatal effects of dissipation and effeminacy upon our public measures.

> I sing the SOFA. I who lately sang
> Truth, Hope and Charity, and touch'd with awe
> The solemn chords, and with a trembling hand,
> Escap'd with pain from that advent'rous flight,
> Now seek repose upon an humbler theme;   5
> The theme though humble, yet august and proud
> Th'occasion — for the Fair commands the song.
>   Time was, when cloathing sumptuous or for use,
> Save their own painted skins, our sires had none.
> As yet black breeches were not; sattin smooth,   10
> Or velvet soft, or plush with shaggy pile:

1 An epic opening. Cf. Pope, *The Dunciad*, 1:1–3 and note.
2 *Truth, Hope and Charity* Three moral satires in Cowper's 1782 volume.
4 Cf. 'my adventurous song, / That with no middle flight intends to soar', *Paradise Lost*, 1:13–14.

7 *the Fair* Woman.
10 *were not* Cf. Joseph Warton, *The Enthusiast*, 99. Cowper inverts Warton's celebration of the primitive.
11 *plush* 'Cloth having a nap longer and softer than that of velvet' (*OED*).

The hardy chief upon the rugged rock
Wash'd by the sea, or on the grav'ly bank
Thrown up by wintry torrents roaring loud,
Fearless of wrong, repos'd his weary strength.   15
Those barb'rous ages past, succeeded next
The birth-day of invention, weak at first,
Dull in design, and clumsy to perform.
Joint-stools were then created; on three legs
Upborne they stood. Three legs upholding firm   20
A massy slab, in fashion square or round.
On such a stool immortal Alfred sat,
And sway'd the sceptre of his infant realms:
And such in ancient halls and mansions drear
May still be seen, but perforated sore   25
And drill'd in holes the solid oak is found,
By worms voracious eating through and through.
    At length a generation more refined
Improv'd the simple plan, made three legs four,
Gave them a twisted form vermicular,   30
And o'er the seat with plenteous wadding stuff'd
Induced a splendid cover green and blue,
Yellow and red, of tapestry richly wrought
And woven close, or needle-work sublime.
There might ye see the pioney spread wide,   35
The full-blown rose, the shepherd and his lass,
Lap-dog and lambkin with black staring eyes,
And parrots with twin cherries in their beak.
    Now came the cane from India, smooth and bright
With Nature's varnish; sever'd into stripes   40
That interlaced each other, these supplied
Of texture firm a lattice work, that braced
The new machine, and it became a chair.
But restless was the chair; the back erect
Distress'd the weary loins that felt no ease;   45
The slipp'ry seat betray'd the sliding part
That press'd it, and the feet hung dangling down,
Anxious in vain to find the distant floor.
These for the rich: the rest, whom fate had placed
In modest mediocrity, content   50
With base materials, sat on well tann'd hides
Obdurate and unyielding, glassy smooth,
With here and there a tuft of crimson yarn,
Or scarlet crewel in the cushion fixt:
If cushion might be call'd, what harder seem'd   55
Than the firm oak of which the frame was form'd.
No want of timber then was felt or fear'd
In Albion's happy isle. The lumber stood
Pond'rous, and fixt by its own massy weight.

21 Cf. Satan's backward look at Heaven 'undetermined
square or round' (*Paradise Lost*, 2:1048).
22 Alfred (849–901), King of the West Saxons.
30 *vermicular* 'sinuous' (literally 'worm-like').
35 *pioney* The peony has large globed flowers, popular on
embroidered seat-covers.

54 *crewel* A thin worsted yarn of two threads, used for
embroidery.
57–8 The navy's demand for oaks was insatiable. See
Yardley Oak, 96n. *Albion* Britain; so called from the
chalk cliffs of Sussex and Kent (Lat. *alba* = 'white').
See 520–1.

But elbows still were wanting; these, some say,   60
An Alderman of Cripplegate contrived,
And some ascribe the invention to a priest
Burly and big and studious of his ease.
But rude at first, and not with easy slope
Receding wide, they press'd against the ribs,   65
And bruised the side, and elevated high
Taught the rais'd shoulders to invade the ears.
Long time elapsed or e'er our rugged sires
Complain'd, though incommodiously pent in,
And ill at ease behind. The Ladies first   70
'Gan murmur, as became the softer sex.
Ingenious fancy, never better pleas'd
Than when employ'd t'accommodate the fair,
Heard the sweet moan with pity, and devised
The soft settee; one elbow at each end,   75
And in the midst an elbow, it receiv'd
United yet divided, twain at once.
So sit two Kings of Brentford on one throne;
And so two citizens who take the air
Close pack'd and smiling in a chaise and one.   80
But relaxation of the languid frame
By soft recumbency of outstretched limbs,
Was bliss reserved for happier days. So slow
The growth of what is excellent, so hard
T'attain perfection in this nether world.   85
Thus first necessity invented stools,
Convenience next suggested elbow chairs,
And luxury th'accomplished SOFA last.
    The nurse sleeps sweetly, hired to watch the sick
Whom snoring she disturbs. As sweetly he   90
Who quits the coach-box at the midnight hour
To sleep within the carriage more secure,
His legs depending at the open door.
Sweet sleep enjoys the Curate in his desk,
The tedious Rector drawling o'er his head,   95
And sweet the Clerk below: but neither sleep
Of lazy Nurse, who snores the sick man dead,
Nor his who quits the box at midnight hour
To slumber in the carriage more secure,
Nor sleep enjoy'd by Curate in his desk,   100
Nor yet the dozings of the Clerk are sweet,
Compared with the repose the SOFA yields.
    Oh may I live exempted (while I live
Guiltless of pamper'd appetite obscene)

---

61 *Alderman* Chief officer of a ward in the City of London
   (here Cripplegate). A symbol of bourgeois dignity.
78 *Kings of Brentford* Characters in the Duke of
   Buckingham's play, *The Rehearsal* (1671), still popular.
79–80 Cf. Lloyd, *The Cit's Country Box*, 3–6.
82 *recumbency* 'lying down' (Lat. *recumbo*).
85 *nether* 'lower'.

89–102 A parody of Eve's evening hymn in *Paradise Lost*,
   4:641–56 ('Sweet is the breath of morn').
91 *coach-box* The driver's seat.
93 *depending* 'hanging down' (Lat. *dependeo*).
94 *desk* Anglican churches sometimes featured a triple
   arrangement of pulpit, reading desk, and clerk's desk,
   one above the other.

From pangs arthritic that infest the toe 105
Of libertine excess. The SOFA suits
The gouty limb, 'tis true; but gouty limb
Though on a SOFA, may I never feel:
For I have loved the rural walk through lanes
Of grassy swarth close cropt by nibbling sheep, 110
And skirted thick with intertexture firm
Of thorny boughs: have loved the rural walk
O'er hills, through valleys, and by rivers brink,
E'er since a truant boy I pass'd my bounds
T'enjoy a ramble on the banks of Thames. 115
And still remember, nor without regret
Of hours that sorrow since has much endear'd,
How oft, my slice of pocket store consumed,
Still hung'ring pennyless and far from home,
I fed on scarlet hips and stoney haws, 120
Or blushing crabs, or berries that imboss
The bramble, black as jet, or sloes austere.
Hard fare! but such as boyish appetite
Disdains not, nor the palate undepraved
By culinary arts, unsav'ry deems. 125
No SOFA then awaited my return,
Nor SOFA then I needed. Youth repairs
His wasted spirits quickly, by long toil
Incurring short fatigue; and though our years
As life declines, speed rapidly away, 130
And not a year but pilfers as he goes
Some youthful grace that age would gladly keep,
A tooth or auburn lock, and by degrees
Their length and color from the locks they spare;
Th'elastic spring of an unwearied foot 135
That mounts the stile with ease, or leaps the fence,
The play of lungs inhaling and again
Respiring freely the fresh air, that makes
Swift pace or steep ascent no toil to me,
Mine have not pilfer'd yet; nor yet impair'd 140
My relish of fair prospect; scenes that sooth'd
Or charm'd me young, no longer young, I find
Still soothing and of power to charm me still.
And witness, dear companion of my walks,
Whose arm this twentieth winter I perceive 145
Fast lock'd in mine, with pleasure such as love
Confirm'd by long experience of thy worth
And well-tried virtues could alone inspire —
Witness a joy that thou hast doubled long.
Thou know'st my praise of nature most sincere, 150
And that my raptures are not conjured up
To serve occasions of poetic pomp,
But genuine, and art partner of them all.

---

105 *pangs arthritic* Painful inflammation of the joints (Gk.
arthron = 'joint'). Gout was linked to overindulgence,
though it was usually hereditary.
120 *hips ... haws* Fruits of the wild rose and hawthorn.

121 *crabs* Crab-apples.
137 *The* That (*1785*).
144 *companion* Mary Unwin.

How oft upon yon eminence, our pace
Has slacken'd to a pause, and we have borne   155
The ruffling wind scarce conscious that it blew,
While admiration feeding at the eye,
And still unsated, dwelt upon the scene.
Thence with what pleasure have we just discern'd
The distant plough slow moving, and beside   160
His lab'ring team, that swerv'd not from the track,
The sturdy swain diminish'd to a boy!
Here Ouse, slow winding through a level plain
Of spacious meads with cattle sprinkled o'er,
Conducts the eye along his sinuous course   165
Delighted. There, fast rooted in his bank
Stand, never overlook'd, our fav'rite elms
That screen the herdsman's solitary hut;
While far beyond and overthwart the stream
That as with molten glass inlays the vale,   170
The sloping land recedes into the clouds;
Displaying on its varied side, the grace
Of hedge-row beauties numberless, square tow'r,
Tall spire, from which the sound of chearful bells
Just undulates upon the list'ning ear;   175
Groves, heaths, and smoking villages remote.
Scenes must be beautiful which daily view'd
Please daily, and whose novelty survives
Long knowledge and the scrutiny of years.
Praise justly due to those that I describe.   180
    Nor rural sights alone, but rural sounds
Exhilarate the spirit, and restore
The tone of languid Nature. Mighty winds
That sweep the skirt of some far-spreading wood
Of ancient growth, make music not unlike   185
The dash of ocean on his winding shore,
And lull the spirit while they fill the mind,
Unnumber'd branches waving in the blast,
And all their leaves fast flutt'ring, all at once.
Nor less composure waits upon the roar   190
Of distant floods, or on the softer voice
Of neighb'ring fountain, or of rills that slip
Through the cleft rock, and chiming as they fall
Upon loose pebbles, lose themselves at length
In matted grass, that with a livelier green   195
Betrays the secret of their silent course.
Nature inanimate employs sweet sounds,
But animated Nature sweeter still
To sooth and satisfy the human ear.

154 *eminence* A hill on the west side of Olney. The walk
Cowper follows in 154–366 is described in *Cowper,
Illustrated by a Series of Views, in, or near, the Park of
Weston-Underwood* (*CI*), published December 1804; the
plates were sold separately to be bound into editions of
his poems.
163 *Ouse* The Great Ouse, on which Olney stands, runs for
156 miles and enters the Wash below King's Lynn.

173–4 The churches of Clifton Reynes and Olney
respectively.
183 *tone* 'The degree of firmness or tension proper to the
organs or tissues of the body in a strong and healthy
condition' (*OED*). Cf. *Yardley Oak*, 85.

Ten thousand warblers chear the day, and one   200
The live-long night: nor these alone whose notes
Nice-finger'd art must emulate in vain,
But cawing rooks, and kites that swim sublime
In still repeated circles, screaming loud,
The jay, the pie, and ev'n the boding owl   205
That hails the rising moon, have charms for me.
Sounds inharmonious in themselves and harsh,
Yet heard in scenes where peace for ever reigns,
And only there, please highly for their sake.
  Peace to the artist, whose ingenious thought   210
Devised the weather-house, that useful toy!
Fearless of humid air and gathering rains
Forth steps the man, an emblem of myself,
More delicate his tim'rous mate retires.
When Winter soaks the fields, and female feet   215
Too weak to struggle with tenacious clay,
Or ford the rivulets, are best at home,
The task of new discov'ries falls on me.
At such a season and with such a charge
Once went I forth, and found, till then unknown,   220
A cottage, whither oft we since repair:
'Tis perch'd upon the green-hill top, but close
Inviron'd with a ring of branching elms
That overhang the thatch, itself unseen,
Peeps at the vale below; so thick beset   225
With foliage of such dark redundant growth,
I call'd the low-roof'd lodge the *peasant's nest*.
And hidden as it is, and far remote
From such unpleasing sounds as haunt the ear
In village or in town, the bay of curs   230
Incessant, clinking hammers, grinding wheels,
And infants clam'rous whether pleas'd or pain'd,
Oft have I wish'd the peaceful covert mine.
Here, I have said, at least I should possess
The poet's treasure, silence, and indulge   235
The dreams of fancy, tranquil and secure.
Vain thought! the dweller in that still retreat
Dearly obtains the refuge it affords.
Its elevated scite forbids the wretch
To drink sweet waters of the chrystal well;   240
He dips his bowl into the weedy ditch,
And heavy-laden brings his bev'rage home
Far-fetch'd and little worth; nor seldom waits,
Dependent on the baker's punctual call,

200 *one* The nightingale.
202 *Nice* 'precise'. Cf. Milton's distinction between profuse nature and 'nice art', *Paradise Lost*, 4:241–3.
203 *kites* The red kite, once common in England.
205 The jay and magpie both chatter noisily.
211 *weather-house* 'A toy hygroscope [for indicating humidity] in the form of a small house with figures of a man and woman standing in two porches; by the varying torsion of a string the man comes out of his porch in wet weather and the woman out of hers in dry' (*OED*).
221 *cottage* 'This farm house is on a small estate belonging to a Mr Chapman; it was completely obscured by the elms that surround it, only three of which now remain, the rest having been felled, about four or five years since' (*CI*, 33).

To hear his creaking panniers at the door,   245
Angry and sad and his last crust consumed.
So farewel envy of the *peasant's nest*.
If solitude make scant the means of life,
Society for me! thou seeming sweet,
Be still a pleasing object in my view,   250
My visit still, but never mine abode.
   Not distant far, a length of colonade
Invites us. Monument of ancient taste,
Now scorn'd, but worthy of a better fate.
Our fathers knew the value of a screen   255
From sultry suns, and in their shaded walks
And long-protracted bow'rs, enjoy'd at noon
The gloom and coolness of declining day.
We bear our shades about us; self depriv'd
Of other screen, the thin umbrella spread,   260
And range an Indian waste without a tree.
Thanks to Benevolus — he spares me yet
These chesnuts ranged in corresponding lines,
And though himself so polish'd, still reprieves
The obsolete prolixity of shade.   265
   Descending now (but cautious, lest too fast)
A sudden steep, upon a rustic bridge
We pass a gulph in which the willows dip
Their pendent boughs, stooping as if to drink.
Hence ancle deep in moss and flow'ry thyme   270
We mount again, and feel at ev'ry step
Our foot half sunk in hillocks green and soft,
Rais'd by the mole, the miner of the soil.
He not unlike the great ones of mankind,
Disfigures earth, and plotting in the dark   275
Toils much to earn a monumental pile,
That may record the mischiefs he has done.
   The summit gain'd, behold the proud alcove
That crowns it! yet not all its pride secures
The grand retreat from injuries impress'd   280
By rural carvers, who with knives deface
The pannels, leaving an obscure rude name
In characters uncouth, and spelt amiss.
So strong the zeal t'immortalize himself

---

251 *never mine abode* 'The house, since Cowper wrote, has been altered, by removing the thatch, and covering the roof with tiles; and the inconvenience it was subject to, from the want of water, has been obviated by sinking a well' (*CI*, 33).

252 *colonade* 'an avenue between two rows of well-grown chesnuts' (*CI*, 35).

254 *Now scorn'd* Taste in garden design had turned against straight lines, and colonnades of trees were no longer fashionable. In his poem *The English Garden* (1772) William Mason recommended removing 'the long cathedral isle of shade' as a 'cruel task, / Yet needful' (1:320, 332–3).

262 *Benevolus* 'John Courtney Throckmorton, Esq., of

Weston Underwood' (Cowper's note). *spares me yet* By the time Cowper's poem was published the colonnade had been felled.

265 *prolixity* 'excessive length' (Lat. *prolixus* = 'stretched out'), commonly used of a tedious narrative.

267 *sudden steep* 'The descent, through the Colonnade, is aptly described by Cowper, the fall of the ground being extremely precipitant and abrupt' (*CI*, 35).

276 *pile* Both 'heap of money' and 'large building'.

278 *alcove* 'This structure is a sexagon, of a light and graceful form, composed of wood: it was erected about fifty years ago' (*CI*, 37).

282 *rude* Cf. Gray, *Elegy*, 16.

Beats in the breast of man, that ev'n a few 285
Few transient years won from th'abyss abhorr'd
Of blank oblivion, seem a glorious prize,
And even to a clown. Now roves the eye,
And posted on this speculative height
Exults in its command. The sheep-fold here 290
Pours out its fleecy tenants o'er the glebe.
At first, progressive as a stream, they seek
The middle field; but scatter'd by degrees
Each to his choice, soon whiten all the land.
There, from the sun-burnt hay-field homeward creeps 295
The loaded wain, while lighten'd of its charge
The wain that meets it, passes swiftly by,
The boorish driver leaning o'er his team
Vocif'rous, and impatient of delay.
Nor less attractive is the woodland scene 300
Diversified with trees of ev'ry growth
Alike yet various. Here the grey smooth trunks
Of ash or lime, or beech, distinctly shine,
Within the twilight of their distant shades;
There lost behind a rising ground, the wood 305
Seems sunk, and shorten'd to its topmost boughs.
No tree in all the grove but has its charms,
Though each its hue peculiar; paler some,
And of a wannish grey; the willow such
And poplar, that with silver lines his leaf, 310
And ash far-stretching his umbrageous arm.
Of deeper green the elm; and deeper still,
Lord of the woods, the long-surviving oak.
Some glossy-leav'd and shining in the sun,
The maple, and the beech of oily nuts 315
Prolific, and the lime at dewy eve
Diffusing odours: nor unnoted pass
The sycamore, capricious in attire,
Now green, now tawny, and 'ere autumn yet
Have changed the woods, in scarlet honors bright. 320
O'er these, but far beyond, (a spacious map
Of hill and valley interpos'd between)
The Ouse, dividing the well water'd land,
Now glitters in the sun, and now retires,
As bashful, yet impatient to be seen. 325
   Hence the declivity is sharp and short,
And such the re-ascent; between them weeps
A little Naiad her impov'rish'd urn

---

288 *clown* 'ignorant rustic'.

288–325 Cowper composes a 'prospect', a feature of eighteenth-century topographical poetry, here perhaps representing Nature's supreme artistry (cf. 417–21).

289 *speculative* 'suitable for observation'. 'The Alcove, being open in three divisions, presents as many distinct, though not equally extensive, prospects' (*CI*, 38–9). One of these is engraved facing p. 39.

296 *wain* 'haycart'.

302 *Alike yet various* Cf. Pope, *Windsor-Forest*, 16.

311 *umbrageous* 'giving shade'.

324–5 Cf. *Windsor-Forest*, 17–20.

328 *Naiad* Nymph of a river or spring. 'This little Naiad is nothing more than a narrow channel to drain the hollow; and we cannot repress our admiration of the unbounded powers of figurative poetry, which can raise the minutest trifle to the appearance of dignity and consequence' (*CI*, 39).

All summer long, which winter fills again.
The folded gates would bar my progress now,   330
But that the Lord of this inclosed demesne,
Communicative of the good he owns,
Admits me to a share: the guiltless eye
Commits no wrong, nor wastes what it enjoys.
Refreshing change! where now the blazing sun?   335
By short transition we have lost his glare
And stepp'd at once into a cooler clime.
Ye fallen avenues! once more I mourn
Your fate unmerited, once more rejoice
That yet a remnant of your race survives.   340
How airy and how light the graceful arch,
Yet awful as the consecrated roof
Re-echoing pious anthems! while beneath
The chequer'd earth seems restless as a flood
Brush'd by the wind. So sportive is the light   345
Shot through the boughs, it dances as they dance,
Shadow and sunshine intermingling quick,
And darkning and enlightning, as the leaves
Play wanton, ev'ry moment, ev'ry spot.
　　And now with nerves new-brac'd and spirits chear'd   350
We tread the wilderness, whose well-roll'd walks
With curvature of slow and easy sweep,
Deception innocent — give ample space
To narrow bounds. The grove receives us next;
Between the upright shafts of whose tall elms   355
We may discern the thresher at his task.
Thump after thump, resounds the constant flail,
That seems to swing uncertain, and yet falls
Full on the destin'd ear. Wide flies the chaff,
The rustling straw sends up a frequent mist   360
Of atoms sparkling in the noon-day beam.
Come hither, ye that press your beds of down
And sleep not: see him sweating o'er his bread
Before he eats it. — 'Tis the primal curse,
But soften'd into mercy; made the pledge   365
Of chearful days, and nights without a groan.
　　By ceaseless action, all that is, subsists.
Constant rotation of th'unwearied wheel
That nature rides upon, maintains her health,

333 *Admits me* 'the poet … was favoured by Sir John Throckmorton with a key, that he might, at all times, obtain ready access' (*CI*, 40).

338–9 Cowper alludes to his poem, *The Poplar Field* (*Gentleman's Magazine*, January 1785): 'The poplars are fell'd, and adieu to the shade / And the whispering sound of the cool colonnade. / The winds play no longer, and sing in their leaves, / Nor the Ouse in its bosom their image receives'.

351 *wilderness* A wooded garden with serpentine paths. It still survives at Weston Underwood (as part of a zoo),

with the memorial urns which Cowper inscribed to Throckmorton's dogs.

354 *grove* 'A deeply-shaded, winding path … leads through the Wilderness, and brings us to the Grove, whence we pass a handsome gate to the village of Weston' (*CI*, 43).

357–61 Cf. the less picturesque description in Duck, *The Thresher's Labour*, 31–63.

359 *ear* Ear of corn.

363–4 God's imposition of labour on Adam: 'In the sweat of thy face shalt thou eat bread' (Genesis, 3:19).

367 Cf. Dyer, *The Fleece*, 3:24.

Her beauty, her fertility. She dreads   370
An instant's pause, and lives but while she moves.
Its own revolvency upholds the world.
Winds from all quarters agitate the air,
And fit the limpid element for use,
Else noxious: oceans, rivers, lakes, and streams   375
All feel the fresh'ning impulse, and are cleansed
By restless undulation; ev'n the oak
Thrives by the rude concussion of the storm;
He seems indeed indignant, and to feel
Th'impression of the blast with proud disdain,   380
Frowning as if in his unconscious arm
He held the thunder. But the monarch owes
His firm stability to what he scorns,
More fixt below, the more disturb'd above.
The law by which all creatures else are bound,   385
Binds man the lord of all. Himself derives
No mean advantage from a kindred cause,
From strenuous toil his hours of sweetest ease.
The sedentary stretch their lazy length
When custom bids, but no refreshment find,   390
For none they need: the languid eye, the cheek
Deserted of its bloom, the flaccid, shrunk
And wither'd muscle, and the vapid soul,
Reproach their owner with that love of rest
To which he forfeits ev'n the rest he loves.   395
Not such th'alert and active. Measure life
By its true worth, the comforts it affords,
And theirs alone seems worthy of the name.
Good health, and its associate in the most,
Good temper; spirits prompt to undertake,   400
And not soon spent, though in an arduous task;
The pow'rs of fancy and strong thought are theirs;
Ev'n age itself seems privileged in them
With clear exemption from its own defects.
A sparkling eye beneath a wrinkled front   405
The vet'ran shows, and gracing a grey beard
With youthful smiles, descends toward the grave
Sprightly, and old almost without decay.
    Like a coy maiden, ease, when courted most,
Farthest retires — an idol, at whose shrine   410
Who oft'nest sacrifice are favor'd least.
The love of Nature, and the scenes she draws
Is Nature's dictate. Strange! there should be found
Who self-imprison'd in their proud saloons,

372 *revolvency* 'capacity for revolution'. This is the earliest example recorded by *OED*.

374 *limpid* 'transparent'.

382–4 Cf. 'The oak clings to the rock, and just as far as it reaches loftily to the airs above, it stretches its roots down to the underworld ... so the hero's will remained steadfast' (*Aeneid*, 4:445–9). The oak had come to symbolize British nationhood: Sambrook (p. 70) compares *Rule, Britannia* (1740), 14–15: 'the loud blast that tears the Skies / Serves but to root thy native oak'. Cf. Dyer, *The Fleece*, 3:350–2.

385 *The law* Nature.

405 *front* 'forehead'.

Renounce the odors of the open field   415
For the unscented fictions of the loom.
Who satisfied with only pencil'd scenes,
Prefer to the performance of a God
Th'inferior wonders of an artist's hand.
Lovely indeed the mimic works of art,   420
But Nature's works far lovelier. I admire —
None more admires the painter's magic skill,
Who shews me that which I shall never see,
Conveys a distant country into mine,
And throws Italian light on English walls.   425
But imitative strokes can do no more
Than please the eye, sweet Nature ev'ry sense.
The air salubrious of her lofty hills,
The chearing fragrance of her dewy vales
And music of her woods — no works of man   430
May rival these; these all bespeak a power
Peculiar, and exclusively her own.
Beneath the open sky she spreads the feast;
'Tis free to all — 'tis ev'ry day renew'd,
Who scorns it, starves deservedly at home.   435
He does not scorn it, who imprison'd long
In some unwholesome dungeon, and a prey
To sallow sickness, which the vapors dank
And clammy of his dark abode have bred,
Escapes at last to liberty and light.   440
His cheek recovers soon its healthful hue,
His eye relumines its extinguish'd fires,
He walks, he leaps, he runs — is wing'd with joy,
And riots in the sweets of ev'ry breeze.
He does not scorn it, who has long endur'd   445
A fever's agonies, and fed on drugs.
Nor yet the mariner, his blood inflamed
With acrid salts; his very heart athirst
To gaze at Nature in her green array.
Upon the ship's tall side he stands, possess'd   450
With visions prompted by intense desire;
Fair fields appear below, such as he left
Far distant, such as he would die to find —
He seeks them headlong, and is seen no more.
     The spleen is seldom felt where Flora reigns;   455
The low'ring eye, the petulance, the frown,
And sullen sadness that o'ershade, distort,
And mar the face of beauty, when no cause
For such immeasurable woe appears,
These Flora banishes, and gives the fair   460
Sweet smiles and bloom less transient than her own.
It is the constant revolution stale

---

417 *pencil'd* 'painted'.
420–1 Cf. Joseph Warton, *The Enthusiast*, 47–59.
425 *Italian light* Many English painters were visiting Italy
     at this period, and Italian landscapes were fashionable.
447–54 'A disease incident to sailors within the tropics,

characterized by delirium in which the patient, it is
said, fancies the sea to be green fields, and desires to
leap into it' (*OED*, s.n. 'Calenture').
455 *spleen* See headnote to Finch, *The Spleen*. *Flora* Roman
     goddess of flowers and spring.

And tasteless, of the same repeated joys,
That palls and satiates, and makes languid life
A pedlar's pack, that bows the bearer down. 465
Health suffers, and the spirits ebb; the heart
Recoils from its own choice — at the full feast
Is famish'd — finds no music in the song,
No smartness in the jest, and wonders why.
Yet thousands still desire to journey on, 470
Though halt and weary of the path they tread.
The paralitic who can hold her cards
But cannot play them, borrows a friend's hand
To deal and shuffle, to divide and sort
Her mingled suits and sequences, and sits 475
Spectatress both and spectacle, a sad
And silent cypher, while her proxy plays.
Others are dragg'd into the crowded room
Between supporters; and once seated, sit
Through downright inability to rise, 480
'Till the stout bearers lift the corpse again.
These speak a loud memento. Yet ev'n these
Themselves love life, and cling to it, as he
That overhangs a torrent, to a twig.
They love it, and yet loath it; fear to die, 485
Yet scorn the purposes for which they live.
Then wherefore not renounce them? No — the dread,
The slavish dread of solitude, that breeds
Reflection and remorse, the fear of shame,
And their invet'rate habits, all forbid. 490
    Whom call we gay? That honor has been long
The boast of mere pretenders to the name.
The innocent are gay — the lark is gay
That dries his feathers saturate with dew
Beneath the rosy cloud, while yet the beams 495
Of day-spring overshoot his humble nest.
The peasant too, a witness of his song,
Himself a songster, is as gay as he.
But save me from the gaiety of those
Whose head-aches nail them to a noon-day bed; 500
And save me too from theirs whose haggard eyes
Flash desperation, and betray their pangs
For property stripp'd off by cruel chance;
From gaiety that fills the bones with pain,
The mouth with blasphemy, the heart with woe. 505
    The earth was made so various, that the mind
Of desultory man, studious of change,
And pleas'd with novelty, might be indulged.
Prospects however lovely may be seen
'Till half their beauties fade; the weary sight, 510
Too well acquainted with their smiles, slides off
Fastidious, seeking less familiar scenes.
Then snug inclosures in the shelter'd vale,
Where frequent hedges intercept the eye,

471 *halt* 'lame'.
477 *cypher* 'nonentity', 'mere token'.

482 *memento* 'memento mori' (reminder of mortality).
507 *desultory* 'wavering'.

Delight us, happy to renounce a while,   515
Not senseless of its charms, what still we love,
That such short absence may endear it more.
Then forests, or the savage rock may please,
That hides the sea-mew in his hollow clefts
Above the reach of man: his hoary head   520
Conspicuous many a league, the mariner
Bound homeward, and in hope already there,
Greets with three cheers exulting. At his waist
A girdle of half-wither'd shrubs he shows,
And at his feet the baffled billows die.   525
The common overgrown with fern, and rough
With prickly goss, that shapeless and deform
And dang'rous to the touch, has yet its bloom
And decks itself with ornaments of gold,
Yields no unpleasing ramble; there the turf   530
Smells fresh, and rich in odorif'rous herbs
And fungous fruits of earth, regales the sense
With luxury of unexpected sweets.
        There often wanders one, whom better days
Saw better clad, in cloak of sattin trimm'd   535
With lace, and hat with splendid ribband bound.
A serving maid was she, and fell in love
With one who left her, went to sea and died.
Her fancy followed him through foaming waves
To distant shores, and she would sit and weep   540
At what a sailor suffers; fancy too
Delusive most where warmest wishes are,
Would oft anticipate his glad return,
And dream of transports she was not to know.
She heard the doleful tidings of his death,   545
And never smil'd again. And now she roams
The dreary waste; there spends the livelong day,
And there, unless when charity forbids,
The livelong night. A tatter'd apron hides,
Worn as a cloak, and hardly hides a gown   550
More tatter'd still; and both but ill conceal
A bosom heaved with never-ceasing sighs.
She begs an idle pin of all she meets,
And hoards them in her sleeve; but needful food,
Though press'd with hunger oft, or comelier cloaths,   555
Though pinch'd with cold, asks never. — Kate is craz'd.
        I see a column of slow-rising smoke
O'ertop the lofty wood that skirts the wild.
A vagabond and useless tribe there eat

---

517 Cf. 'short retirement urges sweet return' (*Paradise Lost*, 9:250).

519 *sea-mew* 'seagull'.

520 *hoary head* The chalk cliffs ('hoary' = greyish white).

527 *goss* 'gorse'.

534–56 Thanking Joseph Hill for an engraved print of Kate, Cowper wrote: 'I cannot say that poor Kate resembles much the Original, who was neither so young nor so handsome' (24 May 1788).

559 *useless tribe* Ever since the 1530 statute banishing them from England gipsies had been associated with casual theft, pickpocketing and deception (through their fortune-telling). Described in Blackstone's *Commentaries* (the standard legal textbook) as 'wandering impostors and jugglers', they became a topic of public debate when laws against them were repealed in 1783.

Their miserable meal. A kettle slung 560
Between two poles upon a stick transverse,
Receives the morsel; flesh obscene of dog,
Or vermin, or at best, of cock purloin'd
From his accustom'd perch. Hard-faring race!
They pick their fuel out of ev'ry hedge, 565
Which kindled with dry leaves, just saves unquench'd
The spark of life. The sportive wind blows wide
Their flutt'ring rags, and shows a tawny skin,
The vellum of the pedigree they claim.
Great skill have they in palmistry, and more 570
To conjure clean away the gold they touch,
Conveying worthless dross into its place.
Loud when they beg, dumb only when they steal.
Strange! that a creature rational, and cast
In human mould, should brutalize by choice 575
His nature, and though capable of arts
By which the world might profit and himself,
Self-banish'd from society, prefer
Such squalid sloth to honorable toil.
Yet even these, though feigning sickness oft 580
They swathe the forehead, drag the limping limb
And vex their flesh with artificial sores,
Can change their whine into a mirthful note
When safe occasion offers, and with dance
And music of the bladder and the bag 585
Beguile their woes and make the woods resound.
Such health and gaiety of heart enjoy
The houseless rovers of the sylvan world;
And breathing wholesome air, and wand'ring much,
Need other physic none to heal th'effects 590
Of loathsome diet, penury, and cold.
    Blest he, though undistinguish'd from the crowd
By wealth or dignity, who dwells secure
Where man, by nature fierce, has laid aside
His fierceness, having learnt, though slow to learn, 595
The manners and the arts of civil life.
His wants, indeed, are many; but supply
Is obvious; placed within the easy reach
Of temp'rate wishes and industrious hands.
Here virtue thrives as in her proper soil; 600
Not rude and surly, and beset with thorns,
And terrible to sight, as when she springs,
(If e'er she spring spontaneous) in remote
And barb'rous climes, where violence prevails,
And strength is lord of all; but gentle, kind, 605
By culture tam'd, by liberty refresh'd,
And all her fruits by radiant truth matur'd.
War and the chace engross the savage whole.
War follow'd for revenge, or to supplant

---

569 *vellum* Fine calfskin parchment used for important documents, including pedigrees. Gipsies traced theirs to Egypt, hence the name.

588 *sylvan* 'woodland'.

608 *War and the chace* Cf. Pope, *Windsor-Forest*, 43–84.

The envied tenants of some happier spot,   610
The chace for sustenance, precarious trust!
His hard condition with severe constraint
Binds all his faculties, forbids all growth
Of wisdom, proves a school in which he learns
Sly circumvention, unrelenting hate,   615
Mean self-attachment, and scarce aught beside.
Thus fare the shiv'ring natives of the north,
And thus the rangers of the western world
Where it advances far into the deep,
Towards th'Antarctic. Ev'n the favor'd isles   620
So lately found, although the constant sun
Cheer all their seasons with a grateful smile,
Can boast but little virtue; and inert
Through plenty, lose in morals, what they gain
In manners, victims of luxurious ease.   625
These therefore I can pity, placed remote
From all that science traces, art invents,
Or inspiration teaches; and inclosed
In boundless oceans never to be pass'd
By navigators uninformed as they,   630
Or plough'd perhaps by British bark again.
But far beyond the rest, and with most cause
Thee, gentle savage! whom no love of thee
Or thine, but curiosity perhaps,
Or else vain glory, prompted us to draw   635
Forth from thy native bow'rs, to show thee here
With what superior skill we can abuse
The gifts of providence, and squander life.
The dream is past. And thou hast found again
Thy cocoas and bananas, palms and yams,   640
And homestall thatch'd with leaves. But hast thou found
Their former charms? And having seen our state,
Our palaces, our ladies, and our pomp
Of equipage, our gardens, and our sports,
And heard our music; are thy simple friends,   645
Thy simple fare, and all thy plain delights
As dear to thee as once? And have thy joys
Lost nothing by comparison with ours?
Rude as thou art (for we return'd thee rude

---

615 *circumvention* 'deviousness' (Lat. *circumvenio* = 'go round').

620 *favor'd isles* The widely scattered islands of Polynesia had been explored by James Cook on his three voyages into the Pacific, 1768–79. They included the Society Islands (Tahiti, Raiatea, etc.), the Friendly Islands (Tonga), the Cook Islands, and Hawaii ('found' by Cook in 1778, and the place where he was murdered the following year).

627 *science* 'knowledge'.

633 *gentle savage* Omai, a native of Raiatea brought to

England in 1774 and fêted by London society. He was received by the King, was painted by Sir Joshua Reynolds, played chess, impressed Samuel Johnson, and dined in the best company. In 1776 he was taken home on Cook's last voyage.

641 *homestall* 'homestead'.

642 *state* 'ceremonial'.

644 *equipage* Coach and horses, with attendants. *gardens* The public pleasure gardens of Vauxhall, Ranelagh, etc. Cowper is returning to his opening theme of the progress from primitive simplicity to sophistication.

And ignorant, except of outward show) 650
I cannot think thee yet so dull of heart
And spiritless, as never to regret
Sweets tasted here, and left as soon as known.
Methinks I see thee straying on the beach,
And asking of the surge that bathes thy foot 655
If ever it has wash'd our distant shore.
I see thee weep, and thine are honest tears,
A patriot's for his country. Thou art sad
At thought of her forlorn and abject state,
From which no power of thine can raise her up. 660
Thus fancy paints thee, and though apt to err,
Perhaps errs little, when she paints thee thus.
She tells me too that duely ev'ry morn
Thou climb'st the mountain top, with eager eye
Exploring far and wide the wat'ry waste 665
For sight of ship from England. Ev'ry speck
Seen in the dim horizon, turns thee pale
With conflict of contending hopes and fears.
But comes at last the dull and dusky eve,
And sends thee to thy cabbin, well-prepar'd 670
To dream all night of what the day denied.
Alas! expect it not. We found no bait
To tempt us in thy country. Doing good,
Disinterested good, is not our trade.
We travel far 'tis true, but not for nought; 675
And must be brib'd to compass earth again
By other hopes and richer fruits than yours.
    But though true worth and virtue, in the mild
And genial soil of cultivated life
Thrive most, and may perhaps thrive only there, 680
Yet not in cities oft. In proud and gay
And gain devoted cities; thither flow,
As to a common and most noisome sewer,
The dregs and fæculence of ev'ry land.
In cities foul example on most minds 685
Begets its likeness. Rank abundance breeds
In gross and pamper'd cities sloth and lust,
And wantonness and gluttonous excess.
In cities, vice is hidden with most ease,
Or seen with least reproach; and virtue taught 690
By frequent lapse, can hope no triumph there
Beyond th'atchievement of successful flight.
I do confess them nurs'ries of the arts,
In which they flourish most. Where in the beams
Of warm encouragement, and in the eye 695
Of public note they reach their perfect size.
Such London is, by taste and wealth proclaim'd
The fairest capital of all the world,
By riot and incontinence the worst.

658 *his country* England. The irony is strong here.
674 *Disinterested* 'without selfish motives'.
679 *genial* 'productive'.
684 *fæculence* 'filth'.
686 *Rank* 'offensive'.
691 *lapse* In the stronger sense of 'fall' (Lat. *lapsus*).

There, touch'd by Reynolds, a dull blank becomes   700
A lucid mirror, in which nature sees
All her reflected features. Bacon there
Gives more than female beauty to a stone,
And Chatham's eloquence to marble lips.
Nor does the chissel occupy alone   705
The pow'rs of sculpture, but the style as much;
Each province of her art her equal care.
With nice incision of her guided steel
She ploughs a brazen field, and clothes a soil
So sterile with what charms soe'er she will,   710
The richest scen'ry and the loveliest forms.
Where finds philosophy her eagle eye
With which she gazes at yon burning disk
Undazzled, and detects and counts his spots?
In London; where her implements exact   715
With which she calculates computes and scans
All distance, motion, magnitude, and now
Measures an atom, and now girds a world?
In London; where has commerce such a mart,
So rich, so throng'd, so drain'd, and so supplied   720
As London, opulent, enlarged, and still
Increasing London? Babylon of old
Not more the glory of the earth, than she
A more accomplish'd world's chief glory now.
    She has her praise. Now mark a spot or two   725
That so much beauty would do well to purge;
And show this queen of cities, that so fair
May yet be foul, so witty, yet not wise.
It is not seemly, nor of good report
That she is slack in discipline. More prompt   730
T'avenge than to prevent the breach of law.
That she is rigid in denouncing death
On petty robbers, and indulges life
And liberty, and oft-times honor too
To peculators of the public gold.   735
That thieves at home must hang; but he that puts
Into his overgorged and bloated purse
The wealth of Indian provinces, escapes.
Nor is it well, nor can it come to good,

---

700 Sir Joshua Reynolds (1723–92), President of the Royal
    Academy and the most eminent portrait-painter of his
    day; in 1779 Cowper had addressed a poem to him.
702 John Bacon, RA (1740–99), sculptor of public
    monuments. He had recently sent Cowper an engraving
    of his memorial to William Pitt, Earl of Chatham
    (1708–78), Prime Minister and supreme orator.
706 *style* The stylus of the engraver.
709 *brazen field* The copper plate.
712 *philosophy* Scientific inquiry.
719 *mart* 'trading-place'.
722 *Babylon* The wealthy civilization destroyed by God
    after Belshazzar's blasphemy (Daniel, 5), a symbol of
    corrupt luxury.

730–1 London's lack of discipline and effective crime
    prevention had been starkly illustrated by the Gordon
    Riots of June 1780, when mobs ruled the streets (in
    Cowper's words 'a Metropolis in flames, and a Nation
    in Ruins').
735 *peculators* 'embezzlers'.
736–8 By 1785 England had more than 150 capital offences,
    including theft. Cowper contrasts the fate of petty
    criminals with the dubious fortunes acquired by
    administrators of British India such as Lord Clive and
    Sir Thomas Rumbold. The failure of a parliamentary
    bill against Rumbold in 1783 caused a scandal (see
    Baird and Ryskamp, 2:348–9).

That through profane and infidel contempt   740
Of holy writ, she has presum'd t'annul
And abrogate, as roundly as she may,
The total ordonance and will of God;
Advancing fashion to the post of truth,
And cent'ring all authority in modes   745
And customs of her own, till sabbath rites
Have dwindled into unrespected forms,
And knees and hassocks are well-nigh divorc'd.
   God made the country, and man made the town.
What wonder then, that health and virtue, gifts   750
That can alone make sweet the bitter draught
That life holds out to all, should most abound
And least be threatened in the fields and groves?
Possess ye therefore, ye who borne about
In chariots and sedans, know no fatigue   755
But that of idleness, and taste no scenes
But such as art contrives, possess ye still
Your element; there only, ye can shine,
There only minds like yours can do no harm.
Our groves were planted to console at noon   760
The pensive wand'rer in their shades. At eve
The moon-beam sliding softly in between
The sleeping leaves, is all the light they wish,
Birds warbling all the music. We can spare
The splendor of your lamps, they but eclipse   765
Our softer satellite. Your songs confound
Our more harmonious notes. The thrush departs
Scared, and th'offended nightingale is mute.
There is a public mischief in your mirth,
It plagues your country. Folly such as your's   770
Graced with a sword, and worthier of a fan,
Has made, which enemies could ne'er have done,
Our arch of empire, stedfast but for you,
A mutilated structure, soon to fall.

743 *ordonance* 'systematic arrangement'.
748 *hassocks* Firm prayer-cushions.
754–6 Cf. Robinson, *The Birth-day*.

766 *satellite* The moon.
774 *mutilated* The independence of the American colonies
   had been recognized at the Peace of Versailles, 1783.

Yardley Oak

Line 3 indicates a date of composition during 1791 (later than February, if Cowper had indeed completed exactly sixty winters); but the poem's echoing of Erasmus Darwin's *Economy of Vegetation*, which Cowper was reading in June 1792, makes the latter date more likely (Richard N. Ringler, 'The Genesis of Cowper's "Yardley Oak"', *ELN*, 5 (1967), pp. 27–32). The text given here is transcribed from the unique autograph MS in the Cowper and Newton Museum, Olney (for details see Baird and Ryskamp, 3:314). It was discovered by William Hayley, who printed it in *The Life, and Posthumous Writings, of William Cowper, Esqr* (1803–4), 3:409–16.

   The poet had two favourite oak trees which were

the destinations of his walks, and there has been much confusion in distinguishing them. Cowper took John Johnson to see the Yardley Chase oak (the poet himself measured it as 22 feet, 6 inches in girth), and this according to Johnson was 'perfectly sound'; in the nineteenth century it became known as 'Cowper's Oak' and was standing, still sound and clearly not hollow, in 1937 (see the photograph prefixed to volume four of *The Victoria History of the County of Northampton*). The older second tree, at Yardley Lodge (28 feet, 5 inches), was reported by Johnson to be 'quite in decay – a pollard, and almost hollow. I took an excrescence from it in the year 1791, and if I mistake not, Cowper told me it was said to have been an Oak in the time of the Conqueror' (Johnson–Hayley, 6 January 1804). This battered survivor, the subject of Cowper's poem, was engraved for the frontispiece to Hayley's *Supplementary Pages to the Life of Cowper* (1806) from a painting 'drawn from nature' in December 1804; it clearly shows the stout, hollow and shattered tree of Cowper's poem (110–12).

The text would seem to represent the beginnings of a longer meditative poem in which Cowper, seated on the roots of the oak (139–43), plays the oracle. Whether it would have extended into a personal or a historical meditation, or into some mix of private and public, is impossible to say; the excised passage (144–66) and the lines that follow (167–84) suggest these two possible emphases. In describing his heroic survivor Cowper looks to Milton for an appropriately venerable Latinate vocabulary and a sometimes gnarled syntax – the poet is throughout conscious of old linguistic roots. Despite its worn-out shell the tree represents a deep commitment and endurance which outbrave the onset of rottenness and corruption.

Survivor sole, and hardly such, of all
That once lived here thy brethren, at my birth
(Since which I number threescore winters past)
A shatter'd vetran, hollow-trunk'd perhaps
As now, and with excoriate forks deform,   5
Relicts of Ages! Could a mind imbued
With truth from heav'n created thing adore,
I might with rev'rence kneel and worship Thee.
It seems Idolatry with some excuse
When our forefather Druids in their oaks   10
Imagin'd sanctity. The Conscience yet
Unpurified by an authentic act
Of amnesty, the meed of blood divine,
Loved not the light, but gloomy into gloom
Of thickest shades, like Adam after taste   15
Of fruit proscribed, as to a refuge, fled.
　　　Thou wast a bawble once; a cup and ball
Which babes might play with; and the thievish jay
Seeking her food, with ease might have purloin'd
The auburn nut that held thee, swallowing down   20
Thy yet close-folded latitude of boughs
And all thine embryo vastness, at a gulp.
But fate thy growth decreed. Autumnal rains
Beneath thy parent tree mellowd the soil
Design'd thy cradle, and a skipping deer   25
With pointed hoof dibbling the glebe, prepared
The soft receptacle in which secure
Thy rudiments should sleep the Winter through.
So Fancy dreams. Disprove it if ye can

5 *excoriate* 'stripped of bark' (Lat. *excoriatus*); *deform* 'misshapen'.
6 *Relicts* 'remnants' (what has been left behind: Lat. *relictus*).
10 *Druids* Priests of the old British religion in Roman times who venerated the oak groves in which they worshipped. Cowper draws a contrast with the reward ('meed') of Christian forgiveness through Jesus's crucifixion ('act of amnesty').
16 *proscribed* 'forbidden'. In *Paradise Lost* Adam cries: 'O might I here / In solitude live savage, in some glade /

Obscured, where highest woods impenetrable / … spread their umbrage broad' (9:1084–7).
17 *bawble* 'mere trifle'; *cup and ball* 'A toy consisting of a cup at the end of a stem to which a ball is attached by a string, the object being to toss the ball and catch it in the cup' (*OED*).
21–2 Cf. Thomson, *Spring*, 99–101.
26 *dibbling the glebe* 'making holes in the soil'.
28 *rudiments* 'parts which are the foundation of later growth' (*OED*).

Ye Reas'ners broad awake, whose busy searce   30
Of argument, employed too oft amiss,
Sifts half the pleasures of short life away.
Thou fell'st mature, and in the loamy clod
Swelling, with vegetative force instinct
Didst burst thine egg, as theirs the fabled Twins   35
Now stars, two lobes protruding paired exact.
A leaf succeeded, and another leaf,
And all the elements thy puney growth
Fost'ring propitious, thou becam'st a twig.
Who lived when thou wast such? Oh could'st thou speak   40
As in Dodona once thy kindred trees
Oracular, I would not curious ask
The Future, best unknown, but at thy mouth
Inquisitive, the less ambiguous Past.
By thee I might correct, erroneous oft,   45
The Clock of History, facts and events
Timing more punctual, unrecorded facts
Recov'ring, and mis-stated setting right.
Desp'rate attempt till Trees shall speak again!
　　Time made thee what thou wast, King of the woods.   50
And Time hath made thee what thou art, a cave
For owls to roost in. Once thy spreading boughs
O'erhung the champain, and the num'rous flock
That grazed it stood beneath that ample cope
Uncrowded, yet safe-shelterd from the storm.   55
No flock frequents thee now; thou hast outlived
Thy popularity, and art become
(Unless verse rescue thee awhile) a thing
Forgotten as the foliage of thy youth.
　　While thus through all the stages thou hast push'd   60
Of tree-ship, first a seedling hid in grass,
Then twig, then saplin, and as century rolled
Slow after century, a giant bulk
Of girth enormous with moss-cushion'd root
Upheav'd above the soil, and sides imboss'd   65
With prominent wens globose, till at the last
The rottenness which Time is charged to inflict
On other Mighty Ones found also Thee —
What exhibitions various hath the world
Witness'd of mutability in all   70
That we account most durable below!
　　Change is the diet on which all subsist
Created changeable, and Change at last
Destroys them. Skies uncertain, now the heat
Transmitting cloudless, and the solar beam   75
Now quenching in a boundless sea of clouds,
Calm and alternate storm, moisture and drought

30 *searce* 'sieve'.
34 *instinct* 'impelled', 'animated'.
35 *fabled Twins* Castor and Pollux, the twin brothers of
　Helen of Troy, were born to Leda in a single egg; they
　became identified with the constellation Gemini.

41 *Dodona* A sanctuary of Zeus in Ancient Greece where
　prophecies came from a sacred oak.
53 *champain* 'level and open landscape'.
54 *cope* 'covering', also a priestly vestment.
66 *wens globose* 'globe-like swellings'.

Invigorate by turns the springs of life
In all that live, plant, animal, and man,
And in conclusion mar them. Natures threads,   80
Fine, passing thought, ev'n in her coarsest works,
Delight in agitation, yet sustain
The force that agitates not unimpaired,
But worn by frequent impulse, to the cause
Of their best tone their dissolution owe.   85
  Thought cannot spend itself comparing still
The Great and Little of thy lot, thy growth
From almost nullity into a state
Of matchless grandeur, and declension thence
Slow into such magnificent decay.   90
Time was, when settling on thy leaf a fly
Could shake thee to the root, and time has been
When tempests could not. At thy firmest age
Thou hadst within thy bole solid contents
That might have ribb'd the sides or plank'd the deck   95
Of some flagg'd Admiral, and tortuous arms,
The shipwrights' darling treasure, didst present
To the four quarter'd winds, robust and bold,
Warp'd into tough knee-timber, many a load.
But the axe spared thee; in those thriftier days   100
Oaks fell not, hewn by thousands, to supply
The bottomless demands of contest waged
For senatorial honours. Thus to Time
The task was left to whittle thee away
With his sly scythe, whose ever-nibbling edge   105
Noiseless, an atom and an atom more
Disjoining from the rest, has unobserved
Atchieved a labour, which had far and wide,
(By man performd) made all the forest ring.
  Embowell'd now, and of thy antient self   110
Possessing nought but the scoop'd rind that seems
An huge throat calling to the clouds for drink
Which it would give in riv'lets to thy root,
Thou temptest none, but rather much forbidd'st
The fellers toil, which thou could'st ill requite.   115
Yet is thy root sincere, sound as the rock,
A quarry of stout spurs and knotted fangs
Which crook'd into a thousand whimsies, clasp
The stubborn soil, and hold thee still erect.
So stands a Kingdom whose foundations yet   120
Fail not, in virtue and in wisdom lay'd,
Though all the superstructure by the tooth

---

85 *tone* Cf. *The Task*, 1:183 and note.

86 *spend* 'exhaust'.

94 *bole* 'trunk'.

96 *Admiral* 'flagship'. Sambrook (p. 59) notes that 'the hull of an average 74–gun warship consumed the equivalent of sixty acres of century-old oak'.

99 *knee-timber* 'Knee-timber is found in the crooked arms of oak which by reason of their distortion are easily

adjusted to the angle formed where the deck and the ship-sides meet' (Cowper's MS note).

100 *thriftier* 'less wasteful'.

101–3 'Perhaps alluding to the Earl of Northampton selling timber in Yardley Chase in order to meet the expenses of a Parliamentary election' (Sambrook, p. 310).

115 *requite* 'reward'.

116 *sincere* 'sound', 'uncorrupted' (Lat. *sincerus*).

Pulverized of venality, a shell
Stands now, and semblance only of itself.
    Thine arms have left thee. Winds have rent them off   125
Long since, and rovers of the forest wild
With bow and shaft, have burnt them. Some have left
A splinterd stump bleach'd to a snowy white,
And some memorial none where once they grew.
Yet Life still lingers in thee, and puts forth   130
Proof not contemptible of what she can
Even where Death predominates. The Spring
Thee finds not less alive to her sweet force
Than yonder upstarts of the neighbour wood
So much thy juniors, who their birth received   135
Half a millennium since the date of thine.
    But since, although well-qualified by age
To teach, no spirit dwells in thee, nor voice
May be expected from thee, seated here
On thy distorted root, with hearers none   140
Or prompter save the scene, I will perform
Myself, the oracle, and will discourse
In my own ear such matter as I may.
    Thou, like myself, hast stage by stage attain'd
Life's wintry bourn; thou, after many years,   145
I after few; but few or many prove
A span in retrospect; for I can touch
With my least fingers' end my own decease
And with extended thumb my natal hour,
And hadst thou also skill in measurement   150
As I, the Past would seem as short to thee.
Evil and few — said Jacob — at an age
Thrice mine, and few and evil, I may think,
The Prediluvian race, whose buxom youth
Endured two centuries, accounted theirs.   155
'Short-lived as foliage is the race of man.'
'The wind shakes down the leaves, the budding grove'
'Soon teems with others, and in spring they grow.'
'So pass mankind. One generation meets'
'Its destin'd period, and a new succeeds.'   160
Such was the tender but undue complaint
Of the Maeonian in old time; for who
Would drawl out centuries in tedious strife,
Severe with mental and corporeal ill,
And would not rather chuse a shorter race   165
To glory, a few decads here below?
    One man alone, the Father of us all,

123 *Pulverized* 'ground to dust'; *venality* 'corruption'.
144–66 These lines are crossed out in the MS.
145 *bourn* 'destination'.
147 *span* The span of the hand: 'thou hast made my days as
    it were a span long' (Book of Common Prayer).
152 'And Jacob said unto Pharaoh, The days of the years of
    my pilgrimage are an hundred and thirty years: few and
    evil have the days of the years of my life been' (Genesis,
    47:9).

154 *Prediluvian* 'before the Flood'.
156–60 'The lines mark'd with inverted commas are
    borrowed from my own Translation of Homer Iliad 6.
    Line 175' (Cowper's MS note).
160 *period* 'end'.
162 *Maeonian* Homer.
167 *One man* Adam.

Drew not his life from woman; never gazed
With mute unconsciousness of what he saw
On all around him; learn'd not by degrees,   170
Nor owed articulation to his ear;
But moulded by his Maker into Man
At once, upstood intelligent, survey'd
All creatures, with precision understood
Their purport, uses, properties, assignd   175
To each his name significant, and, fill'd
With Love and Wisdom, render'd back to heav'n
In praise harmonious the first air he drew.
He was excused the penalties of dull
Minority; no tutour charged his hand   180
With this thought-tracing quill, or task'd his mind
With problems; History, not wanted yet
Lean'd on her elbow, watching Time, whose course
Eventful should supply her with a theme;

171 *articulation* 'power of speech'.
176 *his name* 'Whatsoever Adam called every living
creature, that was the name thereof' (Genesis, 2:19).

180 *charged* 'entrusted', 'burdened'.
181 *quill* 'quill pen'.

On the Ice-islands seen floating in the Germanic Ocean

Cowper began a Latin poem, *Montes Glaciales*, on 11 March 1799, and he completed this English translation of it on the 18th. John Johnson recalled that it was prompted by a newspaper report 'which he had heard me read to him, some weeks before, without at the time taking any notice of it' (Robert E. Spiller, 'A New Biographical Source for William Cowper', *PMLA*, 42 (1927), pp. 946–62; p. 960). The report has not been traced. The poem continues Cowper's interest in organic growth, this time of a malign, invasive and portentous kind. The text given here is that of the autograph manuscript in the Hannay Collection, Princeton University Library. The poem was first printed in William Hayley, *The Life, and Posthumous Writings, of William Cowper, Esqr* (1803–4), 2:383–5.

What portents, from what distant region, ride
Unseen, till now, in ours, th'astonish'd tide?
In ages past, old Proteus with his droves
Of sea-calves sought the mountains and the groves,
But now, descending whence of late they stood,   5
Themselves the mountains seem to rove the flood.
Dire times were they, full-charged with human woes,
And these scarce less calamitous than those.
What view we now? more wond'rous still! Behold!
Like burnish'd brass they shine, or beaten gold,   10
And, all around, the pearl's pure splendour show,
And, all around, the ruby's fiery glow.
Come they from India, where the teeming Earth
All-bounteous, gives her richest treasures birth?
And where the costly gems that beam around   15
The brows of mightiest Potentates abound?
No. Never such a countless dazzling store
Had left unseen the Ganges peopled shore.

Title *Germanic Ocean* The North Sea.
  3 *Proteus* A Greek sea-god who brought his herd of seals
  ashore at noon (*Odyssey*, 4:385–424).

Rapacious hands and ever watchful eyes
Should sooner far have mark'd and seized the prize.   20
Whence sprang they then? Ejected have they come
From Vesvius' or from Ætna's burning womb?
Thus shine they self-illumed, or but display
The borrow'd splendours of a cloudless day?
With borrow'd beams they shine. The gales that breathe   25
Now land-ward, and the currents' force beneath
Have borne them nearer, and the nearer sight,
Advantaged more, contemplates them aright.
Their lofty summits crested high they show
With mingled sleet and long-incumbent snow;   30
The rest is ice. Far hence, where, most severe,
Bleak Winter well-nigh saddens all the year
Their infant growth began. He bade arise
Their uncouth forms, portentous in our eyes.
Oft as, dissolved by transient Suns, the snow   35
Left the tall cliff to join the flood below,
He caught and curdled with a freezing blast
The current ere it reach'd the boundless waste.
By slow degrees uprose the wond'rous pile,
And long successive ages roll'd the while,   40
Till, ceaseless in its growth, it claim'd to stand
Tall as its rival mountains on the land.
Thus stood, and, unremoveable by skill
Or force of man, had stood the structure still,
But that, though firmly fixt, supplanted yet   45
By pressure of its own enormous weight
It left the shelving beach, and with a sound
That shook the bellowing caves and rocks around.
Self-launched and swiftly to the briney wave,
As if instinct with strong desire to lave   50
Down went the pond'rous mass. So bards have told
How Delos swam th'Ægæan Deep of old.
But not of ice was Delos; Delos bore
Herb, fruit and flow'r; She, crown'd with laurel wore
E'en under wintry skies a summer smile,   55
And Delos was Apollo's fav'rite isle.
But, horrid wand'rers of the Deep! to you
He deems Cimmerian darkness only due;
Your hated birth he deign'd not to survey,
But, scornful, turn'd his glorious eyes away.   60
Hence — seek your home — nor longer rashly dare
The darts of Phœbus and a softer air,
Lest ye regret too late your native coast,
In no congenial gulph for ever lost.

22 Vesuvius, the volcano near Naples, had been especially active in 1794; the 1780 eruption of Etna, on the east coast of Sicily, features in Cowper's poem, *Heroism*.
50 *lave* 'bathe'.
52 *Delos* The small Greek island, birthplace of Apollo and sacred to him. According to legend it rose from the sea at the behest of Poseidon and floated on the surface until chained to the sea-bed by Zeus.
58 In Homer (*Odyssey*, 11) the Cimmerii live on the edge of the world in perpetual darkness.
62 *Phœbus* Apollo as the sun god.

The Cast-away

Cowper began writing his last original poem on 19 March 1799, the day after completing *On the Ice-islands*. He translated it into Latin the following August. See Charles Ryskamp, *The Cast-away* (Princeton, 1963). The incident that prompted Cowper occurred on 24 March 1741 when Commodore Anson's ships were rounding Cape Horn during their circumnavigation of the world; it is described in Richard Walter, *A Voyage Round the World ... by George Anson* (1748), pp. 79–80: 'one of our ablest seamen was canted over-board; and notwithstanding the prodigious agitation of the waves, we perceived that he swam very strong, and it was with the utmost concern that we found ourselves incapable of assisting him; and we were the more grieved at his unhappy fate, since we lost sight of him struggling with the waves, and conceived from the manner in which he swam, that he might continue sensible for a considerable time longer, of the horror attending his irretrievable situation.'

The text that follows is that of the autograph manuscript in the Hannay Collection, Princeton University Library. The poem was first printed in William Hayley, *The Life, and Posthumous Writings, of William Cowper, Esqr* (1803–4), 2:214–17.

Obscurest night involved the sky,
    Th'Atlantic billows roar'd,
When such a destin'd wretch as I
    Wash'd headlong from on board
Of friends, of hope, of all bereft,   5
His floating home for ever left.

No braver Chief could Albion boast
    Than He with whom he went,
Nor ever ship left Albions coast
    With warmer wishes sent,   10
He loved them both, but both in vain,
Nor Him beheld, nor Her again.

Not long beneath the whelming brine
    Expert to swim, he lay,
Nor soon he felt his strength decline   15
    Or courage die away;
But waged with Death a lasting strife
Supported by despair of life.

He shouted, nor his friends had fail'd
    To check the vessels' course,   20
But so the furious blast prevail'd
    That, pitiless perforce,
They left their outcast mate behind,
And scudded still before the wind.

Some succour yet they could afford,   25
    And, such as storms allow,
The cask, the coop, the floated cord
    Delay'd not to bestow;
But He, they knew, nor ship nor shore,
Whate'er they gave, should visit more.   30

---

7 *Chief* George Anson (1697–1762), later Admiral Lord Anson; he returned with a rich prize after capturing a Spanish galleon. *Albion* Britain.

22 *perforce* 'of necessity'.
27 *coop* Wicker basket used in catching fish.

Nor, cruel as it 'seem'd, could He
   Their haste, himself, condemn,
Aware that flight in such a sea
   Alone could rescue *them*;
Yet bitter felt it still to die   35
Deserted, and his friends so nigh.

He long survives who lives an hour
   In ocean, self-upheld,
And so long he with unspent pow'r
   His destiny repell'd,   40
And ever, as the minutes flew,
Entreated help, or cried, Adieu!

At length, his transient respite past,
   His comrades, who before
Had heard his voice in ev'ry blast,   45
   Could catch the sound no more;
For then, by toil subdued, he drank
The stifling wave, and then he sank.

No poet wept him, but the page
   Of narrative sincere   50
That tells his name, his worth, his age,
   Is wet with Anson's tear,
And tears by bards or heroes shed
Alike immortalize the Dead.

I, therefore, purpose not or dream,   55
   Descanting on his fate,
To give the melancholy theme
   A more enduring date,
But Mis'ry still delights to trace
Its semblance in anothers' case.   60

No voice divine the storm allay'd,
   No light propitious shone,
When, snatch'd from all effectual aid,
   We perish'd, each, alone;
But I, beneath a rougher sea,   65
And whelm'd in deeper gulphs than he.

45 Cf. Gray, *Ode on a Distant Prospect of Eton College*, 39.
61 'And he arose, and rebuked the wind, and said unto the sea, Peace, be still. And the wind ceased, and there was a great calm' (Mark, 4:39).

Charlotte Smith (1749–1806)

Along with William Lisle Bowles, Charlotte Smith helped establish the sonnet form as a medium for articulating subjective experience in terms of the natural world. By 1796 Coleridge (who admired both poets) could write that to complain of egotism in a sonnet was 'to dislike a circle for being round'. In Smith's hands the form became a vehicle for expressing the frustrations of her lifelong struggle for personal and financial independence. She was the daughter of a landed gentleman, Nicholas Turner of Bignor Park, Sussex, but when her father remarried in 1764 (Charlotte's mother having died when she was three) she was herself married off, aged fifteen, to Benjamin Smith, the son of a West Indies merchant. Smith was feckless, unfaithful and bad tempered, and encumbered Charlotte with twelve children and mounting debts. For a time she lived with him in the King's Bench Prison (where Christopher Smart had ended his days) and later near Dieppe in northern France, where he had gone to escape his creditors. Nine children survived to maturity (one of whom became a baronet and Governor of Jamaica), and the plight of her large family was made worse by the will of her father-in-law, who died in 1776. His bequest of considerable property to Charlotte's children was entangled in legal disputes for the rest of her life, and to her mounting anger and frustration no money was released by the trustees until long after her own death. Her poems served as a means of giving vent to feelings of fatalistic melancholy, but also to relieve her dire financial situation. In 1788 she finally separated from her husband, and she and her children settled until 1793 in Brighton on the Sussex coast. Smith's small collection of *Elegiac Sonnets* (1784) had been well received, and by 1789 an expanded fifth edition was published through a highly successful subscription. Further editions followed, and a second subscription volume in 1797. Rather more lucrative were the ten novels she produced within a single decade, beginning with the popular *Emmeline* (1788), and including *The Old Manor House* (1793), and her most political novel *Desmond* (1792), which expresses Smith's early enthusiasm for the French Revolution. Her struggle to survive by the efforts of her pen had many admirers, but others grew tired of the angry self-justification of her prefaces in which the narrative of her woes was regularly updated. Her democratic sympathies also aroused suspicion, not allayed by her longer poem, *The Emigrants* (1793), in which she expressed disillusionment with developments in France. She remained prolific and determined, but financial security was never achieved and things became harder through her increasing ill health. She died shortly after her husband in 1806, and the following year saw the publication of *Beachy Head*, a meditative topographical poem which reiterates many of the themes of her earlier work. After Charlotte Smith's death her sister spoke of her natural wit and cheerfulness; but the self projected in her most influential poems is a more vulnerable one, highly sensitized both to nature's gentle details and to its destructive potential.

Sonnet: Written in the Church Yard at Middleton in Sussex

Sonnet 44 was one of those added for the fifth edition of *Elegiac Sonnets* (1789), p. 44, the text given here. In her appendix Smith notes: 'Middleton is a village on the margin of the sea in Sussex, containing only two or three houses. There were formerly several acres of ground between its small church and the sea; which now, by its continual encroachments, approaches within a few feet of this half ruined and humble edifice. The wall, which once surrounded the church yard, is entirely swept away, many of the graves broken up, and the remains of bodies interred washed into the sea: whence human bones are found among the sand and shingles on the shore' (pp. 79–80). Smith revisits this churchyard in her *Elegy*.

> Press'd by the Moon, mute arbitress of tides,
>   While the loud equinox its power combines,
>   The sea no more its swelling surge confines,
> But o'er the shrinking land sublimely rides.
> The wild blast, rising from the Western cave,
>   Drives the huge billows from their heaving bed;
>   Tears from their grassy tombs the village dead,

5

---

1 Cf. 'while overhead the moon / Sits arbitress' (Milton, *Paradise Lost*, 1:784–5).

2 *equinox* The equinoctial gales are common in Britain during late September–early October.

And breaks the silent sabbath of the grave!
With shells and sea-weed mingled, on the shore
  Lo! their bones whiten in the frequent wave;   10
  But vain to them the winds and waters rave;
They hear the warring elements no more:
While I am doom'd — by life's long storm opprest,
To gaze with envy, on their gloomy rest.

Sonnet: To Fancy

Sonnet 47 was added for the fifth edition of *Elegiac Sonnets* (1789), p. 47, the text given here. Smith sees her move from innocence to experience stoically in terms of the 'false medium' of imagination which exaggerates both delight and pain.

Thee, Queen of Shadows! — shall I still invoke,
  Still love the scenes thy sportive pencil drew,
When on mine eyes the early radience broke
  Which shew'd the beauteous, rather than the true!
Alas! long since, those glowing tints are dead,   5
  And now 'tis thine in darkest hues to dress
The spot where pale Experience hangs her head
  O'er the sad grave of murder'd Happiness!
Thro' thy false medium then, no longer view'd,
  May fancied pain and fancied pleasure fly,   10
    And I, as from me all thy dreams depart,
Be to my wayward destiny subdu'd;
  Nor seek perfection with a poet's eye,
  Nor suffer anguish with a poet's heart!

2 *pencil* 'artist's paintbrush'.

4 Cf. Akenside, *The Pleasures of Imagination*, 1:372–7 and note.

Sonnet: The Gossamer

Sonnet 63 was added for the two-volume eighth edition of *Elegiac Sonnets* (1797), 2:4, the text given here. In her appendix Smith notes: 'The web, charged with innumerable globules of bright dew, that is frequently on heaths and commons in autumnal mornings, can hardly have escaped the observation of any lover of nature – The slender web of the field spider is again alluded to in Sonnet 77' (2:92).

O'er faded heath-flowers spun, or thorny furze,
  The filmy Gossamer is lightly spread;
Waving in every sighing air that stirs,
  As Fairy fingers had entwined the thread:
A thousand trembling orbs of lucid dew   5
  Spangle the texture of the fairy loom,
As if soft Sylphs, lamenting as they flew,
  Had wept departed Summer's transient bloom:
But the wind rises, and the turf receives
  The glittering web: — So, evanescent, fade   10
Bright views that Youth with sanguine heart, believes:
  So vanish schemes of bliss, by Fancy made;
Which, fragile as the fleeting dreams of morn,
Leave but the wither'd heath, and barren thorn!

7 *Sylphs* Smith's sonnet echoes Pope's description of the sylphs in *The Rape of the Lock*, 2:59–68.

11 *sanguine* 'cheerfully hopeful'.
13 *dreams* Changed in later editions to 'dews'.

Sonnet: On being cautioned against walking on an headland overlooking the sea, because it was frequented by a lunatic

Sonnet 70 was added for the two-volume eighth edition of *Elegiac Sonnets* (1797), 2:11, the text given here. Smith's Walpole allusion adds a dramatic element to the poem. In II.iii of *The Mysterious Mother* the castle porter warns the Countess not to go out into the storm, to which she replies: 'Wretches like me, good Peter, dread no storms. / 'Tis delicate felicity that shrinks, / When rocking winds are loud, and wraps itself / Insultingly in comfortable furs, / Thinking how many naked objects want / Like shelter and security'. This parallel with Shakespeare's *King Lear* (notably III.iv.28–36) perhaps extends to the sonnet.

Is there a solitary wretch who hies
　　To the tall cliff, with starting pace or slow,
And, measuring, views with wild and hollow eyes
　　Its distance from the waves that chide below;
Who, as the sea-born gale with frequent sighs　　　　　　5
　　Chills his cold bed upon the mountain turf,
With hoarse, half utter'd lamentation, lies
　　Murmuring responses to the dashing surf?
In moody sadness, on the giddy brink,
　　I see him more with envy than with fear;　　　　　　10
He has no *nice felicities* that shrink
　　From giant horrors; wildly wandering here,
He seems (uncursed with reason) not to know
The depth or the duration of his woe.

11 "''Tis delicate felicity that shrinks / When rocking winds are loud." (Walpole)' (Smith's note, 2:93). The lines occur in Horace Walpole's play, *The Mysterious Mother* (1768), II.iii.5–6, spoken by the guilt-ridden and despairing Countess of Narbonne. *nice* 'over-sensitive'.

Elegy

Smith's elegy in a country churchyard could hardly be more different from Gray's: the suppressed energies of his poem here burst out destructively, and the turf heaves in a dramatic way (62). There are also ironic echoes of that other great elegy, Milton's *Lycidas*, in which a drowned friend is mourned. The poem was first included in the fifth edition of *Elegiac Sonnets* (1789), pp. 52–6, in the text given here (later editions add more capital letters and exclamation marks). A note in the Appendix summarizes the narrative: 'This elegy is written on the supposition that an indigent young woman had been addressed by the son of a wealthy yeoman, who resenting his attachment, had driven him from home, and compelled him to have recourse for subsistence to the occupation of a pilot, in which, attempting to save a vessel in distress, he perished. The father dying, a tomb is supposed to be erected to his memory in the church yard mentioned in Sonnet the 44th. And while a tempest is gathering, the unfortunate young woman comes thither; and courting the same death as had robbed her of her lover, she awaits its violence, and is at length overwhelmed by the waves' (pp. 81–2).

"Dark gathering clouds involve the threatening skies,
The sea heaves conscious of the impending gloom,
Deep, hollow murmurs from the cliffs arise;
They come — the Spirits of the Tempest come!

"Oh! may such terrors mark the approaching night   5
As reign'd on that these streaming eyes deplore!
Flash, ye red fires of heaven, with fatal light,
And with conflicting winds, ye waters roar!

"Loud and more loud ye foaming billows burst!
Ye warring elements more fiercely rave!   10
Till the wide waves o'erwhelm the spot accurst
Where ruthless Avarice finds a quiet grave!"

Thus with clasp'd hands, wild looks, and streaming hair,
While shrieks of horror broke her trembling speech,
A wretched maid — the victim of despair,   15
Survey'd the threatening storm and desart beech,

Then to the tomb where now the father slept
Whose rugged nature bade her sorrows flow,
Frantic she turn'd — and beat her breast and wept,
Invoking vengeance on the dust below.   20

"Lo! rising there above each humbler heap,
Yon cypher'd stones *his* name and wealth relate,
Who gave his son — remorseless — to the deep,
While I, his living victim, curse my fate.

"Oh! my lost love! no tomb is plac'd for thee,   25
That may to strangers eyes thy worth impart;
Thou hast no grave, but in the stormy sea,
And no memorial but this breaking heart.

"Forth to the world, a widow'd wanderer driven,
I pour to winds and waves the unheeded tear,   30
Try with vain effort to submit to heaven,
And fruitless call on him — 'who cannot hear.'

"Oh! might I fondly clasp him once again,
While o'er my head the infuriate billows pour,
Forget in death this agonizing pain,   35
And feel his father's cruelty no more!

"Part, raging waters part, and shew beneath,
In your dread caves, his pale and mangled form;
Now, while the demons of despair and death
Ride on the blast, and urge the howling storm!   40

"Lo! by the lightenings momentary blaze,
I see him rise the whitening waves above,
No longer such as when in happier days
He gave the enchanted hours — to me and love.

6 *deplore* 'lament'.
16 *desart beech* 'empty beach'.
22 *cypher'd* 'carved'.
32 Cf. Gray, *Sonnet on the Death of Richard West*, 13. In a
note Smith quotes lines 13–14 of Gray's 'exquisite
Sonnet', adding: 'in reading which it is impossible not
to regret that he wrote only one' (Appendix, p. 82).

"Such, as when daring the enchafed sea,   45
And courting dangerous toil, he often said,
That every peril, one soft smile from me,
One sigh of speechless tenderness, o'erpaid.

"But dead, disfigur'd, while between the roar
Of the loud waves his accents pierce mine ear,   50
And seem to say — Ah! wretch, delay no more,
But come, unhappy mourner — meet me here.

"Yet, powerful fancy bid the phantom stay,
Still let me hear him! — 'Tis already past;
Along the waves his shadow glides away,   55
I lose his voice amid the deafening blast.

"Ah! wild illusion, born of frantic pain!
He hears not, comes not from his watery bed;
My tears, my anguish, my despair are vain,
The insatiate ocean gives not up its dead.   60

"'Tis not his voice! Hark! the deep thunders roll;
Up-heaves the ground; the rocky barriers fail;
Approach, ye horrors that delight my soul,
Despair, and Death, and Desolation, hail!"

The ocean hears — The embodied waters come —   65
Rise o'er the land, and with resistless sweep
Tear from it's base the proud agressor's tomb,
And bear the injured to eternal sleep!

45 *enchafed* 'roused to anger'. Cf. 'the enchafed flood'   53–5 Cf. Pope, *Eloisa to Abelard*, 236–8.
(*Othello*, II.i.17).

William Lisle Bowles (1762–1850)

During his long and undramatic life Bowles remained in many people's eyes the author of youthful sonnets. He was never to match their critical success or recapture that moment when his voice excited a whole generation of aspiring young poets. The son of a Northamptonshire vicar, he went to Winchester College in 1776 where the headmaster Joseph Warton encouraged his poetic talents, and the Wartonian influence was strengthened when in 1781 he was elected to a scholarship at Trinity College, Oxford, where Thomas Warton was senior fellow. He left Trinity in 1787, and after being disappointed in love 'sought forgetfulness' by becoming 'a wanderer among distant scenes'. According to his later memoirs the sonnets were composed in his head and not written down till he returned. Bowles persuaded a publisher at Bath to bring out a hundred copies of *Fourteen Sonnets, Elegiac and Descriptive. Written During a Tour* (1789), and these proved so successful that a second edition, heavily revised and extended to twenty-one sonnets, was published later that year as *Sonnets, Written Chiefly on Picturesque Spots, During a Tour*. Other works followed, including *Monody Written at Matlock* (1791), *St Michael's Mount* (1798), and several lengthy historical poems such as *The Spirit of Discovery* (1804) and *The Grave of the Last Saxon* (1822). In 1792 he finally took his degree and entered into holy orders, becoming Vicar of Bremhill, Wiltshire, in 1804. Here he lived until the end of his life, 'greatly beloved by his parishioners'. Bowles returned to public notice with his ten-volume edition of Pope (1806) which denigrated the poet for lacking poetic imagination. Lord Byron came to Pope's defence and the resulting Byron–Bowles controversy was one of the most significant critical debates of the age.

The influence of Bowles's sonnets on Coleridge, Wordsworth and Southey has been well documented. Their effect on the sixteen-year-old Coleridge was especially remarkable: he was so excited by them that he made more than forty transcriptions for friends (evidently of the extended second edition, the texts given here), considering them 'of a style of poetry so tender and yet so manly, so natural and real, and yet so dignified and harmonious' (*Biographia Literaria*, 1817). Nor was this a brief enthusiasm: seven years later he had twenty-eight of his own and his friends' sonnets privately printed to be bound up with Bowles's. In the Preface to this rare pamphlet Coleridge offers an interesting definition of the sonnet as 'a small poem, in which some lonely feeling is developed'. He goes on: 'but those Sonnets appear to me the most exquisite, in which moral Sentiments, Affections, or Feelings, are deduced from, and associated with, the scenery of Nature. Such compositions generate a habit of thought highly favourable to delicacy of character. They create a sweet and indissoluble union between the intellectual and the material world. Easily remembered from their briefness … these are poems which we can "lay up in our heart, and our soul" … Hence, the Sonnets of BOWLES derive their marked superiority over all other Sonnets; hence they domesticate with the heart, and become, as it were, a part of our identity.'

Sonnet: Written at Tinemouth, Northumberland, After a Tempestuous Voyage

Sonnet 3. The site of the castle and ancient priory of Tynemouth is a rocky coastal promontory jutting into the North Sea, 8 miles east of Newcastle. In revising this poem for the second edition of his *Sonnets* (Bath, 1789), p. 12, Bowles rewrote the last three lines, which originally read: 'Whilst the weak winds that sigh along the deep, / The ear, like lullabies of pity, meet, / Singing her saddest notes of farewell sweet.' It was revised further for later printings. The following is the second edition text.

> As slow I climb the cliff's ascending side,
> Much musing on the track of terror past,
>   When o'er the dark wave rode the howling blast,
> Pleas'd I look back, and view the tranquil tide,
>   That laves the pebbled shore; and now the beam 5
> Of evening smiles on the grey battlement,
> And yon forsaken tow'r that time has rent: —
>   The lifted oar far off with silver gleam
> Is touch'd, and the hush'd billows seem to sleep!
>   Sooth'd by the scene, ev'n thus on sorrow's breast 10

A kindred stillness steals, and bids her rest;
  Whilst sad airs stilly sigh along the deep,
    Like melodies which mourn upon the lyre,
    Wak'd by the breeze, and as they mourn, expire.

13 *lyre* The Aeolian harp, a stringed instrument producing harmonic sounds as the air plays across it.

14 *expire* Includes the sense of 'breathe out' (Lat. *expiro*).

Sonnet: To the River Wensbeck

Sonnet 5. The River Wansbeck (as it is now spelt) rises in the Northumbrian fells and enters the North Sea north of Newcastle. Lines 4–13 of this sonnet were completely rewritten for the second edition, p. 15, the text given here.

As slowly wanders thy sequester'd stream,
  WENSBECK! the mossy-scatter'd rocks among,
  In fancy's ear still making plaintive song
To the dark woods above, that waving seem
To bend o'er some enchanted spot, remov'd   5
  From Life's vain scenes; I listen to the wind,
  And think I hear meek sorrow's plaint, reclin'd
O'er the forsaken tomb of one she lov'd! —
Fair scenes, ye lend a pleasure, long unknown,
  To him who passes weary on his way —   10
  The farewell tear, which now he turns to pay,
Shall thank you, — and whene'er of pleasures flown
  His heart some long-lost image would renew,
  Delightful haunts! he will remember you.

1 *sequester'd* 'secluded'.

Sonnet: Written at Ostend. July 22, 1787

Sonnet 13. Except for the addition of the date in the title, no substantive changes were made for the second edition, p. 23, the text given here. Like Sonnet 3 this poem is characterized by distancing effects of both space and time. The Belgian coastal town of Ostend is notably absent.

How sweet the tuneful bells' responsive peal!
  As when, at opening morn, the fragrant breeze
  Breathes on the trembling sense of wan disease,
So piercing to my heart their force I feel!
  And hark! with lessening cadence now they fall,   5
And now, along the white and level tide,
They fling their melancholy musick wide;
  Bidding me many a tender thought recall
Of summer-days, and those delightful years
  When by my native streams, in life's fair prime,   10
  The mournful magic of their mingling chime
First wak'd my wond'ring childhood into tears!
  But seeming now, when all those days are o'er,
  The sounds of joy, once heard, and heard no more.

5 *cadence* 'The fall of the voice' (Johnson).

10 Cf. Thomas Warton, *Sonnet: To the River Lodon*, 9, 13.

Elegy Written at the Hot-Wells, Bristol

Here Bowles extends the mood of his sonnets into a meditative poem. He chooses the quatrain of Gray's *Elegy* and uses that famous text to create a background memory, consistently echoing its rhythms, rhymes and phrasing, but without allowing it to intrude too specifically. More directly nostalgic are his allusions to Thomas Warton's Lodon sonnet about vanished youth, and to Milton's lost paradise. Bowles's subject is the spa of Hotwells, at Clifton on the outskirts of Bristol, and the consumptive cases that were attracted to its warm spring (76°F). In the poem human and natural merge into each other, and life-giving air and water run through the poem. Bowles's disembodied vision gains irony as he mourns the passing of a generation that included the poets Russell and Headley, both his friends. It is addressed to William Howley, who recuperated sufficiently to become Archbishop of Canterbury 1828–48. The poem was first published as a quarto pamphlet, *Elegy Written at the Hot-Wells, Bristol. Addressed to the Revd. William Howley* (Bath, 1791), the text given here.

> The morning wakes in shadowy mantle grey,
>   The darksome woods their glimmering skirts unfold;
> Prone from the cliff the falcon wheels her way,
>   And long and loud the bell's slow chime is toll'd.
>
> Now gains the struggling light upon the skies,   5
>   And far away the glist'ning vapours sail;
> Down the rough steep the accustom'd hedger hies,
>   And the stream winds in brightness through the vale!
>
> How beauteous the pale rocks above the shore
>   Uplift their bleak and furrow'd aspect high;   10
> How proudly desolate their foreheads hoar,
>   That meet the earliest sunbeam of the sky!
>
> Bound to yon dusky mart, with pennants gay
>   The tall bark, on the winding water's line,
> Between the riven cliffs plies her hard way,   15
>   And peering on the sight the white sails shine.
>
> Alas! for those by drooping sickness worn,
>   Who now come forth to meet the gladsome ray;
> And feel the fragrance of the tepid morn
>   Round their torn breast and throbbing temples play!   20
>
> Perhaps they muse with a desponding sigh
>   On the cold vault that shall their bones inurn;
> Whilst every breeze seems, as it whispers by,
>   To breathe of comfort never to return.
>
> Yet oft, as sadly-thronging dreams arise,   25
>   Awhile forgetful of their pain they gaze;
> A transient lustre lights their faded eyes,
>   And o'er their cheek the tender hectic strays.
>
> The purple morn that paints with sidelong gleam
>   The cliff's tall crest, the waving woods that ring   30

---

9 *rocks* St Vincent's Rocks overhanging the River Avon. Cf. Yearsley, *Clifton Hill*, 126n.

13 *mart* 'trading-place': the port of Bristol, upstream from Hotwells.

22 *inurn* Cf. 'the sepulchre, / Wherein we saw thee quietly inurn'd' (*Hamlet*, I.iii.48–9).

28 *hectic* 'flush'. The word also evokes the 'hectic fever' of consumption.

With charm of birds rejoicing in the beam,
    Touch soft the wakeful nerve's according string.

Then at fond memory's sad and silent hour,
    A thousand wishes steal upon the heart;
And, whilst they meekly bend to Heaven's high power,   35
    Ah! think 'tis hard, 'tis surely hard to part —

To part from every hope that brought delight,
    From those that lov'd them, those they lov'd so much!
Then fancy swells the picture on the sight,
    And softens every scene at every touch.   40

Sweet as the mellow'd woods beneath the moon,
    Remembrance lends her soft uniting shades;
Some natural tears she drops, but wipes them soon,
    The world retires, and the dim prospect fades!

Airs of delight, that soothe the aching sense,   45
    Waters of health, that through yon caverns glide,
O kindly yet your healing powers dispense,
    And bring back feeble life's exhausted tide!

Perhaps to these grey rocks and mazy springs
    Some heart may come, warm'd with the purest fire;   50
For whom bright Fancy plumes her radiant wings,
    And warbling Muses wake the lonely lyre.

Some beauteous maid, deceiv'd in early youth,
    Pale o'er yon spring may hang in mute distress;
Who dreamt of faith, of happiness, and truth,   55
    Of love — that virtue would protect and bless.

Some musing youth in silence there may bend,
    Untimely stricken by sharp sorrow's dart;
For friendship form'd, yet left without a friend,
    And bearing still the arrow at his heart.   60

Such was lamented RUSSEL'S hapless doom,
    The lost companion of my youth's gay prime;
Ev'n so he sunk unwept into the tomb,
    And o'er his head clos'd the dark gulph of time!

Hither he came, a wan and weary guest,   65
    A softening balm for many a wound to crave;

---

31 *charm* 'song'. Cf. 'With charm of earliest birds'
    (Milton, *Paradise Lost*, 4:642).
43 Adam and Eve leaving Paradise: 'Some natural tears
    they dropped, but wiped them soon' (*Paradise Lost*,
    12:645). The ending of Milton's epic ('They hand in
    hand with wandering steps and slow, / Through Eden
    took their solitary way', 12:648–9) is echoed in lines 81,
    98 and 96.

49–52 Cf. Gray, *Elegy*, 45–8.
61 Thomas Russell (1762–88), Bowles's friend at
    Winchester and Oxford, died of consumption at
    Hotwells. His posthumous *Sonnets and Miscellaneous
    Poems* (1789), edited by William Howley, were much
    admired by Wordsworth.

And woo'd the sunshine to his aching breast,
    Which now seems smiling on his verdant grave!

He heard the whispering winds that now I hear,
    As, boding much, along these hills he past;   70
Yet ah! how mournful did they meet his ear
    On that sad morn he heard them for the last!

So sinks the scene, like a departed dream,
    Since late we sojourn'd blythe in WYKEHAM's bow'rs,
Or heard the merry bells by *Isis'* stream,   75
    And thought our way was strew'd with fairy flow'rs!

Of those with whom we play'd upon the lawn
    Of early life, in the fresh morning, play'd,
Alas! how many, since that vernal dawn,
    Like thee, poor RUSSEL, in the ground are laid.   80

As pleas'd awhile they wander'd hand in hand,
    Once led by friendship on the spring-tide plain,
How oft did Fancy wake her transports bland,
    And on the lids the starting tear detain!

I yet survive, now musing other song   85
    Than that which early sooth'd my thoughtless years;
Thinking how days and hours have pass'd along,
    Mark'd by much pleasure some, and some by tears!

Thankful, that to these verdant scenes I owe,
    That he whom late I saw all-drooping pale,   90
Rais'd from the couch of sickness and of woe,
    Now lives with me these mantling views to hail.

Thankful, that still the landscape beaming bright,
    Of pendent mountain, or of woodland grey,
Can wake the wonted sense of pure delight,   95
    And charm awhile my solitary way!

Enough: — Through the high heavens the proud sun rides,
    My wand'ring steps their silent path pursue
Back to the crouded world, where fortune guides;
    CLIFTON, to thy white rocks and woods Adieu!   100

74 Winchester College was founded by William of
    Wykeham in 1382.
75 *Isis* The River Thames at Oxford.
76 Cf. T. Warton, *Sonnet: To the River Lodon*, 3.
79–80 Bowles also wrote an elegy on his Oxford friend
    Henry Headley (1765–88), the poet and literary
    scholar.

83 *bland* 'gentle'.
90 *he* Howley.
92 *mantling* 'enveloping'.
95 *wonted* 'customary'.

Anna Seward (1742–1809)

'The Swan of Lichfield', as she became known, was the daughter of Thomas Seward (1708–90), a Canon of Lichfield Cathedral, and from 1754 until her death she lived in the Bishop's Palace there. Tall, handsome and with a good voice, she was made much of by her father's friends and she flourished in the town's cultured society. This included the poet and physician Erasmus Darwin (grandfather of the celebrated Charles), who encouraged her poetic ambitions. She began writing sentimental coterie verse before making the vital transition to a more public voice. It was with the publication of an *Elegy on Captain Cook* (1780) and the popular *Louisa, A Poetical Novel* (1784) that she made her mark more widely. Seward rarely visited London, partly because of the needs of her ailing father; but in her Staffordshire home the Swan glided and hissed very effectively. As a frequent contributor to the magazines, especially the *Gentleman's Magazine*, she gained prominence as a literary celebrity, patroness and controversialist, who was always willing to let her critical views be known in prose or verse. She directed corrective criticism at writers as diverse as Dr Johnson (for his dislike of Milton and Gray), Cowper (for his unpatriotic cynicism) and Charlotte Smith (for her views on the sonnet). Of liberal outlook in politics and religion, Seward was one of many early supporters of the French Revolution who became horrified by the Terror of 1793–4, and this caused her to denounce her former friend Helen Maria Williams. She was an admirer of William Hayley, Thomas Warton and later of Walter Scott, and helped to encourage the work of younger writers. Many of her poems are addressed to friends and acquaintances and are of an occasional nature. Her *Llangollen Vale, With Other Poems* (1796) was followed by *Original Sonnets* (1799), to which she added a critical preface advocating the formal constraints of the 'regular' or 'legitimate' sonnet and its 'nervous' (i.e. sinewy) style which 'partakes of the nature of Blank Verse, by the lines running into each other at proper intervals'. In her own poems Seward moved away from a regular smoothness towards a more 'nervous' verse of this kind, and this is evident in her blank-verse *Colebrooke Dale*. Her enthusiastic admiration for Milton and Shakespeare also leaves its mark. Seward's posthumous *Poetical Works*, 3 vols (Edinburgh, 1810) were collected and edited by Walter Scott.

Colebrooke Dale

Coalbrookdale, Shropshire, a narrow picturesque valley on the River Severn, was the cradle of the Industrial Revolution. Abraham Darby had founded the ironworks there in 1709, and these expanded greatly under his son and grandson, attracting other industries. Arthur Young reported in 1776: 'This neighbourhood is uncommonly full of manufactures, among which the principal are the potteries, pipe makers, colliers and iron works … The whole process is here gone through from digging the iron stone to making it into cannons, pipes, cylinders, &c. &c. All the iron used is raised in the neighbouring hills, and the coal dug likewise … Mr Darby in his works employs near 1000 people, including colliers' (*Annals of Agriculture*, 4 (1785), pp. 165–7). Like many visitors Young was fascinated by the contrast between nature and art, beauty and sublimity: 'Colebrook Dale itself is a very romantic spot, it is a winding glen between two immense hills which break into various forms, and all thickly covered with wood, forming the most beautiful sheets of hanging wood. Indeed too beautiful to be much in unison with that variety of horrors art has spread at the bottom: the noise of the forges, mills, &c. with all their vast machinery, the flames bursting from the furnaces with the burning of the coal and the smoak of the lime kilns, are altogether sublime, and would unite well with craggy and bare rocks, like St. Vincent's at Bristol' (p. 168). Seward's poem engages with this duality: the loss of the old poetic landscape is set against the exhilaration of the new technology and its transformative effects. Appropriately the language moves between the lyric note of the early Milton and the more convoluted sublimities of *Paradise Lost*.

The poem was first published in Seward's *Poetical Works* (1810), 2:314–19. That text is a substantial revision of an earlier version, of which a transcript survives (headed 'written Augt. 1790') in the Bodleian Library, Oxford, MS Pigott d. 12 ('Unpublished Verses Written by Anna Seward'), pp. 13–17. This transcript was made after July 1791 (see note to line 58), and is the text given here. The only changes are our expansion throughout of '&' to 'and'. Seward's sonnet *To Colebrooke Dale* (*Original Sonnets* (1799), p. 65) reads as a condensed version of the poem's opening paragraph.

Scene of superfluous grace, and wasted bloom,
O violated Colebrooke! in an hour
To Beauty inauspicious, and to song,
By Plutus brib'd, the Genius of thy shades,
Amid thy grassy Lanes, thy wood-wild Glens,   5
Thy Knoles precipitant, thy Rocks, and Streams
Slumbers; — while Tribes, with shoulders bent, and broad,
Keen eye, and cheek fuliginous, invade
Thy soft, romantic, consecrated scenes:
Haunt of the Woodnymph, that, with airy step,   10
In Times long vanish'd, thro' thy pathless groves
Rang'd; — while the pearly-wristed Naiads lean'd,
Braiding their moist locks o'er thy silver flood,
Shadowy, and smooth. — What tho' to *vulgar* eyes
Invisible, yet oft the piercing gaze   15
Of the rapt Bard in every opening Glade
Beheld them wander; — saw, from the pure wave
Emerging, all the watry Sisters rise
Weaving the fountain-lilly, and the flag,
In wreaths fantastic for the tresses bright,   20
Of amber-hair'd Sabrina. — Now we view
Their fresh, their fragrant, and their silent reign
Usurpt by Cyclops; — hear, in mingled tones,
Shout their throng'd Barge; their ponderous Engine clang
Thro' thy coy Dells; while red the numerous Fires,   25
With umber'd flames, bicker on all thy Hills,
Dark'ning the Summer's Sun with columns huge
Of thick sulphureous smoke, which spread, like palls
That screen the Dead, upon the sylvan robes
Of thy aspiring Rocks, pollute thy Gales   30
And stain thy glassy waters. — See in Troops
Thy dusk Artificers, with brazen throats,
Swarm on thy Cliffs, and clamor in thy Dells,
Steepy, and wild; — ill suited to such guests.
 Ah! what avails it to the Poet's sense   35
That the large stores of thy metallic veins
Gleam over Europe; transatlantic Shores
Illumine wide; are chang'd in either Ind
For all they boast, hot Ceylon's breathing spice,

---

4 *Plutus* Wealth personified (Gk. *ploutos*).

6 *Knoles* 'small hills' (knolls).

8 *fuliginous* 'blackened with soot' (Lat. *fuligo* = soot).

12 *Naiads* Water-nymphs.

12–21 These lines echo the Spirit's invocation of Sabrina, a nymph of the River Severn ('the silver lake'), in Milton's *Masque*: 'Sabrina fair / Listen where thou art sitting / Under the glassy, cool, translucent wave, / In twisted braids of lilies knitting / The loose train of thy amber-dropping hair' (858–62).

23 *Cyclops* The one-eyed giants of Greek myth, workmen of Hephaestus, God of fire.

25–8 Cf. 'on all sides round / As one great furnace flamed, yet from those flames / No light, but rather darkness visible' (*Paradise Lost*, 1:61–3). The nocturnal fires of Coalbrookdale were a frequent subject for sublime painting.

26 *umber'd* 'A word of Shakespears wh. means *shaded*' (MS note). Cf. 'Fire answers fire, and through their paly flames / Each battle sees the other's umber'd face' (*Henry V*, IV.i.chorus). *bicker* 'flicker'.

32 *Artificers* 'labourers'; *brazen throats* 'loud voices' (Cf. 'the brazen throat of war', *Paradise Lost*, 11:713).

38 *chang'd* 'exchanged'.

Peruvian gems, Brassillia's golden ore   40
And gums odōrous, which the white-rob'd Seer,
With warbled orizons, on Ganges' brink
Kindles, when first his Mithra's living ray
Purples the Orient! — Ah! the traffic rich,
With equal auspices, might Britain send   45
From Regions better suited to such aims,
Than from her Colebrook's Muse-devoted Vales,
To far resounding Birmingham; the boast,
The growing London of the Mercian Plains;
Where philosophic Science leads her Sons   50
To guide th'attentive Artist's glowing hand;
Plan the vast Engine, whose extended arms,
Heavy, and huge, on the soft-seeming breath
Of the hot Steam rise slowly; till, by cold
Condens'd, it leaves them soon, with ringing roar,   55
Down, down to fall precipitant. Nor these,
Known tho' their names in every Land, nor these
Our second-London's *only* boast; — the Sage,
Who trac'd the viewless Aura's subtle breath
Thro' all its various powers, there bending feeds   60
The lamp of Science with the richest oil
That the Arch-Chymist, Genius, knows to draw
From Nature's stores, or latent, or reveal'd.
      Thus grac'd with Intellect, as gay in wealth,
While neighboring Cities waste th'unfruitful hours,   65
Careless of Art, and Knowledge, and the smile
Of every Muse, expanding Birmingham
Commands her aye-accumulating Walls
From month, to month, climb up th'adjacent Hills,
Creep on the circling Plains, now here, now there,   70
Divergent; — change the Hedges, Thickets, Trees,
Upturn'd, disrooted, into mortar'd Piles,

41 *gums odōrous* Cf. 'Groves whose rich trees wept odorous gums and balm' (*Paradise Lost*, 4:248).
42 *warbled orizons* 'melodiously sung prayers'.
43 *Mithra* Persian god of the sun, the Roman Mithras.
45 *equal auspices* 'similarly happy outcome'.
48–9 Nucleus of the early Industrial Revolution 1760–1800, Birmingham's population doubled during the period to 70,000. Mercia was the midland kingdom founded in the sixth century.
50 *her Sons* 'Messrs. Bolton, Watt, Keir' (MS note, also *1810*). Matthew Boulton (1728–1809), the engineer who founded Birmingham's Soho works in 1762, Boulton's partner, James Watt (1736–1819), pioneer of the steam engine, and James Keir (1735–1820), chemist, in charge of the Soho works from 1778, were all members of Birmingham's Lunar Society, a group of twelve committed to the development of new principles and processes ('philosophic Science').
52–6 'Viewed the furnaces, forges, &c. with the vast bellows that give those roaring blasts, which make the whole edifice horribly sublime' (Young, 1776).

58 *Sage* 'Docr. Priestley – the event was then unforseen wh. exiled him from Birmingham. What pity that religious & political sophistry shd. have estranged him from his philosophic [i.e. scientific] studies!' (MS note, omitted from *1810*). Joseph Priestley (1733–1804), scientist and theologian, had been driven from Birmingham by the 'Church and King' riots of July 1791, when as a radical sympathizer his house was destroyed by the mob. He moved to London, finally emigrating to America in 1794. In 1774 he was the first to describe oxygen (which he called 'dephlogisticated air').
69 A 1790 Birmingham advertisement offered at Summer Hill 'a range of elegant and uniform building, comprising fifteen houses, along the declivity of the beautiful hill' (Conrad Gill, *History of Birmingham*, 1 (1952), p. 122). In 1799 Birmingham Heath was enclosed and eight streets built on it. Cf. Dyer, *The Fleece*, 3:326–40.

The Street elongate, and the formal Square.
　　So, with intent transmutant, Chymists bruise
The shrinking leaves, and flowers, whose steams saline,　　75
Congealing swift on the Recipient's sides,
Shoot into crystals; — and the Night-frost thus
Wave after wave incrusts. — Warn'd by the Muse
If this the wide-extending Town shou'd draw
Her dusky Bands from uncongenial Scenes,　　80
And sylvan Colebrooke's winding Vales restore
To Beauty, and to Song; content to bring
From less inchanting Climes her rattling stores
Massy, and dun; ah! if no more from thence
She gluts the avidity of Commerce, see　　85
Grim Wolverhampton kindles smouldering fires,
And Sheffield smoke involv'd! — dim where she stands,
Circled by lofty Mountains, that condense
Her dark, and spiral wreaths to drizzling rains,
Frequent, and sullied; as the neighboring Wilds　　90
Ope their swart veins, and feed her cavern'd flames;
While to her dusky Sister sullen yields
Long desolated Ketley's livid breast
The ponderous metal. No aerial Forms
There wove the floral crown, or smiling strech'd　　95
The shelly sceptre; — there no Poet stray'd
To catch bright inspirations. — Albion, blush!
And *thou*, the venal Genius of these Groves
With thy soil'd pinions thy apostate head
Veil!, that hast thus thy beauteous Charge resign'd　　100
To Habitants ill-suited; — hast allow'd
Their rattling Forges, and their hammer's din,
And hoarse, rude throats to fright the sacred Train,
Neriads, and Dryads; — the soft woodland song
Silence; — dissolve the raptur'd Poet's spell,　　105
And to a gloomy Erebus transform
The destin'd Rival of Tempean Vales.

75 *saline* 'salty'.
81 *sylvan* 'woody'.
84 *dun* Dull greyish brown.
85 *gluts the avidity* 'indulges the greed'.
86 *Wolverhampton* A centre for metal manufacturing 12 miles north-west of Birmingham, and 15 miles east of Coalbrookdale.
87 *Sheffield* Steel-making town on the edge of the Yorkshire Pennines; it held a monopoly in the cutlery trade.
91 *swart veins* Black seams of coal.
92 *dusky Sister* 'Wolverhampton has the greatest part of her iron from Ketley, a dreary Wild in Shropshire' (MS

note, also *1810*). Ketley is some 4 miles north of Coalbrookdale.
93 *livid* 'leaden-coloured'.
97 *Albion* Britain.
98 *venal* 'corrupted'.
99 *pinions* 'wings'; *apostate* 'treacherous'.
104 *Neriads* This confounds 'Naiads' (water-nymphs) and 'Nereids' (the sea maidens of Greek myth); *Dryads* Wood-nymphs.
106 *Erebus* In Greek myth the dark approach to Hades.
107 *Tempean Vales* See Akenside, *The Pleasures of Imagination*, 1:295–305.

Sonnet: To the Poppy

Seward's Sonnet 71 was probably written in 1789 (her sonnets appear to be chronologically ordered and no. 72 is so dated). The text is that of the poem's first printing in *Original Sonnets* (1799), p. 73. In her preface Seward notes: 'The Sonnet is … the best vehicle for a single detached thought, an elevated, or a tender sentiment, and for a succinct description. The compositions of that order now before the Reader, ensued from time to time, as various circumstances impressed the heart, or the imagination of their Author, and as the aweful, or lovely scenes of Nature, arrested, or allured her eye' (p. vi). This sonnet offers another rather different glimpse of nature's vulnerability.

> While Summer Roses all their glory yield
>   To crown the Votary of Love and Joy,
>   Misfortune's Victim hails, with many a sigh,
>   Thee, scarlet POPPY of the pathless field,
> Gaudy, yet wild and lone; no leaf to shield   5
>   Thy flaccid vest, that, as the gale blows high,
>   Flaps, and alternate folds around thy head. —
>   So stands in the long grass a love-craz'd Maid,
> Smiling aghast; while stream to every wind
>   Her gairish ribbons, smear'd with dust and rain;   10
>   But brain-sick visions cheat her tortur'd mind,
> And bring false peace. Thus, lulling grief and pain,
>   Kind dreams oblivious from thy juice proceed,
>   THOU FLIMSY, SHEWY, MELANCHOLY WEED.

2 *Votary* 'devotee'.
6 *flaccid* 'loosely hanging' (Lat. *flaccus* = 'drooping').

10 *gairish* 'over-decorative' (garish).
13 *juice* Opium.

Mary Robinson (1758–1800)

'Perdita' Robinson, the noted beauty and favourite actress of her day, was born Mary Darby at Bristol, the daughter of a whaling captain who neglected his family. She moved with her mother to Chelsea where they ran a girl's school for a while. In 1774 Mary married Thomas Robinson, a clerk with 'prospects' who turned out to be a rakish spendthrift, and their child was born seven months later. After a period of stylish living the husband and young wife and infant daughter found themselves in the King's Bench Prison for debt. During her ten months there she wrote poems and found an influential patron in the Duchess of Devonshire, to whom she presented her *Poems* (1775). Mary's great beauty and fine voice captivated David Garrick, the manager of Drury Lane Theatre, who introduced her to the stage as Juliet in December 1776. Many hearts were broken and she rapidly became the focus of male adoration, whether playing the chaste Lady in an adaptation of Milton's *Masque*, or the great Shakespeare heroines. It was her appearance as Perdita in Garrick's adaptation of *The Winter's Tale* in December 1778 that caused an adoring Prince of Wales (later George IV) to write to her in the guise of Florizel, and she became installed, though only for a year, as the Royal Mistress, quitting the stage in 1780. When the prince's affections moved elsewhere she was bought off with an annuity of £500. She remained heavily in debt for the rest of her life.

Robinson seemed to have achieved a permanent relationship with Colonel Banastre Tarleton, MP, with whom she lived in France for a while, but the liaison proved fitful and her husband never divorced her. She returned with her daughter to live in England in 1788. At this stage her poetry tended towards the lyric form, and as 'Laura' and 'Laura Maria' she took part in the sentimental intimacies of Della Crusca (Robert Merry) and his circle, the fruit of which was her *Poems* (1791), a volume supported by six hundred subscribers including the Prince of Wales. She later turned against her sentimental 'coterie' poetry. From 1792 she eased her financial troubles by publishing novels spiced with incidents thought to be from her own career, and there was a considerable demand for them in France where she was known as 'La Belle Anglaise'. A second volume of *Poems* appeared in 1793, and she wrote several longer pieces including a social satire, *Modern Manners* (1793), and a sonnet sequence, *Sappho and Phaon* (1796), which charted the struggles between reason and passion and led to her other nickname of 'the English Sappho'. In the 1790s she mixed in radical circles and became friendly with Coleridge, Godwin and Mary Wollstonecraft, and from 1798 she contributed poems to the *Morning Post*, including verse that recovered the satiric voice of Pope and Swift and developed it in interesting directions. Since about 1783 Robinson had suffered a degree of paralysis in her lower limbs, and towards the end of her life this severely crippled her. She died at a cottage in Windsor Park on Boxing Day, 1800. Her *Memoirs* (1801) and three-volume *Poetical Works* (1806), which included many unpublished poems, were edited by her daughter.

London's Summer Morning

A poem obviously indebted to Swift's *A Description of the Morning*. The aural and visual details have moved out of Swift's mock-pastoral context, but the life of the streets goes on much as in 1709, with the smart and dingy, trim and tattered side by side. Everything is open and on display: only the surreptitious lawyer has something to hide. The poem first appeared in the *Morning Post*, 23 August 1800. Text from *Poetical Works* (1806), 3:223–4.

Who has not wak'd to list the busy sounds
Of summer's morning, in the sultry smoke
Of noisy London? On the pavement hot
The sooty chimney-boy, with dingy face
And tatter'd covering, shrilly bawls his trade,   5
Rousing the sleepy housemaid. At the door
The milk-pail rattles, and the tinkling bell
Proclaims the dustman's office; while the street
Is lost in clouds impervious. Now begins
The din of hackney-coaches, waggons, carts;   10
While tinmen's shops, and noisy trunk-makers,

Knife-grinders, coopers, squeaking cork-cutters,
Fruit-barrows, and the hunger-giving cries
Of vegetable venders, fill the air.
Now ev'ry shop displays its varied trade,   15
And the fresh-sprinkled pavement cools the feet
Of early walkers. At the private door
The ruddy housemaid twirls the busy mop,
Annoying the smart 'prentice, or neat girl,
Tripping with band-box lightly. Now the sun   20
Darts burning splendour on the glitt'ring pane,
Save where the canvas awning throws a shade
On the gay merchandize. Now, spruce and trim,
In shops (where beauty smiles with industry,)
Sits the smart damsel; while the passenger   25
Peeps thro' the window, watching ev'ry charm.
Now pastry dainties catch the eye minute
Of humming insects, while the limy snare
Waits to enthral them. Now the lamp-lighter
Mounts the tall ladder, nimbly vent'rous,   30
To trim the half-fill'd lamp; while at his feet
The pot-boy yells discordant! All along
The sultry pavement, the old-clothes-man cries
In tone monotonous, and side-long views
The area for his traffic: now the bag   35
Is slily open'd, and the half-worn suit
(Sometimes the pilfer'd treasure of the base
Domestic spoiler), for one half its worth,
Sinks in the green abyss. The porter now
Bears his huge load along the burning way;   40
And the poor poet wakes from busy dreams,
To paint the summer morning.

12 *coopers* Cask makers and repairers.
20 *band-box* Cardboard box for millinery.
25 *passenger* 'passer-by'.
32 *pot-boy* 'tavern boy'.

38 *Domestic spoiler* 'housebreaker'.
39 *green abyss* The lawyer's bag used for legal documents (lawyers became known as 'green-bags'); here he is buying stolen goods cheap.

The Poet's Garret

The scene is a reworking of the Grub-Street garret of Pope's *Dunciad*, 1:115ff, with which it repays comparison. The poem also recalls William Hogarth's satirical plate, 'The Distrest Poet' (1737); but here there is no starving baby. Robinson's poet can turn his hand to anything from heroic drama to riddles and street ballads, and (it is hinted) to classical or Gothic styles. Matter and spirit co-exist: he has food and drink, and a sentimental cat for company, and his narrow room remains a place of hope and restless imagination. The poem was printed in *The Wild Wreath* (1804), edited by Robinson's daughter. The following text is that of *Poetical Works* (1806), 3:233–5.

Come, sportive fancy! come with me, and trace
The poet's attic home! the lofty seat
Of the heav'n-tutor'd nine! the airy throne
Of bold imagination, rapture fraught
Above the herds of mortals. All around   5

2 *attic* An ironic pun on *Attic* ('classically elegant': Athens was the capital of Attica).

3 *nine* The classical Muses.

A solemn stillness seems to guard the scene,
Nursing the brood of thought — a thriving brood
In the rich mazes of the cultur'd brain.
Upon thy altar, an old worm-eat board,
The pannel of a broken door, or lid   10
Of a strong coffer, plac'd on three-legg'd stool,
Stand quires of paper, white and beautiful!
Paper, by destiny ordain'd to be
Scrawl'd o'er and blotted; dash'd, and scratch'd, and torn;
Or mark'd with lines severe, or scatter'd wide   15
In rage impetuous! Sonnet, song, and ode,
Satire, and epigram, and smart charade;
Neat paragraph, or legendary tale,
Of short and simple metre, each by turns
Will there delight the reader.
               On the bed   20
Lies an old rusty suit of "solemn black," —
Brush'd thread-bare, and, with brown, unglossy hue,
Grown somewhat ancient. On the floor is seen
A pair of silken hose, whose footing bad
Shews they are trav'llers, but who still bear   25
Marks somewhat *holy*. At the scanty fire
A chop turns round, by packthread strongly held;
And on the blacken'd bar a vessel shines
Of batter'd pewter, just half fill'd, and warm,
With Whitbread's bev'rage pure. The kitten purs,   30
Anticipating dinner; while the wind
Whistles thro' broken panes, and drifted snow
Carpets the parapet with spotless garb,
Of vestal coldness. Now the sullen hour
(The fifth hour after noon) with dusky hand   35
Closes the lids of day. The farthing light
Gleams thro' the cobwebb'd chamber, and the bard
Concludes his pen's hard labour. Now he eats
With appetite voracious! nothing sad
That he with costly plate, and napkins fine,   40
Nor china rich, nor fork of silver, greets
His eye or palate. On his lyric board
A sheet of paper serves for table-cloth;
An heap of salt is serv'd, — oh! heav'nly treat!
On ode Pindaric! while his tuneful puss   45
Scratches his slipper for her fragment sweet,
And sings her love-song soft, yet mournfully.
Mocking the pillar Doric, or the roof
Of architecture Gothic, all around

---

6 Cf. Gray, *Elegy*, 6.
17 *charade* 'riddle'.
21 Cf. 'customary suits of solemn black' (*Hamlet*, I.ii.78).
30 Samuel Whitbread (1720–96), founder of the brewing firm.
34 *vestal* 'chaste'.

36 *farthing light* The cheapest candle.
45 *Pindaric* A lofty lyric ode. For examples see Isaac Watts, *The Adventurous Muse*; Anne Finch, *Upon the Hurricane*; or the odes of Gray and Collins.
48 *Doric* One of the orders of classical architecture.

The well-known ballads flit, of Grub-street fame!   50
The casement, broke, gives breath celestial
To the long dying-speech; or gently fans
The love-inflaming sonnet. All around
Small scraps of paper lie, torn vestiges
Of an unquiet fancy. Here a page   55
Of flights poetic — there a dedication —
A list of dramatis personæ, bold,
Of heroes yet unborn, and lofty dames
Of perishable compound, light as fair,
But sentenc'd to oblivion!
           On a shelf,   60
(Yclept a mantle-piece) a phial stands,
Half fill'd with potent spirits! — spirits strong,
Which sometimes haunt the poet's restless brain,
And fill his mind with fancies whimsical.
Poor poet! happy art thou, thus remov'd   65
From pride and folly! for in thy domain
Thou can'st command thy subjects; fill thy lines;
Wield th'all-conqu'ring weapon heav'n bestows
On the grey goose's wing! which, tow'ring high,
Bears thy sick fancy to immortal fame!   70

61 *Yclept* 'called' (a medieval touch. Cf. 49).
62 *potent spirits* Probably laudanum, a tincture of opium.

68–9 A goose quill pen, and suggesting the more heroic arrow feathers.

The Birth-day

Royal birthdays were the occasion for fashionable display and finery. This evening scene shows the arrivals for the 'birth-night' ball (Cf. Pope, *The Rape of the Lock*, 1:23). This is another poem showing Robinson's eye for powerful satiric detail, here sharpened by a moral indignation that culminates in her allusion to King Lear's meeting with 'poor Tom'. The text is that of *Poetical Works* (1806), 2:338–40.

Here bounds the gaudy gilded chair,
    Bedeck'd with fringe, and tassels gay;
The melancholy Mourner there
    Pursues her sad and painful way.

Here, guarded by a motley train,   5
    The pamper'd Countess glares along;
There, wrung by poverty and pain,
    Pale Mis'ry mingles with the throng.

Here, as the blazon'd chariot rolls,
    And prancing horses scare the crowd,   10
Great names, adorning little souls,
    Announce the empty, vain, and proud.

1 *chair* 'bounds' suggests this is a one-horse chaise, rather than the still fashionable sedan chair.
9 *blazon'd chariot* A light four-wheeled carriage with forward facing seats, here decorated ('blazon'd') with an aristocratic coronet. Perdita Robinson 'was to be seen daily in an absurd chariot, with a device of a basket likely to be taken for a coronet, driven by the favoured of the day, with her husband and candidates for her favour as outriders' (*DNB*).

Here four tall lacquies slow precede
  A painted dame, in rich array;
There the sad shiv'ring child of need
  Steals barefoot o'er the flinty way.

15

'Room, room! stand back!' they loudly cry,
  The wretched poor are driv'n around
On ev'ry side, they scatter'd fly,
  And shrink before the threat'ning sound.

20

Here, amidst jewels, feathers, flow'rs,
  The senseless Duchess sits demure;
Heedless of all the anguish'd hours
  The sons of modest worth endure.

All silver'd and embroider'd o'er,
  She neither knows nor pities pain;
The Beggar freezing at her door
  She overlooks with nice disdain.

25

The wretch whom poverty subdues
  Scarce dares to raise his tearful eye;
Or if by chance the throng he views,
  His loudest murmur is a sigh!

30

The poor wan mother, at whose breast
  The pining infant craves relief,
In one thin tatter'd garment drest,
  Creeps forth to pour the plaint of grief.

35

But ah! how little heeded here
  The fault'ring tongue reveals its woe;
For high-born fools, with frown austere,
  Contemn the pangs they never know.

40

'Take physic, Pomp!' let Reason say,
  'What can avail thy trappings rare?
The tomb shall close thy glitt'ring day,
  The BEGGAR prove thy equal there!'

13 *lacquies* 'footmen'.
41 Take physic, pomp, / Expose thyself to feel what
  wretches feel' (*King Lear*, III.iv.33–4).

Helen Maria Williams (?1761–1827)

After the death of her father in 1769 Williams moved to Berwick-upon-Tweed, where she and her sister were educated by their mother. But her provincial life ended in 1781 when she returned to London with the manuscript of a verse tale, *Edwin and Eltruda*, published the following year. As the author of a fashionable legendary narrative she was welcomed into literary circles and soon had a wide acquaintance that included Samuel Johnson, Anna Seward, the Wartons, Elizabeth Montagu and Charlotte Smith. One side of her poetic output was represented by sentimental sonnets and occasional pieces, and the other by ambitious poems on public and historic themes, *Ode on the Peace* (1783), *Peru* (1784) and *Poem on the Slave Bill* (1788). A highly successful two-volume edition of her *Poems* (1786) was followed by an expanded collection in 1791. Like many British writers and intellectuals Williams welcomed the French Revolution in 1789, and her enthusiasm is evident in *The Bastille*, a poem included in her novel *Julia* (1790). On a visit to France that year she witnessed the popular rejoicing at the Festival of the Federation, and celebrated the new liberty in her *Letters written in France in the Summer of 1790*. This inaugurated the work for which Williams is best known, a series of chronicles published in London between 1790 and 1819 in which she follows the latest developments in France. She returned to the continent in July 1791 and finally settled there for good the following year. Her Paris salon attracted French politicians and British radicals, and she became friends with Thomas Paine and Mary Wollstonecraft (who was amused by her hostess's formality: 'Her manners are affected, yet her simple goodness of heart continually breaks through the varnish'). Williams was an active supporter of the Girondin party of Danton and Madame Roland, and when the Jacobins triumphed in October 1793 she was imprisoned and in danger of being guillotined. Having seen Danton, Roland and other friends led off to execution she was fortunate to be released, and in 1794 she set off on a six-month visit to Switzerland, only returning after the fall of her enemy Robespierre. By this time most of her acquaintance in England had turned against her, shocked at the tenacity with which she clung to her libertarian beliefs during the Terror, and the British reviews reviled her as a disgrace to her sex. Her reputation there also suffered from her relationship with the extreme radical John Hurford Stone (1763–1818), who divorced his wife for her in 1794. At first a supporter of Napoleon, Williams grew increasingly disillusioned with France's imperialist ambitions; but finally she and Stone became naturalized French citizens in 1817. She died at Paris in 1827.

To Dr Moore

The poem first appeared in Williams's *Letters from France* (2nd edn, 1792), 2:10–13, with the full title *To Dr Moore, in answer to a Poetical Epistle written by him, in Wales, to Helen Maria Williams*, and this is the text given here. Reprinting it in her *Poems on Various Subjects* (1823) she added the date 'September 1791'. In her picture the French peasantry are gathering the fruits of their new freedom, and the violence of revolution has given way to a scene of pastoral innocence and community like that nostalgically evoked in Goldsmith's *Deserted Village*. From line 43, however, the tone shifts as Williams engages with the current Revolution Controversy of 1790–1 and echoes its polemical imagery. She attacks Edmund Burke's conservative *Reflections on the Revolution in France* (1790) in terms similar to the anti-Burke writings of Thomas Paine (*Rights of Man*), Mary Wollstonecraft (*A Vindication of the Rights of Men*) and James Mackintosh (*Vindiciæ Gallicæ*), in which Burke is seen as the reactionary defender of an old Gothic feudalism. Like them, Williams wants to replace Burke's romantic Gothic structure with an enlightened neoclassicism recalling democratic Greece and republican Rome.

John Moore (1729–1802), Scottish physician, novelist and travel writer, was a close friend of Williams's and had been addressed in an earlier epistle (*Poems* (1786), 2:1–20) in which she expressed personal gratitude for his 'healing art' and for his encouragement of her literary efforts. This later verse-letter reflects Moore's radical sympathies and his support for the early stages of the French Revolution, 1789–92. However, in his *Journal During a Residence in France* (1794) Moore describes his horror at witnessing the September massacres of 1792, and his realization that one tyranny had been replaced by another. Williams's poem can only have reminded him of his own early hopes for French liberty. In *Letters from France* it is introduced as follows: 'When we drew near Orleans, we saw the country, as far as the eye could reach, covered with grapes, and men, women, and children employed in gathering the vintage. This scene gave me a new image of plenty, a new aspect of the riches of nature, which it was impossible to contemplate without the most pleasing emotion. But a description of the vintage will perhaps read better in verse, than prose; and I shall therefore send you a copy of a rhyming letter which I have written to my friend Dr Moore on this subject.'

While in long exile far from you I roam,
To sooth my heart with images of home,
For me, my friend, with rich poetic grace,
The landscapes of my native isle you trace;
Her cultur'd meadows, and her lavish shades, 5
Her winding rivers, and her verdant glades;
Far, as where frowning on the flood below,
The rough Welsh mountain lifts its craggy brow;
Where nature throws aside her softer charms,
And with sublimer views the bosom warms. 10
 Meanwhile, my steps have stray'd where Autumn yields
A purple harvest on the sunny fields;
Where, bending with their luscious weight, recline
The loaded branches of the clust'ring vine;
There, on the Loire's sweet banks, a joyful band 15
Cull'd the rich produce of the fruitful land;
The youthful peasant, and the village maid,
And feeble age and childhood lent their aid.
The labours of the morning done, they haste
Where the light dinner in the field is plac'd; 20
Around the soup of herbs a circle make,
And all from one vast dish at once partake:
The vintage-baskets serve, revers'd, for chairs,
And the gay meal is crown'd with tuneless airs;
For each in turn must sing with all his might; 25
And some their carols pour in nature's spite.
 Delightful land! Ah, now with gen'ral voice
Thy village sons and daughters may rejoice.
Thy happy peasant, now no more a slave,
Forbad to taste one good that nature gave, 30
Views with the anguish of indignant pain
The bounteous harvest spread for him in vain.
Oppression's cruel hand shall dare no more
To seize with iron gripe his scanty store;
And from his famish'd infants wring those spoils, 35
The hard-earn'd produce of his useful toils:
For now on Gallia's plain the peasant knows
Those equal rights impartial Heav'n bestows.
He now, by freedom's ray illumin'd, taught
Some self-respect, some energy of thought, 40
Discerns the blessings that to all belong,
And lives to guard his humble shed from wrong.
 Auspicious Liberty! in vain thy foes
Deride thy ardour, and thy force oppose;
In vain refuse to mark thy spreading light, 45
While, like the mole, they hide their heads in night;

---

31 The sense seems to demand a second 'no more' here.
37 *Gallia* France.
43 *thy foes* Burke's *Reflections* (1790) and its defenders.

45 Burke attacked rationalist philosophy as 'this new-sprung modern light'.

Or hope their eloquence with taper-ray
Can dim the blaze of philosophic day;
Those reasoners who pretend that each abuse,
Sanction'd by precedent, has some blest use.   50
Does then some chemic power to time belong,
Extracting, by some process, right from wrong?
Must feudal governments for ever last?
Those Gothic piles, the work of ages past;
Nor may obtrusive reason boldly scan,   55
Far less reform the rude mishapen plan;
The winding labyrinths, the hostile towers,
Whence danger threatens, and where horror low'rs;
The jealous draw-bridge, and the moat profound,
The lonely dungeon in the cavern'd ground;   60
The sullen dome above those central caves,
Where lives one tyrant, and a host of slaves?
Ah, Freedom, on this renovated shore,
That fabric frights the moral world no more!
Shook to its basis, by thy powerful spell,   65
Its triple walls in massy fragments fell;
While, rising from the hideous wreck, appears
The temple thy firm arm sublimely rears;
Of fair proportions, and of simple grace,
A mansion worthy of the human race.   70
For me, the witness of those scenes, whose birth
Forms a new era in the storied earth;
Oft while with glowing breast those scenes I view,
They lead, ah friend belov'd, my thoughts to you!
Ah, still each fine emotion they impart,   75
With your idea mingles in my heart;
(You, whose warm bosom, whose expanded mind,
Have shar'd this glorious triumph of mankind;
You, whom I oft have heard, with gen'rous zeal,
With all that truth can urge, or pity feel,   80
Refute the pompous argument that tried
The common cause of millions to deride;
With reason's force the plausive sophist hit,
Or dart on folly the quick flash of wit.)
Too swift, my friend, the moments wing'd their flight,   85
That gave at once instruction and delight;
That ever from your ample stores of thought
To my small stock some new accession brought.
How oft remembrance, while this bosom bleeds,

53–66 In *Reflections* Burke had used the image of an old
castle to represent France's sense of continuity with its
past: 'Your constitution ... suffered waste and
dilapidation; but you possessed in some parts the walls,
and in all the foundations of a noble and venerable
castle. You might have repaired those walls; you might
have built on those old foundations.' For Williams, this
Gothic edifice symbolizes tyranny, like the Bastille
which had been stormed on 14 July 1789.

60 'Since the destruction of the building, many
subterraneous cells have been discovered underneath a
piece of ground which was enclosed within the walls of
the Bastille' (Williams, *Letters written in France*).
76 *idea* 'image'.
83 *plausive sophist* 'one who praises with false arguments'.

My pensive fancy to your dwelling leads;   90
    Where, round your cheerful hearth, I weeping trace
The social circle, and my vacant place! —
    When to that dwelling friendship's tie endears,
When shall I hasten with the "joy of tears?"
    That joy whose keen sensation swells to pain,   95
And strives to utter what it feels, in vain.

A Hymn written among the Alps

The poem forms part of Williams's *A Tour in Switzerland* (1798), 2:16–19, where it concludes chapter 22, and was later included in her *Poems on Various Subjects* (1823), pp. 293–8. Williams came to Switzerland expecting to find the fabled haven of liberty, but was disillusioned by the reality of a country 'where liberty, of which so vain a boast has been made, is so little understood; where the absolute restraint put on the press, and the intolerance exercised with respect to religious opinions, have stifled every attempt to promote a more liberal education, and softer, more benevolent and enlarged sentiments' (2:272). If human institutions once again disappointed Williams, the physical Switzerland opened to her 'a new world of ideas' (2:277). Earlier in chapter 22 she quotes Rousseau: 'The general impression felt by those who scale the higher mountains, where the air is pure and subtile, is a greater easiness in breathing, more lightness in the body, and more serenity in the mind. – Meditation assumes, in those regions, something of a character great, and sublime, proportioned to the objects which strike us; something of tranquil rapture, remote from all that is selfish, or sensual' (2:7). Williams records her strenuous climb to one of the great glaciers: 'While my fellow travellers amused themselves by wandering over that world of ice ... I sat down on the border of the Glacier, to enjoy the new and magnificent vision around me. On the right, rocks and mountains of ice, arose in dread and sublime perspective; before me, St Bernardin lifted its barren and uncovered top ... I employed the hours of meditation in throwing together the new images ... into the form of an hymn' (2:8–10). The fact that the poem is a single unfolding sentence is stressed by the punctuation of lines 4 and 8. The 1798 text is given here, but with the numbering of the stanzas removed.

Creation's God! with thought elate,
    Thy hand divine I see;
Impressed on scenes where all is great,
    Where all is full of thee!;

Where stern the Alpine mountains raise   5
    Their heads of massive snow;
Whence, on the rolling storm I gaze,
    That hangs — how far below!;

Where, on some bold stupendous height,
    The eagle sits alone;   10
Or soaring wings his sullen flight
    To haunts yet more his own;

Where the sharp rock the chamois treads,
    Or slippery summit scales;
Or where the whitening snow-bird spreads   15
    Her plumes to icy gales;

1–4 Cf. the opening of Thomson's *Hymn* appended to *The Seasons* (1730): 'These, as they change, Almighty Father, these, / Are but the *varied* God. The rolling Year / Is full of Thee'.

13 *chamois* Mountain antelope.

Where the rude cliff's steep column glows
    With morning's tint of blue;
Or evening on the Glacier throws
    The rose's blushing hue;   20

Or where by twilight's softer light,
    The mountain shadow bends;
And sudden casts a partial night,
    As black its form descends;

Where the full ray of noon, alone   25
    Down the deep valley falls;
Or, where the sun-beam never shone
    Between its rifted walls;

Where cloudless regions calm the soul,
    Bid mortal cares be still;   30
Can passion's wayward wish controul,
    And rectify the will;

Where midst some vast expanse, the mind
    Which swelling virtue fires,
Forgets that earth it leaves behind,   35
    And to its heaven aspires;

Where far along the desart-sphere
    Resounds no creature's call;
And undisturbing mortal ear,
    The Avalanches fall;   40

Where, rushing from their snowy source,
    The daring torrents urge
Their loud-toned waters headlong course,
    And lift their feathered surge;

Where swift the lines of light, and shade,   45
    Flit o'er the lucid lake,
Or the shrill winds its breast invade,
    And its green billows wake;

Where on the slope, with speckled dye,
    The pigmy herds I scan,   50
Or soothed the scattered *chalets* spy,
    The last abodes of man;

Or, where the flocks refuse to pass,
    And the lone peasant mows,
Fixed on his knees, the pendant grass,   55
    Which down the steep he throws;

---

28 *rifted* 'split apart'.
53–6 'We spied the inhabitants of the various cottages …
    hanging on the steeps like goats, to turn the swath

[scythed hay], and leaving us to wonder by what
ingenuity the grass was first mowed' (*Tour*, 2:2).

Or where the dangerous pathway leads
   High o'er the gulph profound;
From whence the shrinking eye recedes,
   Nor finds repose around;   60

Where red the mountain-ash reclines
   Along the clefted rock;
Where firm, the dark unbending pines
   The howling tempests mock;

Where, level with the ice-ribb'd bound,   65
   The yellow harvests glow;
Or vales with purple vines are crown'd
   Beneath impending snow;

Where the rich minerals catch the ray
   With varying lustre bright,   70
And glittering fragments strew the way,
   With sparks of liquid light;

Or, where the moss forbears to creep,
   Where loftier summits rear
Their untrod snows, and frozen sleep   75
   Locks all th'uncoloured year;

In every scene, where every hour
   Sheds some terrific grace,
In nature's vast, overwhelming power,
   THEE, THEE, my GOD, I trace!   80

65–8 Cf. Pope, *The Dunciad*, 1:78.

Bibliography

A selected list of editions (poems and letters), biographies and bibliographies of poets included in this volume.

MARK AKENSIDE

The Poetical Works of Mark Akenside, ed. Robin Dix. Madison and Teaneck: Farleigh Dickinson University Press; London: Associated University Presses, 1996.

Mark Akenside: A Biographical and Critical Study, by Charles T. Houpt. Philadelphia, 1944 (reprinted New York: Russell and Russell, 1970).

ANNA LAETITIA BARBAULD

The Poems of Anna Letitia Barbauld, ed. William McCarthy and Elizabeth Kraft. Athens: University of Georgia Press, 1994.

Memoir of Mrs Barbauld, including letters and notices of her family and friends, by Anna L. Le Breton. London, 1874.

A Memoir, Letters, and a Selection from the Poems and Prose Writings of Anna Barbauld, by Grace A. Ellis, 2 vols. Boston: J. R. Osgood & Co., 1874.

WILLIAM LISLE BOWLES

The Poetical Works of William Lisle Bowles, ed. George Gilfillan, 2 vols. Edinburgh: James Nichol, 1855.

A Wiltshire Parson and his Friends. The Correspondence of W. L. Bowles, ed. Garland Greever. London: Constable & Co., 1926.

ROBERT BURNS

The Poems and Songs of Robert Burns, ed. James Kinsley, 3 vols. Oxford: Clarendon Press, 1968.

The Letters of Robert Burns, ed. J. De Lancey Ferguson, 2nd edn edited by G. Ross Roy, 2 vols. Oxford: Clarendon Press, 1985.

A Biography of Robert Burns, by James Mackay. Edinburgh: Mainstream Publishing, 1992.

A Bibliography of Robert Burns, by Joel W. Egerer. Edinburgh and London: Oliver & Boyd, 1964.

A Burns Companion, by Alan Bold. Houndmills and London: Macmillan, 1991.

THOMAS CHATTERTON

The Complete Works of Thomas Chatterton, ed. Donald S. Taylor, in association with Benjamin B. Hoover, 2 vols. Oxford: Clarendon Press, 1971.

A Life of Thomas Chatterton, by E. H. W. Meyerstein. London: Ingpen and Grant, 1930.

The Marvellous Boy: The Life and Myth of Thomas Chatterton, by Linda Kelly. London: Weidenfeld & Nicolson, 1971.

A Bibliography of Thomas Chatterton, by Murray Warren. New York: Garland Publishing, 1977.

MARY COLLIER

The Thresher's Labour by Stephen Duck. The Woman's Labour by Mary Collier, ed. E. P. Thompson and Marian Sugden. London: The Merlin Press, 1989.

WILLIAM COLLINS

The Works of William Collins, ed. Richard Wendorf and Charles Ryskamp. Oxford: Clarendon Press, 1979.

The Poems of Gray, Collins, and Goldsmith, ed. Roger Lonsdale. London and Harlow: Longman, 1969.

Thomas Gray and William Collins. Poetical Works, ed. Roger Lonsdale. Oxford: Oxford University Press, 1977.

The Life of a Poet. A Biographical Sketch of William Collins, by P. L. Carver. London: Sidgwick & Jackson, 1967.

WILLIAM COWPER

The Poems of William Cowper, ed. John D. Baird and Charles Ryskamp, 3 vols. Oxford: Clarendon Press, 1980–95.

William Cowper: The Task and Selected Other Poems, ed. James Sambrook. Longman Annotated Texts. London and New York: Longman, 1994.

The Letters and Prose Writings of William Cowper,
  ed. James King and Charles Ryskamp, 5 vols.
  Oxford: Clarendon Press, 1979–86.
William Cowper. A Biography, by James King.
  Durham, NC: Duke University Press, 1986.

GEORGE CRABBE

George Crabbe: The Complete Poetical Works, ed.
  Norma Dalrymple-Champneys and Arthur
  Pollard, 3 vols. Oxford: Clarendon Press, 1988.
Selected Letters and Journals of George Crabbe, ed.
  Thomas C. Faulkner, with the assistance of
  Rhonda L. Blair. Oxford: Clarendon Press,
  1985.
*George Crabbe and his Times 1754–1832. A Critical
  and Biographical Study*, by René Huchon,
  trans. Frederick Clarke. London: John Murray,
  1907.

STEPHEN DUCK

*The Thresher's Labour by Stephen Duck. The
  Woman's Labour by Mary Collier*, ed. E. P.
  Thompson and Marian Sugden. London: The
  Merlin Press, 1989.
Stephen Duck: The Thresher-Poet, by Rose M.
  Davis. University of Maine Studies, ser. 2, no.
  8. Orono, Maine, 1926.

JOHN DYER

The Poetical Works of Armstrong, Dyer, and Green,
  ed. George Gilfillan. Edinburgh, 1858.
Poet, Painter and Parson: The Life of John Dyer,
  by Ralph M. Williams. New York: Bookman
  Associates, 1956.

SARAH FYGE EGERTON

Eighteenth Century Women Poets, ed. Roger
  Lonsdale. Oxford and New York: Oxford
  University Press, 1989, pp. 26–7.

ANNE FINCH

Poems, ed. Myra Reynolds. Chicago: University of
  Chicago Press, 1903.
Anne Finch and Her Poetry. A Critical Biography,

by Barbara McGovern. Athens and London:
  University of Georgia Press, 1992.

JOHN GAY

John Gay. Poetry and Prose, ed. Vinton A.
  Dearing, with the assistance of Charles E.
  Beckwith, 2 vols. Oxford: Clarendon Press,
  1974.
The Letters of John Gay, ed. C. F. Burgess.
  Oxford: Clarendon Press, 1966.
*John Gay: A Profession of Friendship. A Critical
  Biography*, by David Nokes. Oxford: Oxford
  University Press, 1995.

OLIVER GOLDSMITH

Collected Works of Oliver Goldsmith, ed. Arthur
  Friedman, 5 vols. Oxford: Clarendon Press,
  1966.
The Poems of Gray, Collins, and Goldsmith, ed.
  Roger Lonsdale. London and Harlow:
  Longman, 1969.
The Collected Letters of Oliver Goldsmith, ed.
  Katharine C. Balderston. Cambridge:
  Cambridge University Press, 1928.
Oliver Goldsmith, by Ralph M. Wardle. Lawrence:
  University of Kansas Press, 1957.

THOMAS GRAY

The Complete Poems of Thomas Gray, ed. H. W.
  Starr and J. R. Hendrickson. Oxford:
  Clarendon Press, 1966.
The Poems of Gray, Collins, and Goldsmith, ed.
  Roger Lonsdale. London and Harlow:
  Longman, 1969.
Correspondence of Thomas Gray, ed. Paget
  Toynbee and Leonard Whibley, 3 vols. Oxford:
  Clarendon Press, 1935. Reprinted, with
  additions by Herbert W. Starr, 1971.
Thomas Gray. A Biography, by R. W. Ketton-
  Cremer. Cambridge: Cambridge University
  Press, 1955.

SAMUEL JOHNSON

The Poems of Samuel Johnson, ed. David Nichol
  Smith and Edward L. McAdam, 2nd edn.
  Oxford: Clarendon Press, 1974.

Samuel Johnson: The Complete English Poems, ed.
    J. D. Fleeman. London: Allen Lane, 1974.
The Letters of Samuel Johnson, ed. Bruce Redford.
    The Hyde Edition, 5 vols. Princeton: Princeton
    University Press, 1992–4.
Boswell's Life of Johnson, etc., ed. George Birkbeck
    Hill, revised by L. F. Powell, 6 vols. Oxford:
    Clarendon Press, 1934–64.
Samuel Johnson, by Walter Jackson Bate. London:
    Chatto & Windus, 1978.
The Life of Samuel Johnson. A Critical Biography,
    by Robert DeMaria, Jr. Oxford and Cambridge,
    MA, 1993.

MARY JONES

Eighteenth Century Women Poets, ed. Roger
    Lonsdale. Oxford and New York: Oxford
    University Press, 1989, pp. 155–6.

MARY LEAPOR

*Mary Leapor: A Study in Eighteenth-Century
    Women's Poetry*, by Richard Greene. Oxford:
    Clarendon Press, 1993.
Eighteenth Century Women Poets, ed. Roger
    Lonsdale. Oxford and New York: Oxford
    University Press, 1989, pp. 194–5.

ROBERT LLOYD

*The Poetical Works of Robert Lloyd ... To which is
    prefixed an account of the life and writings of the
    author*, by William Kenrick, 2 vols. London,
    1774.

JAMES MACPHERSON

The Poems of Ossian and Related Works, ed.
    Howard Gaskill. With an introduction by Fiona
    Stafford. Edinburgh: Edinburgh University
    Press, 1996.
Fragments of Ancient Poetry (facsimile of 1st edn,
    1760), introd. John J. Dunn. Augustan Reprint
    Society 122. William Andrews Clark Memorial
    Library, 1966.
*The Sublime Savage. A Study of James Macpherson
    and the Poems of Ossian*, by Fiona J. Stafford.
    Edinburgh: Edinburgh University Press,
    1988.

LADY MARY WORTLEY MONTAGU

*Lady Mary Wortley Montagu. Essays and Poems,
    and Simplicity, a Comedy*, ed. Robert Halsband
    and Isobel Grundy. Oxford: Clarendon Press,
    1977.
*The Complete Letters of Lady Mary Wortley
    Montagu*, ed. Robert Halsband, 3 vols. Oxford:
    Clarendon Press, 1965–7.
The Life of Lady Mary Wortley Montagu, by
    Robert Halsband. Oxford: Oxford University
    Press, 1956; Galaxy Books, 1960.

THOMAS PARNELL

Collected Poems of Thomas Parnell, ed. Claude
    Rawson and F. P. Lock. Newark: University of
    Delaware Press; London and Toronto:
    Associated University Presses, 1989.
Thomas Parnell, by Thomas M. Woodman.
    Boston: Twayne Publishers, 1985.

AMBROSE PHILIPS

The Poems of Ambrose Philips, ed. M. G. Segar.
    Oxford: Blackwell, 1937.

JOHN PHILIPS

The Poems of John Philips, ed. M. G. Lloyd
    Thomas. Oxford: Blackwell, 1927.

JOHN POMFRET

Poems, in volume 8 of *The Works of the English
    Poets*, ed. Alexander Chalmers, 21 vols.
    London, 1810.

ALEXANDER POPE

*The Twickenham Edition of the Poems of Alexander
    Pope*, ed. John Butt et al., 11 vols. London:
    Methuen; New Haven: Yale University Press,
    1939–69.
The Poems of Alexander Pope, ed. John Butt.
    London: Methuen, 1963.
Alexander Pope, ed. Pat Rogers. The Oxford
    Authors. Oxford and New York: Oxford
    University Press, 1993.

The Correspondence of Alexander Pope, ed. George
  Sherburn, 5 vols. Oxford: Clarendon Press,
  1956.
Alexander Pope. A Life, by Maynard Mack. New
  Haven and London: Yale University Press, 1985.
A Concordance to the Poems of Alexander Pope,
  compiled by Emmett G. Bedford and Robert J.
  Dilligan, 2 vols. Detroit: Gale Research
  Company, 1974.
*Pamphlet Attacks on Alexander Pope, 1711–1744: A
  Descriptive Bibliography*, by J. V. Guerinot.
  London: Methuen, 1969.

MATTHEW PRIOR

The Literary Works of Matthew Prior, ed. H.
  Bunker Wright and Monroe K. Spears, 2 vols.
  Oxford: Clarendon Press, 2nd edn, 1971.
Matthew Prior, Poet and Diplomatist, by Charles
  Kenneth Eves. New York: Columbia University
  Press, 1939.

MARY ROBINSON

*Memoirs of the Late Mrs. Robinson, written by
  herself*, ed. M.E. Robinson, 4 vols. London,1801.
The Lost One: A Biography of Mary Robinson, by
  Marguerite Steen. London: Collins, 1937.
Eighteenth Century Women Poets, ed. Roger
  Lonsdale. Oxford and New York: Oxford
  University Press, 1989, pp. 468–70.

RICHARD SAVAGE

The Poetical Works of Richard Savage, ed.
  Clarence Tracy. Cambridge: Cambridge
  University Press, 1962.
An Account of the Life of Mr. Richard Savage, by
  Samuel Johnson (1744), ed. Clarence Tracy.
  Oxford: Clarendon Press, 1971.
*The Artificial Bastard. A Biography of Richard
  Savage*, by Clarence Tracy. Toronto: University
  of Toronto Press, 1953.
Dr. Johnson and Mr. Savage, by Richard Holmes.
  London: Hodder and Stoughton, 1993.

ANNA SEWARD

*The Poetical Works of Anna Seward, with extracts
  from her literary correspondence*, ed. Walter
  Scott, 3 vols. Edinburgh, 1810.

Letters of Anna Seward, ed. A. Constable, 6 vols.
  Edinburgh, 1811.
A Swan and her Friends, by E. V. Lucas. London:
  Methuen, 1907.
Eighteenth Century Women Poets, ed. Roger
  Lonsdale. Oxford and New York: Oxford
  University Press, 1989, pp. 311–13.

CHRISTOPHER SMART

The Poetical Works of Christopher Smart, ed.
  Marcus Walsh and Karina Williamson, 6 vols.
  Oxford: Clarendon Press, 1980–96.
Jubilate Agno, ed. W. H. Bond. London: Rupert
  Hart-Davis, 1954.
The Annotated Letters of Christopher Smart, ed.
  Betty Rizzo and Robert Mahony. Carbondale &
  Edwardsville: Southern Illinois University
  Press, 1991.
Christopher Smart, Scholar of the University, by
  Arthur Sherbo. Michigan State University
  Press, 1967.
*Christopher Smart. An Annotated Bibliography
  1743–1983*, by Robert Mahoney and Betty W.
  Rizzo. New York and London: Garland
  Publishing, 1984.

CHARLOTTE SMITH

The Poems of Charlotte Smith, ed. Stuart Curran.
  Women Writers in English 1350–1850. New
  York and Oxford: Oxford University Press,
  1993.
Charlotte Smith, Poet and Novelist, by Florence
  Hilbish. Philadelphia, 1941.
Eighteenth Century Women Poets, ed. Roger
  Lonsdale. Oxford and New York: Oxford
  University Press, 1989, pp. 365–7.

JONATHAN SWIFT

The Poems of Jonathan Swift, ed. Harold Williams,
  3 vols. Oxford: Clarendon Press, 1958.
Swift. Poetical Works, ed. Herbert Davis. London:
  Oxford University Press, 1967.
Jonathan Swift. The Complete Poems, ed. Pat
  Rogers. Harmondsworth: Penguin Books,
  1983.
Jonathan Swift, ed. Angus Ross and David
  Woolley. The Oxford Authors. Oxford: Oxford
  University Press, 1984.

The Correspondence of Jonathan Swift, ed. Harold
Williams, 5 vols. Oxford: Clarendon Press,
1963–5.
Swift. The Man, His Works, and the Age, by Irvin
Ehrenpreis, 3 vols. London: Methuen,
1962–83.
*Jonathan Swift, A Hypocrite Reversed. A Critical
Biography*, by David Nokes. Oxford: Oxford
University Press, 1985.

JAMES THOMSON

James Thomson. The Seasons, ed. James Sambrook.
Oxford: Clarendon Press, 1981.
*James Thomson, 1700–1748. Letters and
Documents*, ed. Alan D. McKillop. Lawrence:
University of Kansas Press, 1958.
James Thomson, 1700–1748. A Life, by James
Sambrook. Oxford: Clarendon Press, 1991.

JOSEPH WARTON

Odes on Various Subjects (facsimile of 1st edn,
1746), introd. Joan Pittock. Scholars'
Facsimiles & Reprints. Delmar: New York,
1977.
Odes on Various Subjects (facsimile of 1st edn,
1746), introd. Richard Wendorf. Augustan
Reprint Society vol. 197. William Andrews
Clark Memorial Library, 1979.
*Biographical Memoirs of the Late Revd. Joseph
Warton, D.D.*, by John Wooll. London: Cadell
and Davies, 1806.
*Joseph and Thomas Warton. An Annotated

Bibliography, by John Vance. New York and
London: Garland Publishing, 1983.

THOMAS WARTON

*The Poetical Works of the Late Thomas Warton,
B.D.*, ed. Richard Mant, 2 vols. Oxford: Oxford
University Press, 1802.
The Correspondence of Thomas Warton, ed. David
Fairer. Athens and London: University of
Georgia Press, 1995.

ISAAC WATTS

The Works of the Rev. Isaac Watts, D.D., revised by
G. Burder, 9 vols. Leeds, 1812–13.
Isaac Watts: His Life and Works, by Arthur P.
Davis. New York: Dryden Press, 1943.

HELEN MARIA WILLIAMS

Eighteenth Century Women Poets, ed. Roger
Lonsdale. Oxford and New York: Oxford
University Press, 1989, pp. 413–14.

ANN YEARSLEY

*Lactilla, Milkwoman of Clifton. The Life and
Writings of Ann Yearsley, 1753–1806*, by Mary
Waldron. Athens and London: University of
Georgia Press, 1996.

Index of Titles and First Lines